A SUMMER OF
MASS MURDER

A SUMMER OF MASS MURDER

1941 Rehearsal for the
Hungarian Holocaust

George Eisen

Purdue University Press • West Lafayette, Indiana

Copyright 2023 by Purdue University.
Printed in the United States of America.

Cataloging-in-Publication Data available from the Library of Congress.
978-1-61249-775-4 (hardback)
978-1-61249-776-1 (paperback)
978-1-61249-777-8 (epub)
978-1-61249-778-5 (epdf)

An electronic version of this book is freely available, thanks to the support of libraries working with Knowledge Unlatched. KU is a collaborative initiative designed to make high-quality books Open Access for the public good.

Cover image: Holocaust by bullets in the Soviet Union. Courtesy of the United States Holocaust Memorial Museum Photo Archives.

For the memory of two brothers, Samu and Karcsi, whose story is told in this book.

For my mother, Ibolya-Breindel, who has never hesitated to fight injustice.

For my grandchildren, Amaris, Baila, Calder, and Aviva,
with a message to remember the story of the Holocaust.

Finally, with special love to my wife, Cynthia.

"The Holocaust is integrally and organically connected to the Vernichtungskrieg, to the war in 1941, and is organically and integrally connected to the attempt to conquer Ukraine."
TIMOTHY SNYDER, HISTORIAN

༄

"The 1941 deportation was a Jewish as well as a national trauma."
RANDOLPH L. BRAHAM, HOLOCAUST HISTORIAN

༄

"Everything that one might have considered once unthinkable, there it happened to us."
LÁSZLÓ ZOBEL, SURVIVOR

༄

"One only wonders how people who consider themselves Hungarians and Christians as well as responsible administrators are not afraid of the retribution that their lawless actions might precipitate."
MARGIT SLACHTA, RESCUER

CONTENTS

	List of Illustrations	viii
	The Main Characters: *Survivors, Witnesses, Rescuers, Perpetrators*	xi
	Author's Note	xv
	Preface	xvii
1.	Prologue: A Primer to the Holocaust	1
2.	The *Ostjuden*: The Galicianer in the Hungarian Imagination	16
3.	Galicia: An Exile into the Unknown	49
4.	Kamenets-Podolsk: The Anatomy of a Massacre	84
5.	Galicia 1941–1942: The Delirium of Murder	126
6.	Weapon of War: Rape and Sexual Violence	164
7.	Return from the Abyss: Rescue and Survival	178
8.	Opening Old Wounds: Responsibility and Consequences	217
9.	Requiem for a Deportation: Unanswered Questions	243
	Epilogue: Looking for Closure	259
	Acknowledgments	265
	Notes	269
	Bibliography	341
	Index	361
	About the Author	381

ILLUSTRATIONS

XVIII	FIG P.1 Galicia and surrounding region, August 1941.
XXIII	FIG P.2A AND P.2B Two brothers, Samu, with a customary bottle of wine, and Karcsi (standing on the left), who was the "quiet one." *Courtesy of George Eisen.*
44	FIG 2.1 Hungary's territorial gains, 1938–1941.
57	FIG 3.1 Collecting Jews for transportation to the train station in the city of Hust in Carpathian Ruthenia. Picture by Erzsébet Szapáry. *Courtesy of the Hungarian National Museum/Photo Archives.*
61	FIG 3.2 Delivering the Jews to the cattle cars for transfer to the transit camp in Körösmező. Picture by Erzsébet Szapáry. *Courtesy of Memorial de la Shoah.*
67	FIG 3.3 Picture of Captain Nándor Batizfalvy from the National Central Alien Control Office (KEOKH). *Courtesy of Ester Horompoly.*
72	FIG 3.4 Hungarian Jews arriving in Skala: "The Jews were dumped alongside of the road . . . the soldiers got tired of transporting them . . . the only thing remaining for them is the ditch by the road. At last this tolerated them." July 23, 1941. *Hungarian National Museum/Photo Archives, courtesy of Béla Somló.*
72	FIG 3.5 Deportees abandoned by the Hungarian military in Skala. While the women tended to the children, the "men sat on the ground with vacant stares looking into the distance." July 23, 1941. *Hungarian National Museum/Photo Archives, courtesy of Béla Somló.*
87	FIG 4.1 Decree by the military commander of Kamenets-Podolsk: "All Jews over 10 years old to wear at all time a white armband with the 'Zionist-Star' on the right arm." July 24, 1941. *United States Holocaust Memorial Museum, courtesy of the State Archives of Khmel'nyts'kyi Region, Ukraine.*
87	FIG 4.2 Decree by the military commander of Kamenets-Podolsk: ". . . from August 9, 1941, all Jews must move into the Old Town Ghetto." August 8, 1941. *United States Holocaust Memorial Museum, courtesy of the State Archives of Khmel'nyts'kyi Region, Ukraine.*
89	FIG 4.3 The final decree by the military commander of Kamenets-Podolsk, before the mass murder: "From now on, selling food for Jews is forbidden; Jews are forbidden to purchase food outside of the Old Town. The guilty will be severely punished." August 24, 1941. *United States Holocaust Memorial Museum, courtesy of the State Archives of Khmel'nyts'kyi Region, Ukraine.*

ILLUSTRATIONS IX

94 FIG 4.4 Orinin: Former Soviet fortification served as mass grave for over two thousand Hungarian deportees. August 26, 1941. *Courtesy of George Eisen.*

99 FIG 4.5 Reichsführer SS Heinrich Himmler converses with SS Obergruppen Führer Alfred Wunnenberg. To Himmler's immediate right is Friederich Jeckeln. *United States Holocaust Memorial Museum Photo Archives, courtesy of James Blevins.*

102 FIG 4.6 A day before the massacre: "All the Hungarian Jews were transferred to the new town, to the barracks near the train station." August 26, 1941. *United States Holocaust Memorial Museum Photo Archives, courtesy of Ivan Sved.*

104 FIG 4.7 Marching to the mass execution: "German soldiers armed with whips stood 10 steps apart and beat the Jews who ran past them." August 27–29, 1941. *United States Holocaust Memorial Museum Photo Archives, courtesy of Ivan Sved.*

105 FIG 4.8 In front of the mass graves: Hungarian Jews are waiting for their final fate. August 27–29, 1941. *United States Holocaust Memorial Museum Photo Archives, courtesy of Ivan Sved.*

114 FIG 4.9 The Jeckeln reports sent to Heinrich Himmler: The sum of three days of murder. August 30, 1941. *Courtesy of Military Central Archive, Military Historical Archive Prague fund Kommando stab "Reichsführer SS, 1941–1943."*

120 FIG 4.10 General Friedrich Jeckeln: The profile of a mass murderer. *United States Holocaust Memorial Museum Photo Archives, courtesy of Bundesarchiv.*

148 FIG 5.1 Police Battalion 133 in Kolomea. *Courtesy of www.military-archive.com.*

150 FIG 5.2 A Letter by a defense witness for Anneliese Leideritz. Hessisches Staatsarchiv. *Courtesy of Hans Peter Trautmann.*

165 FIG 6.1, 6.2, AND 6.3 The three phases of mass murder of women and children: collection, undressing, and execution. *United States Holocaust Memorial Museum Photo Archives, courtesy of Instytut Pamieci Narodowej.*

176 FIG 6.4 The Gestapo building in Stanisławów: The SS brothel was located on the fourth floor of the building. *Courtesy of the Ghetto Fighter's House and Museum, Israel/The Photo Archives.*

183 FIG 7.1 László Zóbel was twenty-four years old when he was deported to Galicia with his mother. After wandering in Galicia, they were smuggled back to Budapest by a Hungarian intelligence officer. *Courtesy of George Eisen.*

186 FIG 7.2 Elizabeth Lubell and her mother, Brona Buchsbaum. She escaped from the Kolomea Ghetto with the help of smugglers that her parents hired. The parents remained behind and were among the last Jews to be shipped to Belzec extermination camp and killed. *Courtesy of Barbara Lubell.*

208 FIG 7.3 Herbert C. Pell, the American ambassador in Hungary. *Public Domain, courtesy of the US National Archives.*

211	Fig 7.4 Head of the Order of the Sisters of Social Service Margit Slachta, parliamentarian, politician, and rescuer. Named as Righteous Among the Nations by the State of Israel.
213	Fig 7.5 Baroness Erzsébet Szapáry, representative of one of the leading aristocratic families. She participated in rescue activities with Margit Slachta and Edith Weiss. Named as Righteous Among the Nations by the State of Israel. *Courtesy of the Hungarian National Museum/Photo Archives.*
214	Fig 7.6 Baroness Edith Weiss, daughter of the richest man in Hungary, Manfred Weiss. She was actively participating in the rescue activities with the Jewish leadership in Hungary. *Courtesy of Daisy Strasser.*
224	Fig 8.1 Two gendarmes with German soldiers. Courtesy of Dr. Sándor Szakály.
234	Fig 8.2 General Henrik Werth, the chief of staff of the Royal Hungarian Army in the first phase of the war. He was responsible for the collection and transportation of the Jews to Galicia. He died in a Soviet prison in 1952. *Courtesy of Dr. Sándor Szakály.*
235	Fig 8.3 Ámon Pásztóy, the former head of National Central Alien Control Office (KEOKH). He provided the legal framework for the deportation. Pásztóy was sentenced and executed for his crimes in Budapest in 1949. *Courtesy of the Állambiztonsági Szolgálatok Történeti Levéltára.*
237	Fig 8.4 As the Hungarian prime minister in 1941, László Bárdossy carried the ultimate responsibility for the 1941 deportation. He was convicted and executed in 1946. *Fortepan, Public Domain, courtesy of Judit Mészáros.*
240	Fig 8.5 Government Commissioner of Carpathian Ruthenia Miklós Kozma assumed full responsibility for the deportation of two-thirds of those who were transferred to Galicia.
245	Fig 9.1 The site of the mass murder: Memorial Park in Kamenets-Podolsk. *Courtesy of George Eisen.*
252	Fig 9.2 Portrait of a religious Jewish farmer from Carpathian Ruthenia, his wife, and six of his children. The family was expelled to Galicia, returned, and then, in 1944, killed in Auschwitz. The farmer, Chaim Simcha Mechlowitz, became immortalized as the farmer in Roman Vishniac's collection *A Vanished World. United States Holocaust Museum, Courtesy of Lisa Wahler.*
262	Fig E.1 The painful memories of eight-year-old Valentina, who witnessed the Kamenets-Podolsk mass murder. *Courtesy of George Eisen.*
264	Fig E.2 Peaceful serenity: The Hungarian graves in Orinin, hidden in the former Soviet military fortification. July 26, 1941. *Courtesy of George Eisen.*

THE MAIN CHARACTERS OF THE STORY
Survivors, Witnesses, Rescuers, Perpetrators

Cipora Brenner, survivor of the Stanisławów ghetto. Her testimony of the "Bloody Sunday" massacre is perhaps the most complete and moving description of the fate of, and tribute to, all those murdered in the New Cemetery of Stanisławów. She also survived Auschwitz.

Elizabeth Lubell, survivor of Galicia and the 1944 Holocaust in Hungary, she was one of the last escapees from the Kolomea Ghetto, leaving her parents. Her harrowing flight and survival, and reconnecting with her future husband, could be the material for a film epic.

László Zobel, survivor from Budapest who, with his mother, was able to escape from Kolomea with the assistance of an enterprising Hungarian counterintelligence agent. He survived the Holocaust after serving in the notorious forced labor service and passing the last year of the war in a Hungarian prison. His mother died in Auschwitz.

৵

Béla Somló, Jewish driver attached to the Royal Hungarian Army. His diary and photographs from 1941 provide an authentic testimony of the plight and fate of the deportees and the Jewish communities in Galicia.

Valentina, the flower seller of Kamenets-Podolsk. She was eight years old during the three-day massacre of 22,600 Jews, August 27–29, 1941. An eyewitness of the carnage, she gave testimony about the event.

৵

Margit Slachta, the head of the Order of the Sisters of Social Service, politician, and member of parliament. She was instrumental in bringing the information of the excesses of the deportation and consequent murders in Galicia to the highest echelons of the Hungarian leadership as well as to the Hungarian and International Red Cross. For her rescue work in 1941 and 1944, she was named by the State of Israel as Righteous Among the Nations.

COUNTESS ERZSÉBET SZAPÁRY came from one of the most exclusive aristocratic families in Hungary. She joined Margit Slachta and Edith Weiss in their efforts to stop the deportation and help those who remained in Galicia, and she maintained close contacts with the Hungarian and the International Red Cross, and directly with the American Embassy in informing the world about the atrocities taking place in 1941. She was named by the State of Israel as Righteous Among the Nations.

BARONESS EDITH WEISS, a Jewish activist and the daughter of the richest man in Hungary, Manfred Weiss, she had access to the highest echelons of the Hungarian state bureaucracy. While the family converted, she remained Jewish and became a leader of the Jewish community in Hungary. She cooperated closely in the rescue activities with Margit Slachta and Erzsébet Szapáry.

☙

LÁSZLÓ BÁRDOSSY, served as the prime minister of Hungary from April 1941 to March 1942. With his full support, the Council of Ministers approved the deportation. His contact with the American ambassador Herbert C. Pell did not moderate his views toward the expulsion. He was sentenced to death by the People's Court in Hungary and executed in 1946.

FERENC KERESZTES-FISCHER, the Hungarian minister of interior. He opposed the deportation in 1941, yet it took him a month stop it, and he did not stop the periodic expulsions of escapees from Galicia until the fall of 1942.

MIKLÓS KOZMA, government commissioner of Carpathian Ruthenia and one of the initiators of the mass deportation. Among all the perpetrators, he was to only one to express remorse for his actions just before his death in the fall of 1941.

ÁMON PÁSZTÓY, the head of the Külföldieket Ellenőrző Országos Központi Hatóság (National Central Alien Control Office, abbreviated KEOKH). He was responsible for the deportation and the follow-up official policies of preventing the escapees in their deperate efforts to return from Galicia. He was sentenced to death by the People's Court in Hungary and executed in 1949.

GENERAL HENRIK WERTH, the chief of staff of the Royal Hungarian Army. A strong proponent of the deportation, he provided the resources of the army to collect and carry out the removal of the deportees to Galicia. He died in a Soviet prison in 1952.

GENERAL FRIEDRICH JECKELN, whose name is associated with the main milestones of mass murder that took place in Eastern Europe. After Kamenets-Podolsk, he became a central character in the largest killing in the Holocaust in Babi Yar and later in the Rumbula Forest in Riga. He was sentenced to death by a Soviet court and executed in 1946 in Riga.

CAPTAIN HANS KRÜGER, head of the Gestapo in Stanisławów, perhaps the most "productive" mass murderer in the General Government, estimated to have killed over one hundred thousand Jews and Poles, including three thousand Hungarian deportees. He was sentenced to life imprisonment in West Germany but was freed after several years.

FIRST LIEUTENANT PETER LEIDERITZ, head of the Gestapo in Kolomea. Under his authority, more than seventy thousand Jews were murdered, including close to three thousand Hungarian, Czech, and German Jews. He was sentenced to death and executed in 1949 in Poland.

And Two Brothers

SAMU AND KARCSI, two unpretentious characters in this book. Samu, born April 12, 1913, and married with three daughters, was a wagon driver, close to the lowest rank on the socioeconomic ladder of contemporary Hungary. Karcsi, the older brother, was born a year earlier on January 27, 1912. A tailor by trade, he was removed from the rough and tumble world of Samu. The only testimony of their last day together came from a Hungarian soldier with the final words of Samu: "I cannot leave my brother."

AUTHOR'S NOTE

For the sake of consistency and historical accuracy, the text uses original Polish and Hungarian place names for cities and towns that were common prior to the war. It also helps to recreate a flavor of a lost era and world. As borderlands, Carpathian Ruthenia and Galicia's locations meant the constant shifting of national boundaries also forced rapid transition from language to language. There are several instances that various towns in the Soviet Union were renamed after historical personalities or Soviet leaders. The reader can find the multiple usage of names of cities and locations in the index.

PREFACE

GALICIA OCCUPIES A UNIQUE PLACE AND TIME IN THE HISTORY OF THE Holocaust. The summer of 1941 ushered a chain of events in this so-called borderland that had no precedent in the rapidly unfolding history of the Holocaust. By thrusting more than twenty thousand Hungarian Jews, who were deemed alien—without proper citizenship papers, or just for being Jews—across its eastern border into Galicia, the Hungarian government set a new "first" in Hungarian history as well as in the evolution of the Holocaust. It was a unilateral action by the Hungarians, neither requested by German military authorities nor warranted either by military or economic rationale.

Through four subsequent stages, the transfer into Galicia and a succession of bloodbaths across this region, this book brings into focus the story of these Hungarian Jews and the fate of their Galician coreligionists who tried to provide them shelter. The collection and expulsion of thousands of people, with corresponding brutality and often lawlessness, set the stage for the unfolding genocide. The killing and robbing of the unloaded and abandoned Jews by Ukrainian irregular forces was followed by an unprecedented mass murder by bullets in the town of Kamenets-Podolsk. Between 14,000 and 16,000 Hungarian Jews were among the 23,600 murder victims in the Kamenets-Podolsk massacre—an apt and unique opening salvo for the Holocaust and later Final Solution. The third phase, coordinated campaigns of "population reduction" by murder in various ghettos and settlements—interspersed with "culling" operations that further reduced the number of Hungarian Jews in various towns—was conducted by German stationary security forces during the fall of 1941 and the spring of 1942. The final stage, ushering in the Final Solution, was the transportation of the remnants in cattle cars, together with their Galician brethren, to Belzec. This foreshadowed an introduction to the concept of large-scale industrial murder that later was perfected in Auschwitz. This sealed the fate of these deported Hungarian Jews.

The 1941 deportation and mass murder of more than twenty thousand Hungarian Jews should not be viewed as a mere part of *Hungarian* history. It is *transnational*. The events may seem disparate, but in the end, they are interrelated. Their significance lies in the fact that they offer a unique vantage point from which to view the lurches and bumps on the road to the Final Solution. But on the scarred landscape of the Hungarian

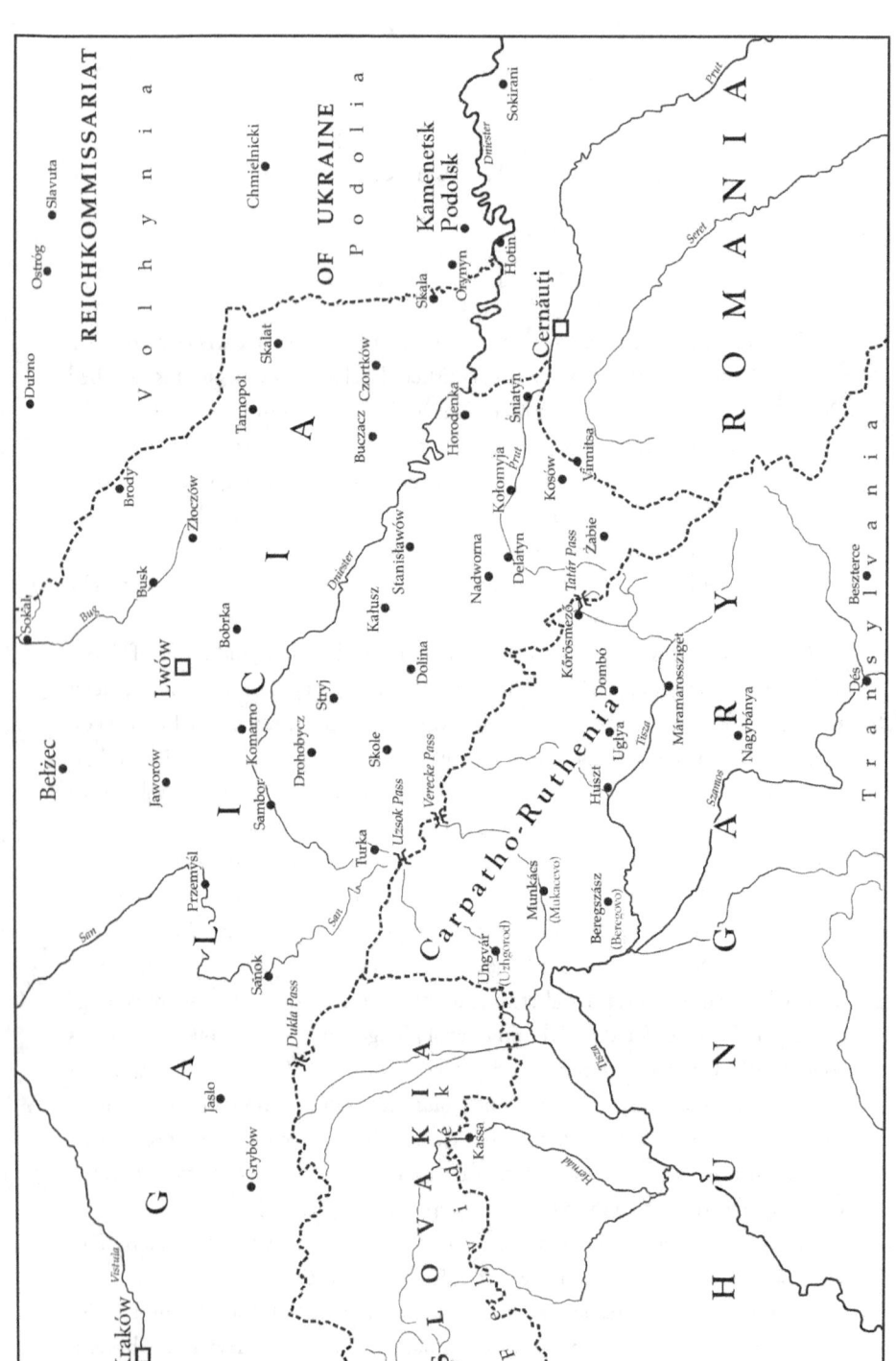

FIG P.1 Galicia and surrounding region, August 1941.

and Jewish history, these events also stand out as a portentous milestone that points toward the final phase of the Hungarian Holocaust in 1944. Substantial new material and the reexamination of known sources helps us to reconstruct not only a bloody chapter in Holocaust history, but also a contentious episode of Hungarian and transnational history.

This is by all account the hardest and most challenging book I have ever written, perhaps because it also harbors a personal dimension—my two family members included among those expelled and murdered. Thus, the book transcends the confines of traditional historiography. It aims to present penetrating questions about morality, culpability, and responsibility by giving voices to both victims and perpetrators. The general contours of the story of the deportation and the extermination of the deportees are not a complete "black hole" in Hungarian historiography. However, it has never been fully explored in Hungary and is largely unknown in international Holocaust literature. The immediate puzzle that confronts the researcher is the rationale: Why did Hungarian authorities opt to expel thousands of people in 1941? And why to Galicia? How does this defining episode fit into the Hungarian and general Holocaust narrative? Equally important is the question as to how the behavior of the main perpetrators in Galicia, the mass murderers who were able to combine murder with sadism and greed, conformed to the Nazi ideology of extermination as well as to their dichotomy on morality? How can one reconcile Himmler's dictum of "kill but remain decent"?

Thus, to comprehend atrocity we need to borrow from disciplines that do not always interlace with historical research. One can find answers only by engaging in a multidisciplinary approach. Similarly, Hungarian Jewish history is not a conventional narrative. In understanding its flow, or rather its unpredictable twists, we need to possess, as the German term *Einfühlung* would dictate, the intellectual and emotional ability to place ourselves within the perspectives of a specific period, culture, and intellectual system. It requires psychology, cultural studies, and sociology as well as historical methodology. Equally important is the fact that in this case, the personal and the professional are inexplicably intertwined.

In fact, this book was not originally planned. It is the final product of a personal pilgrimage to a remote town in Ukraine. It started with four professors who set out from Uzhhorod, Ukraine, in the spring of 2008 on a 283-mile journey to Kamenets-Podolsk, a faraway town on the border of Galicia and Podolia. I was one of the professors. I asked my three Ukrainian colleagues from Uzhhorod National University—Nataliya Kubiniy, Vasyl Miklovda, and Mykhaylo Pityulych—to join me, both as colleagues and personal friends, on a trip to explore a small corner of my family's history. Nataliya's English was perfect, while Vasyl and Mykhaylo spoke only Ukrainian. I wanted to find out, by tearing open a painful chapter of this history, how and why two brothers—my uncles—were murdered in this dusty, nondescript Podolian town in the summer of

1941. It was a harrowing road, even with a car, to retrace the journey of the two brothers and thousands of other Hungarian Jews toward their final destination and mass murder. The landscape was dull, flat, and gray as we passed little villages and dilapidated settlements along the rutted and potholed roads. The most immediate impression was of its featurelessness—wide and empty. My quest was one with no discernable pattern or goals. Why had I come to Kamenets-Podolsk? What did I think I was going to find in this town, which was dramatically reshaped by many decades of communist rule?

The murder site was surrounded by tall, slowly decaying, yellowish, communist-style apartment buildings, built as the city spread outward during the postwar decades. These apartments, cracked, broken, and peeling, as if prematurely aged, seemed to obliterate the past. It was a town that forgot its own history. Or, maybe, was it too tired and worn down to remember all the atrocities—Stalinist or Nazi, interchangeably?

Here was a mass grave, completely surrounded by a modern town. Enclosed by a low wrought-iron fence, thanks to the Israeli government, the murder site was adjacent to a small market and a children's playground. The memorial monuments in various languages stood in stoic silence. A lonely garland graced one of them. The place was deserted, seemingly oblivious of its history and significance.

Standing in front of one of the monuments, the sole visitor, I was enveloped in silence; I still was not sure why I was there and what I was hoping to accomplish, nor did I know exactly what I was looking for and what I wanted to find. After all, I knew little beyond family lore about the fate of my two uncles, Samu (Samuel) and Karcsi (the Hungarian nickname for Charles), and their final hour. My drive to see the site where the lives of thousands of Jews were extinguished within the span of three days, the two brothers among them, seemed more like a pilgrimage than a scholarly exploration. Visiting a mass grave, where thousands of nameless victims were murdered, demands a forensic passion, as there are multitudes of layers of politics, culture, and, above all, psychology—both that of the victims and of the executioners. I was reminded of the American historian Jill Lepore's dictum: "All historians are coroners."[1] To sift through these layers, one needs imagination to picture the terrifying final moments of the victims and the hardened faces of the executioners pulling the trigger, again and again.

Monuments have never moved me; they are impersonal and cold. But, then, an unexpected and serendipitous encounter changed everything. It opened the first crack in a dam that soon became a torrent of information. As I turned my gaze toward my three travel companions, who waited discreetly in the distance, staying behind not to intrude on a private moment of grief or contemplation, I noticed their excitement as they waived frantically. They had found in the adjoining market a simple flower seller, Valentina, who, I came to realize, was an eyewitness herself. She was a seven- or eight-year-old Ukrainian peasant girl at the time, from a small village adjacent to the murder site that took the lives of 23,600 people.

As Valentina recounted her memories, tears streaked down her worn face. Our questions opened long-repressed memories that suddenly burst forth. This was perhaps the first time she was asked to share her suppressed memory fragments. She was there. During the mass shooting. An eight-year-old girl—a mere child. She watched as "the columns of Hungarians [were] ordered to the edge of the mass pit and shot." In her soft, lilting Ukrainian cadence, she described the nights when "we heard the moans of the wounded who were buried alive. . . . There were cases when people who were thrown into the ditch alive later climbed out, only to jump back in, because they thought that they were on the 'other side.' They went insane." Her father's horses were requisitioned after the massacre to tamp down the hastily shoveled soil over the heaving, undulating graves filled with victims still alive.[2]

I hugged her, almost instinctively. At this moment, I understood that besides those who were killed, and grieving family members who knew somewhat sketchily their loved ones' final fate, there were other unwitting victims in this brutal phase of history, the so-called Holocaust, or more poignantly, the Shoah. I also realized that I had to come back to this ill-fated town, which became synonymous with mass murder, to ask many more questions of Valentina and of myself.

Meeting her was like a message in a bottle, tossed into the ocean of time that washed up on the dunes many years later. I opened this "bottle," and this was the moment that I decided to explore the story of the deportation where two brothers disappeared forever. It signaled a transition from a personal quest to an in-depth scholarly inquiry.

That was also the moment this book was conceived.

But there was a second crack in this proverbial dam, which had a major influence on my decision to explore the deportation and mass murder of Hungarian Jews in the summer of 1941. Almost by chance, I stumbled upon a work that changed my view of writing this book. Daniel Mendelsohn, in his book *The Lost: A Search for Six of Six Million*, made me realize the importance of the human dimension and corresponding narrative in writing history—the victims' voices need to be heard. As he so adroitly proved, the chasm between the personal and the historical can be bridged. The final product, this book, is not a mere history of the Holocaust, but a multidimensional view of the fate of thousands of people who were swept up and away in this tragic moment.

The main challenge was, of course, to reconcile the scholarly with the personal. It's never easy. As a scholar, I have written and spoken about the Holocaust extensively: books, articles, lectures. On the other hand, the Holocaust on the personal level is not unfamiliar to me. I also carry its DNA. Having been born in Hungary during the war, I became a part of its narrative. And this narrative is a painful one, which can either be repressed and never mentioned, as many did during the postwar decades in Eastern Europe, or shared with future generations to fulfill the biblical commandment: "Don't forget the things that you saw with your own eyes and so that they do not fade from your mind as long as you live. And make them known to your children and to your children's children."³

The ability to process and deal with this trauma was often an individual choice. Many refused to share their Holocaust experience because of fear of anti-Semitism or to repress painful memories. After the fall of the Soviet Union, suddenly everything opened up with often heartbreaking results. When a grandmother wears long-sleeve dresses all her life, a grandson could not have guessed that she tried to hide the number that was tattooed on her arm in Auschwitz. Even her daughter did not know that they were from an Orthodox Jewish family. It was a rigorously maintained and self-imposed silence.⁴ The Hungarian government, following the example of the Soviet Union, was also complicit in this silence about the public memory of the Holocaust in the hope that the wounds of the past would not impede the building of a utopian proletarian paradise. Based on the Stalinist dictum that one should not "divide the dead," social scientists wrote Jewish victims out of history books. In reading contemporary reports by the Soviet Investigating Commission of Nazi Crimes, one is struck by the fact that no Jews are mentioned, but only "peaceful Soviet Citizens." Consequently, a whole generation grew up without an awareness of their family's fate in the Holocaust or even that they were Jewish.

Fortunately, my family belonged to the group that resisted the temptation to remain silent. For me the Holocaust always lurked in the background. I grew up with its stories, spellbound by the yarns told during the long evenings, far into the night. They were tales of pain, humiliation, hiding, defying, heroism, and, above all, fighting for survival. The words about my father's incarceration in the Mauthausen concentration camp and my mother hiding under false identity with Christian papers, and with two children, in Budapest were casually woven into a tapestry of survival at all costs. There was nothing hidden, nothing cloaked in protective euphemism, and yet the tone of these stories remained subdued, almost understated, without a sense of rancor, accusation, or a quest for revenge. I was perhaps more incensed about the stories than were my father and mother.

Wrapped within these wartime accounts, there was a story of two brothers who were swept up in the looming genocide, never to return. They were killed in a faraway place, mentioned in hushed tones only, Kamenets-Podolsk. The word "genocide," like the term "Holocaust," fails to fully convey the enormity of the crime of which they became victims. Cesarani struggled with this definition, noting that "it might be too broad, encompassing many national and racial groups besides the Jews." In Israel, the Hebrew word "Shoah" is preferred, used widely for the first time in Claude Lanzmann's magisterial documentary. It connoted utter devastation, a world in flames, consumed by an inferno. Ian Kershaw's words reverberate in this context: "the murder of Europe's Jews was the lowest point of mankind's descent into the abyss of inhumanity."⁵

The two brothers were deported and killed ostensibly for not being Hungarian citizens. They were simple people, born in Budapest, one eking out a living by working with horses and wagons and the other a tailor. With three little daughters, Samu was married to a Christian woman with impeccable Hungarian roots. Karcsi was the older one, the tailor by trade. In family stories, and by looking at old sepia photographs, Samu was the outgoing one, the drinker, a ladies' man, with a radiant smile, deep-set blue eyes, and often with a bottle of wine in his hand. About Karcsi we know the least. He was the introvert, the quiet one, never married. Their story just didn't add up in my mind. Neither was my grandfather's fate of being arrested and hauled off at the same time to an impromptu collection camp in Budapest, waiting for transfer to Galicia. His second wife accompanied him (voluntarily or by force, we do not know). Leiser, as he was called by everyone, was born, indeed, in Galicia. But being over seventy years old and ill, he should have been exempted by law. Only through my mother's fearless intervention was he sent home, where he would die several months later, perhaps of a broken heart over losing two sons and his wife, and maybe knowing the exact details of their final moments.[6]

I argued with my mother. They were Hungarians, just like my father—why was he not taken? Later, I discovered that my father was saved by a bureaucratic oversight. I also came to know that my father wanted to go also, upon hearing official rumors that in Galicia "there are free houses and employment" that would be distributed to those who were being sent there. Thankfully, he was sternly warned not even to think about this. Two years later, I was born.

FIG P.2A AND P.2B   Two brothers, Samu, with a customary bottle of wine, and Karcsi (standing on the left), who was the "quiet one." *Courtesy of George Eisen.*

But then, there was a third approach for making sense of the trauma of the Holocaust in which the conflict between faith in God and the Holocaust became central. Through the haze of the rapidly disappearing decades, I can still remember an encounter between one of our neighbors, a highly emotional, Seventh-day Adventist woman, and an official, perhaps thirty years old, who was sent by city hall to assess the value of her house. The neighbor lady loudly, almost hysterically, invoked the name of God, which she often did, imploring the official to remember God and how he would punish them if her property was confiscated. There was a moment of silence. Then, the woman from city hall turned to our neighbor sternly: "You should not talk to me about God! I was in Auschwitz.... After Auschwitz, there is no God. There cannot be a God." This moment, etched indelibly in my memory as a seven- or eight-year-old, reminds me of Primo Levi's reasoning that in the absence of God, the world itself becomes void of humanity. Auschwitz became perhaps the ultimate metaphor of this "absence of humanity without a god" or the "silence of god amidst atrocity" for many survivors.

This memorable outburst brings me to several questions. Why are we fixated on Auschwitz? Is it because of the audacity of industrial murder cloaked in impersonality and facelessness? Or because the process was hidden from the world and "hygienically" conducted almost like a clinical trial in a medical experiment? If we view the Holocaust in its totality, this sense of an "absence of god" could not have been more obvious than during the first two years of the war and the first phase of the Holocaust when people were murdered by bullets, face-to-face, one by one. It was in Eastern Europe, far away from the probing eyes of the world. Here, there was no need, as in Western Europe, to take the Jews somewhere else to kill them. Entire local communities were co-opted to do the dirty work of the Nazi executioners. These were "the neighbors," as Daniel Mendelsohn so insightfully phrased, "the intimates, with whom the Jews had lived side by side for centuries, until some delicate mechanism shifted and they turned on their neighbors."[7] Or, in the same light, the Hungarian neighbors who didn't protest, who looked away or even lined up, waiting to see what was available for plunder as the family being deported filed out of their home.

The Holocaust was not just a historical event. It was a test for our humanity and soul. The storyline of this book is full of this void of humanity and futile search for God. These killings in the East reduced extermination to its bare essence. Yet, if we dissect the "Holocaust by Bullets," as Father Patrick Desbois coined it, we can still see a well-orchestrated process—the proverbial German obsession with orderly conduct that started with digging the ditches a day before by Jews or Ukrainian forced labor, who also covered the mass graves. The Germans were preoccupied, meanwhile, with an evening planning session prior to the Aktion,[8] a hearty breakfast, and a final "corporate meeting" after the mass murder to evaluate the efficiency with which the extermination was carried out. This established a certain cadence and ritual for murder.

And let's not forget an important ingredient of these mass murders: bottle upon bottle of schnapps, consumed before, during, and after the murders. In Galicia, the image of an SS officer orchestrating the killing and running up and down in the front of the mass grave with a gun in one hand and a bottle of vodka in the other is rooted in reality, not in cinematic fiction.

In researching and writing this book, I often was faced with utter incomprehension about the rationale for actions that, in retrospect, cannot be rationalized. I came to realize that the Nazi rationale and justification for mass murder that overlaid the ideology of mass extermination of inferior races, not only Jews, exemplified a distorted worldview. In Galicia, even this "cosmic struggle" was interspersed with the unbridled urge for plunder.

On the other side of genocide is the question of the eager participation of the Ukrainian paramilitary forces, who harbored no ideology, tormenting and butchering defenseless Hungarian refugees, mainly women, children, and elderly, and their own Jewish neighbors. But the Hungarian motives for expelling thousands of people, and then preventing them from escaping, remained the most puzzling mystery. The recurring questions on my mind were obviously unanswerable. What was it all for? This spate of unbridled violence, costing the lives of thousands of people? I wondered what they were thinking—all these well-educated officials, masquerading as statesmen, officious, petty, regional bureaucrats, and the legendarily brutal gendarmerie that managed the expulsion? A sense of frustration hit me every time, for there are no answers that can explain the human avarice, depravity, and shortsightedness that enveloped this first stage of the Hungarian Holocaust.

_I_

PROLOGUE
A Primer to the Holocaust

ON A HOT DAY IN LATE AUGUST 1941, THE SUN ROSE ON A RAGGED STREAM of people clutching their most precious possessions as they left the demolished barracks where they spent the night outside the city of Kamenets-Podolsk, in what is now western Ukraine. There were thousands of them: children and babies held in their mothers' arms, rabbis carrying Torah scrolls, elderly grandparents struggling to keep pace with younger family members. Their captors formed a cordon through which the weary group marched, and those who moved too slowly were beaten.

In the middle of the winding column were two brothers walking side by side. A Hungarian soldier, walking along the column, turned to the younger one, "I know you, Samu. I can save you. I can procure a Hungarian uniform for you." The younger brother replied, "Thanks, but I cannot leave my brother." As they struggled up the low hills outside of the city, they could hear gunfire. Few knew for sure what lay ahead, but a palpable sense of fear ran through the group. Finally, they reached an open area marked by four huge craters, the remnants of munition explosions left behind by the retreating Soviet Army. There, the truth became apparent: Today they would die.

The Hungarian soldier, a simple porter in civilian life, followed the column to the murder site, witnessing the final moments of the two brothers. The younger one, Samu, was shot through the head, stumbling into the crater. The older brother, Karcsi, jumped into the mass grave alive, following his brother.[1]

What none of them knew, what they could not know, is that the tragic and violent ending of their lives was only the beginning of an even greater horror—for this would be the largest mass murder, held in the opening phase of the Holocaust in Eastern Europe. Over three days, more than 23,000 Jews, many of them Hungarian, were shot and killed or wounded, and buried—many of them still alive—in the munition craters. This is their story.

"A CLEANSING ACTION"

The Hungarian Holocaust cuts a wide panorama in the public imagination. Most images focus on trainloads of prisoners speeding toward Auschwitz, with its smoke- and flame-belching chimneys. It was in the summer of 1944. These images, though, reveal only the final chapter of the Hungarian Jewish tragedy—the extermination in gas chambers. The mass deportation of Jews from Hungary to the neighboring Galicia[2] region, and extermination of more than 20,000 of them there in the summer and fall of 1941, an opportunity presented by the hostilities between Nazi Germany and the Soviet Union, is lesser known, yet equally lethal. It was an extermination by bullets, a prelude and an introduction to the main act of genocide three years later. While we know some details about the event, it remains a fragmented story.

As the second chapter lays out, this deportation, and the consequent extermination campaign, did not emerge in a vacuum. Paraphrasing Holocaust historian Peter Hayes, one can note that hostile acts against a minority are based on ideas—how the majority perceives a minority—and circumstances that enable this majority to carry through its "murderous intentions."[3] In this instance, both factors were in alignment in Hungary. The ideology of restricting immigration from the east and the consequent clamor for expulsion of those deemed "foreign elements" was a common staple in Hungarian body politics since the late nineteenth century. During the postwar period, though, this demand galvanized into a dynamic momentum partly because of the unique, internal political undercurrents in Hungary, and partly because of Nazi ideological influences of the 1930s. The reviled "Galicianers,"[4] a catch-all term that exemplified these "foreign elements" in common parlance, could be blamed for all the ills and problems of Hungarian society. In some ways, the question during the interwar period was not if, but when to find the right "circumstance" for their transfer to a country, a territory, or a region that would be willing to accommodate this influx.

The outbreak of hostilities on the eastern flank of Europe between Nazi Germany and the Soviet Union provided this highly awaited "circumstance." On June 22, 1941, Nazi Germany launched Operation Barbarossa, invading the Soviet Union. German military planners envisaged a rapid collapse of the communist state within a few weeks. The war unleashed a chain of events in Europe and the world unparalleled in human history. The upper echelon of the Hungarian general staff was aware of the German leaders' intentions.[5] In the hopes of safeguarding the territories Hungary reannexed and occupied between 1938 and 1941, and in light of political jockeying vis-à-vis Romania, Hungary joined Germany against its eastern neighbor five days later. Neither Hitler nor the German military had asked for such military assistance. However, following an air raid allegedly by Soviet planes on June 26, 1941, in Kassa (Košice in Slovakian), a provincial town in Upper Hungary, Hungary pounced on the opportunity to join the military invasion. Some speculation exists that the air attack was instigated by Germany to give Hungary a casus belli for joining war. Hungary was eager to join the war, which was strongly supported by the Hungarian military and political establishment, with or without the prodding of Nazi Germany. On June 27, 1941, Hungary declared war on the Soviet Union.[6]

The next day, the Royal Hungarian Army, represented by the "Carpathian Corps" (*Kárpát Csoport*) crossed the border, advancing far into Ukraine, and later, southern Russia. Attached to the German 17th Army, the Carpathian Corps' initial goal was to relieve the pressure on the German units and rapidly advance to the Dniester River by securing its bridges. By July 6, they controlled large swaths of Galicia and its forward units, reaching the town of Kamenets-Podolsk on July 10, 1941.[7] As a consequence, Hungary gained territorial control of southern and eastern Galicia, and a corresponding window of opportunity for cross-border expulsion of the so-called undesired foreigners, stateless refugees, or "alien" Jews, Christian family members from mixed marriages, and even a few "troublesome" Ukrainians. Interestingly enough, the word "deportation" was never used in official parlance. Just as with Nazi phraseology, the words that pop up repeatedly were "resettlement," "repatriation," and "cross-border removal."

The rather seamless transition from idea to action incorporated the collection of these Jews, their transportation to Galicia, and the final, abrupt dumping of the expellees along forests, meadows, and dirt roads. Chapter three provides an overall picture of the decision-making process that led up to the expulsion as well as the actual modus operandi in accomplishing this transfer. While the German military onslaught against the Soviet Union indirectly became a significant factor in the relocation of these Hungarian Jews, German authorities were vehemently opposed to their moving into a war zone that had not been stabilized or pacified. The area was still contested territory eyed by Germany as an extended "Lebensraum."[8] A flurry of German diplomatic communications, military cables, and personal interventions protesting the usage of Galicia as a dumping ground for Hungarian Jews demonstrated the marked displeasure of Germany against Hungary's and Romania's actions.

Hungarian participation in the war created optimal conditions for implementing a wave of ethnic cleansing, a phrase coined later and, in another context, on Hungarian soil. The idea of expelling these Jews was common in Hungarian political discourse, and was largely supported by societal consensus. However, to make this happen, three central political, military, and administrative figures—Miklós Kozma, the government commissioner of Carpathian Ruthenia[9]; Lieutenant General Henrik Werth, the chief of general staff of the Royal Hungarian Army; and Ámon Pásztóy, the director of the Külföldieket Ellenőrző Országos Központi Hatóság (National Central Alien Control Office—hereafter KEOKH)—were indispensable. They were the catalysts in promoting, authorizing, and finally implementing the deportation. The prime minister of Hungary at the time, László Bárdossy, was supportive of the concept, assuming the role of an enabler in the unfolding expulsion.

While Kozma initiated the idea of cleansing Jews from Carpathian Ruthenia, geographically the closest province to Galicia, the general staff under the leadership of Werth had a much more ambitious design for getting rid of as large a number of Jews as physically possible. Consequently, other regions joined almost immediately. The central role KEOKH played in offering a legal framework for the expulsion, as well as the general policy outline for it, will be discussed in chapter two. The Hungarian army, on the other hand, provided a plan of implementation and the operational "muscle" for the transfer. A directive by General László Dezső, dated July 9, 1941, prior to the removal, gives a clear picture of the preparation for the planned course of action. One of the most staunchly pro-Nazi officers on the general staff, Dezső instructed the invading troops for "the expansion of its military control of the occupied territory as long as possible ... for the transfer of *undesirable populations such as Jews and Ukrainians*."[10]

The number of expelled can only be approximated, with estimates ranging from 17,500 to 40,000. Official records originating from the files of KEOKH show a more precise number of 17,656, which corresponds with its account about the number of registered Polish and Russian nationals. But this number included non-Jewish individuals also.[11] The demographics of the expelled might be more precisely defined. Approximately two-thirds of those transferred to Galicia came from Carpathian Ruthenia and northern Transylvania. We can add to that thousands of Jews who were collected in Budapest along with a large number of foreign nationals and international refugees from internment camps.

The authorities in Budapest maintained a relatively accurate account of those deported from the capital—estimated at around four thousand. However, they had little control over or knowledge of those whom the military and law enforcement authorities uprooted in the provinces. This was especially true for the military-controlled zones in Carpathian Ruthenia and Transylvania, where entire villages were emptied of their Jewish population—Hungarian citizens included. Military trucks collecting the deportees often proceeded directly to Galicia from the train station with their human cargo and bypassed the registration protocol in the official transfer camp located in Körösmező.

Chapters four and five explore the catastrophe that rapidly overtook Galicia, in part because of the influx of thousands of Hungarians; this influx unhinged an already precarious ethnic mélange in the territory, partly because of emerging Nazi policies making Galicia "*Judenrein*." These murders encompassed a full year. Within a half year, a large majority of the deportees were executed in unmarked graves, in forests, and on the banks of the Dniester River by Ukrainian irregulars, or shot over freshly dug mass graves and ditches by Nazi execution squads. Many also perished from hunger, maltreatment, and the vicissitudes of wandering across the large expanses of Galicia.

These two chapters provide an account of the final three stages of the saga that include the practical solution for such an unexpected and unwanted influx of Hungarian Jews; an unprecedented mass murder in Kamenets-Podolsk; follow-up massacres in Galicia in the fall of 1941; and the introduction of industrial annihilation of hundreds of thousands of people by gas in the spring of 1942. Thus, this deportation had unintended but dire consequences, both for Hungarian Jewry and for the evolution of the idea and implementation of the Final Solution.

The dry statistics of population displacement cannot convey a sense of the death, destruction, suffering, and misery entailed in the removal. "Emigration" conjures an orderly move, with well-packed luggage and well-laid plans. The state of being evicted from one's home, with a coffer and three days of food, is something else entirely; there is no common word for it. It is the state of knowing nothing—not how long the journey will last, nor what its final destination might be, nor how one will recognize that destination when it is reached.

The term "ethnic cleansing" is a relatively modern expression. The idea, however, is not. While the dictionary definition implies "systematic killing... of national, ethnic of religious group," it does not have to end in genocide—though it often does. The idea also connotes the removal or exiling of people who, besides the potential physical trauma, are also exposed to mental anguish and psychological shock. It erases a collective memory, a sense of belonging to a national community, a local neighborhood, and a home.

Something very similar happened to the expelled Jews from Hungary. The cross-border transfer of more than 20,000 persons, turning them into refugees in an alien land, cannot be viewed as an out-of-the-ordinary phenomenon—at least not in the context of World War II. Huge demographic shifts accompanied by mass murder were the hallmark of both Soviet and Nazi designs and policies.[12] Following the example of Nazi Germany, all its allies engaged in some form of exchange or forced relocation. In expelling hundreds of thousands of Jews, Romania was a glaring example.

"Ethnic cleansing" on a gigantic scale was an intrinsic part of the war. The expulsion of Jews from Hungary reflected the prevailing norms of the time. The deportation itself did not emerge either in a political vacuum, without an ideological foundation, nor did it lack an indispensable precedent. An equally comprehensive transfer of Serbs and Jews from the southern region of Hungary (Délvidék), in the former Yugoslav area of Backa, to German-occupied Serbia presented this precedent. While there were obvious differences in the motivation and rationale between these two events, the "southern" population transfer served as a prelude and model for the Hungarian military and the Hungarian political leadership for the Galicia action.[13]

In Hungary, and to a large degree in Romania, the persecution and expulsion of Jews was conducted independently from German policies—indeed often against German wishes in both cases. These satellite states, ignoring German requests, used the unfolding war to find their own solution for their "Jewish Question." The Hungarian action—expelling thousands of people—was an "ethnic cleansing" in the true sense of the word. Indeed, one of the architects of the deportation in Carpathian Ruthenia used the term "cleansing action" in describing the collection and transfer of the Hungarian Jews to an "unknown" destination.

As chapter two will present it, the story of this Hungarian-initiated deportation can be traced back to a political and intellectual ambivalence in the second half of nineteenth century toward the westward movement of Jews from the *shtetls* of Galicia, at that time an Austrian province. They were considered, for all practical purposes, Austrian citizens, hence it might be termed as internal movement. While the large majority of these migrants ended up in America, sizeable populations also reached Vienna, Berlin, Paris, London, and to a lesser degree Budapest. In Europe, the question of the *Ostjuden* [Eastern Jews], as they were called, created a political firestorm, both for respective governments and for the established and more assimilated Jewish communities. The majority of these migrants lived in three outlying regions of Hungary: the southern provinces of former northern Hungary (Felvidék), Carpathian Ruthenia, and northern Transylvania (Erdély), forming a semicircle around the periphery of the country. The fulcrum of the deportation concentrated on these regions, and especially in Carpathian Ruthenia.[14]

In answering the question as to why the Jewish communities, especially those on the periphery, were singled out for expulsion, it is misguided to consider it purely on "religious" grounds. By the late 1930s, "Jew" metamorphosed from a religious to a racial-national designation. As the Hungarian chief of general staff, it was Lieutenant General Werth's idea to make Hungary an ethnically homogeneous state through a surge of ethnic cleansing that would have encompassed other, much larger national minorities on a massive scale within the borders of the newly reshaped Kingdom of Hungary—a population transfer of close to seven million people. While this initiative was embraced by the upper echelon of the military cadre, the civilian segment of the government refused to adopt it. Indeed, when Werth finally forwarded this proposal to the prime minister, he called him "an irresponsible lunatic."[15]

But anti-Semitism and racism weren't the sole factors; there were multitudes of victims besides Jews with problematic identities and multiple motives for their removal. The identification of the "Galicianers" for removal did not stem solely from religious hatred or racist ideology, or even from the politics of ethnicity. It was a uniquely Hungarian chapter of the Holocaust that unfolded independently from the Nazi design. It was not based on strict racial doctrine, for it had its own dynamics and rationale.

There was interdependence and interaction among racism, political expediency, and diverse economic factors in the 1941 deportations—along with greed and economic causality. Mass expulsion was profitable on the local level. As Aly Götz phrased it, it came from "the least desirable of the seven deadly sins: Envy."[16] Yet, we cannot ignore its political usefulness to governmental circles either.

The momentum for expulsion successfully blended racial and political anti-Semitism with blatant and often petty economic opportunism. A contemporary observer summed it up this way: "There were many who dreamed about misappropriating a Jewish pharmacy, and others about Jewish estates, and some just about a Jewish apartment."[17] The successive anti-Jewish laws that aimed to curb Jewish economic and cultural dominance in Hungary were most severely enforced in the periphery of the country. Revoking Jewish business licenses, confiscating commercial and agricultural enterprises, and dismissing Jews from public employment had disastrous effects on the economic situation in these areas. Coincidentally, these regions were the most impoverished and backward regions, and Jews were the nascent middle class.[18]

A substantial majority of those deported had settled in Hungary in the later decades of the nineteenth century. Yet the deportation also included Jews who had been living in Hungary for many decades but never obtained citizenship documents, European refugees with Nansen passports[19] (who escaped into Hungary after the German annexation of Czech lands in Austria and elsewhere in Western Europe, and were placed in internment camps), scores of Ukrainians who were considered politically unreliable, and many Jews who were in possession of citizenship papers.[20] Because of a rapid increase in intermarriages in the 1920s and 30s, especially in Budapest, Christian family members were also caught in this dragnet.

The civil administration and military authorities conducted the expulsion with unparalleled cruelty and callousness. It led to a subsequent wave of mass murder, both by Ukrainian paramilitary forces and Nazi extermination squads. The collection, transportation, and haphazard dispersion of more than 20,000 deportees across a wide swath of Galicia was, as the American ambassador had also voiced, lawless and against international conventions. Within half a year, 90 percent of the expellees, sharing the fate of the local Jews, were floating dead on the Dniester River or shot in mass graves—randomly murdered by Ukrainian militias or systematically executed by SS squads who were ably assisted by the Ukrainian police forces and German Order (Reserve) Police Battalions.

WHY GALICIA

It was not a coincidence that Galicia became the dumping ground for a large number of people. Galicia has always been a "contested territory" with a complex web of nationalities, religions, and identities. To use Anne Applebaum's characterization, it was a typical "borderland," where borders were erased and redrawn like pencil lines. It later became a veritable "bloodland." Nazi officials entertained a much darker image. SS-Gruppenführer (Major General) Fritz Katzmann, one of the architects of the Nazi genocide in the region, described it: "Galicia, by virtue of the universally familiar term 'Galician Jew,' was a speck on the surface of the earth best known for its Jews. Here lived, in large compact masses, a world of its own whichever supplied the next generation of world Jewry."[21]

The evolution of Galicia from "borderland" to "bloodland," as Timothy Snyder coined it, is interesting. Somewhat larger than the area of Massachusetts, it was populated by an ethnic mélange of Ukrainians, Poles, and, of course, Jews. At that time, it was a seething cauldron of ethnic, religious, and national enmity. The addition of thousands of Hungarian Jews further inflamed this rivalry. Violence against Jews was not new in this area; it had been part of the political landscape since the dissolution of the Austro-Hungarian Monarchy and presaged the horrors of the 1940s.[22]

The invasion of the Soviet Union by the Wehrmacht changed all this overnight.

The subsequent implementation of genocide in Galicia occurred in three waves, as mass murder engulfed Ukraine and other regions of the Soviet Union, closely adhering to the chronology, ideological premise, and dynamics of the Holocaust. There was a discernible pattern in the radicalization of Nazi policies in genocide. The first wave, corresponding roughly with August and September 1941, ran parallel to the commencement of hostilities and the rapid advancement of the German military. The extermination units closely followed the fighting groups, liaising and coordinating with them on their plans for the extermination in Ukraine. The military, in turn, requested and logistically supported these security forces "to deal with security problems in rear areas." Initially, the methods of killing were haphazard and experimental. These killings were personal—face-to-face. This phase occurred as regional leaders implemented a wave of murders that followed a broad mandate from Berlin, but under the watchful eyes of Himmler. Undoubtedly the largest atrocity, collectively labeled the "Kamenets-Podolsk massacre," gave an "identity" and cognitive association to the cross-border removal of Hungarian Jews. Within a three-day span, August 27–29, 1941, 23,600 victims, among them an estimated 14,000 to 16,000 Hungarians, were shot and dumped into mass graves.[23]

Following the Kamenets-Podolsk massacre, and with the transfer of power from military to civilian administration at the end of the summer, a second wave of extermination by Nazi security services commenced with equal ferocity in southern and eastern Galicia. Disparate killing units, led by mid-level SS officers who relied on a host of law-enforcement agencies, fanned out across the area, slaughtering more than half a million Jews in the last five months of 1941. That included the remnants of the Hungarian expellees. Though not as well known or documented, this signaled the systematic ghettoization in Galicia, which could have been accomplished only by reducing the Jewish population. The murders reached a crescendo in the middle of October when a coordinated decimation of communities occurred. The reduction in the size of the ghettoes through mass shootings wasn't carried out by *Einsatzgruppen* [mobile killing units operating behind the front lines] or the Wehrmacht, but by security officials, along with reserve police battalions, with the enthusiastic cooperation of local German municipal administrations. This stage is best characterized as "community-based" extermination, in which the local Ukrainian auxiliary police assumed a supporting role in the unfolding campaign of murder. In the Nazi plans, the ghetto became inextricably tied to the policy of genocide. This wave swept up the remaining survivors among the deportees. During this second upsurge in murder, the fate of the deportees diverged from the local Jewish communities. The Nazi death sentence hung over both. But the deportees were invariably the first target of extermination.

The third and final wave of extermination, the total annihilation in Galicia, taking with it the last remnants of Hungarian refugees, introduced the concept of the Final Solution—industrialized murder. It was written by the transports to the extermination camp in Belzec in 1942.[24] This was mandated by the decree from the Wannsee Conference in Berlin on January 20, 1942. Although by that time only a fraction of the Hungarian Jews was still alive, they inextricably became an integral part of the Final Solution.

There was a corollary phenomenon in this deportation that has rarely been discussed, yet is equally important. Chapter six describes the wave of rapes and sexual violence, some might use the term "sexualized violence," that accompanied, or rather preceded, the actual killings. This silence in the scholarly literature is partly due to a paucity of testimonies by the *victims* themselves. But equally important factor was the silence by the *perpetrators* about their crimes during the Holocaust. Finally, there was a reticence to open such a painful topic by scholars—mainly men. Indeed, such open discussion about this topic commenced only recently, and mostly by female scholars.

THE HOLOCAUST CONTEXT

There is a wide range of questions connected to the 1941 Hungarian deportation. The most immediate one is how the idea of deporting thousands of people—who were well-integrated into Hungarian society and culture—came about. As noted, the Hungarian military played a crucial role in the collection and deportation of the Jews. Examining Hungarian governmental directives and regional administrative policies sheds further light on motivation and rationale. A corollary question that needs to be addressed is how this deportation fits into a broad historical context. The Hungarian deportation and the ensuing murders in Galicia were instrumental in influencing the Nazi plans for the full extermination of European Jewry. But were they an aberration or a predictable part of a pattern? How did the Hungarian actions during the summer and fall of 1941 influence the evolution of the Final Solution? And if they served as a catalyst that presaged and triggered the Holocaust in Ukraine, what were the consequences and role of the deportation in igniting the fuse?

As noted earlier, the 1941 expulsion is not a completely unexplored chapter of the Hungarian Holocaust. However, neither an in-depth analysis based on personal recollections of the events, nor a comprehensive and interdisciplinary account about the deportation and murders, nor the placement of the event in the context of the unfolding Holocaust been written. Nor have the accounts of survival, rescue, and ultimate responsibility been explored.[25]

This is also a narrative that transcends the narrow confines of Hungarian history. There are several compelling reasons for exploring this story: (1) this deportation and subsequent mass killing introduced quantitative and qualitative "firsts" in the annals of the Holocaust—it was the first instance when the number killed reached five digits; (2) it introduced for the first time a new concept of "total" genocide: men, women, and children were systematically murdered; (3) Hungarian authorities also expelled international refugees who were accorded asylum, in clear contravention of international norms; (4) the massacre in Kamenets-Podolsk, was initiated and directly requested by the German military as a response to the influx of destitute refugees, implicating it fully in the unfolding genocide. The Wehrmacht's cooperation with the SS in implementing genocide reflected the understanding between Heinrich Himmler and the leadership of the Wehrmacht in solving the "Jewish problem"[26]; and (5) finally, the entire expatriation, culminating in bloodbaths of unprecedented magnitude, became almost instantaneously known not only to various Jewish communities in Galicia, but also within Hungary, the British, American, and Soviet governments, and, later, the international press.

There are many sources for exploring this tragedy: trial transcripts, personal narratives of survivors, and recently discovered documents, all of which offer new windows for our understanding. On the ground level, during the deportation of Hungarian Jews, soldiers or forced labor personnel serving in the Royal Hungarian Army were also intimately acquainted with the details of the Galician nightmare. They often met their Jewish neighbors or their own families in Galicia. The indigestible horror of the Holocaust sinks deeper in the human consciousness with a "personalized dimension" to the tragedy. It is natural to want to look at both the victim's and the executioner's points of view. For one glimpse of the tragedy, we have a group of prisoners from the ghetto in Nadwórna forced to return to the site of the massacre eight month later, tasked with piling more dirt over the killing sites that already held their families. Many of the buried were Hungarians. Coming close to the ravine, a ghetto prisoner remembers "we saw a chewed-off hand, pointing towards heaven, stick out of the mass grave ... raised like an accusation against God and men."[27]

The trial proceedings against policemen and SS officers who actively participated in the massacres provide the details of the technical elements that allowed the mass murder to happen. But very little remorse. The "personalized" angle is seen in the image of a soldier with an initial ambivalence in killing Jewish babies, which rapidly escalates into a routine when "by the tenth try I aimed calmly and shot surely at the many women, children, and infants.... Infants flew in great arcs through the air, and we shot them to pieces in the air before they fell into the ditch and water."[28]

This soldier saw the killing of the infants as a sport, a form of target shooting and amusement, rather than an efficient elimination tactic. We know with the clear knowledge that children and babies were routinely thrown into the pits alive. As testimony from those in Rovno illustrate, "they did not shoot the children—they didn't want to waste the bullets—and instead just hurled them live directly into the pit."[29] This can be viewed against the lists of executed Jewish children on the meticulously typewritten reports of the *Einsatzgruppen*.

There were also eyewitnesses. The yellowed and hand-written pages of their testimonies, deposited in archives in the Soviet Union, are valuable. More recently, a witness who was a mere child at the time had to face their childhood trauma in describing the murder site as an "anti-tank ditch freshly filled, that where the Jews were shot. The earth was still moving, it [looks] like it was breathing as if they were not all dead."[30] These are unwitting participants and sometimes victims as well, who provide the connecting filament between the two. Their reports illuminate with a human touch a complex historical reality. The Ukrainians who were forced by the Germans to dig or cover the mass graves in 1941 are also the witnesses who were present at the opening of the same graves in 1944. Standing in front of an open pit in Kamenets-Podolsk, holding the remains of Hungarian Jews in 1944 for whom "there was nobody to cry," a member of the investigative committee saw "the corpse of a little boy, buried alive.... This can be seen by the pose as his little hands were cupping his head, his knees brought up to his chin, his back bent as he tried to lift the weight on top of him."[31] Thanks to these witnesses, we can verify the mind-numbing statistics of the Soviet investigators that during the killing process "35 percent of the victims were shot dead on the spot, 50 percent of the people were injured, and 15 percent were buried alive."[32]

These somewhat impersonal numbers also reflected exiled Hungarians. This, in turn, brings into focus the complex question of what could have been done to stop the deportation and save the remnants. Corollary to that is the thorny issue of primary responsibility. As chapters six and seven chronicle, in some ways rescue and responsibility present two sides of the same story.

The great paradox facing Hungarian history is to explain how the land of "wonderful opportunity" for Jews in the second half of the nineteenth century transformed within several decades into a land that irrevocably banished them, and three years later sent them to the gas chambers. From a judicial vantage point, the Hungarian government became complicit in mass murder by launching the 1941 deportation and the follow-up refusal to repatriate the survivors, Jews, and their Christian family members alike. This was done in spite of the fact that they were privy to information about the genocide taking place in the recently conquered territories. In retrospect, the 1941 deportation stands as a testament to the follies of a dysfunctional political system that pursued short-term political gains by subscribing to a "culturally constructed" perception, a mirage of its own creation, about an internal enemy, the "Galicianer." This mirage distorted historical realities and contravened international norms and laws.

In Hungary proper, save a few voices of conscience and individual attempts at rescue, there was initially an eerie silence. This silence—perhaps disbelief would be a better word for it—was grippingly expressed by Elie Wiesel in the image of Moishe the Beadle who returned from the inferno of Galicia to a wall of silence. The removal of these unfortunate people went smoothly. There were no burning synagogues, no broken storefronts, no looted stores, mass riots, or demonstrations—only disappointed provincial officials who complained that the job was not completed because of the shortage of time for removing the entire Jewish community.

This lack of response rapidly gave way to a concerted momentum to modify or stop altogether the expulsion. The Jewish community, under the leadership of Baroness Edith Weiss, made every effort to intervene, mainly behind the scenes, to limit the scope of deportation first and, afterward, to assist the thousands who were abandoned in Galicia. For some, like Margit Slachta, one of the most respected moral and religious voices of the times, a raised and accusing finger was not enough. She also posed the question of moral responsibility. As early as July 29, 1941, she addressed this issue in a letter sent directly to the wife of the reigning head of state, Miklós Horthy. She minced no words in labeling the deportation as "the defilement of the Christian religion and Hungarian honor." As one of the pivotal figures in the efforts of stopping the removal and rescuing the exiles, her unsparing letter bring into focus Hungary's accountability.[33] She was not alone in questioning the moral and legal underpinning of the deportation. Besides the leaders of the Jewish community, parliamentarians, civic leaders, some members of the aristocratic elite, and, equally significant, the American ambassador Herbert C. Pell also joined in Slachta's efforts to stop the deportation.

Mass murder is not a twentieth-century invention, but, in the Holocaust, it is the tragic hallmark of the century. When viewed against the background of Europe's relatively peaceful period after 1815, the first half of the twentieth century seems like a sharp drop into an unprecedented moral chasm—a descent into apocalyptic violence. Even if we discount the carnage of World War I and the Stalinist purges, we have to contend with an estimated 55 million who died in World War II. The centrality of the Holocaust, with six million Jewish victims within this 55-million-person total, is undisputable. Given the countless atrocities and massacres, as well as the inimitable specter of genocide, the mass deportation of more than 20,000 people in these tumultuous times might seem a minor matter if not for its dire consequences.

The Nuremberg Trials are perhaps the most visible demonstration of holding those that designed, initiated, and perpetrated atrocities accountable. We are all familiar with the main architects of the Holocaust: Hitler, Göring, Goebbels, Himmler, and many others. The newly minted words "genocide," "crimes against humanity," and the "Holocaust" are themselves also a testimony for an emerging awareness that something tragic and extraordinary happened during this war for which routine expressions would not suffice. Intertwined in this new awareness was the issue of responsibility.[34]

Research into the Hungarian Holocaust and the 1941 deportation poses unique challenges. Chapter eight, about the perpetrators of the deportation and their ultimate responsibility, is a needed conclusion for the book, but here we have a recognition problem. After all, the names of those responsible for the Galician deportation, such as László Bárdossy, Henrik Werth, Ámon Pásztóy, Miklós Kozma, and many others, in Hungary are not an immediate informational commodity for the uninitiated—especially outside Hungary. Yet, these Hungarians were as much, or perhaps more, responsible for the early phases of the Hungarian Holocaust as the Nazi murder squads. There was a rather short postwar window through which the Hungarian courts attempted to call upon those responsible for war crimes in general and the 1941 deportation in particular. The Hungarian People's Court, as judicially weak as it might have been, made concerted efforts to address their guilt or innocence. And there were many officers, regional administrators, and government officials who ensured that the vision of these leaders become a bloody reality, but they were never brought to justice.

Finally, we also encounter vocal and sometimes unwitting saviors amid the destruction, who are slowly fading into the mist of history yet coming to life, for a fleeting moment, through the voices of these survivors in the videos. With a full communist takeover of Hungary, ideology and enforced silence limited access to their stories—mostly for political reasons.

In recent years, the investigation of the Holocaust has fostered innovative approaches toward understanding the political as well as individual motivations for mass murder. This book presents a micro-history centered on a pivotal "first": the opening act of the Hungarian Holocaust and its far-reaching consequences for the evolution of the Final Solution. Yet even a micro-study needs a wide canvas: a multiplicity of experiences and motives to accommodate the nuances of the 1941 deportation.

After the fall of communism, this subject remained the domain of a handful of Hungarian historians. Writing history in Eastern Europe, though, can turn into a re-imagining of the past as painted on a black-and-white canvas. Snyder's question is pertinent: "Can truthful historical accounts resist the gravity of politics?" He provides no answer, but the question implies that there is an inherent danger in seeing history as the instrument of the present, in which national histories are, as Applebaum opined, "re-appropriation of history." As is frequently the case in Eastern Europe, everyone feels victimized in some form or another—both on the individual and national levels. This hinders national soul-searching for the crime of expelling thousands of innocent people or becoming complicit in their murder.

This "national soul-searching" becomes even more complicated, because during the waves of extermination in Galicia, Jews were not the only victims and Germans were not the only enemies. The main goal of the Nazi plan was to eradicate Jews. But during the occupation, Ukrainians massacred Poles, Germans massacred Ukrainians and Poles, and Ukrainians massacred Ukrainians.[35] Without overinflating the indigenous anti-Semitism, the Holocaust, including the murder of Hungarian Jews, would not have been as successful or even accomplishable without local assistance.[36] Add to that an uneasy alliance with conflicting priorities among the three invading armies: Germany, Romania, and Hungary.

The psychological and political underpinnings of the deportation, as well as the corollary governmental and military policies, highlight the uneasy alliance between Germany, Romania, and Hungary. There is also the question of how the Hungarian deportation fit into the German design of the Holocaust in Ukraine. This Holocaust was a "remarkably low-tech and non-capital intensive" affair; by the time the death factories of Treblinka, Chelmno, Majdanek, and Auschwitz began to function, more than million and a half Jews had been killed in the occupied territories in the east.[37]

In Snyder's phrase, Auschwitz has the power to blunt the face-to-face "individuality" of the killing during this early period. Holocaust by bullets was raw murder. It took place within communities where neighbors knew neighbors and, often enough, the accomplices were acquainted with the victim. In the process, the whole communal entity became co-opted for murder. A complex interaction of four "players" can be identified: the victim, the executioner, the witness, and, sometimes, the rescuer.[38]

This book is based on extensive archival research, interviews, and corresponding literature across countries and languages, incorporating many hitherto unknown documents that present uncharted territory in Holocaust scholarship. Along the way, readers will hear the voices of the victims who survived the bloodbath, but not the trauma; look at the images of the perpetrators whose motivation for murder is still a riddle; and read the long-forgotten testimonies of contemporaries, not simple bystanders, swept up in the nightmare unwittingly, who recorded the horror in simple words. Built on a historical narrative, the book attempts to share human voices and a history of human feelings. We can weave major and complex stories, but it is the human element that cements them truly together.

After examining the history of the 1941 deportation and the consequent mass murder, the most pertinent question might not be why it happened, but how could it happen in the first place? Historians have written a great deal on the regional implementation of genocide and its links with Nazi policies of extermination. Yet we still know very little about what took place in communities that came under German occupation, especially in Galicia.[39] By expanding our attention from the ominous shadow of the largest mass murder, in Kamenets-Podolsk, to the smaller towns and communities where the deported Hungarian Jews intermingled and lived, the question as to where the Hungarian Jews fit in the policies of the Holocaust finds its answer. This book is guided by the maxim that history contains one kind of truth and human stories another, and that only the combination of the two can create a comprehensive picture and add texture to this tragic historical event.

2

THE *OSTJUDEN*

The Galicianer in the Hungarian Imagination

"...this greedy hatred of the Jews did not burst into flames all at once; its acrid smoke hung over Hungarian life already for decades."[1]

THIS CANDID ASSESSMENT BY SÁNDOR MÁRAI, ONE OF THE MOST ASTUTE observers of the Hungarian social and political scene in the 1930s and 1940s, well sums up the evolution of an image of the hated Galicianer, in the six decades leading up to World War II and the Holocaust. There is an old axiom that in order to be able to exclude socially, to expel, or to exterminate a group of people, a political culture needs to create an image of the "other." While this image might be a caricature, it must convey all the presumed negative features a group has assigned to it.

The creation of such an image was a prerequisite for the 1941 Hungarian deportation to Galicia. Indeed, the idea of an imminent danger to "Hungariandom" by an unchecked wave of Jewish immigration from the East goes back to the middle and second half of the nineteenth century.[2] During the following half century, this notion metamorphosed into the more concrete representation of a hated figure, the Galicianer, who must be expelled from the body of the nation.

The stereotype of the Galicianer is not a Hungarian invention. Indeed, it was a European phenomenon, across the continent. The Swiss philosopher and social observer Denis de Rougemont summed up this well as "the difference between the 'liberal European' type and the 'vulgar arrogant' Jew who, by implication, always emanated from Eastern Europe."[3] *Ostjuden* is a German label attached to such Jews, who tried to escape from the pogroms of Czarist Russia. But this label also applied to the Galicianers—Jews who were searching for economic salvation from the poverty of Galicia, an Austrian province at the time. The alarm over the mass movement of more than two million Jews from an economically and culturally backward corner of Eastern Europe permeated the intellectual body politics on both sides of the Atlantic. The largest wave of emigration from Galicia in the later part of the nineteenth century impacted mostly America. Bernard Wasserstein's quip might hold true that to be called a

"Galitzianer was for long not much of a compliment... [and] denoted folksy backwardness and at times also a petty mercantile mentality and moral shiftiness."[4] However, in Central Europe at the turn of the century, and especially between the two world wars, this perception took a darker and more sinister tone. The quote supporting the chapter heading exemplifies this evolution from exclusion to extermination. It was based on virulent backlash against an alien population movement emanating from the Austrian province of Galicia—its destination Central and Western Europe, and America.

The appearance of the Galicianer in Hungary held a special Hungarian twist that was reflective of the country's retarded social and industrial development. Hungary of the late nineteenth century was in a paradoxical position as it faced the stream of newly arriving Jews from across the Carpathian Mountains. This internal migration, from Austrian-controlled Galicia into Hungary—effectively from one province to the next—was powered by economic opportunism. It was different from other foreign influx at the time. These immigrants, the first Jewish wave from Galicia, willingly and wholeheartedly identified with Hungarian national aspirations, rapidly assimilating to Hungarian culture and language. Conversely, Hungarian society was in dire need of numerical superiority in a multinational empire, as well as a viable and robust middle class. Thus, Jews were a most welcome addition to the mélange of ethnicities in this multiethnic and multilingual country,[5] but while they were obviously needed, the picture was infinitely more complex and paradoxical.

A rift within the fractious Jewish establishment, with palpable interdenominational tensions among the assimilated Neolog (reformed) and more traditional Orthodox Jews, also divided the community. The two main branches of Judaism, and corresponding communal organizations, were established in the late nineteenth century in Hungary along religious lines. Socially, the liberal and modernist Neologs were more inclined toward fully integrating into Hungarian society with less restrictive Jewish worship and intermarriage. They were largely the representative body of urban, assimilated middle- and upper-class Jews. This assimilated segment, from the perspective of cosmopolitan Budapest, viewed with a degree of ambivalence, bordering on disdain, the "backward" Jewish masses in the provinces.

THE AGE OF CONVERGENCE

The relationship of the Hungarian population and the Jews started as an unprecedented success story in the second half of the nineteenth century, based on a common platform of Hungarian and Jewish aspirations. From an economic point of view, the decades preceding the Great War were an especially successful period in which Jews played a critical role. Although the war of independence fought against the Habsburg Empire in

1848–1849, in which the Jewish community fully identified with Hungarian national objectives, was unsuccessful, Hungary became a constitutional monarchy as a result of a comprehensive political accommodation in 1867 between Austria and Hungary. Consequently, the empire was renamed the Austro-Hungarian Monarchy.

In its new form, Hungary could reap the benefit of direct access to Western European culture, industry, and economic development. Jewry became the necessary agent for rapid industrialization, establishment of financial institutions, and educational reform. Along the way, the Jews transmuted into a key economic and cultural force—establishing a viable and strong middle class and a corresponding financial and industrial empire. Due to their high birth rate, which was above the national average, and the steady flow of emigration from the East, the number of Jews in Hungary proper increased exponentially.[6]

Parallel to this Austro-Hungarian "accommodation" in 1867, a corresponding Hungarian-Jewish "compromise," aptly labeled a "renaissance," took place. The Hungarian government granted full emancipation to Jews with corresponding civil and political rights. It recognized them as Hungarians of the Jewish faith. From then on, the word "Jewish" was eliminated from official statistics and government publications.[7] This was followed in 1895 by the "Law of Recepció," which recognized the Jewish religion officially as one of the religions accepted in the state, and accorded rights enjoyed by the Catholic and Protestant churches. The ratification of this law was enacted despite vigorous objection from the Catholic Church. Many of these progressive policies were advanced by the Hungarian aristocratic ruling elite. In conjunction with the liberal spirit of the age, Hungarian politicians understood the crucial role Jews could play in the modernization of Hungary. In a socially, educationally, and economically backward country, which was divided into a thin aristocratic layer and a huge mass of inured peasantry, the role of a viable and functioning middle class was assigned to the Jews.

The ruling circles had a vested interest in granting Jewish emancipation and equality, for a rather practical reason. Because of the apparent demographic imbalance in this multinational empire, where Hungarians constituted less than half of the total population, the Jewish community, numbering close to a million people, became the tipping point for Hungarian domination. By accepting the rapidly expanding Jewish community as Hungarians, the Hungarian population acquired a slight majority, 51.4 percent, at the turn of the century. Again, an economic rationale, combined with national priorities, played a crucial role in this drive for Jewish emancipation.[8]

Because of these farsighted policies, Jews rapidly acquired a leading role in the creation of financial institutions, the establishment of industry, and the setting up of an economic infrastructure for Hungary's agricultural sector. One of the lesser-known contributions of this rapidly assimilating community was their advancement in secondary and higher education. The first generation of Jewish peddlers and traveling salesmen was followed by offspring who gained university degrees in much larger numbers than would be indicated by their percentage in the general population.

The change was dramatic. While their representation in certain fields such as industry, finance, and trade by the end of the nineteenth century was remarkable, their number in the liberal professions was equally impressive. In the first decade of the new century, 45 percent of lawyers, close to 50 percent of doctors, and similar number of journalists belonged to the Jewish faith. Jews were considerably overrepresented in academia as well. Perhaps the best reflection of the quest for assimilation by the well-educated segment of the Jewish establishment was the change in the ratio of Hungarian-speaking Jews within ten years. The proportion of individuals whose mother tongue was Hungarian grew from 63.8 percent to 76.9 percent among those of the Jewish faith. Simultaneously, the percentage of those officially registered as German, but whose mother tongue was, in fact, Yiddish, dropped from 33.0 percent to 21.7 percent.[9]

The assimilation was especially significant among the urban, Neolog Jewry with a strong anchor in Western culture and thought. Reflecting a cultural drive of "Magyarization," many of these same Jews dropped their German family names, adopting Hungarian ones. Conversion to Christianity also gained momentum. As a sign of full assimilation, those who changed their religion could pursue careers in public administration as well as in the military.[10] Numerous Jews directing industrial companies and financial institutions were awarded nobility for their contribution to Hungary. Intertwined with this wave of conversion, intermarriages with the nobility, especially by the Jewish "financial aristocracy" and industry leaders, also became prevalent.

On the other hand, members of the Orthodox and Hasidic Jewish communities, living mainly in the northern and eastern parts of the country, insisted on their distinctive clothing and customs. They interacted with the surrounding population mainly in business or official matters. They retained Yiddish as their spoken language within the family and religious institutions. The observation of Eleanor Perényi, the daughter of an American diplomat who married into one of the leading families of local nobility in Carpathian Ruthenia in the late 1930s, is instructive regarding the social situation of the Jews. Although they were the ultimate middle class in Carpathian Ruthenia, "the Jews were isolated in the community, partly from discrimination, but partly, too, because they kept their character so strongly."[11] Yet the same observer also noted that these "Jews were pro-Hungarian," and even these socially and culturally isolated Jewish communities maintained a staunchly nationalistic orientation. They communicated in Hungarian in public discourse and enrolled their children in Hungarian schools in much higher numbers than did their non-Hungarian neighbors.

Not everyone viewed these developments as positive or welcome. By the later years of the nineteenth century, rapid modernization and corresponding economic prosperity could not hide a simmering social tension within society. These tensions were partly due to rapid industrialization and a correspondingly lopsided distribution in the workforce that was based on religious affiliation. This social phenomenon was not particularly Hungarian, for it was noticeable across Central and Western Europe, yet the rapidly deepening division between the robust Jewish and fledgling Christian middle classes in Hungary was much more concrete and visible.

As social observers of the Hungarian scene opined, a collision course, if not an open conflict, between the two middle classes was only a matter of time. At the turn of the century, the Catholic People's Party became the main proponent of anti-Semitism. Its rationale for anti-Jewish sentiments was based on the notion that Jews were the promoters of anti-Christian and destructive ideas embedded in liberalism and socialism. Jewish intellectuals and their allegedly harmful influence were a particular target for unrestricted attack. Those in aristocratic circles, who intermarried in growing numbers with the Jewish upper bourgeois, glossed over these emerging fault lines—partly for the national economic interest and partly because of the Jewish community's wholehearted identification with Hungarian national aspirations. Nevertheless, this emerging division and simmering resentment carried the seeds of a potential social conflict, rapidly evolving into a racial conflict, which came into full force during and after World War I.

CRACKS IN THE EDIFICE: CREATING THE IMAGE OF THE "OTHER"

While there were pockets in the periphery where religious and Yiddish life was more entrenched, those emigrants who settled in Hungary during the second half of the nineteenth century had become well integrated into Hungarian society by the outbreak of the war. Thus, the subsequent appearance of the Eastern Jew with the traditional kaftan, sidelock, and beard, mainly in the margin of the country but also in the capital, was not a sign welcomed either by the well-to-do Jewish establishment or by the escalating voices of anti-Semitic circles. By the outbreak of the war, anti-Semitic sentiments became more vocal and organized, but the animosity toward the Easterners came into full force during the war years because of a second wave of Galicianers, a steady influx of legitimate war refugees from Galicia and later Transylvania. Thus, the concern that these newcomers were "conquering the country," reinforced repeatedly by anti-Semitic intellectuals, exploded during and after World War I. By the late 1930s, this idea evolved into a permanent subject within the general political discourse.

In reality, Jewry in Hungary was never a uniform or united community—either religiously or socioeconomically. It was composed of three large groups, divided by history, economy, and culture. The Jews of the northwestern districts (Oberland), of Austrian and Moravian origin, spoke German or a western dialect of Yiddish; the Jews of the northeastern districts (Unterland), mostly of Galician origin, spoke an eastern dialect of Yiddish; and of the Jews of central Hungary, the overwhelming majority spoke Hungarian. This last group settled in this region as early as the seventeenth century.

The bulk of the Galicianers arrived in Hungary at the end of the nineteenth century, as a first wave, settling down mainly in the northeastern and eastern provinces of the country.[12] The Jews of Old Hungary were less religious and more assimilated. Equally important was the socioeconomic demarcation between the two groups. While the rich Jewish bourgeois and middle class were concentrated in Budapest and other major towns, a large segment of Jews, and especially the Galicianers, led their lives mostly along religious lines in the provinces. These could be identified, an observer noted in 1942, as "mostly proletarian small Jews in their masses." This was the area where Jews engaged in agriculture, plus, there was a narrower but "economically more elevated stratum above them: the group of innkeepers, tenants and salesmen."[13]

Thus, an intercommunal rift within the Jewish establishment was based both on the socioeconomic level and religious orientation, and was also evident in the territorial distribution of Hungarian Jewry. Jews living in bigger towns mostly belonged to the reformist trend, or Neolog branch of Judaism. They made concerted efforts to assimilate and integrate fully into Hungarian society. However, on the periphery, orthodox communities, intermingled with various Hasidic "dynasties," were much more traditional in observing religious tenets and constituted the majority.

A marked resentment by those assimilated Jewish communities with a Western cultural orientation against these already existed in the nineteenth century, but it was a European problem, not a particularly Hungarian one. The socially integrated Jews felt a sense of embarrassment about their backward coreligionists; they also felt threatened by looming competition from these newcomers. Gustav Landauer summed up this concern about the impact of Eastern Jewish immigration on the already-assimilated community: "their own assimilation has not stabilized enough yet, so that another influx [of Jews] would be warranted."[14] Although he was speaking specifically about the situation in the German culture sphere, it could be applied equally to the well-established and well-integrated Hungarian Jewish establishment. As was the case in the neighboring countries, the ambivalence and insecurity on the part of the well-assimilated and culturally integrated Jews toward their East European coreligionists reflected a marked unease about Hungarian society's perception of the Jews in general. The stereotypes that Hungarian Jews themselves created about East European Jews reflected their own evolving self-perception and conflicting national identity. Just as in Germany, the Hungarian Jewish resentment of the *Ostjuden* reflected the insecurity of a group that had only recently gained membership in the national community.[15]

This Jewish insecurity was fueled and reinforced by politically charged anti-Semitism that emerged in the last decades of the nineteenth century. Societal division, as the Dreyfus Affair[16] elicited in France, could not arise in Hungary. Nevertheless, it was at this time that the first cracks began to appear in harmonious coexistence, which gradually turned into deep faults by 1918. Instead of framing or limiting anti-Semitism as a purely political discourse, as was the case in France and Germany, in Hungary it assumed more national-religious and economic overtones.

This concentrated on multiple fronts, targeting Jewish domination in the economic and cultural sphere by political and social movements. The Jews became scapegoats because "they filled the positions which the gentry considered beneath their rank." Moreover, since they formed the engine of capitalist development, it was easy to assign all the faults of capitalism to them.[17]

As a newly evolving political philosophy, anti-Semitism revolved around the social teachings of the church. As it was noted, anti-Semitic individuals belonging to the Catholic People's Party, founded in 1894, were especially active. Young priests, among others, formulated their critique of the existing political and economic system, the evils and vices of which they assigned mostly to the Jews. The leading ideologue of this movement was Ottokár Prohászka, a theologian and Catholic bishop, who would become one of the intellectual leaders of Hungary after World War I. He cogently framed this philosophy in 1893: "the Jewish immorality, the lack of conscience, the distorted spiritual values, which has only perverted notions of what is good, beautiful, and moral ... sees Christians as the enemy." Elsewhere, he openly noted, "We do not perceive anti-Semitism as a racial or religious reaction, but as a social, business-related one." Thus, in his criticism of the Jews, he counterposed capitalism, in which utility and profit-making are the goals, with Christian values.[18]

Prohászka's views became progressively radicalized during and after the war, but individuals from clerical circles were not alone in decrying Jewish influence in industry, finance, and the free professions. They were joined by a small but influential group of intellectuals who called themselves "civil radicals." In the name of "progress," they became vocal critics of the liberal capitalist system from the opposite direction of the clerics, considering it conservative, nationalist, and oppressive. In an inherent contradiction, these intellectual circles attacked the Jewish "bourgeoisie" with special venom because they saw this broad group as exemplifying "liberal capitalism" and its support of the "ruling feudal class."

The fact that this intellectual cadre included Jews like Oszkár Jászi, a firebrand with a Jewish background, is an interesting twist of Jewish and Hungarian history. Jászi wrote in 1912 that "It is without exaggeration to state that the power of Jewish usury—whose representatives we should be looking for not only in village saloons, but especially and mostly in the big and prestigious banks of Budapest—had never been so overwhelming in the country; the most fanatic followers of István Tisza [the prime minister] should be looked for not only in the financially ruined members of the country gentry, but also among the Jews craving for honours and nobility."[19] By 1917, Jászi's views and those of his followers became radicalized to the extent that he could assign all societal ills that encompassed "usury," "unfair competition," "internationalism and cosmopolitanism," "financial capitalism," and "cultural liberalism," or "coffee-house culture" to Jews.[20]

This political philosophy, coming from a respected clergyman, reflected a reality in which the traditional negative image of the Jew of "blood libels" underwent a process of "secularization" by becoming a figure responsible for all negative aspects of modernity. The complexity of these arguments was compounded by a desire to differentiate between the Galicianers and the assimilated community. The radical personalities around Jászi made this distinction between the two groups by claiming that those who fully embraced Hungarian culture should not "be considered parasites," while those who adhered to "their ancient ways" represent the true "parasites."[21] There were clear differences with obviously discordant views within these philosophical circles. Nevertheless, the emerging voices of discontent remained on the intellectual and sometimes the parliamentary level, without exerting discernible influence on the public discourse.

Nonetheless, the questions about the authenticity of the "Hungarianness" of the Jews, which was composed of diverse groups and still on its way to full assimilation, was challenged, again and again. This is the period, in the early years of the 1910s, when the full-blown figure of the Galicianer enters the Hungarian national consciousness. The relationship of Jews and non-Jews was still harmonious, but the fragility of their coexistence was increasingly evident. A major and extraordinary catastrophe was needed to launch the dissemination and institutionalization of anti-Semitism and its prime representation in the figure of the Galicianer. This catastrophe was World War I.

A CONVENIENT SCAPEGOAT: GOOD JEWS AND BAD JEWS

Historians have often proposed that just as World War I gave revolutionaries their chance, it also spawned the seeds of counterrevolutions that led, in turn, to World War II. As an unmitigated disaster for the Austro-Hungarian Monarchy, the defeat in World War I signaled a watershed moment in Hungarian–Jewish relations. At the conclusion of the hostilities, Hungary was on its knees, impacted by rampant inflation and poverty, coupled by the trauma of the collapse of greater Hungary.

The defeat precipitated three corollary national traumas in which Jews were placed in the center. First, the radical right—intellectuals and parliamentarians—jointly tried to justify the hardship at home and the defeats on the battlefields by creating a mythical yet insidious internal enemy, the Jews. Just as in Germany, "the stab-in-the-back" myth was a convenient explanation. The second consequence was equally traumatic when the war was followed in Hungary by a short-lived but brutal experiment with a communist dictatorship. It was conveniently labeled the Red Terror, in which Jews played a significant role. Finally, this was followed by a counterrevolution, the White Terror. It exacted a bloody revenge in which Jews, as the assumed fomenters of the Red Terror, became the primary victims.

However, the ultimate and most dramatic consequence of the war was the dismemberment of the country by the Treaty of Trianon. The treaty was the peace agreement signed in 1920 to formally end World War I between the Allies and Hungary, the latter being one of the successor states to the monarchy. Robert Gerwarth noted the whiplash effect that the treaty had on the defeated Hungary. It regulated the status of an independent Hungarian state and defined its borders. It left Hungary with only 28 percent of the territory that had constituted the prewar Kingdom of Hungary. Its population was 7.6 million, only 36 percent of the prewar kingdom's population of 20.9 million. One of the most unfortunate side effects of this treaty was an introspective search for a scapegoat by a tired and dispirited country.[22]

British author Antony Julius captured the essence of anti-Semitism, and the parallel creation of a scapegoat, when he defined it as "a way imagining Jews, a pernicious, elaborate fiction, and not just a series of theorem about the Jewish people."[23] During the war, leaders of Hungarian Jewry forcefully showcased Jewish patriotism and full identification with the Hungarian nation. The Jewish press, led by the premier news organ of the community (*Equality*), made every effort to reassure the public that Jews, along with Catholics and Protestants, were in a common front against the hated Czarist Russia and its virulent anti-Semitism. Fiery editorials showcased news about Czarist atrocities by the advancing Russian troops in parallel with Hungarian Jewish heroism on the battlefield. The leaders of the community wanted to preempt any accusation that the Jews were trying to evade military service, and that when they were sent to the front, they were bad soldiers.

By the second year of the war, however, the hopes for a rapid victory evaporated and the economic burden of the conflict increasingly impacted Hungarian society. Mirroring a deep-seated frustration and resentment, public life became a breeding ground for unsubstantiated rumors and open allegations. These revolved around Jewish financial, commercial, and industrial domination, in parallel with their political influence, which gave them unfettered access to military contracts as primary suppliers of the army. The charge of war profiteering from these contracts, coupled with a growing shortage of commodities and money supply, became a catchword not only for radical intellectual circles, as it was before the war, but across the political spectrum and the public at large. Perhaps the most often repeated accusation was that Jews shirked military service, or if they were drafted, they benefited from clerical assignments far from the dangers of the front line.[24]

The level and toxicity of the polemics increased exponentially as the war dragged on. The persuasive assessment of Péter Bihari that by "1916–1918, the Jewish Question penetrated every pore of Hungarian society" well describes the atmosphere of the later war years.[25] But, perhaps the most toxic element within these charges was the appearance of the second wave of refugees flooding Budapest, directly from Galicia, starting in 1914. These were the authentic Galicianers in language, attire, and religious orthodoxy. At first, the presence of the bearded masses with sidelocks and kaftans in Budapest sparked more curiosity than enmity; it presented to cosmopolitan Budapest an interesting spectacle. From late autumn 1914, however, accusations began to emerge, without distinguishing between the rich or the homeless Jews among them, about their increased burden to society. Their appearance reinforced the old, negative images of trading and peddling Jews, or in the common parlance the "Khazars," a term that rapidly became interchangeable with "Galicianers." Correspondingly, the Khazar was depicted as an alien creature, "with shifty eyes red beard, and alien costume."[26] A Hungarian historian's comment that the "appearance of these refugees in Hungary made a disastrous impact" is an apt description of the contemporary public perception.[27] If a Jewish refugee was poor, he was called a "parasite," and if he was rich, he was labeled a "usurer." When inflation spiraled out of control, Galician Jews became "profiteers," and later they were blamed for the shortage of commodities.

Because of Russian victories at the outset of hostilities, Jewish masses occupying both Galicia and Bukovina fled across the Carpathian Mountains. They were Austrian citizens, so many of them were able to reach Vienna, Moravia, Bohemia, and Hungary. While accurate estimates are hard to find, contemporary reports placed the number of Galician refugees in Hungary in the autumn of 1914 at around 15,000 to 25,000 people.[28] In the hope of a rapid victory in the war, Hungarian Jewish organizations extended support to the new arrivals. Yet, the already assimilated community viewed them with some derision and condescension. There was a real concern that these Galicianers—in their torn clothes and with their strange, "backward," and "superstitious" lifestyle—would be associated with the well-integrated and cosmopolitan Jews of Budapest. This concern was somewhat justified, for these newcomers became the tangible incarnation of an image that lurked in the recesses of the Hungarian imagination even before the military conflict. Besides their outward appearance, these people did not speak Hungarian, they did not identify with Hungarian national aspirations, and they did not serve in the armed forces.

While Austria refused to underwrite the support of the refugees trapped in Hungary, and the Hungarian government did not consider it their problem, a temporary resettlement was implemented. The government called upon the refugees of

Austrian nationality, not all of them Jewish, to report to designated collection points from which special trains transported them to Czech territory in Moravia in the second half of April 1915. Although the transports reduced the number of emigrants in the Hungarian capital, this action did not solve the issue of the Galician war refugees, for many of them preferred to remain legally in the country. These were escapees who had found a job in Hungary when the country struggled with labor shortages during the war. Two additional groups could also stay in Hungary legitimately: wealthy refugees who did not depend on others' financial support, and rabbis and teachers who were supported by the Jewish community of Pest after the state benefit was no longer provided.

This resettlement of refugees had a calming effect, however temporary, on the public discourse in 1915. However, the polemics were reignited as a consequence of a renewed Russian military campaign, the Brusilov Offensive, and the Romanian invasion in Transylvania a year later, when a new wave of refugees, both Jews and non-Jews, streamed across the Carpathian Mountains from Galicia and Transylvania.[29] This new flare-up had far-reaching consequences not only for the new refugees themselves, but also for the original emigrants from the nineteenth century and their descendants. An evolution took hold of the public imagination as an increasing number of people became labeled as Galicianers, linking the notion of the usurer and profiteer not only with the newly arrived refugees, but also with those whose ancestors had arrived from the East in the nineteenth century. By that time, thousands of them had been born in Hungary, becoming respected citizens and productive members of the middle class. Thus, the idea of a continuous "Galician influx" became the central theme of Eastern European and Hungarian anti-Semitism.

While in the first two years of the war the intellectual conversation concentrated on "kaftan-wearing profiteers," as the military tide turned against Austria and Hungary, the public debate also lurched toward more ominous tones in which a general "Jewish Question" emerged. The influx of the Galicianers became a component in this newly framed and expanded blame game for the military reverses and the economic hardship on the home front. Before the war, racist anti-Semitism was confined to the fringe of radical politics. By the third year of the armed conflict, however, it had entered into the mainstream. Parliamentary debates became increasingly contentious and vitriolic, with Jews described as "profiteers," "wheeler-dealers," and "shirkers."[30] The daily press reflected this trend with articles that expanded the issue of the Galicianers within the context of the overall "Jewish Question."

By 1917, the contours of a differentiation between "good Jews" and "bad Jews" emerged in which the former signified the culturally assimilated true "Hungarian" Jews, while the latter were the traditional (i.e., Orthodox or Hasidic) Jews. The specter of a failed process of assimilation due to the recurrent waves of immigrants from Galicia and, to a lesser extent, from Bukovina, consumed the public imagination. A riveting book, aptly titled and published in 1917 queried leading intellectuals and clerics about their views pertaining to the question. The majority, among them Jászi, spoke of deep pessimism about the potential of integration of the Jewish masses, the Galicianers, into the mainstream. One respondent squarely placed the problem in economic focus by suggesting that "the incarnation of the capitalist worldview is also Jewish." The majority implied that the assimilated segment had been overwhelmed by the influx of the eastern elements. A political commentator went as far as claiming that there were good Jews, bad Jews [the Galicianers], and a third group, which conformed outwardly to Christian values practiced in Hungary and Europe. This is the first time that a clear delineation emerged between the Galicianers as a race and the assimilated segment as a religion.[31]

Another influential thinker and law professor from Nagyvárad (Oradea, Romania), Péter Ágoston, interjected an additional element into this intellectual debate by assigning guilt for "dual loyalty" on the part of the assimilated community, since they supported their coreligionists against the interests of the Hungarian nation. As an antidote, he proposed "sealing the borders against immigration and expulsion of alien Jews from the country."[32] That this clamor for expulsion reached Parliament should not come as a surprise. Several representatives openly advocated that while the war was raging, "they can still be expelled on the basis of an extraordinary legislation and perhaps such a new act can be submitted to the Parliament." Otherwise, this unassimilable multitude "will lead to both social and national catastrophe."[33]

To the credit of the governmental authorities, they made every effort to contain anti-Semitic agitation, both in Parliament and on the streets. From genuine concern that such agitation would be divisive in the face of the military threat, the long-serving prime minister István Tisza called for national unity by forcefully denouncing anti-Jewish voices during the debates in Parliament. His main concern was that racial exploitation of religious divisions during the war could impact society's cohesion. Simultaneously, he banned newspapers that promoted the anti-Semitic agenda.

In spite of such injunctions, though, the "Jewish Question" became a central topic of discussion in the mainstream media. The Catholic press represented the media's preoccupation with this topic in declaring that the "Jewish Question has become one of the most pivotal problems and central challenge for the future of Hungary."[34] We can quote again Prohászka's words in declaring that "As we are getting closer to the front lines, the more numerous are the Christians while the Jews are remaining far back in the hinterland. The Christians are sacrificed while the Jews are saving their hides for the future benefits of Hungarian culture."[35]

While the regular citizenry vociferously questioned the Jewish commitment to the war, the rampant corruption, and the presence of the Galicianers in Hungary, the government of Tisza and subsequent premiers appointed several Jewish politicians to high-level governmental positions. The significance of these appointments cannot be understated, for it served as a psychological reaffirmation of their acceptance, integration, and assimilation at a time when the loyalty of the Jews and their belonging to the Hungarian nation was increasingly questioned.[36]

Successive governments followed in Tisza's footsteps in decrying anti-Semitism, yet they reminded the Jewish community not to express solidarity or extend support to the emigrants. A month before the military collapse, Sándor Wekerle, one of the last prime ministers, informed Parliament that the "repatriation of the Galicianers is under way, within the confines of the law."[37] These cautiously formulated words aimed to assuage the concerns of the representatives. Parallel with this announcement, though, raids by law enforcement agencies were launched across the country, and especially in northern Transylvania and Carpathian Ruthenia, for ferreting out and identifying Galicianers. These raids did not spare even towns close to the Hungarian capital. Contrary to the promise of the prime minister of adherence to the legal code, the raids were accompanied by beatings, abuse, and plunder.[38] This dramatic change in the atmosphere toward the Jews in the summer and fall of 1918 accurately reflected a change in popular public sentiment on the street level.

As the war reached its final moments, frustrated people in the heartland and the masses of returning soldiers from the front needed an explanation for the military defeat. The Jews, and specifically the Galicianers, became the convenient scapegoats. The liberal era, which had started with the Austro-Hungarian Compromise of 1867, and which can be characterized as a mutually beneficial partnership between Hungary's ruling elite and its Jewish minority, came to an inglorious end. Perhaps the most cogent argument from this era belongs to a contemporary witness who dryly observed that "When the Jew-haters talk or write about Galicianers, they do not just mean those few hundreds of Galician refugees who are stuck here, but in fact the children and grandchildren of yesterday's Galicianers, i.e. the entire Jewish community of Hungary as it is, fathers and sons included."[39]

The conclusion of World War I created a complex and troubled world. The consequent treaties, as Kershaw pointedly noted, were "to reward support for the Entente [the winning powers] during the war and to punish the vanquished enemies."[40] Perhaps no country lost as much territory and population as Hungary. While 72 percent of its territory was transferred to newly created states, more than three million Hungarians ended up in the newly created Czechoslovakia, Yugoslavia, and Romania. Among these Hungarians, there were more than three hundred thousand Jews.

A country does not necessarily need an ethnic or religious scapegoat to explain national misfortunes, but it sure helps. Like all nations losing a war, Hungary needed to find an explanation. Just like Germany, where Hitler honed to perfection an excuse for German defeat, Hungary identified the Jews as the main culprit for the loss. But the accusation started much earlier, as the year that followed the end of the war was a tumultuous one in the newly independent Hungarian Republic. It declared independence on November 16, 1918, severing its partnership with the Habsburg royal house.

However, there were no major celebrations and no corresponding declarations. A political vacuum became palpable. The new regime was beset by labor unrest, a disorganized mass of frustrated, dissatisfied soldiers returning from the battlefields, a dispirited middle class, and, more importantly, a rapidly shrinking country. While the government, under the leadership of a liberal aristocrat Count Mihály Károlyi, implemented reforms, the loss of the major industrial base around the outlying provinces, as a consequence of dismemberment of the country by the winning powers, robbed Hungary of its economic vitality and power.[41]

Károlyi faced an unwinnable situation in holding together a country teetering on economic collapse. Beyond the economic despair, the psychological trauma of losing large swaths of the country paralyzed society. His short-lived and ineffectual government, cobbled together with the participation of social democrats and civil radicals, could not cope with the challenges both from within and without.

Abandoned by the victorious powers, the ability to govern slipped rapidly out of Károlyi's grasp toward the radical left, which seized the opportunity to assume full control on March 21, 1919, establishing the Hungarian Soviet Republic. The small but well-organized communist party, under the leadership of Béla Kun, instituted a sweeping restructuring of Hungarian society. This included the purging of aristocrats, bankers, factory owners, and even small businessmen, commonly labeled as the "exploiters of the people." The Jews, being the middle and upper middle class, were the most affected in the corresponding nationalization drive. Concomitantly with the expropriation of wealth, the new regime instituted a reign of fear, hence the moniker "Red Terror," aimed at the "class enemies" of the people. This "Red Terror" was often identified in the following decades as "Jewish Terror." Conversely, the label "bourgeois" was also equated with being Jewish.

The Jewish presence in both the Károlyi government and in the upper ranks of the communist dictatorship was conspicuous. It was especially overwhelming in the latter. These Jews represented the new political elite, which came from the ranks of social democrats and other politically left-oriented movements. In the ranks of the social democrats, the highly educated Jewish intellectuals were in the majority. In both cases, though, these leaders had left the fold of the Jewish religion or community either through conversion or by subscribing to communist ideology. Kun's admission that although he was born Jewish, he rapidly converted to being a "socialist and communist," was an apt description for the entire leadership. Not surprisingly, almost all these leaders, divorced from their Jewish roots, bore Hungarian family names. Conversely, very few came, as it was later falsely touted by right-wing circles, from "Galicianer" background.[42] In fact, communist elite troops, the Red Guards, followed the order of the People's Commissar for the removal of thousands of Galician Jews to Poland.[43] Although the communist revolution was short-lived, it stamped its mark on a cross section of society. The Red Terror did not differentiate between a Hungarian aristocrat, a Jewish industrialist, or a small shopkeeper.[44] Their wealth was confiscated, and they were indiscriminately persecuted or sometimes executed.

The first Hungarian proletarian dictatorship was finally toppled by the victorious alliance (Triple Entente) via the intervention of Romanian troops. The National Army, gathered in the southern town of Szeged and led by Miklós Horthy, a naval admiral in World War I, launched a parallel attack with the aim to clear the country of communist forces. Realizing the failure of the communist experiment, on August 1, Kun resigned and fled the country along with several other communist leaders.[45]

Within six month, after consolidating his grip on a territorially truncated, dispirited, and economically devastated country, Horthy was elected officially as "Regent of the Kingdom of Hungary" by Parliament on March 1, 1920. His condition of almost absolute power was granted by this legislative body; however, the emergence of Horthy as the de facto leader of Hungary did not stop a wave of murderous retribution, commonly branded as the "White Terror," which swept through the country. The indiscriminate extrajudicial killings by paramilitary units, loosely aligned but outside the control of the national army, and atrocities perpetrated by them, dwarfed anything the Red Terror had inflicted during its three-month siege. The torture and killings encompassed a cross section of society, from communist party functionaries to shopkeepers, and from lawyers to major landowners. Now "Jew" and "communist" became interchangeable, exacting a horrendous toll on the Jewish community.[46]

These atrocities did not escape the attention of the victorious powers, which dispatched a military delegation to investigate this wholesale slaughter. They also caught the attention of the ruling circles around Horthy, which demanded stability and a focus on reconstruction. Finally, by 1921, the situation in Hungary calmed down enough to implement a "national conservative" government that provided political stability during the interwar years by rejecting political extremes of both the left and the right. It identified itself as Christian, mainly based on the doctrine of the Roman Catholic Church. Its national mission was to rectify the injustice of the Treaty of Trianon by territorial revision. How much the new regime practiced the "Christian values" that it vocally professed during the interwar years is an open question, for often the term "Christian" simply meant "non-Jewish."

Attempts to rebuild the country were hindered by the loss of major industries and a population base with corresponding markets located in the lost provinces. The added influx of hundreds of thousand refugees from these territories, mainly from the ranks of aristocracy, county administrators, and the professional class, tested the capacity of the country to absorb these new arrivals. It also hindered the ability of the country's leading elite to restart the economy as well as introduce badly needed social reforms. In addition to the burden of caring for the Hungarian victims of the war—invalids, orphans, and widows—the state had to tend to the needs of the refugees streaming across the borders.

One of the rallying points in this national emergency was finding and assigning blame for this turn of events. While anti-Semitic sentiments could have had palliative psychological effects as they provided an immediate explanation, they could not, in the long run, resolve the complex demographic and economic malaise facing Hungarian society. It was a political balancing act. However anti-Semitic the political leadership may have been or seemed to be during the interwar years, it had to reconcile itself to the notion that the Jewish community was crucial for the reconstruction of a badly fractured country. Valdemar Langlet, a Swedish observer of Hungary during the 1930s, provided a candid yet unsparing picture in which aristocrats controlled the reins of power by privilege, while Jews, many of them converts, held the industrial and financial power by hard work. He also quoted a rather sobering statistics that "85 percent of the vast estates which were left to Hungary after the Peace Treaty [Trianon] now belong to Jews," and, conversely, these estates "yield both better crops and larger income than when they were in the Magnates' [aristocrats'] hands." He was rather surprised and gratified by the assessment of a Hungarian aristocrat who, "anti-Semite himself, nevertheless maintained that Hungary could not exist without Jews . . . they are a necessary evil and their commercial talents are an indispensable factor of the life of the country. They may be [an] ulcer on society, but the ulcer cannot be removed without endangering the patient's life."[47]

Thus, Hungarian society had to reconcile itself with recognition that while a "Jewish Question" might not be immediately solvable, it could be managed. The solution that emerged immediately after the ruins of World War I, reflecting the intellectual trends during the war, was to divide the community into "good" and "bad" Jews. It should not come as a surprise that the "good" Jews comprised the bankers, landowners, and industrialists, while the "bad" Jews were those in the provinces who remained religious. During his American lecture tour in 1921, Count Pál Teleki, who served as prime minister in several governments, reassured his audience that he was not against "the Jewish religion or Jews." Rather, his animus was anti-Galicianer. He addressed this by drawing an unmistakably sharp line between the assimilated Jews and the Galicianers: "It is much more a question of immigration, and antagonism towards a certain group of foreigners who turned against the nation. . . . Bolshevism in Hungary was led and directed by these foreigners. Of course, there were Jews of older Hungarian origin, just as there were Hungarians taking part in the Bolshevist movement, but the hatred of the people was aroused by the Galicianers."[48]

This ideological line, coming directly from one of the leading Hungarian politicians of the interwar years, reflected and permeated the intellectual fabric of the governing elite across the political spectrum. It conveyed the notion that assimilation as a social and psychological experiment had stalled, if not outright failed, and those who succeeded in conforming to Hungarian culture and political aspirations remained in the minority. The "eastern Jews," those who emigrated from Galicia to the border region, the Galicianers, constituted the majority. They remained unassimilable and therefore needed to be excised, sooner or later, from the body of the nation.

Equally ominous, this ideology signified a shifting political discourse from religiously communal toward a racial definition of a large segment of the Jewish community. This racial definition, coupled with a notion of failed assimilation, emerged most clearly, again, in the influential voice of Bishop Ottokár Prohászka in the early years of the 1920s. For him there could not have been a differentiation between the old and new Jews; the assimilation of the established Jewish community was superficial and not sincere, and emotionally unrelated to the Hungarian state and society. Thus, they remained a foreign entity: "How can we assimilate and mix together the alien Jew with the Hungarian while erasing the anthropological and racial differences? [The Jew] was alien and remains alien. He spoke Hungarian, but he was feeling Jewish. He lived in Hungary but stuck in his Jewish existence. They created a community within the community."[49]

For Prohászka there was no compromise Teleki, a savvy politician and an avowed "anglophile," differed in that he harbored a large degree of class-based anti-Semitism. However, as a pragmatist, he understood that economic realities of contemporary Hungary dictated political expediencies when the country was in dire need of the wealthy segment of the Jewish community—many of them with a title of nobility, intermarried with the aristocracy, and in control of the banking system as well as industrial production. He, and a whole cadre of politicians during the 1920s and 1930s, proscribed to this notion of duality within the Jewish community. While Horthy openly professed himself an anti-Semite in 1920, he recognized the value of the Jewish contribution to Hungary by the 1930s: "the Jews contributed singlehandedly more to the economy of Hungary than all the people on the extreme right combined."[50]

Consequently, an irreparable schism developed within Hungarian society and within the Jewish community, which divided Hungarian Jewry not only along lines of religious orthodoxy, but also along educational and economic lines. The assimilated segment was made up of moderately religious, if not already converted, highly educated Jews representing middle- and upper-class values. They were factory owners and bank executives whose elimination would have imperiled the economic foundation of the Hungarian state. The other group, the Galicianers, included those who presumably had failed to identify with Hungarian nationalist objectives. The allegation that during the revolutions of 1918–1919 the Jews were behind the communist dictatorship and temporarily seized political and economic power was tempered by assigning the blame exclusively to the Galicianers. One of the leading figures in Hungarian politics during the 1920s, considered a moderate at the time, summed up this perception in a parliamentary speech: "The respect that we feel toward the old and patriotic Jewry cannot stop us stating that the first and second-generation immigrant Galician Jews brought to us a proletarian dictatorship."[51]

Contemporary scholarly and popular literature was not immune to this fixation. One of the most venerated Hungarian historians between the two world wars, Gyula Szekfű's views are especially representative. Writing in the mid 1930s, he openly placed the blame on the doorstep of Hungarian Jewry for their failed assimilation and, consequently, for the communist dictatorship. In his view, the influx of the Galicianers subverted not only the assimilation process, but drove a wedge between Hungarians and assimilated Hungarian Jews who "held out their hands to their racial relatives in the name of brotherhood ... and letting their love for their kind flow freely, they surrendered themselves and their higher culture to the strangers flooding in."[52] The subtext of dual loyalty, as well as the betrayal of Hungarian and European Christian culture along the way, is intimated in his pronouncements. The question as to how much his work influenced public perception, or how much it reflected it, is a moot point. In the Hungary of the 1930s, the Galicianer issue became more and more the political hobbyhorse not only of the extreme right, but also of the general public.[53]

Simultaneously, the collective designation for the Galicianers became more flexible. Based on political pragmatism, it was inflated in subsequent decades from those who directly arrived from Galicia in 1914, to those whose ancestors originated from the east and their descendants. Thus, second- or even third-generation Hungarians were lumped into this category. Finally, the term encompassed almost everyone from the provinces, even those who might have lived in an area for many decades and professed full identification with Hungarian nationalist sentiments, but clung tenaciously to their religious or folk way of life.

The trappings of a functional parliamentary system could not slow the emergence of a virulent form of anti-Semitism both in the parliamentary debates and in the public discourse. During deliberations in the Hungarian Parliament in the 1920s, the distinctions became more and more blurred between Jews who had arrived after 1914—the "real Galicianers"—and those who had lived there for a long time, but who, in the opinion of the ruling circles, had not sufficiently assimilated into the Hungarian population. In public life, this term evolved to encompass every Jew whose Hungarian affiliation was questioned. This attitude was also reflected by the fact that right-wing parliamentarians deliberately inflated the number of "eastern" Jews to an almost absurd extent.[54]

Statistical data contradicted the claim for a large Galician influx. Yet, even a scientifically based counterargument could not change minds. Leading statistician Alajos

Kovács, who could not be accused with philo-Semitism, provided one in 1922. He stated that emigration from Hungary prior to World War I dramatically outpaced immigration from the East. His assessment was revisited almost a century later by Walter Pietsch, who reconfirmed Kovács' findings.[55]

Recent regional studies place the number of eastern Jews who settled in Hungary or continued to other destinations between 60,000 and 70,000. However, many of these emigrants viewed Hungary and Austria as transit stations to their final destination, which was America. By some estimates, America absorbed more than two million Jews from Eastern Europe between 1881 and 1920, which included a quarter of a million from Galicia alone. Eastern Jews ending up in Western Europe also accounted for around 300,000.[56]

THE LEGISLATION OF HATE

The ruling circles understood the negative economic ramifications of the "Jewish Question." Nevertheless, the radicalization of the political discourse after the war demanded anti-Jewish action. Count István Bethlen, a long-serving prime minister in the interwar years, staunchly believed that mindless anti-Semitism would be contrary to the interest of the country. He was perhaps the most eloquent in expressing the division in Hungarian society toward the Jewish community. On December 17, 1925, at the Parliament he stated: "Those Jews who identify themselves with Hungarians . . . I consider as Hungarians. . . . On the other hand, I also have to say that there are some Jews in this country who have declared themselves a separate race by not adopting the interests of this nation in the past or present."[57] Not surprisingly, Bethlen considered the Galicianers among the latter: a separate race, and not a religious entity. Thus, the Galicianer, eastern Jew, or "alien" Jew, as was used interchangeably, continued to preoccupy the Hungarian public as economically harmful, politically subversive, and culturally unassimilable.

The failure of Jewish assimilation was especially emphasized. During a parliamentary debate, a representative expounded on the difference between the Jewish and German communities in Hungary by postulating that "Jewry is Hungarian-speaking but in mentality foreign, the German minority (Swabians) is foreign-speaking, but in spirit Hungarian."[58] As early as this dictum, it was recognized that a safety valve that could neutralize growing societal and economic pressures—especially among the younger Christian segment of society that had little prospect for advancement—had to be found.

To defuse the explosive situation within the country, the leadership, coming from the ranks of old-style aristocrats with a strong anchor in the prewar parliamentary system, opted for a change through legislative means. With the influx of officials from the detached territories, an "over-production" of the educated class was the most immediate concern. Thus, the change that seemed the least disruptive economically and most expedient politically was to target the issue of an educational imbalance that tilted toward the Jews in higher education. Voices during the war had already addressed this educational disparity between Jews and Christians. Again, Bishop Prohászka's intellectual influence was decisive. His was not the only voice to claim that while Christian university students heroically fought on the battlefield, Jews flocked to the universities to occupy the empty benches. His thinking aligned well with the nationalist-intellectual undercurrents that advocated the granting of preference to Christian youth who would reclaim Hungarian culture and economic vitality from Jewish domination. Perhaps not coincidentally, the universities were a hotbed of Hungarian nationalism and anti-Jewish movements, where Jewish students were exposed to taunting and beating. The premier student association was the Ébredő Magyarok Egyesülete (Association of Awakening Hungarians)—its flyer openly "declared war on the Jewish race."[59]

The implementation of anti-Jewish policies started with a legislative action on July 22, 1920, when the Hungarian Parliament began to debate Act XXV. The law passed with a great majority. The "*numerus clausus*," as it became commonly known, did not mention Jews. By declaring, though, that "the proportion of members of the various ethnic and national groups in the total number of students should amount to the proportion of such ethnic and national groups in the total population," the act clearly targeted Jewish students, because it effectively adjusted their enrollment to their percentage in the general population, which was 6 percent.[60]

While the law could not reduce the endemic unemployment among the Christian intelligentsia and professional classes, it served as a psychological panacea for the government and the new political elite.[61] The initiative was the brainchild of Count Pál Teleki, prime minister at the time. While he was cautious not to present it officially as anti-Galicianer legislation, his view about a "struggle for life and death" between "Christian Hungarians" and "Eastern Jews" did not leave much to one's imagination. The significance lay in the fact that it gave the government an opportunity to limit access to certain religious-racial groups out of political considerations and expediencies. Thus, this law had an important role in presaging future anti-Semitic legislative actions, also the hallmark of Count Teleki, in the late 1930s, and the singling out of a specific group for deportation.[62]

Almost parallel with the "*numerus clausus*," and perhaps not coincidentally, laws were promulgated for the internment and expulsion of individuals who were viewed as a rather loosely defined threat to national security and economic prosperity. The two decrees that were enacted in succession in 1920 were broad in scope, without mentioning the Galicianers.

The first decree singled out Jews who fled to Hungary during and after the war. Subsequently, this hunt expanded to Jews on the eastern periphery of the truncated Hungary who had been living in the country for a long time. The rationale was wrapped in wide-ranging legalistic language indicating "dubious nationality," "subverting the economic interest of Hungary," and "posing danger to national security."[63] A subsequent decree (20,000/1920) was more specific in that it ordered the internment and expulsion of foreigners and, among them, those persons belonging "to the Jewish race" who had arrived in Hungary after January 1, 1914.[64] This national paranoia extended to the political leadership, who believed that the influx of Jews fomented a general unrest that swept over the country in the early 1930s.

Corresponding with these parliamentary actions and interminable discussions about the Jews who "invaded" Hungary from the east, practical actions for ferreting out such undesirables were launched across Hungary by law enforcement agencies. Their mandate was to identify persons without proper residence permits as well as thwart illegal immigration from the east. Throughout this decade, periodic sweeps by police and the gendarmerie ranged from outright arrests to summons to police stations for a review of citizenship status. The target of these raids included houses of worship, public markets, and schools, and encompassed not only purported Galicianers, but also veterans of the Great War.

The number of foreigners detained in these raids hovered around 1,000—which may testify to the fact that a major influx of foreigners into Hungary was nonexistent during the interwar years. Decree 20,000/1920 was more symbolic, a theoretical proposition rather than practical solution, because deportation of foreigners was not an option. While in 1919 there was a sizeable resettlement of Jews of foreign nationality from Hungary to Poland, by the 1920s neighboring countries refused to accept refugees.[65]

THE ROAD TO GALICIA

The second half of the 1930s ushered in a sequence of interconnected political developments that dramatically changed the Hungarian national discourse regarding Jewry and Galicianers. The political upheaval that changed Europe dramatically, if not the world as a whole, was the emergence of Nazi Germany as the dominant power in Central and Eastern Europe. One of the immediate impacts of the ascending Nazi regime was the ideological reinforcement of radical right-wing movements across the continent.[66] On the practical level, though, it also precipitated a demographic disaster, with thousands of refugees attempting to find safe haven. Hungary became one of their prime destinations. With its growing military might, Germany also assumed a prominent role as a power broker in the regional rivalries of Central and Eastern European countries. With the support of Germany, Hungary benefited the most from the redrawing of the borders and reannexing some of the territories lost after the war. Finally, the German example of dealing with its own Jewish population also provided a blueprint for the countries of the region as a solution for their own "Jewish Question."[67]

These developments coincided with a changing political climate in Hungary, which transitioned from reflecting by and large the aristocratic elite to representing the middle and upper classes. While the government toned down its attacks toward assimilated Jewry, the venom toward the Galicianers increased. The views of Gyula Gömbös, who served as prime minister between 1932 and 1936, and who is credited with the trend toward fascism in Hungary in the interwar period, is instructive of this evolution. In 1925 he openly labeled the segment of Jews as subversive "whose father had come here from Galicia or who has come from Galicia himself."[68] In his inaugural address as premier before the Parliament in 1932, he softened his tone, declaring "that part of the Jewish community which acknowledges a common fate with the nation, I wish to consider my brethren just as much as my Hungarian brethren. I saw some Jewish heroes during the war.... I know prominent Jewish men who pray as I do for the destiny of Hungarians." Then, with a twist, he condemned "that part of the Jewish population which does not want to or is not able to integrate into the national social community."[69] As to what to do with this segment of the population, he did not shy away from advocating for the repatriation of the Galicianers.

Gömbös died in 1936. Already during his premiership, the influence of Nazi Germany as the dominant ideological model for the countries in Central Europe dramatically changed the political landscape of the region. Central Europe saw the rise of radical right-wing racial politics. In Hungary, the national discourse about Jews in general and this dangerous minority of "alien" Jews among them turned shriller and more uncompromising. Just like across Europe, the image of the "alien" in Hungary evolved from national-religious discourse toward the politics of race. One only needs to look at the words of the head of the Hungarian Reformed Church, Bishop László Ravasz, during the deliberations for the impending First Jewish Law in 1938: "Judaism is not a religion.... Judaism is a race, with strong racial characteristics which prevent assimilation."[70]

This ominous evolution can be attributed equally to the political changes taking place in Central Europe at the time, and to the political radicalization within Hungary itself. Thus, the motivation and preoccupation with the "alien Jews" came from outside and from within Hungary itself. Again, Nazi Germany's ideological influence cannot be denied. However, its racist policies on the practical level also had an immediate effect on neighboring countries. After Hitler's ascendance to power in 1933, Germany became the dominant factor in the refugee crisis engulfing Europe. Its discriminatory policies had immediate effects in precipitating a continent-wide exodus of Jews from

Germany proper first, soon to be followed by Jews from Austria, the Czech protectorate, Slovakia, and even France and the Netherlands. Many of these so-called stateless Jews attempted to find asylum in Hungary. This influx from the West did not escape the attention of the radical right in Parliament, which conveniently labelled these Western refugees as "the new Galicianers who want to settle down in Hungary."[71]

Perhaps the weightiest factor in this national obsession with the "Jewish problem," as a prime minister at the time termed it, was the increase in the number of Jews within the newly drawn borders of Hungary. The reannexation of some of the lost territories in the later years of the 1930s, and the corresponding increase in the total number of Jews, provided a convenient excuse for anti-Jewish legislation.

In successive political and military steps, Hungary regained control over provinces in Upper Hungary, Carpathian Ruthenia, northern Transylvania, and, finally, the southern tier of the country. While reconstituting the historical boundaries of Hungary added sizeable Slavic, Romanian, and Serbian minorities in the millions, Hungarian policymakers saw the most vexing issue to be the addition of a sizeable number of Jews residing in these regions. These Jews considered themselves staunch Hungarian patriots, yet carried the stigma of being political aliens and economically harmful. Though still only 6 percent of the general population, the government exploited this numerical increase in the Jewish population in pushing through their legislative agenda.[72]

Concurrently with these demographic developments, we can see an ideological shift in the government toward the far right of the Hungarian political spectrum. This development was partly due to the efforts by the ruling circles to outflank the radical right, which was guided by Nazi ideology toward the Jews by adopting in milder form of their political goals. The ruling class also believed that some of the new anti-Jewish policies, cloaked in anti-Galicianer rhetoric, were necessary to mollify the Christian middle class. By the late 1930s, the overwhelming majority of the Hungarian political elite, along with the popular voice, wished for and even demanded an economic and cultural realignment toward Christian Hungary.

While no perceptible pressure by Nazi Germany was in evidence, it would be a mistake to discard its ideological imprint. It provided a model for the consequent introduction of three anti-Jewish legislations for purging Jews from the free professions, restricting their role in culture, and reducing their control and numbers in the economic and financial sphere. This legislative process started in the spring of 1938 and lasted until 1941.[73] Within these three years, legislation evolved from a relatively mild realignment of Hungarian economy and property laws into a strict adherence to the numerical percentage of Jews in Hungarian society in the distribution of jobs and ownership.

This process was accompanied by a fateful evolution of the community from a religious entity to a racial one. The first Jewish law did not deal with this division. The second one, however, followed the German model in clearly defining Jewishness based on parents and grandparents.[74] Finally, by 1941, the Third Jewish Law culminated in the adoption of the Nazi definition of race defilement, which governed even private life and employment between Christians and Jews. As in 1920, the year the legislation was introduced, the fingerprints of Teleki could be seen in drafting and introducing for parliamentary approval all three of these legislative actions. The justification for these anti-Jewish measures, commonly labeled as the "Jewish Laws," harkened back to the "insidious influence" of the Galicianers.

Echoes of the Galicianer image ran through the parliamentary debates, or rather, the one-sided justification for this legislative process. The minister of religion and education launched the first salvo: "Jews ... live a separate, peculiar life, with a separate, peculiar ideology; and they are considered as aliens by the Hungarians."[75] What is notable in his speech is how much this statement dispenses with a nuanced approach toward the "good Jew" and the "bad Jew." In his second term as prime minister, Teleki's role in promoting anti-Jewish policies overshadowed all the other politicians. His preoccupation with "foreign Jews," as noted earlier, was exacerbated by the addition of 330,000 Jews in the newly acquired territories between 1938–1941. This was especially true of the annexation of Carpathian Ruthenia, where the percentage of Jews came close to that of the local Hungarians, around 15 percent, in the general population prior to 1941.[76] The uniqueness of the region also manifested itself in the large number of Jews who were engaged in agriculture—the largest percentage in Europe.

In addition, the major cities were overwhelmingly Jewish. The fact that the proportion of religiously conservative "easterners" increased significantly within the Jewish population was exploited for justifying these laws. Indeed, one of Teleki's main arguments for limiting Jewish influence was that the addition of so many Eastern Jews overwhelmed the thinly spread assimilated segment, rendering the assimilation process a failure.

As the prime minister, he did not need special inducement for his anti-Jewish feelings or rhetoric. One historian depicted him as "a deep-rooted anti-Semite, the most unaccommodating anti-Jewish politician of the period."[77] Yet, he was a savvy politician, who belonged to the ruling aristocratic families in the Hungarian Parliament. He was also regarded as a leading intellectual, one who believed in racial determinism.

Unfortunately, his views were not beyond the mainstream, since a large segment of the aristocracy and the leadership subscribed to similar precepts. His race theory was not based on the Nazi model of anti-Semitism. As one of the preeminent historians of the period opined, while "he was determined to curtail Jewish dominance in Hungarian life, he had no intention of exterminating them."[78] He openly challenged Hungarian Jews who "must choose between Hungary and their co-religionists, who are foreign to us and infiltrated into the country."[79] With this, he repeated the charge of dual loyalty for the assimilated Jewry. More importantly, in his justification for the Second Jewish

Law, he made no differentiation between the established community and "the Eastern Jews, an oriental race, which due to its long history of isolation is more different and more unassimilable than any other kind. We have treated them with western democratic principles. That is the Hungarian problem that needs to be solved."[80]

One of the unfortunate by-products of the emphasis on collective guilt and responsibility for the "sins" of the "Galicianer" Jews, perceived or real, was a split within the Jewish community itself. The Jewish leaders in the provinces blamed the emotional and intellectual disconnect with the more assimilated community concentrated mainly in Budapest and major population centers in the provinces. There was an unstated sense that the leadership in Budapest did not represent the needs and interests of the more traditional Jews in the newly incorporated territories. As for the assimilated Jews, instead of seeing through the subterfuge of crafty politicians like Teleki, they turned against the Eastern Jews. We cannot find a more poignant example of this rift than the fiery speech by Dr. Lajos Láng, a noted Jewish financier, during a heated parliamentary debate in the upper chamber of the Parliament on the further economic restrictions for Hungarian Jews seen in the Second Jewish Law. Representing the assimilated segment of Hungarian Jewry, he rejected the planned anti-Jewish legislation by stating that "it stigmatizes us, who have resided in this country for the past three hundred years, speak Hungarian, think Hungarian, and have nothing in common with the so-called eastern—caftan-wearing Jews."[81]

Regrettably, he did not understand, or did not want to understand, that according to these laws, the economic marginalization of the Jewish community affected all persons equally and that the onus on the Galicianers was only an excuse. As a consequence, more than 200,000 people lost their employment all across the Jewish community. The law especially impacted the Jews in the outlying regions. Not surprisingly, when the Jewish laws were submitted by the government and discussed in the House of Representatives, no distinction emerged between the assimilated Jews and the Galicianers. The message was that these anti-Jewish legislative actions were made necessary because the eastern influx in the nineteenth and early twentieth centuries that blocked the assimilation process of Jews who had been living in Hungary for centuries.

The prime minister invoked an even weightier accusation, which was directed toward the established Jewish community—the grave sin of dual loyalty: "No doubt Hungary has had a Jewish community which has lived here for centuries.... The rootlessness of these masses... and the fact that the Jews who have lived here for a long time ... felt a stronger sense of affiliation with these newcomers than with the non-Jewish population of the country."[82]

These statements only reinforced a sense of dilution of the Hungarian identity among the established community by the influx of thousands of Jews, who were considered, for all practical purposes, stateless easterners. In justifying the anti-Semitic measures, a minister in the government placed the burden for the Galicianers' sins on the established Jewish community: "The earlier ones [Jews] tried to adjust themselves to the public spirit, but the newcomers live separated, thus Hungarians regard them as aliens.... Therefore, those Jews who have been living here for long also have a vested interest in solving this question. For that is the only way to assure a peaceful coexistence and the quelling of the anti-Semitic atmosphere now prevalent all over Europe."[83]

There was an urgent need for implementing a comprehensive policy of managing and regulating these two parallel problems: the steady stream of Jewish refugees from the West and a parallel but more substantial "Galicianer problem" in Hungary itself. From policy formulation to practical solutions, the road was short. The most immediate question remained how to handle the influx of refugees from the west. Many of these international refugees viewed Hungary as a way station to future destinations. Consequently, these refugees from the Nazi-controlled territories were conveniently funneled into a series of internment camps. A more long-range and much larger problem for the Hungarian leadership was the addition of the more than 300,000 Jews from the reannexed territories. It had to find a regulatory agency that could ferret out these two loosely interconnected issues.

To regulate immigration, promulgate citizenship policies, and monitor alien residents, an administrative unit within the Ministry of Interior was established in 1930: National Central Alien Control Office (Külföldieket Ellenőrző Országos Központi Hatóság, abbreviated KEOKH).[84] Modeled after the Swiss immigration agency, Fremden Büro, the unit mainly concentrated its activities in Budapest, with some provincial outposts around the country. By the later years of the decade, it evolved from a gray regulatory agency within the Ministry of Interior to a dreaded institution, arbiter of the fate of thousands of people.

The office reported directly to the minister of interior. As an alien control agency, its personnel viewed anyone who could not present their citizenship papers or attempted to enter the country, even via legitimate means, with open suspicion. The office also had the authority to launch police raids for suspected populations. The appalling violence accompanying these raids against suspected Eastern Jews presaged the horrors of the 1941 Galician deportation.

COUNTING DOWN AND FINDING THE RIGHT OPPORTUNITY

The succession of three Jewish laws and various other regulations unleashed a process that, by defining the community in racial terms, inevitably led to and sped up the momentum for the 1941 deportation. During the enactment of the Second Jewish Law, the issue of the Galicianers became a lever against the Jewish community as a racial entity. It intractably connected the fate of large numbers of Jews, some of them possibly Galician in origin, with those who had already settled in Hungary for several generations and lived in perfectly legitimate conditions.

The stipulations of the second Jewish law in regard to the annulment of naturalization indicated that the establishment of citizenship was becoming a subject of political considerations. It was accompanied by calls for a review of the citizenship of all "Galician" Jews as well as a call for "those tribal Jews who should emigrate from the country in the first place because they do not identify themselves with Hungarians either in language, taste or culture."[85] Perhaps the most uncompromising view about the prevailing political sentiments in the Hungarian Parliament was voiced by one of the radical conservative deputies who advocated for a cessation of efforts to assimilate the Jewish community because they are unassimilable and, rather, "expel it to the last person."[86]

The issue of citizenship thus became a legal tool for removal from the country when an opportunity presented itself, which generated a deep concern in the Jewish community. Pieter Judson noted that during the Austro-Hungarian monarchy, a sense of nationality or citizenship was not necessarily strong or well-defined in the population, and served more as a political umbrella than an official designation.[87] After the conclusion of World War I, a large segment of the minority population, and especially the Jews in the successor states, defined themselves as Hungarians. But assimilated or traditional, Hungarian Jews believed that being born in a multinational Austro-Hungarian monarchy automatically granted protection before the law.

The Jewish response to the successive anti-Jewish decrees—which limited options for citizenship—and to the economic difficulties that resulted from the Jewish Laws, was setting up two organizations. The Hungarian-Jewish Assistance Committee (Magyar Izraeliták Pártfogó Irodája, abbreviated MIPI) handled issues relating to the status of refugees streaming into the country from newly occupied German territories, as well as the citizenship issues of Jews from the successive territorial expansions of Hungary itself. The humanitarian-economic cost resulting from the anti-Jewish legislation of the late 1930s, mainly impacting the lower socioeconomic strata of the community, was addressed by the Hungarian-Jewish National Aid Action (Országos Magyar Zsidó Segitő Akció, abbreviated OMZSA). These quintessential self-help institutions were unique in that they were able to unite and represent a bitterly fragmented, fractious Jewish community along economic, demographic, as well as theological lines. One of the preeminent historians of this subject well summed up MIPI's significance in uniting Hungarian Jewry: "MIPI was of fundamental importance not only in the invaluable aid it provided but to the internal history of Hungarian Jewry."[88]

With the emergence of Nazi Germany and an escalating refugee crisis across Europe, the rapidly shifting national borders in the waning years of the 1930s and the parallel problem of citizenship became an all-European issue. Arbitrary reclassification of Jews as non-citizens by the tens of thousands happened almost simultaneously in Romania, Slovakia, and Poland.[89] In Hungary, KEOKH became the gatekeeper and final arbiter of thousands of people who got swept up in its dragnet, as it ferreted out "alien" Jews and "stateless" refugees arriving from various countries. Because these countries ceased to exist as sovereign states, the refugees had no clear citizenship status, which implied that there was no legal recourse to repatriate them to their "home" countries.

Moreover, individuals who sought refuge from Nazi persecutions in Hungary had little chance to be granted international refugee status. While this designation was mandated by the League of Nations, and was also ratified by Hungary, it was conveniently ignored by the authorities. This wave of refugees from Nazi Germany and its rapidly expanding empire—Austria, Czechoslovakia, and Yugoslavia—ranges from 8,000 to 10,000 men, women, and children, who were shunted into internment camps across Hungary.

The only exception to this policy were Polish military units and civilians streaming over the northern border after the defeat of Poland by Nazi Germany and the Soviet Union. All other nationalities wanting to enter Hungary, even with legal documents, were viewed with suspicion if not outright hostility. Thanks to Hungary's traditional ties with Poland and an aristocracy that intermarried with Polish nobility, an estimated 100,000 Jews and Christians were welcomed with open arms. Perhaps the key factor in accepting and ultimately saving several thousand Polish Jews along the way was that these refugees "were removed from the KEOKH's scope of authority between 1939 and 1945."[90]

A much more encompassing concern for the government was the dramatic increase in the number of Jews as a consequence of territorial revisions in which Hungary was the largest beneficiary, with corresponding reformulation of its demographic composition. While some of its neighbors lost Jewish population, Hungary doubled the number of Jews residing there. Thus, the two critical elements in the citizenship question, and a visceral concern of the ruling political elite in Hungary, were this increase in the number of Jews residing within the newly redrawn borders, and the continuous arrival of Jewish refugees from the west and neighboring states. One of the leading politicians of the era summed up this new reality in stark terms by suggesting that the Jewish community was a "life threat" for Hungary. In a political speech, he claimed that "with the incorporation of the new territories, the proportion of the Jews changed for the worse. ... Therefore, we need to reassess also our views in this matter."[91] This reassessment led to tragic consequences. There was no territory or country to which this population could be transferred. The citizenship status of a large segment of Hungarian Jewry, especially in the upper provinces, northern Transylvania, and Carpathian Ruthenia remained at best tenuous.

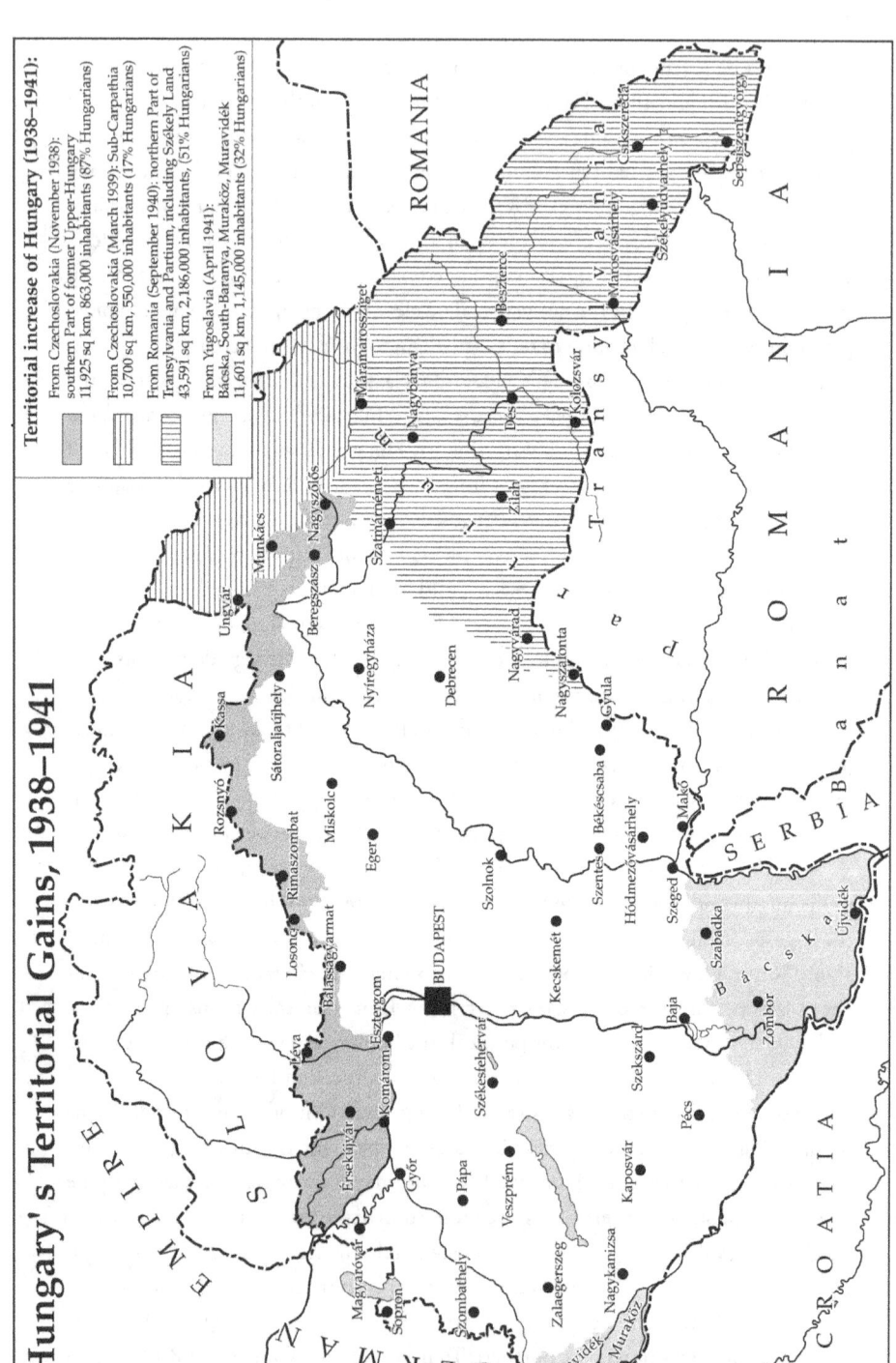

Fig 2.1 Hungary's territorial gains, 1938–1941.

Such practices were mini-rehearsals for future cross-border removals that would encompass a much larger population. A blatant example of such removal was reported by the American Jewish Joint Distribution Committee (JDC), on November 8, 1938, to its headquarters in New York. It concerned the arbitrary expulsion of thousands of people, mostly Jews, across the Hungarian border by Slovakian authorities as a consequence of the territorial revision between the two countries. As the report noted, paramilitary forces "seized Jewish citizens, who were mostly from the ceded border districts, placed them in trucks, which were requisitioned for this purpose ... and took them at night across the new border, where they were dumped in open fields or forests." It estimated that between 8,000 to 10,000 Jews ended up in no-man's-land. Such expulsions from a border region precipitated a tit-for-tat response from the neighbor. Most often, Jews bore the brunt of these reciprocal expulsions. The Hungarian response was predictable: it transferred 3,000 Jews to Slovakian territory.[96]

Less than two years later, attempts to transfer Jews from Hungary to Romania and the Soviet Union encompassed scores of people. Thanks to Margit Slachta's tireless efforts in exposing and halting the deportation, these action attracted more attention, including that of the Ministry of Interior, the Ministry of Defense, and the Parliament. These initiatives of local military commanders centered around the Transylvanian town of Csikszereda (Miercurea Ciuc in Romanian), which made repeated attempts to transfer local Jews to neighboring countries. Romania rejected this influx, repatriating the Jews to the no-man's-land where they languished for several days during the bitter winter. Those who were dumped across the Soviet border disappeared without a trace—perhaps transported to the Gulag. These ad hoc attempts, without any coordination by the respective ministries and the foreign countries involved, continued sporadically until 1942. Based on a flurry of directives from Ámon Pásztóy, the head of KEOKH, the involvement of this department in these initiatives, actively or tacitly, is beyond doubt.[97]

While the number of expellees in this case was relatively small, these cross-border removals were eerily similar to and bore the hallmark of the much more comprehensive deportation to Galicia in the summer of 1941. This group included a few individuals who might have lacked full citizenship, but the majority possessed proper papers, or were born and lived in this region all their lives, going back several generations. The authorities cynically demanded special payment, labeled "community service," which was a form of extortion, and then deported these Jews nonetheless. Highly decorated veterans from World War I also were bundled in the group. Authorities gave half an hour to prepare, with the Jews allowed to bring a limited supply of personal belongings. Many families included only women and children, because the fathers and sons were serving in the Hungarian military.

The main players in this drama were the same ones who a year later impacted, positively or negatively, the deportation to Galicia. Ámon Pásztóy, as the head of KEOKH, fully endorsed these steps, and Miklós Kozma, as the government commissioner of Carpathian Ruthenia, acquiesced to them. A follow-up investigative report by Arisztid Meskó, who, as the police commissioner of Carpathian Ruthenia became the main planner of the 1941 deportation from this region, whitewashed the whole affair. Finally, Slachta, who later became instrumental in saving Jews in 1941 and during the main phase of the Hungarian Holocaust in 1944, became one of the lone voices to alert the country's leadership about the travesty taking place in northern Transylvania.[98]

These loosely coordinated early attempts to forcibly remove people in the middle of winter, and without due process, might be considered as isolated initiatives by overzealous local commanders. On the other hand, we cannot discard the likelihood that they did not take place in an intellectual or a political vacuum. If one can draw some conclusion from this and other reports about cross-border population transfers, they might be predictive of future deportations to come. They were crude, inefficient, and almost bumbling undertakings. In any case, neighboring countries refused to cooperate. However, they foreshadowed the potential of removing a population when and where the opportunity presents itself.

Thus, the 1941 expulsion of over 20,000 people was a predictable event. A report by JDC in early 1940 estimated that 2,800 foreign nationals and 10,000 refugees resided in Hungary. The report expressed concerns about the Hungarian authorities' "demand that these Jews should leave urgently the country.... The Hungarian authorities insist further on removing the so-called illegal refugees, who entered Hungary without passport or visa."[99] It concluded that it would be only a matter of time when this will happen. This opportunity came much faster than the policymakers in Budapest and the provinces could have foreseen.

By 1941, a vocal chorus clamoring for expulsion emanated not only from the fringes of the political right, but also from a civil administration, the military, and ministers in the government itself, especially from the chief of staff and the minister of defense. The main impediment was the lack of identifiable countries or a designated territory where authorities could dump their unwanted Jews. Although negotiations were initiated in 1939 and 1940 with Romania and the Soviet Union "for the admission of Jews of Galician origin," the two countries adamantly refused.[100] Yet unceasing pressure by a wide segment of Hungarian society demanded the removal. This was especially true in the provinces where the "unassimilable" Jews resided. Not coincidentally, in these areas the Jews were also dominant in the economy.[101]

From the point of view of the ruling elite in the provinces, connecting racism and economic opportunism was both natural and went hand-in-hand with getting rid of a loathed minority. The demand for expulsion reached an especially high pitch in

Carpathian Ruthenia, where Kozma openly complained to the prime minister about the constant pressure and open intrigues against him from local circles. Not surprisingly, he had to address the issue of the Galicianers head-on, which he did repeatedly. As a member of the political elite who maintained contacts with civilian and military leaders, and had direct access to the leader of Hungary, Miklos Horthy, his views were an accurate barometer of the prevailing intellectual winds within the Hungarian political power structure. We can see in his pronouncements an evolution to the solution of the problem of the Galicianers.

During the early stages of his tenure as government commissioner, in a speech in the fall of 1940, he declared his intention to adhere to existing laws, which didn't stipulate expulsion. In October of the same year, though, he recognized that the only solution for the local Jewish Question was removal.[102] By early 1941, he wrote that "I would be very happy to relocate them somewhere, but for the time being it is not possible."[103] In a speech in May of the same year, he admitted that there were no immediate remedies for the Jewish Question. "So, what can we do?" he said. "Sending them to reservations, introducing ruthless regulations such as throwing them into the river, and so on, is not a possibility. As long as they are here, we can, of course, implement very strict and comprehensive policies of controlling them . . . either way, they are here and will remain here. And as long as they are here, this question cannot be solved. . . . Ultimately and substantially, the Jewish Question at this moment cannot be solved, but it can be held in check until the end of the war provides a solution to this issue."[104]

This prophetic last sentence, in which the looming war provided a context for expulsion, might not have been as innocent as it seems. This pronouncement can be placed less than two months before the Nazi attack against the Soviet Union, and two months before the start of the deportation. Based on dispatches from the Hungarian embassy in Berlin that placed the start of the war in mid-June, Kozma might have been privy to information that the outbreak of the war was imminent. The Hungarian emissary to Berlin, Döme Sztójay, relayed back to Budapest the information, quoting German military sources, that that the chances of the breakout of a German-Soviet war were growing. In his report from June 3, he wrote that "the launching of the German military operation is to be expected by the middle of this month [June]."[105]

Germany's intentions of attacking the Soviet Union were not a well-guarded secret in Berlin. The American military attaché, along with his counterparts in various embassies, were aware of the preparations for the impending attack against the Soviet Union and openly talked about them. Consequently, the Hungarian general staff and Lieutenant General Henrik Werth, as the chief of staff, were also aware of these plans. Following Germany's attack on the Soviet Union on June 22, 1941, and Hungary's declaration of war on the side of Nazi Germany five days later, this opportunity, finally, materialized. A large swath of territory across the Carpathian Mountains in eastern and southern Galicia came under Hungarian control, and Hungarian governmental and military circles wasted no time in utilizing this chance for the expulsion of thousands of Jews.

A fateful transformation took hold of Hungary. The image of the Galicianer suddenly metamorphosed into a living thing; it became a tangible target. Within two weeks from the outset of hostilities, and with alarming efficiency, the cattle cars started to roll and disgorge their human cargo by the thousands on the train platform of the small, nondescript town of Kőrösmező, high up in the Carpathian Mountains, on the Hungarian and Soviet border. Incarcerated in a transit camp in Havasalja, several kilometers from the town, the Jews were transported from there by the Hungarian military, fifty trucks a day, across the border to a mysterious land named Galicia, a place where neither history nor geography forms a boundary.

3

GALICIA

An Exile into the Unknown

"Everything that one might have considered once unthinkable, there it happened to us."

SITTING IN THE LIVING ROOM OF LÁSZLÓ ZOBEL, A SURVIVOR OF THE 1941 deportation, these few carefully chosen words in well-balanced, soft cadences sum up his two-months of wandering with his mother in Galicia. Betrayal, endless trudging, hunger, murder, and salvation from an unexpected source led him to ponder these experiences and lessons for a lifetime. I have seen already the video of his testimony, along with those of other surviving witnesses to the carnage in Galicia, before meeting him in Budapest. As in the video, he repeated this sentence again, slowly, as to give additonal weight to his words.

Belying his age, a centenarian, tall, erect, with a mane of white hair and sparkling, intelligent eyes, his story was told in sparse prose, hiding a barely disguised bitterness. With a razor-sharp memory, he recalled precise dates, times, locations, and names. But, reclining on the sofa with crossed arms, he refused to employ superlatives. And, while he chose his words carefully, the word *gazság* was repeated again and again.

This quintessental Hungarian word connotes equally depravity, villainy, and wickedness, aimed perhaps to convey the feeling of betrayal by seemingly irrational governmental policies that led to the deportation, the chaotic, borderline criminal conduct of the Hungarian military that implemented it, the plunder of the defenseless deportees by the accompanying gendarmes, and the local gentile janitor in Budapest who promptly informed the police upon Zobel's escape from Galicia, leading to his incarceration in an internment camp. He did not neglect to place some responsibility on the Jewish communal leaders who initially acquiesced to the deportation, and who later refused to fully believe in his story. His words conveyed more disappointment than rancor or anger. Yet, he repeatedly used this word, *gazság*, for he carried a deep wound that time couldn't heal, even after seventy-eight years.

Although he endured a harrowing two-month-long, aimless wandering in Galicia, interspersed with Ukrainian atrocities and abuse by Hungarian military personnel, Zobel was one of the fortunate ones to return and tell his story. His journey, though, is not unique, but rather emblematic. He, like the many thousands of his fellow deportees, went through a process that started with labels for creating the image of the Galicianer. In turn, this process evolved into legal exclusion, dehumanization, and, for many, death by bullets.

First, Zobel lost his job in 1938 as a consequence of the First Jewish Law. Although he used a Hungarian passport when he traveled in Europe, that was followed by the revocation of his citizenship. Overnight, he became a stateless person and was forced to report regularly to the offices of KEOKH. Finally, he was arrested during a routine identity check on August 5, 1941. The next day the inevitable happened; he was shipped, together with his mother—whose citizenship papers were in order—to the transit camp in Kőrösmező and consequently to Galicia. He remembers this day well—August 11, 1941.[1] Coincidentally, it was three days after the ministerial order that was deliberately ignored by the commander of the transit camp, and which explicitly forbade border transfer to Galicia.

A VENEER OF LEGALITY

The first official announcement for the impending expulsion was issued on July 12, 1941, by the newly appointed director of KEOKH, state councilor Dr. Sándor Siménfalvy. In contrast to the prevailing political clamor for expulsion, encouraged by the radical-right press, the general tone of this key piece of communication seems almost restrained. What was perhaps most noteworthy about the announcement's language is that it did not mention expulsion or deportation. Neither were Jews, Poles,[2] or Russian citizens specified as the target. The term *Galicianer*, the key villains in Hungarian mythological narrative, was also absent. The announcement was succinct and to the point in alluding to the "changing foreign political conditions" that could facilitate in the near future the "removal of unwanted foreigners or foreign citizens." The memorandum merely instructed all police authorities to commence with the "registration" of these individuals within three days with due legality and diligence. The guidelines concluded that the director "will issue the proper instructions relating to the foreign nationals upon the receipt of the reports."[3]

This directive did not emerge in a vacuum. Its importance lies in the fact that it established a legal framework, however nebulous, for the commencement of the expulsion. Otherwise, it is hard to ascertain its practical impact because by the time it was issued, the wheels of deportation were in full gear and the preparation for the collection of Jews in Carpathian Ruthenia was already underway. And while KEOKH's administrative participation in the project was deemed necessary and crucial, the initiative and operative power to launch the deportation was not within its purview. To embark on such a momentous political endeavor, the planning and execution of it had to come right from officials much higher in the governing hierarchy who had direct access to the highest levels of the Hungarian government.

Almost immediately and parallel with the onset of hostilities on June 22, 1941, and Hungary's entrance into the war several days later, feverish consultations began between the military leadership and high-level officials in the provinces to utilize this opportunity for the expulsion of unwanted populations, specifically Jews. The war opened a long-coveted door for cross-border removal. Recent Holocaust scholarship, supported by newly discovered documents, places this proposal unfailingly on the shoulders of the military establishment. The most ardent pursuer of the expulsion, and not just Jews, was Colonel-General Henrik Werth, the chief of staff of the army. His aims coincided with those of Miklós Kozma, the government commissioner of Carpathian Ruthenia.

While Kozma's territorial focus was narrow, limited to the eastern counties bordering the Soviet Union, his was the central spark that unleashed the removal.[4] Werth's plans were much more ambitious. Such sweeping views of a comprehensive solution for minorities, in which the "Jewish Question" was only one component, were shared by the entire general staff. A revealing diplomatic dispatch by the Hungarian military attaché in Berlin addressed to the general staff resonated this line of thinking. Utilizing the Hungarian occupation of Galicia, it proposed four key points. Two dealt specifically with minorities: (1) it could offer a prominent opening for the repatriation from Hungary of all those who infiltrated from north of the Carpathian Mountains [i.e., Galicianers], and (2) it would be also "very convenient for transferring vocal and unreliable '*tót*' [Slovaks] and '*oláh*' [Romanians] living in Hungary."[5]

Werth harbored an almost pathological impulse for the deportation not only of the Galicianers, but of the entire Jewish community; however, for the time being, he also had to abandon the idea of expelling millions of Romanian and Slovakian minorities along with the whole Jewish community, despite periodically advocating for this step. He was forced to focus his attention on the removal of Jews from the border provinces. Within a few days, though, he expanded the ranks of the intended expellees with foreign nationals from internment camps. A contemporary report by the American Jewish Joint Distribution Committee estimated the number of such foreign nationals between 2,600 and 2,800, with 10,000 stateless Jews.[6] At this time, no mention was made of Jews living in the interior of the country or those residing in Budapest.

To maintain a sense of legality, the proposal for the cross-border removal of Jews with "Polish and Russian citizenship" needed the approval of the Council of Ministers under the leadership of the prime minister, László Bárdossy. By the time of this meeting of the cabinet, Hungarian troops, represented by the Carpathian Corps [Kárpát Csoport] were deep in Galicia.[7] As one of the central characters in the unfolding deportation, Ámon Pásztóy recalled during his postwar trial that the "decree of expulsion was initiated by Henrik Werth, who was not a member of the Council of Ministers, but at that time was also present. On the basis of his suggestion, this proposal was presented to the Cabinet as a motion by Károly Bartha, then minister of defense."[8]

The intervention of Kozma might also have been a key element in the evolution of the initiative, for he was in direct communication with the office of the prime minister as well as the minister of interior. In the last days of June 1941, he openly intimated that a solution for the Jewish Question was impending: "We will see in the future a definite improvement because *those groups that are not comfortable due to political or racial reasons in Carpathian Ruthenia will have the opportunity to return soon to places where they could entertain hopes for a better existence and find a homeland more suitable to their allegiance.*"[9]

These words were a mere preamble for the decision by the government. The seal of approval by the Council of Ministers for the deportation was almost a formality, a rather anticlimactic affair. During the meeting, the focus was mainly on Carpathian Ruthenia. Since no detailed notes have survived about the deliberations, we are in the dark about individual ministers' explicit views about the initiative. Subsequently, it was approved with the sole objection coming from the Minister of Interior Ferenc Keresztes-Fischer.

In an effort to assuage his concerns, Bartha reassured those present with the promise that "resettlement from a military point of view is well-prepared and the displaced persons, with the support of the Hungarian military administration, will be supplied all the prerequisites which is necessary for the reconstruction of a devastated territory and the launching of their new existence." There were also promises made about resettling the deported Jews in recently abandoned homes to a place where "they can engage in agriculture." In an effort to align KEOKH's policies with that of the defense ministry, the official line emphasized that in Galicia, empty villages, houses, and furnished apartments would be waiting for the new settlers. There was also a promise made that "these Jews will not be exposed to any danger because they will be under the protection of the Hungarian army stationed in Galicia."[10]

As we will see later, if these egregious claims weren't consciously mendacious, they were purposefully misleading, or at best wishfully blind. One of the perverse aspects of this misinformation campaign was that the idea was deliberately circulated to the public. More importantly, a rosy future with abandoned houses, empty villages, and abundance in employment opportunities waiting for the expellees in the newly conquered territories was aimed mainly at the Jewish leadership. The aim was to reassure leaders that the removal would benefit the expellees. In reality, the stringent regulations of carrying 30 kg, bringing with them only the essential items, and a meagre 30 pengő was not a promising omen that a successful existence in Galicia was planned for the unfortunates.

Such announcements and rumors were disseminated at the outset of the deportation, aiming to alleviate any concern on the part of the Jewish communities in the provinces and the leadership in Budapest. It worked for a while. Commentaries in the contemporary press to the effect that Jews should be removed and would find livelihood opportunities in the occupied territories reinforced this misinformation campaign. They might also be a clear testimony to that fact that the impending removal was not a secret.[11] The most outlandish example was the call by the subprefect [*alispán* in Hungarian] of Máramaros County, in northern Transylvania, Dr. Gábor Ajtay, for "voluntary" emigration from this eastern border region. On July 8, 1941, he urged local residents to return to their birthplace where they could engage in agriculture. To complete this rosy picture, the authorities also promised that "assistance" would be forthcoming.[12]

This call was an unwelcome intrusion on Kozma's turf, which he deeply resented. A contemporary report noted that the subprefect planned the transfer of 30,000 people just from his county alone, and regardless of their citizenship. This offer was not coordinated with any governmental entity in Budapest and certainly not with the three main officials entrusted with the removal. Kozma intimated in one of his reports, addressed to the prime minister, that such private initiatives, such as that of the hapless Ajtay who had obviously overstepped his authority, should not be tolerated. Nevertheless, it showed that even mid-level administrators could, and were keen to, remove large number of people and dismiss in the process any legal constraint.[13]

Following the cabinet's approval, preparations began almost immediately. Three entities—the government commissioner, KEOKH, and the military—were entrusted with carrying out the expulsion. They proceeded along three parallel lines. In spite of some degree of cooperation that was needed for accomplishing the expulsion, there was an element of interdepartmental competition among them. They interpreted the governmental missive independently and loosely on their own terms. During the deliberations of the cabinet, the well-rehearsed official line was (as Siménfalvy from KEOKH testified in his trial) to address the issue of citizens with "Polish and Russian" nationality. Indeed, a sequence of official communiqués from KEOKH followed this line. However, for the next two weeks new groups were added almost daily—and arbitrarily—for removal, often ignoring resident permits or full Hungarian citizenship not only in the provinces, but also in Budapest.[14]

On the one hand, it was an operation of the Ministry of Interior, represented by KEOKH and its ambitious "gray eminence" Pásztóy. Kozma, on the other hand, ran a fully independent campaign in Carpathian Ruthenia that was assisted by local police and the gendarmerie. Finally, the military was supposed to be the conduit for transporting the collected Jews over the border from a transit camp. However, Werth could not stay idle while the two other organizations became fully operational, and unilaterally expanded the population who must be expelled.

It is not easy to create a clear, chronological outline of the unfolding deportation. The main perpetrators were running parallel operations, reported to different superiors, and often bypassed their direct supervisor. When opportunity presented itself, Kozma, Werth, and Pásztóy pounced on it, often without clear coordination among them. The chain of communications, crisscrossing the political landscape in the first two weeks of July, betrays an understated rivalry among the three main individuals.

Tracing the chain of events, we first note a diary entry by Kozma, dated July 4, celebrating the successes of the Hungarian Army on the Eastern Front. The entry also informs us those communications were started with the military for expulsion from a five-kilometer-wide border zone. Then, he cryptically, though with authority, notes that the impending action will include the expulsion of "Jews with foreign citizenship; young single Jews; ... forcibly, voluntarily." The note about *"young single Jews"* was a new twist and signaled a disturbing trend in the implementation of the cabinet's mandate. Another overlooked recommendation by Kozma was aimed at Ukrainian nationalists who escaped across the border. He advocated stripping their citizenship and expelling their families. This showed that new groups could be added, on the whim of the main architects, to the agreed upon governmental order.[15]

An order from the general staff three days later, on July 7, followed. It instructed the commander of the Carpathian Corps, Lieutenant General Ferenc Szombathelyi, to coordinate with Kozma for "the immediate removal of non-Hungarian Jews, immigrated from Galicia to Carpathian Ruthenia, to recently occupied Galicia." Then, the order requested a contingency plan, a blueprint, for the potential expulsion of "non-citizen Jews" (foreign nationals) from the interior of the country *"and foremost those from the internment camps—in agreement with the government—to Galicia."*[16]

This was another new milestone. These foreign nationals were not the hated Galicaners and not from Carpathian Ruthenia. They included citizens of various countries who found sanctuary in Hungary as well as those holding Nansen passports.[17] The claim of an "agreement with governmental authorities" is perhaps the most spurious declaration in this document. There is no evidence that he coordinated this step either with Keresztes-Fischer, the interior minister, or KEOKH. Werth was notorious for taking unilateral actions without official consultations or approval. This might have been one of them. As noted earlier, he instructed one of the most staunchly pro-Nazi officers on the general staff, General László Dezső, on July 9, 1941, to issue a directive to the Carpathian Corps. The directive sets the logistical contours of the expulsion, ordering the military to expand "its control of the occupied territory as long as possible for the transportation of captured military hardware, food, gasoline, and rubber as fast as possible and, on the one hand, for the transfer of *undesirable populations such as Jews and Ukrainians*."[18]

Not far behind, the trail of communication lead to the prime minister's office. On July 10, 1941, Kozma informed Bárdossy about the impending cross-border transfer as a fait accompli: "Next week I will put across the border non-Hungarian citizens, infiltrated Galicianers, *exposed Ukrainian agitators, and Gypsies*. The details have already been finalized with Bartha, [Secretary of Defense], Szombathelyi, and the commander of the army corps in Debrecen."[19] In addition to designating new groups for removal, the words "across the border" betrayed the signal for the practical phase of the deportation in specific and unambiguous terms.

In fact, it would seem that the authorities in the capital had no objections to his plans because on the next day, July 11, his diary noted with a degree of satisfaction that "Pest [Budapest] started to move and follows me in this new situation." He reiterated in his cursory style that the removal is aimed at "1. Foreign nationals; 2. Military zone; 3. Ukrainian agitators; 4. Gypsies."[20] No reply from the prime minister has survived. The only sign that the prime minister might have had some concerns was a cryptic note in Kozma's diary on July 16; however, these communications show that Bárdossy was updated and knew that the plans for deportation were expanded to others than the Galicianers.

A subsequent memo from Kozma, dated on July 12, 1941, parallels KEOKH's instruction but is much more advanced in planning, and indicates that the deportation is about to start. The only unanswerable question is whether Kozma meant the collection or the actual transfer of the Jewish population across the border. The fact that it gives details about the handling of property left by the deported Jews, and already speaks of them in the past tense, points to the arrest of the unfortunates before or around July 12. In comparing this statement with the KEOKH memo, also dated on July 12, which requests only the *registration* of those to be deported, we can conclude that collection was in full momentum by that time and without discernable coordination or assistance from Budapest. Not coincidentally, the Hungarian military had occupied Kamenets-Podolsk the previous day.[21]

Finally, KEOKH was also ready to spring into action. Two days after the first memorandum, Sándor Siménfalvy sent out a second, more pointed announcement addressed to police prefects and authorities. This mentioned Jews specifically, though "Polish and Russian nationals" and below the age seventy for men and sixty for women. He also set down guidelines that limited the luggage to absolute necessities, including food provisions for three days so that the deportees "would not cause shortages in local food supplies," and identified who should care for the property left behind. This last proviso was a misnomer, for the gathering was undertaken at such a dizzying speed that the deportees, plucked out with a half hour of preparation time, were unable to make any orderly arrangement for transferring their property. A revealing report also indicated that there were villages where the entire Jewish population was deported, leaving all their property behind without any lawful transfer or guardianship.[22]

Frantic preparation of lists as to who should be expelled started late—somewhere in second half of July 1941. KEOKH had a rather rudimentary list, mainly relating to Budapest and the internment camps. In its catalog, the number of Polish- or Russian-born aliens numbered only 6,000.[23] Therefore, additional masses of Jews had to be declared stateless even if they had no connection with Poland or Russia. To expedite the deportation so that "the removal could proceed unhindered," he also dispatched one of his trusted lieutenants, a police officer in the rank of captain, Nándor Batizfalvy, to the hastily organized transit camp on the Hungarian-Soviet border.[24]

How this police officer could expedite the process was not spelled out. As it is, the transit camp rapidly evolved into a humanitarian nightmare. Under the jurisdiction of the military, it was located several miles from the town of Kőrösmező, in Havasalja, and was among three planned collection points, but the only one that became operational. The official name of the approximately 1.5-acre area enclosed by a muddy, clay lath fence was "Royal Hungarian Military Collection and Transit Camp Number 104." Not surprisingly, it was anything but what the defense minister promised when he declared during the meeting of the ministers, "the resettlement from a military point of view is well-prepared." For the next five weeks this created a gridlock in the process, overwhelming the capacity of the primitive camp. As the trains started to funnel thousands of unfortunate deportees to the site, it became clear that it turned into a bottleneck, and, consequently, a catastrophe. This foreshadowed the unmitigated disaster that the follow-up transportation to the east turned out to be.

Set up in a former sawmill, the camp consisted of a large, rudimentary shed that could house only several hundred people, at best. There were days when the camp housed over three thousand people. Thus, many of them were forced to stay outdoors in the open air, unsheltered against the rain and the wind. The site lacked basic amenities for the people incarcerated there. Through the eyes of a thirteen-year-old survivor, we learn that the camp had "no water available at the site and we had to fetch in pails from quite a distance away [from the river].... We used this water for drinking only—there was never enough left to bathe in or wash our clothes." Since the military refused supply food for the prisoners, hunger became rampant. Nutrition was limited to "a bowl of soup a day." László Zobel arrived at the camp on August 8 and was deported across the border on August 11. During these three days he received no food.[25]

Many families with children and the elderly slept in the open on the muddy ground; a survivor summed up the overall conditions in the camp as "frightful and horrible; especially during the nights, the children's crying amidst the moaning and groaning of the elderly were unbearable."[26] Only by the intersession of Jewish welfare agencies in Budapest, and donations by local Jewish communities, were they able to survive. The guards treated the detainees with utmost brutality. Their behavior is well-illustrated by the fact that the soldiers were equipped with clubs, which were not part of the standard army equipment. These sticks, as Margit Slachta, mother superior of the Order of Sisters of Social Service, sarcastically remarked, were canes, but not for a "stroll in the park." Her fact-finding delegation of concerned parliamentarians and religious personalities could not ignore the dismal conditions and the abuse the military personel in the camp meted out to the defenseless people.

The detainees were not allowed to approach the fence, especially when their relatives or lawyers bringing citizenship certificates appeared around the camp. It often happened that these concerned visitors were also detained and consequently interned or outright deported to Galicia. Batizfalvy and the representatives of the civil administration could not prevent these abuses because the camp at Havasalja and the territory east were declared military zones. Their scathing assessment of the site and its arbitrariness, contrary to all legal constraint, can be summed up in their own words: "you could boldly write on the gate of the camp, *Lasciate ogni Speranza* [Abandon all Hope]."[27]

Kozma didn't concern himself with such trivialities and minutiae. His rapid-fire communications with the prime minister's office indicate that the cross-border "evacuation" of Jews from Carpathian Ruthenia started on Monday, July 14, 1941. His request for financial assistance on the same day from Keresztes-Fischer, the minister of interior, claiming that "the removal is underway and can't be stopped," supports this fact.[28] The urgency in his tone might reveal that the assembling and transportation of Jews to the transit camp was brutally efficient, wide-scale, and labor-intensive. It was conducted with a ferocity befiting the gendarmerie and corresponding capriciousness by local officials, reflecting an attitude that interior ministry directives did not have to be enforced in Carpathian Ruthenia. They interpreted the expulsion as they saw fit.

FIG 3.1   Collecting Jews for transportation to the train station in the city of Hust in Carpathian Ruthenia. Picture by Erzsébet Szapáry. *Courtesy of the Hungarian National Museum/Photo Archives.*

Two days later, Kozma's diary reveals that "the transfer is continuing since Monday." He obviously meant the transfer of Jews to Galicia. The diary made no mention of any similar efforts in collecting various populations from other parts of the country. The military records also remained devoid of any information regarding the evacuation from the eight internment camps spread across the interior. However, Kozma didn't stop there. He expanded the ranks of those to be removed with Jews who were serving in the forced labor companies that were attached to the military.²⁹ On July 15, he appealed to the regional military headquarters, mentioning for added weight his cooperation with Lieutenant General Szombathelyi, noting that "it was found that Jews with foreign nationality, whose expulsion is warranted, currently perform labor service. I request from the regional command... to remove from their units immediately those Jews who are serving in the military but without Hungarian nationality."³⁰ Apparently, this name-dropping worked. The local commander dismissed these servicemen. What seems immediately obvious is that Kozma finally discarded the original designation for expulsion of the Polish and Russian citizens, and resorted to a general term of foreign nationality. As for the targeted labor-servicemen, and because of the shortage of time, the majority were not sent to Galicia. Their families, on the other hand, were not spared. They were forwarded without these servicemen's knowledge to the transit camp in Körösmező and, consequently, trucked east.³¹

Meanwhile, KEOKH's slow approach for jump-starting the collection of the targeted population paled in comparison with Kozma's frantic activism. The first explicit order for the "immediate detaining of Polish and Russian stateless persons to be expelled" and their "direct transfer to Kőrösmező" came from KEOKH on July 19, 1941. The fact that the author of this communication, Dr. Sándor Siménfalvy specified "Polish and Russian" but omitted Jews did not disguise the fact that the order aimed to deport Jews only.³² By that time the transfer of deportees from Carpathian Ruthenia, northern Transylvania, and the internment camps were in full swing. Suddenly, the veneer of judicial legitimacy evaporated. And so did any form of civility.

"A PICTURE THAT IS FITTING DANTE'S INFERNO"

Margit Slachta served as the leader of the previously noted delegation of clerics, civic leaders, and parliamentarians visiting Carpathian Ruthenia in early August 1941. She minced no words in a devastating report to the highest echelons of the Hungarian leadership. The main points of this report were also sent, through the Hungarian Red Cross several month later, to the International Red Cross in Geneva. Through

Countess Erzsébet Szapáry, it also filtered into the American ambassador's reports to Washington. It described the conditions in the region concerning the local collection, transportation to the transit camp, and border transfer of the wretched multitude of desperate Jews.

She headed an eclectic group that included, in addition to Margit Shlachta, Count György Apponyi, a member of the parliament, Dr. Imre Szabó, papal councilor and Catholic priest, and Countess Erzsébeth Szapáry.[33] The participation of Countess Szapáry was especially noteworthy. Two surviving pictures taken by her demonstrate the process of collection and transport of the unfortunates. As one of the leading members of the Hungarian-Polish Refugee Committee and also the Hungarian Red Cross, she was well-connected with upper strata of Hungarian society. In a status-conscious country such as Hungary at the time, police and military authorities in Kőrösmező were unable to rein in her activism for saving lives on the ground. Their whirlwind tour of Carpathian Ruthenia, besides the transit camp, for an investigative report during the high point of the deportation in early August, yielded a damning indictment of Hungarian governmental policies, societal indifference, and an avaricious local officialdom.

Describing the individual despair of the victims as they mounted the military trucks to train stations headed to the transit camp, the ruthlessness of the gendarmerie in smothering any opposition or feeling of sympathy, and the single-minded drive by overzealous public administrators in the provinces, it is a harrowing document to read. Their final conclusion that "as Hungarians, we cannot abide by the tarnishing of the Hungarian honor that these atrocities represent" summed up well the ethical conundrum that enveloped the entire wave of deportation.[34]

The report by no means overdramatized the events taking place on the periphery of Hungary. The campaign encompassed every settlement and village in Carpathian Ruthenia, the adjacent region of Upper Hungary (today Slovakia) and northern Transylvania. The expulsion itself can be summed up as a sweep that was ruthlessly comprehensive, utterly chaotic, and capriciously executed. One can notice, even at first glance, glaring disconnects between the guidelines specifying "Polish and Russian nationals," issued in Budapest, and the policies introduced by mid-level officials for the nightly or early morning raids by the feared and loathed gendarmerie, who brutally swooped down on unsuspecting residents. The short time limit for preparation, ostensibly for the prevention of escape, was intentional. Arisztid Meskó, the feared state police councilor in Carpathian Ruthenia, admitted that "originally he wanted to give 6 hours ... for packing and transferring their property, etc., but was forced to shorten this time for one hour, because, according to him, many escaped." He should have known this, because he was entrusted with drafting the rules and regulations in the province that governed the expulsion.[35]

The arrest usually started with a five-o'clock knock on the door. The list of names, prepared in advance, was not always adhered to, and was followed by a terse command to pack the necessities, secure food for three days, and proceed under guard to an assembly point—a synagogue, a schoolhouse, or even a central square in the village. There was no place for an appeal, protest, or thought of resistance. The arrested were transported to a train station almost immediately. While there were reports of escapes—three villages are mentioned explicitly—resistance, active or passive, was almost nonexistent. As an example, the Carpathian Ruthenian village of Irhóc (Vilhiv'ce in Ukrainian) was raided: "about 500 people, most of the 850-person community, were classified as 'stateless and arrested.'" While a sizeable number escaped to the mountains, most of them voluntarily gave themselves up.[36]

There might have been three loosely interconnected reasons as to why no resistance or mass escapes occurred. First, the official Jewish leadership in Budapest tacitly acquiesced to the removal of the "Polish and Russian" nationals and exhorted the Jewish masses to cooperate in doing that. Also, there was no opportunity to find adequate hiding places for traditionally large families. Finally, individual efforts of escape were constrained by family ties and unfamiliarity with the mountains. The Jewish family credo of staying together—no matter what—was a binding principle. The example of Max Solomon, who made an escape attempt, is instructive for an additional motive. Upon the arrest of his family in the village, he headed for a safe place in the hills. However, an explicit threat to the family by the gendarmerie of brutal retaliation, conveyed from his mother via a childhood friend, convinced the fifteen-year-old to rejoin the family the next day.[37]

The first stage was the rapid assembly and removal of the often arbitrarily collected population. A typical description of the procedure by a survivor from the town of Mukachevo (Munkács in Hungarian), who was able to return after wandering for over a year in Galicia, conveys the harrowing experience. Starting with a knock on the door at five o'clock in the morning, he was given half an hour to pack a suitcase, with a governmental prescribed allocation of only 30 pengő [$6 USD].[38]

The trauma of being plucked from familiar surroundings, leaving a home with a little bundle, and facing an uncertain future reverberates in the testimonies of survivors. Irene Weiss, twenty-two years old at the time, reflects the attitude of an adult: "Within two hours we had to leave our entire life behind us." On the other hand, a single act of forcibly evacuating one from a home that served as the ultimate constant in a child's life, coupled with witnessing the humiliation of powerless parents, was perhaps the most ingrained and resonant moment in a child's eyes on the road to being turned into a refugee. Solomon was emotionally compelled to revisit repeatedly such a moment during his testimony. It was perhaps the most distressing point for him in this entire ordeal. Looking skyward, almost talking to himself, he remembered: "You never experience things like this that out of this place you were born, raised ... all your family from generations to generations, you have some horses, chickens, and a little dog ... it was like somebody hit you on the head."[39]

The process of arrest and removal was deliberate and blatant abuse. Uniform guidelines or their enforcement for the deportation were rarely adhered to. While orders from Budapest, clearly proscribed the target population, neither Kozma in Carpathian Ruthenia nor other middle-level administrators observed these guidelines. Arbitrary arrests based on enmity toward a family and a reprieve due to a bribe or business connection run parallel.[40] In one village they gave a week to prepare, while in most places the expulsion from one's home was immediate. The executing authorities very rarely, if at all, troubled with the examination of citizenship papers or considered mitigating circumstances.

In one village, like Drahovo (Kövesliget in Hungarian), almost the entire Jewish population of three hundred families were collected in the village school before being forcefully marched to the train station. In this case, all the wives and children were exempted because the husbands were away in the military's forced labor companies. But even here, there was a caveat. The women had to procure marriage certificates, which in many cases were not available. Since Jews in the eastern provinces, deeply religious, often did not enter their marriages in civil registers, having been officiated by a rabbi, this condition was often a problem.[41]

On the other hand, several miles from Drahovo, in the town of Irshava (Ilosva in Hungarian), the entire population was carted off regardless of the military service. In

FIG 3.2   Delivering the Jews to the cattle cars for transfer to the transit camp in Körösmező. Picture by Erzsébet Szapáry.
Courtesy of Memorial de la Shoah.

Upper Hungary [today Slovakia], like in Moldava nad Bodvou (Szepsi in Hungarian), similar scenes took place. All women and children were sent to the transit camp in Kőrösmező while the men were away in labor companies serving in the Hungarian Army. Corruption in implementing the expulsion was rampant. In one of the most egregious examples, the chief magistrates in several towns collected the citizenship papers from the local inhabitants and then unceremoniously shipped them, deemed as "aliens," directly to Kőrösmező.[42]

The list for abuses of power would not be complete without quoting from the aforementioned report by Margit Slachta. She informed the government in Budapest that the authorities in Carpathian Ruthenia also carted off children who were only relatives and happened to visit families from other towns: "At present, these children from other parts of Hungary are somewhere in Galicia, if they are still alive. And their parents are tearing their hair out to find them, because they know that they'll never be found again."[43]

In such an environment, the orderly transfer of property, as was stipulated by guidelines of the Ministry of Interior or Kozma himself, became only an illusion. Perhaps as a consequence of the American ambassador's protestations to the prime minister, on July 30 a new directive spelled out specifically that in the future only "Jews whose Polish and Russian origins could be verified by information already in our possession, or by future investigation," could be expelled. Then the memorandum expanded the rank of expellees by adding those aliens who possessed residency permits.[44] This new document, though, made no impression or impact on the conduct of the provincial administration, or, for that matter, on the military.

Sometimes, local authorities, such as a deputy sheriff or a subprefect of a region, arbitrarily emptied entire villages of their Jewish inhabitants, leaving homes, property, and domestic animals without a caretaker. One of the unenforceable orders promulgated by Kozma was that an individual from the Jewish community should be designated as a warden for the properties left behind. An exasperated county official, in turn, pointed out that in many villages the entire Jewish community was taken away. No one was left to guard the abandoned property. The removal happened so quickly that there was no time to transfer a house or the cattle left behind—not even the keys to the house—to a trusted friend or family member. In one instance, the arresting gendarme himself demanded a distraught mother with gun against her head hand over the keys for her home. It's not hard to figure out that this "protector of the law" had some plans for this property.

Contrary to the promises made by the minister of defense or some provincial officials, the most traumatic phase of the expulsion, before the border crossing to Galicia, was the transportation to the transit camp in Kőrösmező. If one entertained any illusion for an orderly transfer and human compassion in doing so, it rapidly evaporated in the reality of being sealed in a cattle car for several days without food or hygienic amenities. It was especially true for the outlying provinces. In many ways, these inhuman conditions in the cattle wagons presaged the notorious train rides to Auschwitz three years later, during the main chapter of the Hungarian Holocaust. The interminable journeys in these sealed and fully packed wagons from the provinces—lasting sometimes five to six days, without food, water, with an overflowing bucket of human excrement, and the stench of dead bodies—very rapidly brought home the realization that "this was a dead train," and the first inkling that the deportation could lead to inevitable death. Yaffa Rosenthal remembered six or seven dead people in her wagon: "They were packed like 70 or 90 people.... They put a small pail for everybody to use as needed, there was no toilet, no water, no food, except what you took along.... People were dying. They could not open the door to let the dead be put out any place. It was summer, it was the smell.... In our car there were six or seven dead people. It was horrific. Yet the people were praying and praying and praying... that's when I became a non-believer."[45]

While the Jewish communities along the train routes often came out to extend water and food to the unfortunate prisoners, the gendarmes guarding the train often prevented even that help. An impromptu informational network functioned, though, because often minutes after arrival in a station "several Jewish men and women appeared to distribute fruit, bread, and water."[46] A communication from the Hungarian train system, addressed to the Ministry of Interior, launched a complaint about this practice, claiming that the "local Jewish communities are waiting for the Jewish expellees with food and presents. This often turns into a festive celebration." Then, the writers requested the intersession of the ministry that in the "future such gatherings, or receptions should not have been repeated."[47]

Budapest was a different story. While thousands were collected and shipped to Kőrösmező, in the capital the levers of justice, or often injustice, worked differently. Corruption in obtaining citizenship papers became widespread. Large numbers of applications for validating citizenship were shelved and intentionally delayed in the offices of KEOKH. A well-placed bribe, however, could expedite the process. Even the final arbiter of the expulsion, Ámon Pásztoy, was accused of influence peddling. A low-ranking Hungarian officer noticed this contradiction in meeting Hungarian Jews, who were forced close to the line of the Carpathian Mountains on the Galician side by German pressure. He acerbically noted in his diary that this multitude "are wandering like nomads, begging, brutalized and murdered by Ukrainian bands.... I had an unpleasant feeling, of seeing young women with pure Christian faces, half-Jews.... A 14 years-old, blond, purely Aryan looking girl, they have resided 70 years in our country, and now because of paper-problems she is expelled by herself—fatherless, a half-Jew." The officer bitterly condemned the policy of targeting the "little people and why not the rich Jews. Sudden enthusiasm and utter disorder." His observation was not far from the truth. The bulk of the deportees were "poor Carpathian Ruthenian Jews with their pitiful bundles."[48]

In Budapest, the real deterring factor for open brutality, comparable to that in the provinces, was the presence of international press organizations, diplomatic observers, and the official Jewish leadership. It dictated a more nuanced approach toward Jews who were deemed to lack proper papers. The arrests of those whose documents were not in order, or were suspicious, was masked more in a façade of civility and seemed more refined than in the country's periphery. In Budapest, laws were also more carefully observed than in the provinces. The example of my grandfather, who was rescued from the collection center by my mother, is enlightening. He was over seventy years old, a fact that legally exempted him from deportation by law. Yet the collection of Jews in Budapest was equally comprehensive, fast, and uncompromising. The brutality of the provinces was absent, for the most part, since it was conducted by detectives from KEOKH, which relied on the assistance of local police forces. These police forces, in turn, often knew the targeted individuals. Frequently, arresting officers from the district precinct had no information about the ultimate goal of the arrest and reassured the detained individuals that they could return home after a cursory check of their credentials. This was often the approach in other major cities. Living in Budapest, my uncle Samu was on a first-name basis with the policeman from the neighborhood precinct who came to his apartment with an invitation to a brief review of his documents. Upon his attempt to bring a coat, the policeman waved him away with the promise that he would be home by dinner. He never returned. This gives us a hint that he did not go voluntarily, like some who believed in the official propaganda in Budapest that a better life awaited in Galicia with houses, land, and work. That might also be the reason that his wife, Tildi, decided not to join him with their three daughters on this fateful journey. A very similar experience befell Peninah Kaufman in Kassa (Kosice in today's Slovakia), a sizeable town in the Upper Provinces. The policemen reassured her mother, "there is no reason to bring a thing... only a few questions and you will be free." Consequently, the family was transferred to an internment camp and from there to the transit camp in Kőrösmező.[49]

Detectives from KEOKH, augmented by these police forces, fanned out to collect the Jews with prepared lists, but random identity checks in coffeehouses or on the streets also netted hundreds of Jews daily, some of them with resident permits and citizenship documents, who were summarily carted off to collections points across the city. Such raids did not escape the attention of the representatives of the New York-based Jewish relief organization the American Jewish Joint Distribution Committee, and, consequently, the American press.[50] Through them, the Jewish media became aware of the deportation. Reports by the Jewish Telegraphic Agency (JTA), headquartered in New York, noted on July 22, 1941, that "passengers on each train reaching Budapest from the interior of Hungary are examined as to their identity, in order to prevent *stateless and Polish Jews* escaping to the Hungarian capital from the provincial towns where they live in constant fear of deportation."⁵¹ Several days later it reported that even hospitals were not spared. On August 4, the JTA sent a dispatch, quoting German newspapers, that "hospitals and sanatoriums throughout Hungary are being raided by the police and Jewish patients are being dragged from there for deportation to Nazi-held Galicia." Health resorts that were "patronized by elderly Jews" were also targeted.

The fear was palpable; it gripped the city. The news dispatch stressed that "it is no longer safe for a Jew to appear in the street. All Jews are stopped by police and asked for citizenship certificates. Those who have no such certificate with them, are immediately arrested. On the other hand, the authorities refuse to issue such certificates to Jews even if they are bona-fide Hungarian citizens."⁵² Like many of the arrested, László Zobel was stopped on the street for a routine identity check, upon which he was promptly transferred to the central synagogue that served as one of the collections points. He was taken without a chance of gathering his meager belongings. Within two days, he was on his way to Kőrösmező.

Contrary to the international media, Hungarian newspapers in Budapest were rather celebratory in their announcements about the success of the deportation. Reporting on the raids in the capital and the provinces, several of them noted that "until now, twelve-thousand Galicianers were removed from he country... and the arrests and expulsion will continue until the country will be fully cleansed."⁵³ The daily papers in the provinces followed suit in reporting the deportation in positive tones.

State councilor Siménfalvy from KEOKH broadened the net in Budapest to include the "maximum number of individuals," which specifically encompassed those who held permanent resident status. Their number is estimated in the thousands. Just as in the provinces, nightly raids in Budapest became the preferred method of arresting entire families. The element of stealth and surprise served the raiding parties well. These Jews from Budapest were perhaps the most traumatized among the refugees. Many of them, having been plucked out of a comfortable middle-class existence in a European metropolis, encountered a wholly incomprehensible situation.

There were seven temporary collection centers set up in the Hungarian capital—mainly synagogues and Jewish institutions, such as the two orphanages for boys and girls. Was it the Jewish community in Budapest that offered these temporary holding centers to the thousands of interned, or an arbitrary and unilateral decision by KEOKH for calming down the international reverberations for the deportations? Either way, placing the community in such an awkward situation was an expedient solution for the authorities. It implicated the Jewish leadership in the deportation, and placed the expenses of feeding and housing, rather conveniently, upon the shoulders of Jewish organizations. And, unlike in the provinces where the expulsion was immediate, in Budapest those arrested were held for several days. This gave an opportunity for a farewell visit from the family, like Samu's wife and their three daughters. It also gave precious time to find a legal recourse, like in the case of my grandfather, for appealing the expulsion.

However, this was a rare exception. For one well-established furrier from the inner-city there was no such an option. He was awoken in the middle of the night and transferred with his wife and fifteen-year-old daughter within a half hour to one of the main synagogues of the city. Several days later, they were on their long journey to exile. In a chance encounter deep in Galicia with a Hungarian soldier, the despondent father confided that his "father settled in Budapest around 1867. He was already born there, and cannot speak anything but Hungarian. His wife was also born in Hungary."[54]

The transportation of the deportees from Budapest to Kőrösmező was also more discrete than in the provinces. Every day, after several hundred were collected, second-class carriages were coupled to ordinary passenger trains. László Zobel remembered that the accompanying guards had no objections to let the passengers accept food from the Jewish communities along the train route. This courteous manner, however, changed dramatically upon arrival to their final destination, Kőrösmező. At that time, all pretense was dropped. There were no international observers nor the press to contend with. The only counterweight for the rampant abuses was the already mentioned representative of KEOKH, Captain Nándor Batizfalvy, who was assigned to review citizenship papers and made valiant efforts to curtail some of the excesses. His authority, however, was limited to the train station where the majority of the deportees disembarked—the camp itself was a military zone. He was assisted by two detectives and the representatives of the Hungarian-Jewish Assistance Committee (Magyar Izraeliták Pártfogó Irodája, MIPI) for ferreting out the unlawfully deported Jews and providing them with travel papers for their return. Those who worked with him in the transit camp—the representatives of MIPI and the delegation led by Margit Slachta—paint a picture of heroic rescue work, an uphill struggle, striving against the obstruction by the military commander of the camp.[55]

His task was not enviable. Because of the rapid delivery of thousands of Jews, he soon became overwhelmed. The office of the government commissioner of Carpathian Ruthenia was also actively hindering the rescue work. Following several cables, the ubiquitous Arisztid Meskó reinforced this by personally visiting the transit camp with corresponding threats and intimidation of Batizfalvy.[56] The camp itself was under full military control. The commander of the camp, Lieutenant Colonel Rudolf Orbán, openly refused to cooperate and, often, obstructed or outright counter-commanded the work of Batizfalvy. His announcement that "from the camp Jews have only one way to go: Galicia" well sums up his attitude.

Fig 3.3 Picture of Captain Nándor Batizfalvy from the National Central Alien Control Office (KEOKH). *Courtesy of Ester Horompoly.*

Military personnel, mainly from the ranks of the gendarmerie, took over from regular police forces, and a rigorous search and thorough examination commenced at the platform. All items of value were confiscated. A survivor recounted how detailed and systematic was such a hunt, which included bodily and luggage searches. This might have been a local initiative, but it was an officially sanctioned plunder. They were "looking for valuables and currency.... One family was beaten for hiding a gold watch on a chain and several rings; this was discovered when a policeman dipped his bayonet into a jar of jam and pulled out the hidden valuables."[57]

To comprehend the desperate situation of the newly arriving detainees, we should resort again to the description provided by the delegation led by Slachta: "If one has really seen the despair on the faces of the people that have been brutally plucked out of their homes, transported like cattle to an unknown destination, probably to their death, and one who was a witness to the hopeless silence, that is more meaningful than any word, with which they walk toward their inevitable doom, this image, that is so fitting of Dante's Inferno, will remain in one's memory for the rest of his life."[58]

The delegation's visit took place on August 10, two days after the issue of the explicit instruction from Budapest for the immediate cessation of the deportation. By that time, though, testimonies filtering back from the occupied territories already painted a grim picture of the dire situation awaiting the expellees. The delegation was cognizant of the looming threat over the fate of the unfortunates in Galicia. By August 10, the date of the visit of the transit camp, the atrocities taking place in Galicia became common knowledge. Their report gives painful details of the full scope of the expulsion in Carpathian Ruthenia—from the large number of "houses that were boarded up" in the villages and towns, to the brutality of the gendarmerie, and from the meticulous search of the deportees for valuables, to the final act of mounting the trucks for the journey into the unknown.

The trucks were loaded with as many as possible, "75 or a 100 . . . standing on the truck like herrings, pressed together."[59] This concluding moment was especially etched in the minds of the observers: "we also saw the tragic image of the truck convoy in the pouring rain, without tarpaulin, as they were leaving the camp and heading out toward Galicia, loaded with the unfortunates who lost all hope."

THE EXPULSION: "JOURNEY ACROSS THE 'DARK MOUNTAINS'"

The mystical "Dark Mountains"—the Carpathians—are a semicircle of towering mountain ranges encircling Hungary, straddling the border between Hungary proper and the interminable steppes of Ukraine. It was through them that the deportation proceeded toward Galicia. In the minds of the expellees, they loomed both as a physical and psychological divide. The range's narrow passes and forbidding primeval forests presented a formidable physical barrier in both directions. It also signified an irretrievable crossing between east and west, between home and exile, and between the familiar and the unknown.

This divide also denoted in the minds of the deportees, especially those from cosmopolitan Budapest, a transition from civilization to a forbidding territory that they had never seen before. Indeed, the picture of Galicia that emerges in the memories of the survivors is extremely dark—a bleak landscape, populated by poor, depressed, and embittered people who were ready to settle scores. A Hungarian military observer dryly noted: "There is a sense that in Kamenets-Podolszk we have left Europe behind. . . . In the so inviting villages from the distance, misery, poverty, hunger and millions of flies beckon us. Neither letter nor microphone nor camera can convey the true reality. . . . Even if a visual recording could give back some of it, the stench that comes out of that misery would be missed, and we wouldn't be able to express it in any way."[60]

Finally, the realization that one became a stateless refugee by crossing a line was perhaps the hardest to rationalize. There is no word in English for the state of being a refugee. Immigration to new countries anticipates an orderly move, with passport and visa, well-stocked luggage, and final destination plans. Losing one's home within a half hour and being transported to an unknown destination without provisions is something else entirely. In the words of Elisabeth Åsbrink, "Existence has exploded."[61] The Hungarian refugees in Galicia knew nothing—not how long the journey would last, nor what their final destination would be, nor how one would recognize the end of the journey when it was reached.

From the start, the transportation was chaotic, ill-planned, and carried through haphazardly at breakneck speed. The ensuing chaos in loading up the trucks had dire consequences. A report by MIPI provides graphic details of how families were separated during the utter confusion of the rapid transfer: "parents are not connected with children, children with the parents and there is a concern that during the evacuation they are deposited in different locations." This report might have been the source of the scathing statement made by the American ambassador to László Bárdossy in his memorandum on July 24: "children are separated from their mothers, husbands are separated from wives and children, and wives and children are deported while the husbands and fathers are absent working in the labor camp."[62]

During the loading, a father protested to the military personnel of this separation. He was reassured that they would meet up at the end of the journey: "all of them will go to the same place."[63] Of course, it was a patent lie. Cipora Brenner's family was also split; father and brother were sent in different directions while she, her sister, and her mother wandered in Galicia, ending up in one of the most notorious murder sites, the ghetto of Stanisławów. As the report somewhat prophetically predicted, "because the evacuation is taking place to various regions of Galicia, they [the parents and children] will never see each other in this life."[64] Not surprisingly, in many Galician communities, the hundreds of separated children found home in orphanages hastily arranged by the local Jewish communities.

A reserve second lieutenant, Alajos Salamon, in October 1941, framed this criticism of the military leadership about the conduct of the deportation: "short-lived enthusiasm, on the one hand, lack of order and any system, on the other."[65] One can only wonder how a relatively low-level officer was able to grasp so well the essence of the failure of the deportation. On average, fifty military trucks were allocated for the transfer of the expellees from the transit camp to any given direction in Galicia. In addition, there were instances of forcing the expellees across the border on foot. The pace was dictated by the availability of trucks, which were also needed to supply the rapidly advancing troops through a bottleneck of a road across the mountain. In a note jotted down by one of the officers attached to the commander of the corps, Lieutenant General Ferenc Szombathelyi, he complained that the requisitioning of the required number of trucks for the deportation "interfered with the reinforcement of the troops on the front."[66]

By the time the cross-border removal started, Hungarian forces had reached the farthest point in their advance—Kamenets-Podolsk on the border of Galicia and Podolia. The troops controlled a large swath of Galicia, which made the continuous dispersal of the Hungarian Jews across the land much easier. However, there was no settlement plan or clear rationale for where and when a convoy stopped. The overall idea, as Kozma has pointed out, was to deposit the refugees as far as possible from the border and, preferably, across the Dniester River, which provided a natural barrier for potential attempts to return to Hungary. Since there was no master plan developed for such an undertaking and the bridges were blown up by retreating Soviet troops, truck drivers accompanying officers and military gendarmes deposited the people all across the region by whim in the Hungarian-controlled zone.

Eyewitness testimonies by survivors, locals, military officers, and members of forced labor battalions paint a uniform and vivid picture of the routine indifference and callousness with which the military authorities deposited the unfortunates across Galicia. The transports reached their distant destinations either by direct marches through hundreds of miles or by shipping them to Kolomea first, and from there by train, or more often by foot, to various end points. If I want to retrace the journey of my two uncles from Budapest to the transit camp in Körösmező, and from there to Kamenets-Podolsk, their final destination, I can only estimate the general direction and the means of reaching it. From Budapest, the Jews were transported by train, then mostly by trucks to Kolomea. As the headquarters of the Hungarian Army located in Kolomea, it became an important transit point to Kamenets-Podolsk. Max Solomon described arriving in Kolomea by truck, then continuing by train to Horodenka. From there, long marches awaited the deportees, mostly in the direction of Kamenets-Podolsk.[67]

A survivor's recollection of the long line of trucks disgorging their living cargo and the utter despair of those deposited provides a snapshot of the process: "During the journey we noticed that some of the trucks stopped. We thought they had stopped for a break. We travelled up to Chortkov, where our truck came to a halt as well. We had to get off, and the first lieutenant who escorted us said that there was a castle nearby, and that we should go there for accommodation.... Of course, it was not true."[68]

Baruch Milch, a Jewish country doctor from Tluste, Galicia, observed with disbelief the caravans of trucks passing by his home. He jotted down in his diary, as he termed, the "terrible sight." He observed that

> for two weeks in a row, groups of trucks, 5 to 10 cars, full of Jews, the elderly, the cripples, women and small children, were driven under an army escort or the Hungarian police [military gendarmes] in white gloves and comical costumes, in hats with long feathers tucked in. They were left in little towns and villages on the other side of the Dniester [River] starting all the way from Kamieniec Podolski. Sometimes they were dumped from the trucks in some woods or field, from which they made their way in waves to the nearest small towns. Often the Hungarian soldiers robbed them of everything, but they were tormented the most by Ukrainian peasants, who waited

for them in bands everywhere on roads and fields, robbing and killing without mercy.[69]

It was a well-rounded summation of the Hungarian deportees' tragic odyssey, which did not escape the attention of Hungarian military personnel either. An eyewitness from a Hungarian motorized unit recalled in his diary an unexpected meeting in Skala, on July 23, 1941, with a newly deposited, or rather, dumped, group of Jews, many of them from Budapest. Having served as a driver, he might have been himself Jewish. His immediate impression of the group was of "tired, sad, civilians... haggard elderly, children dragging bundles, tearful, hesitant women.... The men, sitting on the ground, are blankly staring into the distance." He still grappled with this sight, almost a month later, when he recalled this disconcerting meeting: "Perhaps the most shocking encounter was again with the Jews... beneath the trees by the roadside, they were sitting along a drainage ditch, whole families, old people and children, because the lorries, that had not received any instructions, got tired of carrying them further into Russia ... therefore the only thing that remained for them is the trench along the road, at least that tolerated them."[70]

These are accounts by outside observers. They cannot convey the personal pain, the sense of betrayal, which was the most devastating for those cast off. The bewildering realization that the end of the road led into a void as the group of refugees got off the trucks reverberates in a bitter comment by a survivor: "So this is what Hungary, our homeland did to us: they dropped us off in the forest of an entirely strange country and our transporters fled without an explanation. They were much too cowardly to tell us openly that we had been kicked out and abandoned."[71]

The scenes depicting the arrival of various groups are eerily similar: "They dropped us off in a meadow, in the middle of nowhere," a lone survivor recalled. "We were perhaps three hundred people. We set down on the edge of a drainage ditch." In this case, an accompanying military gendarme gave them a not-so-subtle warning: "This is your country now, and here is your messiah. Do not drink from the water because the wells are poisoned and do not try to return home because you will be shot! With that, he left us there."[72] From this and all accounts, a certain predictability filters through about the dispersal.

At the end of the unplanned journey, almost invariably at the side of the road along a meadow or a forest, a thorough search of the deportees included robbing the unfortunates of whatever was still left from the earlier searches in the transit camp. Moshe Deutsch described the scene upon arriving at Kamenets-Podolsk: "Hungarian gendarmes watched over us all night. At dawn the men were ushered into a nearby church, and the gendarmes closed the doors on us. They took us out, one by one, and commanded us to raise our hands as they searched our pockets and robbed us of our money,

FIG 3.4 Hungarian Jews arriving in Skala: "The Jews were dumped alongside of the road... the soldiers got tired of transporting them... the only thing remaining for them is the ditch by the road. At last this tolerated them." July 23, 1941. *Hungarian National Museum/Photo Archives, courtesy of Béla Somló.*

FIG 3.5 Deportees abandoned by the Hungarian military in Skala. While the women tended to the children, the "men sat on the ground with vacant stares looking into the distance." July 23, 1941. *Hungarian National Museum/Photo Archives, courtesy of Béla Somló.*

coins, and watches." A similar experience befell László Zobel, who, along several hundred deportees, was stripped all valuables "in a shed in Horodenka."[73]

"THEY PULL FROM THE DNIESTER JEWISH CORPSES DAY AFTER DAY..."

We do not know the identity of the writer of the report that contained this sentence. It was dated August 30, 1941—some six weeks after the start of the deportation. It conveyed a horrifying experience after the Hungarian military trucks disgorged their human cargo. The *sichacks*, as the Ukrainian irregular forces were called, often rough bands of young toughs, and sometimes peasants, clad in black shirts, pounced almost immediately on the defenseless multitude for free plunder.[74] Armed with old rifles and knives, they encountered little resistance from the women, children, and elderly—the majority of the expellees. Sometimes they offered protection for money, which rapidly evolved into increased demands for payment. The expellees became both wards of and easy prey for the Ukrainian irregulars.

Besides the impulse for plunder, rape, the lust for power, and a deep-seated anti-Semitism, there were no ideological motivations for the ensuing wave of murders perpetrated by the Ukrainian militia. The immediate conflict between the two groups raises a fundamental question about inserting a foreign population into a system that was not ready to absorb them. In addition, Galicia was a fertile ground for ethnic discontent. By the time of the commencement of the deportation, bloody anti-Jewish riots were erupting across the region. Fueled by accusations that the Jews wholeheartedly supported the Bolshevik regime, these riots were also encouraged by the German military forces. They reminded the local population that after the Red Army's entrance, in September 1939, the Soviet system was introduced in this region, which aimed to eradicate any semblance of Ukrainian nationalism. Consequently, tens of thousands were deported to the far east of the Soviet Union. Part of the Jewish population welcomed the new regime at first, because for them Communism seemed like a sort of emancipatory offer. The weightiest accusation that was leveled against the local Jewish communities was the "complicity" in the murder of political prisoners before the pullback by Soviet forces. Thousands of such prisoners were shot to death. Their corpses had to be dug out by the local Jewry.[75]

Thus, the Germans viewed this as an opportunity for the Ukrainian masses to vent their simmering resentment and frustration by launching violent anti-Jewish pogroms. A horrified Hungarian officer recorded in his diary on the first day of the occupation (July 4, 1941) of Kolomea about a pogrom that was orchestrated by German military authorities: "everyone is beating up everyone... they are collecting and concentrating the Jews in the central park for dismantling the statues of Lenin and Stalin, while unceasingly beating them... while I want to save a crying Jewish girl, a German soldier has threatened me with his submachine gun... in the ensuing mayhem, she was able to escape."[76]

This episode took place less than a week before the start of the deportation from Hungary. Similar scenes left their mark on the pages of the extant diaries of Hungarian military officers from every corner of Galicia. A Hungarian military observer identified these "irregular forces as armed national guards wearing yellow-blue armbands [who] often committed atrocities against the population, especially against the Jews, and took revenge on those against whom they held a grudge for some reason."[77] To their credit, the Hungarian military's attitude toward such disturbances was overwhelmingly negative, putting an end to anti-Jewish excesses under their occupational authority almost immediately. However, for the despoiling and random massacres of the aimlessly wandering groups of Hungarian Jews by marauding gangs of Ukrainian irregular forces, there was rarely protection.

We have no estimates as to the number of Hungarian Jews who were slaughtered by Ukrainian paramilitary groups. In assessing contemporary reports by Hungarian military officers and Ukrainian observers, an estimate in the thousands might be correct. The surviving accounts present in graphic detail the horrific pictures of Jewish corpses floating down the Dniester River. But descriptions of mass executions, the shooting of entire families, or groups of men pulled out of the meandering columns in ravines or prepared mass graves also provide a sobering reminder of the various forms of the carnage that took place in Galicia in July and August 1941.

Not surprisingly, the native population resented the unwanted intrusion of thousands of foreigners, especially Jews, which rapidly escalated into interethnic clashes. A poignant example for such conflict is described by the already quoted country doctor. During a visit to a sick patient in a small village, thus trusted and somewhat protected by the Ukrainian population, he encountered several hundred Hungarian Jews. They were facing an agitated peasant population of a small village, perhaps thirty households. The pandemonium that could have developed into a bloody conflict between the villagers and the deportees was averted by the doctor who learned, to his utter surprise and consternation, that "Hungarian soldiers unloaded the Jews in the village, told them that it was theirs—houses, fields, and all—and left in gales of laughter." The soldiers reassured the deportees that "this village is designated for them, and these fields and houses will be theirs."[78]

The doctor wrote, "On one side of the open square stood about 300 Hungarian Jews, women, the elderly, and children with bundles. One corpse already lay among them, above whom a young woman was crying—as I later learned, [it was] the wife of the murdered—and next to them, the wounds of other men and a woman were being treated." By the time the doctor averted further bloodshed and defused the situation, several Hungarians had been shot, killed, and wounded. Upon the pleas of the deportees, the doctor successfully bribed the Ukrainian paramilitaries to accompany the column to the neighboring town, from which they were chased further east by the next day.

This accidental skirmish was temporarily resolved, but in the general atmosphere of anti-Semitism, the local inhabitants felt hostility toward the newcomers arriving unexpectedly and in droves. Fear, exacerbated by the scarcity of food, also played a role. Based on information received from the deportees, a report by MIPI noted that "in many . . . places the remaining Ukrainian population objects already to the staying of the Jews transported there; they were driven out from many villages, and they were forced to run away into the woods . . . the Ukrainians do not want to let the Jews in at all in their villages, they drive us away from everywhere, and even our life is in danger."[79] This report, posted on July 23, relatively early in the deportation, and forwarded to the Hungarian government, was only the precursor of more detailed descriptions of the atrocities taking place in Galicia. Upon approaching the first Ukrainian village, László Zobel was introduced almost immediately to the horror: "They [the local Ukrainian militia] thought we were their enemies . . . so they attacked us at once and started shooting at us and several of us were injured and one of us even died."[80]

The narrative of the endless marches from village to village and from town to town was interspersed with periodic killing sprees upon a stop or during the nights. A member of a large group, estimated at close to two thousand people, Yaffa Rosenthal's testimony sums up this nightmare:

> Wherever we went, we went by walking carrying bundles, carrying the sick people. . . . As we walked, we were big, big transport. When they gave us sometimes a rest, anybody who did not get up fast enough was killed right there. There was a young man, I don't know his name, he was 14- or 15-years old boy. He carried his mother who had very swollen legs, she had problems walking. He carried her on his shoulders for about 3-4 days. And one time she could not get up fast enough, they killed her right there, in front of the son. They would not let him bury her. They left her on the site of where we were. . . . Anybody who fell or did not go along fast enough were killed on the road.[81]

Again, it's hard to find ideological principles for such escalating waves of violence. The words of the Hungarian poet Miklós Radnóti come to mind: "I lived on this earth in an age when man was so depraved that he pursued murder for pleasure, not just for complying with orders."[82] But, then, where inhumanity starts and where it ends is, at best, a nebulous proposition. Is it when little girls are raped and mutilated "beyond recognition," as encountered in contemporary reports, or when the Dniester overflowed with Jewish corpses that literally clogged up the river? Idl Feuer testified after the war that "early in August of 1941, Jewish refugees from Hungary came to Tlumacz, some 1,200 to 1,500 of them. Tlumacz Jews who were ready to help the refugees were sent with them to the same camp, in the direction of Horodenka. Later we learned about the fate of these Hungarian refugees: they were tied in groups with barbed wire and cast into the Dniester. Ukrainians lying in wait on the banks of the river grabbed the survivors and threw them back again."[83]

Perhaps not by coincidence, Ukrainians butchered local Jews the same way. In many villages along the Dniester virtually each and every Jew was slaughtered. They were herded from the villages to the river, where hands and feet of the elderly were tied with barbed wire. Additionally, "they tied stones to the children and pushed them into the middle of the Dniester from a ferry. The profound hatred felt for the Jews is well reflected by the fact that only a local priest was willing to help the doomed—but only if the drowning Jews promised to convert to the Christian faith."[84]

It became almost routine for the Hungarian exiles to be hounded from village to village with little respite. The accompanying militia members worked in shifts, replacing one crew with a fresh team from town to town. For the unfolding atrocities committed by the militia, often transcending human imagination, it is hard to find rational explanation. It is also hard to find the right word for the periodical "culling" of the men from the transports along the march or collecting them from the villages that they stopped in for a night.

Moshe Zelmanovits, nine years old at the time, remembered the long, arduous journey of several hundred people through forests and villages interspersed with daily killings. While the leaders of the militia were overseeing the march from horseback, the common militiamen accompanied the column on both sides. Those on horseback specifically targeted the tall and strapping fellows in the column, shooting them as they walked without any provocation. As Zelmanovits surmised, this was "a deadly form of attrition" to eliminate any potential problem or resistance from the men.

Along the march, passing village after village, they distributed scores of refugees in each settlement with the aim of making them work for the local farmers. Without giving a reason, three days later, in the middle of the night, they took the Zelmanovits family and several additional refugees, sixteen people altogether, to an outlying area and "simply, they shot us into a ravine." The story, however, did not end there. The father, sensing what would happen, "threw himself on the ground . . . as they started firing. I stood behind my brother Ezra, who, got a bullet in the back, which passed through him and grazed my side. He fell on me and, apparently, he knocked me into the mass grave. I thought, that's it . . . that is death. I didn't feel pain, I didn't feel anything." The militia concluded its ghastly task by covering the grave with branches and leaves. Finally, the young boy and his father were able to climb out of the mass grave, deathly silence all around them, by holding onto tree roots and low branches. They left behind seven members of their family. In recalling these events, Zelmanovits' voice was calm, almost detached, without rancour or bitterness. He never asked or gave thought to the central question: what was their motive for this mass murder?[85]

It was not an easy task to find shelter in the summer of 1941 in Galicia. A survivor remembered, in 1945, that the large group she and her immediate family was traveling with stopped at Chortkov—a large town in eastern Galicia. Upon finding shelter in a synagogue and being warned that Ukrainian bands routinely murdered Hungarian Jews, "young peasant boys came with weapons and took most of the men, but many women as well. We never saw those people again.... We hid the other men in the wardrobe; that was how we stayed in there crammed together and in unspeakable panic. For anyone could attack us and go unpunished."

Apparently, Chortkov was especially dangerous for Hungarian refugees, because another survivor's story supports this testimony. Cipora Brenner remembered how "they came and rounded up the men, 200 people. They took them outside the town. They made them dig a pit and buried them alive. We learned this the next day from a Christian butcher who was coming into the town. He told us that he saw a covered pit and papers lying around it. He took them to the Jewish community. Then the fate of the 200 men was revealed. Later they dug up the pit and saw that the men had not been shot to death, but buried alive."[86]

One group found temporary respite from the endless wandering in two villages, after having been made to march in columns from village to village. On August 8, which was a Friday, "the Hungarian Jews were driven out from the two villages at about 20 km from each other. Between lines of Ukrainian peasants, they were beaten brutally during the length of their march with cudgels [so] that about 15 of them died and all the others were injured (with broken arms and ribs, etc.)." Jewish doctors who treated the wounded could not provide medicine for the injured since pharmacies were forbidden for the Hungarian Jews. The source that described this macabre scene was a Hungarian labor serviceman who witnessed firsthand this death march.[87]

Complementing the horrors was the gnawing hunger that became an ever-present companion of the exiled. The original missive limiting the deportees to three days' worth of food ensured that hunger was a constant torment for the roaming groups or individual families. The contents of their bundles quickly vanished during the forced migration, and after a few weeks of wandering, the personal belongings of the deportees were exchanged for food. After that everything was bartered, and then only begging remained.

Yaffa Rosenthal recalled that the Ukrainian militiamen "did not give us any food or drinks. Sometimes we stopped on the places where there were waters. We drank what we could grab on the fields."[88] A Hungarian soldier, encountering groups of Jews around

Kamenets-Podolsk, recorded in his diary of seeing "great number of Jews, wandering in masses, with an escort, of course. It is like seeing the living garbage of humanity marching to the gallows. Many of them, especially women, in rags but wearing jewellery and with lips painted red, ask you for bread in Hungarian, and they would be willing to pay any price for it."[89] As we will see later, the German commandant of the city promised to supply food but never delivered it to the rapidly swelling Hungarian refugee population. By the time of this diary note, in the second half of August, the commandant had forbade the purchase of food items by Hungarian Jews.

In a letter to relatives, smuggled out by a labor serviceman, a deportee raised a rhetorical question: "what we carried along with us has allowed us to survive for a month. *And then what?* . . . We are destined to starve to death; that will be our fate." There was a going rate for objects to be exchanged. Clothing had the highest value. A suit would buy its seller a chicken. The price for a family to be taken over to the western bank of the Dnieper by boat, for those who made the decision to return to Hungary, was a winter coat.[90] A survivor remembered vividly that on their way back to Hungary, in a last-minute escape from extermination, her mother bartered her camisole, the last item that she had for an exchange, for a pitcher of milk. That saved the two of them.[91] Thus, survival hinged on one's ability to exchange objects brought with them from home. When the deportees ran out of items to be bartered, though, they had no choice but to beg.

After they had been abandoned by the Hungarian soldiers, the deportees encountered them only sporadically. Based on a few accounts, these encounters generally still proved to be useful and sometimes even lifesaving for the deportees, because the soldiers not only gave them food, but sometimes helped them to find accommodation, and reined in the violent Ukrainian militia. They were also instrumental in creating a communication lifeline between the deportees and their families in Budapest and elsewhere. Finally, some soldiers were willing to smuggle deportees back to the mother country, some driven by money, others by humanitarian impulses.

But there were also cases when the soldiers forced them to work for the army. When the Dniester flooded, washing away the military equipment stocked along the riverbank, the soldiers drove not only the local Jews into the river's strong current, but the deportees lingering in the area, too, so that they could save the valuable supplies. When a pontoon bridge was washed away by the rapid currents, the Hungarian deportees were forced to tow the ferry substituting for the structure. When the new bridge was mounted, the soldiers let the Jews go.[92]

Members of the Jewish labor companies viewed the torment endured by their Hungarian coreligionists, and sometimes their own immediate families, with a mixture of sympathy and a sense of powerlessness. One of them wrote: "When we stop somewhere, hundreds and hundreds surround us for bread; whatever we can collect we distribute among them, but what is it compared to the needs? For the sake of illustration, here is a typical scene: We bartered cigarettes for raspberries, and we dumped the bad ones. Grown-up people picked them all up from the ground, stuffing them into their mouth—they are on the verge of starving to death."[93]

Complicating the situation of the Hungarian refugees was a steady stream of Romanian Jews who were expelled from Bukovina, which later also reached Kamenets-Podolsk. Marion Samuel characterized it as "two rivers meet, the Romanian and Hungarian Jews . . . united."[94] Both group were left to their fate, rejected by the Ukrainians and the Poles, and persecuted by armed militias.

In this bleak landscape, the only ameliorating factor for the plight of these Jews was the support of the local Jewish communities, who extended badly needed humanitarian aid to the refugees. Sometimes, though, their numbers and the neverending columns were overwhelming even to major Jewish population centers. During the deportations 700 to 800 Jews arrived daily in the region situated 200 to 300 kilometers away from Hungary, because most of the deportees were taken beyond the Dniester. An example of the magnitude of this humanitarian disaster, conveyed in a letter by a woman to relatives in Budapest, described the arrival of a group of two thousand people in the region of Kamentsk-Podolsk. While the German commandant ordered the newly arrived to leave the area immediately, the local Jewish community, comprising mainly of women, children, and the elderly, was powerless to extend any humanitarian help.[95]

HELPING HANDS

During the early stages of the expulsion, the wandering multitude was met with a genuine sense of bewilderment. The dramatic entrance into a town by the refugees, often joined by thousands of Romanian Jews expelled from Bukovina, left everlasting, though perplexing, impressions on the host communities.

Contemporary accounts routinely designated the refugees as Carpathian Ruthenian or "Carpatoros" in the local lingo. While the refugees included those from various foreign countries, from the upper and eastern Hungarian provinces, and a sizeable number from Budapest, for the Ukrainian Jews they were all deported from the camp in Carpathian Ruthenia. Their initial ambivalence rapidly metamorphosed into a sense of urgency for a call to action, especially by Zionist youth groups. Saving lives often hinged on finding an immediate host family with some contacts in the local Ukrainian power structure who were willing to share accommodation and food with the refugees. Making contact with these families was facilitated by the fact that most of the Jews, at least from Carpathian Ruthenia, spoke or understood the language of the local Jews, Yiddish. Some were also able to communicate in Rusyn, a Ukrainian regional language that was spoken on both sides of the Carpathian Mountains.

The number of refugees crossing daily into the little or midsize towns was staggering. In the town of Borshchiv (Borszczów in Polish and Austrian), for example, "within two weeks approximately seven to eight thousand Hungarian Jews went through the city." Most of the Jews traveled on foot. Some of them were housed overnight in tobacco warehouses. Responding to the humanitarian needs, the community brought "cooked food and bread" and later "hired wagons to take the old and weak to the border [Kamenets-Podolsk]." Complicating this humanitarian gesture, almost simultaneously, some Jews who had escaped pogroms in Romania started to arrive. Unfortunately, "most of them had perished on the way."[96]

Even in relatively small towns, such as Mielnica, the local community responded to the plight of the expellees with immediate aid: "The Hungarians brought to Mielnica several truckloads of Jewish refugees from Carpatoros. These refugees were starved and weak, shoeless and threadbare, and had been robbed and beaten on the way by the Ukrainians. The Jews of the town aided the refugees as much as their means allowed, inviting them into their homes, feeding them, and collecting clothing for them."[97]

The rapidly emerging Jewish Councils (*Judenrat*) and ghettos—set up upon German order—also provided badly needed support. From Kolomea to Skala, from Horodenka to Kosów, and from Nadwórna to Buczacz, public kitchens, distribution of clothing, and housing assistance were extended to the refugees. Equally important was the establishment of orphanages for the hundreds of children who were separated from their parents, or, in the later stages, whose parents were murdered. One of the unforeseeable consequences of these hastily arranged shelters for the children, though, was the tragic fact that orphanages became death traps during the final liquidation of the ghettos.[98]

The Jewish leadership in Kolomea made special efforts to create liveable conditions for the deportees. They were given soup and bread for breakfast and lunch, and they could spend the nights in the corridors of the building of the religious community. Kolomea was unique in Galicia. Having the headquarters of the Royal Hungarian Army might have had some moderating, though limited, influence. Also, in addition to the Hungarians, Jews from Austria, Czechoslovakia, Slovakia, and Germany made the town an international refugee hub. Altogether, two thousand of them crowded the town. They were placed with host families who shared accommodation, food, and clothing. Among the children there were one hundred orphans who posed a special problem because they understood only Hungarian.[99]

There are dramatic descriptions of their arrival in Stanisławów, mainly from the Máramaros region, which straddled Carpathian Ruthenia and Transylvania. A diary note about their entrance into the city is especially gripping: "The refugees were in a dreadful situation: broken, worn-out, frail, hungry, ill, and destitute, since they have been plundered en-route by the Hungarian [military] and Ukrainian population."

Initially, they were housed in religious institutions and synagogues. However, the swelling of their numbers as more and more groups were directed to this city forced the Jewish Council to move them to the Rudolfsmühle, a flour mill that was owned by Samuel Rudolf, an unfinished building several stories high. "This building turned into the house of death, due to hunger and the cold... About 1,000 sick and frail Jews lived in this building until the main Aktion of March 31, 1942, they were the first to be killed in the Aktion."[100] While the *Judenrat* formed a "health committee to lighten their lot," and organized a communal kitchen and other necessary facilities, the local Jewish community faced such challenges that "very little was done for the Hungarian Jews." Abraham Liebesman's diary conveys in tragic details their fate: "their lot was constant hunger, cold, not enough clothing to cover their bodies, exposed to all sorts of sickness like typhoid, dysentery, they were short on everything, hardly any similar situation on earth."[101]

Indeed, the deteriorating social and humanitarian conditions in the host communities and in the rapidly mushrooming ghettos, German food restrictions, and periodic killings imposed a reduction and elimination of support to the Hungarians—dictated by an almost atavistic or natural instinct to give preference to the host community. In Stanisławów, the *Judenrat* understood that by their own power alone they could not sustain support for the Hungarian refugees. This city held the largest concentration of Hungarian Jews after Kamenets-Podolsk, around 2,300 in number. In their letter to the Hungarian Jewish Baroness Edith Weiss, the *Judenrat* appealed for assistance, describing the rapidly deteriorating conditions in the city in which the local community's needs could not be met, as well as the situation in the Rudolfsmühle. It is unknown if this appeal was honored by the baroness or MIPI, but we have information about her appeals to both the Hungarian and the International Red Cross for support of the deportees already transferred to Galicia.[102]

The fact that the entire region was under military administration, first Hungarian, and then German, might have excluded any potential for organized support from Hungary. Most of the surviving sources about the fate of the deportees came from main population centers like Kolomea, Stanisławów, and Kamenets-Podolsk. An interesting memoir from a rather ordinary Ukrainian village, Bilah Solta (Bil'che Zolote in Ukrainian), provides a unique vantage point of the column of Hungarian Jews passing through a small village where no organized leadership, like a Jewish council, could provide assistance: "These were religious and poor families, taking care of many hungry and tired children." The group was escorted by the Ukrainian paramilitaries who "allowed them a short rest in the village. They seemed worn out, pitiable and the hunger struck them hard." The local Jews were "afraid to come out" at first, until one of their leaders decided to act by contacting the only moral authority in the village, the local priest. He, in turn, ordered the people in charge to allow the distribution of the refugees among the Jewish families in the village. The respite was temporary, though, because the paramilitaries forced them to continue their deadly journey: "They were deported to the depth of Ukraine, there they were killed. Many of them died of hunger, others died during the war."[103] The cryptic allusion of "there they were killed" implied that the massacres across the region, and which culminated in Kamenets-Podolsk, took their deadly toll on the Hungarian refugees.

THE FINAL DESTINATION

Kamenets-Podolsk was the end destination. We cannot ignore the question as to why and how thousands upon thousands of Jews from Hungary ended up in this faraway place. The direct distance between the transit camp in Kőrőmező and Kamenets-Podolsk is around 150 miles. However, the majority of the deportees were led through circuitous routes, without a clear target destination in mind, which often took two to three weeks and ended up in various towns where they shared the fate of the Jews of Galicia.

The stated aim of the Hungarian military and political leadership was to deposit the thousands of expellees as far as possible from the Hungarian border. This translated, as we can learn from correspondence and reports, into removing the Jews over the Dniester River, which provided a natural barrier for desperate attempts of return. It is difficult to ascertain the reason for selecting Kamenets-Podolsk for the destination, because no explicit or implicit military correspondence survived that could point to a central missive selecting this nondescript border town, a former tzarist outpost, on the border of Galicia and Podolia. Part of the answer might lie in the fact that Kamenets-Podolsk was the farthest point in the short Hungarian military conquest. Indeed, many Jews were deposited there by columns of military trucks, brusquely ordering them to proceed to the "castle," which in reality was an imposing tsarist fortress.

The majority of people, though, were mercilessly driven by Ukrainian militiamen across eastern Galicia, through muddy "country roads, some of them walking 40 km on foot . . . with their bundles. . . . I saw one who was holding a bundle even between his teeth, it was pouring, and he was barefoot."[104] Unfortunately, these words of a Hungarian labor serviceman do not reveal the reason as to why these Ukrainian bands also drove the ill-fated Jews toward Kamenets-Podolsk. But, by the second half of August, a large segment of these so-called repatriated Jews, close to two-thirds of the exiles, arrived and finally settled into a precarious existence in an already overcrowded, poverty infested, and plague decimated ghetto located in the Old Town of Kamenets-Podolsk. At first, the local Jewry made every effort to accommodate the newly arrived Hungarians in synagogues, community halls, and private homes. The deportees were also able to secure provisions by bartering in villages around the city with local peasants.

By the middle of August, though, when everyone had to move into the newly created ghetto in the Old Town, the full weight of overcrowding, poverty, hunger, and epidemics erased any distinction between Hungarians and locals. On August 26, 1941, the Hungarian Jews "were lined up in rows in military fashion and taken to the destroyed train station.... Rabbis with Torah scrolls led [this procession], followed by mothers with their children, and ill and old people supported [by others]. All the people moved along with difficulty; the majority of them believed that they were going to be returned home."

They did not know the final destination of their journey, though, since they were reassured, somewhat nebulously, that they were going to be relocated—even as far as Odessa or maybe taking a train home. Instead, the next morning,

> they were driven out of the barracks with rubber clubs and taken to an open field where there was a ravine surrounded by hills. There all of them were shot by SS men.... [The site of the three days massacre] was full of smoke coming from the constant shooting. Many people were thrown into the grave while still alive, some of them having been wounded only slightly. Several days afterward, both day and night frightful noises were heard from the graves. Then SS men forced peasants from the surrounding villages to cover the graves. The railway workers said that the earth was heaving for several days.[105]

Orchestrated by a hitherto unknown SS general, Friedrich Jeckeln, this massacre set a new high in the rapidly evolving waves of mass murder. This three-day "event" also heralded a new phase in the Holocaust: the total annihilation of Jews as well as the opening salvo in the Hungarian Holocaust. Thus, these 23,600 victims, among them 14,000 to 16,000 Hungarian deportees, became a statistic in the art of mass murder and, in turn, the history of the Holocaust.

4

KAMENETS-PODOLSK
The Anatomy of a Massacre

"Look at this man. He is a typical Jew that must be exterminated so that we Germans can live." This was the concluding sentence of a rather theatrical speech given by one of the most notorious mass murderers of the Holocaust, SS General Friedrich Jeckeln. As one of the participating policemen recalled in his own trial twenty years later, Jeckeln spoke these words after the three-day slaughter that extinguished the lives of 23,600 people in Kamenets-Podolsk: "I still remember that about 6 Jews were kept back for the end of the shooting. These 6 Jews were ordered by Jeckeln to stand between two bomb craters. Then J[eckeln] made a short speech to us. I remember, I believe, that during his speech he pointed specifically to one Jew, who was wearing a grey suit and who made a particularly respectable impression. In very dramatic manner he referred to this Jew by name."[1]

IN FINDING A RATIONALE FOR MASS MURDER, PERPETRATORS OFTEN RESORT to existentialist reasoning that borders on theatrical pathos. The executioners must, after all, find justification for a horrendous crime. The quote above constitutes an ideological summation for three days of carnage. The mass murder took place between August 27 and 29, 1941, during which four huge pits, craters from a series of ammunition explosions, were filled to the brim with murdered Hungarian, Romanian, and local Jews. This quote, allegedly by Jeckeln, Höhere SS und Polizeiführer (Higher SS and Police Leader, HSSPF) for southern Russia at the site of the slaughter, was his justification for genocide accross the occupied territories against "inferior" races.

The message these words implied was a war in which the Jew as a cosmic enemy with diabolical power must be eradicated. They also faithfully reflected the world vision of Hitler, and that of the Nazi leadership, of a final cataclysmic struggle between National Socialism and Judeo-Boshevism. A revealing picture of smiling German soldiers with a large hand-painted sign is eerily reminiscent of Jeckeln's pronouncement: "The Russians must die so that we can live." It is dated October 2, 1941.[2]

This massacre, the largest until that point in the history of the Holocaust, existed at the intersection of ideology, economics, and personal ambitions operating within the Holocaust. The Hungarian deportation itself cannot be viewed strictly within a Hungarian context—it must be looked at against parallel policies of expulsions sweeping across Europe. Neither can we see the mass murder of these expelled Jews and Christian family members as an isolated incident of genocidal politics. The Kamenets-Podolsk mass murder, taking place in a relatively insignificant town, is important not only as a horrifying historical episode, but also in what it says of the Nazi politics of genocide as it swept across a whole continent.

On June 30, 1941, the Hungarian forces designated as *Kárpát-Csoport* (Carpathian Corps) crossed the Soviet border and rapidly reached the Dniester River—a line crucial for the fate of many of the deported. By July 10, the Hungarian Rapid Deployment Force (*Gyors Hadtest*), embedded within the Carpathian Corps, reached Kamenets-Podolsk in Podolia Province. We can identify the commencement of the mass arrests, collection, and expulsion of the Hungarian Jews to around that date. The fulcrum of their eastward movement within Galicia was in Kolomea, where the headquarters of the Royal Hungarian Army was located. Many of those expelled were transported directly or through circuitous wanderings to Kamenets-Podolsk. Equal numbers were deposited arbitrarily across Galicia and then force-marched hundreds of miles on foot to reach the same destination.

Concentrated in the ghetto, located in the Old Town together with their Romanian and local coreligionists, they were murdered at the end of August 1941. Among the total number of murdered there were also two thousand Romanian Jews from Bukovina. They had either escaped originally with the Red Army or were forced across the Dniester River by Romanian forces, following the explicit order of the Romanian dictator, General Ion Antonescu. While the Germans were able to repulse a column of Jews expelled across the Dniester by the Romanians at Yampol, a second column, mainly from Bukovina, reached Kamenets-Podolsk around August 20, 1941. Kamenets-Podolsk, in the words of Christopher Browning, became "the destination of mass deportation by Romanian and Hungarian authorities, before the formal transfer of the city to the civil administration [i.e., German] on September 1."[3]

Although relatively small, the city had importance for the three allies—Germany, Hungary, and Romania. Kamenets-Podolsk enjoyed a strategic location as a Tsarist outpost of the Russian Empire, straddling the border between Galicia and Podolia. Allocated to the Russian Empire during the partition of Poland in 1793, the town had never benefited from the architectural and cultural influences of Habsburg Austria, like Lemberg-Lwów (Lviv), for example, which controlled the western half of Galicia for more than a hundred years. Like all towns in the region, it already had a sizeable Jewish population who lived alongside Polish, Ukrainian, and Armenian inhabitants. While it might have been strategically placed, the city was a nondescript, drab former garrison town, with a massive fortress overlooking the Smotrych River. By the time of the transfer of power from military to German civilian control and owing to the influx of tens of thousands of expellees, Jews comprised close to 75 percent of the local population.

THE GHETTO

The decision by the military commandant of the city, *Oberstleutnant* (Lieutenant Colonel) Josef Meiler, to establish a large ghetto in Kamenets-Podolsk on August 9, 1941, was more out of necessity than a matter of official policy. Ghettoization did not commence in Galicia or Podolia until the latter part of the year. The drive was directly influenced by the large influx of Jews from Hungary. The official German estimate of Hungarian Jews deposited in Kamenets-Podolsk by mid-August hovered around 11,000 people. However, a more realistic appraisal, based on Hungarian and Galician sources, puts the number at around 16,000. Not surprisingly, so many "refugees" unbalanced the German military's logistical and supply system by diverting scarce food supplies from the Wehrmacht to civilian consumption.

Two conflicting forces were at work that created this logistical quagmire. Hungarian authorities were determined to expel the maximum number of Jews, specifically to this Podolian *shtetl*. This came into direct conflict with German military interest in solidifying their grip on a region that teemed with the struggling remnants of the defeated Red Army as well as a sizeable local Jewish presence. The Hungarian deportees became an almost instantaneous irritant and pawn in Hungarian–German relations, something that can be seen in internal German military communications. The unregulated influx created sanitary as well as food supply problems for which the military authorities were not prepared.

The city came under German military administration on July 11, 1941. This was followed by the establishment of the first makeshift ghetto on an island in the Old Town on July 20, 1941, with corresponding and routine discriminatory policies—among them requiring the wearing of a distinctive white armband with a blue "Zionist star" in the middle, instituted by the Wehrmacht in every town and city. It also applied the Nuremberg Laws' definition of "who is a Jew."[4]

The final removal of the entire Jewish population of Kamenets-Podolsk and surrounding environs into this designated *jüdische Wohnungviertel* (ghetto) was to be accomplished, the Feldkommandant decreed, "by August 9, 1941 at 3:00 PM." The announcement also specified that local Jews moving into the enclave "were limited to bring with them only fifty kilograms of luggage per person ... and [to facilitate] the creation of a five-member Judenrat." Finally, it forbade the residents "to leave the enclave without written official authorization."[5]

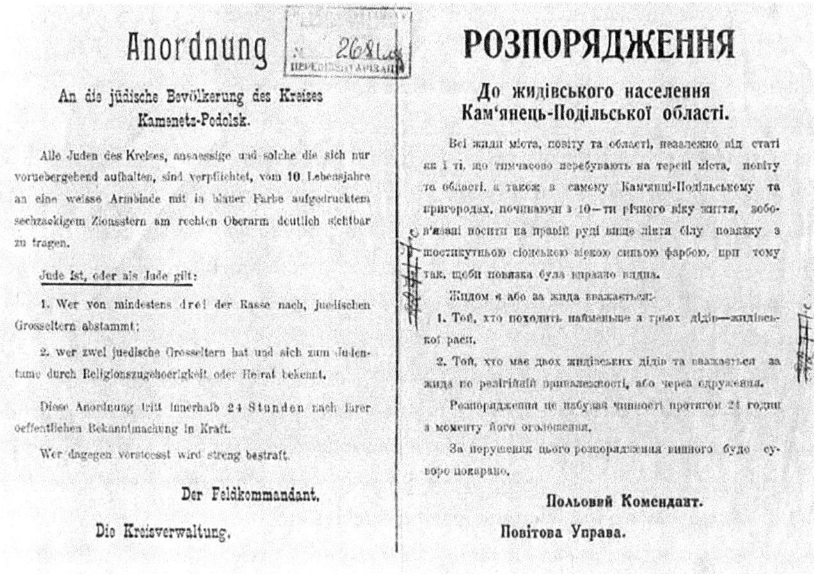

Anordnung

An die jüdische Bevölkerung des Kreises Kamenetz-Podolsk.

Alle Juden des Kreises, ansaessige und solche die sich nur voruebergehend aufhalten, sind verpflichtet, vom 10 Lebensjahre an eine weisse Armbinde mit in blauer Farbe aufgedrucktem sechzackigem Zionsstern am rechten Oberarm deutlich sichtbar zu tragen.

Jude ist, oder als Jude gilt:

1. Wer von mindestens drei der Rasse nach, juedischen Grosseltern abstammt;

2. wer zwei juedische Grosseltern hat und sich zum Judentume durch Religionszugehoerigkeit oder Heirat bekennt.

Diese Anordnung tritt innerhalb 24 Stunden nach ihrer oeffentlichen Bekanntmachung in Kraft.

Wer dagegen verstoesst wird streng bestraft.

Der Feldkommandant.

Die Kreisverwaltung.

РОЗПОРЯДЖЕННЯ

До жидівського населення Кам'янець-Подільської області.

Всі жиди міста, повіту та області, незалежно від статі як і ті, що тимчасово перебувають на терені міста, повіту та області, а також в самому Кам'янці-Подільському та пригородах, починаючи з 10—ти річного віку життя, зобов'язані носити на правій руці вище лікта білу повязку з шостикутньою сіонською зіркою синьою фарбою, при тому так, щоби повязка була виразно видна.

Жидом є або за жида вважається:

1. Той, хто походить найменьше з трьох дідів—жидівської раси.

2. Той, хто має двох жидівських дідів та вважається за жида по релігійній приналежності, або через одруження.

Розпорядження це набуває чинності протягом 24 годин з моменту його оголошення.

За порушення цього розпорядження винного буде суворо покарано.

Польовий Комендант.

Повітова Управа.

FIG 4.1 Decree by the military commander of Kamenetsk Podolsk: "All Jews over 10 years old to wear at all time a white armband with the 'Zionist-Star' on the right arm." July 24, 1941. *United States Holocaust Memorial Museum, courtesy of the State Archives of Khmel'nyts'kyi Region, Ukraine.*

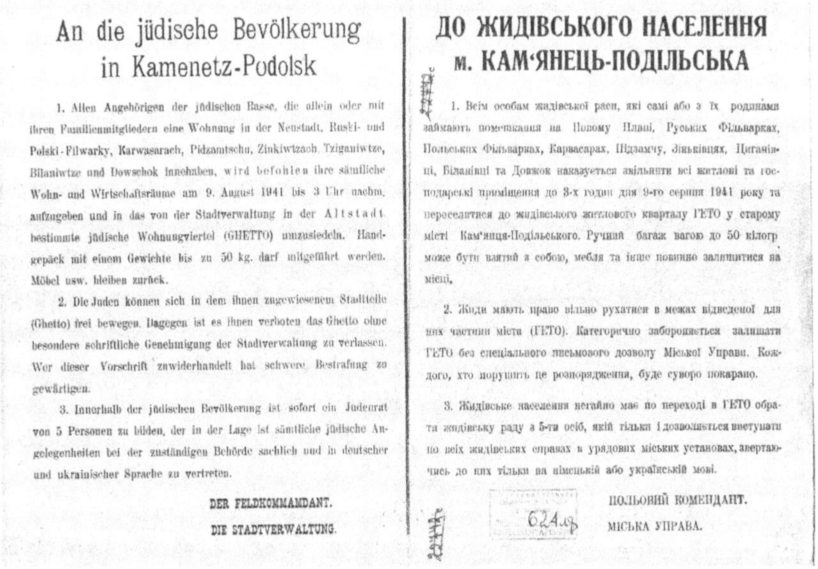

An die jüdische Bevölkerung in Kamenetz-Podolsk

1. Allen Angehörigen der jüdischen Rasse, die allein oder mit ihren Familienmitgliedern eine Wohnung in der Neustadt, Ruski- und Polski-Filwarky, Karwasarach, Pidzamtschu, Zinkiwtzach, Tziganiwtze, Bilaniwtze und Dowschok innehaben, wird befohlen ihre sämtliche Wohn- und Wirtschaftsräume am 9. August 1941 bis 3 Uhr nachm. aufzugeben und in das von der Stadtverwaltung in der Altstadt bestimmte jüdische Wohnungviertel (GHETTO) umzusiedeln. Handgepäck mit einem Gewichte bis zu 50 kg. darf mitgeführt werden. Möbel usw. bleiben zurück.

2. Die Juden können sich in dem ihnen zugewiesenem Stadtteile (Ghetto) frei bewegen. Dagegen ist es ihnen verboten das Ghetto ohne besondere schriftliche Genehmigung der Stadtverwaltung zu verlassen. Wer dieser Vorschrift zuwiderhandelt hat schwere Bestrafung zu gewärtigen.

3. Innerhalb der jüdischen Bevölkerung ist sofort ein Judenrat von 5 Personen zu bilden, der in der Lage ist sämtliche jüdische Angelegenheiten bei der zuständigen Behörde sachlich und in deutscher und ukrainischer Sprache zu vertreten.

DER FELDKOMMANDANT.

DIE STADTVERWALTUNG.

ДО ЖИДІВСЬКОГО НАСЕЛЕННЯ м. КАМ'ЯНЕЦЬ-ПОДІЛЬСЬКА

1. Всім особам жидівської раси, які самі або з їх родинами займають помешкання на Новому Плані, Руських Фільварках, Польських Фільварках, Карвасарах, Підзамчу, Зіньківцях, Циганівці, Біланівці та Довжок наказується звільнити всі житлові та господарські приміщення до 3-х годин дня 9-го серпня 1941 року та переселитися до жидівського житлового кварталу ГЕТО у старому місті Кам'янця-Подільського. Ручний багаж вагою до 50 кілогр може бути взятий з собою, мебля та інше повинно залишитися на місці.

2. Жиди мають право вільно рухатися в межах відведеної для них частини міста (ГЕТО). Категорично забороняється залишати ГЕТО без спеціального письмового дозволу Міської Управи. Кожного, хто порушить це розпорядження, буде суворо покарано.

3. Жидівське населення негайно має по переході в ГЕТО обрати жидівську раду з 5-ти осіб, якій тільки і дозволяється виступати по всіх жидівських справах в урядових міських установах, звертаючись до них тільки на німецькій або українській мові.

ПОЛЬОВИЙ КОМЕНДАНТ.

МІСЬКА УПРАВА.

FIG 4.2 Decree by the military commander of Kamenetsk Podolsk: ". . . from August 9, 1941, all Jews must move into the Old Town Ghetto." August 8, 1941. *United States Holocaust Memorial Museum, courtesy of the State Archives of Khmel'nyts'kyi Region, Ukraine.*

A report from Lieutenant Colonel Meiler, dated on August 13, 1941, was more specific. It detailed the necessary steps for segregating the Jews from the surrounding population. The report to the army headquarters was very specific, also, about Hungarian presence in the city. "In KP all Jews were requested recently to leave the new parts of the city and move into the old-town—as their future ghetto. They could take only 50 kg luggage per person. The old town was evacuated by the Ukrainian population. As it was reported, 3,000 recently deported Jews by the Hungarians are in the old city already. Their further treatment [return] has been requested, but no decision has yet been taken. The demand of these Jews on the food supply poses an unwanted burden on the city."[6]

The ghetto was not a hermetically enclosed entity with fences and guarded gates; it was accessible by one easily guarded bridge. In the early stages, the residents, including Hungarian refugees, could leave the zone in their quest for food in the neighboring villages. The ghetto was more of a designated area to which the rapidly expanding influx of refugees was funneled and local Jews relocated.

Upon arriving in the city, the Hungarian refugees, especially those from Budapest, made every effort to establish some semblance of a functioning civil society. The German military commandant (Feldkommandant Meiler) made a promise to supply the ghetto with adequate food. This was never done. On August 24, 1941, the Jews living in the ghetto were expressly forbidden, in German, Hungarian, and Ukrainian: "(1) to purchase food outside the ghetto; (2) Jews who buy food-stuff outside the ghetto (Altstadt) will be severely punished; and (3) all food-stuff will be confiscated, and the person will be punished."[7]

Neither the town nor the new ghetto was designed for the mass of destitute and brutalized people that moved there. Indeed, for the military authorities, this solution was only temporary. Unlike Poland and the Baltic, there had never been any desire in Ukraine to set up proper ghettoes, but only temporary "storage facilities" for Jews waiting for the Final Solution.

Some of the local inhabitants, mainly the young men of military age, escaped from the city with the retreating Soviet Army, leaving behind the elderly, women, and children. Prior to the war, the Jewish inhabitants of the city ranged around 14,000—38 percent of the total population. It is estimated that the establishment of the ghetto, with the influx of large number of Jews from neighboring communities as well as those deported from Hungary in July and August, led to a total of 28,000 Jews being compressed into the Old City. More than half of them came from Hungary.

The town was impacted dramatically by fighting in which many houses were destroyed and the entire district made uninhabitable. A Hungarian officer described the scene upon entering the town on July 10: "the city is destroyed by the German air force ... unburied corpses under the ruins ... large segment of the population fled."[8]

Bekanntmachung

Mit dem heutigen Tage ist jeder Verkauf von Lebensmitteln an Juden verboten.
Juden, die ausserhalb der Altstadt Lebensmittel einkaufen, werden bestraft.
Bei Verkäufen von Lebensmitteln an Juden werden die Lebensmittel beschlagnahmt
und der Verkäufer wird bestraft.
24. 8. 1941.   Der Feldkommandant.

Hirdetmény

A mai naptól kezdve élelmiszerek eladása zsidók részére tilos.
Azok a zsidók, akik az óvároson kivül élelmiszert vásárolnak, szigorúan
megbüntettetnek.
Zsidók részére történö élelmiszer - eladásnál az élelmiszert elkobozzuk es az eladót
megbüntetjük.
24. 8. 1941.   Tábori parancsnokság.

ОГОЛОШЕННЯ

З сьогоднішнього дня продаж різних продуктів жидам недозволяється.

Жиди, які будуть купувати продукти за межами старого міста караються.

Куплені продукти за межами старого міста конфіскуються, продавець каратиметься.

24. 8. 1941 року.   Польовий Комендант.

FIG 4.3 The final decree by the military commander of Kamenetsk Podolsk, before the mass murder: "From now on, selling food for Jews is forbidden; Jews are forbidden to purchase food outside of the Old-Town; The guilty will be severely punished." August 24, 1941. *United States Holocaust Memorial Museum, courtesy of the State Archives of Khmel'nyts'kyi Region, Ukraine.*

Later reports and letters by soldiers, victims, and survivors that reached the Hungarian capital paint a horrifying picture of a demographic and humanitarian nightmare. A survivor from Uzhgorod (Carpathian Ruthenia) remembered that "There was [were] no beds at all. In this time in Kamenets-Podolsk there was you can imagine as we lived—maybe six, ten, thirteen, fourteen people in one room and we all slept on the floor and there was no kitchen to cook... we lived, you know, like animals, like animals. We slept on the floor, we didn't have beds, we had nothing."[9]

Although the conditions seemed dire upon arrival, a quest for some semblance of order was initiated by the new arrivals. They set up three committees: one for communication "with the German military command, the second with the Hungarian military command, and the third to look after local matters."[10] As the days went by, though, the situation deteriorated to the point that the German military became alarmed about a possible outbreak of widespread epidemic and infectious diseases. The specter of a typhus epidemic was especially threatening because of the polluted water supply. Their concerns were not unfounded; reports indicate that diarrheal infections were rampant among the refugees. Frantic German reports sent to Berlin underlined these conditions not only in Kamenets-Podolsk, but also in the Romanian sector. The daily log by a Hungarian artillery regiment on August 18 and 19, 1941, conveys in dramatic hues the desperation of the deportees and the German apprehension. The first report on August 18, 1941, noted that "There are many Jews here, especially women in rags, they ask for bread in Hungarian, wearing jewelry and with lips painted red. They would give any money for it. Some count their steps with the ultimate desperation shown on their faces, others are crawling on the road collapsed from exhaustion and hunger. Others bandage the wounds on their feet with rags from their clothes. Tiny children are crying, collapsing from hunger." A second log was more general and included a description of the situation along the Dniester River: "The Jewish quarter of the city is full of deported Jews, among them many are from Budapest; they live in unspeakable squalor, they come and go in scanty attire, the streets stink, unburied dead bodies are lying in some houses. The water of the Dniester is infected, here and there corpses are washed up on the bank of the river. The crews are forbidden to leave the camp, drinking the water is forbidden, contact with the population is forbidden."[11]

The threat of a full-blown epidemic explains why the German military authorities became alarmed by the seemingly intractable situation in the city as well as by the thousands of destitute refugees roaming the countryside. This quandary is reflected vividly in German military communications directly to the headquarters of General Karl von Roques,[12] commander of the rear areas of Army Group South. They requested intercession with the Hungarian government to halt and reverse the deportation policies. On July 28, 1941, a message was sent to von Roques: "Hungarian Jews are delivered from Hungarian concentration camps [internment camp] by trucks to the regions of

Buczacz, Czortków, and Kamenets-Podolsk. Ukrainian population in turmoil. These Jews must forcibly return. Division 444/Ia requests that Hungarian authorities be given appropriate instructions."

Correspondingly, communication with Hungarian authorities was established by Major-General Kurt Himer,[13] who served as the liaison officer for the OKW (*Oberkommando der Wehrmacht*—Supreme Command of the Armed Forces) in Budapest in 1941. He was informed by his Hungarian counterpart on July 30, also forwarded to von Roques, that "these Jews are not Hungarian citizens. They escaped to northeastern Hungary from the Soviets two years ago. They are returned now to their native land again." This was a patent lie.

The trail of communication did not end here. A characteristically terse note in Kozma's diary informs us of a meeting as late as September 16, 1941, between General Himer and Kozma, presumably about Hungarian efforts to resume the deportation.[14] A follow-up frantic communication by Security Division 444 to headquarters on July 31, 1941, was even more alarming: "the number of Jews increased by the influx of Jews expelled from Hungary, of which 3,000 have arrived in the last few days. Feeding them is proving a major challenge, danger of epidemic also exists. Immediate order for their evacuation is urgently requested."[15]

By the first week of August, thousands more joined the ranks of the expellees in the city. A deportee's letter sent back to Hungary on August 4, 1941, indicates a surreal situation in which German authorities were making every effort to get rid of the Hungarian Jews while the Hungarian government had steadfastly rejected them. It also underscores the German dilemma: "After 5 days of terrible sufferings, we arrived [2000 people] to the city of Kamenic Depolski [Kamenets-Podolsk]. Near the Russian border. No sooner had they deposited us; the German commander informed us that we must leave the city by tomorrow morning. . . . It's incomprehensible that the Hungarian authorities deport us here and the German authorities in turn expel us."[16]

Devoid of housing and logistical support capable of sustaining such a large number of people, setting up the ghetto was a German military-made humanitarian disaster. It became a slow death sentence to thousands of Hungarian expellees and local Jews. A report from the city two weeks later, sent by Feldcommandant Meiler, reiterates almost word for word this assessment with a warning about a looming likelihood of famine: "As it was reported, there are already 3,000 recently expelled Jews from Hungary reside in the Altstadt for whom a decision of removal has still not have been made. The feeding of these Jews poses a particularly unwanted burden for the city . . . the Jews are used by the mayor in work details for daily services [only cleanup], that are in the public interest."[17]

Compounding this crisis, the administration of the city within the general reorganization of the newly occupied territories was scheduled to be transferred from

German military to civilian control on September 1, 1941. This gave an additional level of urgency to finding a solution to the ghetto. These diverse factors leading up to the Kamenets-Podolsk mass murder reinforces the notion that the genocide doesn't emerge in a vacuum.

ORININ: THE ANTECHAMBER OF DEATH

The sporadic and randomized execution of thousands of Hungarian Jews by German detachments commenced prior or very close to the destruction of the Kamenets-Podolsk ghetto. One example, almost unknown in the annals of the Holocaust, specifically singled out Hungarian Jews. It took place in Orinin (Orynyn in Ukrainian) on August 26, 1941. Based on the testimonies of Hungarian and Galician survivors, and supported by the findings of the Soviet State Commission investigating Nazi atrocities around Orinin, the number of Hungarian Jews killed was estimated to be over two thousand. At the time, local Jews were unharmed. The target of extermination was explicitly the Hungarians.[18] It foreshadowed the mass murder in Kamenets-Podolsk by a day.

Zvi (Hermann) Zelikovitch, a thirteen-year-old boy, recounted after the war a tortuous and dramatic journey across Galicia with a group of fellow Jews, mainly from Máramaros County in Carpathian Ruthenia. Upon arriving in Orinin they were housed in a large barn and with local Jewish families. On a sunny morning, this respite from the long wandering came to an abrupt halt. They were told to assemble next to a picturesque meadow with the promise that they would be repatriated to Hungary. In the recollection of this young boy, though, the elation of returning home soon evaporated:

> Suddenly three or four trucks appeared. Some 60 or 70 German soldiers armed with pistols climbed out of the trucks. This was the first time I had ever seen German soldiers. These soldiers were part of the SS, but I learned this only later ...
>
> ... three private automobiles stopped. We were standing in the field by the road not far from the cars. The soldiers immediately fell into formation while I watched them, not standing with my parents. I stood alone to see the soldiers and their formation. I remember well thinking that I liked the formation.
>
> Then all of a sudden, I heard screaming. The soldiers leaped up onto the trucks, taking out machine guns and still I understood nothing of what was happening. Everything happened in seconds. I stood there and watched as they unloaded the machine guns. It just never occurred to me what was about to happen.

The horror began—the killing horror. The German soldiers began firing. I heard terrible screaming from all directions: "Shema Yisroel, Shema Yisroel" from thousands of Jews, exactly how many I cannot say.[19]

Four teenage boys, including Zelikovitch, were able escape into the cornfields. Thus, they would not witness the second and main phase of the mass murder. For that, we recount the testimony of sixteen-year-old Max Solomon (Mayer Slomovitz) from a small village in Carpathian Ruthenia. The goal of the initial gunfire was not the immediate extermination of the assembled Jews, for no ditches or mass graves were prepared in advance. It was only aimed to control the thousands of terrified people who were led, in groups of three hundred, from the scenic field to military fortifications that were blown up by the retreating Soviet forces several miles away. In describing the final hellish scene, the surviving Solomon didn't need to resort to superlatives. The systematic killing of the refugees from ten o'clock in the morning until eight o'clock in the evening, as they were shot into a deep trench, filled with water from burst pipes, leaves little to the imagination. In the words of the survivor, "two Germans sitting by a large machine gun, one was feeding it, one was shooting.... There was a huge-huge piece of steel across that bunker." As the killing unfolded, "people did not look like people ... you see only shadows; people had no faces, you could see only shadows. They march approximately 50–100–150 people on the piece of steel [in succession]. Some of them been hit some of them not hit, some of them killed some of them wounded but everyone goes and you can just see that everyone is falling into the water ... water, water, water, still water." His words, spilling out in staccato, convey a surreal scene of bodies filling up the watery grave. These words, like a string hanging in the air, have the force of poetry—the ars poetica of mass murder.

Two thousand Hungarian Jews were murdered within ten hours. As the evening and silence descended on the killing field, the dazed sixteen-year-old, wounded slightly in the head by a grazing bullet, stumbled on top of the dead and the wounded who by then completely filled the watery trench: "as he recalled, he was found and instructed by a Ukrainian woman, who gave him her blouse, to turn to the left and escape into the cornfield. The boy, stunned and disoriented, turned to the right, facing two hundred Ukrainian militiamen who silently parted as the boy escaped. They might have seen an apparition."[20]

The most immediate question is how the massacre in Orinin was connected to and presaged the much more massive bloodletting in Kamenets-Podolsk. What was the rationale for this mass murder a day before that of Kamenets-Podolsk? Orinin, a small, nondescript Podolian shtetel, with a sizeable Jewish population, is located less than fifteen miles northeast from Kamenets-Podolsk. While no military records survived,

FIG 4.4   Orinin: Former Soviet fortification served as mass grave for over two thousand Hungarian deportees. August 26, 1941. *Courtesy of George Eisen.*

this mass murder might have been precipitated by a concern on the part of the German military command that the thousands of Jews would continue from Orinin to the already overcrowded quarters in Kamenets-Podolsk, which could complicate the planned extermination of the ghetto. Was it, then, a preemptive massacre before the main event in Kamenets-Podolsk? As we will see, the decision to eliminate the ghetto in Kamenets-Podolsk, on August 25, preceded the Orinin massacre by a day. Being in Berdichev at the time, Friedrich Jeckeln was not present at this event, but we know from testimonies that the perpetrators belonged to an SS detachment. In reviewing the situation reports of the 1st SS Brigade, under Jeckeln's direct command, it seems likely that they were involved in this massacre.

There is, however, an information gap between the August 15 and 25, 1941. Jeckeln's radio messages confirm that in this period the brigade was continuously shooting Jews in this geographic area.[21] Thus the timing of the Orinin massacre on August 26 is by no means a coincidence. The systematic extermination of the Hungarian deportees by killing squads started prior or almost simultaneously with the mass murder at Kamenets-Podolsk. This preplanned massacre signaled a definite shift in Nazi policies as to how to resolve the Hungarian refugee question within the context of the general annihilation of Soviet Jewry. The common thread between the slaughters in Orinin and Kamenets-Podolsk, besides the close geographic proximity of the murder sites, were the Hungarian expellees, and, of course, the ubiquitous Friedrich Jeckeln.

DECISION AND RATIONALE FOR MASS MURDER

Three sets of direct documents, all connected to Jeckeln, stand as opening and closing statements to the massacre in Kamenets-Podolsk. The first contains the minutes of a meeting held on August 25, 1941, sent to Berlin two days later. This remains the only source that indicates a previously arranged agreement between the German military and civilian authorities, and the Wermacht's complicity in—and endorsement of—a drastic solution (i.e., mass murder) to the refugee problem. The second set, containing three reports of the massacre's daily toll, was sent by the perpetrator of the massacre, Jeckeln, directly to Heinrich Himmler. Finally, a short sentence at the end of a lengthy operational situation report, sent on September 11, 1941, and composed by the chief of the security police (Sicherheitsdienst or SD) from Einsatzgruppe C, alludes to the final outcome of the just-concluded genocide: "in the course of 3 days 23,600 Jews were shot in Kamenets-Podolsk by a Kommando of the Higher SS and Police Leader ["South"]."[22]

This first document, the meeting minutes, marks a tragic turning point in the fate of the deportees crowded into the Old Town ghetto. It can be dated to a crucial meeting of high-level German officers and civilian administrators in Vinnitsa (Vinnytsia in Ukrainian) on August 25, 1941. Held in the headquarters of the OKH (Army Supreme Command), the gathering's main agenda was the coordination of details for the impending transfer of the newly created area of Reich Commissariat Ukraine from military to civilian administration.[23]

Based on the composition of the participants, which included officers from the top echelon of Rear Army Group South representing General Karl von Roques and high-level civilian administrators from the Ministry of Eastern Territories, headed by Erich Koch, the meeting was an important milestone in the war. Major Hans Georg Schmidt von Altenstadt (department head for War Administration, Office of the Quartermaster General) presided over the meeting. Additional participants included Colonel Ernst-Anton von Krosigk (chief of the General Staff of the Commander of the Southern Army Area Rear), Assistant Secretary Justus Danckwert (chief of the Administrative Branch within the Army Administrative Group), Paul Dargel (head of the Political Department in the Reich Commissariat Ukraine, and representative of the Reich Commissioner Erich Koch), two representatives of the Ministry of the Eastern Territories in the rank of councilor—Dr. Walter Labs and Captain Dr. Otto Brautigam—and a Major Wagner.[24]

One of the most surprising facts emerging from this meeting was Meiler, the military commandant of Kamenets-Podolsk, was not invited. Indeed, he was kept in the dark about the decisions taken until the commencement of the actual murder. Among the discussion points on the agenda was a single paragraph succinctly addressing the arrival of Hungarian transports, the looming humanitarian and health crisis they posed, and the proposed solution to this problem. The minutes of this meeting, transferred to Berlin on August 27, 1941, contained an ominous paragraph: "Major Wagner explained... near Kaimenez-Podolsk [sic], the Hungarians have pushed about 11,000 Jews over the border. In these negotiations, up to the present, it has not been possible to arrive at any measures for the return of these Jews. The Higher SS and Police Leader (SS-Obergruppenführer Jeckeln) hopes, however, to have completed *the liquidation of these Jews* by the 1.9.1941."[25]

This short paragraph unequivocally singled out the Hungarian deportees for "liquidation." The minutes were highly confidential, presumably for the top echelon of the Nazi hierarchy, yet they dispensed with the euphemistic terms so characteristic to the Final Solution. They did not cloak their intent in bureaucratic euphemisms as "transfer," "resettlement," "removal," or "special treatment" (*Sonderbehandlung*) to sanitize the act of murder. The word "liquidation" left little to the imagination. There was also none of the usual justification for the murder of civilians, such as eliminating the "Judeo-Bolshevik threat," "Partisan activities against communication lines," or "the inability to support refugees." This signaled the end of the slow death in the confines of the ghetto—an untenable situation of squalor, pestilence, and hunger. It also conveyed an unmatched cynicism by the Wehrmacht officers for solving a problem that they themselves had created. We can understand the last sentence of this fateful document only if we put the Kamenets-Podolsk massacre within the context of the rapidly shifting Nazi policies—not as an end itself, but as part of an emerging trend of total annihilation. In other words, it was not an exception, but an essential part of a rapidly evolving policy of comprehensive and systematic extermination of the Jewish population in Ukraine.

The factors that led to this meeting and its tragic consequences are worth exploring. The only person who was not present in this meeting—though he is mentioned by name—and who promised to implement the ensuing mass murder, was Jeckeln. The matter-of-fact tone of the report implies that the decision to liquidate the ghetto had already been made prior to this meeting and cleared with all parties concerned. More importantly, it seems certain that this had to have been made in direct consultation with General Karl von Roques and perhaps with the office of quartermaster general of the army, Eduard Wagner. It was in line, as Timothy Snyder notes, with the fact that "By late August 1941, nine weeks into the war, the Wehrmacht had serious concerns about food supplies and the security of the rear. Murdering Jews would free up food."[26]

We can draw a direct line between Nazi policies and the extermination of the ghetto because this concern was prominently on the minds of both General Wagner and General von Roques, commander of the rear areas of Army Group South. General von Roques agreed that the Jews should be exterminated as a "binding guiding principle." He reiterated his full support for this process, short of Wehrmacht active participation in the killings, on September 1, 1941: "Executive measures against certain parts of the population (in particular against Jews) are expressly reserved to the forces of the Senior SS and Police Leader.... The right to object does not exist for the subordinated headquarters with regard to measures carried out by the SD detachments."[27]

As for the impending massacre in Kamenets-Podolsk, he specifically instructed the commandant of the city, Meiler, not to get involved or assist the SS: "The Wehrmacht has nothing to do with the whole action." In question of logistical support, the SS was "subordinate" to the army and coordinated their operations with army commanders in their area of responsibility. But this directive implied a subservient relationship between the Wehrmacht and the office of the SS police leader as far as the extermination of civilian populations were concerned.[28]

This was not the only massacre in territories under von Roques' control for which he was implicated after the war. But Wagner may have played an even more overarching role—economically rather than ideologically. Although he was not present at the fateful meeting in Vinnitsa, his drafting of regulations with Reinhard Heydrich in March 1941 fit well with that meeting's resolutions. They ensured that the army and special murder attachments would cooperate in executing Soviet Jews. According to this agreement, the German Armed Forces High Command military agreed that "within the framework of the instructions and upon their own responsibility, the Sonderkommandos are entitled to carry out executive measures against civilian population."[29] This laid down the framework for mass annihilation in which various security agencies of the Third Reich, not just the Einsatzgruppen, and the Wehrmacht shared responsibilities for "pacification" in the newly occupied territories.

Because of the rapid northward advance of the German military, no units of Einsatzgruppe C functioned in southern Galicia. Instead, the mass murder was entrusted to a much more potent and capable murder mechanism—that of the office of the HSSPF, which was augmented by police battalions and local auxiliaries. Altogether the six battalions subordinated to HSSPF Russia South (led by Jeckeln) killed considerably more Ukrainian Jews than Einsatzgruppe C and Einsatzgruppe D combined.[30] Wagner's responsibility for the decimation of the civilian population, as well as millions of Russian POWs, lay in the fact that he bore the burden of securing a continuous supply of war matériel, including food, in a time of limited and over-stretched resources.[31] In order to achieve this, he fully implemented the Hunger Plan (*der Hungerplan*), a system that ensured that German military was given priority in food supplies at the expense of the inhabitants of the German-occupied Soviet territories. The plan relied on the premise that the German Army would feed itself by living off the land in the territories it conquered in the eastern regions of the Soviet Union.

Wagner's directives to reduce food supplies for the civilian population and POWs resulted in the deaths of millions during the war. The reduction of food for Jews, who were prohibited from purchasing eggs, butter, milk, meat, or fruit, was the most severe.[32] In this light, the earlier quoted announcement on August 24, 1941, forbidding the purchase of food by the ghetto residents in Kamenets-Podolsk, makes sense. It amounted, though, to a death sentence. This was a well-calculated design by the German authorities that aimed for the decimation of the population. Implementing mass murder in Kamenets-Podolsk—in fact *requesting* it—was a noticeable escalation of the extermination process and an early example of Wehrmacht officers' cooperation with the SS. It reflected the general understanding between Heinrich Himmler and the leadership of the Wehrmacht on how they would solve the "Jewish problem," both from ideological and economic vantage points.[33]

Himmler's direct influence in the turn of events for the deported Jews was evident in his consultative meeting with the top military brass on July 20 in Lviv (Lwów). During this trip, he conferred with von Roques to hammer out a general policy laying down the framework for the respective roles in the extermination—specifically that of the 1st SS Brigade under Jeckeln's command.[34] This reflected an expansion of the extermination process in the occupied areas as they moved from sporadic killings of Jewish men and those who "abetted the Bolshevik system"—which amounted to same—to wholesale and indiscriminate executions of men, women, and children. While it is not known what they discussed that day, the Hungarian Jewish Question might have been raised by General von Roques.

By early August, Heinrich Himmler, as the *Reichsführer SS*, directly communicated with the three appointed Higher SS and Police Leaders, *SS-Gruppenführer* Hans-Adolf Prützmann (responsible for the Baltic states and northern Russia as HSSPF *"Rußland-Nord"*), *SS-Gruppenführer* Erich von dem Bach-Zelewski (in charge of Belorussia as HSSPF *"Rußland-Mitte"*), and *SS-Obergruppenführer* Friedrich Jeckeln (in control of southern Russia and Ukraine as HSSPF *"Rußland-Süd"*), about Hitler's "wishes" for expediting and expanding the extermination process. There is still some disagreement among scholars on whether a written directive, a *führerbefehl,* pertaining to this issue was ever issued by Hitler. We know, though, that all communications between Himmler and his trusted henchmen were limited to verbal instructions. During his Riga trial, Jeckeln testified that Himmler's exact words were: "it is my order, which is also the Führer's wish." For Jeckeln and the other Nazi functionaries down the rungs of the annihilation mechanism, the *führerbefehl* alleviated all "legal" or "moral" questions or qualms.[35]

Jeckeln's responsibility for the extermination of the ghetto is another piece of the puzzle that must be put into context. In a multilayered Nazi bureaucracy, with internecine rivalry among various security agencies, armed services, and personalities, he

FIG 4.5 Reichsführer SS Heinrich Himmler converses with SS Obergruppen Führer Alfred Wünnenberg. To Himmler's immediate right is Friederich Jeckeln. *United States Holocaust Memorial Museum Photo Archives, courtesy of James Blevins.*

served as personal representative of the Reichsführer SS in southern Ukraine and directly commanded a staff company (*Kommandostab*) with representatives from almost every branch of the SS. In times of need, he could also tap into the various branches of the security services, such as the *Ordnungspolizei* (ORPO, Order Police—often referred as Reserve Police), Gestapo (secret police), *Sicherheitsdienst* (SD, security service), *Sicherheitspolizei* (Sipo, security police), *Schutzpolizei* (*Schupo*, municipal police), and available SS combat unit (1st SS Brigade). SS combat units answered to their immediate chain of command and would only be requisitioned by the Higher SS and Police Leader in the event of an emergency. Supplementing these forces, Jeckeln, and many officers engaging in the mechanism of annihilation, relied on specifically recruited *Volkdeutsche* (ethnic German) units, *Hilfspolizei* and *Schutzmann* (Ukrainian militias and police officers), and even on the participation of the border guard units (*Grenzpolizei*), and the humble railway police (*Bahnschutzpolizei*).

In discussing the mechanism of annihilation, we cannot ignore the ease with which SS officers of every rank could co-opt not only these branches of the Nazi law enforcement apparatus, but also civilian departments of the local administration. The mainstay of Jeckeln's genocidal activities, though, was *Ordnung Polizeibattalion* (Reserve Police Battalion) 320, one of the five police battalions that were subordinated to him, with the aim of facilitating the repression and murders carried out under his command. The initial role for the members of the battalion was to collect those to be murdered and surround the murder site. This rapidly evolved into an active participation in the murder itself.

Until the Kamenets-Podolsk massacre, the pace of extermination in southern Galicia was below the rate of other regions. The fate of the Hungarian Jews in Galicia, and particularly the slaughter of those in Kamenets-Podolsk, cannot be separated, as Peter Longerich aptly stated, from the "general radicalization of German *Judenpolitik* in August and September 1941."[36] This sudden spike in the pace of extermination can be traced back to the competing dynamics of personalities, egos, and aspirations of the central characters in the unfolding drama, as well as the exigencies of conditions on the ground.

In a meeting on August 12, 1941, Himmler instructed Jeckeln that alongside Jewish men, women and children should be shot as well—thus breaching a psychological barrier for the executioners. More importantly, Himmler berated Jeckeln about falling behind in "productivity," in the number of executions in comparison with fellow Higher SS Police Leaders, including Erich von dem Bach-Zelewski in the center and Hans-Adolf Prützmann in the Baltic states.[37]

Albert Hartl, who opted out of mass murder, observed after the war that some of the officers entrusted with mass exterminations "were very ambitious and they wanted to report the highest possible shooting figures to Berlin."[38] Not coincidentally, British intelligence analysts who had intercepted messages reporting daily killings came to the same conclusion: "the leaders of the three sectors [the three HSSPFs] stand somewhat in competition with each other as to their 'scores.'" As we will see in the succeeding chapters, even lower ranking SS officers stationed in Galicia were competing ferociously with each other for the highest murder tally. Jeckeln possessed a cut-throat personality. He showed ambition and drive in planning extermination. During the four long years of the war, he became arguably the single most inventive mass murderer in the Eastern theater. As Mallmann persuasively suggested, since Himmler was not satisfied with Jeckeln's progress when the HSSPF South reported to him on 12 August 1941, he might have offered the mass killing of Hungarian Jews as a solution.[39]

This is only an assumption, but if true, it gives the Vinnitsa meeting new meaning. It might now be considered a crucial step in the escalation of genocide in Ukraine in which the Hungarian expellees were both immediate victims and pawns. As Christopher Browning surmised, it might have served as the "starting block" for the Final Solution.[40] Following this conference, the unprecedented three-day massacre of the 16,000 Hungarians, several thousand Romanians, and approximately 4,000 to 5,000 local Jews commenced on Wednesday, August 27, 1941. Based on recollections of survivors, Hungarian military personnel, court testimonies by perpetrators, and Ukrainian witnesses, we can reconstruct the entire affair almost minute by minute.[41]

THREE DAYS IN AUGUST: ON THE EDGE OF THE ABYSS

Once the decision was made to eliminate the ghetto, the mass killing was primarily a matter of logistics. The massacre started with the collection of the Hungarian deportees who were to be murdered in the first two days. The day leading up to the bloodbath, August 26, gives a glimpse into the mindset of the perpetrators, as well as the perceptions of the victims.

The minor discrepancies in the recollections of the witnesses don't detract from the fact that a well-tested Nazi misinformation ploy served as a prelude. A terse announcement was posted on August 25 in the Old Town stating that all Hungarian Jews should assemble in a certain location early on August 26 "for relocation to a more convenient place or even an imminent return to Hungary."[42] Deliberately deceptive and unrealistic rumors were also circulated about the possibility of removal to Palestine. Prior to their departure from the ghetto, the chief of the Ukrainian police demanded from the "Jews 40,000 pengő [a large amount of Hungarian money], which was to be collected by the morning of August 26." The sum was promptly collected.

Eyewitnesses recorded the slowly moving procession on early Tuesday morning, August 26, 1941, to the train station in the new part of Kamenets-Podolsk:

> they were given two hours to get ready for the journey. They were lined up in rows in military fashion and taken to the destroyed train station. Rabbis with Torah scrolls led [this procession], followed by mothers with their children, and ill and old people supported [by others]. All the people moved along with difficulty; most of them believed that they were going to be returned home. They were taken to demolished barracks [the former NKVD barracks] near the train station and were held there under guard . . . on the pretext that they were waiting for a train.[43]

They were housed overnight in the barracks, where "they were locked in and no one was allowed to leave the building" under the threat of death. In fact, "a woman gave birth during the night" and one man from Kassa (Kosice) who dared to leave "the building for water was killed by the guards." The next day, "at 5 AM two German soldiers went through each hall and ordered all [the Jews] to assemble outside but to leave all their belongings behind. Two other German soldiers ordered all the Jews who were German subjects to remain."[44]

The journey to the murder site started in the morning of August 27, 1941. It was a sunny Wednesday: "German soldiers armed with whips stood 10 steps apart and beat the Jews who ran past them."[45] The first day and a half was specifically dedicated to the

FIG 4.6 A day before the massacre: "All the Hungarian Jews were transferred to the new town, to the barracks near the train station." August 26, 1941. *United States Holocaust Memorial Museum Photo Archives, courtesy of Ivan Sved.*

murder of the Hungarians. By late afternoon of the second day, the time had come to destroy the local Jewish community; the collection and murder of the Jewish population settled into a routine. There was no need to hide the truth. Of course, the recognition that the march would lead to death did not make it less terrifying for the victims. There were instances when the executioners could not "process" the number of those condemned to death and groups were sent back to the city. On the second day of the massacre, many local Jews were forced out to join the death march. A seventeen-year-old girl, a city resident, recounted her terror when she was marched to the massacre site, then taken back because there were too many candidates for murder. Several hours later, she was again returned to the execution site.

> On August 28, 1941 at dawn, they started to drive the Jews out of their apartments, telling to take with them their most valuable possessions. We were driven out of our apartment to the square, where we were surrounded by Germans and *Hungarians*. Whoever of us carried bags on our shoulders was beaten and [our bags] were thrown aside. Later, we were lined up 6-8 in a row and told that the way was going to be difficult and long and, therefore, there was no point in taking many belongings with us. We were taken first in the direction of Polskie Folwark, (Polish Farm) [where] we were divided into two

groups. One group was taken through Polskie Folwark toward a pit while the other was stopped at a bridge near a rock and ordered to lie down. We sat down, while those who were tired lay down. In the meantime, the Germans set up machine guns ... Some "schutzmanner" [Ukrainian auxiliary police] were there as well. After they had ordered all this to be done, the Germans surrounded us and started to take pictures of us. *Then they took us back to the Old Town....*

At several minutes past noon, we were once again assembled in the center of the city. I asked the policemen "Where is that part of the people who were taken away? My parents were among them." "You are going to be evicted from the city" he replied.... After the people were assembled, we were taken to Polskie Folwark. Those unable to walk were beaten. There were German trucks and those who had been beaten were lifted up, put into trucks, and driven to the shooting site. On the way, I understood that we were going to be shot and all those walking [with me] understood this as well.[46]

A fact that should not escape attention in this testimony is that this is the first instance that Hungarian military involvement, however peripheral it might have been, is mentioned relating to the Kamenets-Podolsk mass murder. The contemporary reports of Hungarian soldiers on leave, and testimonies of survivors taken by the Soviet Extraordinary State Commission between May 15 and 30, 1944, repeatedly placed Hungarian forces at the murder site in cordon duties. Yet we can assume with certainty that they had no idea about the final fate of the deportees. Just like the members of the Reserve Police Battalion 320 who became part of the genocide, they believed that the Hungarian and local Jews were to be relocated.[47]

By the second day of the massacre, however, it is hard to believe that anyone had any illusion about the fate of the assembled Jews. Supporting these testimonies is the only surviving collection of four photographs taken by Gyula Spitz, a Jewish driver in the Hungarian Army.[48] These grainy pictures are genuinely horrifying in their simplicity and candor. They document the three stages of destruction: the collection, procession under German escort, and the final station before the slaughter. Judging by the attire of the marchers, these were Ukrainian Jews, which also indicates that they could have been taken in the second or third day of the slaughter. The looming presence of the German police troops in one of the pictures also reinforces the original descriptions. No gruesome brutality can be seen, and no luggage is carried; there is only a devastating and overwhelming sense of resignation. In testifying to the Soviet Extraordinary State Commission[49] after the liberation of the city, a Ukrainian Christian "saw a neighbor who used to live in the same courtyard as I did, a certain Mrs. Shvartsman, her husband, their daughters Liza and Basya, and their relatives, *who went arm-in-arm, silently,*

FIG 4.7 Marching to the mass execution: "German soldiers armed with whips stood 10 steps apart and beat the Jews who ran past them." August 27–29, 1941. *United States Holocaust Memorial Museum Photo Archives, courtesy of Ivan Sved.*

without uttering a sound, their heads lowered toward the ground. Liza, who saw me, waved to me and shouted: 'Senia, we are doomed.'"⁵⁰

The final segment of the march to the murder site was accompanied by ferocity and violence to stamp out any inclination for resistance: "the old people who could not move and lagged behind were beaten to death by Germans, afterwards they were picked up by carts that followed, loading 20–30 people into each cart and transporting them, as I know, to the shooting site."⁵¹ The victims were forced to run a gauntlet of policemen and to surrender their valuables and clothing in subsequent stations. Testimonies of the perpetrators, both German and Ukrainians, paint a clear picture of the process. A member of the Reserve Police Battalion 320, the unit that was intimately involved in the collection and the shooting, testified in the trial of the police officers on January 4, 1961:

> I spoke to some Jews.... The Jews asked me about the destination of their journey. The Jews were convinced they were going to be resettled. *At that time, I myself did not know that the Jews were going to be shot.* From talking to the Jews, I also thought that, indeed, this was going to be a resettlement. We took the Jews out of the city. We moved about one kilometer or a bit more out of the city. I cannot say today what direction it was. We were going through impassable territory. There we encountered our cordon. We saw from far away many

people standing in that area. From afar we also heard shooting from submachine guns. We took the Jews through the cordon formed by policemen. There were already several thousand Jews on the other side of the cordon. Thereafter, following orders, we reinforced the cordon.⁵²

In reality, there were two cordons. The outer perimeter, set up by the Ukrainian auxiliaries, was connected by a corridor, a so-called hosepipe, to the second cordon, manned by German Order Police. The recollection of one of the *Schutzmanner* (Ukrainian policemen) who participated in the roundup and guarding of the condemned provides a detailed picture: "The cordon around the shooting site consisted of two circles, the first of which, consisting mainly of Germans, was right at the graves and encompassed the place where people about to be shot were undressing, while the second, consisting of the *schutzmanner* from the 2nd company, surrounded the whole area and was located at a distance of 100–150 meters from the first circle."⁵³

FIG 4.8 In front of the mass graves: Hungarian Jews are waiting for their final fate. August 27–29, 1941. *United States Holocaust Memorial Museum Photo Archives, courtesy of Ivan Sved.*

The location of the murder site, the final destination, was some distance from the train depot and the city itself, a moderately hilly area northeast of the city. The area was pockmarked by four huge craters, the remnants of colossal explosions of munitions depots by the retreating Soviet Army. These became mass graves, with "a diameter of about 20–30 meter and a depth of about 5–6 meter," and were expanded and enlarged by slave labor prior to the executions. One of the most striking aspects of the atrocity was the fact, as eyewitnesses reported, that the killers were not discreet about their task and made no effort to conceal the mass murder from the local population. In any case, it would have been almost impossible to do so, because Ukrainian policemen were an integral part of the killing machine. Neighbors, familiar with some of the local victims and living in close proximity to the killing fields, could see and hear the terrifying sounds and view the spectacle from their homes. We also know that Hungarian soldiers were able to loiter around the killing pits unhindered. Or were they present in a military capacity? We don't know. Because of the shocking magnitude of the carnage, the murders became common knowledge across Galicia almost immediately, and shortly thereafter in Budapest.

In this light, we might ponder the question as to how could a Hungarian corporal, a humble porter from Budapest, witness the ultimate fate of my two uncles? We know that he was also able to observe their final moments, but one should also pose the ultimate question: In what capacity? Was he merely a curious observer? A murder-tourist in contemporary parlance? Or was he ordered to collect the Jews, including Samu and Karcsi, and lead them to slaughter? Or, perhaps he had to serve as a cordon personnel before the final act? Unfortunately, there are no easy answers. About one thing we can be sure—he was in close proximity and served as an intimate eyewitness. He could see how Samu was murdered by a single bullet to the head, and how Karcsi jumped into the pit after his brother alive. And the porter could recount this directly to my family. He could not answer, though, the rhetorical question if Karcsi's ultimate action was spurred, in this terrifying moment, by his desire to defy the executioner? Wanting to die on his own terms? Or perhaps only Karcsi himself understood, to quote a German Nazi officer, that "Death is not so bad, the agony before is worse."[54]

Jeckeln flew to Kamenets-Podolsk from his headquarters in Berdichev (Berdychiv in Ukrainian) in his small Storch plane in late afternoon, August the 26, or the next morning to personally supervise the extermination. An experienced pilot, he often commuted between extermination sites and his command center.[55]

Upon arriving, he lost no time in proceeding to the site of the impending mass murder and, simultaneously, setting up the teams of shooters comprised mainly of his own staff. He had ordered the Reserve Police Battalion 320, under the leadership of Major Kurt Dall, and Ukrainian policemen and auxiliaries (*Schutzmannschaften*), to serve as cordon personnel. Because of the short notice, only Company 1/320 and 2/320, commanded by Captain Alfred Weber and Captain Hans Wiemer, respectively, were able to arrive in time from their base in Proskurov—some fifty miles away—to participate in the collection and escort of the Jews. Under the command of Captain Heinrich Scharwey, the third company (3/320) would reach the site of the slaughter midday on August 28, becoming embroiled in the killings almost immediately.

Reserve r Police Battalion 320, consisting of approximately five hundred policemen, was set up in the Berlin–Spandau area in February 1941 and transferred to Galicia in the latter part of June. Unfortunately, no exhaustive research—such as Browning's study of *Reserve Police Battalion 101*—has been conducted on the demographic composition, ideological orientation, and motivation of Battalion 320. Our limited information about the members of the battalion comes from their trial in the 1960s.

The battalion's recruits and their motivation to join the police force was reflective of the majority of ORPO recruits across the spectrum. Most of these men were neither overtly political nor true believers in Nazi ideology. Nor did they harbor any deep hatred of Jews. Their participation in this and a string of subsequent massacres has clear implications for our understanding of the willingness of "ordinary Germans" to carry out killings.[56] The initial execution team members were from a unit formed especially for this task by Jeckeln from among his personal bodyguards, a guard platoon from his Stabskompanie/HSSPF "Russland-Süd," and his support staff. In times of "manpower shortage," it was not uncommon for Jeckeln to try to persuade even his drivers to join a mass shooting. For many, this was their first occasion to participate, willingly or through coercion, in mass murder.[57]

While there are some minor discrepancies in the testimonies as to when Reserve Police Battalion 320 became actively involved in the slaughter, we know that by the second day, members of the third company were also forced to participate in the shootings. At least twelve members of the battalion became part of the four-member execution squads. They were part of more than a quarter million German Order Police who operated in Eastern Europe during the war. The units that were subordinated to Jeckeln, as Dieter Pohl opined, "killed considerably more Ukrainian Jews than Einsatzgruppe C and Einsatzgruppe D combined."[58]

Considering the single-minded zeal with which the Nazis pursued the murder of the Jews, the extermination of 1.5 million victims in a relatively short time should not come as a surprise. Rather, the real surprise might be the fact of how little manpower was required to accomplish this. Browning remarked that "SS and Police Leader[s] (SSPF) were given the task but not the men to carry it out. They had to improvise by creating ad hoc 'private armies.'"[59] Not surprisingly, Jeckeln often had to face a shortage of willing executioners as he worked to recruit for the *Erschiessungs-kommando*—execution squad. The Kamenets-Podolsk massacre amply demonstrates that he was a ruthless master of improvisation. Yet without local Ukrainian police and auxiliary forces, perhaps

Hungarian troops as cordon personnel, and the active participation of the police battalion in the annihilation process, mass extermination could have not been as successful or even as feasible.

The mass murder in Kamenets-Podolsk was neither smooth nor tidy; it was not a "sanitized" affair. Mass murder never is. In contradiction to the testimonies of members of Reserve Police Battalion 320 in their postwar trial, there were many glitches and breakdowns with moments of chaos and internal conflict. The *Sardinenpackung* method of execution, invented later by Jeckeln, had not yet been "refined" or "perfected" for mass scale. It reached its full implementation in Babi Yar and the Rumbula Forest in Riga, where victims were ordered to lie down on the already murdered and were executed from close range.[60]

So, when considering the number of victims and relatively limited available executioners, the three-day slaughter was chaotic and messy. "There were no doctors who could verify the victims' death," one of the executioners recalled during his trial. "I still remember how one Jew was shot not fatally and lost consciousness. When he recovered consciousness, he screamed that he had been shot. He then received the *coup de grace*. The execution lasted from 10 hours in the morning until 16 hours in the afternoon on the first day." This witness was not a professional soldier, but the head of the motor pool of Jeckeln's staff company.[61]

Since this massacre happened in the early stages of the Holocaust and the Hungarian Jews were not as traumatized as they would later become, they went to the slaughter compliantly, despite the merciless beatings. As they arrived at the execution site, they were funneled through a corridor with blows raining down on them, ordered in stages to hand over their money and valuables, their shoes, and finally, to undress. They were taken in groups to the huge craters and brought down by submachine gun fire at the edge of the mass graves. Execution squads of four men for each grave worked in shifts, while police units cordoned off the site. A member of Jeckeln's staff who personally participated in the slaughter recalled during his murder trial that the executioners "were armed with submachine guns, apparently Czech-made. The execution squads consisted of policemen and SS-men." Other sources state that Russian-made weapons were the preferred tools of the murderers because of their large magazines, which held a clip of fifty rounds of ammunition and could be fired singly or automatically.[62]

While some of the victims were killed outright, many were only wounded slightly, and some jumped or were thrown into the pits alive. Several eyewitnesses, both victims and perpetrators, described the terror. One of the survivors "saw a grave across which planks had been laid, and the Germans standing around. The people approaching the grave were forced by the Germans to run along the planks; they were beaten with sticks and rifle butts and fell alive into the grave." Corroborating this account is a contemporary comment by a Hungarian military engineer who was a witness to the massacre:

"Platforms had been erected at the rims of the pits. The Jews were ordered to climb the platforms and face away from the pits. Machine guns were pointed at them. In this manner, the Jews met their demise."[63]

A Ukrainian woman who dared to sneak with a friend as close as possible to view the grim spectacle "could see how the children, women, and men were forced to undress and to jump into the grave in groups of 10. Some of them *resisted* since they did not want to undress. They were beaten with rifle butts, stabbed with bayonets and dragged by their legs and arms, were pulled to the grave. The babies were snatched away from their mothers and stabbed with bayonets." To add an infernal hue to this scene, "[The site of the massacre] was full of smoke coming from the constant shooting. Many people were thrown into the grave while still alive, some of them having been wounded only slightly."[64]

Finally, interspersed with the monotone staccato of the submachine guns were the cries of the victims that were heard miles away: "I heard shots from automatic weapons and terrible, penetrating cries of the people that was like an inhuman roar." Ukrainians, women, and children from the Kamenets-Podolsk train station area, who were living in a cellar about a kilometer from the murder site, reported horror of the groans and cries that they heard from far away. A Hungarian survivor, who was reprieved at the last minute, remembered this roar for the rest of his life: "People [were] screaming. You can imagine—15,000 people. Everybody was screaming."[65]

That the killing did not go smoothly can be gleaned from the fact that the killing squads at first were limited to Jeckeln's own *Stabskompanie* and were severely shorthanded. Without the infusion, under coercion, of members of the Reserve Police Battalion 320, especially on the second and third days, it would have been difficult to finish the grisly undertaking. This was a baptism in mass murder for the members of the battalion.

There was an element of psychology in the Nazis' preparations for mass shooting that included, alongside a large supply of schnapps, the withholding of information until the last minute. Even SS men were rarely notified in advance about their imminent participation in an execution. For example, members of Jeckeln's staff company were alerted only in the evening before "that [they] were going to an execution." Policemen who were ordered to be part of an execution team were not informed about the impending mass murder until the last minute. Members of Reserve Police Battalion 320 "did not know that the Jews were going to be shot" even on the morning of the massacre, and some policemen were not aware that they were escorting the Jews to their gruesome and imminent demise.[66]

A Ukrainian policeman described the dynamics of the extermination in his trial in 1944: the executioners "'worked' in shifts: when one of them got tired, he went to rest.... He was replaced by another [accomplice]. In this way, they changed shifts throughout the shooting. The henchmen, and not only the henchmen, were strengthened by schnapps all the time... ate a sandwich, drank some schnapps, smoked a cigarette and then, went back to 'work.'"[67]

Since the shooting brought the executioners nearly eye-to-eye with their victims, even hardened SS men found it difficult. In ruminating on the moral complexities of mass murder, Michael Burleigh noted that "many of the shooters vomited, either because of the blood and the brains flying around or because they had consumed too much schnapps."[68]

The copious flow of alcohol became an integral ingredient for the killing process. Hermann K., a member of Jeckeln's staff, shows the ambivalence that drove the shooters to alcohol: "Jews were constantly brought to it [the grave]. Some of them had to lie down, others we killed by a shot in the back of the head while they were standing. There were men, women, and children, *but I only shot men*. There were no breaks. I often moved away from the grave when *my nerves could not stand it anymore and I tried to shirk this assignment*."[69] We should add that this SS man also augmented his resolve by drinking schnapps before returning to the firing line.

In order to convince the policemen to shoot unarmed civilians, a psychological and mental barrier had to be broken—a transformation had to take place. During their trials, these same policemen freely admitted that their participation was voluntary, yet a certain collective psychological coercion and pressure was needed to enter and remain in the killing field.[70]

Among the members of the battalion, only one policeman from the third company voiced his objection to the impending murder. While the first two companies of Reserve Police Battalion 320 served as cordon personnel, augmented by Ukrainian auxiliaries, the third company, upon arrival, became part of the execution teams. This member of the battalion reported at a hearing in 1960 how First Lieutenant Heinrich Scharwey had given an anti-Semitic lecture to his men to justify the annihilation of the Jews: "I remember a speech by our company leader, Scharwey, before the assembled men that the entire battalion will be used in a Jewish action in Kamenets-Podolsk. From his speech, it was clear that the Jews were to be shot.... Anyway, he tried through his speech to convince us of the necessity of this shooting."[71]

At the same time, Scharwey also gave the option to refrain from the killing, the policeman remembers: "He could not give any of us individually the order to take part in the shooting." The same policeman requested to be relieved from participating in mass murder, invoking the Hague Convention: "I called Scharwey's attention to the Hague Convention pertaining to Land Warfare and invoked the provision[s] contained therein whereby it was not allowed to shoot at defenseless people, and also to my not being able to reconcile this with my conscience. I further called his attention to the fact that during my training in Eilenburg I had been instructed about The

Hague Convention.... I am not aware that other company members requested to be exempted themselves."[72]

Records consistently show that those who refused to engage in the killing process did not suffer negative consequences or punishment for their refusal. This raises the question, why didn't more soldiers ask to be waived from participation? During their trials, all admitted that their participation in this massacre was wholly voluntary. In retrospect, it is impressive that Scharwey accepted this policeman's reasoning and released him from the slaughter. Unfortunately, he was the only one who requested to be exempted by invoking individual conscience. The rest of the battalion of middle-aged reserve and active policemen, with no identifiable ideological or political motives, decided to participate and "continued to kill, week after week."

For Jeckeln's personnel, on the other hand, this was not an option. He coerced his staff company with various means, including outright threats and intimidation. In one sharp exchange, he snapped at a reluctant Einsatzgruppe commander: "I have thought and considered this very carefully, and if I catch somebody who objects to this [mass killing] or breaks down, then he will also be shot."[73] Not surprisingly, at least twelve members of the battalion joined thirty SS and security police personnel from Jeckeln's staff company as the core of the execution squads.

While Jeckeln could not force his will on the policemen in the battalion, his vociferous demand for more productive participation in the killing process sparked an angry exchange with Major Kurt Dall, the commander of the battalion. We do not know the outcome of this exchange. This argument, though, transcended the issue of individual policemen dodging or unable to continue the killing. It may have been about lines of authority. While assisting the Higher SS and Police Leaders, these police battalions were technically under the command of *SS-Oberst-Gruppenführer* and *Generaloberst* of the police (ranks equivalent to *Colonel General*) Kurt Daluege, chief of the national uniformed *Ordnungspolizei* (Order Police). Thus, Major Dall had full authority over the conduct of his subordinates.[74]

Overall, though, Jeckeln himself held the ultimate authority, with all the arbitrariness and capriciousness fitting an SS general. The four mass graves were in the bend of a low hill that served as Jeckeln's command post. From this vantage point, he could overlook the slaughter in the company of *SS-Sturmbannführer* (MAJOR) August Meier, the representative of Einsatzgruppe C, and Major Kurt Dall, commander of Reserve Police Battalion 320. Some reports also placed *SS-Brigaderführer* and *Generalmajor der Polize* Gerret Korsemann[75] with Jeckeln on the massacre site as he prepared for his role as the future HSSPF of the Caucasus. Finally, there were also several Wehrmacht officers from General von Roques' staff who joined the spectacle out of sheer curiosity. The three company commanders, Captain Alfred Weber (1/320), Captain Hans Wiemer (2/320), and Captain Heinrich Scharwey (3/320) meanwhile supervised the extermination.

From his perch, he made the decision of life or death, who should be saved and who should be destroyed. An officer from his command company who was a member of the execution squad recalled in his trial that on the first day of the massacre "a young girl around the age of 20 years old and a small boy around the age of 12 appealed to *Sturmbannführer* Meyer [Meier] that they were not Jews and that he grants them life. Meyer then spoke with Jeckeln and the two were released. I still remember how the boy was overjoyed and jumped up because his life has been spared. Also, the girl was very happy."[76] We can identify with certainty *Sturmbannführer* Meyer with Major August Meier, which adds an interesting dimension to this story. He was assigned to Jeckeln's staff company as the representative of Einsatzgruppe C and was an authentic mass murderer in his own right. But even an SS major could not grant a reprieve from death without Jeckeln's approval.[77]

Albert Fein, a thirteen-year-old Hungarian boy from Uzhgorod (Ungvár in Hungarian) in Carpathian Ruthenia, recalled standing in front of Jeckeln, waiting on a life-or-death decision from "the General." Amid the raging massacre all around him, his testimony is almost surreal. After his mother, a blond with Aryan features from Austria, speaking in perfect German, was able to convince one of the policemen that she was Christian and German, the family, with four children, were hauled to see Jeckeln. After hastily getting rid of his traditional Jewish undergarment (*Tallit-katan*), Fein reports "we left there. My two sisters, they were blonde, I was blonde, and my mom was blonde, and my father was dark haired, and my brother was dark haired. The general looked at us for profile, you know, from side to front, speaking to my mother.... I don't know what he was thinking. He says, 'Back. Take them back.'"[78]

Indeed, it's hard to fathom, even in retrospect, as what propelled Jeckeln to make a decision of life or death. What was both impressive and disturbing about him was his absolute emotional detachment. We can see in him a task-oriented person, a problem solver, who accomplished what needed to be done without bothering about the content. In his motivation to murder, it's hard to discern an overarching philosophical foundation. Yet his split-second decision that non-Jews should not be executed was anchored in pure ideology—an ideology that was denuded of any moral, emotional, or human dimension.

After three days of murder, he accomplished what he had come to do. As the murder pits overflowed and even as people still moved under the mass of corpses, Jeckeln got into his small Storch plane and flew back to his headquarters in Berdichev. A somewhat disgruntled Ukrainian auxiliary policeman testified three years later that the German participants "took for themselves the possessions of the people who were shot."[79] One final point that escaped Jeckeln's attention—or perhaps he did not want to be bothered by a mundane detail—was the covering and recovering of the mass graves. As a matter of policy, this was often left to Jews who might have dug the trenches themselves that now held the bodies of their families. Subsequently, they were shot themselves. The journalist Adam Gopnik perceptively noted "that was the true image of the Holocaust, more so than the trains running in time to industrialized gassings and burnings."[80]

In this case, though, there were no Jews left alive. Peasants from neighboring villages, factory workers, and concentration camp inmates were hastily assembled by force for covering the scene of the crime. The work was genuinely traumatic, causing indelible psychological marks on the participants. A Ukrainian policeman remembered that "several days afterward, both day and night, frightful noises were heard from the graves. Then SS men forced peasants from the surrounding villages to cover the graves. The railway workers said that the earth was heaving for several days."[81]

For survivors and eyewitnesses, it was hard to convey in words the immediate aftermath of the carnage. An eight-year-old Ukrainian girl remembered that "the Germans brought in horses to tramp down the soil. At night, we heard the moans of the wounded who were buried alive... the earth quivered in tremors." Returning Hungarian soldiers and Jews from the forced labor companies testified that the "earth moved up and down over the graves for days."[82]

ORDNUNG MUSS SEIN!

A preoccupation with German punctuality: "Order must prevail!" Based on Jeckeln's final tally in his Operational Situation Report, sent directly to Heinrich Himmler from the killing fields, within three days a total of 23,600 Jews, among them an estimated 14,000 to 16,000 Hungarian Jews and their Christian family members deported from Hungary, were murdered.[83] This final report was dated August 30, 1941. In fact, the meticulous *SS-Obergruppenführer* updated the *Reichsführer* daily about the progress of the extermination. Reading the previous three daily reports, dated August 27, 28, and 29, respectively, and comparing them for discrepancies with the final report, reveals much about the changing numbers, about Jeckeln's vanity, and about the need for praise from Himmler. The daily telex and radio communications for reporting the murder tally lists 4,200 victims for August 27; 5,000 for August 28; and 7,000 for August 29. It concludes with "the total number of Jews liquidated in the Kamenets-Podolsk action is around 20,000."

The three reports offer an interesting evolution in Jeckeln's allocation of credit for the mass murder. The first dispatch lists both Reserve Police Battalion 320 and Jeckeln's commando staff as the perpetrators. The next day he names Reserve Police Battalion 320 as solely responsible for the shooting. Finally, on the last day, he credits solely his staff company and his own leadership with completing the grisly task: "Staff Company Higher SS and Police Leader for Southern Russia under command of SS-*Obergruppenführer* Jeckeln completed Kamenets-Podolsk operation [...] Successes:

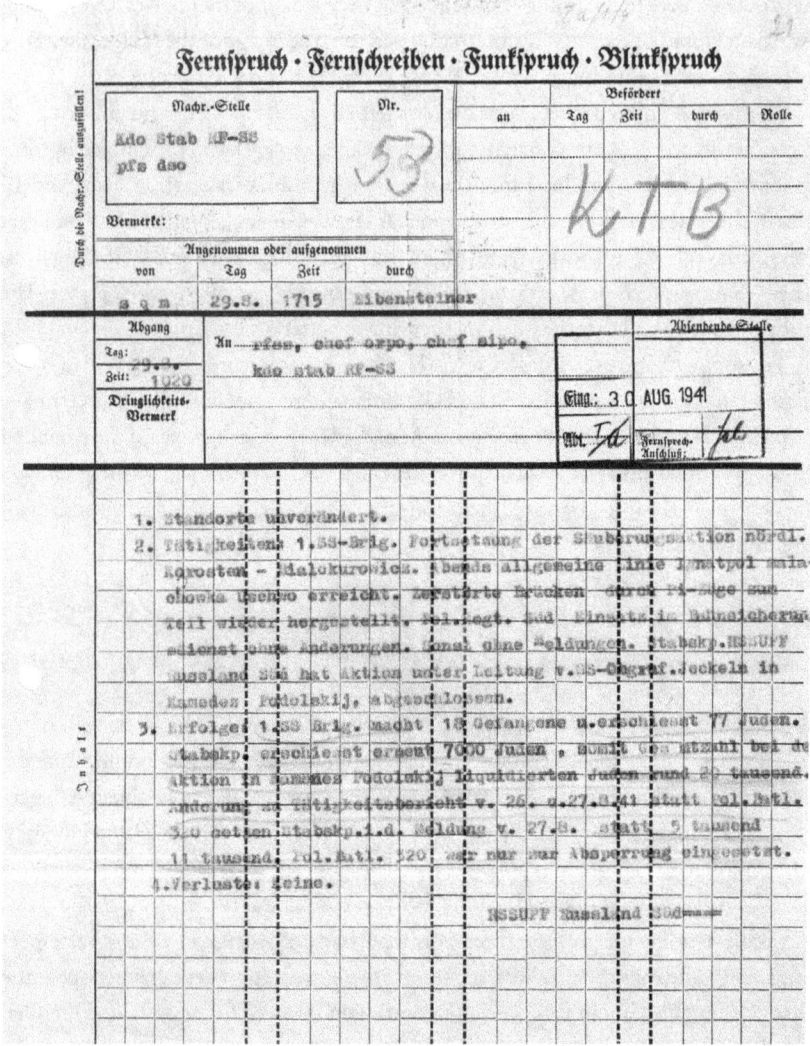

FIG 4.9 The Jeckeln reports sent to Heinrich Himmler: The sum of three days of murder. August 30, 1941 *Courtesy of Military Central Archive, Military Historical Archive Prague fund Kommando stab "Reichsführer SS, 1941–1943."*

[...] Staff Company shot another 7,000 Jews, thus total number of Jews liquidated in Kamenets-Podolsk operation around 20 thousand. Amendment to activity reports of 26 and 27.8.41 instead of Reserve Police Battalion 320 insert Staff Company, in the report of 27.8 instead of 5 thousand 11 thousand. Reserve Police Battalion 320 was only used for cordoning [the site]."

A subsequent radio communication by Jeckeln on August 30, however, amends the earlier information. The battalion's role is ignored completely, and the final number of Jews murdered is fixed at 23,600. A final note about the massacre, dated September 11, 1941, was drafted not by Jeckeln, but by the chief of the Security Police and SD from Einsatzgruppe C. This routine Operational Situation Report USSR No. 80 contained a curt summation: "in the course of 3 days 23,600 Jews were shot in Kamenets-Podolsk by a Kommando of the Higher SS and Police Leader ["South"]."[84]

Holocaust scholars did not fail to notice the discrepancy between the original number of 20,000 victims and the hastily revised one that rounded up the figure to 23,600. One possible explanation is that Reserve PoliceBattalion 320 moved back to its headquarters in Proskurov (Khmelnytskyi in Ukrainian) after the massacre. Before that, however, the battalion took a detour to the town of Minkowice (Minkovt'syi in Ukrainian), thirty-seven miles northwest of Kamenets-Podolsk. Again, Jeckeln's exceptional logistical and organizational abilities prevailed. On the morning of August 30, 1941, all of the Jews of Minkovice were assembled in the town square, led to three pre-dug pits a mile east of the town, and shot to death with the assistance of Ukrainian policemen in groups of ten to fifteen people. A follow-up radio message from Jeckeln on August 31, 1941, dutifully informed the *SS-Reichsführer* of this action by Reserve Police Battalion 320, which ended the lives of 2,200 Jews. On the following day members of the battalion shot approximately 700 Jews in Zwianczyk (Zhvanchik Velikiy in Ukrainian) and 380 in Sokolec, both located about eighteen miles northeast of Kamenets-Podolsk.[85]

There is no information about the number of Hungarian deportees who might have been the victims in these corollary massacres. We must rely on German Operational Situation Reports, which only provides the number killed; however, based on the random dispersal of the killings across the region, we can assume that many could be included in the final tally. Did Jeckeln incorporate this number in his final report, augmenting the total number of those killed in the mass murder to 23,600? The proximity of these towns to Kamenets-Podolsk might give us a clue that Hungarian Jews were part of these massacres as well.

As for the police battalion, the first massacre in Kamenets-Podolsk was the opening round in their participation in a long string of mass executions across southern Galicia. After the baptism in mass murder, perhaps the second wave of massacres in Minkowice and elsewhere came more easily, signaling the inevitable descent of Reserve Police Battalion 320 into genocide. The exploits of the battalion did not end here, though. After several days, the group was called back to patrol the mass graves in Kamenets-Podolsk, searching for those who escaped from the murder pits. Compounding this ghastly task, they were asked to deal with plundering Ukrainians.[86]

AN OPEN SECRET

Almost simultaneously with the report sent to the desk of Heinrich Himmler, the British secret service successfully decoded Jeckeln's missives and informed the government in London about the unprecedented scale of the slaughter in Kamenets-Podolsk. They were not alone, though, in their intimate knowledge of the atrocity. As it was mentioned earlier, a steady stream of detailed reports by horrified and traumatized Hungarian officers, common soldiers, and forced labor personnel provided evidence that the Royal Hungarian Army was eminently present during the carnage. The executioners performed their grisly task openly, and Hungarian military units moved unhindered across the entire area. Not surprisingly, German military dispatches to Berlin expressed a marked unease about the presence of allied military personnel across Galicia and their tendency for "murder tourism." They took pictures and openly reported on war crimes committed by the German Army.[87]

That raises the question of what was the extent of the participation of the Royal Hungarian Army in the carnage, either as bystanders or accomplices? We have already mentioned the role Hungarian units played in the collection of the Jews on August 28, in the Old Town. Other Soviet sources from regional archives support this and note that Hungarian soldiers served as cordon personnel and even participated in the killing process.[88] We know that Reserve Police Battalion 320 originated in Berlin. Dieter Pohl, a German historian, is the only one who specifically mentions the fact that "Police Battalion 320 was reinforced by an ORPO company of ethnic Germans from the Baltic region."[89] The testimonies of the German participants during their trial emphasize that the murder squads consisted of four: three staff company members and one policeman per murder squad, all German. But the best source for refuting direct Hungarian participation in the slaughter comes directly from Jeckeln himself. During his trial in Riga, he was clear about not using non-German personnel, since such an undertaking needed the mental toughness and effectiveness of an SS man.[90]

This reduces the question of Hungarian complicity, then, to a supporting role—specifically to cordon personnel—and not the killing itself. But one detail is undeniable: soldiers, officers, and, curiously enough, Jewish drivers attached to the military units were also present at the mass murder, personally witnessed it, and subsequently provided detailed reports back to affected families, Jewish organizations, and government officials. Gábor Mermelstein, a Jew who served as a truck driver in the Hungarian military, observed the mass murder in real time: "we saw hundreds of people undressing ... we passed a row of maple trees—practically above the multitude of naked corpses ... suddenly we noticed a square shaped pit where people were lined up. Hundreds of innocent people were machine-gunned down. I will never forget what I saw and felt: the frightened faces, the men, women, children marching into their own graves without resistance. I was terrified, outraged, and overwhelmed by grief at the same time."⁹¹

The role of Jewish military drivers in channeling information about the atrocity was especially crucial. Their accounts, although somewhat sketchy, filtered into the intelligence reports of the Hungarian military: "according to drivers attached to the military, German soldiers and Ukrainian militiamen wanted to drive further large number of Jews who were removed from Hungary. The Jews resisted the military upon which they 'shot several of them.'"⁹² A more detailed account by such a driver, Izidor Salzer, noted that "on August 27–29 the Ukrainian militia and Hungarian military units escorted the Jews out of the area under the idea of relocating them to a different region." In describing the "defenseless, frantic, and horror-stricken crowd" streaming toward their doom, he did not need superlatives. His account corroborates testimonies of local Jewish and non-Jewish eyewitnesses.⁹³

Although its author is cloaked in anonymity, a brief but contemporaneous report, dated August 30, 1941, also presents the distinct likelihood that perhaps a representative of a Hungarian Jewish organization, was also "on the ground" and in the vicinity of the slaughter. The description itself ranges from the atrocities committed by Ukrainian paramilitaries along the Dniester River to the direct description of the three-day massacre in Kamenets-Podolsk. The report is the one that supplied the estimated number of deportees, between 14,000 and 16,000 who were murdered during these three days. The language, narrative, and painful details all testify to the fact that this author was present:

> They chased them with rifle butts and whips to where they received the final redemption from further suffering in the form of a bullet by a German submachine gun. No one troubled to check if they were dead; as one fell into a pit, a moment later the next followed, and so on, until the pit filled up to the brim. When it was full, they covered the grave even if there were still many alive, and the same game continued, at the next pit. The popping sound of the machine gun is still on my mind after 3-4 days and I will perhaps never forget it as long as I live. The August 27-28 will be a Yahrzeit for the Jews because 15,000 innocent people have lost their lives in this city... among them many Hungarians. It is constantly on my mind. God be merciful to us all.⁹⁴

This and other reports were accurate both in the portrayal of the massacre and the number of victims. The world became almost instantaneously aware of the carnage that was taking place in Galicia and its Hungarian Jewish angle. Headlines such as "Jews Dragged from Hospitals in Hungary for Deportation to Nazi-held Galicia," "Thousands of Jews Killed in Ukraine by Nazis; Bodies Floating in Dniester," and others by the Jewish Telegraphic Agency (JTA) left little to the imagination. Quoting

Hungarian officers, these dispatches informed the American public about the extent of the carnage: "Thousands of Jewish corpses are floating in the waters of the Dniester River, in the Nazi-occupied Ukraine, as a result of massacres of Jews carried out by German soldiers in cooperation with Ukrainian bands.... The officers, shocked by the horrible scenes, estimated that tens of thousands of Jews were massacred in the Kamenetz-Podolsk region.... Among the dead are at least 15,000 Hungarian Jews." One of the officers "also estimated that among those killed in Kamenets-Podolsk region were 8,000 Galician Jews."[95]

This number accurately reflected the final total given by Jeckeln. In a letter dated October 20, 1943, and sent to Palestine, a writer reported similar statistics: "In this way, twenty-five thousand Jews were at that time in Kamenets-Podolsk executed."[96] The English-, Yiddish-, and Hungarian-language Jewish press in New York and London also picked up this news.[97] During the trial of one of the main architects of the deportation, Ámon Pásztóy, a figure of 20,000 was mentioned. We can also glean from this testimony that through military reports and direct testimonies by KEOKH personnel, the office was also appraised on the continuous massacres and the final mass murder committed in Kamenets-Podolsk. The de-facto head of KEOKH, Dr. Sándor Siménfalvy, promptly reported this information to the minister of interior.[98]

In reviewing the extant files of the US Department of State, it is clear that the American Embassy in Budapest, and especially Herbert C. Pell, the envoy extraordinary and minister plenipotentiary of the United States were privy to the situation in Galicia. Consequently, the US Department of State was also informed in detail.[99] The Americans had reporters and diplomatic and military personnel in Budapest to collect information about Nazi atrocities, at least until early 1942. One of the quirks of Hungarian policy was the fact that the JDC, through which information reached Geneva, Lisbon, and Washington unhindered, could function undisturbed. The ever alert and watchful British secret service, on the other hand, relied on electronic means for gathering information about the monstrous deeds committed in Kamenets-Podolsk and elsewhere by Jeckeln and Reserve Police Battalion 320. As mentioned earlier, they were able to decode the communications between Jeckeln and Himmler, his direct superior, and apprised Churchill routinely on the magnitude of the exterminations. By October of the same year, the press in New York and London reported the carnage committed in Galicia in relatively precise details.[100]

The Jewish communities across Galicia also became aware almost instantaneously of the mass murder as straggling survivors, some of them literally climbing out of the mass graves, and traumatized eyewitnesses reached cities, towns, and villages. The bloodbath was sobering and disturbing news to the Jews of Galicia and sent a shockwave through the communities. A note from Borshchiv reflects this apprehension: "We became aware of this [Kamenets-Podolsk] right away from the few who survived. The shooting of these Jews was the first major action in our region, and it made a horrible impression."[101] Many of these communities harboring the refugees from Hungary had viewed the influx of the deportees as "insurance" against extermination. Hungarian troops often curbed Ukrainian excesses or stopped pogroms against Jewish communities in Galicia. The murders at Kamenets-Podolsk now sent a portentous message of tragic things to come. Some reports referred to a day of mourning declared by various Jewish communities across the region.

From the German military's point of view, we must also ask how much detail filtered back to von Roques' headquarters about Kamenets-Podolsk? An unexpected angle came to light during war crime trial of von Roques in Nuremberg that could address the question of how much he knew about the massacre. It is evident that he fully acquiesced to the role the security forces played in the euphemistically called "pacification" actions (i.e., extermination). The directive, dated September 1, 1941, provides clear proof of that. During the trial, though, the curious fact that Jeckeln "usually had his headquarters in the same locality as the defendant and frequently dined with him and his officers" did not escape the prosecutors' attention. The prosecutors reminded von Roques that he had to have known intimately the details of the murder since "on 2 September [1941] von Roques' chief of staff [Colonel Ernst-Anton von Krosigk] had a conference at the headquarters of Army Group South in which the figures 'concerning the settlement of the Jewish Question in Kamenets-Podolsk' were discussed."[102] Additional critical evidence about his knowledge of the extermination came through the military commandant of the city, Lieutenant Colonel Josef Meiler. He recalled during his interrogation in 1959 that the general was aware of the impending action. Given these documents, we can assume with a degree of certainty that von Roques was meticulously debriefed on the massacre taking place on his operational territory.[103]

Kamenets-Podolsk unleashed a chain of events of calamity-defying description. It constitutes a milestone and stepping stone in turning sporadic episodes of mass killings into an organized genocide. It marked an irretrievable transition from the so-called *Judenpolitik* to *Vernichtungspolitik*, thanks also to the implicit collaboration—or rather to the non-opposition—of the leadership of the Wehrmacht. This signified a point of no return on the road to the Final Solution.

"SPECIALIST FÜR DIE 'ENDLÖSUNG' IM OSTEN"

As the title of an article about Jeckeln, Richard Breitman, well sums up a man who was dedicated to his mission: "The Specialist for the 'Final Solution' in the East."[104] Jeckeln was not an ordinary murderer. By all accounts, he was a genuinely fanatical believer in the Nazi doctrine of mass extermination. His career in the Nazi hierarchy contains some impressive milestones. His rise through the SS ranks was meteoric. But then, he knew Hitler personally, overseeing his security details on several occasions and dining with him. We also know that he was one of Himmler's most trusted senior officers in implementing his policies in occupied Eastern Europe. Bennet's characterization of him as one of "the principal 'field managers' of the Final Solution to the Jewish problem" is an apt one.[105] It reflects his record as one of the most ruthless, ambitious, and prolific mass killers in the history of the Third Reich.

A powerfully built man with penetrating blue eyes, he was personally responsible for ordering and organizing the deaths of more than 100,000 people by bullets. Kamenets-Podolsk was only an inaugural salvo in his career. A summary situation report from September 25, 1941, stated that Jeckeln's men executed a staggering number of Jews, specifically 44,125 people, within a four-week span between August and September.[106] This was followed by larger massacres in Babi Yar, Rumbula Forest in Riga, and elsewhere. Yet, during his trial in Riga in 1946, he was not even called to account about his actions in Kamenets-Podolsk. The prosecutors did not realize at the time his central role in the extermination of Hungarian Jews in the summer of 1941. During the trial, Jeckeln showed no emotion at all. His answers were clear and precise—he admitted everything put to him. On February 3, 1946, he was hung for his crimes in Riga.[107]

Evidence of Jeckeln's thoughts, feelings, and moral questionings of his actions, an "ego document," never surfaced during his interrogation in Riga in 1946. Beyond the

FIG 4.10   General Friedrich Jeckeln: The profile of a mass murderer. *United States Holocaust Memorial Museum Photo Archives, courtesy of Bundesarchiv.*

cold facts, the trial records reveal very little about the person. But in reading Bennett's short biography, the recollections of his court-ordered translator in his trial in Riga, and the reflections of comrades in arms in 1965, one comes away with the notion that sentimentality was not part of his psychological makeup. He was totally dedicated to the task at hand: killing the "enemies of the Third Reich." He managed atrocity denuded of emotions and devoid of moral standards. Fritz Blaschek, a fellow SS officer, intimated during his trial that "Jeckeln was not simply obeying orders—he was personally motivated in his campaign of murder against the Jews."[108] When he was asked why he felt that he had to be personally present at the exterminations, Jeckeln's exact words were: "the shooting of thousands of people... is always a heavy burden for the men, and the Leader must be present." Yet, as his translator noted in a documentary, "one sensed a certain charm... other than that, he was a totally cold-blooded man... a man who had ordered people to death."[109] The medical officer of his staff company summed him up best in describing him as "a genuine psychopath."[110]

Like many of his contemporaries in the Nazi extermination machine, his impulses and aspirations were cloaked in utter mediocrity. Among the coterie of mass murderers in the Holocaust, Jeckeln was perhaps the least educated, with only one semester at university. In another time he might have been no more substantial than a grey *apparatchik* in a nondescript office, if not a total failure. Yet he assumed a role as the ultimate arbiter of life and death. The Nazi party provided him with a framework, and just as it was for many of his fellow mass murderers, the victims remained mere statistics. The enduring image, painted by Hanna Arendt specifically about Eichmann as an ordinary man, doesn't fit Jeckeln. He was far from a thoughtless functionary simply performing his duty. He proceeded quite intentionally from a set of tenaciously held Nazi beliefs. His was a consciously wrought racial "ethics," one that pitted as an ultimate value the survival of one's own blood against that of the Jews.[111]

Yet, Jeckeln had to deal with his own personal insecurities, pride, and ambition. His first wife, from whom he was bitterly divorced, was half-Jewish, with an Aryan mother and a Jewish father, which might explain his visceral anti-Semitism. Then he had three children from this marriage who were categorized as *mischlinge*—a Nazi derogatory definition of partially Jewish—and who also served in the Wehrmacht.[112] He not only had to compete with his two fellow HSSPFs for the attention and approval of Himmler, but also with the rival agencies within the multilayered security and military establishment. While he was one of the flag-bearers for murder in the occupied Soviet Union, second-string SS personnel were equally lethal in their extermination drive, even if they could not equal his numbers and ferocity. One only needs to remember the words of the first Gestapo head, Rudolf Diel, who "confided" in Martha Dodd, the daughter of the American ambassador to Berlin, William Dodd, in the mid 1930s: "everyone in the Nazi hierarchy distrusted everyone else, how Göring and Goebbels loathed each other and spied on each other ... 'a vast and complicated espionage, terror, sadism and hate, from which no one, official or private, could escape.'"¹¹³

It is probable that, like that of many of his fellow SS men, Jeckeln's relationship with Himmler featured utter and unconditional subservience, with a continual need for reassurance. The dictum of Peter Longerich that Himmler gathered around him a corps of dependent personal loyalists characterizes Jeckeln well. These were officers "who committed themselves to Himmler because he offered men limited gifts, of which only ruthlessness was indispensable, unique opportunities for advancement from relative humble circumstance."¹¹⁴ He may have craved Himmler's approval much like Himmler craved Hitler's. Felix Kersten, personal physician of the powerful *Reichsführer*, noted in his diary that "an unfavorable comment by Hitler on one of his [Himmler's] measures were enough to upset him thoroughly and produce violent reactions which took the form of severe stomach pains."¹¹⁵ He diagnosed him as a divided and cowardly man, completely subservient to Hitler.

So, too, did Jeckeln clamor for the respect and approbation of his superior officer. As we have seen, there was an instantaneous spike in mass exterminations as the tangible result of Jeckeln's meeting on August 12, 1941, with Himmler who scolded him for not being energetic enough in the business of mass murder. The *Reichsführer* was obviously not satisfied with Jeckeln's progress. His communication with Himmler about the final results of the slaughter in the last days of August, then, was to demonstrate that Jeckeln "was in charge and that his 'commando unit' carried out the action."¹¹⁶

Again, if we recount his behavior during his trial in Riga, we come away with a sense that he willingly admitted everything and took responsibility for everything. He did not present excuses; in the words of his interpreter, "he was a very clear thinking man, a competent man." The final testimony of the same interpreter might provide an apt summation of Jeckeln: "A man can be cultured, which Jeckeln wasn't, but he can be highly cultured and still behave this way.... But neither culture nor education nor artistic leanings can exclude it."¹¹⁷

CONCLUSION TO A MASSACRE

The original record of the critical Vinnitsa meeting on August 25, 1941, clearly implied that Jeckeln would "liquidate" 11,000 bothersome Hungarian Jews. Per the recollection of one of the participants in the mass murder, Captain Hans Wiemer, Jeckeln similarly reassured the officers of the battalion on the eve of the mass murder that specifically Hungarian Jews would be the explicit target of the impending extermination. He justified this by adding that those to be killed would be future partisans and, in any case, by killing them they would also eliminate international Jewry.¹¹⁸ True to his promise, the first two days were fully dedicated to the extermination of the Jews from Hungary and Romania. It might be reasonable to assume that the killing of thousands of local Jews was a spur-of-the-moment decision, prompted by his desire to report and take credit for the highest number of killed. But then, he was not only a prolific but also an opportunistic killer.

In searching for answers to the human dimensions of the carnage, it should not boil down, as mass murders often do, to mere statistics. This stunning number of those killed and the magnitude of the massacre does not truly reflect the lives lost or the suffering endured. However, in looking for reassurance and testimonies of survival, there is precious little that can be found. The majority of those who were able to climb out of the murder pits under the cloak of darkness were hunted down by patrols of Reserve Police Battalion 320. But a few struggling survivors, among them a twelve-year-old boy, would tell their heartrending tales to local Jewish communities.

Friday, August 29, 1941, was the final day of the carnage. As the sun slowly set over the killing fields of Kamenets-Podolsk, thirty-two dazed survivors huddled together amid the eerie sounds and cries of the many who were still alive in the mass graves. Among those who survived by pretending to be Christians was twelve-year-old Albert Fein and his family. They were among the few who were saved by ingenuity, quick thinking, a quirk of fate, and a policeman from Reserve Police Battalion 320. The Fein family was pulled away from the mass grave after a brief, inconclusive inspection by Jeckeln himself, and their escape spoke to the notion that survival in the Holocaust was utterly unpredictable, and often due to sheer luck as much as to deft thinking. The policeman leading them through the cordon, after being ordered by Jeckeln to "take them back," curtly deflected any challenge by claiming, "The General says to take them back." He instructed the family to sit on the side of the field for the entire afternoon, without a reassurance of whether they would be spared or not. Soon they were joined by a dozen Jews from Gheorgheni (Gyergyószentmiklós) in northern Transylvania and others, all claiming to be Christians. As Albert Fein exclaimed in his interview about their escape, "miracles can happen." "We were sitting there and waiting. There [were] people coming, you know, asking us, 'What, you are sitting here? If this is the case, we are not Jews. We are not Jews either,' and they sit, sit down beside us. This way we had thirty-two people. . . . They came from Gheorgheni . . . the General was on—there was a plane—a small plane—he left. So, the whole command was in this person, this soldier's hand, and he says, 'I will take you back to the barracks. . . . I will take you back to the barracks.' And he took us back. First of all, we were all hungry like dogs. [We] didn't eat the whole day, so he brought for us from the kitchen food. He brought food and he gave his name; his name was Josef Swintek. And he says he has been from Berlin."[119]

It is tempting to ask if Josef Swintek really believed that those thirty-two people were non-Jews. While it might seem almost inconceivable, we want to believe that he knew that these were Jews yet wanted to save them. In reading the Operational Situation

Report by Jeckeln, though, it was clear that the perpetrator of the massacre did not entertain such a question. One recurring scene in the eyewitness accounts is that of the victims jumping or the children being flung into the mass graves alive. By doing this, they may have been expressing a fear of death, but they also denied the murderer the right to kill. It allowed the victim to control his or her own fate. Again, one cannot escape the question as to what motivated my older uncle, Karcsi, to jump into the mass grave alive. Was it fear or, perhaps, defiance of the executioner? After all, many exercised this last act. As we mentioned earlier, a Soviet forensic medical commission's findings from 1944 support this based on a record from the village of Plebanowka in the Tarnopol region, not far from Kamenets-Podolsk. Upon opening the mass graves, it found that "thirty-five percent of the victims were shot dead on the spot. Fifty percent of the people were injured, and fifteen percent were buried alive."[120]

Upon recapturing Kamenets-Podolsk in the spring of 1944 and opening several mass graves from the 1941 and 1942 massacres, Soviet authorities conducted painstaking investigations with graphic reconstruction of the victims' final moments. As we peruse the pages of testimonies of the simple Ukrainians who were forced by the Germans to cover and recover the mass graves in 1941, and the same individuals who were also present at the opening of the mass graves in 1944, it becomes obvious that the human imagination has limitations in comprehending mass extermination. Nikolai Tupenko, a Ukrainian Christian who was taken at gunpoint with his coworkers to one of the murder pits to bury the victims, described his experience in grisly yet touching details during his testimony to the Soviet Extraordinary State Commission on May 19, 1944:

> In August 1941 executioners came to our brewery, where I was a worker, and selected 14 people, including me, to cover the graves. They took us at gun point. The people from Hungary were shot at the former Polish cemetery. They forced us into a ditch, where we were guarded until all the Hungarians [Hungarian Jews] were taken to the grave. I did not see the shooting... but only heard the sound of shots from automatic rifles. After the shooting was over, we were taken to the pit where the Hungarians were killed and ordered to bury them. I saw a terrible picture, which became permanently engraved in my memory—this was the work of the brutal fascists. Some people in the grave were still alive. The image of a Hungarian girl about 14 years old was especially imprinted [in my mind], she was lying in the grave although she was still alive. A middle-aged man, also still alive, was lying above her. We were told to take away some of the earth and to step aside. Germans from the killing unit dragged them [out of the grave], shot them, and threw them back into the grave. The middle-aged man was still able to raise his head; he begged to be killed and not be buried alive. I was not conscious of throwing earth on top of them. If any of us stopped out of

shock at what was happening, he was beaten with a rifle butt to hurry and cover the grave now filled with people. When we finished covering the grave, in some places the earth over the grave heaved. Apparently, there were people still alive, who were being suffocated or suffering death throes. After we were sent away, three [more] graves were filled solely with [the bodies] of Hungarians."[121]

The eyewitness accounts of opening the same graves indicate the enormity of the suffering of the victims in their final moments. Standing in front of one of the murder sites of Hungarian Jews in 1944 for whom "there was nobody to cry," a member of the investigative committee saw "a mother so tightly pressing her child against her breast, that they are not separated from each other even after the final moment.... Here the bodies of an entire family: father, mother, three children" and "the corpse of a little boy, buried alive, thrown alive into the pit with the dead. This can be seen by the pose as his little hands were cupping his head, his knees brought up to his chin, his back bent as he tried to lift the weight on top of him."[122]

One cannot find a better elegy for those who were murdered at Kamenets-Podolsk than the testimony of another Ukrainian who was forced, like Nikolai Tupenko, to come to the grave site in the middle of the carnage: "I, an old man, was taken with a shovel close to the pits where the Hungarians were being shot. I trembled when I realized that now I have to fill the hole.... I particularly remember a woman with a child in her arm, pressing the child close to her heart, afraid of parting with him. But a German came up to her and snatched the child, throwing him like a ball in a great arc into the pit. The woman, covering her face with her hands, jumped after the child alive."[123]

The recollection of this unwitting participant, and in some way a victim himself, might be a fitting commemoration of the 23,600 Jews killed in the summer of 1941. The carnage in Kamenets-Podolsk cannot be viewed as single atrocity with its own rationale, but as part of a far greater tragedy that would play out in the ensuing years. With the backdrop of war between Nazi Germany and Soviet Russia, the specter of this massacre stands out as a landmark on the road to total annihilation. Perhaps the most eloquent yet concise summation of this event belongs to the German historian Dieter Pohl who named it the "turning point in the Final Solution."[124]

The influx of Hungarian Jews and their consequent murder was a defining moment on two levels: an integral component of the unfolding Holocaust and, simultaneously, a spark and catalyst for follow-up bloodbaths. This is not to say that it precipitated the wave of annihilation engulfing Eastern Europe. The plans and actions for that were already in motion in Berlin and, consequently, by the combined forces of the Wehrmacht and a multitude of killing units. Rather, it validated and intensified the process, showing that murder on a gigantic scale was feasible and, at the same time, pointing toward larger massacres and human tragedies to come in Galicia and the East.

5

GALICIA 1941–1942

The Delirium of Murder

"Death was their tool and life their toy."

THIS POWERFUL SENTENCE WAS UTTERED IN THE NUREMBERG PALACE OF Justice's quiet, wood-paneled courtroom in 1947 during the trials of twenty-two leaders of the Einsatzgruppen who were responsible for the wholesale murder of Jews, Gypsies, and others in the Soviet Union. There was poetic justice in this dramatic moment, which belonged to a Hungarian-born, twenty-seven-year-old Harvard educated Jew who was the American chief prosecutor. Benjamin Berrell Ferencz hailed from northern Transylvania, from one of the little villages in the Carpathian Mountains from which many of the Jewish inhabitants were sent to Galicia in 1941.[1]

The Einsatzgruppen were not involved in the annihilation of Hungarian Jews either in Kamenets-Podolsk or anywhere else in Galicia. The only mention of their encounter with the Hungarian deportees was made in a German Situational Report, which indicated that they pushed one thousand Hungarian Jews back across the Dniester to the line of the Carpathian Mountains when the 10th Hungarian Pursuit Battalion transported them over the river.[2] Their murderous deeds, though, can serve as an apt summation for the fate of the Hungarian deportees and their Galician brethren in 1941 and 1942.

Every mass murder has its own dynamics. The three-day Kamenets-Podolsk carnage was undeniably one of the defining moments in the debut of the Holocaust in Ukraine as well as the apogee of a Hungarian Jewish tragedy in 1941. It was a "raw atrocity" neither equaled in numbers nor in ferocity in the annals of genocide until that point, yet this massacre was not an anomaly within the unfolding annihilation process. It had an ominous prequel, for it was not a coincidence that, almost simultaneously with Kamenets-Podolsk, on August 26, 1941, SS troops unleashed a bloodbath in Orinin (also in Podolia), which harbored close connections with Kamenets-Podolsk. Both mass murders aimed to eliminate the wandering hordes of Jews expelled from Hungary. This spasm of killings also had a likely common fingerprint: that of Friedrich Jeckeln.

Orinin and Kamenets-Podolsk were only the opening salvo in the unbridled savagery that gripped the region. By German estimates, up to seven thousand Hungarian Jews remained in the Galician district after these two "signature" massacres. They were mainly concentrated in the southern tier, in Nadwórna (Nadvirna in Ukrainian), a small town in the southeast of the district, Kolomea, and Stanisławów.[3] Thus, the character, dynamics, and pace of mass murder changed in the following months. We might characterize the pivotal massacre in Kamenets-Podolsk as a "targeted" carnage with a utilitarian and "problem-solving" rationale—a pivotal moment on the road to total genocide—the jumpstart of the Final Solution.[4] The tragic role the Hungarian influx played in igniting it is undeniable. Kamenets-Podolsk was as "professionally" conducted as mass murder could be, at least in comparison to the ensuing bloodletting in the region in the fall of 1941.

By October 1941, a dramatic shift took place in the extermination process in which the almost detached professionalism of Jeckeln that could be summed up by Wendy Lower's statement, "he was notorious for 'getting the job done,'" was replaced by an orgy of killings that often bordered on chaos. This new phase, the "building blocks" toward the Final Solution, aimed to decimate the Jewish communities by unleashing waves of murder not only across the District of Galicia, but Ukraine as a whole. This period combined the "joy" of mass executions with corruption on every level. The executioners cloaked the carnage in racial and political terms, but they were able to bring this in sync easily with their visceral and almost pathological lust for brutality, murder, and outright thievery.

Thus, it was also an unbridled opportunity for personal enrichment and greed masquerading as ideology. The main players in this slaughter, Ukrainian irregulars and Nazi security agencies, exhibited an almost sadistic joy in torturing and killing the defenseless masses on the long and dusty roads of Galicia and in the shtetls and ghettos. This was not conducted in accordance with Himmler's dictum of killing but not enjoying it—that is, conducting the killings professionally, without sadistic pleasure or, in the parlance of the SS, "remaining decent."[5]

THE GATHERING STORM

The situation in Galicia during the summer and fall of 1941 was complicated and the influx of Hungarian Jews made it even more complex. While Jews were the specific targets of extermination by the German security agencies, aided by Ukrainian paramilitary forces, they were not the only victims. After the elimination of the Jews, Nazi officers' attention was to refocus on Poles and other perceived enemies of the Third Reich. Yet the Germans were not the only murderers. As the extermination of the Hungarian deportees and local Jewish communities began, an internecine war that was accompanied by a systematic ethnic cleansing flared up between Poles and Ukrainians, between nationalist Ukrainians of Bandera and the perceived "Bolsheviks." It was a time for settling scores. Adam Gopnick has observed so perceptively that the unfolding bloodletting in Eastern Europe of the fall of 1941 was a "convulsion in a long-disputed territory, in which everyone killed everyone."[6]

The period between September 1941 and March 1942 might be identified as a time of mass murder by bullets in Galicia. During that period, the Nazi plans for extermination became systematic, consistent, and premeditated. By 1943, though, the inauguration of a new and more efficient death by gas in Belzec rapidly superseded this form of genocide. The conditions for the implementation of the Final Solution in the District of Galicia, and within it the fate of the Hungarian Jews, lurched forward with the transition from German military to civilian rule on September 1, 1941. This was also the start of a most resourceful alliance between the understaffed security apparatus and the German civil administration for implementing the unfolding Holocaust. Christopher Browning noted that "without the active support of mayors, city councils, housing offices, and a plethora of local administrators, the identification, expropriation, and ghettoization of the Jewish population ... would have exceeded the limited logistical capabilities of German occupation agencies."[7] This phase saw the reduction of the Wehrmacht's participation, directly or indirectly, in the extermination process. Instead, civilian authorities became complicit and often directly involved in mass murder. They often supplied the transportation of the doomed to the murder pits. In Stanislawów, the German city administration provided the tracks for transferring the Jews to the New Jewish Cemetery for slaughter. In Buczacz, the tracks transporting the Hungarian expellees and the local Jewish intelligentsia to their execution bore the clear mark of "Für die deutsche Winterhilfe"—German Winter Relief. In Kolomea, the Kreishauptmann went far beyond that. Claus Volkmann became an active participant in the extermination of the Hungarian Jews.[8]

As part of transferring the territories into civilian control, the District of Galicia became incorporated into the General Government as its fifth district, administered directly from Lwów (Lviv in Ukrainian, Lemberg in German). Parallel to this transition and filling the power vacuum created by the removal of Hungarian military control, security teams of seasoned SS officers were dispatched from Lwów to Stanislawów and Kolomea.

We can attribute the wholesale annihilation of Jewish communities across southern Galicia, and the Hungarian deportees along with them, to these "second-tier" SS men with regional authority. They followed the general dictum emanating from the headquarters of Major General Fritz Katzmann, who was appointed as Higher SS and Police Leader of the District of Galicia. Joining him in stage-managing the unfolding genocide were two well-educated, high-ranking SS officers, SS Senior Colonel and Police Colonel Dr. Karl Eberhard Schöngarth and Major Dr. Helmut Tanzmann, who headed the Security Police in Lwów from August 1, 1941.

Jeckeln's reputation had been cemented by his role in masterminding mass murders in Kamenets-Podolsk, Babi Yar, and Riga. While these three officers could not match the productivity of Jeckeln in murder, they were equally notorious for being ruthless and prolific murderers. Fritz Katzmann was not as well educated as many of his contemporaries in the officers' rank. Yet, because of his party fealty, he rose rapidly in the ranks and was promoted to major general of police on September 26, 1941. One of his commanding officers from his early years in the SS called him "unusually ambitious ... full of the fighting spirit ... a fanatical political soldier."[9]

Schöngarth and Tanzmann, on the other hand, were both displaced intellectuals, well born and university educated with degrees in law. Schöngarth's approach to murder was especially instructive: he ordered his commanders to follow his example in individually shooting Jews during executions—there was no option except to participate. Following such an episode, he made a speech: "You saw how it was done. Every man should join in the shooting. I will shoot anyone who doesn't agree. I will back up every SS Führer who shoots a man for not obeying my order."[10]

The first priority for the security leadership in Lwów was to stabilize the border region adjacent to Carpathian Ruthenia and Bukovina, in Romania. This demanded a rapid expansion of security services in southern Galicia. This had, as we will learn later, direct connection with the Hungarian decision to transfer Jews to Galicia. In turn, the most immediate question is how this influenced Hungarian policies toward the deportation, and how this new security establishment impacted the fate of the already deposited deportees from Hungary.

The rapidly evolving administrative structure and corresponding policy of genocide became clear during the trial testimony of one of the main architects of the Holocaust in Galicia, Captain Hans Krüger. He testified in 1968 that the decision to secure the border and destroy Galician Jewry, and with it the remnants of the Jews deported from Hungary, was made in Lwów in early July 1941. As head of the security services reporting to Katzmann, Dr. Schöngarth instructed him to set up a branch office of the Regional Command of the Security Police.[11] Two weeks prior to Krüger's arrival, an advance unit of six men, under the command of Oskar Brandt, was dispatched to Stanisławów for establishing security presence parallel to the Hungarian military's departure.[12] By mid-September, a whole network of police stations, border stations, and security offices came rapidly into existence along the line of the Carpathian Mountains thanks to the efforts of Krüger and his soon-to-be-arriving subordinate First Lieutenant Peter Leideritz. The rationale was clear. Setting up these outposts (*Grenzpolizei-Kommissariat*) along the lines of the Carpathian Mountains, in Tatarow, Wyszkow, Śniatyn, Zabie, and other locations,[13] indicated the paramount importance of creating a buffer zone between the Galician communities and Hungary. Its explicit aim was to prevent any further transfer of Hungarian Jews into the General Government

Thus, Krüger and Leideritz became the undisputed rulers of life and death for large swath of Galicia. The main control was concentrated in the offices of the Sipo[14] in Stanislawów and Kolomea. To shore up the operation in Kolomea, reinforcements consisting of thirty-five men of the Vienna *Schutzpolizei* (*Schupo*) arrived in September. Beside Kamenets-Podolsk, these districts were the main regions where Hungarian Jews streamed in large numbers. In addition to blocking the border region, these command posts dictated the implementation of the first stage of the Holocaust across Galicia. Roving murder squads, pulled together from various border stations, security agencies, and local civil administrations, were dispatched to smaller towns and villages to finish the periodical cleansing actions. The hallmark of this stage of the unfolding genocide in Galicia could be found in the multilevel and overlapping authorities of Nazi bureaucracy. Top-down directives might have been issued, but they did not prescribe the mode of implementing the killings by these leaders. Local commanders acted with a surprising degree of autonomy. As one historian phrased it: "it was largely left to the judgment of the individual administrator how he would deal with 'his' Jews." Replacing the mobile extermination units, stationary security offices across the region were able to pursue their own "*Judenpolitik*," with corresponding killing operations.

Hungarian Jews were not the only concern of the incoming security agencies. To a lesser degree, these forces also faced Jewish refugees from the south, from Bukovina. Considering the massive Romanian expulsion of hundreds of thousand Jews from Bukovina and Bessarabia, their alarm was justified. However, the most vexing issue remained the large and sustained transfer of Jews from Hungary. Thus, the border security was given an overlapping command by Tanzmann to Krüger to immediately execute everyone routinely returned by the Hungarian border authorities. These included Hungarian Jews who had been captured by Hungarian border guards while attempting to flee and were sent back over the border as well as escaping Galician Jews from the ghettos, who desperately tried to find shelter in Hungary or Romania. The first shooting of about "100 young people up to 35 years of age, which was handed over by the Hungarian authorities, took place in December [1941] at the Wyszkow Pass." Similar instructions were given to other border posts facing Romania.[15]

From the beginning, one of the chief mandates of the Nazi security apparatus—in fact a rationale for their existence—was the implementation of the rapidly evolving Final Solution. Within its context, the Hungarian Jewish influx assumed a special place. The fall of 1941 can be identified as a qualitative marking point in the solution of the "Jewish Question" in the Galician region. As the pulse of genocide in the following several months accelerated with a rapid escalation of the killings, its character moved from spontaneous massacres to the systematic and utilitarian decimation of the Jewish population headed to the newly created ghettos or concentrated in large towns.

Again, the guiding rationale for the implementation of this policy, as Krüger explained in his pretrial interrogation of June 26, 1962, was: "when the heads of the various branch offices were installed by the new commander in Lwów, SS-Lieutenant Colonel [Helmut] Tanzmann, specific areas were assigned, and then the guidelines for work were set down.... Jews not suitable for deployment as laborers were to be shot on a regular basis, because space was no longer available."[16]

Without dismissing the underlying racial myopia as a base for the extermination of Jews, and Russian soldiers as well, an equally weighty factor was the German concerns about food shortages during 1941 and 1942. As a rule, the people of the conquered territories were condemned to a drastic reduction in food supply. The Jews were subjected to forced starvation and, later, outright killing. For example, the March 31, 1942, "*Gross Aktion*" in Stanisławów was precipitated by German concerns that "there were too many Jews to be fed. They decided that there is only food enough for 8,000 Jews."[17] As a side note, the Hungarian refugees who were housed in the *Rudolfmühle* (Rudolf's Mill), a "warehouse" for those marked for death, were, by that time, dying daily from systematic starvation. The ghetto administration was not able to supply food even for their own population. Christian Gerlach argued persuasively that worry over food shortages sharply accelerated the mass killings.[18] Yet these concerns were a reinforcing, not a primary, motive for murder. And since they realized that such shootings could not be organized overnight, the plan was that the residential areas set aside for the Jews should be progressively reduced. This poses the question as to how the influx of thousands of Hungarian Jews impacted the precarious communal balance in various Galician communities?

REFUGEES FROM "*KARPATOROS*"

With the commencement of German civilian rule, an estimated 30,000 to 40,000 Jews were killed in the District of Galicia alone by the end of 1941.[19] Among the murdered in this sweep, the number of Hungarian Jewish victims can be placed at over 5,000. Because the majority came from or via Carpathian Ruthenia and adjacent areas, their common designation by the locals was "*Karpatoros*." These peripatetic Hungarians, chased and hounded from town to town, were viewed by the emerging security establishment as a nuisance that needed to be eliminated. This is also the moment when the fate of the Hungarian Jewish expellees intertwined with that of the Jews of Galicia. Here may be an answer to one of the enduring questions that has occupied historians:

Why was the District of Galicia the first in the General Government to exterminate its entire Jewish population?

Concurrently with the formation of civil authority, a sizeable number of the Hungarian Jewish survivors found themselves, after long and tortuous treks on foot, in the already crowded Jewish shtetls, thus increasing the Jewish population of cities and towns. In turn, these destitute masses strained the local humanitarian resources of the Jewish communities who were themselves under economic distress.

In tracing the fate of the Hungarian expellees across the region, we need to reexamine the follow-up phase to Kamenets-Podolsk, the implementation of the second and third waves of extermination in Ukraine. These subsequent phases coincided with a unique evolution within the Nazi administrative hierarchy from a centralized to a diffused power structure. By the fall of 1941, as Richard J. Evans perceptively noted, Nazi power ceased to be vertical. It was not taking its cues in every detail solely from Berlin. As German soldiers, policemen, and civilian authorities spread themselves thin over the occupied territories, mid-level security officers interpreted their role and mandate in administering the territories relatively independently.[20]

The Galician Jews looked on the long columns from "*Karpatoros*" slowly winding through their towns, flanked by club-wielding, gun-toting Ukrainian paramilitaries, with compassion and a marked degree of trepidation. The town of Skala was located along one of the routes through which Hungarian Jews were funneled toward Kamenets-Podolsk. At the end of July, "the Jews of Skala saw the heartbreaking march of thousands of Jews from Carpathian Ruthenia, guarded by Ukrainians, taken to the old Russian border and from there to Kamenets-Podolski. The Skala Jews collected food and clothes and provided them with carts to carry the exhausted. All those people perished in massive killings in the environs of Kamenets-Podolsk."[21] Not everyone, though, ended up in that city. Thousands of them were directed, instead, to Kolomea, Horodenka, Czortków, Nadwórna, Delatyn, Kosów, Zablotow, Jaremcze, Kuty, Buczacz, and other locales where they shared inextricably in the fate of their local coreligionists. A letter, dated on November 13, 1941, openly informed relatives in Budapest that death became so ubiquitous that "we almost ignore it." By working for the German military, the writer held a special pass that temporarily protected him, but he was also aware that whenever the roaming Gestapo men decided, "they empty a street where Jews live and take the people away though we don't know where. They allegedly are executed."[22]

The majority, mainly from the Máramaros region of Carpathian Ruthenia, reached Stanislawów in early August. The concentration of these refugees increased the local population. This led to a regular sequence of slaughter, culminating in one of the most notorious mass murders in the General Government on October 12, 1941. In writing about the extermination of Jews in the District of Galicia, Thomas Sandkuehler noticed that a pattern emerged when the ghettos as designed were "much too small from the outset to accommodate all the Jews of the city. This brought on hunger and disease. *Added to this was a widespread famine due to the flooding and the deportation to this area of Hungarian Jews, only part of whom had been deported to the Ukrainian city of Kamenets-Podolsk and shot there.*"[23]

The extermination drive in the fall of 1941, sweeping unremittingly across Eastern Europe, culminated in October and November with a daily killing rate that surpassed that of Kamenets-Podolsk. This, of course, impacted not only the District of Galicia. One can detect a centralized course of planning emanating from Berlin via Kiev. Probably it was not a coincidence that almost parallel with massacres in this district, a sudden surge in mass murder was occurring in many locations, hundreds of miles away, as far as Dnepropetrovsk, Krivoy Rog, and other locales in Eastern Ukraine, by mid-October. The launching of the Holocaust in Galicia, though, started in August and September, earlier than other regions.[24]

The next six months can be characterized as filled with overlapping murder waves that lurched toward the Final Solution: the ultimate annihilation of the Jewish community. They ranged from the elimination of the intellectual strata of various communities (*Intelligenz Aktion*) in the first week after the establishment of the German civil administration, to intermittent "culling" of specific groups within the Jewish community, mainly those expelled from Hungary and other European countries, and to large-scale "signature" massacres in mid-October and early November that gave focus to the genocide taking place in the General Government.

Under the psychological and physical stresses of German rule, the Hungarian influx into various communities complicated precarious intercommunity dynamics. Upon their arrival, the local Jewish community would extend spontaneous assistance to the worn out and traumatized multitude by establishing a tentative support system that included food distribution, housing, and orphanages. Orphanages were especially important because of the many families broken up during the military transportation to Galicia or the Ukrainian murder sprees.

This supportive arrangement rapidly disintegrated under the weight of an unremitting reduction in food supply and living space in the ghettos. The refugees (essentially) became a burden to the ghetto leadership.[25] Baruch Milch summed up well this evolution: "The remaining Jews [Hungarians], who were able to settle among the local Jews in various ways, were vegetating terribly. They communicated with great difficulty with their mother country, they quickly used up capital and valuable property, which they had with them, as a foreign element in these lands they were always the first to be exposed to all manners of danger—whether burdened with forced labor, or round-ups for lagers, or in actions [*Aktionen*]. Our Jewry had enough work with itself, so that the committees, initially bringing them help, quickly ceased their work."[26]

The German demands for forced labor and, at the final stages, the systematic delivery of Jews to the slaughter, further eroded any semblance of unity within the community. The impact on the fraying communal solidarity because of the fate of the Hungarian expellees was incremental but inevitable. Eliza Binder in Stanislawów expressed this frustration of not being able to help: "an immense hatred awakens in me.... Still, it's mostly about those Hungarian Jews. Besides them, isn't it true that each day they put twenty hunger victims into a common grave?"[27] Since they had no anchor in the host communities, and they had no means to bribe officials, they were the ones sent by the Jewish Councils (*Judenrate*) to satisfy the ever-increasing Nazi demands for slave labor or to death. A survivor, trying to reach the Hungarian border, was specifically warned not to register in the Horodenka *Judenrat* for aid, because "it sends the Hungarian refugees to German work camps." One illuminating event was the building of a 1,360-mile-long "trans-Ukrainian highway," the infamous *Durchgangstrasse IV* (DGSIV), in which Hungarian deportees also played a prominent role.[28]

Finally, the Hungarians were also the first ones to be marked for extermination within the various communities. The Jewish police in the ghettos had to fill a quota of Jews for the routinely conducted decimation, *Aktionen*, or their own family would be target for execution pits. Intercommunity cooperation or moral standards under these circumstances dissolved in the face of extreme conditions. The quote of a survivor from the Bolechow ghetto (Bolekhiv in Ukrainian) well sums up the general view of the Jewish police: "I was more afraid of them than anybody."[29] They often delivered the Jews of "*Karpatoros*" first. And, within these concentric circles in the rapidly fractured Jewish communities, the "foreign" Jews, those who were either expelled by the Germans in 1939 or transported from Hungarian internment camps, were perhaps the most defenseless, as they were on the bottom of the socioeconomic scale. These same international refugees viewed the "poor" and "religiously backward Jews" of Galicia with a degree of cultural superiority if not disdain. Blanca Rosenberg's sharp words resonate in this context: "But even after that, they wanted nothing to do with the rest us [poor Polish Jews]."[30] While these "foreign Jews" had very little common ground or connection to the Hungarian Jews, there was an even deeper cultural divide with the local communities. As a result, they had almost no chance for survival.[31]

CULLING THE DEPORTEES: "*INTELLIGENZ AKTIONEN*"

The transition to German civilian control and setting up the security establishment signaled the second wave of extermination, commencing in late August and early September. It was invariably inaugurated by a decimation of the intellectual and political leadership of the Jewish community and, to a lesser degree, the Polish intelligentsia—hence the term *Intelligenz Aktion*. This was the opening salvo in the annihilation process for many towns and cities in the District of Galicia.[32] That is also the procedure SS-Captain Hans Krüger employed in launching the Galician Holocaust.

Krüger looms large in the successive wave of murders engulfing the region. By some estimates, he was singularly responsible for the murder of more than 70,000 Jews and the deportation of another 12,000 to death camps within the span of sixteen month. What is most astonishing is that he could accomplish this with a small cadre of men, sometimes as few as twenty-five, and a minimum of resources. But he could augment his security team with a wide array of human resources from security agencies, including a large contingent of Ukrainian auxiliaries,[33] teams of ethnic Germans, railroad police (*Bahnpolizei*), and even the youngsters from the Hitler *Jugend*. Notably, Krüger had at his disposal a *Volksdeutsche* (ethnic German) unit recruited from Hungary that routinely participated in the exterminations. He also established a unit recruited from Romania.[34] However the backbone of the successive "*Judenaktionen*" was Reserve Police Battalion 133, which participated in the collection, transportation, cordon duties, and the killing of the Jews. Finally, the logistical support of the German civil administration was also a contributing factor. Nevertheless, his accomplishments in genocide, at least in comparison with the *Einsatzgruppen* with a much larger cache of human resources, is gruesomely impressive.[35]

Krüger's transfer to Stanislawów to organize the Final Solution in Galicia coincided with the influx of Hungarian Jews into the region. It was a well-calculated move on the part of his superior, Dr. Schöngarth. He could not have selected a more dedicated Nazi officer for such a task. Several weeks later, he was joined by SS-First Lieutenant Peter Leideritz, who assumed command of the *Grenzpolizeikommisariat* Kolomea. As it was noted earlier, these two officers crafted an impressive record in genocide. They were well-seasoned killers with prior mass shootings on their résumés.[36] In turn, the two of them soon became the most productive executioners in the District of Galicia, if not in the entire General Government. Under their leadership, security teams from Stanislawów, Kolomea, and the various border stations fanned out to villages and towns where only German civilian authorities were stationed for periodical small-scale slaughters. There was a fierce rivalry between the two as to the number of exterminations. Both also harbored an enthusiasm for the art of plunder. It became common knowledge that they blatantly emptied the homes of their Jewish and Polish victims of all valuables upon their arrest and the inevitable executions.[37]

Krüger's arrival in Stanislawów on August 1, 1941—parallel with the influx of thousands of Hungarian Jews in the city—was anything but uneventful. Wasting no time, he unleashed an immediate spate of killings, the so-called *Intelligenz Aktion*, starting the next day, August 2, 1941.

Anticipating his arrival, an order by the Gestapo was issued on July 29 to the *Judenrat* to compile a list of the Jewish intellectuals listed by profession. This included doctors, lawyers, teachers, and religious leaders. Poles and Jews of the professional and educated classes were ordered to report to the police under the guise of registering for work placement. The *Judenrat* refused to make this selection and give a list to the Germans. During the selection, the captain did not hide his omnipotent power over the frightened intellectuals, some of them members of the *Judenrat*, by introducing himself: "*Ich bin der Herr von Euer Leben und Tod*" (I am the Master of your Life and Death).[38] He lived up to his words. By the time of his transfer sixteen months later, he had made Stanislawów "*Judenfrei*." This included the destruction of close to 3,000 Hungarian exiles.

On August 4, he followed through on this pronouncement by shooting approximately five hundred Jews and ninety-nine Poles in the forest near the village of Pawelcze. The killers followed the well-rehearsed playbook of the SS in assuming operational control of a city. It was a short and lethal introduction to the second phase of the "Holocaust by bullets," which by and large escaped the attention of historians. The aim of these "*Intelligenz Aktionen*" was first to decapitate the leadership of both the Jewish and, to a lesser degree, Polish communities, and second to instill physical and psychological terror in the community.

Hans Krüger's candid admission during a conversation with the Polish Countess Karolina Lanckoronska, whom he arrested as a member of the Polish underground in 1942, is instructive of this modus operandi of the Gestapo. "When we march into a city," Krüger boasted, "we always have lists, prepared in advance, of people who have to be arrested." And, in this rare moment Krüger also proudly admitted to her his involvement in one of the most infamous examples of an "*Intelligenze Aktion*," that of the executions of the leading intellectuals in Ukraine—the killing of the Lwów professors.[39] It might be that this "confessional" moment was driven by his belief that the countess would not leave his prison alive. No one ever did. Nevertheless, it was a tactical error on his part, for the countess survived, thanks to the intervention of the Italian Royal House. His indiscretion later contributed partly to his downfall and consequent transfer; his transgression being not the killing itself, but "betraying secret information."[40]

Reminiscent of the rationale for the *Intelligenz Aktion*, and still within the framework of the second wave, was the practice of targeting specifically Hungarian Jews and with them other refugees from various European countries—many of them from Hungarian internment camps. These killings were conducted through the closing months of 1941 and spring of 1942. They might be termed "culling or cleansing actions," with a goal of reducing the size of the ghettos as well as savings in the corresponding food supply.

The weekly killings of certain numbers of Hungarian Jews, concentrated in Rudolfmühle in Stanislawów, became a ritual for Krüger and other *Sipo* personnel.

In Czortków, the process was more covert. Penina Kaufmann, who was deported with her family from Kassa (today's Kosice in Slovakia) to Czortków, recalled that announcements were posted in winter 1941–1942 for all persons "who were not the residents of the city" (i.e., Hungarian expellees) to report to the building of the *Judenrat*. Realizing that the decree spelled imminent doom for those who obeyed it, five Hungarian families set out the same night on the perilous journey toward the Hungarian border. Their concern was justified because those who reported were exterminated.[41]

In Kolomea, the security services were especially active in ferreting out "foreign nationals." It might be that this general designation was used intentionally as a subterfuge by Peter Leideritz so he would not have to alert the Hungarian Army headquarters in the city when he exterminated Hungarian refugees. As head of the *Sipo* post, the commandant conducted such routine "culling actions." As a perpetrator admitted in his trial, it was done "in three-week intervals." He issued an order on December 23 that "all Jews who possessed a foreign passport were ordered to the Gestapo headquarters for 'registration.'" For full compliance, the announcement promised to repatriate the foreign nationals to "their home countries."[42] Twelve hundred Jews, believing in this ruse, were imprisoned, tortured, and taken to Szeparowce Forest[43] where they were killed. While this was specifically aimed to destroy the expellees from Hungary, German, American, Brazilian, Austrian, Czech, Cuban, and even Peruvian citizens were also mentioned.

A local survivor, Blanca Rosenberg's, recollection of a dialogue with a German Jew who went willingly to the Gestapo with some Hungarians, is a chilling reminder of the vulnerability of the "foreign" Jews who had neither a cultural nor political affinity with the local Jewish community, nor with their fellow deportees from Hungary. This German–Jewish dilemma of believing in German culture, law, and decency, and the inability to adopt to an "alternate" reality—even on the brink of the abyss—doomed them. "I stared at him. 'But you're not going, are you? It's certain death.' 'Don't worry. It'll be all right. After all, we're German nationals. They can't just liquidate us. *Anyway, it's an order*.'" Rosenberg noted that "for him the Nazis weren't German" and even this proud German Jew "in the end, remained loyal to a fiction." The bitter irony of this moment was that neither the Hungarians nor the German Jews understood that this was not Schiller's or Goethe's Germany anymore.[44]

Such monthly culling *Aktionen* in the Kolomea Ghetto continued unabated in 1942: "On 24 January 1942, 400 Jewish intellectuals were imprisoned, tortured, and killed." Among those 400, there were thirty Hungarians and four Romanians who were arrested in Kosów and transported to Kolomea. Finally, between March 9 and 16, 1942, the remaining 2,000 foreign nationals, which included over 600 Hungarians, in addition to Austrian, Czech, Slovak, and German Jews, were exterminated.[45]

Not less significant were the many ongoing extermination operations, on a more limited scale, in almost every corner of Galicia. Because of the deliberate Nazi policy of making the border zone between Hungary and Ukraine "*Judenfrei*," the cleansing of this area was a priority. Many Hungarian Jews were caught up in this deadly dragnet on both side of the border. While conditions were different from place to place, in the Kolomea and Stanislawów districts the hunt for Hungarian Jews was the most intense. It's difficult to reach a reliable estimate about the number of expellees who were murdered in these "culling" operations in the smaller communities. From early October on, though, there was a noticeable shift in the policy of annihilation, focusing on a more comprehensive decimation of the Jewish population. With the aim of reducing their numbers as the implementation of ghettoization commenced, these killings took place prior to setting up the ghettos. Accordingly, directives from the office of SS-Lieutenant Colonel Helmut Tanzmann in Lwów were sent out in early October to the stations in Stanislawów and Kolomea. They instructed Krüger and Leideritz to prepare for a wave of extermination around mid-October that would dwarf in scope and size any previous killings.

DRESS-REHEARSAL FOR MASS MURDER: "*PROBEAKTION*"

The next phase of the Galician Holocaust was launched in the first week of October in a small featureless town, Nadwórna, not far from Stanislawów. Mass killing, as a form of absolute control over thousands of defenseless people, can be hard to renounce. It has an intoxicating power, as its perpetrator becomes an arbiter of life and death. Krüger and many of his fellow officers from the lower ranks tasted the power of murder and remained addicted to it even where there were almost no Jews left to kill. He pursued with equally visceral loathing the Polish community in the Stanislawów District. He singled out for special "treatment" Poles who befriended Hungarian officers. Countess Lanckoronska, who was arrested by Krüger in 1942, noticed a pattern in that "nearly all of them [Poles] were accused of 'having contacts with Hungarians.'"

Considering that the Hungarians were close military allies of the Wehrmacht, one can only guess about the source of his hatred. The only creditable explanation might be found in a recurring theme in his Operational Situation Reports about Polish friendship with the Hungarian military. Another motivation for this "anti-Hungarian" complex might be his humiliation by Lieutenant General Szombathelyi in Kolomea, a notable episode that will be discussed later in forcing him to release a group of doomed Jews.[46]

The main target of annihilation for Krüger and fellow SS officers remained the Jews. Until October 1941, the killings were limited to sporadic massacres—mostly

"*Intelligenz Aktion.*" By mid-October, though, they faced the formidable task of drastically reducing the Jewish population. Krüger had participated in prior murders, but nothing prepared his fellow officers for the magnitude of a large-scale "*Judenaktion.*"

Killing thousands of human beings is a complicated task. It demands advance planning, logistical coordination, the diversion of human resources from other branches of the security services, and, above all, mental conditioning. The active and passive cooperation of the occupied population was equally important for shaping the impending wave of executions. In the end, it was the sheer German persistence, above all, that allowed for the success of the extermination of the Jews of Galicia and the Hungarians with them.

Krüger understood that for a well-planned program of extermination, with a *Grossaktion* in Stanislawów on his mind, there was a need for a dress rehearsal. Nadwórna, with a Jewish population of 5,000, seemed suitable for the first bloodletting. Twenty-five percent of the entire Jewish population was comprised of Hungarian refugees: "1,000 Jewish refugees were brought to Nadwórna from Karpatoros [Carpathian Ruthenia] who had been Hungarian citizens. The Jews of Nadwórna stretched out to them a helping hand, opened a community kitchen and housed them in the synagogue and in private homes."[47] They became the primary targets of the ensuing extermination.

The mass murder was envisioned as a "training exercise" for larger massacres to come. Because of the magnitude of the operation, Krüger brought in reinforcements from the border police, Ukrainian auxiliaries, and Reserve Police Battalion 133. Special efforts were made to foster camaraderie and boost morale prior to the execution. A major dinner with plenty of schnapps was provided for the officers the evening before. There was nothing unique about an evening like this; it was based on the SS manual's instructions on how to condition the mind of the executioners for mass murder.

On the first day of the Jewish holiday of Succoth, October 6, the full-scale extermination began in Nadwórna. Two thousand Jews, among them 500 Hungarian and some Austrian deportees, were concentrated in the main square: "The Germans and the members of the Ukrainian police burst into the homes of the Jews and started to assemble them in the square near the church. On the way [there] many of those who refused to go were killed and those who tried to escape.... In the afternoon trucks arrived and the Jews were transported to the Bukowinka forest," where the victims were ordered to undress before their execution.[48]

The involvement of the German civil administration is notable; the *Kreishauptmann* (County Executive) supplied the trucks. Reserve PoliceBattalion 133, whose 1st and 2nd company were stationed in Stanislawów, also played a vital role in the massacre. Under the command of Lieutenant-Colonel Gustav Englisch, the battalion was transferred from Nuremberg to Galicia in October. It was thrust almost immediately into mass murder.[49]

The slaughter started in the early afternoon and continued uninterrupted until the evening. An official from the municipal services commented that "only SS personnel from Stanisławów, who had come with their boss, Krüger, did the shooting." Indeed, Krüger personally demonstrated, like Schöngarth, how to shoot efficiently. An eyewitness recalled that "during the killing many of them [Jews] were being beaten cruelly, and especially, both the Nazis and their helpers, taunted and physically abused the old, the women, the children and the handicapped. Some of the Jews were buried alive." More than 2,000 of the Nadwórna Jews were killed in this *Aktion* as well as Jews from the surrounding villages: "Among the killed there were also the refugees from Karpatoros" [Hungarian Jews].[50] This was not the only recollection that mentioned the killing of the Hungarian Jews. The most moving epithet belongs to a Galician survivor who was able to escape Galicia and find shelter in Budapest. He was ordered to cover the mass graves again eight months after the murders in Nadwórna, because the site was not covered adequately by the requisitioned villagers, noted that "strewn all over [were] torn prayer books ... some in Hungarian translation; most likely the Hungarian Jews (there were several hundreds of them) who had lost their lives there, had brought these prayer-books from Hungary."[51]

After the guns fell silent, the macabre ritual of the distribution of the worldly possessions of the Jews who had just been murdered, scattered around in heaps, began. There was a pecking order, though. The Germans, members of the police battalions, were the first one to select the most valuable items, after which the Ukrainian auxiliaries could get a few pieces from the discarded garments. They even organized a public auction for the remaining items.

In the evening, the SS officers retired for a sumptuous dinner at the local restaurant, Kazia Hanus—the point of departure from where, that same morning, they had started the liquidation of half of the Jewish population of Nadwórna. It may have been the first, but it was not the last time that these men would celebrate mass murder with a party. There was a festive atmosphere in the air. Edwards Westermann labeled such an event as "Fellowship Evenings" or "Murder Banquets," which not only celebrated the accomplished massacre, but also fostered camaraderie and, reflecting Himmler's comment, "helped to prevent these 'difficult duties' from 'harming the mind' associated with mass murder."[52]

Krüger summed up the events of the day with a cynical quip: "The wedding was a success, but we had not been prepared for such a large number of guests."[53] What he meant was that despite running out of ammunition and the impending darkness that prevented the SS from finishing the job, it was a "successful" *Aktion*. The evening was both a victory celebration and a consultative meeting to assess the operation. Accompanied with the customary heavy drinking, it resembled, in some ways, a business enterprise with a jovial "corporate board meeting" about murder; the discussion centered on lessons learned from this experience, what need to be changed, and constructive suggestions for future massacres to come.

As often with Nazi atrocities, the executioners did not bother with covering the mass graves. In this case, this task was left for the Jewish community: "The next morning, about 200 Jews were fetched from their homes, including me, and brought us to the site of the massacre. They had also brought shovels and lime and ordered us to cover the mass graves. The sight was catastrophic. We hurried along with our work, and then we were allowed to go home again."[54] What made this mass murder different from future *Aktionen* was its purpose: conditioning the executioners. Besides serving as a "dry run" for the much larger Stanislawów massacre a week later, this event marked the actual beginning of the "Final Solution" in the General Government.[55]

"*Wer noch lebt, kann nach Hause gehen, der Führer hat Euch das Leben geschenkt*" ("Those who are still alive can go home, the Führer has gave you the gift of life") were Hans Krüger's closing words on the evening of October 12, 1941, signaling the conclusion of the most notorious and largest massacre in the General Government until then.[56] *Die Blutsonntag* (the Bloody Sunday), as it became known in Holocaust lore, resulted in the murder of an estimated 12,000 people during a short, snowy, and cold afternoon in the New Jewish Cemetery of Stanislawów. After a murder of such a magnitude, Krüger ran out of time to fully accomplish his grisly task. Reprieved at the last minute, for the dazed and traumatized survivors it might have sounded like a bitter irony that the killing had come to an end and they were free to go home. As darkness descended, among the murdered thrown into the hastily dug pits were more than 2,000 Hungarian Jews.

There are several questions that might help to understand the evolution of the tragic fate of these victims. How these Hungarians ended up in Stanislawów? Why their initial hearty welcome by the local Jewish community changed dramatically as time went by? How the Nazi administration viewed them? And, more importantly, why the Hungarians were singled out to be the first ones for the massacre? The Hungarian deportees, by some estimates hovering around 3,000, were the second largest contingent after those in Kamenets-Podolsk. Deported mainly from Máramaros County in Carpathian Ruthenia and northern Transylvania, the first large contingent arrived in this provincial town at the end of July and early August. Their life and death in Stanislawów became an especially grisly memento in the history of the 1941 deportation. Their entrance into the city was a pitiful sight, a genuine shock to the local Jewish community:

> They came by foot, in front the women, others with infants on their breasts and some with beddings, the elderly walking propped up on their canes. A tragic sight, seeing the Eternal Wandering Jew... travelling by foot, they covered the 300 km, they arrived in Stanislawów to share the tragedy with the

local Jews. The Judenrat first put them up in prayer houses and the synagogue, then they were moved to the Rudolfmühle. It was a flour mill, that name was changed to the house of death. From this time, their lot was constant hunger, cold, not enough clothing to cover their bodies, exposed to all sorts of sickness like typhoid, dysentery, they were short on everything, hardly any similar situation on earth."[57]

Additional Hungarian transports arrived periodically to Stanisławów. Their initial and direct treatment by the Gestapo, though, was even more ghastly. Upon arriving in Stanisławów, based on the testimony of a Hungarian prisoner, the Ukrainian guards led them directly to the Gestapo prison where they met SS-Captain Krüger: "This was the first time I saw a German. Until then only Ukrainians.... The first German officer, his name was Krüger. He came with a big dog. We were told to stand in attention—all the men took their hats off. One man didn't take his hat... he was very old and shaky.... This German officer, Krüger, sent his dog on him and tore this man to pieces. That's was our greeting there."

Indeed, it was an apt introduction to a dystopian universe created by Krüger. During ten days in the Gestapo prison, which was known alternately as the "courtyard of the Jews" or "courtyard of death," this Hungarian transport was kept under the open sky without food. When asked how they coped with hunger, Marion Samuel confided that "we didn't feel anything... we were leaning against each other. You didn't talk, you didn't want to waste any energy."[58] Some of the men were asked if they wanted to work and were shipped to an unknown destination—never to be heard from again. The remainder, mainly women and children, were marched off to the *Judenrat*, which directed them to *Rudolfmühle*.

They joined thousands of Hungarian exiles already confined in this building. It was a large, unoccupied redbrick building, several stories high, situated on Halitska Street. This depot, and the building next to it, the former Shutzman factory, housed 3,000 Jews in cramped quarters. Most of the Hungarians remained in that place even afterward, when the ghetto was set up separately. Despite humanitarian efforts by the *Judenrat* and selfless volunteers who "set up a kindergarten... washed them, deloused them.... All those activities were like a drop in the ocean. Because of the cramped conditions and the shortage of supplies, there were catastrophic hygienic conditions. Epidemics broke out just two weeks after the first victims were brought in. Daily 10–20 corpses were removed from the mill, due to starvation and contagious diseases."[59] Consequently, Krüger had set up a brutal mechanism: he had ordered that all sick Jews be murdered there.

By the spring of 1942, the Rudolfmühle became the regular execution site for the Gestapo in their attempts to decimate the ghetto and exterminate the Hungarian survivors from the earlier bloodbaths.[60] Based on a letter from the local Judenrat to

Baroness Edith Weiss, who was from a rich family of Hungarian industrialists and was a noted Hungarian Jewish activist in Budapest, we know that by end of August, 2,300 Hungarian expellees were registered with the Jewish community. The urgent communication sent her on August 28, 1941, emphasized that the city could not cope even with the needs of the local population—not to speak of the newly arrived and destitute refugees from Hungary.[61]

For the Nazi administration, just like in Kamenets-Podolsk, these Hungarians presented an unwelcome complication. A nuisance. Consequently, they directed the refugees to the care of the *Judenrat*. By early fall, though, the Stanislawów Jewish community faced, as was true across southern Galicia, intolerable humanitarian and sanitary conditions. Reflecting back again to Kamenets-Podolsk, this Hungarian influx to Stanislawów influenced and expedited the killing process. It has been proposed by several historians that the large number of Hungarians exacerbated the already tenuous situation, contributing to the specter of famine and disease and indirectly to the subsequent murder.

The Nazi solution to this dilemma used the well-tested scenario: an unprecedented bloodbath. To adjust the number of Jews to available space and food, and the eventual ghettoization, SS and Police Leader Fritz Katzman, in consultation with the Chief of the Security Office Helmut Tanzmann, "ordered the 'superfluous' Jews of the city to be shot." For the Jewish police as well as the Nazi security forces, the most immediate and accessible population for extermination were the Hungarians in the *Rudolfmühle*.

The ensuing bloodletting of October 12, 1941, took place during the Jewish festival of Sukkoth (Hoshana Rabbah) in the New Jewish Cemetery, and created, again, a defining moment in the story of the deportation and the Holocaust. It the largest mass murder in the district of Galicia at that time and was conducted virtually in public. But there is another component of the killing mechanism: a massacre of such proportions under German civil administration was virtually unprecedented in Galicia.

SCHNAPPS AND MASS MURDER: "THE BLOODY SUNDAY"

The shooting started at midday. A member of the *Judenrat*, Juliusz Feuerman noticed almost instantly that "by the way they were leading the Aktion, I realized that this was not their first one, but something well-rehearsed."[62] The lessons learned in Nadwórna served SS-Captain Krüger well. Diaries and survivors' testimonies present a detailed picture of physical and psychological brutality during the mass execution. Nor do they fail to mention that the murderers often held a bottle of vodka during murder operations. Indeed, alcohol served as both a literal and metaphorical lubricant for acts of violence and atrocity. Westermann noted that "the consumption of alcohol was part of a ritual that not only bound the perpetrators together, but also became a facilitator of acts of 'performative masculinity'—a type of masculinity expressly linked to physical or sexual violence."[63]

The preparation for the *Aktion* started, as Abraham Liebesman's diary recounted, on October 10 and 11, when the building department (*Baudienst*) instructed Ukrainian police to dig huge pits in the cemetery. Because the Nazis were concerned that two pits would not be enough for the impending slaughter, a hastily dug third grave was prepared, almost at the beginning of the massacre. While these arrangements were explained as air-raid shelters, the Jewish community rightly understood that an impending *Gross Aktion* might be the real reason. Liebesman dryly noted that "on October the 11 rode Krieger on a [white] horse through the Jewish quarter. Since then whenever an action took place he always rode on a horse through the Jewish quarter."[64]

As customary before a major *Aktion*, a sumptuous dinner was provided to members of Krüger's staff the night before, accompanied by a final conference with his commanders about the orders for the next day's events. On the following morning, a motley assortment of security forces that included, beside his security detail, a *Volkdeutsche* unit, the Ukrainian police, the Reserve Police Battalion 133, and the railroad police, forcibly removed thousands of Jews from their homes, with the instruction to pack their valuables. Clinging to the hope of resettlement, many did just that. Concentrated in the *Ringplatz* market square in the center of town, they were force marched or transported in open trucks to the New Jewish Cemetery, which gave an inkling about the true purpose of the march. However, before transporting the local Jews, the collection of Hungarian Jews from *Rudolfmühle* as well as a large group that arrived in the Gestapo prison a night before started moving in early morning. For them, there was no selection.

Cipora Brenner's insider account from the killing site is perhaps the most comprehensive description by an active participant in the unfolding drama and the horror endured by the local and Hungarian victims. The details are chilling. Her group arrived from Delyatin by trucks a day before the slaughter. After enduring a night of torment and killings in the Gestapo prison, they were transferred directly to the cemetery in the early hours. As they were the first ones, these "early arrivals" were seated along the cemetery wall on the left side of the mass graves, which she credited for saving her and her mother's lives. Her sister, however, was suffocated by hundreds of bodies piling upon her. Groups upon groups from the city filled the space between them and the huge pits, pressing them more and more against the cemetery wall. In the center, between the two large pits, were separate tables with sausage and alcohol set up for the Germans and Ukrainians. In her estimation, from the five hundred freshly transported Hungarians only five survived the massacre.[65]

By all accounts, Fritz Katzmann, the Higher SS and Police Leader of the District of Galicia, assumed a critical role in the decision-making process for the massacre. Prior to the commencement of the execution, a phone call came in the morning, directly from him, officially authorizing the mass shooting. The members of the *Judenrat* and their families were spared. They were separated by the personal order of Krüger and were made to sit on the side of the mass grave, forcing them to witness the unfolding nightmarish scene. Was this a continuation of his "I am the Master of your Life and Death" fixation, exuding omnipotence? Or was it a form of torture and humiliation of the highly educated members of the *Judenrat*?

As they entered the cemetery, the victims were ordered to give up all valuables, which were promptly collected. After undressing, the shooting started by individual executions around one o'clock. Because of the arrival of wave upon wave of victims, however, the rate "of killing individually" became inefficient enough that Krüger ordered the Jews "to get into the ditch on top of the previous victims... and mowed them down by machine gun fire. Not everyone was killed immediately. Dead people were laying together with wounded ones. Small children were not shot, just simply dumped into the ditch... the dead bodies simple choked them."[66] A survivor recounted that amid the carnage, "I saw Krüger running back and forth, exhorting his subordinates to work [kill] 'schneller, schneller' [faster, faster]. In one hand, he held a pistol, in the other a bottle of schnapps.... The Germans and the Ukrainians [*sic*] shot and drank without interruption."[67]

The shooting was accompanied alternately by moments of indescribable drama and silences. As a mother was pleading for pity for her three-year-old daughter, "said the Gestapo, you may live, but your daughter must die. She was holding her daughter against her heart, they killed both of them."[68] Cipora Brenner remembered only an eerie silence, "no crying, not even a voice.... They kept walking between two lines of club-wielding Ukrainians who were beating them toward the grave."[69]

The killing continued into the evening. As night fell over the cemetery, Krüger, determined to finish the job, ordered trucks from the motor pool to illuminate the murder site with their headlights. There were serious concerns, though, on the part of the Gestapo about accidentally shooting their own men, for the executioners were too drunk to aim properly.[70] Around six o'clock, the civilian administrator of the city, *Kreishauptmann* Heinz Albrecht, arrived, stopped the carnage, and ordered those alive to return home. It was a surprising development when a civilian head of the region made the decision to put an end to the carnage.

Krüger declared: "the Führer has granted you life. A hysterical atmosphere prevailed at the cemetery, uncontrollable laughter, cries, lamentation after dear ones all over." By that time, however, the ground of the cemetery was covered by layers of dead bodies who were not shot but died as consequence of the huge number of people crowded and pressed against the cemetery wall. As the executioners drove more and more people toward the mass graves, "everyone tried to move toward the wall, getting away from the pits." One might be tempted to reenvision the terror with which the cornered mass of humanity inside the confines of the cemetery responded to this horrific moment. Human imagination, though, has a natural filter for providing a true picture of the fear and panic.

In the ensuing tumult and panic, hundreds were trampled, crushed, and suffocated under the weight of this compressed humanity. In her testimony, Cipora Brenner captured the chilling and surreal picture of the concluding moments of the nightmare: "I was under several layers of dead people as I heard my mother calling our names. After finding her, we started to look for my sister ... we found her by removing the dead from top of her ... she was still alive. She raised her hand with a faint wave and fell back, 'finished.' We didn't cry, though. My mother pulled me away, 'let's leave that we can tell our story to the world. ...' Can you imagine, a mother is leaving her daughter?" This was the moment that she snapped and began bitterly to sob. This was also a moment of unexpected humanity. A German soldier, he might have been a policeman from Reserve Police Battalion 133, approached her and gently lifted her by the arm, softly imploring her: "My child, you have remained alive (*du bist leben geblieben*), you cannot help her anymore ... leave now and find a man with a beard who should surely be Jewish, he will help you."[71]

As for the members of the *Judenrat*, who were forced to watch the slaughter from beginning to its inglorious end, the spectacle must have been unbearable torment. One member, Juliusz Feuerman, and his family were released by the order of Krüger himself and were sitting on the side of the mass grave along with the rest. He recorded this agony in his diary:

> We set on the ground, not moving, numb and indifferent. Wet snow was falling on us. I looked on at what happening all around us. A few times I had to force myself with all my will to realize that this is an actual reality and not some bad dream. After all, they were throwing into the grave pregnant women, mothers with children at breast, and shooting them continuously.... About 6 P.M. they stopped the execution and let the rest go home. I could hardly get up from the ground. During that one day, I became an old man.... Until now I knew how to work as if I were twenty. I didn't even have a grey hair. That day, my temples became white.[72]

The final act of the day was predictable. Krüger hosted a celebratory feast in one of the town's trendy restaurants. No account has survived as to what was said or given as a celebratory toast. The mass graves were not covered until the next day. A few survivors who were only wounded succeeded in climbing out and returned home under the shelter of darkness. One witness, however, distinctly remembered hearing a faint voice from the grave: "I am a Hungarian doctor... I am still alive..."[73]

THE FLUIDITY OF GENOCIDE

The order for extermination across Galicia originated directly from Lwów, but the planning and implementation remained in the hands of the executioners. Extermination actions continued unabated at regular intervals across Galicia until 1943. The momentum spiked in and around the middle of October. While the largest slaughter took place in Stanisławów, the key players moved from town to town simultaneously with the Bloody Sunday massacre, sharing manpower and expertise with each other. The role of the Reserve Police Battalion 133 was especially significant in this rolling wave of murder. Starting in Nadwórna, the battalion moved to Stanisławów, Kolomea, Delatyn, Jaremcze, Drohovycz, Bolechow, and other towns, leaving destroyed communities in their wake. They also assisted in the final liquidation of the ghettos and prepared transports to Belzec in 1942 from Kolomea and Stanisławów as the Final Solution transited from killing by bullets to death by gas.[74]

The list of communities with a large number of deported Hungarian Jews is a long one and involves almost every town in southern Galicia. There were some notable stations that stood out for the number of victims and ferocity of their killings. What was typical of these successive waves of genocide was how even low-ranking SS officers became the lords of death. The example of Ernst Varchmin, the head of the Border Police Station in Tatarow, is instructive. As a low-ranking *Hauptscharführer* (sergeant), he orchestrated the destruction of the Jewish community of Delatyn and Jaremcze on October 16, 1941. In both towns, there was a substantial Jewish Hungarian presence. With only two German officers under his command, along with several Polish and Ukrainian *Kripo* officers, he needed the manpower of the 3rd Company of Reserve Police Battalion 133 and Ukrainian auxiliaries for the shooting of 1,950 Jews. Geography here had a decisive role in the slaughter, because these were the most southern Jewish communities in the region.[75]

Several days later, it was the turn of the Jewish community of Dolina, west of Stanisławów, where Sergeant Rudolf Müller from the Border Police at Wyszkow Pass commanded a unit that rounded up 3,500 Jews. After a selection in the marketplace, 2,000 Jews were taken to the local cemetery and shot in the usual way. Nevertheless, these were local actions that had to be authorized by higher-ups in the ranks. The common fingerprint for many of these *Aktionen* across the region invariably belonged to one SS officer, SS First Lieutenant Peter Leideritz from Kolomea. He had the rank and the

FIG 5.1   Police Battalion 133 in Kolomea. *Courtesy of www.military-archive.com.*

authority to implement this terror. He played a role earlier in Kosów and Horodenka. Local survivors meticulously recorded murder statistics from both places: "2,088 Jews had been shot [in Kosów] during the preceding two days, including 149 refugees from Hungary." The date was October 18, 1941. Elsewhere, the author reports that the "first Aktion in Horodenka occurred on December 4, 1941. Half of the Jewish population of 4,000 was shot, as were 400 Jewish refugees from Hungary and Romania."[76]

In mid-October around 900 people, both local and deported Jews from Hungary, were shot by death squads in Jablonica.[77] Parallel massacres were perpetrated in Zabie, Zablotow, Jaremcze, Kuty, and Buczacz. In general, the border area was singled out as a priority for stemming the Hungarian tide and securing the border between Galicia and Carpathian Ruthenia. The Hungarian deportees were pushed back closer and closer to the Carpathian Mountains by relentless pressure from German security forces in the opposite direction. A sizeable number of Hungarian victims were caught along this line and swept up consequently in cleansing actions in the smaller communities.

The fate of the Hungarian expellees in Kolomea was somewhat unusual. The town served as a transit point in the endless meandering of the deportees to their final destination in Kamenets-Podolsk. Equally important was the fact that it functioned temporarily as the headquarters of the Royal Hungarian Army. How much this impacted the operational freedom of the Nazi hierarchy toward the Hungarian Jews is not clear. While they shared the fate of their coreligionists, just like everywhere else, in Kolomea they, as "foreign Jews," were singled out for extermination in a separate "special action" on December 23, 1941. This action was attributed to *Kreishauptmann* Claus Volkmann, the county executive; 1,200 Hungarian and Austrian Jews were massacred on this occasion.

This was followed a month later, on January 24, 1942, by a second wave. The number of killed can be estimated over 2,000.[78]

The presence of the Hungarian Army did not impede the head of the Nazi security services, Leideritz, from conducting these killings. Besides these culling and *Intelligenze Aktionen*, the first large-scale massacre coincided with that of Stanisławów. On October 12, 1941, almost in competition with SS-Captain Krüger, 3,000 Jews were murdered in the Szeparowce Forest, near Kolomea. This "signature" *Aktion* did not reach the magnitude of that of the Bloody Sunday. Its brutality, however, matched that of Stanisławów: "A small girl who escaped from the mass grave in the night (she was only wounded) told us that during the execution, the Gestapo people were laughing: 'Faster, faster, we will be late to the evening theater show... and the blood was flowing in streams.'"[79]

Hungarian Jews were also included among those killed in the October 12 mass murder. One of them succeeded in crawling out of the grave, wounded but alive, and returned to the city.[80] Overall, Leideritz's murder rate in the recurring sweeps in Kolomea and its environs came close to that of Krüger's. By some estimates between 70,000 to 100,000 Jews were murdered between 1941 and 1943 under his operational authority. During Leideritz's and his fellow officers' interrogation by American authorities, and later in his trial in Warsaw, several key details came to light that provide a clear picture about the method and scope of his activities in Kolomea. The testimonies of two of his associates, Staff-Sergeants and *Kriminalsekretaers* Alfred Kiefer and Albert Warmann, head of *Kripo*, clearly show that the outmost brutality was combined with a cunning ability to reassure the Jewish community "that the last operation had been the final one and that no harm would come to the remainder of the Jews."[81]

Otherwise, he was well known to viciously beat his victims prior or during the killing operation. A witness recalled that "A popular method of Leideritz was to beat these unfortunate people with a horse-whip until their skin completely peeled away. He carried out the Aktion in the ghetto with utmost sadism by locking people in the houses while setting the buildings on fire through the windows. These scenes were filmed by Leideritz and his officers." We also learn from these confessions that all executions were supervised by Leideritz, who often participated in the shooting personally: "At these occasions, the Sicherheitspolizei [*Sipo*], Kripo, Ordnungspolizei [Reserve Police Battalion 133] were present." The execution squad consisted of four Gestapo men, and to "shoot a batch of a thousand usually took four hours."[82]

These details betray a preoccupation with efficiency. Just like Krüger, the Gestapo chief of Kolomea had to contend with limited human resources while accomplishing a high rate of killing. Unlike Krüger, however, Leideritz had a committed, albeit contentious and competing ally in murder as well as plunder in the person of Claus Volkmann. As the *Kreishauptmann*, he represented the civilian authorities in the region. In contrast to other local administrators in southern Galicia, though, he was an eager and active participant in mass executions. He also took an active part in the deportation of Jews from Kolomea, locals, and Hungarians to Belzec. In a testimony, survivors in the war crime trials of 1947 in Vienna, directly "accused him with the ordering of the liquidation of the Hungarian Jews in Kolomea." He was named among the "leaders of mass murder together with Peter Leideritz."[83]

Postwar investigations revealed that Leideritz had another, rather unlikely partner in Kolomea, his wife, Anneliese Leideritz. Wendy Lower described in her arresting book, *Hitler's Furies: German Women in the Nazi Killing Fields*, how German women became complicit in direct killings in the East, mainly working for the occupational authorities in various administrative roles. Her statement that besides gawking proudly at their "men at work" during mass execution, genocide became also "women's business" could be applied to Kolomea where some willingly pounced on the opportunity to loot and kill.[84] Indeed, these inquiries also implicated Anneliese Leideritz in unabashed seizure of property that belonged to Jews. A fellow officer from Kolomea testified in 1946 that "it should be mentioned that the procurement of things (civilian clothes and uniform) as well as shoes and boots by Leideritz and his wife has taken on such a large volume, that it aroused the envy of most of the members of the department."[85]

According to Jewish witnesses, however, the wife of Peter Leideritz went far beyond gawking or plundering. In 1946, she was accused of murder. Anneliese Leideritz had no official title, no official position in the Nazi hierarchy. For all practical purposes, she was

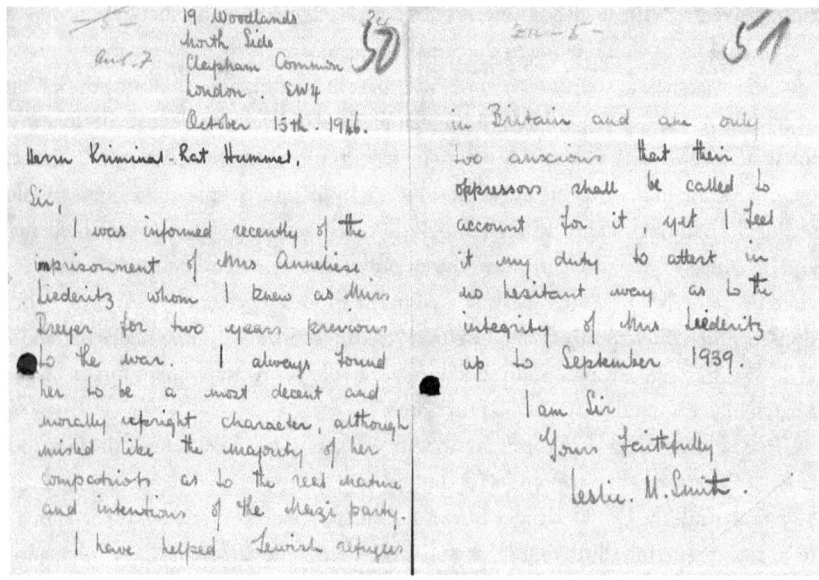

FIG 5.2 A Letter by a defense witness for Anneliese Leideritz.
Hessisches Staatsarchiv. *Courtesy of Hans Peter Trautmann.*

a typical "*Hausefrau*." Yet, Holocaust survivors' testimonies painted a damning picture of a woman who was an overeager volunteer in the business of murder. They present a vivid portrait of this "*Satansfrau*" [wife of Satan], as a survivor titled her, who routinely participated in the whipping and shooting of the Jews while riding a horse in the ghetto and during mass murder in the Szeparowce Forest: "It made no difference to her whether she shot at women and children.... She never entered the ghetto without a revolver or riding whip and she used these without provocation.... Anneliese Leideritz acted during this street action as a supervisor."[86]

Perhaps the most revolting deed attributed to her, as one account described, was the liquidation of the Jewish Orphans' Home on September 9, 1942. The orphanage housed approximately four hundred children, mostly Hungarians whose parents had already been murdered or were now waiting in the wagons for "resettlement" to Belzec. The orphanage was in Ghetto 2, and when this was liquidated, it was planned to move the children into Ghetto 1. By that time, the older children were already on the train. In the morning, before the transfer could take place for the youngest ones, several *Schupo* (city policemen) entered the facility. This fateful morning suddenly turned into perhaps one of the grisliest moments of the Galician tragedy. During the trials of the main characters, Officer Friedrich Knackendoeffel admitted under cross-examination that he was specifically ordered to kill the children.[87] He had taken them to the garden—fifteen of them. Infants were carried out, according to an eyewitness, by Anneliese Leideritz. The children were forced to lie face down on the ground, side by side. Knackendoeffel killed them, one by one, with a bullet to the head. According to this witness, the wife of Peter Leideritz was present in this massacre.[88]

She was arrested on July 31, 1946, in her hometown of Kirch-Beerfurth. Three Kolomea survivors' testimony implicated her in mass murder by placing her in the ghetto as well as the site of the mass murder of the Kolomea Jews in the adjacent forest. Yet these witnesses did not mention her participation in the murders of Jewish children in the orphanage. In their face-to-face encounters they unfailingly identified her as the perpetrator of the crimes of indiscriminate murder. During her interrogation, though, she denied all the charges by stating that "I was never present at a shooting of people, whether they were Jews or from other religions.... And I further deny ever having struck Jews with my riding whip, or ever riding behind transports of Jews."[89]

She willingly admitted to owning a small pistol, a Browning 6.35 mm. It was a gift from her husband in 1943, a year after the massacre in the ghetto, but she insisted that she never used it. Two secretaries working for the SS offices in Kolomea, and a business manager with his daughter, who employed Jewish workers from the ghetto, testified for the defense. The central argument was of mistaken identity in which Herta [Hertha?] Abicht, the secretary of the regional district head (*Kreishauptmann*), Dr. Herbert Gorgon, was identified as the culprit.[90] Other witnesses from the German civil administration supported this claim by testifying that "her behavior described by the survivors was not characteristic to her." The defense lawyer, Franz Haus, on the other hand, has went as far as accusing the survivors of pursuing a vendetta in order to punish her for the sins of her husband.[91]

The American military authorities apparently did not believe her, because she was extradited to Polish authorities, to face a trial in Poland, on December 10, 1947—following her husband, who was transferred a year earlier on December 18, 1946.[92]

COMPETITION IN MURDER: THE TALE OF TWO SS OFFICERS

Christopher Browning aptly sums up the atrocities in Galicia: "the large-scale massacres were concentrated in the southern region of the district and were carried out above all by just two of the Security Police branch offices—Stanisławów and Kolomyja [Kolomea]."[93] Not surprisingly, SS-Captain Hans Krüger and SS-First Lieutenant Peter Leideritz, contending ferociously with each other in the business of mass extermination, and equally for theft and plunder, headed these offices. In turn, they collected a coterie of subordinates who became complicit in mass murder and the full despoliation of the Jews prior to that. An associate of Leideritz openly admitted to his interrogator that "it was the general rule that both the Kripo and Gestapo were allowed to requisition anything they wished of Jewish property. This can explain the terrific amount of loot that subject was able to send home for his own use of his wife, daughter and other relations."[94]

Again, one may recall Jeckeln's impersonal, almost detached style of murder, in which emotions were relegated to the hidden recesses of his mind. But Krüger and Leideritz and other newly emerging killers on every level were drafted from a different cloth. The thread that runs through their bodies connects opportunism, corruption, outright petty thievery, and an insatiable lust for murder. Perhaps an anonymous Polish doctor summed up best this experience, "[It] was like living in a country where all the thieves and gangsters had been let loose."[95]

Mass killing, the absolute power over thousands of defenseless people, can be hard to renounce, for it has an intoxicating power. Both Krüger and Leideritz tasted murder and remained addicted to it even when there were no Jews left. They pursued with equal zeal other perceived enemies of Nazi Germany, like the Poles. However, the Jews from Hungary had a special place in the Final Solution in Galicia. In the hierarchy of those to be killed, they were the most immediate target. For both Nazi officers, they were a nuisance that could not be exploited; there was nothing to barter for their lives. Hungarian military personnel and, consequently, Ukrainian paramilitaries saw to it that they reached an accidental destination utterly destitute, without geographic connection, and without roots in the host community. Thus, in this life-and-death chess game, they were truly dispensable.

We often meet soldiers and SS men in Holocaust narratives who found an ideological justification for their behavior by invoking a rationale cloaked in a cosmic life-and-death struggle between Nazism and the diabolical Judeo-Bolshevism. In a letter to his wife, one of the killers excused his shooting of "women, children, and numerous babies, aware that I have two babies of my own at home, and these hordes would treat them just the same, or even ten times worse, perhaps."[96] But, the majority did not need ideological justification. In Tluste, "Children were thrown into the pits alive, and covered up with the corpses. A German would grab a child by the neck and shout: '*Nimm das dreck und schmeiss herein!*' [Grab the filth and throw it in.] The children were swimming in blood in those pits."[97]

Krüger and Leideritz created and ruled over such a relentlessly dystopian Holocaust universe. From diaries, survivors' recollections, and the postwar trials of Leideritz and, much later, Krüger, they emerge as the personification of evil without discernable political motives. Not that they were devoid ideological motivation. They were able to combine Nazi ideology and the insatiable quest for murder with equal zeal for brutality, and, finally, with a penchant for plunder. The list of Leideritz's crimes during his interrogation in the American Zone included a special paragraph about how he "requisitioned much Jewish property for his own purposes. He accepted huge bribes and presents from the Judenrat of Kolomea and other towns."[98]

While many of his contemporaries in Galicia were court-martialed for their insatiable quest for riches, the question as to how Leideritz was able to evade the watchful eyes of the SS authorities is an intriguing one. His fellow officers' testimonies after the war shed some light on this question. He was very careful not to send packages directly to his home address. He conveniently enlisted his wife's family in hiding the goods from the East. Albert Warmann, head of *Kripo*, informed the American investigator in 1946 that: "From time-to-time he [Leideritz] dispatched very large parcels to Germany, part of them to consignees in Cologne bearing the name of Leideritz." His fellow officer from Kolomea was even more candid: "Leideritz especially accepted a lot of things from the Jews. His wife's name is Anneliese, the wife's parents are called Heim. The parents—they are the foster parents—live in Frankfurt and have a gardening business there." Many of the packages were sent to them.[99]

Leideritz possessed a degree of cynicism that was not easily surpassed even in the surreal Holocaust universe. He brought this "economic opportunism" directly to the killing process itself. In making a policy of billing the various Jewish communities for the expenses involved in the ongoing genocide, he implemented a new concept in the annals of extermination, which later became common practice in Galicia: "self-financing of murder." After each mass killing, the Jewish community was billed for the expenses of the killing itself. After leading the massacre of 2,000 Jews personally in Horodenka, including the 400 Hungarian and Romanian deportees, "Leideritz went to the Jewish Council [*Judenrat*] and presented it with a bill for his expenses—gasoline, bullets, wear and tear on the cars, etc.—in the sizeable sum of 10,000 zlotys, payable within ten hours." In Zablatow, following the murder of 1,000 people, on December 22, 1941, among them 600 Hungarian Jews, and in Tluste, where 3,400 people were shot, his demand was the same. In Tluste, though, the community had to pay also for "the wine that had been drunk up."

That this practice became widespread can be seen in the murder of the Jews, local and Hungarian, in Buczacz. Even a low-level Gestapo officer, Sergeant Kurt Köllner, could introduce a highly detailed bookkeeping system by forcing the *Judenrat* "to pay 20 Zloty for every bullet fired during the action. The amount paid was registered in the Judenrat's accounting books . . . and Thomanek [a mere corporal] would be given a receipt."[100]

It should not come as a surprise that the extermination of the Jews was both understaffed and underfinanced. Most victims, if not buried alive, "died, in a sense, one by one, by single shots to the back of the head or neck, not by machine-gun fire, because of the killers wanted to be as sure as possible that they had not missed or wasted ammunition." Every bullet had to be accounted for. Krüger's modus operandi was exactly the same. After the mass killings of the Jews of Bolechow, north of Stanislawów, the *Judenrat* had to "pay for the ammunition expended [and] . . . beyond that, they forced them to pay 3 kg of granular coffee for labor expenses." Hayes commented that "the Holocaust was not only self-financing but also . . . a profit-making enterprise."[101] Leideritz, Krüger, and with them almost all the security personnel in the District of Galicia, meticulously adhered to this principle by placing the financial burden of murder on the victims.

We can safely assume, of course, that not all the routinely collected funds, wine, coffee, and furs after each murder operation were dutifully remitted to the Reich's treasury—as Himmler has decreed. Plunder in general was the hallmark of the Nazi hierarchy across the General Government; only the extent and quality differentiated the Head of the General Government Hans Frank, who pilfered a Leonardo da Vinci painting before escaping from Cracow, and Krüger who confiscated coats or furniture. The testimony of Countess Carolina Lanckoronska about Krüger's penchant for thievery, small-time and grand, underlines the corruption of the entire SS officer class in Galicia. If the people belonged to the affluent classes, "he would arrest them personally and with his own hands, and before their very eyes, would remove the more valuable contents of their homes—above all whole wardrobes of men's clothing, as well as provisions, while not disdaining silver or linen."[102] Their conduct begets the question of where we can trace a dividing line when mass murder descends from political or racial ideology into the realm of assuring personal pleasure by inflicting pain, murder, and robbery. The trenchant observation of Saul Landau, the American filmmaker, that "the essence of Nazism was not so much ideology but a complex web of corruption, and in order to maintain this corruption, they [Nazis] needed an ideology," well summarizes the events in Galicia.[103] For Krüger and Leideritz such a line between ideology and corruption was blurred completely. Within the SS's profoundly corrupt hierarchy, it was not enough to fulfill a duty. For someone to gain a high position, it was necessary to project and abuse power on every level.

During their service in the District of Galicia, many similarities emerged in their conduct, attitudes, and even their mode of communication. They both aimed to deprive, as the psychologist Herbert C. Kelman phrased it, "groups of human beings of their right to be regarded as human." While their competitive streak was evident, their language, the language of the SS, was strikingly uniform. The introductory words of Krüger to the Jewish community were: "I am the Master of your Life and Death." He exercised this maxim to its full power. In her testimony, Cipora Brenner recalled an almost surreal meeting of a "German officer" riding on a horse in the middle of an *Aktion*. The officer ordered her to follow him. She walked along. "I looked at him and asked, 'would you let me say a few final words?' He answered tersely, 'Do you know where I am taking you? . . . think about that.' I answered, 'Exactly because I know that this is my death sentence, I want to say my final words.' He became silent and I started to talk. Suddenly the officer shouted at me, '*Gehen nach Hause und verstecken*! [Go home and hide].'"

Hers was the desperate monologue of the doomed. What Brenner, an eighteen-year-old woman, did not know at the time, or even during her testimony in 1994, was that her life was spared by none other than the mass murderer Hans Krüger, riding on his white horse. This encounter demonstrated that he was, indeed, the ultimate arbitrator of life and death in the Stanisławów Ghetto. It was no different in Kolomea or elsewhere. As Blanca Rosenberg recounted in her postwar memoir, Leideritz used a curiously analogous exclamation during a selection. She was kicked back in the line of those who were deemed fit enough to work, at least until the next *Aktion*, with the words: "You'll live, damn you. I'll decide on life or death here."

In these two officers' deeds, a picture emerges that defies conventional imagination. One curious fact: no reference was made during their trials to victims deported from Hungary. They were nameless, just like in Kamenets-Podolsk. Their trials, and that of Anneliese Leideritz, twenty years apart, provide an interesting contrast. While the Leideritz couple were handed over and tried by Polish courts in 1947, Krüger was lucky enough to be caught and charged with mass murder in West Germany, where the death penalty was abolished. Their attitudes during their trials differed dramatically. Leideritz and his wife disappeared after the war, only to surface in the American Zone in 1946.

Their arrest was almost anticlimactic. After changing his name to Peter Lewald, Leideritz settled and worked as an unobtrusive farmhand in a neighboring village, periodically visiting his hometown of Kirch-Beerfurth. Unbeknownst to him, a Kolomea survivor patiently watched his ancestral home from across the street in the small village and promptly alerted the American occupational authorities to his presence. After the couple's arrest, American military personnel emptied the house and removed the loot plundered from the Jews of Galicia. It took two truckloads.[104]

While in the early stages of his arrest in Germany, he defiantly claimed that "I never shot or killed any person during my stay in Kolomea and I can say the same for my wife." During his trial in Warsaw, Leideritz exhibited more submissive behavior, bordering on obsequiousness. He repeatedly contradicted himself and his comments in claiming that "it's not true," or that "I was not there at that time." This was easily rebutted by the prosecutors. It is impossible to glean from the official accounts, though, if Leideritz had true remorse for his past deeds. He knew that no mercy could be expected. Leideritz's own fellow officers in the Kolomea Sipo, Kripo, and Gestapo incriminated him, and each other, by revealing inside information about his behavior, murders, blackmail, and plunder. A telling characterization of the attitudes prevailing in Kolomea during Leideritz's rule can be gleaned from the concluding remark of the American military investigator of one of his subordinates in 1946: "He talks about brutalities, murder, and beatings as if he was talking about a tea-party."[105]

By charging him with the murder of 70,000 people, the Polish court sentenced Leideritz to death on November 17, 1947. In turn, he appealed for "a fair judgment." His claim "that he is a victim of the Hitler system," though, was outright rejected by the court, with the rebuttal that Leideritz himself was part of the "Hitler system."[106]

The final act, though, had to wait for almost two years. In his last appeal directly to the president of Poland, he claimed he saved the lives of four Jews. By that time, though, Poland was controlled by the Communist party. Boleslaw Bierut, the staunchly Stalinist president of Poland, and himself a Jew, did not entertain clemency. In his official reply he noted that "The nature of the crimes committed and the extent of the evil is clear enough that the convicted Peter Leideritz deserves no mercy."[107]

The Polish authorities hanged Leideritz in Warsaw on February 22, 1949.

His wife, on the other hand, continued to maintain her innocence, rather forcefully. But, then, Anneliese Leideritz case was much more complicated and less clear-cut. While Jewish survivors from Kolomea described in graphic and dramatic details a woman, identified as Anneliese Leideritz, there were enough contradictions to cast a doubt on their testimonies. Indeed, in reviewing the evidence presented by defense witnesses, including a woman from England, her guilt was not fully proven. As it was mentioned, the specter of "mistaken identity" and the image of Herta ABICHT s the real murderer loomed over the proceedings. Was she confused with this another woman?

Were the revolting deeds in the Jewish orphanage also committed by Herta Abicht? But the most puzzling question, posed by a German historian, could be if Anneliese Leideritz was to "made to atone *'for her husband's serious crimes?'*"[108] The Polish court could not answer these questions. It had serious doubts, though, about the testimonies of the Jewish witnesses. As a compromise, she received a sentence of ten years, with the reasoning that although "under these circumstances, the court doubts about the alleged eyewitnesses' findings regarding the individual and mass killings of Jews or regarding participation in such killings. However, since the beating and mistreatment of the Jews lead to their final annihilation, the court has found the guilt of the defendant (Anneliese Leideritz) proven."[109]

The saga of Anneliese Leideritz, though, did not end here. Upon her appeal for the dismissal of her sentence, and concurrently by the prosecutor to increase it, the court overturned it on May 3, 1950, and, with a curious twist, imposed the death penalty. This in turn, was commuted, again, to ten-year imprisonment in 1951.

She died from tuberculosis at age forty in a prison hospital in Grudziadz—some two hundred kilometres from Warsaw in 1955.

Hans Krüger's trial in West Germany in the 1960s, in the words of Countess Lanckoronska, one the most surprising witnesses, was chaotic. She perceived that with his loud anti-Semitic outbursts during the proceedings, the accused reinforced the impression that his beliefs and behavior had not changed since the Stanislawów days. He regretted nothing and learned nothing. He became and remained silent only when Countess Lanckoronska entered unexpectedly in the courtroom. The face-to-face meeting was dramatic. He hoped that no one could testify against him—no one remained alive. Krüger believed that the countess had also died in the Ravensbrück concentration camp for women: "The Judge turned to the accused and asked him what he had to say, in view of what he had heard from the witness [the countess]. Krüger was silent."[110] He escaped punishment in France where he was sentenced to death in absentia in Lyon on October 6, 1953. His sentence of life imprisonment in West Germany reflected the prevailing judicial climate of the time. He was set free in 1986, two years before his death.

From the fragmentary evidence, it is not easy to produce deep psychological insights into the mindset of either Krüger or Leideritz. About the roots of their hatred for Jews or Poles one can only guess. No interviews were ever conducted with them, comparable to those in Nuremberg, for unearthing their world views or beliefs. Even more surprising, and considering their "achievements" in murder, very little can be found about them in major Holocaust archives. Their legacy should be told, then, through the recollection of survivors, trial minutes, and the investigative works of a few German historians.[111] In perusing the biographies of these officers and their subordinates, the most striking aspect is how low their relative ranks and how uneducated they were. Both

Krüger and Leideritz were disappointing and mediocre individuals. Yet they were elevated to more senior positions in the occupied lands than they could have ever dreamed to hold at home. What unified these two and their subordinates was that they enjoyed the killing, savored the unbridled power over the powerless, and, equally, were there for the loot.

How could such banal and ordinary individuals, with relatively limited human potential, assume a power as arbiters of life and death, as the organizers of mass murder? Peter Longerich suggested that Nazism "offered men of limited gifts, of which only ruthlessness was indispensable, unique opportunities for advancement from relatively humble circumstances."[112] Dieter Pohl summed up the General Government that the Nazi regime placed in the occupied territories as not a "perfectly functioning super-bureaucracy," but rather a "colonial administration that is as corrupt and criminal as it is dilettantish."[113]

WHAT WAS DIFFERENT IN GALICIA?

This last statement poses a challenge for finding a rationale for the behavior of these relatively low-level Gestapo personnel who were entrusted with the implementation of genocide in Galicia. It begets the question of how their behavior conformed to the norms within the murder mechanism of the Holocaust. What was different in Galicia from other districts in the General Government or from other regions in the East? We know from surviving trial records that their conduct contravened the code that governed that of the SS, the Wehrmacht, and the police battalions in Galicia.

In many ways, Galicia was not a typical microcosm for the general handling of the genocide taking place in the East. It was a late comer in the war—almost two years after the outbreak of World War II—and to the General Government. The corollary question is why was the situation in Galicia so ripe for abuse? A German historian opined that in Poland and Belarus a "triangular relationship" existed between the civilian authorities, the SS, and the Wehrmacht. In Galicia it was bilateral, in which the military was absent from the direct killing process. While soldiers of the Wehrmacht became complicit in the extermination of Jews by bullets in Belarus and elsewhere, in Galicia the directive of General von Roque explicitly forbade the direct participation of military personnel in the extermination campaign. Unlike in Belarus, where Wehrmacht complicity in genocide was extensive, they did not participate even in the transportation to or serve as cordon personnel in the murder sites. The *Einsatzgruppen* were also absent from the waves of massacres in Galicia.[114]

The management of the extermination campaign in Galicia rested on the shoulders of a thinly spread security establishment, undermanned by low-level Gestapo officers, and German civil administration. They were assisted in their task by Reserve PoliceBattalions 320 and 133 and Ukrainian auxiliaries. These units were highly mobile, rapidly moving from town to town, without an "anchor" in the day-to-day management of the community, which limited their opportunity for loot. The policemen provided the cordon while the mass shooting was done by the cognoscenti of murder—the "specialists." At best, they could pilfer or share the meager belongings of the victims and sometimes some valuables. The feverish pace of extermination and collection for transport to Belzec, as Christopher Browning described the work of Reserve Police Battalion 101, left little time for finding riches in occupied Poland either.[115] The groundbreaking work of Waitman Beorn regarding the atrocities committed by the soldiers of the Wehrmacht implicates the German armed forces in genocide in Belarus. But the war did not provide the time or opportunity to enrich the rank-and-file common soldiers. His comment that "a long-term association with the murder of the Jews" abetted also the plunder, might be a key to understanding why stationary personnel were able to materially benefit more substantially from the genocide. In Belarus, as he describes it, the civilian authorities, the *Gebiets-kommissars* (regional administrators), were the main beneficiaries of extorting large sums of money from the Jewish Councils, after which they routinely murdered them.[116]

While general directives for the extermination were forwarded from Lwów, the overall deportment of the Final Solution in Galicia was left to men on the ground with a wide berth for its implementation. This independence of action, and corresponding lack of direct supervision was one of the main differences between Galicia and neighboring regions. The officers in these outposts dealt with the Jewish communities directly, for an extended period, and as capriciously as they saw fit.

This direct connection between the Gestapo and a helpless community created a never-ending opportunity for extortion and blackmail, demanding bribes and offering temporary reprieve. This cycle of thievery, as we have seen earlier, went to absurd lengths when morality became an optional commodity among the officers. The fact that Krüger was able to empty entire apartments after the arrest of their occupants should not come as a surprise. But the demand for reimbursement for the expended fuel, ammunition, and coffee with the customary schnapps after mass murder from the decimated Jewish community was a Galician invention—it might have been unique even in the otherwise dystopian universe of the Holocaust.

It seems self-evident that there were shared ideological, social, and emotional motivations for killing a race of "subhumans" across the Nazi universe. The words of Hayes in describing the district leaders in the General overnment who were ideologically committed Nazis, but "often the most incompetent, greedy, or scandal-ridden."[117] However, Galician reality was "site-specific," and murder, plunder, and sexual exploitation freely intertwined in that ideology. One cannot discard an inherent contradiction in the Nazi promotion of group conformity, camaraderie, and the ferociously competitive environment across the Nazi universe. Eric Larson aptly noted that Hitler's Germany was ripe for competing agendas and interests not only by Göring, Goebbels, and Himmler, but in every segment of the security establishment.[118] The competition in Galicia between the main players regarding the number of those murdered and, simultaneously, the opportunity for plunder, was just as fierce. In reading the investigative reports by the American military, one comes away with the sense that camaraderie was not the binding principle. They undermined each other at every turn, including testifying against each other.[119]

Perhaps the best testimony for the rampant bribery and robbery within the ranks of Gestapo officers was the fact that the highest number of SS trials dealing with corruption in the General Government was concentrated in Galicia. From Berlin's perspective, the proceeds of the plunder were intended for the Reich. In an order dated March 18, 1942, and distributed to the SS and police, Himmler warned against withholding "even the smallest amount." In fact, during his speech to SS and police leaders in Posen a year later, Himmler threatened to impose death sentences on anyone within the SS found guilty of keeping "even one Mark."[120] That tells us that "ideology" very rapidly gave way to a code of conduct, which was not compatible with "SS values." It might not be a coincidence that several major players in Galicia became the target of such investigation launched by Himmler himself into the theft of Jewish property in Galicia, in 1943. As a direct consequence, Krüger's superiors in Lwów, SS Brigadenführer Dr. Eberhard Schöngarth, Nazi security police chief, was removed from his post in Poland and sent to Greece. Helmut Tanzmann was only suspended. Again, it's worth to note that these two officers broke the image of the Nazi perpetrators as primitive, poorly educated, proletarian thugs. They belonged to a strikingly homogenous group of young academics, who came from the educated, bourgeois stratum of society, as they started to identify with the Nazi concept of *Volksgemeinschaft*, which labeled Jews as enemies of the people and justified their murder.[121]

At the same time, Hans Krüger also became implicated in several bribery and looting scandals. The official report after the inspection noted that "lots of cash, including gold, and various currencies that included $6,000 was found. Whole boxes with valuable jewels [i.e., diamonds] were found. None of these were registered.... The estimated monetary value alone amounted to 584,195.28 zlotys. The jewels themselves were appraised over one-hundred thousand German Mark." The report also noted that the provenance of the loot was assumed to be the Jewish community.[122]

No studies have explored fully the circumstances leading to his downfall, but one can assume that the impetus for his removal came from inside the ranks. He was openly loathed by his own comrades in arms in Lwów, as Countess Lanckoronska recalled. After conviction by an SS court, he was removed from his post in 1943 and transferred to Dijon, France. To add insult to injury, he was demoted from captain to the rank of second lieutenant.

Finally, and in competition with SS officers, even heads of the civil administration were accused of misappropriating Jewish property or the outright theft of valuables in Galicia. In investigating civilian authorities in Galicia, a Nazi court found that the *Kreishauptmann* of the Nadwórna region took 880–900 wedding rings and five sacks of jewelry, some of it the property of Hungarian Jews, after the mass murder of October 6, 1941. Consequently, this county executive and his secretary were found guilty and executed. The investigative reports by the American military in 1946 noted that the rivalry of Peter Leideritz and Claus Volkmann, the *Kreishauptmann* of the Kolomea region, was also legendary on this account. They genuinely detested each other. The conflict between the two started with the issue of extermination. Leideritz favored the direct extermination of the Jews. Volkmann advocated first taking over Jewish property, and, prior to extermination, demanding payments from the town's Jews. Then, murder. Not surprisingly, Volkmann was also court-martialed and transferred from Kolomea because of endemic corruption.[123]

THE FINAL JOURNEY: BELZEC

The year 1942 saw the introduction of the Final Solution—industrialized murder. By some estimates, one-third of the Jews of Galicia, among them between 2,000 to 3,000 Hungarian Jews who were still alive in Galician ghettos, were transported to and exterminated in Belzec. By late 1942 and 1943, very few Hungarian Jews had survived the militia massacres, mass shootings, starvation, and slave labor. The transition from mass shootings to killing by gas was not clear-cut. Shootings remained a mode of extermination almost until Galicia was declared *Judenrein*. Ongoing executions, especially during roundups for transportation to the extermination camp, or to reduce the population of the ghettos, remained always an option.

The only detailed testimonies that convey the last few months of the Hungarian Jewish odyssey and daily life at that time inside the *Rudolfmühle*, belong to two survivors: Cipora Brenner and Marion Samuel, both from Carpathian Ruthenia. They portray graphic scenes of hunger, pain, and death. The withholding of nourishment, however meager it was, amounted to a form of slow execution. Marion Samuel saw her three-year-old brother dying slowly yet stoically. The prisoners didn't receive food for almost two weeks. While no human life can be reduced to an individual sentence, her words are gripping in their simplicity: "I saw him ... he wasn't crying, just lying there, very quietly and dying day by day." Hiding on the top floor of the building, Samuel was the last survivor of the *Rudolfmühle*. She slowly descended to street level in the morning to an eerily deserted street. The *Rudolfmühle* became empty of its human cargo. The Hungarian Jewish tragedy came to an end in Stanislawów. Having done their job, the Jewish police and the SS disappeared. Discarded clothing littered the street. The last of the Hungarians were carted off to the New Jewish Cemetery to be shot, including her mother. Later she learned that her mother jumped off the truck and also made her way to the ghetto. Reunited, they escaped a month later, embarking on a long, perilous journey toward the Hungarian border.[124]

There were also local witnesses to the extermination of the last Hungarian Jews in Stanislawów on March 31, 1942 (on the eve of Passover 5702). Abraham Liebesman, a doctor in the ghetto, wrote, "at the Rudolfmühle lived a few hundred Hungarian Jews. Those were the worst of the lot. Nobody cared or paid attention to them. When somebody dropped, fainted in the streets, the Ukrainian police and the SS men just loaded them into trucks that cruised in the main streets, they just shot them to death.... This way 1,500 people were liquidated."[125]

A young diarist in the ghetto, Elza Binder, recorded their final journey in touching simplicity: "On the 31st of March they started to search for invalids and old people.... From the attic in which we hid, we could see the transport of the last few of the Hungarian Jews as they were led away from the Rudolfmühle. I saw children, orphans, wrapped up in sheets and the sight was illuminated by houses burning in the ghetto."[126]

Cipora Brenner described the same inferno from her hiding place in an attic in equally dramatic terms: a "horrifyingly beautiful sight." As a helper in the orphanage in *Rudolfmühle*, she witnessed the final collection of the children. To assure compliance with deportation orders, the Germans delivered a truckload of soup, bread, and jam to the starving and emaciated adults and children who, in turn, willingly lined up for their final journey. It was the standard "carrot and the stick" policy used all over the Holocaust universe: "On a Tuesday.... Two days later, they took all the children, hundreds of them, and executed them in the New Jewish Cemetery." Within the six thousand Jews deported from the Stanislawów Ghetto in March, the remaining 1,000 sick and frail Hungarian Jews were the first to be killed in this *Aktion*—shot or sent to Belzec. These destitute Hungarians, broken in body and spirit, were "slowly marching toward the waiting train" taking them to their final destination, the gas chambers of Belzec.[127]

Krüger was able to shunt the Jews from Hungary to a central location, separate from the ghetto, by creating a murder "warehouse" called *Rudolfmühle*. Conversely, no such collection points existed in Kolomea and other ghettos. The Hungarian refugees were distributed among and blended in with the local Jewish families. Thus, successive transports of the local Jewish population to Belzec automatically included Jews from Hungary. For example, German records showed that a thousand Jews from Hungary were dispatched in March 1942 by train from Kolomea and Stanislawów to Belzec. In other cases, like in Czortków, we find only a cryptic note in the transportation logs of August 1943 that the shipment of Jews to Belzec "included many Hungarian Jews."[128]

The only separate institutions that were dedicated to Hungarian refugees in Kolomea and elsewhere were the orphanages. Four hundred older children from the Kolomea children's home, originally set up for Hungarian children separated from their parents in the chaos of transportation or after being by the Ukrainian militia, were deported to Belzec on October 11 and 13, 1942. Their three social workers, one of them also Hungarian, faithfully accompanied them to their final journey. A similar act was described in Horodenka, where a special home was set up for orphaned Hungarian children. As usual, a day before the *Aktion*, the Germans brought a sack of apples for the children, to make the "Jews think that nothing was going to happen.... I found the tables laid out for breakfast with pieces of bread and butter and pieces of apples. The children never had a chance to taste the fruit. They were taken out early in the morning and led to their death."[129]

Mila Sandberg-Mesner survived the Kolomea Ghetto. She recorded in her postwar memoir the fate of one Hungarian family, assigned to her home, and their five-year-old daughter, Éva. Her notes encompass a year in the experiences of the Hungarian deportees in Galicia—from arrival to Kolomea to deportation to Belzec. The parents and Éva came every day to ask for food: "She had big, dark, sparkling eyes trimmed with long lashes. She was always smiling. Her black hair swept down over her little arms in soft beautiful waves. She was full of life, running and playing games, hugging, and kissing her parents, moving, and chattering endlessly." By the winter of 1941, however, only the father and daughter came to the host family. After the mother was killed during a Nazi *Aktion*, "She [Éva] stood there silently. Her big, dark eyes expressed bewilderment. She kept very close to her father and would not leave his side for a moment. She no longer smiled and not a sound came from her little lips." In the spring of 1942, Sandberg-Mesner reported that all the Jews were forced into the ghetto and soon "hunger began to gnaw at our insides." On one gray fall day, the father was killed too: "Éva stood alone in the doorway. Horror and panic reflected in her face."

We can assume that with the hundreds of abandoned children in the ghetto after each murder spree, she was put in one of the children's homes. By that time, though, a dramatic change took hold of the child: "Her beautiful dark hair was gone, shaved to the scalp, but her face remained beautiful. Her wide-open eyes seemed to take up half of her face. The bewildered look was still there. She was swollen from hunger and could barely walk." The end came swiftly with the final round-up of Jews for deportation to Belzec. "On a cold October day" of 1942, she was swept up in the dragnet of 6,000 other people "awaiting to be transported to the gas chambers.... Éva sat on the brown sparse grass, shivering from cold and fright. She was panic-stricken and understood that something terrible was going to happen to her. Now they were going to kill her, just as they had killed her mother and father. Éva was weeping."[130]

6

WEAPON OF WAR
Rape and Sexual Violence

"It is to be mentioned here that the JEWS were stark naked when going to their fate. This applied equally to the women as it did to the men."[1]

THESE WORDS BY ALFRED KIEFER, AN ACTIVE ACCOMPLICE IN THE MASS murder in Kolomea, betray one of the least understood and discussed elements of the deportation and mass executions in Holocaust literature. He stated this matter-of-factly, without remorse or introspection, during his testimony in front of the American war crime invesigator in 1946. Indeed, Kiefer impressed the American officer as one of the coldest murderers he had the chance to interview. Was it a simple act of "stripping of dignity" of the condemned, as a memoirist opined? Or was it just an efficient way of distributing the worldly possessions of the doomed?

Kiefer noted, indeed, that the clothing and valuables were routinely collected and plundered by the executioners and their Ukrainian collaborators. Still, the question looms as to whether there was an underlying, more sinister motive for this prequel to murder? The widespread practice of making the victims undress before they were executed served not only to facilitate the plunder of their clothing and a search for valuables. We know that the process of total dehumanization and sexual degradation of a human being, used against the condemned, was an integral part of the extermination process, and that it did not differentiate between men or women. Marta Havryshko observed that "Sexual humiliation of the Jewish body was an inevitable consequence of the dehumanizing Nazi racial theories." It was an exercise in perverted power to humiliate and debase, which defiled the individual and robbed their identity in the camps, ghettos, on the bank of Dniester River, or in front of the mass graves.[2]

One perhaps needs to reframe this picture of naked rows of human beings standing in front of the executioners. Can we call it a "sexualized murder"? Or "genocidal sexual violence," as Havryshko termed it? It can be construed, of course, also as a means to simply disposses the Jews from their clothing and, sometimes, hidden gold and other

FIG 6.1, 6.2, AND 6.3 The three phases of mass murder of women and children: collection, undressing, and execution. *United States Holocaust Memorial Museum Photo Archives, courtesy of Instytut Pamieci Narodowej.*

valuables, making the looting undoubtedly easier. Either way, it is safe to conclude that sexual violence against Jewish men, women, boys and girls was not just a by-product of the war—it was part of the war itself—and such sexual degradation used against the condemned was prevalent all across the Holocaust universe, practiced by Wehrmacht soldiers, reserve police, SS personnel, the Ukrainian militia, and Hungarian troops, even when there was no material gain or even Jews, involved.[3]

Yet, we know painfully little about this chapter of the Holocaust—especially in Galicia.

Often a missing element in the narratives, we must direct our attention to the sexual humiliation, the acts of rape, and sexual depredation inflicted on men, women, boys and young girls during World War II. Not surprisingly, this is a subject that has always been difficult to face, especially when the winning side of the war, the Soviet Army, also committed such atrocities.[4]

On the other hand, many testimonies by victims have been constructed, perhaps subconciously, to avoid this conflicted area, weaving a veil of silence around personal experiences and histories of the events that often border on the "unspeakable." Sexual degradation of men during their humiliating experiences is even rarer. David Cesarani pointed out that these testimonies "maintain a discreet silence . . . on the sexual exploitation of Jews in ghettos and camps, in hiding and on the run."[5] On the opposite side, SS officers, soldiers, and members of the reserve police battalions rather self-servingly avoided any mention of their specific deeds during their interrogations, which could have incriminated them at their trials after the war. Finally, interrogations of many of the perpetrators, reflecting contemporary cultural attitudes by the interrogators themselves toward sexual exploitation, neglected the exploration of this sensitive subject.

In framing the multiplicity of sexual experiences in Galicia, it might be helpful to review the official attitudes and approaches of the various agencies in the eastern territories toward these issues. Even during the short one-and-a-half years that encompassed the deportation and ghetto existence for Hungarian Jewish women, we can discern a tripartite power structure relating to them. It started with sexual atrocities by Ukrainian irregulars along the long wandering, which followed a ghetto existence in which sexual violence or exploitation routinely occurred. The difference was that the coercive sexual atmosphere in the ghettos was exercised by various power structures within the ghetto hierarchy itself. Finally, the rapidly expanding Nazi security apparatus became involved in sexual slavery, which manifested itself in the establishment of brothels for work camp inmates, Wehrmacht soldiers, and the SS. The SS, entrusted as security personnel, further expanded their depredation of women by individual initiatives.

THE LONG WANDERING

The Ukrainian militia had no ideological or political constraints for rape, sexual torture, and other sadistic practices. These forces were rarely, if at all, supervised or disciplined for any infraction. They remained in the initial phase of the war independent bands of thugs without a central governing mechanism. Thus, they were able to inflict cruelties that we might be able to equate to more recent Yugoslavian or Rwandan conflicts.[6]

In the first phase of the Hungarian odyssey, sexual violence was an integral part of their daily experience inflicted by their Ukrainian guards. This demonstration of sadistic power over defenseless people was inflicted by the Ukrainian paramilitaries during the long marches. Keith Lowe commented that "in the Second World War it was a phenomenon that grew beyond any previously known proportions: more rapes occurred in this way... than during any other war in history."[7] While sexual exploitation of Jewish women was also common among German security personnel, as we will see later, it was overwhelmingly the Ukrainians who imposed the mental and physical agony of rape in the early stages of the deportation during the long treks across Galicia. Lowe's observation holds true in this context that the prevalence of rape is more widespread "where there is a greater cultural divide."[8] This cultural divide was also a prominent factor in the Ukrainian–Hungarian relations. Many Jewish accounts describe the self-satisfaction and smugness of the Ukrainian militia members when they killed or tortured Jews. It endowed them with a sense of unbridled power.

Was it the same cultural divide that guided the relationship between Jews from Bukovina and Romanian soldiers who committed unspeakable atrocities against them? David Cesarani gave special attention to the sexual depredation by Romanian soldiers during the deportation of these Jews to Transnistria. Indeed, if we attempt to find parallel to the Galician savagery, Cesarani's descriptions of the Romanian Army's behavior in Transnistria could come the closest to that of the Ukrainian militia. "Women were raped and murdered as a matter of course by the Romanian soldiers," a witness reported. "During the night, the members of the new detachment and their helpers would pick out girls from the throng and abuse them until dawn. During the day, they managed to make a little money by 'selling' a girl to a peasant."[9]

If we juxtapose this with the Galician experience, the similarities are striking. Thus, rape of young girls on mass scale became the norm. They were especially targeted out of an unbridled sexual sadism by their Ukrainian guards. To explain this phenomenon, psychologists often assuage the trauma of a rape victim by noting that "rape doesn't have anything to do with sex. It's all about power."[10] The previously quoted words of a shocked Hungarian observer in late August brings home the horror of the genocidal sexual sadism taking place: "They pull from the Dniester Jewish corpses day after day, old, young, even children 3 to 4 years old, *but mostly young girls, violated and tortured beyond recognition, that one could not look at them,* our soldiers buried them in unmarked graves ... at the end, they just let them float down the river."[11]

While Hungarian Jewish women were often reticent to provide full details about the sexual torment they endured in Galicia, stories filtered through the memories of the survivors in hushed tones. Marion Samuel started her journey with 2,000 people on a never-ending trek across Galicia. She described the long, interminable trudges from village to village and the terrifying nights that were filled with the screams of women being raped, their cries etched in her mind indelibly. As a defense mechanism, parents did everything possible to save their daughters from rape. They would hide them, dress them in rags, hide or cut their hair, and smear soot on their faces to make them unattractive. Being a teenager, Marion Samuel's mother instructed her to march in the middle of the column and shield her face with huge bulky scarf to protect her from being singled out for rape—all to avoid attracting the attention of the militiamen who preyed on young women.[12]

Simultaneously, young men routinely were pulled out of the transport, "sometimes there were ten, sometimes twenty," under the ruse of taking them to work. Invariably, they never returned. As Samuel learned, the Ukrainians executed them in the forest. Other testimony reinforces this by stating that a form of sexual slavery also existed. Stopping in Czortków, as a survivor recalled in 1945, the Ukrainian paramilitaries took away the "major part of the men" from the transport, "but also several women. We never saw them [the men] again." The women, however, were let go after three weeks: "They were ragged, had no shoes, and were bags of bones. The men who went with them had been all beaten to death."[13] This might have happened due to a desire to eliminate potential challenge and resistance by the men. In a terse allusion to the torment endured during the march, Samuel noted that "in the first three days many committed suicide ... because of the stress almost all the women started menstruating at the same time."[14]

The question as to the dividing line between the act of rape and sexualized violence cloaked in outright sadism has never been defined or addressed by Holocaust literature. Yaffa Rosenthal, from a transport of a 1,000 people that included Hungarian and Romanian expellees, described the senseless killing of a beautiful fifteen-year-old girl from Bukovina (Romania), whose brother had already been killed in the Dniester River. The Ukrainian guard submerged her head over and over in the river. Additionally, they did it to several other girls, and to Yaffa Rosenthal as well. The guard succeeded in killing this young girl in front of Rosenthal. In recalling the moment, she described the horror in a soft, almost inaudible tones. As Rosenthal recounted it, the pain on her face was visible. After fifty-five years, she still remembered vividly the girl's "beautiful dark braids floating on the water."[15]

Hungarian refugees, mostly women, children, and the elderly, were the most defenseless to thwart rape or sexual mistreatment. It could happen along the routes of the long wandering or in the sealed ghettos. In her video testimony, a survivor, who had wandered with her mother and sister from town to town, was stopped in a checkpoint around the town of Delatyn. After brief questioning, she was taken into the guardpost where she was "thrown on the mattress and raped repeatedly." She described an act of unspeakable violence, in a simple sentence, sparse, and clipped to its essence like it might need no more elaboration. The unembellished description of the trauma of being raped by eight guards, four German and four Ukrainian, in a guardpost in the entrance to Delatyn, a small, unremarkable Galician town, might not be able to convey the lifelong trauma of being sexually assaulted. Upon her release: "I came out dirty and filthy from the ordeal," she remembered vividly. As her eyes slowly clouded over, she recalled the moment her mother, without asking what happened in the guardpost, tried to ease her trauma by tenderly wiping her ski pants clean from the filth, softly asking, "Did they beat you?"

In viewing the video of her testimony—the furtive look, eyes darting back and forth between the camera and the interviewer, the short, clipped sentences, teared-up eyes, interspersed with painful silences—she admitted that her ordeal resulted in lifelong trauma, requiring psychological counseling after the war.[16] Interestingly, she gave her testimony in Los Angeles in Hungarian, not in Yiddish, not in Hebrew. Was it, perhaps, on purpose? She spoke in the language of the country that expelled her.

Her torment did not end there. In a desperate attempt to escape toward the Hungarian border, in 1942, she also recalled a jarring episode in which sexual favors were demanded by one of the Ukrainian escorts. The hired Ukrainian, who was a member of a smuggling ring, tried to rape her on their way to the Hungarian border. Upon complaining to the Jewish underground, one of the Jewish labor companies that organized the rescue from Galicia, the smuggler was summarily executed with the rationale that "if he rapes defenseless women, he cannot be trusted and will also be willing to betray the organization."[17]

One cannot write about sexual relations in the Holocaust, forced or consensual, without discussing homosexual encounters. Sexual coercion was not confined to heterosexual partners. This is perhaps the most guarded subject, a taboo among the reminicences of the survivors. Thus, chance meetings in a homosexual context are rarely mentioned in Holocaust literature. In a very carefully crafted note in her testimony, a female survivor from Budapest recounted her lesbian relationship in which the balance of power between Germans and Jews was the central and guiding element. As a member of a cleaning crew in an officer's residence, she came across a German officer who was abusive toward the girls. At the same time, his wife "acted rather humanely to the Jewish girls. It happened to be that, I don't know whether I should mention it, but everything—but she had some tendencies for liking girls." As the deportee phrased, "the question was whether to use this situation to your advantage or not to use it to your advantage.... Sometimes you came to a point when the only thing on your mind was, you are twenty years old, and somewhere along in the sky when you looked up, there is a life yet for people." These were very carefully chosen words, indeed. Were her ruminations an attempt to find justification for a moment in life when one had little control over the next day? In analyzing the possible motivation for such a relationship, Beorn noted that "when Jewish women had the chance to make decisions regarding these relationships, the motivation was almost assuredly survival, the options simpler, but the choices certainly far more agonizing."[18] Indeed, this survivor, in the end, had to make the decision, as she phrased, "whatever is possible but let's survive. It happens to be that that woman helped me a lot to get easier job, to get more food until her husband came into the picture."[19]

IN THE GHETTOS

A particularly sore and sensitive subject area is the fact that not all instances of sexual exploitation were perpetrated by Nazis or their allies. One tends to forget, or perhaps subconsciously avoid, that in the ghettos even the Jewish police or members of the *Judenrat* became complicit in such exploitation. A significant number of cases of rape and sexual coercion, or sexual barter, took place among Holocaust victims themselves. In this case, sexual encounters were not always violent, but based on power relations. Several authors mention, for example, that prostitution in Warsaw, Lodz, and other ghettos was rife—often for food. Even after the war, in a rather unguarded moment, a survivor blurted out an incident in the displaced persons camp when Jewish men 'raided' the women's block, initiating sex.[20]

During the Holocaust, consensual relations offered comfort and escapism. The Jewish police and the fire brigade in the Stanisławów ghetto oversaw the Hungarian Jews in the Rudolfmühle. Cipora Brenner remarked about their nightly visits to find companionship and, along the way, to seduce her and her roommate. She made it a point in her testimony that they both resisted their advances. Even in this case, the relationship was based on power. But, then, it often boiled down to life or death when a policeman or an official could prevent one's deportation to a death camp in exchange for sexual favors. It might be pertinent to remember that in various ghettos, the foreign Jews who had no anchor in the local community were the first ones to be selected for slave labor, delivered for killing "*Aktionen*," or sent to Belzec. Indeed, one of the policemen, with whom she became friends, saved her and hid her during the deportation of the Hungarians, in the spring of 1942, from the Rudolfmühle to Belzec. He also provided her more food and comfort in his own residence. That this relationship also reflected a degree of inequality might be deduced from the fact that she attempted to commit suicide during her time spent hiding in his attic.[21]

Of course, not only Hungarian deportees but local Jewish women were raped, beaten, and subjected to sexual violence. Wendy Jo Gertjejanssen provides a tentative number of women in sexual slavery: "It is safe to assume from the evidence available that the Germans enslaved at least 50,000 women into sexual slavery during World War II, but it is likely that the number is far higher."[22] We do not know how many Jewish women were included in this number, but then, the question as to how much the Nazi doctrine of racial hygiene, which explicitly forbade sexual relations between Jews and Aryans, influenced the practices on the ground, however forced they were, might be a moot one. Again, the words of Havryshko sum up this point: "The notion that sex with a Jewish woman (even coercive) would constitute 'racial defilement' (*Rassenschande*) was not an effective mechanism for preventing rape by Germans because some of them did not consider this rape to be a crime." Indeed, German military authorities established hundreds of brothels across the Reich in which also Jewish women were coerced into sexual slavery.[23] The military culture, with its cult of physical strength, hegemonic masculinity, and dominance over women, highly contributed to sex crimes, especially when it came to gang rape. As feminist scholars point out, in some military groups gang rapes served as a tool for building military brotherhood. Reflecting this attitude by the military, as Richard Evans noted, "the courts dealt with this kind of offence leniently." He presents some revealing statistics in that among "1.5 million members of the armed forces... only 5,349 were put on trial for sexual offences."[24]

This was, however, mainly applicable for the Wehrmacht. SS officers were held to a higher standard. Himmler's dictum explicitly forbade it: "In April 1939, Himmler made it clear in his order on the self-esteem of the folk (*Befehl über die völkische Selbstachtung*) that any connection [sexual contact] with those of non-German populations was forbidden for members of the SS and police."[25] He threatened demotion and discharge for those who did not obey this order.

In Galicia, all racial and ideological inhibitions, dictated by the Nuremberg Laws, rapidly evaporated, if they were taken into consideration at all. Sexual slavery by SS officers became common practice across the occupied territories. It was especially true for stationary security outposts where Nazi officers interacted with the Jewish community. In an interview with a witness in Busk, in western Galicia, Father Patrick Desbois recorded that the commandant of the outpost selected the most beautiful Jewish girl for himself: "Silva, who was very beautiful—wasn't killed straight away. Silva had to live with the German commander." The commander was not alone: "The Germans kept 30 or so very pretty Jewish women that they set to work in the offices of the Gestapo but whom they also used as 'sex objects' for the police [Ukrainian?] and the Germans." It was not an official brothel in the true sense of the word. Of course, the term "sex object" might also be a misnomer, for they were sex slaves in the full sense of the word. This saved their lives temporarily. The witness explained later that all the women became pregnant. A decision had to be made. The Germans, not having the "courage to kill them themselves" before escaping from the rapidly advancing Soviet forces at the end of the war, called in a murder squad from a neighboring town to massacre these women.[26]

In southern Galicia, where the Hungarian Jews were deposited, the acts of rape and sexual violence, against both men and women, became equally endemic. The difference was that the perpetrators in the south would personally kill the rape victims soon afterward. The elimination of these women and girls in these "makeshift" brothels also was fueled by the necessity to remove any potential witnesses to the sexual crimes. An equally weighty factor, just like in Busk, was that "as soon as one of them became pregnant she was exterminated."[27] A case in point was the border police outpost (*Grenzpolizei*) in Sniatyn, just across the Hungarian border. Under the command of SS-Untersturmführer (second lieutenant) Paul Elsner, the outpost was established for blocking the influx of Hungarian expellees, which also included their arrest and summary execution. Reporting to Peter Leideritz, in Kołomea, between September 1941 to February 1942, Elsner instituted a reign of sexual terror in the outpost with the full participation of his staff. Even in a short span of six months, he established and maintained a private "harem" of Jewish women, together with his fellow SS officers, with corresponding orgies, the victims of which he subsequently murdered. His sexual perversion exhibited itself in commanding his dog to attack attractive girls who were ordered to undress prior to the attack. All this to the accompaniment of blaring music from the radio: "The ferocious animal first ripped the girl's dress off and then tore hunks of flesh from her body until she bled to death." Elsner's removal from his command in early 1942 was not due to his deviant sexual activities but, rather, was because he was caught stealing Jewish valuables, for which he was court-martialed.[28]

In close proximity to Sniatyn, in Mielnica, where a large number of Hungarian exiles found refuge, heavily inebriated German border guards roamed the streets, "rioting through the town and harassing Jews whom they happened to encounter in the streets. They broke into houses at night and raped young girls. Many Jews never undressed for the night or simply slept out of their houses until dawn."[29] In this case, alcohol acted as a catalyst to violence and sexual predation. Even a low-level corporal in the Gestapo, such as Paul Thomanek, in Czortków, could demand from the *Judenrat* a supply of alcohol and women for his entertainment.[30]

KRÜGER IN STANISLAWÓW

No studies or references by scholars have raised the question of what role SS-Captain Hans Krüger may have played in instituting sexual terror in Stanislawów and the surrounding areas, nor was any mention made about his deviant sexual activities during the deliberations at his rather chaotic trial in the 1960s. However, memoires and testimonies paint a picture of Krüger as a psychopathic sexual predator, which might have been exceptional even within the ranks of the SS.

Three days after assuming his post as the commander of the Gestapo in Stanisławów, and perhaps as an introduction to things to come, he ordered a sex orgy in which Jewish women doctors and pharmacists were paraded nude and subsequently raped by German officers and Ukrainian militia men. Abraham Liebesman, a noted physician in the ghetto, was personally acquainted with Hans Krüger. As a keen observer of the ghetto scene, his remark that Krüger harbored special "animosity toward well-educated women" was especially poignant. He provides a graphic scene of this orgy that took place on the evening of "Monday the 4th of August . . . the band was playing when they brought in naked women [all physicians] pressed one against the other. . . . Thereafter came in naked men, among them the Rabbi Horowitz, his beard shaven. They forced the old rabbi to make advances to Dr. Zaslawski [a noted physician], when he refused, they beat him up until he was unconscious."[31] The next day, the participants of the evening, almost the entire intelligentsia of the community, were carted off to an adjacent forest near the village of Pawelce and murdered.

Evenings like this, when naked girls and men were forced to dance together, became routine entertainment for the Gestapo in the ghetto. In addition, Krüger demanded cultural activities and theatrical and musical performances for his own entertainment, at least until the spring of 1942, when most of the performers were transported to Belzec.

Reading contemporary testimonies, one comes away with the impression that in addition to sexual sadism toward women, especially well-educated ones, Krüger had a special animus toward rabbis. During his time in Stanisławów, he was able to combine the two, for eerily similar scenes were described about the first *Aktion* in Bolechow. The town, with a sizeable Jewish population, was located close to the Carpathian Mountains, some forty-five miles from Stanisławów. While the initial evening of an *Aktion* of sexualized violence in Stanisławów took place on August 4, the first such operation in the town of Bolechow was relatively late in the wave of murders sweeping through Galicia—October 28, 1941. Until then, the town was spared, by and large, from Nazi atrocities. It's ferocity, though, matched that already described *Aktion* in Stanisławów, and, it was conducted according to Hans Krüger's playbook.

Mainly targeting the town Jewish intelligentsia, the raid collected close to a thousand people of all ages in the *Dom Katolicki* [town hall]. Krüger arrived in the morning, briefly overseeing the arrangements. As he left half an hour later, he handed the command over "to Gestapo Officer Schindler."[32] Based on testimony by a survivor in 1946, and confirmed through interviews by Daniel Mendelsohn, the scenes of that afternoon and evening easily challenge human imagination: "Nine hundred people were packed into the hall. People were stacked on one another. Many suffocated. They were killed in the hall, shot or simply hit over the head with clubs and sticks."

The amusement started around four o'clock in the afternoon. The testimony emphasized that "the rabbis were especially targeted," and that sexual brutalization was not confined to women: "Rabbi Landau was ordered by one of the Gestapo men to stand naked on a chair and declaim a speech in praise of Germany." He was beaten simultaneously and later killed. As a blind piano player played on the stage, the wife of a noted lawyer "had to dance naked on naked bodies." Also, another rabbi was forced to sing and dance, "his eyes running blood," with a naked Jewish girl while beaten by "one of the Gestapo men." His eyes gauged out, the rabbi refused the German command to lie on top of the naked girl, upon which he was killed. "It is said that [the rabbis] were thrown into the latrines."[33]

Why was there a need to design uniquely anti-Semitic sexual torments, in a manner calculated to be particularly humiliating, when the fate of the assembled Jews to be exterminated the next morning was already decided? One psychological explanation is that in order to kill a group of people, you must reduce them, dehumanize them to a state in which you cannot see them as humans.[34] In this sense, increasingly brutal action could be used to convince oneself of his own virulent anti-Semitism, which then provided a justification for exterminating them with corresponding savagery.

These actions raise also some fundamental questions as to how Krüger's behavior reflected Nazi ideology and policies. And if they did not, what was different in Galicia? The directive from Heinrich Himmler as SS-Reichsführer clearly listed among the nine "virtues of the SS man," the "abstinence from alcohol" (*Alkohol vermeiden*). He especially threatened to double punishments for men convicted of crimes committed while under the influence.

As for behavior with women in the east, as we have already noted, Himmler outright forbade sexual intercourse with women of a different race, especially with Jewish women. Any transgressions were to be reported to him personally.[35] While this kind of sexually fueled savagery, prior to the killing of the arrested, was the hallmark of Krüger, sexual crimes were not the sole domain of the SS leadership in southern Galicia. As numerous studies show, they were endemic across the Eastern Theater. One finds a common denominator, though. There was a direct connection between heavy alcohol consumption, mass murder, and sexual violence. Edward Westermann's observation that "acts of sexual violence by SS and police forces were commonplace, and the abuse of alcohol was often a key contributing factor" sums this up well. It provided a bonding experience before the act and a diversion from the horrors of the crime committed afterward. Indeed, alcohol-fueled sexual predation ranged from voyeurism to rape and ultimately murder.

But there was an additional factor in Krüger's modus operandi, which was somewhat unique to southern Galicia. The number of people coerced in these acts of sexualized violence was extraordinary even by SS standards. As several scholars demonstrated, Wehrmacht soldiers committed sexual savagery in Belarus and Poland—mainly directed at a limited number of women. Yet, officers by and large did not condone such behavior or did not initiate it.[36]

The fact that Krüger was never called upon to answer for the sexual crimes committed by him and his security team is at best enigmatic. It shows perhaps a tacit complicity on the part of the security circle of fellow officers around Krüger in a behavior that was blatantly contrary to the SS code of conduct. The answer might lie also in the residual and corollary effects of such unbridled sexual violence. Again, we can rely on Abraham Liebesman's recollection in describing the immediate health results for sexual promiscuousness. As a physician in the Stanislawów ghetto, Liebesman was aware of the rapes and promiscuity of the German officers and Ukrainian policemen, for there was a veritable epidemic of venereal diseases, such as syphilis and gonorrhea, among the Gestapo personnel and the victims. He personally treated Krüger himself, who had several Jewish and Polish mistresses whom he infected with venereal diseases. In turn these women infected other officers as swapping mistresses became common. Unfortunately, for the Jewish sexual victims there was no need for medical treatment. As often was the case, the SS commandant routinely and expeditiously murdered them. Liebesman noted that Krüger was rumored to keep a photo album in which nude girls in various poses were depicted with guns pointed at their head—they were killed regularly.[37] This testimony illustrates that Krüger and fellow officers' behavior exhibited a deviant streak that might have diverged dramatically from the SS code of conduct, mandated by Himmler, but fostered a code of silence.

INSTITUTIONALIZED SEXUAL SLAVERY

One of the corollary effects of the rapidly spreading venereal diseases prompted the Wehrmacht and the SS leadership to address this issue head-on. The most immediate and rational solution was the establishment of several hundred brothels across the Reich and the East. We cannot discount an additional and rather obvious rationale for these brothels—satisfying the soldiers sexual desires or, perhaps more accurately stated, their sexual demands. However, from a health point of view, the weightiest factor for the SS officers was to bring the venereal diseases under control.

German military records inform us that five hundred brothels, catering to camp inmates, Wehrmacht soldiers, and SS officers, were functioning during the war across the

Reich. In the moment, women were coerced to work in them, with the Wehrmacht and security services complicit in the institutionalization of sexual violence. In the District of Galicia, we know of four brothels that were in service: Lwów, Drohobycz, Tarnopol, and Stanisławów. As the highest-ranking officer, the brothel in Stanisławów might have been Krüger's brainchild. While the first attempt, undertaken in November 1941, was not successful, we know that by February 14, 1942, it was fully operational, located in the German Officers' Club.[38] While relegating the administration to company and sanitation officers in the Wehrmacht, usually the field commander was in charge of such institutions. It seems likely that the brothel in Stanisławów was under the jurisdiction of Krüger.

Krüger was transferred from Stanisławów a year later, in early 1943, after the liquidation of the ghetto. The town was declared *Judenfrei*. His transfer was not precipitated by the orgies and by his sexual transgressions against the Reich's racial laws. Rather, his cardinal sin, as seen in the previous chapter, was his predilection for looting and robbing his victims in the ghetto. However, his legacy of sexual slavery continued long after his departure from a "Jew-free" Stanisławów. The brothel centered around the German Officers' Club was housed on the fourth floor of the Gestapo building. By that time, the only Jewish women still alive were those in this brothel.

As it was noted, military brothels were integral part of the Nazi Reich, in concentration camps, cities, and military installations. There was a priority order, though, in setting up this network. Gertjejanssen noted that "women who were less than pretty were

FIG 6.4   The Gestapo building in Stanisławów: The SS brothel was located on the fourth floor of the building. *Courtesy of the Ghetto Fighter's House and Museum, Israel/The Photo Archives.*

sent to the brothels established in concentration camps for male prisoners, the prettier to the Wehrmacht brothels and the prettiest to the SS brothels."[39] It is assumable that the German Officers' Club in Stanislawów could be considered such a "handpicked" SS brothel, because it catered to the local security officers only. The women enslaved in this establishment received more food and better sanitary condition, which included three times a week medical examination for venereal diseases.

We would have no knowledge or information about the brothel's existence and its operational details if not for an unexpected source. Michael Jackson (Jakubovics), a Hungarian Jew from Carpathian Ruthenia, who was drafted into a labor battalion attached to the Hungarian Army, arrived in Stanislawów around December 1943. His reminiscences of being deported in 1941 to Galicia could be the material for a film drama: a stateless Jew in Stanislawów, an escape back to Hungary over the Carpathian Mountains, and being sent back in a military unit to the scene of the "crime" two years later. It may seem a cruel twist of fate that he was drafted a year after his escape from Galicia into the Hungarian Army and transferred back to Stanislawów.

During his stationing there, for close to six weeks, he often worked in a four-story building that housed the German officers' club—entrusted with cleaning the staircases and rooms. Upon wandering to the fourth floor, he inadvertently stumbled upon a brothel staffed by Jewish and Polish women that served the officers. The officers used these young women as sex slaves, in the full sense of the word—without recourse, except suicide. We know that because "after sometimes the girls disappear and never come back.... The women were not allowed to leave the floor... and some of the girls jumped out of the windows." In turn, the Germans installed bars on the windows to stop a rush of suicides by the despondent and traumatized victims.

Since the forced laborers from Carpathian Ruthenia spoke Yiddish among themselves, one of the girls tearfully approached him and confided in him about her life in the brothel. An emotional Jackson recalled in his testimony in 1997 the final words he exchanged with this Jewish girl: "If you survive the war, tell our story, tell the world what these beasts did to us." Michael Jackson later, on camera, concluded his testimony on a tearful note: "My dear Jewish sister, now I am fulfilling your request. I looked into your eyes, and I saw and felt your pain."[40]

7

RETURN FROM THE ABYSS

Rescue and Survival

"I implore you, spare no effort for we are reaching the end together with 2,000 people."[1]

THE OPENING CHAPTER OF THE HUNGARIAN HOLOCAUST DID NOT COME to an abrupt close with the three-day massacre in Kamenets-Podolsk or the genocidal convulsion across Galicia in 1941 and 1942. Desperate efforts by the expellees who survived the massacres to return to Hungary continued sporadically until mid-1943. Officially, the deportation came to an impasse on August 8, 1941, by the direct decree of the Minister of Interior Ferenc Keresztes-Fischer. His directive was sent out to all provinces, instructing both civilian authorities as well as police agencies to cease the transborder expulsion. The telegram's tone is unambiguous: "I forbid the removal of the Jews to Poland [sic] effective immediately... those Jews of Polish and Russian extraction that their expulsion is desired... in the future, only with [my] approval can be expelled."[2] On the original telegram, delivered promptly to Miklós Kozma's office, a curt handwritten note of confirmation stating "I have taken action" was dated August 10, 1941—two days after the original order. During these two days' lag, and even after, the trucks of the Royal Hungarian Army continued to roll unchecked, transporting another 3,859 people to their predictable fate in Galicia.[3]

This was the first time that a direct communication from the minister of interior explicitly forbade the deportation. Yet the fact that his order was delayed and that removal from the provinces continued intermittently long after this decree should also not come as a surprise. This deliberate obfuscation was not the first instance when regional authorities (and even under the nose of the minister) ignored the minister's instructions. His decree on July 30 that limited the expulsion to individuals with Polish and Russian roots, requested by the prime minister and conveyed to the American ambassador three days later, remained a "theoretical proposition." Repeated complaints from the provinces reported disobedience to a sequence of ministerial orders, indicators of an environment ripe for abuses.[4] The blatant disregard of an order to halt the deportation might also be demonstrative of a deep-seated resentment by Hungarian officialdom at not being able to accomplish the complete expulsion of the entire Jewish community. In a 1942 document from Carpathian Ruthenia, a disappointed county commissioner bemoaned the fact that although "the most welcomed governmental decision of 1941 was the transfer of Jews of foreign nationality [to Galicia].... Unfortunately, this action only lasted for 8–10 days [sic] and so Carpathian Ruthenia's biggest question has not been solved."[5]

The flouting of the directive could equally be the result of a dysfunctional political and administrative system, based on privileges and overlapping connections, in which checks and balances were only an illusion. In hindsight, we can also discern "stress fractures" in the political system. There were three distinct jurisdictions, functioning in parallel with each other, which were not clearly delineated and defined. Carpathian Ruthenia was governed by Miklós Kozma who, as government commissioner, ostensibly reported to the regent, Miklós Horthy. As such, he could take autonomous decisions with the proviso that he conferred and updated the government of László Bárdossy. In a surviving memorandum from his office, four days after the minister of interior had already suspended the deportation, he explicitly wanted to explore the possibility of restarting "further shipments of Jews" with the German authorities, effective August 14.[6] He simultaneously proposed the prime minister establish contact with German authorities with the same goal. Two follow-up directives in succession, from August 15 and 17, had to be sent by the head of KEOKH to enforce the minister's earlier injunction.[7]

The Royal Hungarian Army, on the other hand, was fully autonomous in the military areas it controlled in Galicia. It also claimed authority in the border zones adjacent to the newly occupied Soviet Union—including Carpathian Ruthenia and part of northern Transylvania. The minister of interior had no jurisdiction over the military. As an example, the Kőrösmező transit camp, located on the border zone and under military control, functioned undisturbed. Its commander, Lieutenant-Colonel Rudolf Orbán, could disregard the instructions from Budapest with the clear knowledge that he was under the operational authority of a staunchly pro-German chief of staff, General Henrik Werth. So, the military trucks continued to roll with their human cargo long after this ministerial decree. A follow-up instruction by the interior minister, stating that refugees or escaping Galician Jews should not be handed over because of the certainty of execution by the German security services, was also blatantly disregarded by border and military authorities.

As far as late October, with corresponding heavy snows and freezing temperatures in the Carpathian Mountains, border guards routinely returned refugees to their death. Kozma's desperate call to the minister of interior, in October, for urgent intervention with the military leadership for the cessation of cross-border transfer of escaping Jews went unheeded.[8] At the other end of this continuum, military officers could also use their power to save lives. The example of Lieutenant-Colonel Imre Reviczky, who secured birth certificates, interceded with the local gendarmerie, and unilaterally stopped and returned several trainloads of deportees heading toward the transit camp in Kőrösmező, is one of the rare examples of such behavior.[9]

Finally, the land within the country's original boundaries was under the jurisdiction of the Ministry of Interior, but his ministerial orders theoretically would apply to the entire country, including the newly reannexed territories. In retrospect, it seems incredible that even relatively low-level operatives in KEOKH and district administrators could refuse the minister's explicit instruction with impunity. The main architect of the deportation in this region, the state police councilor of Carpathian Ruthenia, Arisztid Meskó, openly boasted to a visiting delegation led by Margit Slachta that "on the personal level he considers the cleansing of his territory from Jews most salutary ... he knows [the order of the minister] but in the territory of Carpathian Ruthenia the laws and legal rulings are governed by different considerations." He bluntly added that the "regulations by the minister of interior apply only to the interior of the country; in Carpathian Ruthenia the sole responsibility rests with government commissioner for such matters. In any case, I [Meskó] drew up the instructions relating to the deportation, developed the plans, and instructed police authorities to exercise the utmost rigor and severity in implementing the 'cleansing action,' *regardless of the individual hardships and tragedies which are not my concern.*"[10]

The most telling sign of the willful contravention of the initial ministerial missive for the immediate cessation of the deportation, from August 8, was, as noted previously, the necessity of sending two follow-up telegrams on August 15 and 17, respectively, to all police agencies and regional KEOKH offices. On August 17, Simenfalvy ordered the "release of alien Jews of Polish and Russian origin that had been slated for expulsion and require them to report once a week in person at their permanent residence." He further requested weekly reports about their progress and the status of the foreign nationals.[11]

However, there was an inherent caveat in the minister's missive. His original telegram spoke only about the cessation of the cross-border transfer. It did not address an equally weighty question: What would be the fate of those marooned in the Galician nightmare or those who desperately wanted to return across the Carpathian Mountains? And, specifically, what should be the fate of those who were able to escape and return to the mother country? László Zobel, one of the survivors of the deportation, succinctly summed up this governmental policy in noting that the "government did not want witnesses to a human disaster they had initiated. It would have been an international admission of a humanitarian tragedy, and a political blunder which would bring into focus the ultimate question of responsibility." Hence the assiduous hunting down of the escapees, returning them to Galicia or locking them away immediately in internment camps.[12]

"I HAVE HEARD ENOUGH!"

This exclamation has been attributed to Keresztes-Fischer upon hearing of the atrocities taking place in Ukraine. Consequently, an order was issued for the cessation of cross-border transfer of Jews to Galicia from the transit camp in Kőrösmező. The Hungarian government was under continuous pressure to moderate its expulsion policy and stop the deportation altogether. Protests by religious and political organizations, individual initiatives, Jewish communal efforts, the American ambassador's intervention, and protest by the US State Department bore fruit.

There are two versions as to how this decision itself came to pass, and it is possible both contain an element of truth. One version comes from the testimony of Dr. Aurel Kern, a ministerial councilor reporting directly to the minister of interior, during the trial of one of the main architects of the 1941 deportation, Ámon Pásztoy. Kern stated that he personally brought the news of the mass murder of the deportees to the attention of Keresztes-Fischer. The enraged minister reacted by "promising an immediate response for this atrocity. It is inconceivable that he would deliver human beings for the slaughter."[13]

Possibly at the same time, the minister heard a report in person from a deportee who was smuggled back to Budapest. This may have been the "final straw" in convincing the minister of interior to suspend the deportation. The plot to inform and influence the minister started out as an individual rescue effort to smuggle back two people who were deported to Galicia. The rescue attempt was initiated by Hansi Brand, a remarkably fearless woman and a Zionist leader, whose sister and brother-in-law were deported within twenty-four hours from Budapest to Galicia. She was assisted by her husband, Joel Brand.[14] As Joel Brand recalled during the Eichmann trial, Hansi insisted on finding someone who could rescue her sister. In a wholly unplanned encounter in one of the many cafés dotting the capital, Joel Brand found a counterintelligence officer, József Krem, who was willing to find and bring back the two for a hefty fee — 10,000 pengő, an enormous sum at the time. The officer made four trips, each time bringing back people who were willing to pay the money for their rescue, until he found the two relatives of the Brands: "He went with his automobile to fetch them. I had only a photograph to give him. But when he returned from there the first time, he had not found my relatives. He was, however, clever or dexterous enough to bring back with him other Hungarian Jews who had been deported there. They had also promised him a lot of money. These Jews told us for the first time clearly about the mass shootings and about the horrors, so that we understood that this was a systematic operation . . . but up to this point had not really believed it."[15]

Joel Brand arranged through an intermediary a meeting directly with Keresztes-Fischer and Hansi Brand's brother-in-law. The intermediary was Samuel Springmann, a mysterious and colorful character in Budapest of the 1940s. He was an influential diamond dealer, who, in spite of being Jewish, had unfettered access to the highest circles of the government as well as the German military intelligence, the Abwher. Brand asserted in his testimony at the Eichman trial that only four people were present at the meeting: the minister, Joel Brand, Samuel Springmann, and Lajos Stern, the rescued brother-in-law. However, it might be more likely that several leaders from the Hungarian-Jewish Assistance Committee (*Magyar Izraeliták Pártfogó Irodája*, MIPI) were also present. Stern told Keresztes-Fischer about the situation in Galicia. Upon hearing the graphic tales of the atrocities and mass killings of local and Hungarian Jews, the minister's alleged response, "I have heard enough," signaled his decision to put an end to the deportation.[16]

There were other factors, of course, that could have played crucial role in this decision. For one, we cannot ignore the role Margit Slachta, supported by several prominent public figures and parliamentarians, may have played in this decision. As the influential head of the Order of the Sisters of Social Service and an astute politician, she had access to the highest levels of the Hungarian government, including the minister of interior. Equally significant was her personal friendship with the wife of the de-facto ruler of Hungary, Miklós Horthy. In forceful words, invoking Christian morality and national pride, she implored the reigning couple to intervene on behalf of the deported. Consequently, she gained an audience with Mrs. Horthy. There are no surviving documents that could testify, indeed, if Horthy became involved in the affair. However, he knew about the events and had continuous communication with his government. Equally important was the sending of her report to the attention of the International Red Cross in Geneva in late 1941, requesting humanitarian assistance for those deported in Galicia.[17]

The intervention of Herbert C. Pell, the American ambassador, in pressuring the prime minister for the cessation of the deportation had also had an impact on Hungarian thinking. The transfer of information to Washington and its dissemination to the American press only reinforced the perception in Budapest that the continuation of this mishandled adventure might be politically untenable.

Finally, the political and military reality on the ground in Galicia—we might also term it an element of "real politics"—might have also influenced the thinking of the government. The territory controlled by the Hungarian military was reduced to a narrow zone that could not permit the delivery of convoys across the Dniester River. An exasperated deputy to the government commissioner in Carpathian Ruthenia conveyed this information to the minister of interior by claiming that until then the deportees' return could be "easily prevented by guarding the crossing-places [Dniester River]." Equally important were the ongoing and relentless German objections, reinforced by the introduction of German military control in Galicia and its incorporation into the

General Government on August 1, to the deportation. Although some Hungarian military presence remained and outposts continued to function in the areas formerly under Hungarian occupation, their operational control was taken over by the Wehrmacht and, consequently, the German security services. This was followed soon after by the transition to German civil administration. Not surprisingly, then, in the deliberations by the Parliament, the loss of control over large swaths of Galicia was listed by the minister as one of the cardinal reasons for the halting of the deportation.[18]

As an interesting footnote to the rescue, a lively trade in human smuggling and the transfer of letters, packages, and money arose among the military personnel stationed in Galicia. József Krem, the counterintelligence agent, continued to pop up periodically in the annals of the 1941 deportation and rescue activities. He routinely conducted his undercover business in the ritzy Café Savoy, a trendy hangout for the rich. According to the testimony of László Zobel, Krem appeared in a sports car in Kolomea on October 3, 1941, dressed in a fitted black leather coat. He was looking for a specific client, whose rich family had paid for his services for transportation back to Budapest. Everything was ready with fake counterintelligence papers, only the intended individual was nowhere to be found. Realizing that the deportee might have been moved somewhere else and not wanting to return empty-handed, the enterprising agent offered to Zobel and his mother transportation across the border for the sum of 5,000 pengő. Zobel masqueraded as a counterintelligence agent, under identity papers provided by Krem, while his mother hid in the luggage compartment of the little sports car, as they deftly made the journey back to Budapest safely.[19]

FIG 7.1 László Zóbel was twenty-four years old when he was deported to Galicia with his mother. After wandering in Galicia, they were smuggled back to Budapest by a Hungarian intelligence officer. *Courtesy of George Eisen.*

Some tales did not end as happily. Enterprising officers of the Royal Hungarian Army repeatedly approached families of the deported to supposedly assist the unfortunates in Galicia. The diary of a young girl, Éva Hyman, mentions the expulsion of her close friend, Márta Münzer, with her parents to Kamenets-Podolsk. She recorded that Hungarian officers often visited the grieving grandmother with offers to deliver money to the deported Münzer family: "A lot of soldiers have already dropped in on them quite a few times, and after asking her for money they told her that they had seen Márta, and her mother too, in some Polish town called Kamenets-Podolsk."[20] The grandmother gave every time, despite the fact that by this time, it was common knowledge that the Hungarian Jews in Kamenets-Podolsk, including the Münzer family, had been exterminated.

THE PERILOUS JOURNEY

The opportunity for flight, survival, and the successful crossing of borders, like all Holocaust experiences, was serendipitous. This might hold especially true in Galicia, an alien land with a hostile population, where the drive to plunder and murder often extinguished all semblance of empathy. Individuals found wandering across the open countryside of Galicia were often denounced and captured. Thus, the journey toward the border had to be conducted during the night while hiding in the fields or forests during the day. One of the critical elements in a successful return was to find a Jewish home in the darkness. Numerous narratives described how the worn-down refugees floundered in the dark, going "from door to door" in order to touch a mezuzah[21] on the doorpost—the sign of a Jewish home. Finding such a home meant a temporary shelter and was often a lifesaver. Yet we also encounter examples of spontaneous assistance even on the part of the feared Ukrainian militia. However, this was more the exception than the rule. Successful escapes were a matter of being at the right time, in the right place, along with a dose of luck and personal resourcefulness. Some decided to take the long road to the Hungarian border on their own. Others were saved by members of the Jewish forced labor companies, or by relatives from Budapest who were rich enough to afford a rescue operation. As mentioned, military officers and enterprising counterintelligence agents had unfettered access to the occupied territories and were paid handsomely for their assistance.

Most of the refugees, however, did not have the financial means or personal connections to be rescued by high-level officers or agents of the Hungarian counterintelligence services. In these prevailing political winds and social conditions, it's a miracle that by some estimates less than 10 percent of the deported, around 2,000 survivors, were able to return, illegally, through the Carpathian Mountains. This number may be inflated because the ratio of survival and successful return of the expellees was low.

Listening to the testimonies of survivors, it is clear that very few were able to return. For instance, from a group of forty that escaped from Czortków, only five individuals could be traced. Another sobering example from a small village in Carpathian Ruthenia shows that from more than 217 Jews deported, only a family of seven and two individuals trickled back. Or consider the fate of one family of twenty-one, also expelled from a small village in Carpathian Ruthenia—only one person came back. This was a woman named Helen Dub who lived in hiding in the forest in a makeshift bunker and returned after the war—she was the only survivor from her family.[22]

Escape was an individual initiative, a decision that often led to tragic consequences. It could signify life and death. The eight-member family of Max Solomon had to split up because of the smugglers' concern that such a large group might attract too much attention. As the first group, the mother and three daughters were dispatched in Ukrainian peasant attire and successfully reached Hungary. The men, however, were caught in the second attempt and, consequently, were killed in the mass execution in Orinin. Max was the lone survivor among three brothers and the father. He realized only after the war that the women miraculously survived the journey and the war.[23]

A somewhat different, though equally harrowing fate befell a family from Budapest. Upon receiving a desperate plea from their daughter languishing in Galicia, with a husband and two children, her parents in Budapest reassured them, "there is a solution, hold out a little longer." Three weeks later, two Ukrainian peasants, Hutsuls, appeared and were ready to lead the family to the Hungarian border, but in order to save them, they had to hand over their children to smugglers. It was April 24, 1942. Since the husband was in no condition to undertake the arduous trip, she decided to entrust the two children to the care of the smugglers to deliver them to Budapest, which they reached safely. Upon her request to send a car, because of her husband's health, the parents were able to arrange a truck, two months later, which brought them to the Hungarian border, which they had to cross with smugglers on foot. After safely arriving in Budapest, they were arrested on July 22, 1942, imprisoned with the threat of cross-border transfer back to Galicia. After bribes, she and the two children were released. Her husband, though, was expelled again and, in the words of the survivor, "disappeared without a trace."[24]

Obviously, the family back in Budapest was able to muster the resources that were needed for such a rescue. The majority of refugees, however, coming from more modest circumstances, especially from the provinces, would not be able to hire rescuers. A letter from Kolomea gives a sobering assessment about the obstacles facing a family with children. The writer informs his relatives in Budapest that the situation is dire: "All our luggage was stolen, and only Rozsi [the nanny that accompanied them voluntarily] succeeded to save her belongings. She sold everything so that the children could be fed, so she remained with very few articles of clothing." The children had winter coats but no gloves and shoes. Basically, the family was destitute. The letter was dated on November

13, 1941, when the daily collection of Jews and their execution was already a familiar routine in Kolomea. Having a special work pass, the anonymous writer reassured his contact in Budapest that in spite of the murders, she should not be frightened, "because I feel that I will escape from this hell and we will reunite in Budapest for starting a new life." Then, the writer pleaded for the family in Budapest to write an appeal and deliver it in person to Miklós Horthy, requesting permission for their return.[25]

Leaving behind loved ones in a ghetto in Galicia, in the last moments before escaping and with the knowledge that this might be the final time they would see each other, required a deep degree of emotional detachment. Elizabeth Lubell, a twenty-year-old woman from Budapest, survived a full year also in the Kolomea Ghetto with her parents. Originally, there were over "20,000 people [Jews] in Kolomyja." By the time of her decision to depart, "there were only a couple hundred left." She knew instinctively that this would be the last time she would see her parents alive. There was an unspoken bond of silence between daughter and mother:

> The last night when I knew that I'm leaving in the morning.... In order to survive you have to lose your—certain feelings disappear from you. But that was the last night and mother just touched me so because she had her own thoughts and I had my own thoughts. The only thing what I remember that I just wanted to—that nobody should touch me and nobody should kiss me. Just to push it away because one more touch and one more kiss, I'm not going to leave.... I never explained it to her but I hope she understood it. Because

FIG 7.2 Elizabeth Lubell and her mother, Brona Buchsbaum. She escaped from the Kolomea Ghetto with the help of smugglers that her parents hired. The parents remained behind and were among the last Jews to be shipped to Belzec extermination camp and killed. *Courtesy of Barbara Lubell.*

when she wanted to touch me, I just like—I pushed it away. I did it in order that I should be able to leave.²⁶

She never saw her parents again. They were deported to Belzec several weeks after her departure and murdered there.

Her experience, harrowing as it was, showed individual daring, sacrifice, and deep faith. Beyond financial constraints, the routes toward the Hungarian border were long and perilous—especially if one considered the crossing of the Dniester River, the most formidable natural barrier. Indeed, this was one of the considerations of Hungarian policymakers for dumping the refugees on the other side of the river. Boatmen were willing to transport the escapees over the raging river for a hefty fee. There was always a well-founded concern, though, that these smugglers would throw the returnees overboard into the river after taking their money.²⁷

Attempts to cross the Carpathian Mountains in late autumn and early winter harbored their own dangers. Besides the challenge of the cold weather and snow, there were recurring reports of massacres of entire families by their Ukrainian guides. By some estimates, half of the escapees, Hungarian and Galician, were murdered by their guides along the way to the border. Rumors were widespread on the Galician side of the border that Hungarian border guards routinely robbed and murdered arrested Jews.²⁸

One Hungarian mother and daughter were captured and imprisoned across the border by a Hungarian unit, alongside Galician Jews. The Galicians, who had attempted the perilous journey across the border, harbored no illusions by that time about their fate. They were resigned. However, the mother and daughter, upon overhearing the guards' detailed discussion in Hungarian about the impending execution of the entire group, made a desperate effort to break out with the help of these Galician Jews. They literally created a human pyramid to reach the window. They were able to escape to safety.²⁹

An unlikely voice of conscience should be interjected. Surprisingly, it came from Carpathian Ruthenia. Miklós Kozma finally became aware of the enormity of the human tragedy that was unfolding on the border. He instructed all officials under his control to "strictly adhere to the minister of interior's explicit instructions" relating to Jews. In his desperate appeal to the minister of interior, on October 22, 1941, for intercession with military authorities, he informed Keresztes-Fischer about the horrors taking place in the "no-man's land where mothers bury their children that died from hunger with their own hands." He also warned the minister of the uncompromising behavior of the military and the gendarmerie, which "continuously transport escapees back to Galicia."³⁰ He was also familiar with the dictum by Major Helmut Tanzmann, as the head of the Security Police in Lwów who ordered the shooting of every returnee, whether Hungarian deportee or a Galician escapee. The German border police carried out this command to the full extent. Elizabeth Lubell's return from Galicia in the autumn of 1942 shows that Kozma's warnings were credible. Part of a group of returnees, the last survivors of the Kolomea Ghetto, could see already the Hungarian border when somebody betrayed them to the German border guards: "we were ten of us who were escaping from the ghetto—they came up, the German guards and they shot everybody on sight." She hid in a hollow three trunk for four days and four nights in the woods, waiting for her rescue. She was the only one who lived to tell the tale.[31]

There were instances when Hungarian refugees joined their Galician coreligionists in attempting to cross the border to Bukovina, with the aim of reaching Chernowitz, on the Romanian side. We know the fate of one group from Mielnica, where some "local Jews and some who were refugees from Hungary attempted to cross the border into Bukovina with the aid of Ukrainian smugglers in exchange for large sums of money. ... Most of the escapees, however, were caught there by the police, brought back to the border point at Sniatyn and handed over to the Germans, who murdered them on the spot."[32] There were other examples of local Jewish assistance for the deportees. In Kosów, the community successfully bribed the German border police to let close to 400 Jews escape back to Hungary. Some were successful while 149 were returned to Kosów by Hungarian authorities, to share the fate of the entire community several months later. What was unique about the Kosów affair is that the Jewish community responded to the German border post in Zabie, which demanded the repatriation of these Hungarian Jews.[33]

The most harrowing part of the trip was the border crossing. A shocking report from October 1941 described how the border guards, the gendarmerie, and even armed youth groups (*levenlék*) hunted for and transferred the unfortunate returnees to no-man's-land, many with proof of their Hungarian citizenship: "In this respect, they know no mercy.... The returnees' situation is beyond shocking. They arrive half-frozen, emaciated, in rags, or sometimes completely stripped of clothing... based on local information the no-man's land is covered with dead bodies that no one can bury anymore, sometimes just covering them with tree branches."[34] Another report by the Hungarian general staff almost at the same time provides exact numbers of Jews for the first two weeks of October who were captured in crossing the border and redeported to Galicia: "The total number reaches two thousand."[35]

A brief note needs to be inserted that can shed light on the behind-the-scenes decision-making process in Budapest. A flurry of directives and proposals by Pásztóy during September might testify to his drive to finish the task that he started in July 1941. His missive to the officials in Carpathian Ruthenia, instructing them by telephone to thwart the return of both Jews and Christians, indicates this uncompromising attitude: "the return of the expelled Jews is non-negotiable, and similarly their Christian family members. The only mode of their return can be through German diplomatic channels."[36] The recognition that military efforts alone would not be sufficient to curtail the number of desperate returnees from recrossing the border propelled him to approach directly the prime minister (also holding the portfolio of foreign minister) with the proposal of a 20–30-kilometer-wide "Jew-free" border zone on the Galician side.[37] Pásztóy's communication, transcending the chain of command with Keresztes-Fisher also advocated for convening a joint German Hungarian governmental commission that could produce a diplomatic solution to the issue of the returning refugees. Upon convoking such a consultative body in Berlin, though, one can sum up the functioning of this committee as mutual recrimination and finger-pointing.[38] While the first communication from the Hungarian Embassy in Berlin started on October 3, 1941, by early November it became clear that no resolution could be reached. Parallel with these rather fruitless diplomatic negotiations, German Hungarian contacts have commenced on the military level on October 11 in Körösmező, on the Hungarian–Galician border. A follow-up meeting at the end of October in Stanisławów, in which SS-Captain Krüger was also a participant, was more productive. It concluded that in case of their unlawful return, "the Jews cannot be handed over but should be interned and later an arrangement could be found for their cross-border transfer."[39] As we have seen, and perhaps reflecting this "arrangement," there were numerous instances when families were sent to internment camps upon their capture, and later transferred back to Galicia—as late as 1943.

CONSPIRACY OF SILENCE

The Hungarian refugees made every attempt to return to Hungary, which was, after all, still home, and familiar territory. But the foreign nationals who were plucked out of Hungarian internment camps or arrested in periodic raids could not do the same. They had no supportive familial network, no friends who could assist them in going underground. Even for those few Hungarian Jews who successfully evaded border patrols and snuck back to their home villages and towns, life did not return to normal. Carrying the psychological and physical scars of the deportation, they were forced silently into hiding for months by the genuine fear of being transported back to Galicia. Their fear was justified. Often the details of the clandestine return of a deportee were kept under wraps for understandable reasons. Some told or wrote about their experiences in Galicia years later. As a Galician survivor later recalled, one of the unexpected escapees was the noted and colorful Hungarian boxer Zsiga Adler, whose girlfriend was able to bribe his way back to Budapest. Ironically, Adler never mentioned this detail during his lifetime.[40]

A vexing aspect of the tragedy was a prevailing "hear nothing, know nothing" attitude during and after the deportation. The Hungarian authorities, naturally enough, did not want eyewitnesses to the crimes. No one in a position of power wanted to face the "inconvenient truth," about a political and humanitarian failure. The public media was also complicit in this silence. Aside from a terse announcement by the Hungarian radio on August 3, 1941, and in some regional newspapers, the mainline news media was silent, or at least circumspect about the deportation and atrocities in Galicia. This reticence was partly due to the strictly enforced military censorship introduced in 1939. There was also, especially on the part of the Jewish press, a self-censorship.[41] They wanted to pursue discrete diplomacy by interceding with various governmental forums and, simultaneously, informing the American Embassy.

On the individual level, relatives and friends were afraid of being arrested for sheltering loved ones, since they risked prosecution themselves. This was not an idle threat. Those caught inside Hungary were either deported back to Galicia, shipped to internment camps, or, in rare instances, were ordered to report weekly to the gendarmerie. In a twisted logic, a family that was able to return in 1942 was sentenced to prison for the crime of "illegal border crossing." Consequently, they were interned for a year. In another instance, the consequences were more lethal. A father, who refused to divulge where the rest of his family was hiding, was beaten so savagely by two gendarmes that he died soon after his release from the internment camp.[42] Some returnees were interned and consequently expelled again to Galicia. A survivor testified during Pásztóy's trial that "we were able to return in the summer of 1942. Following the advice of the Hungarian-Jewish National Aid Action (*Országos Magyar Zsidó Segítő Akció*, OMZSA) we reported to the police upon which we were interned immediately. While my mother and I were freed, my father and brother ... were transferred in September 1942 to Poland [Galicia] again, from where they have never returned."[43]

No one dared to talk openly about the horrors they witnessed and experienced due to an ever-present network of informers. László Zobel, upon his return to Budapest, was denounced to the police by the janitor of his apartment complex almost immediately. Following his arrest, he was sent to an internment camp. Everyone was intimidated into silence. Even the representatives of the Jewish communal organizations, not able to initially comprehend the gravity of the situation, tacitly acquiesced to the governmental directives for the deportation. A rousing homily, delivered by a representative of OMZSA, was seared in Zobel's memory. As the despairing detainees lined up to board the waiting military trucks for the transfer from Kőrösmező to Galicia, he exhorted them "to build a new life in your new homeland with ample of opportunities while remembering with pride and gratitude that you lived in Hungary."[44]

In this light, the silence seems sinister. The survivors who filtered back tried to share their stories of horror, but they were rebuffed by the Jewish communal organizations and the community at large. The words of a survivor that "nobody wanted to believe us" are typical in reconstructing the survivors' post-Galician life. Neither relatives nor the official representatives of Jewish organizations wanted to accept that such events could be taking place. A nine-year-old at the time vividly remembered the violent outburst of a woman who chastised his father "for telling such an unbelievably crazy story."[45] The boy and his father were the only survivors of a group of sixteen, including members of their own family. They climbed out of a mass grave. Their testimony challenged the rational mind and human imagination. Even some seasoned leaders of the Jewish community were somewhat incredulous. Zobel, who was invited by the president to share his experiences at two of the largest Jewish communal organizations, MIPI and OMZSA, faced a mixed reception to his presentation. The majority of those present listened with disbelief and skepticism to the detailed account of atrocities he experienced in Ukraine.[46]

Elie Wiesel wrote, "No one wanted to listen," especially the established Jewish community, which closed its eyes and ears to the pleas of the returnees. His haunting image of Moshe the Beadle is based on the true story of Moshe Lieberman from Wiesel's hometown of Máramaros Sziget in northern Transylvanian. The "*shamesz*" of the Etz Hayim synagogue slowly descends into madness from the trauma of witnessing mass murder. He traveled "day after day, night after night . . . from one Jewish house to the next, telling his story and that of Malka, the young girl who lay dying for three days, and that of Tobie, the tailor who begged to die before his sons were killed." The ultimate tragedy is Moishe's final desperate cry: "I am alone. But I wanted to come back to warn you. Only no one is listening to me."[47]

THE WEHRMACHT, GESTAPO, AND THE ROYAL HUNGARIAN ARMY

The role of the Hungarian occupational authorities and German military and civil administrations in the occupied territories confounds any preconceived assumptions about the Hungarian deportation. One might assume that the entire German military, security, and civilian apparatus was bent on the destruction of the refugees. Additionally, one could entertain hope that the Hungarians were engaged in saving their compatriots, but the situation on the ground was more complex. The German authorities, from self-interest, often made genuine efforts to repatriate the Hungarian Jews in 1941—even giving them travel assistance on German military vehicles.

Hungarian authorities, meanwhile, were equally adamant about returning those who were caught on the border to certain death. Travel documents, the highly valued *Passierschein*, signed by military authorities and district commissioners (*Landkomisar* and *Kreisthauptmann*), were clear testimony that not every German was a murderer. German border posts in Galicia and the General Government sent frantic requests from Krakow and Lwów to Berlin requesting intercession with the Hungarian government for the cessation of the deportation and return of those deported. A memorandum sent directly to Berlin claimed that 20,000 Hungarian Jews had crossed the border at Jablonica Pass and another 17,000 were waiting along the Hungarian side of the border. While this number is an exaggeration, highly inflated, the panic of the official was real.[48] And, to add to the absurdity of the situation, Hungarian officials stubbornly protested this assistance given by German authorities to the returnees. They spared no efforts to intercept the few who attempted to recross the border to send them back to their death. The diary of a Galician doctor recorded that "325 Jews [Hungarian] reached Kosów on the eve of Rosh Hashanah in 1941 [September 21].... The Hungarian Jews spent a short time with us. *Then, at the demand of the German border guard in Zabie, we arranged to have the Jews returned to Hungary.*" The Jewish community bribed the Germans to facilitate their escape: "Some of the Jews managed to cross the river, others were apprehended by the Hungarians and sent back to us. Unfortunately, we have evidence that the returned Jews were executed soon thereafter."[49]

In the middle of the carnage of Kamenets-Podolsk, a surprising document that instructs a mother and son to proceed to the border with military transportation shows the willingness of German officers to save Hungarian refugees. The order was signed by Lieutenant Colonel Meiler, the German military commandant of Kamenets-Podolsk, on August 29, 1941.[50] At almost the same time, Meiler signed travel documents jointly with his Hungarian counterpart, Major László Darnay, for eighteen people, including the already mentioned Fein family. This points to a perplexing contradiction. While the chief executioner in Kamenets-Podolsk, Friedrich Jeckeln, moved with murderous zeal to perpetrate genocide, there were many German administrators in the conquered territories who gave transfer documents and transportation to the Hungarian border.

In retrospect, it is hard to reconcile the contradictions within the Hungarian Army toward Ukrainian abuses and the German killing operation. There were serious German concerns, for example, that Hungarian forces, including the 16th Bicycle Battalion stationed in Kamenets-Podolsk, would intervene in the massacre of Hungarian Jews. Unfortunately, they opted to sit on the sideline and even participated in the collection of the Jews. Yet the Hungarian commander sheltered a Jewish family. To save them, he gave travel papers to an entire group to the border, which included Albert Fein's family and a dozen more Hungarian Jews. They requested permission from the Hungarian commander to travel back to Hungary as Christians,

> and the Hungarian commandant, he had a family—a Jewish family. This means a wife with two sons. Her husband was a wrestler champion in Budapest. This was his friend—the general's. He was not a general, he was a colonel. So, he says, "Okay, I know you are Christians and I'll make out everybody—I make for you papers," and he made papers. Only the problem was

why he made those papers? He wants those—this lady with the two sons to send out in a group... you can't get through if the Germans does not permit us. So we have to make sure that the Germans put stamp on it, you know?[51]

We don't know the identity or the fate of the mother with the two sons, but her chances of crossing the border were grim indeed. Albert Fein remembered that upon arriving at the border, the Hungarian guards brusquely shipped them back to Kolomea—despite the German and Hungarian commandants' document stating that they were Christians and as such given the permission to return to Hungary.

Two interesting factors stand out in this testimony. The immediate one is that the Hungarian commandant had no authority without his German counterpart's signature to release and dispatch the family from Kamenets-Podolsk. The second factor was that they had to declare that they were Christians. As a further contradiction, the commandant of Kamenets-Podolsk, Meiler, was responsible for the establishment of the ghetto, yet he vehemently objected to the massacre. A survivor recounted how his staff saved a group of sixty young Hungarian Jewish workers, among them this survivor, locking them in his headquarters during the mass execution in the end of August. Meiler pointedly refused to participate in or attend the three-day slaughter. Another survivor remembered how common Wehrmacht soldiers were shocked and stunned by the massacre: "they have never seen such a thing."[52]

This confirms the often-mentioned paradox that the attitudes toward extermination were nuanced within the German military, and sometimes even in the Gestapo, which alerted and occasionally protected its Jewish workforce before an impending *aktion* in the ghettos. While we know that the German Army aided and abetted the extermination, it sometimes represented the "human" face of genocide: in these small and rather insulated "work communities," contact with the people whose fate depended on the authorities' sympathy, rage, kindness, or cruelty was frequent, close, and occasionally ambivalent. SS Police Leader Fritz Katzmann, the butcher of Galicia, bitterly complained that "the Wehrmacht authorities in particular aided the Jewish parasites by issuing special certificates without proper control."[53]

Hungarian policies during the war years, both governmental and military, and their approach to the Jews in Galicia as well as to the deportees, was also rife with contradictions. As indicated earlier, the officers on the Hungarian general staff were staunchly pro-Nazi and rabidly anti-Semitic. Chief of Staff Henrik Werth's successor, Colonel General Ferenc Szombathelyi, stated about the general staff: "[it] was Nazi-oriented to its core in its political outlook.... High ranking officers and generals around me were in every respect pro-Germans."[54] There were also repeated instances in which Hungarian troops on the ground, especially the field gendarmes, robbed the deportees upon delivering them to Galicia. The same can be said for their behavior toward the

Ukrainian population. The officer corps and the common soldiery, on the other hand, were much more sympathetic to the plight of the deportees and local Jewry. The six weeks of Hungarian rule over a large area of south and east Galicia provided a sense of security for local Jewish communities against the ferocious anti-Jewish sentiments and violence of the local population. This was in direct opposition to German policies that encouraged the local population to vent their simmering resentment and frustration by launching violent anti-Jewish pogroms all across eastern Ukraine.

Native Jews, remembering nostalgically the benign Habsburg period, viewed the entrance of the Hungarian soldiers with relief, often turning to them for protection against the marauding Ukrainian militias. A young boy's recollection could sum up the general view of the difference between the Germans and the Hungarians: "On the night of July 2nd, the Hungarians entered the town [Tluste]. By the morning they robbed many of the Jewish homes but did not kill." Indeed, Hungarian soldiers routinely entered Jewish homes and confiscated various items with the full permissions of their officers.[55]

A more idyllic view of the occupation from Kolomea, the headquarters of the Royal Hungarian Army, remembered by a Galician survivor who recalled a peaceful moment of the Hungarian occupation: "one beautiful summer evening, soldiers and officers were sitting on the lawn around bonfires.... One soldier picked up a violin and began to play a hauntingly sad melody, The Last Letter [*Utolsó Levél*].... From the balcony where I was standing, I could see men crying. Tears began to run down my own cheeks."[56]

Overall, the Hungarian occupation was a tense calm before the storm—at least in comparison with subsequent Nazi conduct. This was an uneasy military alliance because Hungarian policies at the local levels often led to confrontations with German military personnel, both on a personal and organizational level. On the one hand, Hungarian troops were the first ones to introduce, immediately after entering a town, arm bands for Jews: "ALL JEWISH MEN AND JEWISH WOMEN, anyone over the age of 12 must wear a 10 cm wide bright yellow ribbon on the right arm and on their outer clothing in the streets, roads and public places." It was accompanied by officially sanctioned plunder of Jewish homes that included food supplies, radios, and anything valuable.[57] On the other hand, the Hungarians did not tolerate unbridled violence against the Jewish communities. The German operational reports reflect this as they filtered back not only to the Nazi military headquarters in Berlin, but also reaching the German Foreign Office. First, the behavior of the Hungarian troops created a conflict: "Hungarians confiscated all food, so that the cities of Kolomea and Stanislawów, as well as the Dolina mountain district, will soon face famine, even according to Hungarian information. In Kolomea it was found that Hungarian soldiers were breaking into shops and plundering." What was more grievous is that these reports depicted the Hungarians as "pro-Jewish."

On July 15, 1941, for example, the same report to Berlin clearly pointed a finger at the Hungarian military, which "intervened immediately" if "actions against the Jews were carried out by the militia [Ukrainian]." This might have been the result of a visit by a Ukrainian delegation from Zablotow to "the German command in Lemberg (Lwów) demanding the expulsion of the Hungarians who befriended the Poles and the Jews."[58]

One flashpoint was the influx of thousands of Hungarian Jews into Galicia who were relocated over a six-to-eight-week period by the Hungarians themselves. Although a German Operational Situation Report from August 25, 1941, clearly indicates that there were some negotiations between the two sides, these were purely for the repatriation of the Jews. A Hungarian missive, dated two months later, indirectly reconfirmed that deported Jews who were able to return to Hungary could not be handed across the border again, but should be interned in Hungarian camps.[59] This agreement, however, was never fully implemented, and in reality, Hungarian authorities continued to expel refugees—months or even a year after they successfully returned from Galicia. Thus, the deportation itself was neither coordinated with nor approved by either the German military establishment or the political leadership in occupied Ukraine. The simultaneous expulsion of Romanian Jews in the Southern sector, reaching all the way to Kamenets-Podolsk and further north, complicated German planning even more.[60]

This set the tone for awkward encounters and tense situations between the two allies. As mentioned earlier, simultaneously with the mass murder in Kamenets-Podolsk, an Operational Situation Report noted that "members of the 10th Hungarian Pursuit Battalion have expelled more than 1,000 Hungarian Jews over the Dniester to Galicia. Einsatzgruppe Tarnopol promptly pushed them back."[61] However, these Jews were not allowed across the border into Hungary. The majority of them ended up in towns close to the Carpathian Mountains, which might have saved their lives—at least for the moment. A Hungarian officer met them in Tatarow, close to the border. On October 1941, he recorded in his diary that "as the Germans found these wandering masses inconvenient, they drove them back to the lines of the Carpathians."[62]

One of the immediate disagreements between the two militaries concerned Hungarian unwillingness to cooperate directly with the politics of genocide—at least in their sector of occupation. In Zhitomir, for instance, they stopped an action by the Ukrainian militia against the Jews on July 15, 1941.[63] At almost the same time and closer to the Hungarian border, the Hungarian commander, upon the imprisonment of large number of Jews from the small village of Richka, "immediately had the Jews released. In response, the Ukrainians complained to the Germans that the Hungarians were supporting the Jews ... the upshot was that the Germans replaced the Hungarians with military police of their own."[64]

Such interference into Ukrainian and even German operations against local Jews did not escape the attention of the German security agencies. An Operation Report dryly noted that "the Hungarian army... was apparently patronizing the Poles and the Jews ... the police action launched against the Jews was halted by the Hungarian army"[65] As a matter of principle, Szombathelyi opposed the atrocities against the Jews, and especially Hungarian participation in them. He was convinced that such actions negatively impacted the spirit and morals of the army. Hence, he considered it as his primary task to ensure order in the territory controlled by the Carpathian Group—the occupied territory between the Hungarian border stretching along the Carpathian Mountains and the Dniester River, where military rule was introduced on July 12.[66]

A rather telling episode of a curious encounter, or rather conflict between him and a newly arriving Gestapo attachment in Kolomea from Stanislawów, reverberated in contemporary Jewish documents on the diary pages of his staff officers, as well as his own recollections. True to the well-rehearsed modus operandi of newly arriving German security teams, an immediate bloodbath was planned: a distinct *"Intelligenz Aktion,"* which was orchestrated, most likely, by Hans Krüger himself around mid-July. It aimed to decapitate the Jewish intelligentsia in Kolomea. The SS detachment conspicuously ignored the fact that the headquarters of the Hungarian military in Galicia was located in the town. Szombathelyi cryptically mentioned this affair and his role in saving two hundred Jews from Kolomea "from the hands of the Gestapo, who were to be executed, in spite of the vehement German protestation."[67] This encounter rapidly became the material of legends among the Jews of southern Galicia, inflating the number of those saved even higher. A Hungarian general saved Jews who were in the process of digging their own grave. A contemporary account by a Galician survivor noted that when the Hungarian arrived, "he found the two hundred men, stripped naked, standing before graves they had been forced to dig for themselves ... after a brief exchange between the SS and the Hungarian commander, one of the German officers turned to the men standing in their graves. 'All right. Jew-swine, get your clothes on and get out of here.'"[68]

Two of his staff officers separately recorded this incident—though somewhat differently. In the recollections of his second-in-command, one of the victims' wives, who spoke French with him, "prostrated herself, embracing and kissing the boots" of this officer and beseeching him to secure the release of the group.[69] Upon being informed, Szombathelyi promptly sent another staff officer with an attachment of Hungarian soldiers, in the company of a military judge, in hot pursuit of the Gestapo contingent with the captive Jews. These diary notes confirm the details in a graphic reminder of an impending execution: "The Jews were lying already face down on the ground in groups of four, well covered by thick bushes, 30–40 meters from the road. Their foreheads pressed to the ground, as their hands clasped behind their necks." The timely and forceful intervention resulted in the release of the Jews who, after digging their own graves, were waiting for the coup de grâce. They returned with the Hungarians to Kolomea. While Szombathelyi's action can be construed as outright compassion, it might have also been a prestige and control issue. The notes of his second-in-command betrayed this motive for the Hungarian general was incensed that "the German commandant did not report to him and he had no knowledge of their presence on his territory." He not only demanded the release of the captive Jews, but ordered the SS "to leave the area since it is under his authority."[70]

The rescue of a group of Hungarian Jews in the village of Yazlovets from the hands of the Ukrainian militia, as recounted by László Zobel, might have not been motivated by purely humanitarian impulses either. The timely appearance of a Hungarian detachment stopped the execution of the group. This last-minute reprieve was prompted by the concern for the hundreds of corpses carried slowly by the currents of the Dniester River: "The Hungarian troops noticed and saw that masses of corpses were carried downstream by the River Dniester. There was a pontoon bridge resting on wooden pillars in the territory of Usechko, where these corpses got caught and endangered the bridge itself."[71]

In assessing the Hungarian military's attitude toward the deportees, it is hard to reconcile the official policy, which was uncompromisingly anti-Semitic, especially from the general staff, with individual rescue attempts by common soldiers and officers who were motivated sometimes by greed but often by compassion. Again, Szombathelyi's, views are enlightening because they betray an ongoing disagreement between himself and the general staff about the magnitude and rationale of the deportation. He sounded the alarm on July 14 about the mass expulsion, its wisdom, and it futility, especially without the establishment of consultative channels with the German military authorities. In his letter to the general staff, Szombathelyi suggested that they should ask the opinion of the Germans "before we begin this ambitious and long-term operation [...] lest there should be complications later on."[72] He saw the passing of control of Galicia to the German forces as inevitable and, based on German responses to this unilateral Hungarian action, his words were prophetic.[73]

As for the soldiers on the ground, the repeated warnings against offering assistance to the refugees indicated that common soldiers served as a main conduit of communication between the expellees trapped in Galicia and their families in Hungary. Soldiers also became involved in rescue work. A court-martial of Dr. Béla Deák, a Hungarian second lieutenant, caught while attempting to smuggle a mother and small child, shows that compassion among the soldiery toward the unfortunate refugees existed. Dated August 29, 1941, their permit carried, again, the official signature of Meiler, and the mother and son were listed as Christians. As arranged by the second lieutenant, they were transported on a Hungarian military vehicle to the border. During a meticulous search by border guards, the pair was discovered. The officer was arrested, and mother and child were expelled again to Galicia. The records of the trial also show that the husband died in Galicia and the expulsion across the border was done despite the mother being pregnant with her second child.[74]

The Jewish forced labor companies attached to the invading Hungarian Army became a vital informational pipeline between the deported and their families in Hungary.

A report to the minister of defense noted that family members requested information about, as well as assistance for, their loved ones from members of the labor battalions stationed in Galicia.[75] In turn, these forced laborers viewed the fate of their unfortunate coreligionists with a mixture of bewilderment and compassion. There were conflicting emotions when Jewish drivers in the Hungarian military, who served as regular soldiers and still could wear uniforms, were ordered to report to the transit camp in Kőrösmező to transport their fellow Jews to Galicia. In some cases, while these drivers were serving in the military, their families were deported in spite of pleas to spare them.

A Jewish forced labor company that was stationed in Kolomea in 1941–1942 provided both material and psychological support, albeit temporary, to the beleaguered local Jewish community. While the sympathetic company commander closed his eyes, they shared food, supplied medicine, and provided an informational window to the world.[76] The accidental meeting of deported family members and forced draftees was not uncommon. The story of a family dispatched to the transit camp, and the frantic search by their family members who were serving in the military following the deportation train from station to station, just one step behind, is one of the most heartrending episodes of the expulsion.[77] Samuel Gottesman's sister was also transported to Kamenets-Podolsk while her husband served in the military. The husband's initial effort to locate her by a Rusyn peasant and to smuggle her back was unsuccessful. Finally, on the second try they were able to bring her back through the Romanian border. After her return, though, she spent several months in hiding while separated from her young child.[78]

This shows that a successful escape was not without consequences. One of the forced laborers, who successfully smuggled back two deportees, was later arrested and court-martialed. A memorandum by the general staff, dated February 18, 1942, clearly blamed Jewish military drivers for the smuggling of refugees across the border back to Hungary. It also implemented preventive measures as well as corresponding penalties for such practices. News of the atrocities filtering back to Hungary often came through these forced laborers and regular soldiers as well.[79]

BETWEEN A ROCK AND A HARD PLACE: THE RESPONSE OF THE JEWISH COMMUNITY

The Jewish leadership in Budapest was cognizant of the inevitability of a deportation. The question was not *if* but *when* and *how extensive* it would be. Contrary to governmental announcements, there was no discernable emigration from Galicia across the Carpathian Mountains between the two world wars. Rather, by the end of the 1930s, Jews had been arriving primarily from Germany, Austria, Slovakia, and the Protectorate of Bohemia and Moravia, because of their "foreign" citizenship ending up in neighboring countries. It was obvious that in Hungary, there was an uncertain future for these Jews because they could not prove their Hungarian citizenship with the documentation required by the authorities. As for the ever-quoted Galicianer, it remained in the realm of a neurotic fixation, if not a common staple in the Hungarian political discourse, which only became more vocal with the outbreak of the war. The only imponderable question was how comprehensive the expulsion would be. In gearing up for such a prospect, two organizations were set up at the end of the 1930s: MIPI and OMZSA While MIPI concentrated on the legal issues facing large number of Jews in securing citizenship papers, OMZSA handled humanitarian aid to the rapidly expanding underclass within the Jewish community as a consequence of the Jewish Laws. With the onset of the deportation, though, both organizations were forced to retool and expand the scope of their rescue and relief work. OMZSA's role rapidly encompassed families of the deported who were left behind, especially the aged and the infirm. Such aid was not limited to the distribution of monetary aid for the elderly, but also finding accommodation and food for those who were unable to work.[80]

If we can characterize the initial responses from Jewish organizations to the lawlessness and arbitrariness with which the collection and deportation was carried out in the provinces and the consequent rapidly evolving humanitarian disaster, "circumspect" might be the proper word. Their approach to confronting the issue head-on was confounded by an uneasy relationship between the community and the ruling class. The trope of "dual loyalty" is perhaps a mild expression in this context. On the eve of World War II, governmental circles leveled ongoing and open accusations that the long-established and assimilated Jewish community in Hungary "felt more affinity toward the newcomers [Galicianers] than toward their Hungarian compatriots."[81] By 1941, this accusation of dual, or perhaps outright disloyalty, was entrenched in the common discourse. Even the prime minister at the time, Count Pál Teleki, who was considered staunchly anglophile, wrote that Hungarian Jewry "must choose between Hungary and their co-religionists, who are foreign to us and infiltrated into the country."[82] One of the unfortunate by-products of the emphasis on differences between the "old" and "Galicianer" Jews was a deepening rift within the Jewish community itself. We cannot find a more poignant example for this split than the comment by Dr. Lajos Láng, a noted Jewish financier, during a heated debate in the upper chamber of the Parliament about further economic restrictions on Hungarian Jews. Representing the assimilated segment of Hungarian Jewry, he rejected the planned anti-Jewish laws by stating that "it stigmatizes us, who have resided in this country for the past three hundred years, speak Hungarian, think Hungarian, and have nothing in common with the so-called eastern—caftan-wearing Jews."[83]

It would be a mistake to ignore or minimize this anti-Galicianer sentiment, which was reinforced by a divide between the highly assimilated and traditionally religious communities, within the Jewish community itself. Because of this, the expulsion was accepted initially by official Jewish circles as a necessary evil. The deportation was cloaked in euphemistic terms, such as resettlement and repatriation. The return of stateless Jews to their "homeland" and the refrain of secure employment and housing was aimed to blunt any Jewish communal or international protest. Thus, it was tacitly accepted. The responses by the two leading Jewish organizations reflected this governmental line by terming the expulsion in official Jewish documents as "resettlement," "removal," and "repatriation," or the "return of the foreign Jews to their birthplace."

Jewish officials felt reassured that it would be conducted lawfully, in a well-organized manner. Their official pronouncements were cautious and muted due to a concern that a confrontational approach could hamper their effectiveness in moderating governmental policies. The key word here was "moderating," because there were also Jewish circles who, if not supportive, nevertheless acquiesced to the relocation of the "stateless" Jews. How this translated on the street level can be found in the recollections of Natan Blum, a rabbinical student. After escaping from a horror-filled time in Galicia, including a stint in a slave labor camp, he was arrested again and confined in the central internment center in Budapest. Sharing a cell with a fellow prisoner, he was astounded to hear his Jewish cellmate, who was in the same predicament, openly advocating for his expulsion with the rationale that he was not a true Hungarian. Blum, on the other hand, incredulously posed the question: "How can a Jew do this to another Jew?"[84]

The tone of the Jewish leadership rapidly changed after the dramatic reports from the field offices in the provinces filtered back to Budapest. The list of blatant abuses was a long one, and damning. The reports described the law-breaking by provincial authorities as they collected and transported Jews regardless of the guidelines from Budapest. During the court proceedings after the war, it came to light the pressure the Jewish community, individual and collective, exerted on the main architects of the deportation. Among the officials, Siménfalvy and Pásztóy were specially targeted and repeatedly visited by Baroness Edith Weiss and other prominent leaders of MIPI. A particularly acrimonious meeting between Pásztóy and Margit Slachta, alluded to in a letter to Edith Weiss after the war, left a lasting negative impression on Slachta. They were joined by Károly Rassay and Endre Bajcsy-Zsilinszky, politicians from the opposition in the Hungarian Parliament who also approached Keresztes-Fischer personally.[85]

One of the most influential and vocal figures within the Jewish community, Samu Stern, also directly approached the minister of interior less than a week into the deportation, on July 17, with information about the lawlessness in arresting and dispatching the Jews to the eastern provinces. A successful businessman, holding the honorific title of Hungarian Royal Court Councilor, he had access to the highest levels of conservative aristocratic circles. He noted that the arbitrary policies in "Carpathian Ruthenia and eastern Hungary... expanded to Jewish individuals who, on the one hand, should not fall legally under expulsion procedures, and, the other, who were called upon to prove their citizenship or expanded to those that have clearly proven their citizenship." One of the sore points in this narrative, as Stern pointed out, was the deliberate attempt by the authorities in Budapest, without naming KEOKH, to slow down the review and approval of citizenship applications for thousands of individuals. He summed up his meeting with the minister by requesting a waiver from expulsion for those who are "neither from Poland nor Russia... and especially for the ones whose Hungarian citizenship is verified, or is being verified, or is pending."[86] However, he did not challenge the basic rationale for the expulsion.

The caveat of all these meetings was not that the deportation should be stopped, but only the collection of those that possessed Hungarian citizenship papers or were in the process of obtaining them. Furthermore, the deportation of large numbers of family members who served in labor companies within the Hungarian military was nowhere mentioned. In private meetings, though, this issue was brought up, as we learn from the postwar trial of Pásztóy. In his testimony during the trial, György Polgár, the head of MIPI, indicated that his primary grievance about the accused was that the wives of servicemen in the labor battalions and foreign-born women married to men holding Hungarian citizenship had been also taken away.[87] What neither of these Jewish leaders, or anyone else for that matter, addressed was the deportation of spouses, mainly husbands, from mixed marriages in which the Christian spouse held Hungarian citizenship. At least in Budapest, the Christian spouse children had the option to remain. As in the case of Samu, one could stay or follow their Jewish partner into exile voluntarily.[88]

During the next several weeks, a further and perceptible shift in the Jewish approach toward the deportation became more pronounced. It was prompted by frightening reports now filtering back from Galicia. By early August, the stream of information about the dire economic plight of the deportees and the hellish atrocities committed by Ukrainian irregular forces in the occupied territories moved the Jewish leadership to a more proactive stance. It evolved from protesting the abuses, especially in the provinces, to asking for the outright cessation of the deportations, and from assisting in identifying individuals with Hungarian citizenship at the ramp in Kőrösmező to channeling financial support to the remnants of Hungarian refugees in Galicia.

A report from Galicia on July 23 informed Budapest that "the Ukrainian population already protests the arrival and settlement of the deported Jews. In many places they expelled them brutally from the villages so that they had to find refuge in the forests.... In some places actual pogroms have started."[89] These graphic descriptions of the horrors taking place across the border were disseminated to various governmental entities as well as international channels; however, frantic appeals came also from other Jewish and non-Jewish sources. Slachta has been mentioned already relating to her unstinting efforts to stop the deportation, both on moral and religious grounds. Because of her contacts in the ruling circles, her often quoted report also reached the highest echelons of the Hungarian government as well as international organizations. Her unflinching prose, describing in hellish detail the conditions in Carpathian Ruthenia in general and the transit camp in Kőrösmező in particular, was also brought to the attention of the Jewish leadership, the Hungarian Red Cross, and later the International Red Cross, which suddenly realized that something had gone dramatically wrong.

Such evolution in Jewish thinking can be best understood by reviewing the actions MIPI took during and after the deportation. On July 27, 1941, the organization forwarded a circular requesting information about deported individuals who "possessed Hungarian citizenship," were above the age of seventy, or were seriously ill and "wrongfully removed." This aimed to eliminate the abuses taking place in collecting the Jews for deportation. A week later, on September 2, 1941, they became more proactive. Three regional representatives of MIPI from Carpathian Ruthenia approached Kozma with a set of grievances pertaining partly to the obstacles officials willfully placed on handling or forwarding citizenship applications and the arbitrary withholding of official assistance for crucial documents related to such applications.[90] This was, of course, within the purview of the government commissioner to handle. The two additional points, however, dealt with the desperate situation across the border, which was not a provincial issue anymore. The petitioners rather boldly appealed to the government commissioner for the return of Hungarian citizens who were unlawfully thrust across the border. As for the rest of the refugees, the representatives were looking for permission to supply "doctors, medicine, and extend humanitarian aid." Kozma's response, burying the request in official obfuscation, was predictable. He instructed the three to submit an application that should be directed to the Ministry of Interior but transferred via his office.[91]

After the intelligence about the bloodbaths sweeping across Galicia in October, and with the knowledge of Kamenets-Podolsk that had been wiped out almost completely of the Hungarian exile communities and their Galician coreligionists, the Jewish leadership in Budapest changed tactics again. While they still toed the official line in labeling the transported Jews as evacuees, in reality the proper term should have been "survivors." By November of 1941, they aimed to directly address the plight of these scattered individuals or families who might still be alive—with or without citizenship. Now the time came to fight for the remnants. A circular from November 9, 1941, solicited from the families of the exiles information about the "exact address at present of the 'evacuees' who have been known to you at the time of this letter's arrival." In this case, the aim was to identify and extend financial aid to all refugees across the region. In a surprising twist, MIPI, with the help of the Hungarian Red Cross, and the American Jewish Joint Distribution Committee (JDC)[92] succeeded to convince the ruling circles to allow the actual transfer of letters, packages, and money to the refugees if they could be located. Thus, on a follow-up circular, on November 17, MIPI informed its regional offices across the country that "as a result of our lengthy efforts, we succeeded to move the directorate of the National Bank of Hungary to approve the transfer of M. 30 /thirty marks/ to our co-religionists that were *'relocated'* to Eastern Galicia."[93]

This hard-fought humanitarian transfer system became operational, though on a very limited scale, in the latter part of 1941. Part of the problem was the dramatically reduced number of survivors who were saved from the periodical bloodbaths, conducted either by Ukrainian irregulars or by German killing squads all across the region. By mid-November, the estimated Hungarian "diaspora" could not have been more than several thousand people, at best, dispersed and intermingled with the local population in various ghettos. Another problem was the lines of communication, which were intermittent between the deportees and their family members back in Hungary. While a letter, dated on November 13, 1941, indicated that postal service, though heavily censored, between Galicia and Budapest began to function, the main conduit between the refugees and their family members in Hungary remained soldiers and forced laborers, who were banned explicitly to do so by military authorities. A testimony by a woman from Budapest, with two children and a husband, described how she was able to exchange letters with her parents, conveying their plight, in the spring of 1942. To her surprise, her parents informed her that "they received permission from the Hungarian authorities for the transfer of 40 zlotys [Polish currency] per month."

Just how effective this new initiative was in saving lives in Galicia is at best an open question. By that time, as noted, the deportees still alive were so dispersed and so few in number that locating them was beyond the capabilities of MIPI. In any case, the transfer of this monthly stipend was suspended after a few months, and while it was a lifesaver for this woman and her family, the fate of the other Hungarian refugees, as she summed it up, was grim: "they died one after another from hunger."[94]

Based on communication to and from the Hungarian Red Cross, one may assume that this organization actively supported these humanitarian efforts. While its archives were destroyed during the 1956 revolution, two extant letters requesting its intercession on behalf of the refugees, both in the transit camp and over the border in Galicia, testify to an ongoing cooperation. We know that as early as July 31, MIPI directly approached the organization, encouraged by Baroness Edith Weiss, to extend humanitarian aid to the deportees. Among the list of urgent issues in the transit camp was "health and social care." For those over the border, the list was more expansive, encompassing food and nutritional support, health services, communication, transfer of money, and delivery of care packages.[95]

This communication came on the heels of Slachta's appeal to one of the influential leaders of the Hungarian Red Cross, Countess József(né) Károlyi, who was also a member of the committee dealing with Polish refugees. While cloaked in deferential language so characteristic to a status-conscious society such as Hungary at the time,

Slachta did not mince words. She requested the countess' direct participation in the rescue of Hungarian citizens being removed to Galicia and a more humane approach toward those who by law could be deported. Again, Edith Weiss' name is mentioned in this context. Slachta did not fail to remind the countess of the responsibility of two organizations in this task: the Hungarian Red Cross and the Hungarian-Polish Refugee Committee.[96]

However, neither MIPI nor the Hungarian Red Cross were effective in moving the military authorities controlling Galicia, which were not impressed by such humanitarian concerns and considerations—neither in the transit camp nor in Galicia. As late as January 1942, the Hungarian general staff still threatened soldiers and forced labor men with court-martial for even delivering a letter.[97] The fact that MIPI was able to send monetary support, as short a period as it was, to a selected few was a veritable achievement. Otherwise, with Galicia being a military zone, civilian authorities were rendered powerless. A communication from the US State Department to the headquarters of the JDC in New York on September 26, 1941, summed up well the powerlessness of the Hungarian Red Cross: "The efforts of the Hungarian Red Cross to alleviate the situation have been quite ineffective. We believe that the situation should be made known to the International Red Cross and other groups."[98]

Thanks to Margit Slachta, Edith Weiss, and Erzsébet Szapáry, though, that was not the last word. By early December 1941, the International Red Cross in Geneva was informed about the dire situation of the survivors and, consequently, took up the issue of the Galician deportation and the potential support, if not salvation, of the remnants.

THE INTERNATIONAL DIMENSIONS

In a meeting with the representative of the International Red Cross, an emissary from the Hungarian Red Cross Mary Dobrzensky presented a confidential report on or around December 3, 1941. In the discussion, the number of refugees was appraised at "about 17,500." In order to send "relief supplies to these deportees," the Hungarian Red Cross requested the assistance of the international organization to obtain "prior authorization from the German authorities." In addition, the Hungarians intimated that such a mission should be headed by a representative of the International Red Cross and accompanied by a Hungarian "adjunct delegate." Finally, Dobrzensky emphasized the necessity of obtaining "lists of names of deportees with their addresses, in order to be able to send news to their parents in Hungary." In appealing for international involvement, the Hungarians understood that the government in Budapest would be more amenable to humanitarian involvement if the International Red Cross headed the efforts. Consequently, and reflecting on the urgency of her request, her appeal was referred to the Coordinating Committee for prompt action. Unfortunately, the response within two days was not favorable. The International Red Cross demurred, perhaps justifiably, from getting involved. They defended this inaction with the fact, as they stated in their official reply, that "Galicia, being a war-zone, where they have neither jurisdiction nor power to intervene. It's beyond the organization's mandate." In addition, the rationale for rejecting participation in the support and rescue activities was based on the enormity of the task at hand in the first place and "he [president of IRC] would hesitate to give the impression that we can do something. On the other hand, Hungary is the ally of Germany. It would have been easier for her to obtain something [permission] from the Germans than we could."[99]

The Hungarian efforts did not stop there. On December 14, 1941, a confidential letter from Budapest specifically requested the intercession of one of the influential leaders of the International Red Cross, Dr. Professor C. J. Burckhard, for the support and rescue of the survivors. While the initiator of the four-page plea was Sarolta Lukács, the vice president of the Hungarian Red Cross, the fingerprints of Slachta were all over the document. The deeply passionate appeal was based on the report that was penned by her and the delegation that had visited Carpathian Ruthenia and Kőrösmező four months earlier. Among the issues that the letter emphasized was the need "to send foodstuff, warm clothes, medications and the help of doctors to the deportees who currently lack everything," and "to go on site and make exact lists of the deportees and provide them with news from the family members from whom they are separated." This request and urgent plea unequivocally noted that the initiative needed to come from Geneva [underlined in the original document], because it was impossible to act alone from Budapest. If the initiative came from Geneva, the Hungarian Red Cross could join in. Lukàcs had already appointed a delegate, "Miss Hanna de Végh, who is well informed on the issue as she has worked for the Red Cross specifically on the question of Jewish deportees." Unfortunately, no extant reply can be found in the archives in Geneva. However, one of the ominous comments in the letter is a request to keep all the names of the central actors confidential, for there would be potential retribution and "persecution" in the event of a regime change in Hungary. The writer concludes with a final plea: "I truly hope that some help can be provided to the poor deportees who are victims of the worst tortures and whose situation reminds us that it is our Christian duty and simple humanity to intervene." The letter came from the crème de la crème of Hungarian aristocracy, yet considering that by that time Slachta had been placed under "discreet surveillance" by police authorities, their concern for potential "retribution" if an extreme right-wing political party would come to power was a justified one.[100]

The "internationalization" of information about the deportation did not start with the impassioned appeals to Geneva by the Hungarian Red Cross. The complex role that the JDC played, in partnership with MIPI, from the earliest stages of the expulsion introduced a new dimension to the saga of the 1941 deportation. It was a partnership that started in the late 1930s for extending assistance to thousands of people who needed citizenship papers. It rapidly evolved into providing badly needed humanitarian and financial support for the beleaguered Jewish community in Budapest and the provinces. Finally, it aimed to reach across the border to save the remnants of the Hungarian exiles.

Transcending the humanitarian domain, in the dissemination of vital information and stopping the ongoing atrocities, MIPI aimed to reach two somewhat opposing entities. As we have seen, they made contacts directly and indirectly with various governmental agencies and, especially, with the minister of interior. It was, however, a delicate balancing act. After initial hesitation, the various communal organizations within the Jewish establishment took the initiative of forwarding information emanating from the provinces, mostly from Carpathian Ruthenia, where the most egregious arbitrariness and disregard of governmental directives took place. Consequently, they also supplied firsthand reports on the shocking atrocities against the wandering expellees in the occupied territories.

Equally important was the informational channel that Jewish organizations had established through the JDC with the American Embassy in Budapest and the US State Department in Washington, DC. While the reports to the US State Department were covert, the information provided to Ambassador Pell was aimed to promote an American intervention on the ground. Thanks to this stream of reliable and timely intelligence, the Americans were well acquainted with the Hungarian actions. Working in tandem in the dissemination of intelligence about the situation within Hungary and in Galicia, MIPI and the JDC also had aimed to save the deportees and simultaneously aid their relatives.

If we can reconstruct this information flow, the reports from regional offices in the periphery kept pouring into the offices of MIPI about the conditions under which the collection and expulsion were conducted. On the other hand, military officers and forced labor battalions serving in the territories across the Carpathian Mountains supplied timely information about the appalling circumstances that the deportees were thrust into. Despite strict military censorship, information also poured back about the string of murders committed by Ukrainian irregulars and German murder squads. This knowledge was detailed, time-sensitive, and highly accurate. For example, a report about the Kamenets-Podolsk massacre was dated on August 30, 1941, a day after the conclusion of this infamous mass murder. It also well gauged the number of Hungarian victims. This up-to-date intelligence, straight from the murder sites, was transferred to the branch office of the JDC in Budapest, via MIPI, which collected and summarized it.[101] It's reasonable to assume that MIPI was walking a delicate line not to being accused of any anti-Hungarian activities.

In turn, the JDC representatives in Budapest, Joseph Blum, C. W. J. Newcomb, and later S. Bertrand Jacobson, can be credited with transferring this information to the attention of Pell. Simultaneously, telegrams were sent to Washington, DC, to the US State Department (Division of European Affairs) with the request to forward them to the attention of the JDC leadership in New York. In turn, Paul T. Culbertson, the assistant chief of the Division of European Affairs at the State Department, forwarded a "paraphrased" version of all telegrams to the JDC's headquarters in New York. This last request, however, was somewhat redundant, because New York was well informed about the chain of events in Budapest and Galicia, and made all efforts to respond accordingly. Ultimately, these reports were also brought to the attention of the American Secretary of State Cordell Hull.

Interestingly, JDC representatives did not communicate directly with their European leadership in Lisbon and its head, Morris C. Troper. He was updated on the situation from New York. The reports to Washington about the situation in Hungary and the occupied territories are grim in describing the abuses in the deportation process and the desperate situation of the deportees in Galicia. They urge the JDC to establish "food kitchens, housing, and medical facilities." One repeating motif is "to intercede with all possible authorities including Hungarian representatives in the United States and enlist public opinion." A follow-up communication from August 1, 1941, points out that "it is supremely important that you publicize the situation and bring pressure to bear on the Hungarian Government with a view of stopping further deportation." A week later, the communication advised the JDC to "enlist Hungarian personalities in the United States" who could influence Hungarian authorities.[102]

A second informational channel was with the American Embassy in Budapest and the Ambassador Pell. During Pell's tenure in the Hungarian capital, the American legation became the focal point of anti-German sentiments, especially for the strongly anglophile aristocracy, after the departure of the British envoy from Budapest.[103] The American Embassy staff in Budapest was well informed about the events taking place across Hungary, and especially the collection and cross-border transportation of Jews to Galicia. The atrocities committed there by Ukrainian paramilitary gangs and the systematic annihilation of the Hungarian Jews by SS attachments did not escape their attention either. The ambassador was privy to this intelligence.

During his short tenure from February 11, 1941, until January 16, 1942, the ambassador distinguished himself among American diplomats with a broad intellectual horizon and a deep knowledge of Hungarian history, including the peculiarity of the Hungarian situation in Central Europe, and the inherent inconsistencies in Hungarian–German relations. Yet he was a man of his time, with all its biases, prejudices, and subtle anti-Semitism. His anti-Semitism was not rooted in racial ideas, but more of an upper-class exclusivity, as he came from the wealthy and conservative class.

Yet he was also an internationalist and progressive within the confines of his social class. He recognized early the danger of Nazism and was the leading American proponent of fostering an awareness of the plight of European Jews in the 1930s and 1940s. During his short stint in Budapest, he gained firsthand knowledge of the anti-Semitic policies and the consequent wave of deportations in 1941.[104]

Pell's sources included the confidential reports from the JDC; however, he was well informed about the deportation from other reliable sources earlier—already at the commencement of the deportation. One of the leaders of the Hungarian-Polish Refugee Committee, who accompanied Slachta to Kőrösmező, Countess Erzsébet Szapáry informed him on July 17 that the Hungarian government had been deporting Polish Jews to the territory occupied from the Soviet Union for almost a week. In addition, the American military attaché, who maintained close contacts with Hungarian military officers, was able to tap into corresponding confidential information about the ongoing disaster in Galicia.[105]

In turn, the ambassador wasted no time in informing Secretary of State Cordell Hull about the "transfer [of a] large number of Polish Jews now in Hungary to an area in Galicia now occupied by Hungarian troops." The US State Department thus had immediate knowledge of the mass relocation. By late July, the ambassador was able to fine-tune this information by noting that the group of expellees included Hungarian citizens and refugees from Western Europe.[106]

Concurrently with his communication with Washington, Pell personally delivered a diplomatic missive on July 24, 1941, to László Bárdossy, the prime minister. The

FIG 7.3   Herbert C. Pell, the American ambassador in Hungary. *Public Domain, courtesy of the US National Archives.*

lengthy, five-page memorandum shared the American envoy's concerns with the prime minister about the atrocities taking place in Carpathian Ruthenia and adjacent areas, the situation in Galicia, and policies that contravened international conventions, like deporting international refugees holding Nansen passports. The memorandum was significant because it introduced an international dimension in this human and political drama, and created a direct line of communication between the two relating to the deportation. Bárdossy replied on August 2, reassuring Pell that the "expulsion-decree ... is exclusively applied to Jews of Galician origin ... all measures have been taken for supplying them during their transport." He added that those who were ill or over seventy years of age were "excluded from expulsion." His reply concludes with a reassurance that "a strict order has been given to all competent authorities to strictly respect the expulsion-decree and carefully avoid anything that would be in contradiction with its principles."

In retrospect, it seems that the prime minister was either misinformed or just an incompetent liar, because by that time similar reports from MIPI and other sources had reached the desk of Keresztes-Fischer. Even Pell was skeptical about the prime minister's reply. In his communication with the State Department on August 7, he opined that the reply "puts the case for the Hungarian government in an unduly favorable light."[107]

The American ambassador's protest, though, might have had an unexpected effect on Keresztes-Fischer's decree, which limited the scope of the deportation to Polish and Russian Jews. It was issued by KEOKH on July 30. The ambassador's reports, sent directly to the attention of the secretary of state made those in Washington rethink Hungarian policies. In a highly confidential missive, dated on August 13, 1941, the Royal Hungarian Embassy informed the prime minister about a rather frosty meeting with high-level State Department officials, who were, in the words of the Hungarian diplomats, "unfavorably informed by the American ambassador." During the discussions, one of the American representatives didn't mince words in bringing to the attention of the embassy that the Hungarian actions relating to the deportation were not well received by the America public. He added that this might have an impact on the two countries' relations: "the expulsion of the Jews produced a negative impression in America ... any Hungarian political decisions will be judged and the Hungarian American relations assessed, whether these actions were taken independently by the Hungarian government or forced by circumstances beyond its control."[108]

The sole objecting "diplomatic" voice was Pell's, and it provided an international dimension to the conduct of the deportation and its eventual suspension. His role in pressuring the Hungarians for the cessation of the deportation cannot be underestimated. Interestingly enough, his German counterpart in Budapest, Dietrich von Jagow, followed the activities in the American legation with open suspicions—even resorting to spying.[109] The American diplomat, though, didn't hold back his forceful protestation in his dialogue with the prime minister, which caught the attention of Bárdossy, forcing him to issue a revised directive as to who should be included in the expulsion.

The US State Department recommendation that "we are firmly convinced that Hungarian authorities would be influenced by American public opinion" was a wakeup call for the JDC in enlisting the media. The calls in every dispatch for increasing the American public awareness about the tragedy taking place in the Hungarian provinces and the mass murders in Galicia, and, consequently, exerting pressure on the government in Budapest, finally resulted in a host of revealing articles overseas. The Hungarian newspapers limited their coverage to reporting small episodes during the ongoing collection of the Jews. For example, the Jewish Telegraphic Agency noted on July 22, 1941, that "Budapest Radio today announced that 500 Jews 'mostly of Eastern origin' were arrested during a large scale police roundup." What happened after the arrest and expulsion remained unreported. Indeed, the daily news bulletin by the JTA became the main source of accurate news stories from Nazi Europe and especially regarding the murders in Galicia. In utilizing the testimonies by Hungarian officers directly from the trenches, they provided an accurate picture of the mass extermination of both Hungarian and Galician Jews taking place there.[110]

The Jewish press in America, on the other hand, became a channel through which the whole scope of the unfolding Holocaust became common knowledge in Jewish circles. By late October, reports from the killing fields, disseminated by the JTA, became front-page news in the Jewish press in New York and London. Through headlines in the Yiddish, English, and even Hungarian news outlets in New York, from late October, such as "Jews Dragged from Hospitals in Hungary for Deportation to Nazi-Held Galicia," "Thousands of Corpses in River Dniester," "Slaying of Jews in Galicia Depicted," the extermination of Hungarian Jews became widely known. While in Budapest the Kamenets-Podolsk massacre was discussed in hushed tones, often not believed, in New York, exact numbers of the victims and details of their murder were openly quoted.[111]

How much of this public information campaign changed the chain of events in Budapest or Galicia? It is at best an enigma. By the time these articles hit the streets of New York, the mass expulsions had stopped, and the murders in Kamenets-Podolsk, Stanislawów, Nadwórna, and elsewhere in Galicia had become a painful reminder of a failed Hungarian policy. For the halting of the deportation, Pell's role, from an American perspective, was more crucial. After the declaration of war by Hungary against the United States, the JDC played a limited role. Bertrand S. Jacobson returned to the United States with the rest of the American diplomats after Pearl Harbor and the declaration of war by Hungary. In New York, he was finally able to speak freely. In a press conference in New York City on March 13, 1942, he described in graphic details the mass murders taking place in Russia. On March 15, 1941, the JTA published an excerpt from this press conference by Jacobson. Blum, not being an American citizen, was able to continue as the director of the JDC in Budapest until the summer of 1944, when he was incarcerated in Bergen-Belsen.[112]

THREE UNCONVENTIONAL SAVIORS

Individual efforts inside Hungary to alter the chain of events during and after the deportation were equally important. Among the leading personalities, which included parliamentarians from the opposition parties, concerned church leaders, and leading politicians, the human tragedies of the deportation brought together an unlikely alliance of three exceptional women—Margit Slachta, Baroness Edith Weiss, and Countess Erzsébet Szapáry. They were willing to challenge the political, social, and moral status quo in a conservative society to stop the deportation, extend humanitarian assistance to the expellees, and help their family members who remained destitute inside Hungary.

Although they came from a diverse social, economic, and religious universe, they were well equipped to step into an arena where many of their contemporaries were afraid to go. They also represented three different organizations and constituencies, yet their role and mission intertwined. All three had direct access to the highest levels of Hungarian governmental circles and members of influential organizations such as the Hungarian Red Cross, the Hungarian-Polish Refugee Committee, and MIPI.

FIG 7.4 Head of the Order of the Sisters of Social Service Margit Slachta, parliamentarian, politician, and rescuer. Named as Righteous Among the Nations by the State of Israel.

Slachta was one of the most fearless church leaders in Hungary between the two wars. Elected as the only female member of the Hungarian Parliament in 1920, she was labeled as the only "real man" in the constitutional assembly. She didn't hesitate to challenge the power structure both on moral and legal grounds.[113] As the head of the Order of the Sisters of Social Service, she naturally gravitated toward serving society's oppressed and underrepresented. She was one of the rare Christian voices that openly opposed the Jewish Laws. In the public consciousness, she is mainly remembered for her heroic efforts to save the lives of thousands of Jews in Budapest during 1944, yet her exploits went far back into the 1930s. She stood side by side with the dispossessed Jews who were thrust across the border from Slovakia in the late 1930s—a pawn on an ongoing tit-for-tat over which country could expel more Jews. A year before the 1941 deportation, she was instrumental in alerting Hungarian society, and the government itself, on the expulsion of Jews from the small northern Transylvanian town of Csikszereda. By all accounts, it might have been a dry rehearsal for the much more encompassing Galician expulsion.[114]

Slachta's intrepidity, coupled with a razor-sharp intellect, could confront Ilona Horthy, the regent's wife as to "what will happen if Germany will not win the war?" She posed this question just a month after Hungary entered the war on the side of Hitler's Germany when both the Hungarian and German armies were deep in Soviet Russia. This was the time when Hitler already celebrated with raised glasses the demise of the Soviet Union. Slachta didn't hesitate to remind the reigning couple that there would be inescapable consequences for these crimes against "law, justice, and Christianity."[115] Tamás Majsai assessed Slachta's stance by noting that "in July 1941 she was one among the rare few within the church who knew what their mission should be."[116]

She utilized well her connections both in Hungary and internationally. Her close cooperation and friendship with Countess Erzsébet Szapáry, from one of the leading aristocratic families in Hungary, and Baroness Edith Weiss, from a noted family of Jewish industrialists, bought together an effective front against governmental policies, military intransigence, and the pervasive anti-Semitism of Hungarian officialdom. On February 18, 1969, Yad Vashem recognized Slachta as Righteous Among the Nations.[117]

Szapáry represented the nobility with a strong anglophile orientation. She was a leading member of the Hungarian-Polish Refugee Committee, established at the outbreak of World War II. She was also one of leaders of the Hungarian Red Cross. Her lineage, enhanced by her mother's title as a Polish countess, opened doors in diplomatic circles in the Hungarian capital. The organization saved thousands of Jews from among the Polish refugees—estimated at around 5,000. It provided Jewish refugees from Poland with shelter, money, clothing, and medical help, as well as forged Christian documents.[118] Politically active, she was member of a literary circle, which encompassed

FIG 7.5 Countess Erzsébet Szapáry, representative of one of the leading aristocratic families. She participated in rescue activities with Margit Slachta and Edith Weiss. Named as Righteous Among the Nations by the State of Israel. *Courtesy of the Hungarian National Museum/Photo Archives.*

the entire leadership of the Hungarian-Polish Refugee Committee, including Baroness Edith Weiss. This was established with a strong anti-Nazi orientation in the early 1940s. The group frequently invited the British ambassador to their weekly get-together. After the departure of the ambassador, Szapáry gained direct access to Pell. She provided vital information to the embassy about issues revolving around the deportation, which, in turn, was forwarded to Washington.

Utilizing her aristocratic pedigree, she was equally undaunted in confronting authority in Körösmező. As a member of the delegation to the transit camp, led by Slachta, she did not hesitate to demand that the head of the gendarmerie on site, a colonel, join them and release those who had documents attesting their Hungarian citizenship. Thus, she was able to save scores of people.[119] Her humanitarian work continued, as more Jewish refugees arrived in 1942 and 1943 when the Polish ghettos were liquidated and Hungary was relatively safe.

After the German invasion of Hungary, Szapáry was arrested by the Gestapo for her activities. She survived and immigrated to Switzerland after the war. On April 19, 1998, Yad Vashem recognized Szapáry as Righteous Among the Nations.

The third member of the trio, Baroness Edith Weiss is, in many ways, an enigma. In spite of her prominent role in the Jewish leadership in Budapest during the 1930s and 1940s, and as a leading member of the Hungarian-Polish Refugee Committee, we know painfully little about her. Very few documents, or even a photograph, have survived

FIG 7.6 Baroness Edith Weiss, daughter of the richest man in Hungary, Manfred Weiss. She was actively participating in the rescue activities with the Jewish leadership in Hungary. *Courtesy of Daisy Strasser.*

from the war years that could attest to the wide-ranging rescue activities she had conducted. She came from one of the wealthiest families in Hungary that had decided to convert to Christianity, yet she remained Jewish and assumed communal responsibility for the fate of the Jews in Hungary.[120]

As one of the leaders of MIPI, she confronted the main perpetrators of the deportation, including Ámon Pásztóy, Sándor Siménfalvy, and other officials. Her effectiveness is hard to gauge. She had contacts, like Slachta and Szapáry, in the Hungarian Red Cross.[121] Their appeals to this organization to aid the destitute family members left behind without sustenance and to reach out to those who were deported to Galicia resulted in the involvement of international entities such as the US State Department and the International Red Cross in Geneva.

Edith Weiss' sphere of influence encompassed the entire Hungarian political spectrum, from ministers to church leaders, and from a personal meeting with Pásztóy to an appeal to the Hungarian Red Cross. Her letters and personal meetings with the head of the Hungarian Reformed Church Bishop László Ravasz provide an indication for her comprehensive grasp of the rescue work. In spite of rejecting conversion, she was at ease with the bishop, who was not always pro-Jewish in his political views. Her words in a letter to the bishop paint a horrific picture of the attempted border crossings, with bona fide German permits (*Passierschein*), and the border guards' unwavering policy of rejecting and returning the unfortunates to Galicia: "The starving, depressed, and down-at-heel deportees—perhaps many hundreds or even thousands—are waiting across the border in the no-man's land." Appealing for Christian compassion, she turned to the bishop for his intervention in the repatriation of the few survivors from Galicia. How much this was useful cannot be ascertained, because no reply from the church leader has survived.[122] As for other luminaries from the Catholic or Evangelical churches in Hungary, there were no raised voices or protest of the deportation.

As a key figure in the leadership of MIPI, Weiss was privy to the reports from across the border. The organization rapidly abandoned its original mandate of extending legal assistance to Jews who needed to prove their citizenship, and refocused its efforts, from late summer of 1941 and on, on saving lives and supporting individuals whose family members were deported. In this mission a partnership developed, rather naturally, with the representatives of the JDC. This partnership, in turn, brought on board Ambassador Pell. Equally important was the channeling of these reports not only to Ambassador Pell, but also through the embassy to the American Jewish press.

Weiss's friendship with Slachta became stronger after the war. With the ascendancy of Communism in Hungary, Slachta fled the country at the end of 1948. Both of them settled in the United States, in New York City and Buffalo, respectively. They remained close friends. By that time, though, the tables had turned. Weiss became part of a network that smuggled out Christians, the members of the Order of the Sisters of Social Service who were persecuted by communist authorities in Hungary.

SEARCHING FOR ANSWERS

As one of the preeminent chroniclers of the Hungarian Holocaust phrased it, the 1941 deportation was a Jewish as well as a national trauma. It became a watershed event in the two communities' coexistence. It might have also contributed to the dismissal of Bárdossy as the prime minister half a year later for seriously entertaining the hopes of a continuation of the deportation that might have included the entire Jewish community.[123]

The rescue and protection of Jews during 1941 and 1942 was a heroic effort by those ranging from simple but caring individuals to moral leaders and organizations. Yet it met with limited success. The Galician deportation, which started in July 1941, ended more than a year later. During this year, intermittent transfer of new groups or escaped and consequently arrested Jews to Galicia was conducted by KEOKH or independently by border authorities.

On October 28, 1942, Keresztes-Fischer ordered all authorities to stop the redeportation of Polish-born Jews and other stateless aliens; however, the intermittent transfer to Galicia continued until 1943. By some estimates, only 10 percent of the deported were able to return and resume "normal" lives. Most of the stories of those who rescued Jews or the ones who were able to escape on their own can be gleaned from individual memoirs. Perhaps the most convincing explanation for the paucity of early and more extensive "rescue" literature may be attributable to the taboo on discussing the Holocaust during the Communist period in general. On the other hand, some of the main actors in the rescue efforts in 1941 belonged to religious circles, the aristocracy, and the upper bourgeoisie—an anathema in Eastern Europe after the war, and those heroic stories had to be squashed. It's perhaps telling that the first real mention of Margit Slachta's name and her activities in 1941 was dated 1986, at the twilight of Communism in Hungary.[124]

While newspapers in London and New York openly reported on the massacres taking place in Galicia, international responses to the deportation and its aftermath were limited to the American diplomatic outpost in Budapest and, ineffectually, to the International Red Cross in Geneva. The protestations by Pell introduced an international element in this human and political drama. There was continuous and direct communication between him and Bárdossy relating to the deportation. We know that Keresztes-Fischer's decree, which limited the scope of the deportation to Polish and Russian Jews, was issued on July 30. The memorandum by the American envoy, informing the prime minister of the atrocities as well as the policies contravening international conventions, was dated July 24. The causality is clearly there.

Evaluating the role that Jewish organizations, specifically MIPI, OMZSA, and the JDC, played is a more complicated one. While the JDC had the backing of an American-based international organization, close connection with the embassy in Budapest, and the Department of State in Washington, MIPI was more circumscribed in navigating Hungarian political realities on the ground. The organization had to steer carefully around a fractious Jewish establishment within Hungary itself. One can see a process of radicalization in MIPI's responses as the deportation proceeded. With its limited ability to maneuver, MIPI made valiant efforts to first rectify malfeasance, especially by public officials. Then it aimed to stop the deportation and, finally, to extend support both at home and across the border.

In several initiatives, however, it failed, at least until late 1942. There was never any government-sanctioned return of Jews with Hungarian citizenship from Galicia put into effect. Nor was permission ever given to repatriate Jews who were languishing across the Galician border after being captured by military and police authorities. By some estimates, over 2,000 unfortunates were redeported to Galicia to their certain murder. As an already quoted survivor phrased it, they "disappeared without a trace."

8

OPENING OLD WOUNDS
Responsibility and Consequences

"Wer wird für das alles bezahlen?"

"WHO WILL PAY FOR ALL THIS?" ONE OF THE HUNGARIAN DEPORTees who was forced to dig a mass grave overheard this introspective question uttered by an SS officer in a moment of "soul searching" during the mass shooting of Hungarian deportees and local Jews in Buczacz, Galicia. While his musing is especially poignant considering the enormity of the crime, the echoes of this question reverberate over and over in the story of the 1941 deportation and mass murder. One only needs to recall the similar words of Major Wilhelm Trapp, commandant of Reserve Police Battalion 101: "If this Jewish business is ever avenged on earth, then have mercy on us Germans."[1] While often there are no answers to be found, questioning is an essential part of comprehending the Holocaust. This moment of reflection by a participant in the atrocity indicates a foreboding that there might be consequences for the murders.

This contemplation, however, transcends borders and cultures. The reflections of a Hungarian soldier, a witness, who, upon observing the arrival of hundreds of displaced Hungarian Jews in Ivanovce, raised an imponderable question: "although I tried to forget, the most shocking moment was my meeting these Jews.... It is impossible to comprehend a reality, which so clearly confounds human logic, human compassion, and our own humanity—our way of life.... Our everyday conduct and actions," he wrote on August 18 about the treatment of these Jews. It "created an unsolvable contradiction with our inner most feelings.... And in our minds, each one of us struggled with the silent question; *if this can happen at home with our own families, what are we doing here?*"[2]

Finally, the often-quoted report of a delegation under the leadership of Margit Slachta, the head of the Order of the Sisters of Social Service, that visited Carpathian Ruthenia with the aim of stopping the expulsion, brings home the ultimate contradiction between atrocity and Christian morality. An eyewitness to the relentless round-ups, transportation, and brutal treatment of the unfortunates, Margit Slachta, a deeply religious person, not only asked an existential question but raised an accusing finger:

> Witnessing such cross-border transports is tantamount to the weightiest indictment against our highest authorities that are either irresponsible and devoid of human conscience or motivated by sheer hatred and a desire to gain approval in the eyes of the 'new world order' by deliberately exposing thousands of people to relentless agony and almost certain death. This is done in contravention of both the letter of the law and the spirit of our unwritten moral code. *One only wonders how people who consider themselves Hungarians and Christians as well as responsible administrators are not afraid of the retribution that their lawless actions might precipitate.*³

The questions posed by these four participants—the perpetrators, the witness, and the rescuer—in the unfolding drama could encapsulate the four phases of the Hungarian deportation: expulsion, the long journey across Galicia, waves of mass murder, and escape. These reflections might be the proper epigraph or this story because they present an inner conflict about the moral and ethical underpinning of the 1941 deportation and, indeed, genocide. These moments of reflection by perpetrators, witnesses, and rescuers inject into this account a sudden recognition that these actions of murder will not be forgotten and have far-reaching consequences. The difference between these questioners was that Margit Slachta's soul-searching plea and warning reached the highest echelons of the Hungarian leadership. How much this changed the course of history, though, begets another question. How much did those in places of authority and responsibility understand or care about the gravity and costs of their action?

THE QUESTION OF LOGIC

The musings of these witnesses pose a dilemma about the rationale for the deportation and subsequent genocide in 1941 and 1942. We, of course, could wish that policymakers in the Hungarian leadership would have grappled with similar moral imperatives before embarking on their course of action. There was neither German political or military pressure, nor defendable demographic or economic reasons, for sending thousands of human beings to their death.

Obviously, this was not a mere case of criminal incompetence. The dilemma of the Hungarian authorities was an unwinnable compromise that also became the harbinger, or more accurately a connecting thread, to the full Hungarian Holocaust in 1944. The leadership had implemented, after the spate of killings in Galicia became known, a deliberate policy of denying the return of thousands of victims, with the clear knowledge that this would spell their death sentences. This knowledge did not come only from Jewish or American sources. A direct military communication to the office of the prime minister in September 1941 did not mince words: "the German military in Galicia and the former Soviet territories are continuously executing quite a large number of Jews."[4] With this information at their disposal, the Hungarian general staff still opted to establish a German–Hungarian joint committee for the prevention of infiltration by returning both Hungarian and escaping Galician Jews. In cooperation with the gendarmerie and police forces, the military "investigated numerous cases, handing over the offenders to the respective law-enforcement agencies for prosecution."[5] That this was neither morally justifiable nor defendable did not escape the attention of Lieutenant General Ferenc Szombathelyi in his capacity as commander of the Carpathian Corps, which was mandated to transport the deported Jews to Galicia. By some, in the upper circles of the military, he was considered to be pro-Jewish.[6] While it might be an exaggeration, he was definitely not an anti-Semite. His sobering comment comes to mind as we consider his dispatch to the general staff about the "Jewish Question." His words, drafted in August 1941, reflected his ambivalence toward the deportation and murders that he witnessed in Galicia: "we achieved much more and earlier than the Germans [in Jewish policies] but because we tried to emulate them, we did everything more idiotically. They drained the Jews, dispossessed them, while we want to beat them to death."[7]

There was a marked reluctance on his part, contrary to the chief of staff and the minister of defense, in carrying out the deportation order. An indication of Szombathelyi's ambivalence was expressed in a letter penned to the general staff on July 14, 1941, in which he explained that it was impossible and inadvisable to begin relocation on a massive scale without prior coordination with the Germans: "The organized resettlement of the Jews might run into obstacles, or might not be approved by the Germans." Although he brought up logistics as an issue, he also was motivated by moral considerations in light of his career.[8]

However, there was no lack of willing accomplices in the expulsion of the Jews. For the successful drive behind this policy, the civilian and military authorities could rely on the support of a committed mid-level state bureaucracy. The collection, transportation, and final transfer to Galicia of thousands of people would not have been possible without the enthusiastic participation of an administrative stratum of law enforcement agencies in Budapest and major cities, as well as provincial municipal officials that willingly ignored or outright contravened the laws of the land. They provided the bureaucratic foundation upon which genocide could be built. There were countless examples in the annals of the 1941 deportation of chief magistrates who ignored directives from Budapest and police commissioners who openly dismissed the authority of the Ministry of Interior. The action, or inaction, on the part of the military leadership was criminally negligent at best and deliberately unlawful at worst. One cannot forget the role of the commander of the transit camp, Lieutenant-Colonel Rudolf Orbán, who went beyond military regulations to make a living hell for the suffering multitude before their expulsion across the border. Even more grievous was his obstruction of the officially sanctioned work of Nándor Batizfalvy, the police officer from KEOKH. Batizfalvy was sent specifically to the camp for enforcing KEOKH's directive of limiting the deportation to genuine "Polish" and "Russian" citizens. He was instructed to return all individuals who were deemed to be Hungarian citizens, over seventy years old, and or too ill to be transported. The camp commander's constant interference, restricting, or rather counter-commanding the rescue work of Batizfalvy did not escape the attention of Margit Slachta. For example, the police officer provided the necessary papers for the release of a number of prisoners who were directed to return to their village the next day. During the night all of them were shipped over the border to Galicia.[9]

One can argue, of course, that Hungarian military authorities were not bound by the directives of the Ministry of Interior. However, the colonel's actions exhibit a malice that might be described as genocidal anti-Semitism. And he was not alone. An exasperated Kozma complained in a dispatch to the prime minister that "it's hard to tolerate mentally how even minor subordinates can contravene political initiatives."[10] He should have known; his office flouted, countless times, directives from the Ministry of Interior. Again, Margit Slachta's rhetorical question comes to mind: "One can only wonder that these officials, who consider themselves Hungarian and Christian, and consciencious civil servants, are not affraid of a retribution as a consequence of their illegitimate actions."[11] Apparently, they were not overtly concerned, because one cannot find even a single example in the history of the deportation or its aftermath that any of the perpetrators were called out, disciplined, or brought to justice for their disobedience and outright criminal behavior. Instead, Margit Slachta was placed under "confidential and discreet surveillance" on October 21, 1941, by the central command of the Royal Hungarian Gendarmerie in Budapest.[12] As an outside American observer, again, Eleanor Perényi's words come to mind about contemporary Hungary where "privilege was everything."[13]

In retrospect, the whole tragic affair within the framework of the Holocaust can be only partially attributed to internal pressures within the Hungarian political constellation, where a constant search for scapegoats opened the bottle with the proverbial genie. It found in the image of the foreign Jew an almost neurotic fixation with the "mythic Galicianer." We have discussed extensively in the previous chapters the creation of the image of the "Galicianer"—a political expediency born from racial hatred—which came handily to the political right in Hungary. Thus, the second component was the urgency for neutralizing the radical elements in Parliament as well as the public life.

However, there was a third, equally weighty motive for the deportation to which we have only alluded. The whole idea of the 1941 deportation was also cloaked in an "ethnic purge" that was powered by an economic rationale. To quote again Aly Götz dictum, it was fueled by the "least desirable of the seven deadly sins: Envy."[14]

Sándor Márai, the highly acclaimed Hungarian writer and a keen observer of his country's social and political scene, placed the responsibility squarely on the shoulders of a "ravenous Christian middle class." He minced no words: "This Hungarian middle class that is corrupt to the core still refuses, or doesn't dare to face reality. They dream about some secret new weapon that will fix everything and they will receive a confiscated Jewish property as a reward: that's all they think, understand, and hope."[15] This acerbic comment, written in 1943, describes an internecine encounter between the two "middle classes" in Hungary. It implies, as an observer postulated, that "a showdown between ... the Jewish and non-Jewish middle class was essentially inevitable."[16]

This "showdown" reached its final apotheosis in the almost total destruction of Hungarian Jewry in the spring of 1944. But, to understand this terminus "bookend" for the Hungarian Holocaust, the examination of 1941 is imperative. It harbored the idea of a final reckoning with this "irksome" minority. A revealing document, dated on April 30, 1942, penned by the Sub-Committee for Judicial-Authority of the City Council of Ungvár (Uzhgorod, Carpathian Ruthenia) blatantly advocated the full ghettoization, deportation, and full-scale plunder of local and Hungarian Jewry as a whole—and in the name of Christianity. It could be considered a working blueprint for the actual deportation in 1944. It promulgated the establishment of a central organization, which would implement the expulsion. The town's mayor, in turn, enthusiastically endorsed it and even deemed necessary to forward this memorandum directly to the attention of Minister of Interior Keresztes-Fischer.

To the credit of the authorities in Budapest, though, a terse, handwritten reply acerbically admonished the authors of this document about their unsolicited advice: "Finding a solution to this question is the responsibility of the Hungarian Government. Therefore, we are in no need of your lecture."[17] By that time, the utter pointlessness of the 1941 deportation and the corollary horror was already known. The Hungarian political gravitation toward the West was also in motion. Yet, this document is instructive about the contemporary ideological undercurrents that presaged the final act of the Hungarian Holocaust, with its total economic plunder and physical annihilation of Hungarian Jewry in 1944.

While this conflict was particularly relevant to Budapest and major population centers across Hungary where the two middle classes lived and competed side by side, in the outlying provinces, where Jews constituted the virtual middle class, a demographic reengineering had to take place prior and during the expulsion. There was a concerted effort of transfer and resettle skilled Christian craftsmen and merchants from the interior to the periphery of the country. This, however, was not always successful without infusion of governmental support.

The 1941 annual report by Miklós Hermann, director of the Máramaros County Administrative Authority, acknowledged that "the most welcomed governmental decision of 1941 was the transfer of Jews of foreign nationality [to Galicia]." He also observed, "I am pleased to point out that the most significant and foremost development of the year 1941 was the transfer of industry and commerce in Carpathian Ruthenia to Christian hands." Indeed, the writer considered the "Christianization" of the industry and trade as the biggest achievement of the year: "With the help of the Christian craftsmen and traders that settled down in the territory under my authority, we have achieved that the Jewry has been ousted from all important areas of trade and industry."[18]

Miklós Kozma, who expressed some remorse at the end of his life for the role he played in this ill-fated adventure, and others were in the dark about rational priorities. They devoted themselves to destroying a segment of their society that was the most productive, however Jewish it might be. His policies, coupled with the successive Jewish Laws, decimated the region's already teetering economy.[19] The highly acculturated and assimilated Jews, by some estimates not more than 6,000 to 7,000 people, who were taken from Budapest and the internment camps, were the obvious minority within the displaced population. Jews from Upper Hungary, Carpathian Ruthenia, and Transylvania, on the other hand, from where the majority of the victims hailed, while considered backward, were perhaps the most willingly "assimilating" group within a mélange of a multiethnic communities of Hungarians, Romanians, Ukrainians (Ruthenian or Rusyns), Slovaks, Germans, and Jews.

In contrast to the native population of Carpathian Ruthenia such as the Rusyns, who subsisted in dire poverty from agriculture in rural and inaccessible areas, the majority of the Jewish community, solidly middle class, resided in the cities and towns.[20] Similar demographic distribution could be found in other regions of the periphery. It should not come as a surprise that one of Miklós Hermann's proposals was to deport the remaining Jews from Carpathian Ruthenia and replace them in the cities with the poverty-plagued rural Ruthenian population. "The weightiest administrative problem that my county faces," he wrote in 1942, "can only be resolved with the deportation of the Jews.... Upon removal of the Jews, the Ruthenian population, should be forced by the authorities to replace them in various towns and villages."[21]

In general outlines, he represented the views and economic priorities of a municipal and regional administration, especially in the provinces. Unfortunately, he failed to provide an explanation as to what this rural population, steeped in agricultural poverty, would do or how it would exist in the cities. Nathaniel Katzburg's comment underscores this point: "Carpathian Ruthenia was the only eastern region where a sizeable Jewish proletariat lived."[22] Countering the claim of a community that resisted assimilation, contemporary statistics show that among all minorities, the Jews in this "periphery" were also the most ardent and staunch supporters of the government's Magyarization drive. The American Eleanor Perényi noticed this contradiction: "The Jews, too, were pro-Hungarian. Among all the stupid things the Hungarians did perhaps none was more stupid than their persecution of these people who were so persistently loyal to them."[23] Based on the 1941 census, their number in the general population was about equal to that of the non-Jewish, Hungarian minority. They overwhelmingly identified themselves as Hungarians. Their children attended Hungarian schools in Carpathian Ruthenia and elsewhere in much higher numbers than other minorities, and despite the acute backwardness and poverty in the outlying provinces, they represented an emerging and well-educated middle class as well as a nascent civil society.[24]

This picture was in glaring and dramatic contrast to the common perception of the "backward and deeply religious orthodox Jewry" ingrained in the imagination of the administrative elite, a large segment of the general public, and even the assimilated Jewish community inside Hungary. Within the context of rapidly escalating anti-Semitism, the political pragmatism of neutralizing the extreme right wing of the Hungarian political spectrum played an obvious role in the 1941 deportation. However, in trying to find a more comprehensive explanation, we might also add a virulent strain of anti-Semitism fueled by an insatiable economic opportunism. Since the local Ruthenian population in Carpathian Ruthenia was mainly rural and extremely poor, there was nothing that the authorities could expropriate except land. Thus, the Jewish middle class was deemed a logical and "ripe" target.[25]

The 1941 deportation came on the heels of three pieces of anti-Jewish legislation, and numerous restrictive regulations, enacted from 1938 to 1941, which aimed to curtail, if not wholly eliminate, a Jewish role in Hungarian economic life. The wishful thinking of an organized emigration from Carpathian Ruthenia and other areas was a common staple of the political discourse. By 1941, though, policymakers realized that with the closing of borders across Europe, they could not provide a viable solution to the perennial "Jewish Question." Thus, the mass expulsion of Jews in 1941 was based on the "economic" rationale of expropriation and transfer of Jewish properties and concentration of enterprises into Hungarian Christian hands. The most effective Implementer was the Hungarian military itself, which controlled the newly acquired territories. Chief of the General Staff Henrik Werth openly advocated that Jewish wealth "must be transferred into Christian ownership."[26]

This meant full-scale financial and economic plunder and despoliation. A meticulously drafted memorandum, dated July 25, 1941, and originating in the office of the government commissioner of Carpathian Ruthenia, gives credence to this statement. It provides a list of names of nearly two hundred Jewish residents from the border region of southern Carpathian Ruthenia who should be deported. Not surprisingly, it contains only affluent merchants and manufacturers, outright dispensing with the pretext of "resettling alien, stateless, or 'Polish or Russian Jews.'" Instead, it promulgates full removal of the Jews from the region, making it a "Jew-free" zone, with their property being expropriated. The author of the document does not attempt to hide his underlying motives and rationale for cleansing the region: "we have to expel the repugnant Jews who only exploit visitors to this area.... We need to get rid of the parasitic Jews so that all economic benefits and opportunities of this border region could be transferred into *Christian hands*."²⁷

THE TALE OF TWO ARMIES

An assessment of the role and responsibility of the Royal Hungarian Army and the specific part the Hungarian general staff played in the expulsion leaves little ambiguity. The Hungarian general staff never produced or implemented a policy or plan that directed the military how to resettle the ill-fated expellees in any orderly fashion. Henrik Werth lied to the Council of Ministers in their meeting on July 1, 1941. The aim was, as Miklós Kozma conveyed to the prime minister, to expel the unfortunates beyond the Dniester River, which provided a natural barrier for potential returnees. The military assigned at least fifty trucks per day for transporting the deportees. A military driver observed that "there were no instructions given to the trucks as to a location or destination ... [the soldiers] became tired of taking them any further."²⁸ Seeing the poverty, hunger, and sufferings of the wandering multitude in Galicia, in close proximity to the border, Reserve Second Lieutenant Alajos Alapi Salamon described a picture of utter chaos. He noted in his diary in October 1941 that "there was neither order nor method to this expulsion."²⁹

Coming from these soldiers, both from the lower ranks, this is perhaps the most damning assessment of the role the Royal Hungarian Army played in the 1941 deportation. There is no reason to revisit the never-ending and indeterminate marches from

FIG 8.1   Two gendarmes with German soldiers. *Courtesy of Dr. Sándor Szakály.*

place to place, interspersed with rape and killing sprees by the Ukrainian irregulars. Nor the moments of how the accompanying gendarmes and soldiers routinely robbed the refugees of all valuables. This was especially true for the Jews from Carpathian Ruthenia. One deportee noted in a letter to Budapest a difference between the attitudes of the military personnel toward "poor Jews with side-locks, who are so meek, toward which they are rude" and those that were expelled from Budapest who were accorded more respect. Either way, the common directive sounded like a well-rehearsed command: "Now forward march; anyone who dares to turn back—a bullet to his head!"[30]

The behavior of the gendarmerie by all accounts was rude, brutal, and merciless. While they were not part of the Hungarian military itself, the field gendarmerie reported operationally to the military authorities in Galicia. Their conduct during the arrests, transportation, looting the meager belongings of the deportees, and reported participation in killings is well documented. One of the rescuers, Countess Szapáry, "took out her camera to document the inhuman way the victims of the deportation were loaded on lories: desperate, weeping women and terrified, sobbing children."[31] It also left deep marks on the memories of the survivors. There were numerous instances of soldiers and officers rescuing Hungarian expellees from the hands of marauding Ukrainian bands. But several survivors have also mentioned the participation of the field gendarmerie (*tábori csendőrség*) attached to the Royal Hungarian Army in the killing process itself. By all accounts, regular army personnel "did not pull the trigger," at least not in Kamenets-Podolsk. However, they refused to block the genocide there, which was a distinct German concern. There is also incontrovertible evidence that they were complicit in the collection and leading of the Jews on the second day to the murder site in Kamenets-Podolsk. At least two Hungarian officers partook in the final dinner, celebrating a "job-well-done of three days of murder," which further points to the fact that they were present and witnesses to the genocide.[32]

That German border units engaged in mass killing on the Galician side of the border should not come as a surprise. The extermination of the Jews had become state policy very early in the war against the Soviet Union. Is it possible to say the same about the Royal Hungarian Army? Based on circumstantial evidence and the recollections of survivors, the Hungarian field gendarmerie or border guards might have joined the Germans in their random killings of Jews—sometimes on both sides of the border. For example, in the Galician border town of Dolina, rumors were rife about Hungarian border guards and gendarmes robbing and killing returnees or escaping Jews from towns in Galicia. A member of a forced labor battalion stationed along the Dniester River area recalled after the war that the brother of a fellow laborer confided in him about the murder of his entire family, along with many expellees, by Hungarian gendarmes.[33]

One, of course, did not need to pull the trigger over mass graves to kill. Several sources, independent of each other, reported atrocities along the Dniester River. A

Hungarian soldier recorded in his diary that "large groups were driven into the Dniester to hasten their crossing the river, by Hungarian soldiers who followed the orders of their officers. Only a few succeeded in that." The name of Lieutenant Simon, the commander of a sapper battalion, pops up repeatedly in documents and survivors' testimonies as the initiator of these atrocities. The same sources also mention the hundreds of dead bodies of men, women, and children floating around the bridges of the Dniester.³⁴ Other Hungarian and Galician eyewitnesses supported this description. A member of a Hungarian forced labor company recounted that under the command of "Engineer Lieutenant Simon," "a sergeant from Nyiregyháza, Jenő Király had 17 people thrown into the Dniester, people deported from Hungary." Many of them drowned or were shot. Corroborating and augmenting this account, a Galician survivor's diary tartly noted that the same officer,

> a notorious Hungarian officer with the last name of Simon, stood on the bridge . . . supposedly the son of some count or prince, who often made arrangements with these people that for a certain sum of money he would let them through, but when they arrived at the bridge, he robbed them of everything, threw [them] naked into the river, and shot at them. Far from the bridge, all along the banks of the river, bands of Ukrainians wandered, who did the same things . . . so that the water of the Dniester was pink from blood, and Jewish corpses floated on it like dead fish.³⁵

The Hungarian general staff and its chief, Henrik Werth, was one of the initiators and prime movers of the deportation. In the autumn of 1941, a change of personnel in the command structure of the general staff and the Carpathian Corps did not signal a discernable change in attitude toward the desperate Jews attempting to return to Hungary. There was a deliberate official policy at the highest levels that aided and abetted the killing of the remnants. Even after the Kamenets-Podolsk "affair" became common knowledge, high-level officials made it a priority to prevent the return of the survivors. A report from October 1941 summed up well: "Over the border, similar horrors, like the Kamenets-Podolsk 'pogrom', are continuing unabated. Returnees are reporting that entire villages and settlements are laid to waste in many areas, without regards, just to get rid of them."³⁶

A flurry of military commands, dating from September 23 and 27, 1941, and issued by the new commander of the Carpathian Corps, Major-General Ferenc Farkas, forbade military personnel to offer any assistance to the deportees. This included the transfer of letters, packages, and money between the refugees and their relatives in Hungary proper. It is worth pondering how "Jewry can grievously harm Hungary's national security and national economy with such actions [transfer of letters]," as the Major-General phrased it in his decree. More important, though, was the specific directive, originating from the office of the chief of the general staff, which aimed to stop the smuggling of Jews who were desperately trying to return. The language is even more uncompromising: "My order is to implement the strictest measures for the prevention of such practices and enact the most draconian punishments for those who are guilty of them." This directive was later expanded to the members of the Jewish forced labor companies that forbade even the transfer of letters or inquiries relating to the deportees from concerned family members.[37]

Survivors' testimonies and military court documents indicate the prevalence of human smuggling, both for monetary benefits and from humanitarian impulses.[38] However, the complicity of the Hungarian military's role in the extermination process itself, excluding for a moment the field gendarmerie, is beyond doubt. The role of Hungarian units during the Kamenets-Podolsk massacre, leading the Hungarian and Galician Jews to the slaughter, raises the specter of indirect responsibility in the murder of the deportees or the local Jewish population.[39] The words of the chief of the general staff, via the commander of the Carpathian Corps, carry an ominous weight here because the "strictest measures for the prevention of such practices" meant the executions of those who either attempted to cross the border or who were extradited after crossing the border. The clearly stated policy, pursued by both KEOKH and Hungarian border authorities such as the border police and gendarmerie, was to prevent the reentry of the refugees at all costs. Hungarian Jews who succeeded in recrossing the border or Galician Jews escaping from extermination in the ghettos of Galicia were routinely handed back to German authorities, who subsequently executed them. While a directive in early 1942 explicitly forbade the handing back the escapees, instead sending them to internment camps, all evidence points to the blatant disregard of this order.[40] In more fortunate circumstances, the Hungarian military transported them to Kolomea. This policy did not spare non-Jewish family members who wanted to return from the nightmare of Galicia.

Hungarian soldiers did not commit atrocities comparable to that of the Romanian army in their expulsion of over four hundred thousand Jews to Transnistria. If we can sum up the responsibility of the Hungarian military and civilian authorities, the deportation of the Jews in 1941 to Galicia smacked of a chaotic improvisation, combined with the deliberate intent to net the largest number of deportees. This was combined with a capricious implementation, if not outright incompetence bordering criminal negligence, on the levels of both the law enforcement and military authorities.

An examination of the role the Wehrmacht played in the final fate of the exiled Hungarian community in Galicia demands a more nuanced approach. Outside Galicia, especially in Belorussia (now Belarus), the direct complicity of the Wehrmacht in the extermination is beyond question. The organization became an active participant in mass murder in which a triangular relationship existed between the Wehrmacht, the security forces, and the civilian administrators.[41]

In Galicia, on the other hand, the extermination was based on a bilateral power structure between the SS and civilian authorities. German armed forces did not become involved directly in extermination. Their responsibility, though, is undeniable in initiating—indeed requesting—the murder of Hungarian Jews in Kamenets-Podolsk. Quite telling the rebuff by the German military commander when one of the Hungarian deportees approached him to ameliorate an unbearable situation in the town: "The Jews wanted war—and here it is in all brutality. It is for them to bear all the consequences."[42] The Wehrmacht was often in overall charge of territories where the killings were taking place. They actively requested a solution to the "Jewish Question," as was demonstrated by General von Roque's role in Kamenets-Podolsk. One has to remember that the crucial meeting on August 25, when the fate of the Hungarian deportees and local Jews were announced, was called and chaired by Colonel Oberst Hans Georg Schmidt von Altenstadt, the chief of staff of General von Roque. Beyond that, the material support of the German military for the implementation and conduct of genocide was essential. While von Roque forbade active participation in the Kamenets-Podolsk massacre, his officers were also part of the decision-making process by eliminating the ghetto, and some of them were present during the executions and later in the festive dinner concluding the three days of murder. Wehrmacht troops under von Roque often supplied the rounds of ammunition for the submachine guns used in the massacres in 1941 and 1942.

In the second phase of the extermination during the fall of 1941, which took place in various communities and municipalities, the German civilian authorities replaced the Wehrmacht by eagerly joining forces with the security agencies for the liquidation of entire ghettos and labor camps. The role Volkmann played, for example in the extermination of the Kolomea Ghetto, and specifically the Hungarian Jews, is a glaring example of how complicit civilian authorities could become in perpetrating genocide. On a more passive level, they could extend assistance for the murder process. During the Eichmann trial one of the witnesses recalled that in Buczacz, trucks provided by the local municipality transported the Hungarian victims to the site of the mass executions.[43] The same can be said about the conduct of Bloody Sunday.

The third element used by the occupational authorities was the indigenous paramilitary forces. Considering the thinly spread security network, the role of the Ukrainian auxiliaries, known as *Schutzmannschaft* (Protective Detachments), in the full sequence of the extermination is one of tragic irony, if this is the right word, of the Eastern European genocide. As Finder noted, "the Ukrainian police played an integral part in the German destruction of the Jews."[44] Without them, genocide could have not been carried through. Their nightmarish spree, murdering thousands of deportees along the interminable treks and on the banks of the Dniester River, lives through the recollections of the survivors.

With a deep sense of dread, they talk about the ferocity of the "*Sichaks*" [*Sicz* or *siczownik* were Ukrainian paramilitary formations] who accompanied them on their wandering from village to village, the majority ending up in Kamenets-Podolsk. This Ukrainian part of digging the trenches, collecting the doomed, serving as cordon personnel, covering the graves, feeding the executioners, and hunting down escaping Jews was essential for the successful conduct of the Holocaust in Galicia. They formed by far the largest group of participants. In a curious twist, only a few hapless policemen, who could not escape with the retreating German forces, were tried in Soviet courts for their participation. In their case, there was no mercy. The sentence was invariable death.[45]

Finally, as the "foot soldiers" of the genocide, the role of the Reserve police battalions in the extermination of Jews, and specifically the Hungarians, is well documented. The two main formations, Reserve Police Battalion 133 in southeast Galicia and 320 in Kamenets-Podolsk,[46] became the mainstay of the Holocaust in the District of Galicia and, consequently, the killing of Hungarian Jews. This brings up the question if anyone from these two units was brought to justice for their participation in mass murder in Galicia—and especially that of Kamenets-Podolsk? The answer is no. Neither the *Feldkommandant* of the city, Josef Meiler, nor the participating members of Reserve Police Battalion 320 were called before the law for the death of 23,600 people. Among the close to 400 members, only three were willing to admit that they pulled the trigger. Indeed, neither the officers nor the policemen of Reserve Police Battalion 320, were convicted in their trials in West Germany. The rationale presented by the court was based on the controversial legal principle of the so-called *Befehlsnotsand*, that is, the supposed "necessity to obey," that granted to the defendant the suspension of the proceeding. On the final account, and among the multitude of perpetrators, only von Roque paid with twenty years imprisonment for his indirect participation in the Kamenets-Podolsk mass murder.[47]

An explanation for the human appetite for mass murder doesn't lie in the simplicity or lack of education of a given population. To be sure, Ukrainian irregulars began the gruesome killings of the deportees in the early phases of the expulsion. This was done with unimaginable savagery. Then, there were the hands-on mass murderers of Hungarian Jews in Podolia and Galicia: Jeckeln, Krüger, and Leideritz. All came from relatively modest backgrounds. On the other hand, almost all the high-ranking Nazi officers heading the organized extermination held university degrees. The title of "doctor" was common in front of the name of many killers in the Holocaust. Behind every mass murderer, though, there was a comprehensive mechanism that enabled or facilitated their work.

The burden of guilt, then, can be directed not only toward the executioners, but also to the three entities that were complicit in the process of murder, directly or indirectly: the Hungarian civil administration, the Royal Hungarian Army, and the Wehrmacht, jointly with the Nazi occupation authorities.

ARCHITECTS: FOOLS, COWARDS, AND CRIMINALS

In Hungary, and in many ways in Eastern Europe in general, to borrow William Faulkner's dictum, "The past is never dead. It's not even past."[48]

Often, scholarship is underpinned by the reconsideration—or cynical subversion—of the history of this war and its unseemly shadows, when each nation asserts its victimhood and denies its guilt. Yet we cannot escape the quandary as to how and why these Jews from internment camps, Hungarian cities, and the reannexed territories ended up in Galicia in the first place, and what mechanisms and circumstances precipitated their demise? There is also the question as to how a country with a highly developed legal infrastructure, a functional parliamentary structure, and a proudly stated and emphasized "value system" that was "solidly anchored in Christian values," could perpetrate such a crime?

The list of obedient and often middle-level and overeager officials in the Hungarian civil service, police, and military, who outdid themselves in their zeal to expel the maximum number of Jews, is a long one. Yet a Hungarian historian insightfully noted that often these same officials were also willing to give a hand in saving Jews from deportation and even hiding them in the final phases of the Hungarian Holocaust. Dr. Sándor Siménfalvy, the director of KEOKH, who issued directives for the deportation, is a case in point. He was a compliant civil servant, who could also exhibit humanitarian impulses. And often, when one official made every effort to deport the maximum number of people, his counterpart tried to mitigate the tragedy. It's hard to opine if this came from genuine humanitarian impulses or from the belated recognition that the war was lost and there would be, to quote again Margit Slachta, "a retribution as a consequence of their illegitimate actions?"[49]

In Budapest, some KEOKH's officials, even in the low rank of detectives, could wield almost absolute authority as to who should be deported. Several of them were called on for their crimes after the war by the people's court. The police commissioner of Carpathian Ruthenia, Arisztid Meskó, on the other hand, was perhaps the ultimate representative of such provincial officials, matched only by his unbridled cynicism, in accomplishing the removal. He disappeared without a trace after the war.[50] Finally, one can not forget the commander of the Kőrösmező transit camp, Lieutenant-Colonel Rudolf Orbán, who ordered the cross-border transfer of all Jews, irrespective their citizenship status. He could tear up the citizenship documents and military honors of a highly decorated World War I veteran by declaring: "Mr. Farkas, are you a Jew? Jews are not citizens of this country." In the distance of more than five decades, his daughter still remembered a father who returned from this meeting, a broken man "aged beyond recognition." Orban was never put to trial for his crimes.[51]

The idea and execution of the expulsion illustrated how the law of unintended consequences can work. Preventing the return of survivors, with the knowledge of the ongoing genocide, was the rejection of the onus of such consequences. Among the top echelon of the Hungarian leadership, Keresztes-Fischer was perhaps the only one who openly objected to the deportation. By all accounts, he was not an anti-Semite, and during his career in public service, he also saved Jews.[52] Yet his lack of awareness, if such a thing were possible in 1941, or belief in misinformation, cannot resolve his administration. He repeatedly reassured various interlocutors from Jewish circles, representatives of the Parliament, and the American ambassador about curtailing the excesses in the provinces. He repeatedly issued, via KEOKH, ineffectual instructions for limiting the deportation to Polish and Russian nationals. He was, of course, undermined or blatantly ignored. Yet in his comments, echoing the official line of the prime minister in the Hungarian Parliament in October 1941, he took personal responsibility for the removal. His statement that the cessation of the deportation was a consequence of German pressure and not humanitarian considerations might be attributable to an effort to mollify the radical right in the parliament. He opportunely neglected to mention in his speech, though, the inconvenient truth about the Kamenets-Podolsk massacre, which was known by then not only in Hungary, but across the Atlantic. In this, Keresztes-Fisher and the prime minister have presaged George Orwell's acerbic dictum: "Political language . . . is designed to make lies sound truthful and murder respectable."[53]

The timeline of the period shows that the official decree suspending the expulsion preceded by two crucial weeks the Kamenets-Podolsk massacre. This ominous milestone was followed by a dogged resistance to repatriating the remnants of the deportees, who were systematically exterminated during the fall of 1941. This is against the flow of information from Jewish as well as military sources. A military report ominously stated on September 5, 1941, that "the killing of the Jews in the occupied territories is common knowledge." A belated directive from Keresztes-Fisher, dated on October 28, 1942, more than a year after the Kamenets-Podolsk massacre, finally and categorically prohibited the transfer of "stateless" Jews to Galicia because "the occupying authorities [Nazi Germany] in most cases execute them; so, these people will be taken to their certain death."[54] It was too little and too late. By that time, almost no Hungarian Jews were left alive in Galicia. As a noted historian recently quipped, the Hungarians did not kill, but "you could smell the corpses."[55]

The inevitable question as to who should be directly accountable is a weighty one. It might seem tempting to name the initiators of this insidious idea of uprooting and transporting thousands of people to an uncertain future and later to their certain death. Yet the ideology and motivation were deeply rooted in the fertile soil of a decades-long creation of an image that found ready acceptance across Hungarian society. It seems evident that the deportation, at least from Carpathian Ruthenia, was the personal initiative of Miklós Kozma, the government commissioner there. The active participation of the Hungarian military, and especially the general staff, ensured governmental approval, advance planning, and logistical assistance. But, it's also true that Colonel-General Werth went beyond this mandate. Jews from the interior of the country as well as international refugees from the internment camps, many of them foreign nationals, were of special interest to the chief of the general staff, who unilaterally expanded the ranks of those to be deported, almost immediately following the governmental consent for the removal. Finally, the directives and decrees issued by KEOKH provided the legal framework and "legitimacy" for the project. It seems highly plausible that KEOKH, in turn, unilaterally broadened the scope of the expulsion by using the impending opportunity to add thousands of Jews from Budapest.[56]

It's hard to answer the question of how much this "demographic expansion" was preplanned or the result of a decision by top-level officials on the spur of the moment. But to bring the deportation to fruition, mid-level administrative nomenclature was needed. A surprising document from the investigations by the Hungarian People's Court in May 1945 shed a light on the mindset of the perpetrators who dreamed of the continuation of the expulsion, even after the minister of interior explicitly forbade future deportations. A visit by Captain Hans Krüger to Budapest in September 1941 rekindled the idea in these second-tier KEOKH bureaucrats' minds, raising the question, within the framework of a sumptuous dinner, of restarting the transports to Galicia: "By the invitation of the head of KEOKH, Sándor Siménfaly, who was not present because of political sensitivity, Krüger was hosted for a dinner in one of the trendiest restaurants of Budapest, the Gundel."

During the dinner, the atmosphere was cordial. The Hungarian participants inquired of Krüger if he would be willing to accommodate future transports. The gallant SS officer, obligingly, was amenable to this idea: "In reciprocating the dinner, Krüger, in turn, extended an invitation to the leadership of KEOKH to visit the occupied territories. Again Siménfalvy, for his part, politely declined the invitation." The delegation that finally embarked on this visit in the spring of 1942 comprised mid-level police officials from Budapest and Carpathian Ruthenia and two military officers, some of them intimately involved in the summer deportation itself. During their trip, as Batizfalvy recounted, "the Germans executed within 15 minutes 40–50 Jews as a demonstration by claiming that these refused to work."[57]

Considering the official Hungarian governmental policy line, which halted the deportation in August, the discussions by these low to mid-level officials on the renewal of the deportation is surprising. They obviously reached far beyond their authority. Was it a moral blindness or a "criminal lack of imagination" that came from ruthless ambition? Either way, this was not the first time that explicit decrees by the minister of interior to limit the scope of the deportation, or halt it altogether, were disregarded without bringing the officials to account. They reinforce the axiom that the gears of genocide are more often than not oiled by ordinary bureaucrats. Vasily Grossman, the Russian Jewish writer, might have grasped the essence of this by noting that "totalitarian regimes needed clerks and not believers."[58]

Apparently this amicable and rather "cordial relationship" was not the sole domain of the minor officialdom in KEOKH, for it continued in early 1942 by a joint coordinating committee established for the policy harmonization concerning the Galician refugees "between the Hungarian military and S.S. police authorities in Galicia, and especially with that of Stanisławów." By mid-July of the same year, even the Hungarian military attaché in Berlin entered in the discourse by proposing to Himmler to resettle "illegally" residing Jews in Hungary to Transnistria that was controlled by Romania at the time.[59] In light of SS-Lieutenant Colonel Tanzmann's explicit order to Krüger in early January 1942 to shoot all those who were thrust across the border again by Hungarian authorities, this "policy harmonization" amounted to a death sentence.[60] Indeed, cross-border expulsion of returnees went unabated until the autumn of 1942, and even, then, because of the explicit order by the minister of interior who forbade any additional transfer.

The ultimate responsibility, however, rests on the shoulders of officials hundreds of miles away from Galicia, sitting in board rooms, chairing governmental councils, and dispatching directives. There are four central architects in the planning, implementation, and final execution of the deportation: (1) General Henrik Werth, the chief of the general staff of the Royal Hungarian Army, (2) Ámon Pásztóy, the head of KEOKH, and consequently the Public Safety Section of the Ministry of Interior, (3) Prime Minister László Bárdossy, and (4) Miklós Kozma, the government commissioner for Carpathian Ruthenia.

These individuals cannot be called sadistic brutes, for all of them were highly educated, well-mannered, "normal" human beings. Yet none of them envisaged unforeseeable consequences. There is no way of knowing how much Werth, Pásztóy, and Kozma's motivations and actions were governed by the fact that they were not "ethnic Hungarians"? Both Werth and Pásztóy came from Swabian (German) ancestry, which might explain their identification with the German war aims as well as their deep-seated anti-Semitism. Kozma concealed a deeper secret. A close confidante of Regent Horthy, he belonged to the upper crust of Hungarian society, and carried the title of *Vitéz* (a form of knighthood). One detail, however, remained hidden; he had Jewish ancestry on one side of his family.[61]

Colonel-General Henrik Werth was one of the earliest proponents of a comprehensive "ethnic cleansing," which would have included not only Jews, but the Slavic and Romanian minorities as well. A preeminent Hungarian politician, László Teleki gave voice to his reservations about General Werth's divided loyalties to Regent Miklós

FIG 8.2 Generak Henrik Werth, the chief of staff of the Royal Hungarian Army in the first phase of the war. He was responsible for the collection and transportation of the Jews to Galicia. He died in a Soviet prison in 1952. *Courtesy of Dr. Sándor Szakály.*

Horthy, as the pro-German chief of the general staff and a "non-Hungarian" of "German ancestry," who will fail "to see the great task of preserving the country."[62]

These words were not far from the truth, for Werth repeatedly engaged in unilateral actions connecting Hungary with Nazi Germany, which often were not aligned with the policies of the Hungarian government.[63] He was notorious for bypassing authority in pursuit of political goals, which not necessary were in his range of authority. We know from surviving correspondence that by August 19, Werth took the liberty to directly approach Horthy, bypassing even the prime minister, with a memorandum that advocated the use of the war for a much more comprehensive action than the Galicia deportation, that of the transfer of "all non-Hungarian persons, singling out Romanians, Ukrainians, and the *entire Jewish community*."[64] It was by all accounts an ambitious proposal, aiming to displace close to eight million people. This memorandum, though, was also the last straw for the prime minister. It signaled the fall of Werth, who was dismissed on August 31, 1941.

Indeed, a contemporary observer characterized his leadership as doggedly aiming to politicize the military. It was not a difficult task. The majority of the general staff consisted of officers with pro-Nazi sympathies who, by the way, also came from Swabian background. His central role, along with the minister of defense, in presenting and promoting the idea of expulsion to the Council of Ministers, is a case in point. By claiming that houses, land, and employment opportunities would be waiting for the deportees in Galicia, he deliberately misled the ministers. He also provided the planning and the operational muscle, assisted by an anti-Semitic general staff, for the deportation of

Jews from the beginning. His participation in the meetings of the Council of Ministers provided him the necessary platform and forum to present and push through this idea. But, in emptying internment camps of international refugees, which was never discussed or authorized by the government, Werth directly became complicit in the unfolding genocide in Galicia. On the other hand, his control of the material and human resources of the Royal Hungarian Army gave him the ability to provide the practical means for the deportation of these unfortunate Jews. His dismissal from his post in early September removed him from active management of the deportation itself. His imprint, though, on the functioning of the general staff remained intact. He died in Soviet captivity in 1952.

Ámon Pásztóy, with a doctoral degree in law, was the legal face of the deportation. Although he did not sign the directives and decrees issued by KEOKH, his power behind the scenes was unmistakable. They provided a cover, enveloped in legalistic framework and "governmental legitimacy," for the impending action. It is highly likely that he never personally saw the victims of his policy face-to-face or through the sight of a gun. He did not need to pull the trigger; he personified the quintessential desk murderer. But a desk murderer implies an "unideological bureaucrat," a grey apparatchik,

FIG 8.3   Ámon Pásztóy, the former head of National Central Alien Control Office (KEOKH). He provided the legal framework for the deportation. Pásztóy was sentenced and executed for his crimes in Budapest in 1949. *Courtesy of the Állambiztonsági Szolgálatok Történeti Levéltára.*

who dispassionately implements orders. Rather, he formulated policies and issued orders. Far from merely mechanical and unaware, he was an ordinary mid-level official in the grip of passion—a passion to complete the task that under him became the law of KEOKH and transformed the expulsion into an ostensible act of patriotism. Neither was he Hannah Arendt's image of the trite paper pusher, a prototypical bureaucrat. He was not the model for the "banality of evil"—a detached, unpolitical technocrat. The words "relentless" and "uncompromising" might be apt terms for describing him, as he repeatedly urged his staff to speed up the deportations. In his quest to accomplish the task, he did not shy away from keeping his immediate superior, the minister of interior, in the dark. He communicated directly with the prime minister about deportation policies, urging him repeatedly to solicit German cooperation in securing a Jew-free zone along the Galician side of the border.

The testimonies during his trial regarding his intransigence toward any request for humanitarian intercession—even threatening to resign if he was overruled—make it clear the enormous power a mid-level official could wield in the Hungarian state bureaucracy. At the time of the expulsion, the Hungarians, and among them Pásztóy, were not aware of a design or policy for mass extermination. Even Himmler didn't express at the time his intentions for a full-blown genocide. The onus for him came when the mass murder became common knowledge. We noted earlier that he instructed border authorities about the official policy of the "repatriation of foreign citizens and their Christian family members, who left voluntarily with them . . . is out of the question."[65] A follow-up communication a week later urged the prime minister to intercede through diplomatic channels with the German military authorities across the border to prevent Jews from approaching the border.

It signed, of course, the death sentence for the desperate deportees.

By incidental comments and remarks of contemporaries, a vengeful and vindictive figure filters through—a real Shakespearean villain. In the concluding phase of the deportation, he boastfully informed the prime minister that utilizing the opportunity provided by the war, "I have expelled, in this time, 18,000 Jews from the country."[66] During his trials, however, he denied any involvement. In a cryptic allusion, Margit Slachta, in a personal letter to Baroness Edith Weiss, paints a depressing portrait of Pásztóy. She alludes to a contentious and apparently very unpleasant meeting between the two on the subject of stopping the deportation. It reveals the depth of Pásztóy's commitment to carrying out the expulsion and preventing the repatriation of the survivors.

His prominent role in the 1941 deportation sealed his fate during his postwar trial. While the death sentence for Pásztóy was hanging in the balance, Slachta, a devout Christian, declined to testify on behalf of the defense. In her mind, there were no and could not have been mitigating circumstances for a mass murderer. As she recalled this inimical meeting between the two, in 1941, and its inevitable failure, she concluded: "For me every death sentence is poignant, especially if I knew the person. Pásztóy's fate is often on my mind. . . . I have approached him, since he handled this thing [the deportation] and described to him the events since I did not think I could appeal to him on high moral grounds. His answer then was such that fully supports the impending judgment now."[67] Pásztóy was executed for his crimes on August 10, 1949.

As the prime minister and ultimate decision-maker, László Bárdossy's role in the expulsion was indirect but crucial. Yet, this was not the deciding factor in his death sentence and consequent execution by a firing squad on January 10, 1946.

During his trial, Bárdossy took responsibility for bringing his country into World War II as an ally of Germany in general, and the 1941 deportation in particular. His decision in declaring war on the Soviet Union, alongside Nazi Germany, is still a contentious topic among Hungarian historians. This might have been politically expedient for him, but morally it was untenable. In representing a nation, could he take an introspective look into the question of accountability, culpability, and guilt? Yet, as prime minister, under whose regime the deportation took place, Bárdossy adroitly dodged this question by claiming, "I am responsible but not guilty." As for the specific responsibility for the deportation, his evasive answer was that "I will not deny my responsibility but I could not know everything." These few, carefully chosen words in a

FIG 8.4 As the Hungarian prime minister in 1941, László Bárdossy (on the left) carried the ultimate responsibility for the 1941 deportation. He was convicted and executed in 1946. *Fortepan, Public Domain, courtesy of Judit Mészáros.*

specific moment and circumstance underlines the American ambassador's (Herbert C. Pell) assessment of the prime minister. In a short message to the British ambassador to Lisbon, he characterized Bárdossy as a "very cultivated man with a great deal of diplomatic experience but extremely weak."[68] He might have also added that Hungarian prime minister also harbored a large degree of vanity coupled with corresponding insecurity.

Bárdossy's guilt in launching the Hungarian participation in the war and, consequently, the opening chapter of the Hungarian Holocaust, did not lie only in his acquiescence to the deportation with unforeseeable and unintended consequences—the Kamenets-Podolsk and corollary massacres. The expulsion was obviously politically expedient in Hungary's racially charged atmosphere. It also was welcomed by a large majority of the Hungarian public. And Bárdossy well exemplified this public view that hoped, as a contemporary social observer so incisively noted, for successfully expropriating someone's hard-earned estate and livelihood instead of working hard for it himself. The chronicler of his trial was perhaps somewhat forgiving in his assessment that "the anti-Semitism widely held by the gentile middle-class was shared by Bárdossy."[69] A Hungarian diplomat summed up his character a little more incisively: "he was an ultra-anti-Bolshevik anti-Semite and believed that harmonious cooperation with Germany was a historical necessity."[70] In this context we might contrast his anti-Semitism with that of Teleki, who abhorred the crude anti-Semitism of Nazi Germany. Indeed, Teleki might have not gone to the extreme of sending people to their death or forcing them to remain where their fate was sealed in a mass grave. To underline this comment, one needs to examine Bárdossy's actions after the "official" cessation of the deportation in August. In his dual role as prime and foreign minister, he pursued every effort to block the return of the deportees.

As noted earlier, the establishment of a German–Hungarian joint commission in the fall of 1941, with the goal of preventing the return of refugees to Galicia, made a priority of doing just that. Their meetings, first on October 11 in Kőrösmező, which was followed in Stanisławów on October 26, 1941, were not productive, though. By that time, of course, the German security forces had decimated the exiled Hungarian Jews to such a degree that there was not too much to talk about. A forceful protestation by the chief councilor of the Hungarian Embassy in Berlin to the German Ministry of Foreign Affairs shows that the expulsion and consequent exterminations were not just an accidental episode of the unfolding Holocaust. During a discussion between the two parties about the Galician deportation, the Hungarian representative furiously reproached his German counterpart in claiming that "while the German authorities deport Jews presently from the Reich and Berlin en-masse … to the occupied territories, they are sending back the repatriated [i.e., deported] Jews by us from the areas that we control." He concluded the exchange by pointing out that while the Hungarian government "supplies many thousands of workers for the Reich to increase German production, we receive, in return, Jews."[71]

Bárdossy's culpability, then, might be rooted in his awareness, knowledge, and eventual cover-up of the atrocities. The critical evidence of his full complicity and consequent guilt comes from a speech during a parliamentary debate, together with the minister of interior, in which he justified his action: "Following the capture of Ukrainian territory, we have transferred a significant number of Jews, originally from Galicia. We wanted to evacuate even larger number, but our German friends warned us not to continue for the time being. Naturally, we had to yield to this request."[72]

In a finely etched portrait of the prime minister, a contemporary provides the picture of a complex but conflicted man. His defense at his trial was to deny guilt, assuming only responsibility, "because he was forced to do it." In an eerie coincidence, Hans Frank, the Nazi governor-general in Poland, presented similar argument in Nuremberg during his war crimes trial, claiming that he "reigned but didn't rule."[73] Both arguments were based on a logical fallacy. A string of reports that reached Bárdossy's desk from Jewish organizations, concerned deputies, Miklós Kozma, and the American ambassador, to whom he lied outright, clearly informed him about the flagrant violations taking place in the provinces and the bloody pogroms in Galicia. Such letters to the prime minister didn't mince words: "The fact that lawful Hungarian citizens are being expelled by the thousands from the country will undermine the internal and international confidence in the Hungarian legal system." The writer also appealed to the conscience of the Hungarian nation: "It is not a Jewish interest, but a Hungarian national interest that the Hungarian officials who are responsible for these resettlements, about which hundreds of letters and telegrams provide testimony describing the dreadful horrors resembling Dante's inferno, put an end to it. If for no other reason, the Hungarian nation's thousand-year-old Christian reputation should not be tarnished by it."[74] The American ambassador also alerted him, unambiguously, to the fact that the expellees were exposed to mass murder in Ukraine, and that the expulsion of foreign nationals from internment camps was a distinct "violation of the right of asylum which is generally granted by sovereign countries to refugees."[75]

The most damning point could be that in spite of a clear knowledge of the genocide happening across Galicia—the massacres in Kamenets-Podolsk, Stanisławów, and elsewhere—and repeated warnings by concerned observers, he gave his endorsement to policies that perpetuated the atrocities—all the way until his dismissal on March 7, 1942.[76]

Among the architects of the deportation, only Miklós Kozma died a free man, without facing the justice of history. In many ways, he served as the main actor, a spark, for the deportation. He was also the only one who expressed regret over his responsibility

FIG 8.5 Government Commissioner of Carpathian Ruthenia Miklós Kozma assumed full responsibility for the deportation of two-thirds of those who were transferred to Galicia.

for it. His prominent role in launching the deportation from Carpathian Ruthenia, which he did not have the opportunity to deny, was a disastrous policy with tragic consequences. He inherited a complex position as the government commissioner in the Carpathian Ruthenian region, which has always been a cauldron of seething ethnic politics. He was under relentless pressure by a wide segment of the region's Hungarian population to expel the Jews. This doesn't absolve him from full responsibility for an ill-fated, ill-conceived, and ill-executed policy that resulted in the gruesome murder of thousands of human beings. To sum up his ultimate accountability for the 1941 expulsion, one need only to look at his role in the initiation, expansion, and coordination of the deportation with the political and military leadership, and his staunch opposition to the return of the unfortunates, although in September he was advised about the ongoing murder of the expelled, at least until October 1941.

Mária Ormos' masterful biography of Kozma depicts a conflicted man—torn between his mandate as a high-level official and a degree of humanity. He single-mindedly pursued the expulsion—even going to extremes to expand it. Yet he also realized at the end of his life the horrific outcomes of his actions. In September, he still advocated barring the refugees' return, but by late October he had a change of heart. The atrocities came too close to ignore them. He understood that those responsible for the murders were not only German security forces, but Hungarians as well. As we noted in the previous chapter, his communication on October 22 to the minister of interior, describing in vivid details the atrocities taking place on the border and committed by the Hungarian military and gendarmerie, attested to his change of heart.

He confided to a friend in October 1941 the details of the nightly killings that were taking place close to the border on the Hungarian side and his recurring mental anguish over them. His words are chilling: "Million secrets out there... during the nights, not every day, but the murdered bodies litter the forest... the act itself is on our conscience. Do you understand? We are the ones who are killing them."[77] The panic in his voice delivering this monologue is palpable. Kozma, perhaps recognizing his responsibility, offered this mea culpa to this confidant shortly before his death from a massive heart attack on December 8, 1941. He was gravely ill. But the confession was not just a delusional declaration of guilt by an ill person near death as his biographer proposed. It was an acknowledgment of the failure of a misguided policy, and taking responsibility for the ongoing murders of returning Jews and those escaping from the ghettos of Galicia. If anyone was well informed about such murders committed routinely by the Germans on the Galician side and Hungarian Border Police and the gendarmerie on Hungarian side, the omnipotent government commissioner was.

Although he took to the grave the inconvenient truth about his Jewish ancestry, this detail haunted the family long after his death. Worthy of a Shakespearian drama, he was expelled retroactively from the "Order of Vitéz," a form of knighthood bestowed upon faithful members of Horthy's circle, by the governing body of the organization. The justification stated his Jewish background.[78]

WHAT IS RIGHT AND WHAT IS WRONG?

Hungarian governmental responsibility for the deportation cannot be questioned. It was a unilateral Hungarian action without consent or coordination with German military or civilian authorities in the occupied territories. The 1941 deportation, as we have already noted, was not unique within the context of World War II or the Holocaust itself, but it was a uniquely Hungarian experience—just like the final chapter of the Hungarian Holocaust in 1944.

In the moment the Hungarian authorities deliberately prevented the refugees' return, with the murder of thousands as a direct result, they became also complicit in genocide.

One of the imponderable questions that inevitably emerges is where was Horthy, the ultimate authority between the two wars, during and after the deportation? While he did not immerse himself in the everyday conduct of the government, he maintained some ethical imperatives and, as a Hungarian historian noted, was not a Nazi sympathizer. But he was a selective anti-Semite—maintaining friendship with the Jewish industrial and banking elite. That he knew about the horrors taking place during the deportation and its consequences is at least plausible, if not undeniable. Margit Slachta's letters to Horthy's wife, combined with a subsequent audience, that described in vivid details the situation of the deportees, could have reached him. However, no evidence about his response or intersession to Slachta's pleas has survived.

These events were by no means out of the ordinary in Europe at the time. The Hungarian state could not claim the dubious distinction of being an exception in the annals of World War II. To paraphrase Adam Michnik's dictum about wartime Poland, "the gutter is not a specifically Hungarian phenomenon." Indeed, the scale of expulsion from Hungary in 1941 paled against its neighbors. Romania expelled Jews from territories they invaded or killed them outright—close to 300,000. Slovakia delivered its own Jews to Nazi forces in Poland, although it was not occupied. Bulgaria (whose record otherwise was good) handed over Jews in the captured areas of Thrace and Macedonia. Even the "enlightened" French deported more than 25,000 foreign nationals (refugees) to the Nazis—10,000 of them voluntarily from Vichy's free zone. This action, taken at Vichy's own initiative, was particularly shocking since it meant that French police delivered Jews to the Nazis from an area outside German occupation. There was no other case like this in Western Europe, and few in Eastern Europe.[79]

Nor can we claim that the deportation and the subsequent murder of those deported were events that inevitably precipitated the Holocaust. Although the rough contours of the Final Solution were in the development phase, it was an ongoing process. By the time of the infamous Wannsee Conference on January 20, 1942, close to half a million Jews had already been murdered in the occupied Soviet territories, as well as over 20,000 Hungarian Jews.[80] Rather, the expulsion and influx into Galicia accelerated and expedited the annihilation. It became a spark and catalyst for the subsequent bloodbaths. Finally, this points to a central enigma of the Hungarian Holocaust, which can either be interpreted as premeditated action, like the Galician expulsion, or a barbaric follow-up improvisation to 1944.

9

REQUIEM FOR A DEPORTATION

Unanswered Questions

"How can one forgive and forget?"[1]

STANDING IN FRONT OF A MASS GRAVE LEAVES LITTLE ROOM FOR MORAL contemplation—only a degree of incomprehension. One needs all the power of the imagination to conjure a vision of the site as it was after the murder of thousands of people, when the cries of the victims were extinguished and the guns fell silent. Ian Kershaw's words come to mind: "This was a person with loved ones, not an unfortunate causality of fighting, but someone deliberately killed."[2]

The Jews of Krivoy Rog were murdered on October 14–15, 1941, near the city. Although no Hungarian expellees were included in this carnage, there was a Hungarian soldier, a Jewish driver, who reported it. Upon witnessing the procession of Jews to the slaughter, Béla Somló, the Hungarian soldier, decided to visit the valley of death for the 7,000 Jews of Krivoy Rog a day after the massacre. Acting against military policy, he also took a picture of the mass grave: "On our way back, we decided to swing by the scene of the shootings of yesterday. Wherever the procession passed, pages with Hebrew letters torn from books, black and white prayer shawls, tefillins [phylacteries], a child's sock ground into the dirt ... the gully is filled with earth ... that is not really filled ... or filled ... but not with earth ... the soil only sprinkled on top ... hastily ... sometimes more, sometimes less."[3]

Such horrifying sights were the norm in the Eastern European Holocaust "theater," where those who committed atrocities were not concerned that their actions would be observed and recorded. The scene in Nadwórna, eight months after the slaughter of 2,000 Jews in the Bukowinka Forest, many of them Hungarian, was eerily similar. A local survivor, who later escaped across the border to Hungary, was ordered to recover the mass graves several months later. He noted in his diary: "When we arrived at that vale of tears, we faced a horrible and unforgettable sight. There were enough traces left to see of the awful tragedy that had taken place there about eight months ago. Strewn all over were many torn shirts, underwear, and shredded left-overs of dresses . . . keys, documents, photos. . . . We were gripped by terror and horror when we saw a chewed-off hand, pointing towards heaven, stick out of the middle of the mass grave."

This hand haunted the diarist. It symbolized the evil that had taken place: "That hand, reaching towards heaven from the grave, was raised like a signal of accusation against God and men for the gigantic crime committed here by bestial men."[4] An eyewitness to the exhumation of Hungarians in Kamenets-Podolsk reflected that: "In two of these craters are specifically driven to slaughter the Kamenets-Podolsk foreigners, Jews. . . . Residents of neighboring villages report that after the first filling [covering with soil] of the large elliptical hole, the ground water pushed to the surface and because of the many thousands of corpses it was painted red, and formed a sinister bloody lake."[5]

These comments and observations underline a frightful statistics, which were quoted in the first chapter. The Soviet investigators from the village of Plebanovka concluded that the rate of success in killing the defenseless victims was "35 percent of the victims were shot dead on the spot, 50 percent of the people were injured, and 15 percent were buried alive." Even with the knowledge that children were thrown alive into the graves, the natural question arises as to why was only 35 percent of the executed died immediately? Why was the ground heaving, and moaning and crying could be heard from the trenches several days after the carnage? Part of the answer lies in the number of executions that had to be accomplished with limited human resources and under pressures of time. Again, the image of Krüger running along the mass grave and urging his men to speed up the process comes to mind. This image, though, also reflects a deeper reality. He holds in his hand a bottle of schnapps. Thus, it is reasonable to argue that the additional—or perhaps the main—reason for the low success rate in killing was the amount of alcohol consumed before and during mass murder. In Kamenets-Podolsk, shooters were periodically excused to take a break to drink schnapps before returning to the firing line. During the Bloody Sunday Massacre in Stanisławów, the shooters were so drunk that missing their target became a serious concern.[6]

These Nazi executioners were not too meticulous about the process of murder, mostly wounding the intended victims. As for covering the mass graves, it was even less of their concern. We can find in the annals of the Holocaust that burying the murdered was routinely relegated to the local population or Jews from the ghetto who were forced to cover and later recover the scene of the crime. As the night descended on the freshly filled craters, with thousands of new victims, their pleas from mass graves echoed all through the night.

THE NEVER-ENDING QUESTIONS

These musings of a Hungarian soldier in Krivoy Rog, a hand raised to heaven in Nadwórna, the color of a manmade "lake of blood" in Kamenets-Podolsk, and a voice from the grave in Stanislawów—they may provide an appropriate précis for the deportation of more than 20,000 people from Hungary. But is there a fitting metaphor for such a singular and unfathomable event as the Holocaust? The imagination fails to find an answer.

When writing about the Holocaust, it is tempting to apply a "whiggish" interpretation of history. In other words, in explaining the 1941 deportation and the consequent genocide we analyze it within the background of modern politics. The axiom, coined by the French historian Henry Rousso, stating "the past that will not pass," indicates the attitudes in Central and Eastern Europe toward the events of 1941. Politics notoriously erases stories that do not fit the preferred narrative, reframing past sins to suit the issues and expediencies of today's reality. This is especially true in Hungary, where historical memory has a complicated history of its own. A colleague mused about taking responsibility for the Galician genocide to ask the penetrating question: "How do you wake up from the nightmare of history when you are the nightmare?"[7]

This question begets, of course, a new question. Can we—or rather should we—protect the past from itself? In the popular imagination, the Holocaust is associated with

FIG 9.1 The site of the mass murder: Memorial Park in Kamenets-Podolsk. *Courtesy of George Eisen.*

rapid industrial killings in the death camps. In 1941, however, an entire system, security and civil, became complicit in robbery and murder. Across the region, it became a vertically integrated criminal enterprise. As Father Patrick Desbois noted, "there is no such thing as genocidal purity."[8] While the killing might have been framed as ideological at the start, it rapidly descended into a frenzy of pillaging and plundering. The Nazi murder squads looked at the killings as purification of the race initially, but didn't disdain from sending back to their families looted Jewish valuables. The Ukrainian militiamen were not motivated by ideology; they were there for the discarded garments, extra food, and unending supply of schnapps. The members of the Hungarian field-gendarmerie did not entertain discernable ideological convictions either. They started stripping deportees from their valuables at their homes, following in the camp at Kőrösmező, and finishing somewhere at the end points in Galicia.

After Auschwitz, Galicia is the second largest Hungarian Jewish Holocaust cemetery in the world. But unlike Auschwitz, in Galicia we are forced to see the men, women, and children through the sights of rifles and submachine guns at very close range and within the confines of the host communities. We can observe the process of murder through the micro-lens of well-designed community involvement: digging the graves, collecting the Jews, guarding them at the execution site, covering the mass graves, and even squabbling over the meager possessions of the murdered. In a deposition during his trial, a Ukrainian policeman openly complained to the Soviet investigative commission that the Ukrainians always received the most inferior pieces, not deemed worthy by the Nazi officers.[9] Echoing such sentiment, a Hungarian military report noted with an undisguised envy that "during mass murder of Jews, for example in Kamenets-Podolsk, approx. 27,000, the Germans prevented the Hungarians from getting even the most trivial things, but permitted the Ukrainian population to sell cheaply the loot distributed to them."[10]

In the introduction to this book, I posed questions raised by researching and writing a narrative about the 1941 Hungarian deportation. In the first place, was there a causality between the deportation and the launching of the Holocaust? The obvious answer is no. The Holocaust was already in progress by the time Jeckeln made a commitment to "liquidate" Hungarian Jews in Kamenets-Podolsk. Snyder's assessment of the Kamenets-Podolsk example is close to the truth in that larger massacres only "confirmed the precedent of Kamenets-Podolsk for the destruction of the Jews."[11] In other words, Kamenets-Podolsk taught us that mass murder by simple means is doable.

Was the Hungarian deportation expedited or influenced by the evolution of the Holocaust in general and the Final Solution in particular? The answer is yes, for in one sense there is an underlying interconnectedness. Again, Snyder's words well defined this question by stating that "the Holocaust is integrally and organically connected to the *Vernichtungskrieg*, to the war in 1941, and is organically and integrally connected to the attempt to conquer Ukraine."[12] Using the pretext of eliminating the Hungarian Jews, Jeckeln exterminated around 2,000 Jews from Bukovina and more than 6,000 local Jews also, who might not have otherwise been targeted at that time. On the other hand, during the notorious Bloody Sunday Massacre of 12,000 people, the first 2,000 victims to be exterminated by the Germans were the Hungarians imprisoned in the Rudolfmühle in Stanisławów. The Galician expulsion also had a direct impact on a string of follow-up murders by German forces. Can we draw, then, a connecting line between the precedent setting mass murder in Kamenets-Podolsk and the follow-up massacres across Ukraine? Was there a causality between Kamenets-Podolsk and Babi Yar? Even a more pertinent question; were the Hungarian actions precipitated a chain of events that led to the unleashing of the Final Solution in Europe? The deportation expedited the extermination process, starting in late August and early September, and culminating in several bloodbaths that became ominous milestones in Holocaust history. They signified a transition from the experimental and selective phase of genocide to the systemic approach to murder and, ultimately, to the Final Solution.

How can we fully absorb the complicated lessons of this deportation? It is a narrow slice of the Holocaust universe, taking place in an obscure corner of Eastern Europe, and initiated by rather unfamiliar Hungarian policymakers, at least for the Western public. Yet it carries all the contours of the unfolding genocide. The influx of Hungarian expellees to Galicia was the primary factor, a fuse in the first mass murder in Kamenets-Podolsk. The Hungarian Jews, then, were part of the follow-up destruction of the Jews of Galicia, becoming an integral part of the Final Solution.

It is a quandary as to how and why these Jews from Hungary proper, from Budapest, and the reannexed territories—a semicircle extending from the southern part of former Upper Hungary in the north (Felvidék), Carpathian Ruthenia on the east, and Transylvania in the southeast—ended up in Galicia in the first place? Another weighty question that needs to be addressed is why were the foreign nationals from various internment camps included in the expulsion? As a savvy former diplomat, Bárdossy, the prime minister, should have known that this was contrary to international conventions. Finally, how could a country with a highly developed legal system, a functional parliamentary structure, and a proudly stated and emphasized "value system" that was proclaimed to be "solidly anchored in Christian values," perpetrate such an action? There are no easy answers.

The most immediate answer for the first question might be in the realm of psychology. As we quoted earlier from Peter Hayes, the transition from ideas and perception about a minority to hostile action depend on circumstances that could promote "murderous intentions." The outbreak of World War II and the Hungarian occupation of Galicia provided these circumstances. As for the international refugees, it was a corollary effect in which both KEOKH and the Chief of Staff General Werth teamed up to resolve this issue—rather unilaterally.

And then, there is the additional question of the demographic composition of the expulsion. Thousands of Jews from Budapest and foreign nationals from the internment camps were collected and deported to Galicia. But why the Jews on the periphery, and especially in Carpathian Ruthenia and northern Transylvania, were singled out in overwhelming numbers for removal? While their geographic proximity to Galicia—just over the Carpathian Mountains—may be one reason, a full answer might demand more nuance. With their large masses of Jews who were more traditional than those in the interior of the country, these regions offered something of a Rorschach test for Hungarian society as a whole. It reflected and magnified the vitriol and hate that gripped the Hungarian political landscape. The socioethnic mélange of this region, allied with a distinctly retarded social development where Hungarians were a minority, was conducive to racial animosity. Surrounded by Ruthenian and Romanian peasants, the Hungarians, competing with a devoutly religious, yet staunchly pro-Hungarian Jewish middle class, saw economic ascendancy in despoiling the Jews. The observation of Eleanor Perényi again is authoritative and instructive: "Jews were looked down on, but only because they engaged in all things which in other countries are the province of the middle class.... And as everyone seemed to be either a noble or peasant, business and the professions were gratefully turned over to the Jews. So, of course, were the arts."[13]

There was no single, linear chain of causality for the expulsion, nor was there a clear, ideological rationale. While the political elite was fully aware of the atrocities taking place in the newly conquered territories, it made every effort to placate the Nazi-inspired right in the Parliament by removing the "Easterners." On the local implementation level, however, there were little ideological or political considerations. Their actions were rooted in an ingrained hatred that was deeper than ideology. This hatred formed the basis for attempts to create the "Other," and place the blame on this creature for economic, social, and cultural ills—real or imaginary.

The euphemistic "economic realignment" of Hungary in the late 1930s, cemented by the Jewish Laws, brings the expulsion into even clearer focus. This despoliation can be viewed on the macro level, as the economic transfer from "Jewish to Christian" hands as the Second Jewish Law decreed. By 1941, however, and following the waves of deportation, the economic transfer took a different form. It was not as orderly as the law would have mandated, rapidly deteriorating into unmitigated plunder. A report by a chief magistrate in Carpathian Ruthenia boasted that he "distributed stocks of goods from numerous Jewish warehouses, whose absentee owners cannot be found, to Christian merchants."[14] He knew very well, of course, as to where these merchants disappeared. But, then, one cannot ignore the micro level either, when the looting started at the moment of deportation by the detective who collected the family for immediate removal. Elie Wiesel's words that "what hurts the victim most is not the cruelty of the oppressor, but the silence of the bystander" can so aptly describe the moment when the gentile neighbors lined up to gawk or, rather, to take away various items from the home of the family that is removed. One of them turned to the mother, just being led out of their home and preparing for deportation, to ask, "can we have the bedroom furniture of the little girl for our daughter?"[15]

In this light, the economic motivation for the deportation becomes more rational and understandable. Compared with the interior of the country, civil society, and a viable middle class in the outlying provinces, which were rural and impoverished, especially in Carpathian Ruthenia and northern Transylvania, was weak. In the interior there was a well-entrenched Christian middle class, Hungarian and Swabian German. But in the provinces, Jews constituted both the virtual middle class and a nascent civil society. In these newly reannexed territories, they were also a substantial political demographic counterweight to the Ukrainian, Romanian, or Slovakian majorities. They had a marked Hungarian cultural and political orientation, stubbornly clinging to the memories of the peaceful years of the Austro-Hungarian monarchy. These Jews remembered, with nostalgia, the monarchy as a bulwark that had once held anti-Jewish hatred at bay. During his meanderings in northern Transylvania under Romanian rule in the mid-1930s, the British traveler Patrick Leigh Fermor described his accidental meeting with Hasidic Jews who were in the logging business in the Carpathian Mountains. These devoutly religious Jews insisted on speaking among themselves in "Hungarian rather than Yiddish" and dreamed of the return of a Hungary that practiced a benign Austro-Hungarian tolerance.

During the Romanian years in Transylvania and the days of Czech-Slovak control of Upper Hungary and Carpathian Ruthenia, Jews consistently identified themselves as Hungarians. The Hungarian writer Márai's diary reflected this: "The Jews during the last twenty years have faithfully supported Hungarian interests, in the elections as well as cultural life."[16] In turn, the Hungarian minority was temporarily tolerant of its Jewish counterpart. But after the reannexation there was no need for a counter-balanced minority vis-à-vis the non-Hungarian majority. The prevailing internal deterioration of the political climate would have been a strong impetus for the deportation. But enmity toward the Jews in these reannexed territories were much more toxic and vengeful than in Hungary proper. There, they didn't need the Jews anymore.

One must confront, then, the question of how many and who were this people forced into "exile" to a "bloodland" called Galicia? At first, we can name them as deportees and expellees. However, they rapidly became a multitude of rootless refugees with no rights and no anchor in an alien land. Joyce Carol Oates said that "'A refugee' is, by definition, desperate: he has been displaced from his home, has been rendered stateless, has few or no resources." More importantly, when one is exiled from home and country, this comes with the ultimate price: "there is a loss of identity in the category term refugees."[17] A survivor, six years old at the time, vividly remembered the moment when they were rendered to such a state. The gendarme gave the mother five minutes to be ready, with two children, upon the threat of a gun to her head: "Our life stopped at this moment ... my mother wanted to put the housekeys in her purse. Small detail but I remember clearly as the gendarme took away the keys. If someone ever experiences this, giving the keys to your own home that you lived all your life ... and within five minutes, it's over."[18] The use of the term "refugee" for the displaced persons from Hungary fits well precisely because of the punitive violence it betrays.

Writing in his diary in the town of Tluste in Galicia, the previously quoted doctor grasped this well. He was surprisingly well-informed about who these refugees, 2,000 of them, were:

> It was also about Jews from the Transcarpathian [Carpathian Ruthenia] regions, recently incorporated to the Hungarian state. Later, this ordinance encompassed those with *Nansen* passports, refugees from Austria, Germany, and Poland, even some Jews formerly from the Polish army. An immense chaos occurred there, families were separated and the hearth of homes were destroyed, as there were many mixed marriages between Jews and Aryans or [Hungarian] citizens. . . . These condemned [people] were torn from their homes with absoluteness and guile and driven to Ukraine on trucks in the path of Hungarian armies following the eastern front. Some were taken from their jobs in the daytime, others were woken from their sleep during the night and immediately loaded into cars. Some were allowed to take the most important [items], and others were not. Some were told that they are being taken to be registered, a second group that they are being temporarily interned in lagers, a third group that they are being resettled to other areas of Hungary, and a fourth group that housing and farmlands are prepared for them, as entire cities and villages are deserted and emptied as a result of the Soviets taking away populations.[19]

While this description does not provide numbers, it is a well-rounded summation from an outsider of the identities of the thousands of people uprooted from their homes in 1941. "The bald statistics of population displacement," Ian Kershaw informs us, "like all macro-economic data, are wholly impersonal. They say nothing of the death, destruction, suffering and misery involved."[20] But the statistics provide us with a tangible picture of the magnitude of an atrocity. Since a limited number of records survived the war, we can only estimate. As mentioned in the opening chapter, the official approximation of the deported was 17,656. This number corresponded with the files maintained by KEOKH. An appeal to the International Red Cross for aid for these people in early December 1941, apparently borrowed from the same sources, speaks of similar estimates. Pásztóy openly boasted in a memorandum, sent to László Bárdossy on September 16, 1941, that "until now I have expelled 18,000 Jews." A month later a perhaps more reliable source, a police report from the border region, quoted 19,426 people.[21] The arrests and forced collections in the provinces, however, were more sweeping than the central authorities in Budapest decreed or were informed about. The resulting reports from these outlying areas, demanded by Budapest, if they were sent at all, were at best fragmentary and incomplete.

On the other hand, the transit camp in Körösmező, a "filter" station, was chaotic and often overwhelmed by the incoming Jews, which made an accurate accounting impossible. Originally three collection camps were planned, but only that one was established. Thus, the expellees were often transported directly from the train station to Galicia, bypassing any registration protocol.[22] Finally, we are not informed about an important demographic segment, that of the nearly 3,000 foreign nationals in the internment camps—Czech, Slovak, French, Austrian, German, and even Dutch Jews—who found temporary shelter in Hungary. These camps were under military administration. Military trucks emptied these camps by directly transporting their human cargo across the border. This was obviously, as the American ambassador pointed out, in contradiction to international laws, which might be the reason that the transit camp in Körösmező was intentionally circumvented. On the final account, though, none of these foreign nationals survived.

An estimate by the Joint Distribution Committee, dated on July 16, 1943, placed the overall number of deported as "close to 23,000."[23] Considering the official statistics in Hungary, German military dispatches from the occupied territories, testimonies, and Yizkor books from villages and towns on both sides of the border, 23,000 to 25,000 seems most plausible. These numbers include their extermination along the long treks by Ukrainian irregular forces, and in ghettos by Ukrainian and German killing squads. Just in the four main killing centers of Orinin, Kamenets-Podolsk, Stanislawów, and Kolomea, the number of the victims exiled from Hungary reached 2,000–3,000, 14,000–16,000, 3,000, and 2,000–3,000, respectively. If we add to that the various killing sites in smaller communities, the magnitude of destruction becomes more palpable. And, then, the shadow of Belzec, where the final remnants of Hungarian Jews ended up, looms largely over the killing fields.

TWICE BETRAYED

Reading the testimonies of Hungarian Jews, one realizes that the true writers of Holocaust history are the victims themselves. They depict a Hungarian as much as a

Jewish tragedy. It might not be hyperbole to claim that the deportation to Galicia served as a "dress rehearsal" for a much more ambitious, concluding chapter of the Hungarian Holocaust in 1944. In this case, the past informs the future as 1941 became a prologue and harbinger for a much deeper black hole of horrors, that of the 1944 mass murder of more than 500,000 Hungarian Jews.

This book would not be complete without finding a connecting cord between the introductory and final chapters of the Hungarian Holocaust, 1941 and 1944. The fate of the estimated 2,000 or so survivors from the Galician deportation, and some of the Galician Jews who found temporary shelter in Hungary, might be this cord. After escaping from their harrowing Galician experience, often the sole returnees from their traditionally large Jewish families, they were forced into hiding inside Hungary. While some made a painful effort to rebuild a semblance of normal life, others dispersed all across the country for fear of being forced to return to Galicia. But these same survivors, and Galician escapees, were invariably collected and dispatched under inhumane conditions with their families three years later, in the spring of 1944, mostly to Auschwitz. The large majority of them never returned from the death camps.[24]

In addressing a political controversy, the Auschwitz-Birkenau Memorial and Museum issued a communiqué that might serve as a connection between 1941 and

FIG 9.2   Portrait of a religious Jewish farmer from Carpathian Ruthenia, his wife, and six of his children. The family was expelled to Galicia, returned, and then, in 1944, killed in Auschwitz. The farmer, Chaim Simcha Mechlowitz, became immortalized as the farmer in Roman Vishniac's collection *A Vanished World. United States Holocaust Museum, Courtesy of Lisa Wahler.*

1944—between Galicia and Auschwitz. It indirectly brings into focus the evolution of the Galicianer and the consequent fate of the Hungarian deportees in 1941 and the second phase in 1944: "When we look at Auschwitz, we see the end of the process. It's important to remember that the Holocaust actually did not start from gas chambers. This hatred gradually developed from words, stereotypes and prejudice through legal exclusion, dehumanization & escalating violence."[25] This could imply that Auschwitz might have not come into existence without the foundation of mass murder in the Soviet Union.

There were also unstated differences in these words for the psychological approaches toward mass murder between Galicia and the death camps. The recurring question as to what was the qualitative and quantitative dividing line between the face-to-face murder and the efficiently run death camps? Afterall, both aimed to address the "Jewish Question." The two events, though, need to be distinguished from each other. In Eastern Europe, the killing fields were open for all to see: locals, Hungarian soldiers, and Jewish members of the labor companies. There was a certain emotional underpinning, soothed over by copious amount of alcohol, as the hands-on killers in the "trenches" of Galicia went on about their business.

Max Solomon, a survivor of the Orinin Massacre, vividly remembered a German SS man, apparently the commander of the unit, who, after killing a little girl, aimed to shoot her sister. Because he was too drunk to properly aim, it took him several shots to finish her. Solomon distinctly heard as the officer jubilantly exclaimed amid the slaughter: *"Ich tötete gerade weiteres kleines Mädchen"* ("I just killed another little girl"). A teacher from Orinin, who assisted in opening the mass graves, and upon finding large number of empty bottles in the murder site, tartly remarked in a video interview that "a normal human being cannot accomplish such a thing [mass murder] without alcohol."[26]

In Auschwitz and other death camps, the perpetrators made all efforts to hide the macabre reality both from the incoming Jews and from the world. It was a choreographed process of murder with a corresponding charade of lies and props. No emotional attachment was needed for professionals in mass murder. During his trial in Nuremberg, Rudolf Höss, the commandant of Auschwitz, confided to a psychologist that the attitude to murder in the death camps was total indifference: "Any other sentiment 'never even occurred to us.'"[27]

Most of the returnees experienced both worlds—sometimes with a macabre twist—Galicia and Auschwitz. We can identify three stages of post-Galician exile, between 1941 and 1944, for these fugitives. The term "fugitives" is not a misnomer in this context, for they were labeled as such—hunted, arrested, and expelled again if they were found. It started with a long period (sometimes a year) of underground existence—at least until the official citizenship papers were arranged. In the second phase, reserved explicitly for the men, they were invariably drafted into the Hungarian Army as forced laborer and sent back, often enough, to Ukraine. Although, their destination was not Auschwitz, many of them perished on the Eastern Front or were transferred for slave labor in concentration camps in the second half of 1944.[28]

When we examine the experiences of László Zobel, a twenty-three-year-old, his post-Galician existence might be reflective of the fate of many men returning from Galicia. Upon being smuggled directly into Budapest from Galicia, he was denounced to the police the same day. While he was able to hide initially, his mother was arrested and later deported. Zobel, himself was caught three months later in an identity check on the street, and was sent to an internment camp from which, in turn, he was drafted directly, along with three hundred fellow internees, into the forced labor companies attached to the Hungarian Army. He recalled that two battalions were formed: one for the interned Hungarian Jews, mainly escapees from Galicia, and one for foreign nationals, the majority of them German and Austrian refugees. These foreign nationals, by now stateless Jews, were sent immediately to the Eastern Front, from which no one returned. After decommissioned, Zobel was arrested again and spent the rest of the war in a prison, which might have saved his life. Apparently, the prison guards were more compassionate and protective of their wards than the gendarmerie or the city police. Her mother, on the other hand, was shipped to an extermination camp from which she did not return.

Following his escape across the Carpathian Mountains in 1942, Michael Jackson's life provide another window into many young men's experiences. After having been forced to go underground far away from his family, the long-awaited naturalization papers arrived, which gave him the ability to move unhindered. At least he thought so. During a visit to his parents, the first in almost a year, he was arrested by two detectives in a routine razzia at the train station. Jackson was brutally roughed up, beaten almost beyond recognition in the police station. Following the beating, his citizenship papers, fortunately a copy, were also confiscated. As mentioned in chapter six, less than a year later, he was drafted and dispatched with his battalion to Stanislawów, in Galicia, exactly from where he escaped a year and a half earlier.

The fate of the families of these servicemen was a whole different story. While many of the forced labor men did not reach Auschwitz, their families—women, children, and the elderly who survived Galicia—were not so fortunate. This was the final stage, the deportation of almost the entire Jewish community—starting again in Carpathian Ruthenia—to death camps. The survivors were swept up in this huge "population relocation" from home to ghettos, and from ghettos to Auschwitz—close to 500,000. Among them were the remaining survivors of the Galicia deportation.

The title of a book by Peninah Kaufman-Blum, about enduring both of these deportations, *Paamayim Shoah* [Shoah Twice], is apt in summing up the experiences of the survivors of Galicia, twice in the inferno. In a short memoir written in Hebrew, she chronicled how she and her mother were the only ones from a large family who returned in 1942 from Galicia. Moving almost immediately to Budapest, she became a member of the Zionist underground, which tried to save lives by distributing false birth certificates and identity cards. Although hiding under authentic Christian papers, her mother was nevertheless arrested in a routine identity check. In spite of her daughter's frenetic efforts to locate her, her mother embarked again on a final, and equally deadly, journey to Auschwitz.

If we want to find a metaphor for the fateful journeys into "Shoah twice," we might borrow the story of a family from a small Carpathian Ruthenian village. The odyssey of a woman with a five-year-old son and a husband encapsulates perhaps best the fate of these 2,000 survivors. Upon returning from the death camp in 1945, she described the three stages of their nightmare. It started with their deportation to Galicia in 1941, even though their citizenship application was in its final stage of approval in the offices of KEOKH. It continued with their escape back across the border in 1942, in the back of a one-man car for twenty-six hours: "We were lying motionless in a curled-up position. We had no food or drink... and I was worried that my son would start crying and we have finished." Upon crossing the border safely and feeling relief, "I thought nothing may happen to us, [then] my husband got a nervous breakdown. It was horrible to watch how terror and hiding helplessly destroyed this robust man.... He started to cry uncontrollably, shrieking, and crying loudly." This was the moment when the five-year-old son tried to calm him down and "started to beg him to keep quiet."[29]

The family continued hiding for fear that "someone in town would notice us." On the advice of Jewish officials, they reported to the KEOKH, after several months of living in a forest, to clear up their legal status. There, one of the central characters in the deportation and a notoriously anti-Semitic officer, Dr. Árkád Kiss, ordered their immediate expulsion back to Galicia. Upon the intersession of an official in the Ministry of Interior, it was agreed that they could report to the office every two weeks. Not long after that, the family received their Hungarian citizenship papers and "believed we could stay here. But we were fatally wrong."

In the spring of 1944, the final chapter descended on this family after being deported to Auschwitz. They endured the separation and slow journey of their two children toward the gas chambers. The woman became aware of their final fate through a conversation in the camp. Upon returning from the death camp, she was informed of the death of her husband. She was the only one, a lonely mother, who returned alive. One can see and feel a raw and deep wound that will never heal as her final words in her testimony upon her liberation in 1945 sum up the scope of her personal tragedy: "So, I have no one. Only a brother of mine is alive. You know, if he was not alive, I would throw my life away, which is only suffering and pain for me."[30]

MAKING SENSE OF THE SENSELESS

Sometimes investigating a historical event leads to a moment that can reduce a well-constructed narrative to one focal point. It might be the tired face of an old man from Bukovina with a flowing white beard or a child carried by a mother randomly selected from thousands of tired and trudging Jews in the dusty Galician flatland. But our eyes can also fix on the erect image of a Hungarian soldier serving in the transit camp for Hungarian expellees incarcerated in inhuman conditions at Kőrösmező. Military rifle on his shoulder and a menacing club in his hand, as an eyewitness acerbically commented, "obviously not for substituting for a walking stick," he represents a dramatic contrast between the powerful and the powerless. One can only ponder why he needs a huge club with compliant, thoroughly exhausted old men, women, and children. These pictures are the forceful reminders of the 1941 Hungarian deportation. When we can envision them, we are finally able to see the human dimension of the tragedy.[31]

Long-forgotten files in the regional archive in Beregovo (Beregszász), Carpathian Ruthenia, illuminate well this human dimension, the hidden consequences of the deportation. These files don't talk about suffering, hunger, or mass murder. Instead, they are local school reports to the superintendent of schools that dryly present, page after page, village after village, the dramatic decline in the number or complete disappearance of Jewish children in the public schools. The report from a small village, on August 9, informs the superintendent that "presently, Jewish families are expelled daily from the village. Therefore, it's impossible to ascertain how many Jewish children will enroll in the next school year." The abrupt drop in the number of Jewish students through the entire region in 1941 is a good indicator of the demographic devastation. Academic classes were cancelled, and entire schools eliminated because of students being taken to Galicia with their families. On August 3, a communication from another small settlement notes that "it is my honor to officially report that today the Jews of the village were officially expelled and so school for the Jewish schoolchildren is not required."[32]

Trying to understand the enormity of the crime of killing thousands of Jews and their Christian family members may leave one in the realm of nameless and faceless statistics. In launching and conducting the Final Solution, as Ian Kershaw noted, "the de-personalization of the Jew had been the true success of Nazi politics and propaganda."[33] Standing in front of the mass graves in Kamenets-Podolsk, one wonders why the Soviet investigative committee did not identify the Hungarian victims upon opening the graves. I asked this question of a silently sobbing elderly Ukrainian woman, Valentina, a witness, who was an eight-year-old peasant girl during the massacre. Had they not, after all, killed many Ukrainian victims who were later identified by grieving relatives? Her answer: the Hungarian victims will remain nameless forever, for no one came to claim them or recognize them. No family, no relatives, and not even friends left alive to identify them or recite the words of the Kaddish over these nameless victims: "there was nobody to cry," she said. The true magnitude of the crime hits home only with the recognition of individual names and images.

In 1944, a thirteen-year-old girl started a diary in the Transylvanian city of Nagyvárad (Oradea in Romanian) in which she mentioned the deportation of her best friend three years earlier to Kamenets-Podolsk. Éva's description of losing Márta Münzer is evocative. After going for a bicycle ride with Éva, Márta was called home, leaving her red bicycle leaning beside the gate. By the next morning, they had joined the thousands of deportees heading toward Galicia. Éva writes, "we didn't have the heart to send [the bicycle] to Márta's grandmother... we cried a lot when we saw the two red bicycles standing alongside each other."[34]

She also knew that her friend was murdered in Kamenets-Podolsk: "I thought that bed was the only possible place to die in, but they say that the Münzers also didn't die in bed in Poland; the Germans shot them. Márta's grandmother doesn't know it, because she still keeps cleaning Uncle Münzer's dress-suit on the balcony, and the neighbors say that while she is cleaning, she has conversation with the suit.... All I think about is Márta. She was also just a girl, and still the Germans killed her."[35] In turn, Éva was deported to Auschwitz, where she died on October 17, 1944.

Her words become ever more haunting when considered next to an obscure and long-forgotten deposition by Katalin Hincsuk, herself a deportee from Nagyvárad. Her testimony was taken on May 26, 1944, after the liberation of Kamenets-Podolsk, by the Soviet Extraordinary State Commission investigating Nazi crimes. Hincsuk remembers scores of people whom she met in the ghetto of Kamenets-Podolsk, among them, the "Münzers, husband, wife, and daughter."[36] We know that they were murdered. But, finally, the image of the "daughter," whose name is Márta, as mentioned by Éva, is reilluminated on the yellow archival pages. A child from the many victims comes to life for a fleeting moment. She is not a number or a faceless abstraction anymore.

The opening salvo of the Hungarian Holocaust is a story of many narratives. Or, as a colleague termed it, "a silent history with many unheard voices." It's not easy to find positive moments or heroes, for we encounter both the outer boundaries of human evil and debasement intermingled with moments of compassion. Murderers and collaborators outnumber willing rescuers. Heroic and selfless efforts by Margit Slachta, Edith Weiss, Erzsébet Szapáry, Imre Reviczky, and others are well documented.[37] But there were also nameless individuals who were willing to show human decency in lending a hand in the rescue—common soldiers, forced laborers, and many others.

In the mist of passing decades, the dim shadow of such a simple, obscure, nameless Hungarian porter, a "*tróger*" in Hungarian parlance, who occupied perhaps the lowest rung in society, offered to save one of my uncles, the younger brother, Samu. I have never met him and I don't know his name, but suddenly he assumed a mythical aura—extending a hand for the doomed.

For Yaffa Rosenthal, an unexpected moment of redemption came amid their interminable wandering, interspersed with rape and murder, on a dusty road one night in Galicia. They were awakened, fearing that this would be their final moment, when a Ukrainian priest came and brought everyone "hot potato and milk.... I still taste that potato... even after fifty-five years."[38]

Kaufman-Blum's recollection of a perilous and long trek to the Hungarian border from Czortkov in 1942, and her capture upon crossing it, ends with a moment of illumination. Following their arrest, the Hungarian commander of the border post brusquely ordered the group to be forcibly returned across the border accompanied by a soldier. Yet the voice of this simple soldier, Tamás, who was to lead them back to Galicia upon this stern command shines with humanity. "Go, return to Poland," the soldier shouted threateningly as he looked back to see if the superior officer could hear them. And then, "he turned to us in a soft voice: 'if you go right, two kilometers, there is a portion of the border that is not guarded. There you could cross safely....' then he continued in whisper, 'Don't continue together. It's dangerous. You better separate into smaller groups.'"[39]

EPILOGUE
Looking for a Closure

During my first trip to Kamenets-Podolsk in 2008, I found a proverbial bottle with a message of mass murder, cast out for an accidental discovery. It was the impromptu testimony of Valentina. This bottle was full of scattered memory nuggets—the repressed mental notes of an eight-year-old girl from a period of history that is hard to comprehend and even harder to explain. But after perusing thousands of pages of wartime documents, scholarly sources, interviews, and video testimonies by survivors, including Valentina's memories, I was able to piece together a more comprehensive tableau about what happened in 1941, which placed the content of her words in context.

Still, something was missing from the overall picture of the 1941 deportation. I had a nagging sense of unfinished business, for there were three additional castaway bottles that needed to be found and opened. Was it the need to find a personal angle and perspective? For one, I wanted to discover more about the fate of the two brothers, my uncles, who disappeared in the mass graves of Kamenets-Podolsk. This book's genesis could be attributed to my quest to find some traces of them.

Also, Valentina's short testimony, fragmented as it was, left me with more questions than answers. How could she see so vividly the process of murder? Could I find out more by revisiting Kamenets-Podolsk?

And, finally, there was a third, rather intriguing quest: the not fully explored story of an almost unknown murder site that my research was able to uncover. It was a hitherto unfamiliar story of the mass murder of the Hungarian expellees in the small Podolian town of Orinin.

The most challenging task was the first one. In looking for some clues about the two brothers, I ran into a wall. I suspected that no new details about them would be easily found. I knew that in the provinces, record keeping was only a perfunctory exercise, but how is it possible that no traces could be found of all the thousands of people deported from Budapest? Why did the personnel in KEOKH not keep a list, a tally, detailed records? Yet, and unfortunately, there were no records or lists of deportees that could be found, if kept at all, in various Hungarian archives. Time was of the essence here, also because the number of family members who could have information about my uncles was rapidly dwindling. Age takes its toll. Far back, I had tried to reach out to Tildi, the wife of the younger brother, Samu. She was living by herself at the time, having never remarried. But she refused to talk about the war years. She reflected a pattern of behavior that was characteristic to many victims of Holocaust trauma—evading the painful past with silence. It did not happen if we do not talk about it. Not long after that, she passed away. Beyond that, I was not able to discover any new information. After all, these were two poor brothers with little education, and without an anchor in society where they could leave a trace or historical memory. One of my greatest regrets, in looking back, as a young boy, was not meeting the porter who wanted to save Samu. But, at that time, I did not know how to ask any questions.

Thus, the most immediate priority in finding new information was contacting the surviving daughters of Samu. In the fashionable Café Europe, in Budapest, I sat with Éva, Zsuzsa, and Gita, the three sisters and their children. This was the first and only time that an opportunity presented itself for meeting all three of them at the same time. I hoped for a soul-searching conversation about their father. What could they remember prior to the deportation? Could they recall any details from the days before his arrest and transfer to the transit camp? Were they aware of his final hours? As we sipped strong espresso, I formulated a whole set of questions, which rapidly evaporated as I sensed a feeling of mutual grief that they had never faced or experienced before. As I learned, their mother had wrapped the whole affair in silence. They did not even know that they were Jewish until later in life. Was it a coping mechanism for the loss? Or the mother's deep sense of guilt for not making an effort to save him? As my own mother once bitterly blurted out in an unguarded moment, "She could have saved him." Did she mean the lack of action on the part of Samu's wife? But it might be also likely, as her granddaughter confided in me later, that she was terrified for her daughters' fate for being partly Jewish.[1]

What surprised me the most was the complete lack of information or knowledge about the final fate of their father. As they slowly opened up, decades of denial gave way to memory fragments. The older one, Éva, remembered that their mother shared the moment when Samu was taken away for a promised short examination of his papers, after which he would "surely return." We now know that he was taken from the precinct directly to the central synagogue of Budapest. Zsuzsa, the middle daughter, also remembered vaguely visiting her father in the makeshift internment camp in the synagogue. Nothing more. Yet, it was an opening for rediscovering and sharing with each other a painful past. There was no anger, only long silences as I explained to them the chain of events in Kamenets-Podolsk that led to the final moments of their father and his brother in facing the executioner's gun. The sisters, who had never faced or contemplated this raw truth, now mourned these gaps in our history that could never be fully recovered. In many ways, and hopefully, our quiet discussion, interspersed with somber reflections, provided long-overdue closure for them.

I did not ask about Karcsi, the second brother. There was no reason. He was the tall, slim, silent figure with deep-set, blue eyes, who will remain forever a mystery, slowly fading into the shadows of the millions who were killed in Eastern Europe.

As for my decision to visit Kamenets-Podolsk again, I was not sure what I would find during this new trip and what I would do once I got there. There was no logical reason to visit the murder site—the memorial park had no historical value for the book that would justify a second trip. Yet, something urged me to return. I replayed in my mind Valentina's spontaneous and emotional words next to the little market. I had only sketchy mental notes from this first meeting, and a few hastily scribbled notes for the records. Was this the reason that I wanted to see her and hear her story again? Or maybe I hoped to discover hitherto unfamiliar new details?

Again, I persuaded my university colleagues and one of their assistants, Éva Veres, who spoke Ukrainian and Hungarian, to join me in this new adventure in the hope that we might find some new or "rediscovered memory." We decided to start this visit by stopping first at Kamenets-Podolsk where a noticeable change had taken place. A special organization was formed, called *Chesed Besht*, which was dedicated to the welfare of the small, truncated, and elderly Jewish community in the region. Not surprisingly, it hardly concerned itself with historical memory.

This limited us to visiting and talking with Valentina again. The consequent interview or a rather nebulous reconnect was, at best, introspective. We were the only ones who asked about her experiences during the fateful three-day massacre. Though I did not have explicit questions in mind, by then I was well-acquainted with the details about the intricacies of mass murder and, specifically, that of Kamenets-Podolsk. It was rather a belated opportunity, perhaps, to say thanks for providing the impetus for writing this book.

We had no address or information as to where to locate her. Fortunately, everyone knew the old flower seller at the little market. So, Éva and I set out to find Valentina. My companion, though, was understandably nervous and emotional. While she had no connection to the Holocaust, she proved that it could touch people who had never encountered, on the personal level, this tragedy.

The short stroll from the market to her house opened a gap in time and space—from the center of town with the mass grave, surrounded by aging, communist-style multilevel buildings, to a dilapidated neighborhood of small houses. This short walk finally helped me to see and understand how an eight-year-old child was able to run to the site and observe the minutia of mass murder. Her little Ukrainian village was adjacent to the craters where 23,600 victims were slaughtered within three days—not more than a five-minute walk. The staccato of gunfire must still ring in her ears.

FIG E.1 The painful memories of an eight-year-old: Valentina, who witnessed the Kamenets-Podolsk mass murder. *Courtesy of George Eisen.*

Valentina's little rickety shack, groaning with age and overgrown with weeds, was perhaps her ancestral home. The roof precariously perched on walls flaking and crumbling. In the accompaniment of her two goats, peacefully grazing, she appeared at the iron gate when she saw us coming. Someone had already alerted her that foreign visitors were looking for her. Her smile, though, was the same. She remained the only living memory of the massacre.

There was not too much that she could add, though. There were no new insights. But it helped me to close the circle, reconfirming the painful memories of a child. On my part, my visit was also a belated thank-you for launching me to write this book. As we stood at the gate recounting her experiences, one of the neighbors sauntered over, listening somewhat bemusedly to Valentina's story. She had never heard about the mass murder in her own neighborhood. Five minutes away. Then, she turned to Éva in a whisper with the impromptu suggestion of giving Valentina a few Hryvnia, the Ukrainian currency. She lived in dire poverty. Éva silently opened her purse and pulled out a handful of banknotes.

The third quest was connected with Kamenets-Podolsk as well. I wanted to stop in a little Podolian town, a quintessential *shtetl*, where close to half of the population was Jewish before the war and was situated a mere ten miles from Kamenets-Podolsk. The name Orinin is not commonly known in Holocaust literature.[2] As many of the episodes featured in this book, the story of Orinin came to light by coincidence. In writing about it, I struggled with two main questions. Was it just another grisly episode of the Holocaust? Or was it unique in its own right? The town harbored a hitherto unknown story of mass murder—the murder of over two thousand Hungarian Jews in a destroyed Soviet-era fortification. I discovered this information accidentally through the video testimonies of two survivors from Carpathian Ruthenia, who did not know each other, but independently recounted this tale of the prequel to and the murder itself. Additionally, I was not able to divorce myself from the gripping and highly evocative words of Max Solomon, the sole survivor of the immediate mass murder, describing in detail the event. I knew that I needed to visit Orinin to see the site, partly to corroborate his account as well as to pay homage to the victims.[3]

Indeed, human stories are, as I mentioned earlier, what history is made of. The role of the historian is to corroborate such narratives. During a scholarly discussion between colleagues, a question arose about the credibility and validity of witnesses after fifty years since their actual experiences. This question often presents a scholarly quandary: how can we give credit to human memory and imagination after such a long lapse in time—especially when we are talking about repressed memories? Primo Levi's words of warning resonated in my mind: "Human memory is a marvelous but fallacious instrument. The memories which lie within us are not carved in stone; not only do they tend to become erased as the years go by, but often they change, or even increase by incorporating extraneous features."[4] By that time, though, I had in my possession a third testimony, that of a local resident, Alexandr Shulyk, whose grandfather was a witness (and perhaps himself Jewish). Thanks to a video prepared by Ágnes Moldova in 2018, Shulyk's recollection confirmed the testimony of Max Solomon.

Nevertheless, I had to see the murder site myself—the physical locale. Of course, there was no certainty that the place of murder of the Hungarians would be marked or even known to the local residents. I knew that we might not find a single Jew in this haunted place. Stalin completed the demographic transformation that Hitler did not finish in Ukraine. And, if some Jews survived the Holocaust, perhaps in hiding, or relocated to the town from Russia after the war, they immigrated en masse in the 1970s to Israel or the United States.

Surprisingly, the aforementioned video proved me wrong. As the video produced by Moldova has shown, there were people who remembered the massacre in detail and could pinpoint the site. I wanted to see it myself, in solitude and contemplation. From the reasonably passable road, we could look around, and as far as the eye can see, green fields framed picturesque small groves of trees. This was the murder site. The "Hungarian graves," as the locals dubbed it.

We approached the grove, a few hundred yards from the road, which was described also in the video. Surrounded by cultivated green fields, the grove remained surprisingly

FIG E.2   Peaceful serenity: The Hungarian graves in Orinin, hidden in the former Soviet military fortification, July 26, 1941. *Courtesy of George Eisen.*

unmolested as it was left eighty years ago. It was hiding its secret assiduously. I looked around, somewhat distracted by the serenity around me. It was scenic and peaceful. It was here, the graveyard shaded by towering trees, providing background to semi-broken concrete bunkers—the mass grave of the Hungarian Jews. There was no commemorative stone or even a single sign reminding us what happened here eighty years ago. Overgrown by vegetation, the fortifications kept their secret well as I peeked through one of the entrances to see only darkness. I guess one could have climbed through the opening, but that would only disturb the sanctity of the place. Standing in deep contemplation, I desperately tried to recall the words of the Kaddish, the Jewish memorial prayer for the dead, that I could recite for the victims of this place. But after the first two lines, my memory failed at this crucial moment.

As I slowly retraced my steps toward the car and my waiting companions, trying not to disturb the crops in the field, I knew that this would not be the last time I would visit this grove. Maybe I would return to properly recite the Kaddish, or, perhaps, to set up a memorial for the victims. But, then, the abandoned bunkers could have served as a form of memorial; a soundless reminder for the atrocity that had taken place here some eight decades ago.

In writing this book, this silent grove became personal. A symbolic place for a collective grief for all the victims of the 1941 deportation. Unlike the memorial in Kamenets-Podolsk, impersonal and somewhat pretentious, a place where I hoped or wanted to reconnect with my two uncles, this place spoke to me with its deep and painful silence. I finally felt a sense of connect tinged with deep anguish.

As the car slowly pulled away, I turned around to take one last look as the line of trees rapidly disappeared in the distance. It felt like I am left with a story abandoned in mid-sentence. I knew I would have to return.

TIME FOR THANKS
Acknowledgments

ONE MIGHT ASK THE "UNASKABLE" QUESTION: DO WE REALLY NEED ONE more book on the Holocaust? Hopefully, I framed this book in order to respond to this question. This text explores a rather narrow and unexplored slice of the Holocaust. Yet, its consequences transcend Hungary—the cross-border removal of the thousands of Jews precipitated a chain of events that shaped the Holocaust process. But it also presaged the full Jewish Hungarian tragedy, which followed three years later in 1944.

My journey through archives, institutions, and countless scholarly discussions with colleagues—from Israel to Ukraine, from France to Germany, and from the United Sates to Hungary—for the past eight years have yielded material that is both enlightening and puzzling. There is a long list of individuals who helped along the way or provided helpful hints and suggestions. The first exploratory trip that we made to Kamenets-Podolsk with my three colleagues, and a follow-up visit in which we were joined by Éva Veres, was only an informal introduction. I owe a special debt to them—Nataliya Kubiniy, Vasyl Miklovda, and Mykhaylo Pityulych—for without them this book might have not been written. Of course, our unforeseen meeting with Valentina might also be construed as a form of divine intervention. In the excitement of the moment, we never learned her family name. She will always remain Valentina. Many thanks to her and her tears.

The most crucial information was buried in archives and museums. The list of such institutions is a long one. My access to the video collection of testimonies by Holocaust survivors located in the Steven Spielberg Film and Video Archive (USC Shoah Foundation Institute for Visual History and Education) at the University of Southern California was crucial. It stands out as the most important place, for these interviews painted a rich tapestry of human experiences under often inhuman circumstances. Through this archive I was able to tap into an invaluable reservoir of authentic recollections of the 1941 expulsion. Initially, Lydia Wasylenko from the Syracuse University Libraries was able to help me to view these testimonies. Later, Douglas W. Ballman from USC made accessible all the requested and re-requested videos, thanks to advanced information transfer, directly via the Internet. I appreciate his prompt responses to my frantic emails. His assistance was crucial, for through these testimonies the story of the summer and fall of 1941, a time of unbridled murder, reemerges in vivid colors.

Thanks to these survivors, we encounter the central architects of the murder mechanism. It's worth of repeating that we all are familiar with the immoral monsters—Hitler, Himmler, Goebbels, Göring—in Germany. Thanks to in-depth interviews during the Nuremberg trials, we are also acquainted with their personalities and their psychological profiles. For the general public, or even historians, the "second tier" low-level SS men, like Leideritz and Krüger, who can be credited collectively with hundreds of thousand murders, are, at best, unfamiliar.[1] As for the international audience, figures such as László Bárdossy, Henrik Werth, Ámon Pásztóy, and Miklós Kozma are almost wholly unknown, enigmas outside of Hungary. Yet, these Hungarians were as much, or perhaps more, responsible for the early phases of the Hungarian Holocaust as the Nazi murder squads. And there are many officers, regional administrators, and government officials who ensured that the vision of these leaders become a bloody reality. This where the recollections of the survivors are invaluable. Through them, we encounter the low-level perpetrators as well as vocal and sometimes unwitting saviors amid the destruction, who are slowly fading into the mist of history, yet come to life, for a fleeting moment, through the voices of these survivors in the videos.

General documents and trial records of the executioners from Hungarian, German, Israeli, Polish, and Ukrainian archives tell a detailed story of the intricate process of murder. A collective thanks is due to the United States Holocaust Museum for the support its dedicated staff extended for the completion of this book. Thanks to the digitalization of Ukrainian archives in Galicia, accessible via the United States Holocaust Memorial Museum, we were able to read long-forgotten testimonies of eyewitnesses, confessions of perpetrators, and trial proceedings. In this, I am indebted to Vadim Altskan, historian at the United States Holocaust Memorial Museum. He went above and beyond in accommodating my often challenging requests. Similarly, important assistance was given by the staff of the photo archives and reference desk of the museum: Megan Lewis, Judith Cohen, and Nancy Hartman.

This book would not be complete without the assistance of a group of creative young Hungarian historians who brought to my attention new sources and research. Gyula Kosztyó, who provided primary documents directly from the archives of the Kárpátaljai Területi Állami Levéltár, (KTAL) Beregovo (Beregszász) in Transcarpathia [Carpathian Ruthenia], Ukraine, is one of them. His groundbreaking work on the economic devastation of the region as the consequence of the Jewish Laws also helped to explain the economic rationale for the deportation. Ákos Fóris, a young and creative historian in Budapest, yielded important primary sources, without which some theories would remain in the realm of mere speculation. In addition, his dissertation yielded important background material about the functioning of the Hungarian military on the Eastern Front.

Then there is a list of individuals who assisted me selflessly, due to friendship, professional courtesy, or a genuine belief that this story should be told. Among them a special thank-you is due to Tamás Stark, who provided invaluable material from a host of Hungarian archives and limitless discussions about various aspects of the 1941 deportation. He has been a valuable help in this project from the beginning. Indeed, his access to Hungarian archives was crucial to this book.

My ongoing brainstorming with Tamás Majsai, a pioneer in the exploration of the 1941 deportation, was also important. I consider his groundbreaking works on this theme as a must-read for any researcher of this subject. I not only benefited from his publications on this topic but also from his astute observations. This book would not be complete without his publication of original documents revolving around the deportation. His unique brand of humor was definitely an added ingredient to our scholarly discussions.

Sometimes an accidental connection on the Internet resulted in unexpected benefits. Such was my virtual meeting with Hans Peter Trautmann, a German history enthusiast. He became an important source for hitherto unknown facts about Peter Leideritz, one of the main executioners of the Hungarian and local Jews in Kolomea, Southern Galicia, and his wife, Anneliese Leideritz. Through our correspondence, important details emerged about Leideritz's activities, capture, and transfer by American military authorities to Poland. Also, Trautmann brought to my attention important archival material about the Leideritz couple that can be found in the Hessisches Staatsarchiv Wiesbaden in Germany, and in the Institute of National Remembrance (Instytut Pamięci Narodowej) in Warsaw. In turn, I had the opportunity to connect with a dedicated and helpful archivist in this archive, Grzegorz Perzyński.

Sándor Szakály, director of the VERITAS Research Institute for History and Archives in Budapest, provided material pertaining to communications directly with Berlin about the unilateral Hungarian deportation by German border authorities. Szakály's assistance in locating a key photograph was also an important contribution to this book. Indeed, one of the problematic aspects of the research was finding photographs (or to be more precise, securing permission to use these photographs). I am greatly indebted to Zsuzsa Katona and George Csicsery, both documentary filmmakers; Tamás Ábrahám, a researcher; Daisy Chorin, a survivor and relative of Baroness Edith Weiss; and Angelika Orgona from the Hungarian National Museum.

A book like this could not come to fruition without intellectual discussions in the accompaniment of a good coffee. The topics ranged from the rationale for genocide to the psychological underpinning of the Holocaust, and how "to make sense from the senseless." I am especially indebted to Professor James Hatley for these enlightening dialogues.

A similar note of appreciation is due to my friend and colleague Mary Van Keuren, who meticulously reviewed and corrected the manuscript. She devoted more time than

I asked for in pouring over the material. Her insightful comments and suggestions not only enriched the book, but it shaped, in some degree, the general tone of it. Her observation that I write as a European might be true.

Finally, I am indebted to Dr. Deb Dooley for the review of the final version of the manuscript. By helping to identify grammatical errors and inconsistencies in the text, she provided insightful comments about these issues. Her sensitivity in reading and commenting on this challenging subject made invaluable contributions to the quality of this book.

Special thanks and gratitude are deserved for the survivors. Many of them are not with us anymore. They volunteered their voices to recount painful memories from a dark epoch that many might want to repress. They were willing to share their stories with future generations in the hope of never forgetting and never letting such an atrocity happen again. These survivors provided the most gripping and unforgettable moments by sharing with me, however inadvertently, their anger, pain, and incomprehension for the sufferings and losses they had to endure. The common thread through their narratives were their never-healing psychological wounds. Yet, each individual dealt with this trauma in their own way, and there a special thank-you is due to László Zobel. He was the only one who provided life interviews and in-depth insights, at age one hundred. My meetings, and friendly discussions with him not only enriched this book, but evolved into a delightful friendship.

After finishing the manuscript, I decided to view selected videos and reread extant letters from Galicia to Budapest again, and suddenly came to the realization that I had missed some important details and nuances. An anguished sentence, a furtive look, a long pause, and a painful expression sometime convey more than a long-winded tale. I was especially taken by the testimony of Cipora Brenner. She is multilingual, so her selection in communicating her tragic story in perfect Hungarian surprised me. For me, her choice of the language of her tormentors still remains an enigma. And there were the deeply moving comments and psychological insights of Elizabeth (Erzsébet) Lubell about her survival and flight from the Kolomea Ghetto. Without their testimony, this book would not be complete. Many thanks Cipora and Elizabeth. Theirs and those of other survivors' stories are also remarkable, if often devastating, for their haunting testimonies bring history vividly to life. It reminds me of Marie Colvin's dictum, as a war correspondent, that "war is about what happens to people."[2]

Finally, I should end with my deepest thanks to my wife, Cynthia, who patiently supported my work. Most importantly, her support expressed itself in giving me unfettered time for travel, research, discussions, and writing. She understood that this book had to be written and, as it turned out, is as much her accomplishment as mine. This patience cannot be better expressed than her words of encouragement: "Stop already the research and finish the damn book." While you will not be able to see the final publication of this book, Cynthia, I love you for these words.

NOTES

PREFACE

1. Jill Lepore, "The Deadline," *New Yorker*, July 8 and 15, 2019, 21.
2. Meeting with Valentina, April 18, 2008.
3. Deuteronomy 4:9.
4. The story of Csanád Szegedi, a far-right politician from Hungary, who trivialized the Holocaust and blamed Jews for the wrongs of the world, before finding out that he was one himself, is instructive. See *Népszabadság*, August 6, 2012, https://www.jpost.com/Jerusalem-Report/A-whole-new-Jew-478706.
5. Ian Kershaw, *To Hell and Back: Europe 1914–1949* (New York: Viking, 2015), 369.
6. Rosa, Leiser's second wife, was deported and shared the fate of Karcsi and Samu in Kamenets-Podolsk. The question of why she was not exempted from the deportation because of her age is an intriguing one.
7. Daniel Mendelsohn, *The Lost: A Search for Six of Six Million* (New York: HarperCollins, 2006).
8. The German term "*Aktion*" in Eastern Europe connoted the violent collection and organized mass killing of Jews.

1

1. This story of my two uncles became part of my family lore, talked about on long winter evenings. The returning Hungarian soldier, the simple porter who knew our family well, confronted my father with the details of the tragic scene and the fate of my two uncles there.
2. Galicia is a historical region in Eastern Europe that presently straddles the border between Poland and Ukraine—east of the Carpathian Mountains. The area, which is named after the medieval city of Halych, was first mentioned in Hungarian historical chronicles in the year 1206 as *Galiciæ*. As a typical "borderland" Galicia was controlled prior to 1918 by Austria, between the two world wars by Poland, and was followed by

a short Soviet rule in the eastern part of the province between 1939 and 1941. Larry Wolff, *The Idea of Galicia: History and Fantasy in Habsburg Political Culture* (Stanford: Stanford University Press, 2011). See also Suzan Wynne, *The Galitzianers: The Jews of Galicia, 1772–1918* (Tucson: Wheatmark, 2006).
3. Peter Hayes, *Why? Explaining the Holocaust* (New York: W. W. Norton, 2017), 3.
4. We use the Hungarian spelling for the designation of "Galicianer."
5. American diplomats in Berlin informed the intelligence officers of several embassies, among them the Hungarians, about these German plans. See Andrew Nagorski, *Hitlerland: American Eyewitnesses to the Nazi Rise to Power* (New York: Simon & Schuster, 2015), 298–99.
6. The investigation as to who carried out the air raid against Kassa (Kosice) is still inconclusive, but the general view is that it was a German provocation. See Krisztián Ungváry, *Magyarország a második világháboruban* (Budapest: Kossuth Kiadó, 2010), 7–9. Also, Gyula Kádár, *A Ludovikától Sopronkőhidáig* (Budapest: Magvető, 1978), 384–91.
7. Ungváry, *Magyarország a második világháboruban*, 11–15.
8. The German military also resisted the expulsion of close to 150,000 Serbians, mainly soldiers, from Hungary in the spring of 1941. Lagzi István, "Forgószél a délvidéken 1941-ben (A délvidéki jugoszláv hadsereg katonáinak hazatérése a német hadifogoly táborokból)," *Valóság*, no. 3 (March 2007).
9. It is also important to note that the use of Carpathian Ruthenia for the region is an attempt to provide a neutral term. The nomenclature of the region depends on geographic perspective and political point of view. Thus, from a Hungarian view the region is described as *Subcarpathia* (i.e., below the Carpathians or *Kárpátalja*), while from a Ukrainian and Russian perspective it is referred to as *Transcarpathia* (on the other side of the Carpathian Mountains). As for the locals, they conveniently named the region, *Zakarpats'ka oblast*. "Government commissioner" is not an exact translation for the Hungarian title, Kormányzói Biztos. He was appointed directly by Miklós Horthy as his special representative, governing the region independently and reporting directly to him.
10. Emphasis added by author. It is dated July 9, 1941, prior to the deportation. Hadtörténelmi Irattár és Levéltár (HIL) Magyar Királyi Gyorshadtest, Kárpát Csoport (July 9, 1941), Box I. Kinga Frojimovics, *I Have Been a Stranger in a Strange Land* (Jerusalem: Yad Vashem, 2007), 104–7; Mária Ormos, *Egy Magyar Médiavezér: Kozma Miklós* (Budapest: Polgár, 2000), 753–67; Colonel General László Dezső was executed on June 8, 1949, by the Hungarian government.
11. The office was placed under the direct control of the Ministry of Interior as Department IX. An excellent analysis about the history of this office was provided by Kinga Frojmovics, *I Have Been a Stranger in a Strange Land* (Jerusalem: Yad Vashem, 2007), 233–39. See also, Tamás Majsai's monograph, "A magyar holocaust első felvonása, 1941," *Holocaust Emlékkönyv* (Budapest: TEDISZ, 2008), 306–8.

12. Timothy Snyder, *Bloodlands: Europe between Hitler and Stalin* (New York: Basic Books: 2010); and *Black Earth: The Holocaust as History and Warning* (New York: Crown, 2015). See also Ian Kershaw, *To Hell and Back: Europe 1914–1949* (New York: Viking, 2015), 414–15.
13. Eniko A. Sajti, *Impériumváltások, revízió, kisebbség. Magyarok a Délvidéken, 1918–1947* (Napvilág Kiadó, Budapest, 2004), 190–98. Latest Serbian scholarly literature puts the number of expellees at 25,000. Slobodan Aleksandar Kasas, *Madari u Vojvodini 1941–1946,* (Novi Sad: *Filozofski Fakultet u Novom Sadu*, 1996), 39. Expulsion of Serbs and Jews from Croatia was implemented by the Ustaša Croatian Revolutionary Movement.
14. The name Carpathian Ruthenia is sometimes used for a contiguous cross-border area of western Ukraine that borders with Slovakia, Hungary, and Romania. The people inhabiting this region identify themselves as Rusyns and use the term Transcarpathia—literally "beyond the Carpathian Mountains"—today's western Ukraine. The Felvidék, southern provinces of former northern Hungary, is today in Slovakia, while Erdély or Transylvania is in Romania.
15. Originally Werth bypassed the prime minister with this idea. See Ákos Fóris "A megszállt szovjet területek kérdése a magyar polgári kormányszerveknél" in *Az Első Világháború Irodalmi és Történelmi Aspektusai a Kelet-európai Régióban,* edited by József Péter Fodor, Renáta Marosi, Dániel Miklós, Krisztina Péró, and Roland Szabó (Budapest: ELTE, 2017), 63–83. Also, Miklós Szinai and László Szűcs, eds, *Horthy Miklós Titkos Iratai* (Budapest: Kossuth, 1963), 306.
16. Aly Götz, *Why the Germans? Why the Jews?: Envy, Race Hatred, and the Prehistory of the Holocaust* (New York: Metropolitan Books, 2014).
17. Sándor Márai, *Hallgatni Akartam* (Budapest: Helikon, 2016), 45.
18. Perhaps the most comprehensive work on the economic destruction of Hungarian Jewry during the Holocaust belongs to Kádár Gábor and Vági Zoltán, *Hullarablás, a Magyar Zzsidók Gazdasági Megsemmisítése* (Budapest: Jaffa, 2005). See also Yehuda Don, "Economic Implications of the Anti-Jewish Legislation in Hungary," in *Genocide and Rescue: The Holocaust in Hungary 1944,* ed. David Cesarani (Oxford: Berg Publishers, 1997), 47–76. However, the newest research belongs to Gyula Kosztyó, who analyzed the archival resources in the Kárpátaljai Állami Levéltár in Beregovo. See "Mit vesztett Kárpátalja a holokauszttal? Egy minisztériumi állapotfelmérés elemzése (1939. augusztus)."
19. Nansen passports were internationally recognized refugee travel documents, issued by the League of Nations to stateless refugees. The first Nansen passports were issued following an international agreement reached at the Intergovernmental Conference on Identity Certificates for Russian Refugees, convened by Fridtjof Nansen in Geneva from July 3, 1922, to July 5, 1922, in his role as high commissioner for refugees for the

League of Nations. By 1942, they were honored by governments in fifty-two countries. Approximately 450,000 Nansen passports were provided to stateless people and refugees who needed travel documents but could not obtain one from a national authority.
20. It is important to remember that during the interwar years there was no clear enforcement of a state policy for maintaining citizenship. Proof of citizenship was not needed even for a passport application. By the late 1930s, however, this policy was more rigorously enforced with the proviso that Jews be subjected to a more arduous process, with the aim of limiting their numbers.
21. Anne Applebaum, *East and West: Across the Borderlands of Europe* (New York: Pantheon Books, 1994). Katzmann became higher SS and police leader of *Distrikt Galizien* in August 1941. The report by him as a SS-Gruppenführer, commander of the German SS and police in the District of Galicia, was titled "Lösung der Judenfrage im Distrikt Galizien" (The Solution of the Jewish Question in the District of Galicia), submitted on June 30, 1943, to the SS and Police Chief Friedrich Krüger. *Report by SS-General Fritz Katzmann on the Killing of the Half Million Jews in Eastern Galicia*, edited by Tuvia Friedman (Haifa, Israel: Documentation Institute: 1993).
22. Between 50,000 to 60,000 Jewish civilians were killed between 1918 and 1921 in Ukraine alone. See Kershaw, *To Hell and Back: Europe, 1914–1949*.
23. Perhaps the most comprehensive work about the Holocaust in Galicia belongs to Dieter Pohl, *Nationalsozialistische Judenverfolgung in Ostgalizien 1941–1944* (R. Oldenbourg Verlag München, 1997).
24. Michael Burleigh, *Moral Combat: Good and Evil in World War II* (New York: Harper, 2011), 249–51. Martin Dean, *Collaboration in the Holocaust: Crimes of Local Police in Belorussia and Ukraine, 1941–44* (New York: St. Martin's Press, 2000), 78–81.
25. We can dispense with a lengthy discussion about what previous authors wrote, for it would only detract from the narrative of this riveting yet tragic story. We can identify, though, several scholars who were trailblazers in exploring this painful period in Hungarian history. Perhaps the most prominent work belongs to Tamás Majsai, who combined solid historical research with a sympathy for the victims. See Tamás Majsai, "A kőrösmezei zsidódeportálás 1941-ben," in *Ráday Gyűjtemény Évkönyve*, Vol. IV–V, 59–86, 195–237, and "A Soá Magyarországon 1942-ben," in *Tilalomfák Ellenében*, edited by Tamás Majsai (Budapest: Wesley János Lelkészképző Főiskola, 2010), 83–116. Another notable work was written by Kinga Frojmovics, *I Have Been a Stranger in a Strange Land* (Jerusalem: Yad Vashem, 2007). Surprisingly enough, a short but comprehensive work was done in Italian about this event: "'Seht euch diesen Mann an' Kamenec Podolski 27–29 Agosto 1941," http://www.ordnungspolizei.org/j259/it/articles/5-kamenec-podolski.html. Most recent scholarship belongs to Ádám Gellért and János Gellért, whose work on this subject appeared in several issues of the

BETEKINTŐ, the Online Journal of the Historical Archives of the Department of State Security, and other publications. The first work during the communist period belongs to Arthur Geyer Arthur, "Az első magyarországi deportálás," in *Új Élet naptár 1960/61* (Budapest: MIOK Kiadása, 1960). Additional work of importance belongs to Judit Fejes, "On the History of the Mass Deportation from Carpatho-Ruthenia in 1941," in *The Holocaust in Hungary: Fifty Years Later*, edited by Randolph L. Braham and Attila Pók (New York: Columbia University Press, 1997), 305–27; Ormos, *Egy Magyar Médiavezér: Kozma Miklós*; and, Klaus-Michael Mallmann, "Der qualitative Sprung im Vernightungsprozess, der Massaker von Kamenez-Podolsk Ende August 1941," *Jahrbuch fur Antisemitismus-forschung* 10 (2001): 239–64. Zoltán Tibori Szabó's article, in manuscript form, about deportation from northern Transylvania is also noteworthy, "Zsidók deportálása Észak-Erdélyből 1940-1942-ben," 2021. Finally, Randolph L. Braham's comprehensive work about the Hungarian Holocaust contains a segment about the 1941 deportation to Galicia: *A Magyar Holocaust*. 2 vols. (Budapest: Gondolat, 1981).

26. Peter Longerich, *Holocaust: The Nazi Persecution and Murder of the Jews* (Oxford: Oxford University Press, 2010), 218.

27. Israel Carmi, ed., *Sefer Nadwórna* (Tel Aviv: Nadwórna Community in Israel and America, 1975), 21.

28. David Cesarani quoted from a letter by a Viennese police officer Walter Mattner to his wife, dated on October 5, 1941: *Final Solution: The Fate of the Jews 1933–1949* (New York: St. Martin's Press, 2016), 399. Also quoted by Adam Gopnik, "Blood and Soil," *New Yorker*, September 2, 2015, 100.

29. Jeffrey Burds, *Holocaust in Rovno: The Massacre at Sosenki Forest, November 1941* (Palgrave Pivot, 2013), 135.

30. Recent interview of Efrossinia from Ukraine by Yahad-in Unum, shared by Father Patrick Desbois, https://www.facebook.com/patrick.desbois.71.

31. In interviewing Ukrainian eyewitnesses, the recurring theme was that after opening the mass graves of the Hungarian Jews, they closed them without attempting to identify those killed since no one was there to identify them. The testimony of Professor V. Chernyovsky, May 20, 1944, United States Holocaust Memorial Museum, RG-22. 002M\7021\64\64-799\,799-0186.TIF.

32. B. F. Sabrin, ed., *Alliance for Murder: The Nazi–Ukrainian Nationalist Partnership in Genocide* (New York: Sarpedon, 1991), 278–79.

33. "Slachta Margit Levele Horthy Miklósnénak," in Tamás Majsai, "A körösmezei zsidódeportálás 1941-ben," *Ráday Gyüjtemény Évkönyve*, Vol. IV–V (1984–1985): 205–6.

34. A long-needed book about the postwar awareness of the uniqueness of the crime perpetrated by Germany was written by Philippe Sands, *East West Street: On the Origins*

of Genocide and Crimes Against Humanity (London: Weidenfeld & Nicolson, 2016).
35. A full chapter on the complex coexistence and genocide in Buczacz, Galicia, was described by Omer Bartov, *Anatomy of a Genocide: Life and Death of a Town Called Buczacz* (New York: Simon & Schuster, 2018), 275–88. See also Gabriel N. Finder and Alexander V. Prusin, "Collaboration in Eastern Galicia: The Ukrainian Police and the Holocaust," *East European Jewish Affairs* 34, no. 2 (2004): 100, 108, n. 60.
36. The idea of Galicia as a "bloodland" for Jews was not new. The successive pogroms with their waves of murder, rape, and plunder did not suddenly emerge. From the early twentieth century to the bloody and violent convulsions of the Russian Civil War in the early 1920s, Jews were the targets for murderous violence. By some estimates, between 50,000 to 60,000 Jews were killed in Ukraine alone during the civil war. See, Jeffrey Veidlinger, *In the Midst of Civilized Europe: The Pogroms of 1918–1921 and the Onset of the Holocaust* (New York: Metropolitan, 2021).
37. Father Patrick Desbois, *The Holocaust by Bullets: A Priest's Journey to Uncover the Truth Behind the Murder of 1.5 Million Jews*, trans. Catherine Spencer (New York: Palgrave Macmillan, 2008).
38. The gripping book by Father Patrick Desbois well describes the entire process. See *In Broad Daylight: The Secret Procedures behind the Holocaust by Bullets* (New York: Arcade Publishing, 2018). For active Ukrainian participation in the killings in Miropol, see https://www.facebook.com/groups/342757449166582/permalink/1770875176354795/.
39. Jan Gross and Anna Bikont review the fate of a small community, in microhistory, that was murdered in the Holocaust not by the Germans, but by their fellow citizens. See Jan Tomasz Gross, *Neighbors: The Destruction of the Jewish Community in Jedwabne, Poland* (Princeton: Princeton University Press, 2001), and Anna Bikont, *The Crime and the Silence: Confronting the Massacre of Jews in Wartime Jedwabne*, trans. Alissa Valles (New York: Farrar, Straus and Giroux, 2014). A similarly gripping narrative by Jan Grabowski tells the story of the Judenjagd in Dabrowa Tarnowska, a rural county in southeastern Poland, where the majority of the Jews in hiding perished as a consequence of betrayal by their Polish neighbors: *Hunt for the Jews: Betrayal and Murder in German-Occupied Poland* (Bloomington: Indiana University Press, 2013); Elisabeth Freundlich, *Die Ermordung einer Stadt namens Stanislau: NS Vernichtungs-politikin Polen 1939–1945* (Vienna: Österreichischer Bundesverlag, 1986); Shimon Redlich, *Together and Apart in Brzeżany: Poles, Jews, and Ukrainians, 1919–1945* (Bloomington: Indiana University Press, 2002); the already mentioned Jeffrey Burds, *Holocaust in Rovno: The Massacre at Sosenki Forest, November 1941*; and finally, a recently published work concentrates on Buczacz in Galicia: Bartov, *Anatomy of a Genocide: Life and Death of a Town Called Buczacz*.

2

1. Sándor Márai, *Hallgatni Akartam* (Budapest: Helikon, 2016), 44–45.
2. Concern about the influx of Jews from eastern territories was voiced by Hungarian statesmen such as Count István Széchényi and Lajos Kossuth as early as the mid-ninteenth century, nevertheless, since the emancipation in 1867 the "Jewish Question" was not a substantive political issue in Hungary. See Nathaniel Katzburg, *Anti-Semitism in Hungary* (Tel Aviv: Dvir, 1969), 24–28, 30–32.
3. Julia Boyd, *Travellers in the Third Reich: The Rise of Fascism Through the Eyes of Everyday People* (London: Elliot and Thompson, 2017), 218. One only needs to remember the "Dreyfus Affair" in France or the turn-of-the-century Vienna with its mayor, Karl Lueger, a master of his strategic use of anti-Semitism.
4. Quoted by Bernard Wasserstein, *On the Eve: The Jews of Europe Before the Second World War* (New York: Simon & Schuster, 2012), 26.
5. An excellent analysis of the influx from Galicia belongs to Albert S. Lindemann, *Esau's Tears: Modern Anti-Semitism and the Rise of the Jews* (Cambridge: Cambridge University Press, 1997), 263–70.
6. From 1805 to 1910, the number of Hungarian Jews grew from 125,000 to 910,000. In the same period, the ratio of Jews within the total population increased from 1.8 percent to 5 percent.
7. It was called Act XVII of 1867. The issue of Jewish emancipation had already been raised at parliament as early as 1839–1840. However, it was enacted only during the War of Independence in 1848 by the parliament of Szeged. It was nulled during the backlash following the defeat of the War of Independence against the Habsburg Empire.
8. The Jewish population numbered 910,000 in 1910. See the seminal work of Ferenc Fejtő, *Magyarság, zsidóság* (Budapest: MTA Történettudományi Intézete, 2000), 97–98. Numerous historians across the political spectrum presented similar arguments.
9. The three notable works that discuss this remarkable evolution are Viktor Karády, "Jewish Over-Schooling Revisited: The Case of Hungarian Secondary Education under the Old Regime (1900–1941)," http://web.ceu.hu/jewishstudies/pdf/01_karady.pdf, and Viktor Karády, *Zsidóság, modernizáció, polgárosodás* (Budapest: Cserépfalvi, 1997), 84. Perhaps the most comprehensive and authoritative work belongs to János Gyurgyák, *A zsidókérdés Magyarországon* (Budapest: Osiris Kiadó, 2001), 83.
10. In 1910, Samu Hazai was appointed minister of national defense. János Teleszky became minister of finance in 1912, and Ferenc Heltai was the mayor of Budapest for a short time in 1913.
11. She married Baron Zsigmond Perényi, the son of the first government commissioner of Carpathian Ruthenia. Eleanor Perényi, *More Was Lost, A Memoir* (New York: New York Review Books, 1946), 94, 159.

12. Karády, Zsidóság, modernizáció, polgárosodás, 84.
13. Béla Vihar, *Zsidók a magyar tájban. in Ararát* (Budapest: Országos Izraelita Leányárvaház, 1942), 60.
14. Gustav Landauer, Ostjuden und Deutsches Reich. Zu Juden gesagt, in Im Scheunenviertel. Bilder, Texte und Dokumente, edited by Eike Geisel (Berlin: Siedler, 1986), 34.
15. See the in-depth analysis by Walter Pietsch, "A Zsidók bevándorlása Galíciából," *Valóság* no. 11 (1988).
16. The Dreyfus Affair revolved around a Jewish artillery captain in the French Army, accusing him of espionage for the Germans in the last decade of the nineteenth and early twentieth centuries. The scandal rocked France to its core.
17. Quoted by Sándor Kibédi Varga, "Horthy mint Pilátus," review of *A Horthy-rendszer mérlege*, January 28, 2013, in https://olvassbele.com/2013/01/28/horthy-mint-pilatus-ungvary-krisztian-a-horthy-rendszer-merlege.
18. Quoted in Gyurgyák, *A zsidókérdés Magyarországon*, 297–98. An in-depth discussion about early anti-Semitism within the Catholic church was provided by Randolph L. Braham, "The Christian Churches of Hungary and the Holocaust," http://www.yadvashem.org/download/about_holocaust/studies/BrahamENGPRINT.pdf.
19. Oszkár Jászi, *Huszadik Század*, May 23, 1912, vol. 1, 734–40. The idea of a capitalist economy stepping over traditional lifestyles and moral principles was connected to Jewry not only in Hungary, but in Romania, Russian-Poland, and to a smaller extent, in Austria as well.
20. *A Zsidókérdés Magyarországon: A Huszadik Század Körkérdése*, 2nd ed., publication by *Huszadik Század* (Budapest: Társadalomtudományi Társaság, 1917), 97. A recent article by Leslie Epstein well summed up this age-old contradiction. See "The Milk Can: Who Gets to Trifle with Despair?," *Tablet*, December 7, 2018. Two recent books about the attitudes toward Jews in France and Germany paint a very similar picture. See James McAuley, *The House of Fragile Things: Jewish Art Collectors and the Fall of France* (New Haven: Yale University Press, 2021) and Stephan Malinowski, *Nazis and Nobles: The History of a Misalliance* (Oxford: Oxford University Press, 2021).
21. Károly Méray-Horváth, *Társadalomtudomány mint természettudomány* (Budapest: Athenaeum RT, 1912), 102.
22. Ian Kershaw provides a thorough analysis of the consequences of World War I on the history of Europe: *Hell and Back: Europe 1914–1949* (New York: Viking, 2015).
23. Anthony Julius, *T.S. Eliot, Anti-Semitism and Literary Form* (Cambridge: Cambridge University Press, 1996), 32.
24. There is no reason to provide here a counterargument for these accusations. Janos Gyurgyák presents a comprehensive picture about Jewish participation in World War I: *A zsidókérdés Magyarországon*, 88–98. Hungarian-Jewish participation in the war is

well described by István Deák, *Volt egyszer egy tisztikar. A Habsburg-monarchia katonatisztjeinek társadalmi és politikai története* (Budapest: Gondolat, 1993).

25. Péter Bihari, *Lövészárkok a hátországban. Középosztály, zsidókérdés, antiszemitizmus az első világháború Magyarországán* (Budapest: Napvilág Kiadó, 2008), 252.

26. The most provocative work on this issue can be attributed to Miklós Bartha, *Kazár földön* (Kolozsvár: Ellenzék Könyvnyomda, 1901). The Khazar theory of Ashkenazi ancestry is a hypothesis that Ashkenazi Jews descend from the Khazars—a multiethnic collection of Turkic peoples who formed a semi-nomadic Khanate in what is now southern Russia, extending from eastern Europe to central Asia. Mercator, "A kazárok," *Huszadik Század* 1 (1911): 81.

27. See György Borsányi, "Zsidók a Munkásmozgalomban," *Világosság* 2 (1992): 147. Also, Gyurgyák, *A zsidókérdés Magyarországon*, 95.

28. Similar figures are presented by Lajos Szabolcsi, the editor of *Egyenlőség*, who knew about 25,000 refugees. See *Két emberöltő. Az Egyenlőség évtizedei (1881–1931). Emlékezések, dokumentumok* (Budapest: MTA Judaisztikai Kutatócsoport, 1993), 172. See also Bihari, *Lövészárkok a hátországban*, 152. In contrast, the number of Galician refugees in Vienna was placed around 70,000. See Piotr Wrobel, "The Jews of Galicia under Austrian-Polish Rule, 1867–1918," 14–16, http://easteurotopo.org/articles/wrobel/wrobel.pdf.

29. The Brusilov Offensive, between June 4 and August 10, 1916, was the largest Russian assault during World War I and one of the deadliest in history. John Keegan, *The First World War* (New York: Vintage, 2000), 306.

30. Such anti-Semitic discourse was not characteristic to Hungary alone; similar outbursts were evident in Austria, Germany, and elsewhere.

31. Jenő Csolnoky, A Zsidókérdés Magyarországon: A Huszadik Század Körkérdése, 59, 72.

32. An incisive analysis about Péter Ágoston and his treatise can be found in Gyurgyák, *A zsidókérdés Magyarországon*, 478–82. See also Péter Ágoston, *A zsidók útja* (Nagyvárad: Társadalomtudományi Társaság Kiadása, 1917).

33. It was Péter Ágoston. László Fényes, and Pál Farkas were leading the call for expulsion in the parliament in 1918. *Az 1910. évi junius hó 10-ére hirdetett országgyűlés képviselőházának naplója*, Vol. 40 (Budapest: Athenaeum Irodalmi és Nyomdai Részvénytársulat Könyvnyomdája, 1918), 179. Quoted also by Gyurgyák, *A zsidókérdés Magyarországon*, 281–82.

34. Bihari, *Lövészárkok a hátországban*, 236. The three main papers, *Alkotmány* (Constitution), *Új Lap* (New Page), and *Új Nemzedék* (New Generation) were especially anti-Semitic after the war.

35. Ottokár Prohászka, "Pro juventute catholica," *Alkotmány*, May 26, 1918. Also quoted by Áron Monori, "A numerus clausus és a magyar katolikus sajtó 1919–1920," *mediakutato*, 2003. http://www.mediakutato.hu/cikk/2003_02_nyar/03_numerus_clausus.

36. In 1917, the position of minister of justice was given to a Jew, Vilmos Vázsonyi. Only a convert was able to attain such a high position until then. Vilmos Vázsonyi (born Vilmos Weiszfeld, 1868–1926) was a Hungarian publicist and politician. See Mária M. Kovács, "A kissebbségek nemzetközi jogvédelmének csapdája. Vázsonyi Vilmos és a numerus clauses," *Beszélő*, April 7, 1994, 28–30.
37. The announcement in the Parliament is dated August 7, 1918. *Az 1910. évi junius hó 10-ére hírdetett országgyűlés képviselőházának naplója*, Vol. 40 (Budapest: Athenaeum Irodalmi és Nyomdai Részvénytársulat Könyvnyomdája, 1918), 176.
38. The prime minister condemned the atrocities in no uncertain terms. Reporting on these raids, the mouthpiece of the Jewish community of Budapest, Egyenlőség, noted that they aimed to capture Galician refugees "who had invaded Upper Hungary," see August 10 and 17, 1918. See also Lajos Szabolcsi, "Két emberöltő. Az Egyenlőség évtizedei (1881–1931)," 235–36.
39. These comments belong to a farsighted Zionist intellectual, József Patai, who settled in Israel in 1933. Quoted by László Lugosi Lugo, *A zsidó Budapest*, Vol. 2 (Budapest: Vince Kiadó, 2002), 363.
40. Ian Kershaw, *Hell and Back Europe 1914–1949* (New York: Viking, 2015), 117.
41. Although staunchly left-leaning, Count Mihály Károlyi came from one of the wealthiest aristocratic families of Hungary. His government came into power on October 31, 1918, and lasted less than five months.
42. A comprehensive picture about the leaders of the communist republic and their attitude toward Jewish issues was drawn by Nathaniel Katzburg in his book, *Zsidápolitika Magyarországon, 1919–1943* (Budapest: Bábel, 2002), 31–41. Mátyás Rákosi changed his name from *Rosenfeld*, Béla Kun from *Kohn*, György Lukács from *Löwinger* (he also held a baronial title), Zsigmond Kunfi from *Kohn*, Jenő Varga from *Weisz*, just to mention a few central characters of the communist revolution. See Gyurgyák, *A zsidókérdés Magyarországon*, 111.
43. The Polish ambassador vigorously protested this action. Jenő Landler, the People's Commissar who ordered the expulsion, also came from Jewish background. *Egyenlőség* 38, no. 17 (September 11, 1919): 4–5. See also Géza Komoróczy, "Zsidók a Tanácsköztársaságban," *Szombat*, February 8, 2012.
44. The ratio of Jewish victims left dead by the proletarian dictatorship was about 8 percent. This was about 3 percent higher than the ratio of Jews within the total Hungarian population. Albert Váry, *A vörös uralom áldozatai Magyarországon. Hivatalos jelentések és bírói ítéletek alapján* (A Váci Kir: Orsz. Fegyintézet Könyvnyomdája, 1922), 2.
45. About Miklos Horthy's life and regime, the most comprehensive work belongs to Krisztián Ungváry, *A Horthy-rendszer mérlege. Diszkrimináció, szociálpolitika és antiszemitizmus Magyarországon* (Budapest: Jelenkor, 2012). See also Istvan Deak,

"A Hungarian Admiral on Horseback," in *Essays on Hitler's Europe* (Lincoln: University of Nebraska Press, 2001), 150–71.

46. A contentious debate in Hungary about the toll of the "Red" and "White" terror is still raging. Béla Bodó, "Paramilitary Violence in Hungary After the First World War," *East European Quarterly* 38, no. 2 (2004); Andras Kovacs, "Terror és pogrom, vörös és fehér," http://www.academia.edu/19607504/Terror_és_pogrom_vörös_és_fehér; and Gábor Kádár and Zoltán Vági, "Törvényen kívül: fehérterror és lakossági pogromhullám 1919–1921," *Társadalmi Konfliktusok Kutatóközpont*, http://konfliktuskutato.hu/index.php?option=com_content&view=article&id=146:toervenyen-kivuel-feherterror-es-lakossagi-pogromhullam-1919-1921-&catid=15:tanulmanyok.

47. Valdemar Langlet, *On Horseback Through Hungary*, trans. Barnard Balogh (London: Hutchinson, 1935), 201, 208. Working in the Swedish Embassy during the Holocaust, he is credited with saving many Jews in Budapest by providing Swedish documents. He was inducted in The Righteous Among the Nations at Yad Vashem in 1965.

48. He spoke at the Institute of Politics in Williamstown after his resignation from the premiership. Paul Teleki, *The Evolution of Hungary and Its Place in European History* (New York: Macmillan, 1923), 141–42.

49. Monori quoted from Prohászka's book about the Jewish Question (1920): "A numerus clausus és a magyar katolikus sajtó 1919–1920," *mediakutato*, 2003. Similar accusation of superficiality was voiced by the statistician Alajos Kovács in *A zsidóság térfoglalása Magyarországon* (Budapest: Self-published, 1922), 6.

50. Quoted by Kibédi Varga, "Horthy mint Pilátus," January 28, 2013, in https://olvassbele.com/2013/01/28/horthy-mint-pilatus-ungvary-krisztian-a-horthy-rendszer-merlege.

51. Speech by Count Kunó Klebelsberg (1875–1932), minister of education and religion in 1926. Lajos Szabolcsi, "Két emberöltő. Az Egyenlőség évtizedei (1881–1931)," 376. See also Krisztián Ungváry, "Kitelepítés, lakosságcsere és a holokauszt egyes összefüggései," in *A holokauszt Magyarországon európai perspektívában*, edited by Judit Molnár (Budapest: Balassi Kiadó, 2005), 84–99.

52. Gyula Szekfű, *Három nemzedék, és ami utána következik* (Budapest: Királyi Magyar Egyetemi Nyomda, 1935), 332.

53. Among the noted writers mentioned by the historian Krisztián Ungváry are Dezső Szabó, Géza Féja, István Sinka, János Kodolányi, József Darvas, Imre Kovács, László Németh, and Péter Veres. Quoted by Kibédi Varga, "Horthy mint Pilátus."

54. Among these groups were the *Ébredő Magyarok Egyesülete* (Association of Awakening Hungarians), founded immediately upon the conclusion of the war, and the *Magyar Fajvédő Párt* (The Hungarian Race-Protection Party), founded in 1924. Tibor Zinner, *Az ébredők fénykora, 1919–1923* (Budapest: Akadémiai Kiadó, 1989), 85–86. See also Rudolf Paksa, *A magyar szélsőjobboldal története* (Budapest: Jaffa Kiadó, 2012), 76.

55. Alajos Kovács, *A zsidóság térfoglalása Magyarországon*, 6, 13. This issue of an influx from Galicia was revisited by Walter Pietsch, who came to the same conclusion. See "A Zsidók bevándorlása Galíciából," *Valóság* 11 (1988).
56. The number 60,000 is mentioned by Károly Kocsis and Kocsisné Hodosi, *Eszter, Magyarok a határainkon túl—a Kárpát-medencében* (Budapest: Tankönyvkiadó, 1991), 33. Wrobel, "The Jews of Galicia under Austrian-Polish Rule, 1867–1918," 5. About the influx of Eastern Jews in America, see Haim Hillel Ben-Sasson, ed., *A History of the Jewish People* (New York: Dvir, 1976). See also Irving Howe, *World of Our Fathers* (New York: Harcourt Brace Jovanovich, 1976).
57. The Journal of the Parliament Convened for 16 June 1922, Vol. XXXVIII, 223. For more on that, see his speech delivered before the Parliament on May 11, 1937. The Journal of the House of Representatives of the Parliament Convened for 27 April 1935, Vol. XIII, 64–65.
58. Endre Sós, Európai Fasizmus és Antiszemitizmus (Budapest: Magyar Teka, n.d.), 53. The debate took place on August 7, 1920.
59. In 1923, the government banned the organization. The history of the association was presented by Tibor Zinner, *Az Ébredők Fénykora. 1919–1923*. See also Moshe Y. Herczl. *Christianity and the Holocaust of Hungarian Jewry* (New York: New York University Press, 1993), 43–47, 57–58, and 118.
60. The most comprehensive work about this topic belongs to Mária M. Kovács, *Törvénytől sújtva: a numerus clausus Magyarországon: 1920–1945* (Budapest: Napvilág, 2012). See also Nathaniel Katzburg, *Sefer ha-Shanah shel Universitat Bar Ilan, 4–5* (1956–65), 270–88. See also "Numerus clausus," *Encyclopaedia Judaica* 12, col. 1267–68.
61. The law was originally proposed in 1919 but was enacted only in July 1920. It did not limit, however, the number of Jews in the national economy, cultural-intellectual sphere, or the free-profession. See Gyurgyák, *A zsidókérdés Magyarországon*, 117–23.
62. See Tibor Péter Nagy, "Antiszemitizmus és felsőoktatás-politik—a numerus clausus törvény jelentősége," in *A Zsidó Iskolaügytörténete Magyarországon*, edited by Laszlo Balogh (Budapest: Országos Pedagógiai Könyvtár és Muzeum, 1996), 81–94; and Monori, "A numerus clausus és a magyar katolikus sajtó 1919–1920," *mediakutato*, 2003.
63. Decree n. 4352 of 1920 in Collection of Decrees of Hungary, Budapest, 1920, 674–84.
64. Edit K. Cseh, "A Békés megyei zsidóság történetének levéltári forrásai: Dokumentumok a Békés Megyei Levéltárból" (Gyula: Forráskiadványok a Békés Megyei Levéltárból, 2002), 156.
65. According to the figures of the American Joint Distribution Committee (JDC), about six thousand foreign Jews were removed from Hungary between June 1919 and May 1921 with about thirty transports, mostly to Poland. See Bernhard Kahn's report to the European Executive Council of the JDC in Paris on May 31, 1921. Joint Archives, Collection: Records of the American Joint Distribution Committee 1919–1921, Record

Group: Refugees, File: Refugees, 1921, Item ID: 215097. See also the report of Joseph Marcus, JDC representative in Hungary to the European Executive Council of the Joint Distribution Committee in Paris on March 38, 1921. JDC Archives, in Records of the American Joint Distribution Committee 1919–1921, Record Group: Hungary, Item ID: 220048.

66. The establishment of the Arrow Cross movement in 1935 in Hungary was a good example for this evolution Miklós Lackó, *Arrow-Cross Men: National Socialists 1935–1944* (Budapest, Akadémiai Kiadó 1969).

67. Concurrently with the consolidation of Nazi power and the enactment of race laws, a flood of refugees from the West began to arrive in Hungary, first from Germany and Austria, and after the outbreak of the war, from Poland and Slovakia. Klaudia Farkas, *Jogok nélkül. A zsidó lét Magyarországon, 1920–1944* (Budapest: Napvilág, 2010), 287.

68. As Hungarian premier (1932–1936), he was known for his reactionary and anti-Semitic views. See Gyula Gömbös, *Válogatott politikai beszédek és írások*, edited by József Vonyó (Budapest: Osiris Kiadó, 2004), 296.

69. Gömbös, *Válogatott politikai beszédek és írások*, 414. On the ideas of Prime Minister Gömbös regarding Jews, see also Gyurgyák, *Magyar fajvédők*, 113.

70. His speech was aimed to support the enactment of the First Jewish Law in 1938. Quoted by Herczl, *Christianity and the Holocaust of Hungarian Jewry*, 87 Leaders of the Christian churches, Cardinal Jusztinian Seredy, prince-primate of Hungary and head of the dominant Catholic Church, Evangelical (Lutheran) Bishop Sandor Raffay, and Laszlo Ravasz, bishop of the Reformed (Calvinist) Church, were unanimous in support of the bill.

71. This took place under the Gömbös government. See *Nemzeti Újság*, January 19, 1936. The central organ of Hungarian Jewry, Egyenlőség, continuously reported about various raids and waves of arrests of Jews in the interwar years. See issues of October 9, 1927; November 16, 1935.

72. By some estimates the total number reached 750,000, and by other calculation, 835,000. In 1941, 725,000 persons registered as Jewish. Close to 100,000 more persons came under the jurisdiction of the Jewish Laws. See Tamás Stark, "Adatok a holocaust magyarországi áldozatainak számáról," in *Visszatérés—újrakezdés*, edited by János Botos and Tamás Kovács, (Budapest: Holocaust Dokumentációs Központ és Emlékgyűjtemény Közalapítvány, 2007), 6–18.

73. Although there were additional restrictions and discriminatory policies after the enactment of the third law in 1941, nothing was as wide-ranging as the three Jewish Laws. The most comprehensive work on this subject belongs to Nathaniel Katzburg, *Hungary and the Jews: Policy and Legislation 1920–1943* (Tel Aviv: Bar-Ilan University Press, 1981). A comprehensive work on the three Jewish laws and various corollary anti-Jewish regulations was provided by László Karsai, "Magyarországi zsidótörvények és rendeletek

1938–1945," in *A magyarországi zsidótörvények és -rendeletek, 1920–1944*, edited by Róbert Vértes. (Budapest: Polgár, 2002), http://www.hdke.hu/files/csatolmanyok/09_KarsaiLaszlo_AMagyarorszagi_zsidotorvenyek.pdf.

74. According to the Second Jewish Law, Jews were those who belonged to the Jewish religion and who had one parent or two grandparents who belonged to the Jewish religion at the time of the enactment of the Second Jewish Law. The most substantial discussion of the Second Jewish Law was conducted by László Karsai, "A magyarországi zsidótörvények és—rendeletek," in *A Holokauszt Magyarországon európai perspektívában*, edited by Judit Molnár (Budapest: Balassi, 2004), 140–63.

75. Bálint Homan delivered this as a lead-up to the First Jewish Law. Quoted by Nathaniel Katzburg, *Hungary and the Jews*, 260.

76. Ildikó Orosz and István Csernicskó, *The Hungarians in Transcarpathia* (Budapest: Tinta Publishers, 1999).

77. Ungváry A Horthy-rendszer mérlege. Diszkrimináció. Szociálpolitika és antiszemitizmus Magyarországon, 377.

78. Mária Ormos, *Magyarország a két világháború korában (1914–1945)* (Debrecen: Csokonai Kiadó, 1998), 108.

79. Debate on December 3, 1940. Quoted by Katzburg, *Zsidó Politika Magyarországon, 1919–1943*, 269. Teleki committed suicide on April 3, 1941, in protest of the participation of Hungary in the dismemberment of Yugoslavia.

80. The speech was given on February 23, 1939, by Count Pál Teleki as the justification for the Second Jewish Law. After serving as prime minister, he committed suicide in the spring of 1941. See Felsőházi napló, 1935, 114, https://library.hungaricana.hu/hu/view/OGYK_FN-1935_04/?query=SZO%3D(per%C3%A9nyi)&pg=123&layout=s. See also Braham L. Randolph, *A Magyar Holocaust*, Vol. 1 (Budapest: Gondolat, 1981), 104–7, 125–33.

81. The debate took place on April 17, 1939. Quoted by Katzburg, *Zsidó Politika Magyarországon*, 123–24. How this translated on the street level can be found in the recollection of Natan Blum, "Girush Yehudim Netulai-Ezrahut M'hungaria L'galicia B'shnat 1941," *Yalkut Moreshet* 43–44 (1987): 42.

82. Gyurgyák, *A zsidókérdés Magyarországon*, 144–45. The work of Gábor Kádár and Zoltán Vági, *Hullarablás* (Budapest: Jaffa, 2005) is perhaps the most comprehensive work about economic marginalization of the Jewish community.

83. The speech made several allusions to the removal of some of the "aliens." Quoted in Andor Ladányi, "Az első zsidótörvény megszületése," *Múlt és Jövő* 2 (2010): 105.

84. Perhaps the most comprehensive account on the establishment and function of KEOKH was written by Tamás Kovács, "A Belügyminisztérium rendészeti és karhatalmi feladatai, 1920 és 1944 között," *Pécsi Határőr Tudományos Közlemények*, Vol. X (2009): 161. See also Frojmovics, *I Have Been a Stranger in a Strange Land*, 57–102.

85. Antal Müller, May 6, 1938, Kepviseloi Naplo XVIII, 324. See also The Journal of the National Assembly Convened for 27 April 1935, House of Representatives, Records, XII, 9.
86. Quoted by Gyurgyák, *A zsidókérdés Magyarországon*, 149.
87. See Pieter M. Judson, *The Habsburg Empire: A New History* (Boston: Harvard University Press, 2016).
88. Frojimovics, I Have Been a Stranger in a Strange Land, 12.
89. For a comprehensive account on Romania, see Radu Ioanid, *The Holocaust in Romania: The Destruction of Jews and Gypsies Under the Antonescu Regime, 1940–1944* (Chicago: Ivan R. Dee Publishers, 2000). For Poland, see Jerzy Tomaszewski, "The Civil Rights of Jews in Poland, 1918–1939," *Polin: Studies in Polish Jewry* 8 (London: Littmann, 1994), 115–27.
90. Department IX, wholly independent from KEOKH, handled the civilian refugees from Poland, including Jews, in the Ministry of Interior. An excellent account of this rescue effort was provided by Frojimovics, *I Have Been a Stranger in a Strange Land*, 172–209. For a general work on the subject of Polish refugees during World War II, see Karoly Kapronczay, *Refugees in Hungary*, trans. Eva Barcza-Bessenyey (Toronto: Matthias Corvinus, 1999). See also Csilla Klettner and Tamás Kovács, "A Lengyel Menekültek Magyarországi Fogadtatása 1939 Őszén," *Archivnet. XX Századi Történeti Források* 16 (2016): 4, http://archivnet.hu/menekultkerdes_migracio_magyarorszagon_a_20_szazadban/2._a_lengyel_menekultek_magyarorszagi_fogadtatasa_1939_oszen.html.
91. The politician was Béla Imrédy, the prime minister at the time. Quoted by Braham, *A magyar Holocaust*, Vol. I, 125.
92. Testimony of Kálmán Tomcsányi, state councillor, January 2, 1946, document number 21389/1945; testimony of Dr. Miklós Kátai (Horner), then public prosecutor, document number 21389/1945; testimony of Dr. Gyula Perlaky, 24 January 1946; testimony of Dr. Roland Jacobi, 25 January 1946. Historical Archives of State Security Services (HASSS), 319, V-103599.
93. My own grandparents didn't get married in a civil ceremony. Subsequently, all the children were registered on my grandmother's name. Interestingly enough, they got married officially ten years after the religious one, after which all the children were recognized retroactively. As for the the internal decrees of the Ministry of Interior, see "Investigation in the case of Dénes Zakariás and Accomplices," HASSS 3.1.9, V-138271.
94. This comment was voiced during a heated debate in the Parliament about the Second Jewish Law by a progressive deputy. The Journal of the House of Representatives of the Parliament Convened for 27 April 1935, XXII, Athenaeum, Budapest, 1939, 441.
95. During the trials conducted against KEOKH employees by the People's Courts after 1945, it was revealed that district administrators and notaries routinely asked for bribes for issuing a document or a certificate. Lawyers charged thousands of pengős for the administration of matters related to citizenship. "Trial of Dénes Zakariás and Accomplices," HASSS 3.1.9, V-138271. See also Ignác Romsics, *Magyarország története*

a XX. században (Budapest: Osiris Kiadó, 1999), 192, 198.

96. The timing of this cross-border transfer coincided with the First Vienna Award in November 1938, which transferred territory populated mainly by Hungarians to Hungary. Interestingly enough, these reciprocal expulsions were not mentioned in contemporary Hungarian documents. See "Memorandum on the Position of the Jews in and from the Sudeten German Areas," JDC Archives, 1933–1944, New York Collection, Folder: Czechoslovakia, Subject Matter: Refugees, 1933–1944, Item ID: 468330. The most comprehensive account about these expulsions can be found in Frojimovics, *I Have Been a Stranger in a Strange Land*, 57–102.

97. "Directive No. 395/1941 eln. VIIb. BM. From Ámon Pásztóy," March 1, 1941, MOL, OL K 490. 1. cs. See also Frojmovics, *I Have Been a Stranger in a Strange Land*, 99.

98. See Tamás Majsai, "Egy epizód az észak-erdélyi zsidóság második világháború alatti történetéből," *Medvetánc* 4, no. 1 (1988–1989): 3–33; Tamás Majsai, "The Deportation of Jews from Csíkszereda and Margit Slachta's Intervention on Their Behalf," in *Studies on the Holocaust in Hungary*, edited by Randolph L. Braham (New York: The City University of New York, 1990), 113–63; Boulder and Zoltán Tibori Szabó, "Csík vármegye zsidósága a betelepüléstől a megsemmisítésig," in *Tanulmányok a holokausztról*, edited by Randolph L. Braham (Budapest: Balassi, 2004), 103–42; and György Dupka, "Ne ítéljetek el … Zsidó népírtás, antiszemita üldözés Kárpátalján a náci és a kommunista eszmék nevében, 1938–1991" (Ungvár-Budapest: Intermix Kiadó, 2005), 352.

99. "Memorandum on the Position of the Hungarian Jewry in the Beginning of 1940," JDC Archives, Countries and Regions, Reel 50, 4–5, Frames, 359, 362, 363.

100. Csilla Fedinec, *A kárpátaljai magyarság történeti kronológiája 1918–1944* (Galánta-Dunaszerdahely: Fórum Intézet, Lilium Aurum Könyvkiadó, 2002), 363.

101. Gyula Kosztyo noted in his groundbreaking study that in a survey conducted in 1938, 78 percent of the merchants and 52 percent of tradesmen and artisans were Jewish. Gyula Kosztyó, "Mit vesztett kárpátalja magyarsága a holokauszttal? Egy minisztériumi állapotfelmérés elemzése (1939. augusztus)," forthcoming.

102. Csilla Fedinec, *A kárpátaljai magyarság történeti kronológiája 1918–1944* (Galánta-Dunaszerdahely: Lilium Aurum, 2002), 362.

103. Quoted by Frojimovics, I Have Been a Stranger in a Strange Land, 106.

104. Quoted by Ormos, Egy Magyar Médiavezér: Kozma Miklós, 728, 737.

105. An imminent outbreak of the war was common knowledge in Berlin among various diplomatic outposts. The dispatch was dated on June 3, 1941. Gyula Juhász, ed., *Magyarország külpolitikája a második világháború kitörésének időszakában* (Budapest: Akadémia Kiadó, 1962), 924, 1070, 1097, 1133. See also Ormos, *Egy Magyar Médiavezér: Kozma Miklós*, 1147. About the awareness of American diplomats about the Nazi plans to attack the Soviet Union, see Andrew Nagorski, *Hitlerland: American Eyewitnesses to the Nazi Rise to Power* (New York: Simon & Schuster, 2012).

3

1. Testimony of László Zobel in USC Shoah Foundation Oral History Archives, #51784. As a note of clarification, his expulsion was three days after the explicit instruction by the minister of interior to halt the deportation immediately.
2. The Galicianers were considered by Hungarian authorities as Polish citizens because between the two wars, Galicia belonged to Poland. Hence, the repeated designation as Polish nationals.
3. Sándor Siménfalvy was appointed on July 1, 1941, for the directorship of KEOKH. In turn, the ubiquitous Ámon Pásztóy was elevated to head the Public Safety Section within the Ministry of Interior at the same time. However, he remained a hands-on person in the issue of the deportation. ÁBTL, Decree # 192/1941. Res. VIIb, on July 12, 1941.
4. Tamás Stark brought to my attention that Miklós Kozma's authority did not extend to the whole of Carpathian Ruthenia (Subcarpathia in Hungarian). Nándor Bárdi, Csilla Fedinec and László Szarka, eds., *Kisebbségi magyar közösségek a 20. században* (Budapest: Gondolat Kiadó – MTA Kisebbségkutató Intézet, 2008), 173.
5. I am indebted to Ákos Foris for bringing this dispatch to my attention. MNL K-63 200. cs. 1941-21/28 – 1469/436.k.a.-1941, "A berlini katonai attasé jelentése a július 9–12-i eseményekről," Berlin, July 12, 1941.
6. The foreign nationals included German, Austrian, Czech, Slovak, and Polish Jews. "Countries and Regions," American Jewish Joint Distribution Committee Archives, Reel 50, frames 359, 363.
7. The Carpathian Group sent to the Eastern Front consisted of the Rapid Corps as well as the 8th Border Guard Brigade and the 1st Mountain Brigade. The troops expedited were composed of about 40,000 persons. The Hungarian military forces deployed within the German Southern Army Group crossed the Hungarian-Soviet border on June 28, and by July 8 they had already reached the Dniester River. Thanks for Tamás Stark for this information.
8. Emphasis added by author. During the early phases of the war, Werth routinely participated in the meeting of the Council of Ministers. "Testimony of Ámon Pásztóy," BFL. B-2890/1951, 45–46, July 12, 1945.
9. Csilla Fedinec, *A Kárpátaljai Magyarság Történeti Kronológiája, 1918–1944* (Dunaszerdahely: Forum, 2002), 377.
10. "Testimony of Sándor Siménfalvy," BFL. B-2890/1951, 40–41, March 24, 1948; "Testimony of Nándor Batizfalvy," C.13.2128.P/E4320B#1991/243#2326, in Schweizerisches Bundesarchiv. I want to thank to Ádám and János Gellért for meticulously reconstructing the decision-making process. See "Az 1941. Évi kőrösmezői deportálások, A kitolocolásokat jóváhagyó minisztertanácsi döntés háttere," *Betekintő* 2 (2012), http://www.betekinto.hu/hu/szamok/2012_2.

11. The right-wing press was especially active in this campaign. See *Függetlenség*, July 5, 1941; *Kárpáti Magyar Hírlap*, July 11, 1941; and *Új Magyarság*, July 13, 1941.
12. MNL, K-148, BM elnöki iratok, 1084. cs. File 4. Fedinec, *A Kárpátaljai Magyarság Történeti Kronológiája*, 378. See also *Sefer Marmarosh; mea ve-shishim kehilot kedoshot be- yishuvan u-ve-hurbanah* (The Marmaros Book; In Memory of 160 Jewish Communities), edited by S. Y. Gross and Y. Yosef Cohen (Tel Aviv: Beit Marmaros, 1983, 1996), 93–112.
13. Majsai, "Iratok a kőrösmezei zsidódeportálás történetéhez 1941," Document # 2, 202. In a second, undated memorandum, or an earlier version of the final document, addressed directly to the prime minister, Kozma reproached the happless Ajtay for overstepping his authority.
14. Interrogation of Sándor Siménfalvy, Február 19, 1948. ÁBTL V-122405. 56é and BFL B-2890/1951, 40–41, March 24, 1948. The testimony of Ámon Pásztóy on May 27, 1949, corraboarted this claim. BFL B-2890/1951. 67. Also quoted by Gellért, "Az 1941. Évi kőrösmezői deportálások." Again, an excellent analysis of the process was provided by Frojimovics, *I Have Been a Stranger in a Strange Land*, 109–16.
15. Emphasis added by author. MNL K-429. File, Diary III. "Kozma Miklos Iratai" # 45. July 4, 1941. Also quoted by Ormos, *Egy magyar médiavezér*, 758. The expulsion of Ukrainians, after stripping them from their citizenship, was dated on July 10, 1941. KTAL, K429-1941-871.
16. Kárpátaljai ukrán tisztviselők felhasználása a szükségszerű katonai közigazgatásban és a zsidók kitelepítése Galiciában. In the name of the chief of staff, Lieutenant-General Decleva to the Carpathian Corps., 665./Eln.vkf .kat.közig. 1941. July 7, 1941. MNL K-149, 1941, 6/231. batch, 105. box, 12103. sz. file, 773. See also Laszló Karsai, *Holokauszt* (Budapest: Pannonica Kiadó, 2001), 228.
17. Proof of identity issued to stateless individuals; a certificate recognized by more than fifty countries. The name comes from Fridtjof Nansen (1861–1930), a Norwegian explorer, diplomat, and humanitarian, who was appointed in 1921 as the High Commissioner for Refugees in the League of Nations.
18. Emphasis added by author. Hadtörténelmi Irattár és Levéltár (HIL) Magyar Kiraly Gyorshadtest, Kárpát Csoport, July 9, 1941, Box I. Frojimovics, *I Have Been Stranger in a Strange Land*, 104–7; Ormos, *Egy Magyar Médiavezér: Kozma Miklós*, 753–67; Lieutenant General László Dezső was executed on June 8, 1949, by the Hungarian government.
19. Emphasis added by author. MNL K-429, 38. file. 1653. sz. Quoted by Mária Ormos, *Egy Magyar Médiavezér: Kozma Miklós*, 758. Nowhere mentioned in this memorandum the need for consultation with KEOKH. In a second, undated memorandum, or an earlier version of the final document, addressed also directly to the prime minister, he reiterated the list of those to be removed.

20. Pest is the left side of the capital Budapest, where the parliament is located. MNL K-429. 45. cs. Napló III. July 1, 1941.
21. The most persuasive account is Judit Fejes' article "On the History of Deportations from Carpatho-Ruthenia in 1941," 311. See also MNL Kárpátaljai Kormányzói Biztosának Hivatala, 646/41/eln. K774 file no. 1.
22. MNL, K-774, August 6, 1941. Also quoted by Frojimovics, *I Have Been a Stranger in a Strange Land*, 122.
23. MNL, K-149, 107. doboz /K 149 – 1941 – 8. A well-rounded account of the process is provided by Frojimovics, *I Have Been a Stranger in a Strange Land*, 108–12.
24. This order was part of the already quoted memorandum on July 14, 1941. See MNL, K-149, 107. doboz /K 149 – 1941 – 8/.
25. Max Eisen, *By Chance Alone* (New York: Harper Collins, 2016), 45, and Testimony of Zobel USC, #51784. No reason was given as to why only Kőrösmező was set up. See Memorandum to Miklós Kozma, government commissioner. MNL K-429 Kozma files. Box 39. Max Eisen has no relationship to the author.
26. Moshe Deutsch, "The Ghetto in Kaminits-Podolsk," in *Kaminits-Podolsk & Its Environs*, edited by Abraham Rosen (Tel Aviv, 1965).
27. Majsai, "*Iratok a kőrösmezei zsidódeportálás történetéhez 1941*," Document 19, 223.
28. Telegram to the Minister of Interior, July 14, 1941. MNL K-774, 1941. 1st box 646/1941 eln.
29. According to Act II of 1939, Jews were banned from military service, and they were assigned to work in labor service units. Forced labor service was a form of humiliation because it implied that the military leadership did not consider Jews worthy of armed service. This attitude was decisive when it came to the army's relationship with the local Jewry as well. See Randolph L. Braham, *The Hungarian Labor Service System: 1939–1945* (East European Monographs, 1977).
30. MNL K-774, 1941, 2. 0.646/41. eln. Sz. Document. Quoted by Ádám Gellért and János Gellért, "Az 1941-es deportálások és Csatáry László," *Élet és Irodalom*, August 31, 2012.
31. HIL, 1941, 10. osztály, eln. sorozat, csomó, o. 18. These servicemen were saved by the August 8 directive of the minister of interior, stopping the deportation. They were summoned back to service in their companies. See "VIII. Corps Command to Government Commissioner for Carpathian Ruthenia," August 27, 1941, MNL K-149, Box 107, 1941-8, 5048-18646.
32. MNL K-149 Ministry of Interior, KEOKH 1941 File, Box 107-8.
33. They were joined along the trip by Károly Pakocs, member of the Hungarian parliament.
34. Two pictures taken by Countess Erzsébet Szapáry, and reproduced in this book, well illustrate the brutality of the removal of Jews from their homes and delivery to the cattle cars.
35. Majsai, "Iratok a Kőrösmezei Zsidódeportálás Történetéhez 1941," 224.

36. "A zsidók deportálása Kárpátaljáról Galíciába 1941 nyara," *Társadalmi és etnikai konfliktusok a 19-20. Században*, tarsadalominformatika.elte.hu/tananyagok/dka/lecke25 _lap6.html#hiv11.
37. Interview with Max Solomon, USHMM, Oral History (1993.A.0087.48) RG Number: RG-50.091.0048. Raz Segal mentions three successful escapes from the collection of Jews. *Genocide in the Carpathians: War, Social Breakdown, and Mass Violence, 1914–1945* (Stanford: Stanford University Press, 2016), 81, n. 114, 115, 116.
38. The Hungarian currency until 1945. Its value might be equivalent to USD$2. This estimate is based Gábor Kádár and Zoltán Vági, *Self-Financing Genocide* (Budapest: Central European University Press, 2001), 25–26.
39. Irene Weiss, "Kiraktak minket a semmi közepére," *Népszabadság*, February 1, 2014. Max Solomon, USHMM, Oral History Accession Number: 1993.A.0087.48, RG Number: RG-50.091.0048.
40. Interview with Gabriel Drimer, USHMM, Accession Number: 1997.A.0441.56, RG Number: RG-50.462.0056.Bottom of FormTop of FormBottom of Form.
41. The only records for traditional marriages, conducted by rabbis, was the *Ketubah*—the Jewish marriage contract—which was not accepted by civilian authorities. Sometimes, they were forced to register retroactively. "Társadalmi és etnikai konfliktusok a 10-20. században" tarsadalominformatika.elte.hu/tananyagok/ dka/lecke25_lap6.html#hiv11.
42. Testimony of Miriam Wohlberg interview by Szirtes Andras, https://www.youtube .com/watch?v =YONYnpXS1p8&t=16s. This happened not only in Carpathian Ruthenia, but also in Hungary proper. The responsible official in Putnok was Imre Mogyoróssy. See László Bernát Veszprémy, *Gyilkos Irodák a Magyar Közigazgatás, a Német megszállás és a Holokauszt* (Budapest: Jaffa, 2019) 23, and Majsai, "Iratok a Kőrösmezei Zsidódeportálás Történetéhez 1941," 224.
43. Solomon, Testimony, USHMM, Oral History, accession number 1993.A.0087.48, RG number RG-50.091.0048. See also Samuel Gottesman, USHMM, Oral History Accession Number: 1990.8.10, RG Number: RG-50.063.0010, and Max Eisen, *By Chance Alone*, 41–42.
44. MNL K-149, 107, Box K149 – 1941-8/. It was signed by Sándor Simánfalvy, the head of KEOKH. Also quoted by Frojimovics, *I Have Been a Stranger in a Strange Land*, 114.
45. Testimony of Yaffa Rosenthal in USC #16308.
46. This train ride lasted close to six days, often without food and water. See Max Eisen, *By Chance Alone*, 43.
47. MNL K-149, 802.
48. Salamon, "Katona naplóm. Orosz föld 1941," October 2, 1941. HIL, TGY 3213. The last comment was made by Irene Weiss, "Kiraktak minket a semmi közepére," *Népszabadság*, February 1, 2014.
49. Interview with Zsuzsa and Éva Eisen, June 7, 2013. The family of Peninah Kaufman

Blum was arrested in 1939 and spent almost two years in an internment camp from which they were deported. *Paamayim Shoah* (Raanana: Docostory: 2006), 31. See also Béla Vihar, *Sárga Könyv* (Budapest: Hechaluc, 1946), 12–13.

50. American Jewish Joint Distribution Committee, also known as the JDC, was a Jewish relief organization based in New York City. See Michael Beizer. "American Jewish Joint Distribution Committee," *The YIVO Encyclopedia of Jews in Eastern Europe*, August 19, 2010.
51. Emphasis added by author. Jewish Telegraphic Agency, July 22, 1941.
52. Jewish Telegraphic Agency, August 14, 1941.
53. *Magyar Lapok*, August 5, 1941, and *Pesti Ujsag*, August 5, 1941. In Carpathian Ruthenia, *The Kárpáti Magyar Hirlap* reported on the deportation, July 31 and August 11, 1941.
54. He met the family in Skala, July 23, 1941. "Somló Béla Naplója," HIL, TGY # 2811. The riveting story of Somló's life and his diary was described by Tamás Csapody, "A Naplóíró Somló Béla," *FONS* (2019): 339–402.
55. A comprehensive work on Batizfalvy's activities during the Holocaust still needs to be written. Some depicted him as easily bribable and corrupt, while others depicted him as a savior. His role during the deportation in the postwar trials was presented by witnesses both as positive and negative. See Majsai, "Iratok a Kőrösmezei Zsidódeportálás Történetéhez 1941," Documents # 4, 11, 19, 210, and 222. See the deposition of Dr. Zoltán Arnabász, lawyer on December 4, 1946, and Dr. Ödön Sugár's statement on May 24, 1947. MNL, Documents of Nándor Batizfalvy, 206. On the negative side, see Frojimovics, *I Have Been a Stranger in a Strange Land*, 124.
56. A vicious campaign intimating that he accepted bribes for releasing Jews from deportation was waged against Batizfalvy. Majsai, "Iratok a Kőrösmezei Zsidódeportálás Történetéhez 1941," 199. See also MNL Documents of Nándor Batizfalvy, 220.
57. It is assumable that these searches were conducted by the military gendarmerie (*tábori csendőrség* in Hungarian), which also served, alongside regular military units, in the occupied territories. Max Eisen, *By Chance Alone*, 44.
58. Majsai, "Iratok a Kőrösmezei Zsidódeportálás Történetéhez 1941," 221.
59. Max Solomon, USHMM, Oral History Accession Number: 1993.A.0087.48, RG Number: RG-50.091.0048.
60. *Felvidéki Újság*, 1941, 6. Also quoted by Ádám Gellért and János Gellért, "Menekülés a népirtás elől," *BETEKINTŐ* (Az Állambiztonsági Szolgálatok Történeti Levéltárának internetes folyóirata) (2015), http://epa.oszk.hu/01200/01268/00027/pdf/EPA01268 _betekinto_2013_3_gellert_gellert.pdf.
61. Elisabeth Asbrink, *1947: Where Now Begins*, trans. Fiona Graham (New York: Other Press, 2018), 86.
62. NARA, RG-59 M1206-864-15-814, July 24, 1941.
63. Majsai, "Jelentés A Deportálás Körülményeiről és Javaslat a Visszaélések Mérséklésére,"

(August 3, 1941) in "Iratok a Kőrösmezei Zsidódeportálás Történetéhez 1941," 211. See also Testimony of Cipora Brenner, in the USC Shoah Foundation Visual History Archives, #279.

64. Majsai, "Iratok a Kőrösmezei Zsidódeportálás Történetéhez 1941," 211.
65. Salamon, "Katona naplóm. Orosz föld 1941," HIL, TGY 3212.
66. Endre Siegler, "Az én világom, meg ez a másik," HIL, TGY 3255.
67. He never reached Kamenets-Podolsk. His family was murdered en route to this city in Orinin. László Zobel traveled by train the same route. See Testimony of László Zobel, USC, #51784.
68. DEGOB, Testimony #2067.
69. Baruch Milch, *Can Heaven Be Void?*, edited by Shosh Milch-Avigal, (Jerusalem: Yad Vashem, 2003), 80–81. He recorded these events in the summer of 1943.
70. Diary of Béla Somló, HIL, TGY 2811. Dr. Béla Somló was a driver in the transport company IV/2 attached to the Rapid Deployment Force. His pictures of the deportees provide a most haunting testimony of their plight. Skala is only twenty-five miles from Kamenets-Podolsk.
71. DEGOB, Testimony #2067. Quoted also by Frojimovics, *I Have Been a Stranger in a Strange Land*, 132.
72. Irene Weiss, "Kiraktak minket a semmi közepére," *Népszabadság*, February 1, 2014.
73. Moshe Deutsch, "The Ghetto in Kaminits-Podolsk," 66. See Testimony of László Zobel USC, #51784. A report by MIPI also noted that in the early phases of the deportation, "our own military plundered the transports." Majsai, "Iratok a kőrösmezei deportálás történetéhez," Document #14, 215.
74. The Sich was a paramiltary organization originally established by Austria during World War I. See Paul Robert Magocsi, *The Roots of Ukrainian Nationalism: Galicia as Ukraine's Piedmont* (Toronto: University of Toronto Press, 2002); "Kik voltak a Szicsgárdisták?," July 2, 2008, https://www.karpatinfo.net/hetilap/belfold/2008/07/02/kik-voltak-szics-gardistak.
75. Perhaps the most in-depth work on the complex relationship in Ukraine between various ethnic and national groups belongs to Timothy Snyder, *Black Earth: The Holocaust as History and Warning* (New York: Crown, 2016).
76. Antal Hidi Naplója, HIL, TGY 3370 11. Virtually every bigger settlement in the eastern Galician territories under Hungarian occupation saw some kind of anti-Jewish atrocities and pogroms As the Soviet troops were pulling out, one thousand political prisoners were shot to death. Their corpses had to be dug out by the local Jewry. Not only Jews fell victim to the massacres in the area of Obertyn, but Poles and Ukrainians, too, who had supported the Soviet regime according to the perpetrators. See also Robin O'Neil, "Extermination of the Jews of Galicia, (Galicia, Poland)," PhD dissertation, University College, London, http://www.jewishgen.org/yizkor/galicia/galicia.html.

77. Major Dr. Árpád Toldy, "Csendőrök a Szovjet elleni háborúban," *Csendőrségi Lapok*, 15 (September 1941): 602.
78. Milch, *Can the Heaven Be Void?*, 80–81.
79. Majsai, "Iratok a kőrösmezei deportálás történetéhez," 201, 230.
80. Testimony of László Zobel, USC, #51784.
81. Testimony of Yaffa Rosenthal, USC, #16308.
82. The poem "*Töredék*" (Fragment) was written by Miklós Radnóti, a tragic figure in Hungarian literature, on May 19, 1944. Thanks for Thomas Land for the translation.
83. Testimony of Idl Feuer in Bucharest, April 14, 1945, in Shlomo Bond et al., *Memorial Book of Tlumacz—Tlumacz-Tlomitsch Sefer Edut-Ve-Zkaron* (Tel Aviv: Tlumacz Society, 1976), 122, 136, 139.
84. See Kai Struve, Deutsche Herrschaft, ukrainischer Nationalismus, antijüdische Gewalt: Der Sommer 1941 in der Westukraine (Berlin: Walter de Gruyter, 2015), n. 106.
85. Testimony of Mosheh Zelmanovits, USC, #48229. This account reminds us of the story of Moshe the Beadle in *Night* by Elie Wiesel.
86. See DEGOB Report 2067. Also, Testimony of Cipora Brenner, USC #279.
87. Majsai, "Iratok a kőrösmezei deportálás történetéhez," Document #21, 228.
88. Testimony of Yaffa Rosenthal, USC, #16308.
89. HIL, II. 1693, diary of the 5th mobile artillery battery, August 18, 1941.
90. Majsai, "Iratok a kőrösmezei deportálás történetéhez," Document #30, 237.
91. Peninah Kaufman Blum, *Paamayim B'Shoah* (Jerusalem: Yad Vashem, 2006), 53.
92. László Zobel mentioned it in his recollections that the mass killing going on in the village of Yazlovets located on the eastern bank of the Dniester was stopped by the appearance of a Hungarian platoon. He worked also on the bridge reconstruction over the Dnieper. Testimony of László Zobel, USC, #51784.
93. Majsai, "Iratok a kőrösmezei deportálás történetéhez," Document #23, 228.
94. Testimony of Marion Samuel, USC, #40972. Marcus Lecker, *I Remember: Odyssey of a Jewish Teenager in Eastern Europe*. Vol. 5 (Montreal: Concordia University Chair in Canadian Jewish Studies and the Montreal Institute for Genocide and Human Rights Studies, 1999).
95. Majsai, "Iratok a kőrösmezei deportálás történetéhez 1941," Document #13, 214–15.
96. The border signaled the dividing line between Galicia and Podolia. *The Book of Bortschoff*, trans. Sefer Borszczow, edited by N. Blumenthal (Tel Aviv, 1960).
97. *Pinkas Hakehillot—Encyclopaedia of Jewish Communities, Poland*, Vol. II, Eastern Galicia (Jerusalem: Yad Vashem, 1980), https://www.jewishgen.org/yizkor/pinkas_poland/pol2_00320.html.
98. *An Account of the Jewish Community of Buczacz, Its History and Society, Culminating in Its Destruction during the Holocaust*, edited by Martin Rudner (Ottawa: Carleton University, 1993), http://www.ibiblio.org/yiddish/Places/Buczacz/bucz-p4.htm;

Reuben Prifer described the special efforts in feeding the thousands of refugees crossing Horodenka to unknown destinations. See *Sefer Horodenka*, edited by Sh. Meltzer (Tel Aviv, 1963).

99. A detaialed account can be found in *Sefer Zikaron L'Kehilat Kolomiya V'hasevivah*, edited by Dov Noy and Mordechai Shutzman (Tel Aviv, 1972).
100. The term *Aktion* (plural: *Aktionen*) was used to refer to the brutal roundup of Jews for forced labor, deportation to ghettos and death camps, or to be killed in shooting operations. See Stanislawów, *Pinkas Hakehillot Polin* (Jerusalem: Yad Vashem), 350.
101. Abraham Liebesman, *With the Jews of Stanislawów During the Holocaust*, trans. Sigmund Graubart (Atlanta, 1990) p. 8. There we see individual efforts to ease the misery of the Hungarian Jews.
102. The memorandum is dated on December 14, 1941. "Red-Cross," USHMM, RG-19.045, Reel 12, File G-59/8-346 and C40-42. See also the communications from Margit Shlachta and Baroness Edith Weiss from MIPI. Majsai, "Iratok a kőrösmezei zsidódeportálás történetéhez 1941," Documents # 6 and 10, 203–4, 208–9. In the first communication, dated on July 29, 1941, and addressed to the head of the Hungarian Red Cross, Slachta requested the assistance of the Hungarian Red Cross. Two days later, July 31, an appeal from MIPI, presumably from Baroness Edith Weiss, asked the assistance for the care of the deportees.
103. Abraham Ringel, *A Time to Speak, the Story of my Life* (Jerusalem: Yad Vashem, 2003).
104. Majsai, "Iratok a kőrösmezei zsidódeportálás történetéhez 1941," Document #2, 202.
105. Testimony of N. H in Yiddish about the murder of Jews deported to Kamenets-Podolsk YVA M.49.E/6848, http://www1.yadvashem.org/untoldstories/database/writtenTestimonies.asp?cid=278&site_id=288.

4

1. From the interrogation of Wilhelm W., former member of the 320 Order Police Battalion. Klaus-Michael Mallmann, Volker Riess, and Wolfram Pyta, eds., *Deutscher Osten 1939–1945. Die Weltanschauungskrieg in Photos und Texten* (Darmstadt: Wissenschaftliche Buchgesellschaft, 2003), 87.
2. Reproduced in Tamás Krausz, ed., *A Magyar Megszálló Csapatok a Szovietunióban* (Budapest: L'Harmattan, 2013), 510.
3. Christopher C. Browning and Jürgen Matthäus, *The Origins of the Final Solution: The Evolution of Nazi Jewish Policy, September 1939–March 1942* (Lincoln: University of Nebraska Press, 2004), 291. Moshe Deutsch mentioned Jews from Bessarabia and not Bukovina. See "The Ghetto in Kaminits-Podolsk," in *Kaminits-Podolsk*

& Its Environs, edited by Abraham Rosen (Tel Aviv: Organization of Emigrants from Kaminits-Podolsk and Its Environs, 1965), 65–67. Also, see Deletant, *Hitler's Forgotten Ally: Ion Antonescu and His Regime*, 152, and Angrick, "The Escalation of German-Rumanian Anti-Jewish Policy after the Attack on the Soviet Union," 228. Albert Fein also recalled meeting of Romanian Jews (February 19, 2005) in Voice/Vision Holocaust Survivor Oral History Archive, University of Michigan-Dearborn. Marcus Lecker, a Romanian Jew, is enlightening about his experience in Galicia, *I Remember: Odyssey of a Jewish Teenager in Eastern Europe* (Montreal: Concordia University Chair in Canadian Jewish Studies, 1999).

4. By this definition, "anyone with three Jewish grandparents was a Jew."
5. "An die jüdische Bevölkerung in Kamenetz-Podolsk," in Khmelnitskiy Oblast Records, USHMM Acc 1996.a.0150, reel 4, 434-1-3. The military commandant was Josef Meiler.
6. "Report by Josef Meiler, August 13, 1941" in Khmelnitskiy Oblast Records, Fond 1275, Opis 3, Folder 662. An erudite analysis of the various ghettoization models by Nazi authorities in Ukraine was provided by Wendy Lower in "Facilitating Genocide: Nazi Ghettoization Practices in Occupied Ukraine, 1941–1942," in *Life in the Ghettos during the Holocaust*, edited by Eric J. Sterling (Syracuse: University of Syracuse Press, 2005), 120–44. "An die jüdische Bevölkerung in Kamenetz-Podolsk," in Khmelnitskiy Oblast Records, USHMM Acc 1996.a.0150, reel 4, 434-1-3.
7. Moshe Deutsch, "The Ghetto in Kaminits-Podolsk," 67. "Selected records from the Khmelnitskiy Oblast Records," USHMM, RG-31.078M/4, 434-1-3.
8. Hidi Antal Naploja, 12. The Hungarian command also gave a twenty-four-hour period for free looting (*szabad rablas*) to the troops.
9. Testimony of Albert Fein in Voice/Vision Holocaust Survivor Oral History Archive. See also *Verbrechen der Wehrmacht. Dimensionen des Vernichtungskrieges 1941–1945*, edited by Hamburger Institut für Sozialforschung (HIS) (Hamburg, 2002), 132. For the Romanian expulsion and German responses, see Deletant, *Hitler's Forgotten Ally*, 150–65.
10. Deutsch, "The Ghetto in Kaminits-Podolsk," 66–67.
11. HIL, V. gépkocsizó tüzérosztály hadműveleti naplója (18–19 August 1941). VKF 26/om.eln.1-1941 and HM 463354/16-1941. Quoted in Krisztián Ungváry, *A második világháboru* (Budapest: Osiris, 2005), 177–78.
12. General Karl Jerome Christian Georg Kurt von Roques was indicted and sentenced to twenty years in the High Command Trials in Nuremberg because of his activities in Galicia. He died in prison December 24, 1949.
13. Major-General Kurt Himer served as liaison officer with the Royal Hungarian Army between March and August 18, 1941. He died in Simferopol on April 4, 1942.
14. Aladár Szegedy-Maszák, *Az ember ősszel visszanéz, Vol. 2* (Budapest: Európa Könyvkiadó, 1996), 35, 392. See Alexander Kruglov, "'Yevreiskaya Actzia' v Kamenets-Podolskom,"

Ukrainian Center for Holocaust Studies (Scientific Bulleti, 2005), 46. HIS, 129. Kozma Naplo (Diary of Kozma) MNL K-429 Box 45.

15. USHMM, RG-11.001, Reel 92, 1275/3/667, 49. See also, Dieter Pohl, "The Murder of Ukraine's Jews under German Military Administration and in the Reich Commissariat Ukraine," in *The Shoah in Ukraine, edited by* Ray Brandon and Wendy Lower (Bloomington: Indiana University Press, 2008), 29.

16. It might have been Lieutenant Colonel Meiler who communicated with this Hungarian group. "Kivonat egy ismeretlen feladó által továbbított levélből," August 4, 1941. in Majsai, "Iratok a kőrősmezei deportálás történetéhez 1941," Document #13, 214–15.

17. "Report by Feldkommandatur 183 to Sicherungs-Division 444," August 13, 1941, USHMM, RD 11.001.M13, 1275-3-662.

18. Estimates for the number of murdered ranges between 2,000 to 3,000 victims. Tsvi Zelikovits Testimony, located in the USC Shoah Foundation Oral History Archives, #19436. Moshe Deutsch places the number of victims to 2,000. "The Ghetto in Kaminits-Podolsk," 69. See also *Skala on the River Zbrucz* (New York: Skala Benevolent Society, 1978), 63, 90–91. *Naziskiy Okupatziyniy Regime na Hmelnitziny 1941-1944, Dokumenty I Materiali* (Kamenets-Podolsk: Oyum, 2009), Report No. 105, 201–3.

19. Zvi Zelikovitch, *The First to the Slaughter at Orania, Ukraine 2 ELUL 5701 26 August 1941*, trans. Marc Zell (Rana'ana, Israel: Docostory Ltd., 2005), 15. Zelikovits came from Uglya in Máramaros County, which today is in Ukraine. The story was corroborated by Fanya Gottesfeld Heller, *Love in a World of Sorrow* (New York: Gefen 2015), 60–61. See also *Skala on the Zbrucz: A History of the Former Skala Jewish Community*, 63–64.

20. "Testimony of Max Solomon" (Mayer Slomovitz), August 10, 1984, USHMM, RG-50.091.0048. Interestingly enough the two survivors came from villages only several miles away from each other. Corroborating this testimony was the recollection of Alexander Shulyk in a video, "elaludt az Isten" by Agnes Moldovai (Budapest: John Wesley College, 2018).

21. One source has attributed the carnage to the Einsatzgruppe, but it is unlikely. Tsvi Zelikovit's Testimony, located in the USC Shoah Foundation Oral History Archives, #19436. Deutsch, "The Ghetto in Kaminits-Podolsk," 69. *Naziskiy Okupatziyniy Regime na Hmelnitziny 1941–1944, Dokumenty I Materiali* (Kamenets-Podolsk: Oyum, 2009), Report No. 105, 201–3. See also Longerich, *Holocaust*, 223–25, and *Heinrich Himmler* (New York: Oxford University Press, 2012), 531–32. Yehoshua Buchler, "Kommandostab Reichsführer-SS: Himmler's Personal Murder Brigades in 1941," *Holocaust and Genocide Studies* 1 (1986): 11–25.

22. Yitzhak Arad, *The Einsatzgruppen Reports: Selections from the Dispatches of the Nazi Death Squads' Campaign against the Jews July 1941–January 1943* (New York: Holocaust Library, 1989), 129.

23. Klaus-Michael Mallmann argues that the meeting was taking place in the headquarters of the quartermaster general in Bartenstein, which is in East Prussia. See "Der qualitative Sprung im Vernichtungsprozeß. Das Massaker von Kamenez-Podolsk Ende August 1941," *Jahrbuch für Antisemitismusforschung* 10 (2001): 239.
24. Major Wagner has often been identified by scholars with General Eduard Wagner, quartermaster general of the German Army. However, in light of the fact that Major Altenstadt chaired the meeting, it seems that he represented General Eduard Wagner. German sources were very pedantic in listing the exact rank and title of military personnel. Raul Hilberg, *Destruction of European Jewry* (New York: Harper, 1992), 520. Another person who repeatedly appears in the annals of genocide and was instrumental in the destruction of Ukrainian Jewry was Paul Dargel. He was responsible for Jewish policy in the Reich Commissariat Ukraine. See Dieter Pohl, "The Murder of Ukraine's Jews," in *The Shoah in Ukraine*, 49.
25. Emphasis added by author. The text of the report in English is not reliable. I used the original German document that specifically use the words "die Liquidation dieser Juden." See *Verbrechen der Wehrmacht. Dimensionen des Vernichtungskrieges 1941–1944*, 132. The English translation was published in *Nazi Conspiracy and Aggression, Vol. III* (Washington, DC: United States Government Printing Office, 1946), 210–13. The full title of Jeckeln: SS-Obergruppenführer Friedrich Jeckeln, Höhere SS und Polizeiführer (HSSPF) for Southern Russia. SS-Obergruppenführer rank is equivalent to an SS general.
26. Timothy Snyder, *Bloodlands: Europe Between Hitler and Stalin* (New York: Basic Books, 2010), 200. It seems that the military commandant of the city, Lieutenant Colonel Josef Meiler (Feldkommandatur 183 Field Administration Command or FK 183), was not given advance notice about the planned extermination.
27. Ian Kershaw, *Hitler 1936–1945 Nemesis* (New York: W.W. Norton, 2000).
28. Kershaw, *Hitler 1936–1945 Nemesis, 467*, 959. Bundesarchive, Ludwigsburg (BArchB) 162/1564 pp.172073. Interrogation of Josef Meiler September 25, 1959. Quoted by Ádám and János Gellért, "Egy tömeggyilkosság anatómiája—Kamenyec-Podolszkij, 1941. Augusztus," *Betekintő 4* (2015), 6. *Trials of War Criminals before the Nuremberg Military Tribunals October 1946–April 1949*, Vol. XI (Washington, DC: United States Government Printing Office, 1950), 362, 796.
29. John Michael Steiner, *Power Politics and Social Change in National Socialist Germany: A Process of Escalation into Mass Destruction* (The Hague: Mouton, 1975), 146.
30. Dieter Pohl, "The Murder of Ukraine's Jews under German Military Administration and in the Reich Commisariat Ukraine," in *The Shoah in Ukraine*, edited by Ray Brandon and Wendy Lower (Bloomington: Indiana University Press, 2010), 40.
31. By July 30, 1941, the German Supreme Command realized that they exhausted their resources. As Army Chief General Franz Halder confessed in his diary: "We have

underestimated the Russian colossus." See Paul Kennedy, *Engineers of Victory: The Problem Solvers Who Turned the Tide in the Second World War* (New York: Random House, 2013).

32. The plan, also called *"der Backe-Plan,"* was much wider, encompassing Germany as a whole. Alex J. Kay, "'The Purpose of the Russian Campaign is the Decimation of the Slavic Population by Thirty Million,' The Radicalization of German Food Policy in Early 1941," in *Nazi Policy on the Eastern Front, 1941* (Rochester: University of Rochester Press, 2012), 101–29. Snyder, *Bloodlands: Europe Between Hitler and Stalin*, 161–63. Quoted in Pohl, "The Murder of Ukraine's Jews," 34, 411. See also Adam Tooze, *The Wages of Destruction*, (New York: Viking, 2007), 482–83.

33. A directive by Himmler dated May 21, 1941, stipulated the assignment of Higher SS Police Leaders in the army group rear areas. See *Trials of War Criminals Before the Nuremberg Military Tribunals*, Vol. XI, 1241 (NOKW-2079).

34. Peter Longerich, *Heinrich Himmler*, 531–32; and *Holocaust: The Nazi Persecution and Murder of the Jews* (Oxford: Oxford University Press, 2010), 218. Snyder, *Bloodlands: Europe Between Hitler and Stalin*, 200. Pohl, "The Murder of Ukraine's Jews," 28. Kruglov, "'Yevreskaya Actzia' v Kamenets-Podolskom," 43–48. As a war criminal, after the war General Karl von Roques was sentenced to twenty years imprisonment and died in 1948.

35. Richard Rhodes, *Masters of Death: The SS-Einsatzgruppen and the Invention of the Holocaust* (New York: Random House, 2002), 206–7.

36. Longerich, *Holocaust, the Nazi Persecution and Murder of the Jews*, 217.

37. Wendy Lower, "The Holocaust and Colonialism in Ukraine: A Case Study of the Generalbezirk Zhytomyr, Ukraine, 1941–1944," in *The Holocaust in the Soviet Union Symposium Presentations* (Washington, DC: Center for Advanced Holocaust Studies United States Holocaust Memorial Museum 2005), 4. See also Fóris Ákos, A magyar megszálló politika a szovjet területeken 1941–1944, dissertation, Eötvös LOránd Tudományegyetem, 2021, 285.

38. Rhodes, *Masters of Death: The SS-Einsatzgruppen and the Invention of the Holocaust*, 124–25; *The Good Old Days: The Holocaust as Seen by Its Perpetrators and Bystanders*, edited by Ernst Klee, Willi Dressen, and Volker Riess (New York: Konecky, 1991), 85. Another officer, Erwin Schulz, also refused to participate in mass murder.

39. Mallmann, "Der qualitative Sprung im Vernichtungsprozess," 239, 246–47.

40. Christopher R. Browning, "When Did They Decide?," *New York Review of Books*, LXIX 5, March 24, 2022, 29–31.

41. The three days of the murder are not uniformly accepted. The corresponding reports about the number of victims were deposited by Jeckeln in the early mornings of August 27, 28, and 29, 1941, respectively. According to Klaus-Michael Mallmann, they are most likely referring to the previous day. Some historians follow him here. Others note that

the deed was committed on August 27 and 28, or from August 27 to 29, and finally, from August 28 to 31, 1941. In reading testimonies, we tend to accept August 27 to 29, 1941. Interestingly enough, one of the memorial monuments over the mass grave gives the starting date for the massacre on August 26. Evidence for Nazi crimes was collected by the Soviet Extraordinary State Commission for the Determination and Investigation of Nazi and their Collaborators' Atrocities in the USSR (ChGK). It was established in 1942. Many of the documents were transferred to Yad Vashem in Israel.

42. Browning, "When Did They Decide?," 29–31.
43. Testimony of Katarina (Ekaterina) Ginchuk (in German), Report of the ChGK, Kamenets-Podolsk, GARF 7021-64-799, copy in Yad Vashem Archives YVA JM/19711. Her name was also spelled Hintschuk—she and her family were deported from Nagyvárad (Oradea) by successfully claimed to be Christians. Similar testimony was given by Albert Fine. Voice/Vision Holocaust Survivor Oral History Archive, 25. Izidor Salzer testimony reinforces this impression. See Béla Vihar, *Sárga Könyv* (Budapest: Hechaluc, 1946), 12–14.
44. Testimony of Katarina (Ekaterina) Ginchuk, Yad Vashem Archives YVA JM/19711.
45. Testimony of N. H. (in Yiddish), Yad Vashem Archives YVA M.49.E/6848. A Hungarian document from August 30, 1941, reinforces these accounts. See Majsai, "A kőrösmezei deportálás 1941-ben," 229.
46. Emphasis added by author. Testimony of Klara Moskal, Report of the ChGK, Kamenets-Podolsk (May 16, 1944), GARF 7021-64-799, copy YVA JM/19711. Similar scenes of brutality were provided by Ksenia Prodanchuk—see note 31. This was the turn of the local inhabitants. The video testimony of Ilya Kelmanovich is perhaps the most heartrending. "Murder of Kamenets-Podolsk Jews at the Munitions Depot," Yad Vashem, April 8, 2014, http://www.youtube.com/watch?v=XYolUFgfFIA.
47. Their presence during the massacre and their role in the collection of Jews for the murder pits is well documented. Vihar, *Sárga Könyv*, 12–14. It escalated later to a more active role in the extermination. See Krisztián Ungváry, *Magyar megszálló csapatok a Szovjetunióban, 1941–1944* (Budapest: Osiris, 2015).
48. Gyula Spitz, who was a taxi driver in a suburb of Budapest, was drafted into the army and assigned to a regular unit instead of being forced into the Forced Labor Companies, in which he served as truck driver, from 1940 to 1942. He died in Mauthausen concentration camp. The pictures are located in the USHMM. "Örökre fülébe csengtek a jajkiáltások," *Népszabadság*, October 12, 1996.
49. The State Extraordinary Commission for the Determination and Investigation of Nazi and their Collaborators; Atrocities in the USSR (ChGK) was established in November 1942 to investigate the damage caused to civilians, public organizations, factories, and state institutions in the USSR. In addition, the ChGK collected evidence of Nazi war crimes and evaluated damage to the economy in Soviet territories liberated from Nazi occupation.

50. Ungváry, *Magyar megszálló csapatok a Szovjetunióban, 1941–1944*.
51. Testimony of Ksenia Prodanchuk, Report of the ChGK, Kamenets-Podolsk (May 13, 1944) GARF 7021-64-799, copy YVA JM/19711.
52. Emphasis added by author. From the interrogation of Wilhelm W., former member of the 320 Reserve Police Battalion, January 4, 1961, in Klaus-Michael Mallmann, Volker Riess, and Wolfram Pyta, eds., *Deutscher Osten 1939–1945. Die Weltan-schauungskrieg in Photos und Texten* (Darmstadt: Wissenschaftliche Buchgesellschaft, 2003), 87.
53. From the interrogation of the former auxiliary policeman Ivan Chaykovskiy, Report of the ChGK, Kamenets-Podolsk GARF 7021-64-799, copy YVA JM/19711. Other sources mention a triple cordon. Quoted by Aryeh Baruch Weiss, *Ha-dunah ha-adumah, massa el he-avar derechk ha-tebach b'kametsk podolsk* (Jerusalem: Yad Vashem, 2008), 82.
54. "Es war oft auch recht lustig," *Der Spiegel* 42 (1995): 96.
55. Jeckeln was trained as a pilot during the last years of World War I. See Richard Breitman, "Friedrich Jeckeln, Specialist für die 'Endlösung' im Osten," in *Die SS: Elite Unter dem Totenkopf* (Paderborn: Ferdinand Schöningh), 267–75.
56. The pioneering study of Christopher R. Browning, *Ordinary Me:, Reserve Police Battalion 101 and the Final Solution in Poland* (New York: Harper-Collins, 1992), provides a glimpse into the role of the police units in the extermination of Polish Jewry. The depth and breadth of the involvement of Reserve Police Battalion 320 in the genocide in the Soviet Union came to light in their trials in the 1960s. See Stefan Klemp, "*Nicht ermittelt*" *Polizeibataillone und die Nachkriegsjustiz Ein Handbuch* (Essen: Klartext Verlag, 2005), 284–89.
57. See http://www.fold3.com/page/286160993_riga_ghetto. Based on the testimony of one of his drivers, Johannes Zingler, this became especially evident during the trials of the main participants in the Riga massacres.
58. Pohl, "The Murder of Ukraine's Jews under German Military Administration," 40. These policemen had received regular military training but were exempt from the draft. Richard Breitman, *Official Secrets* (New York: Hill and Wang, 1998), 30. Arad estimated the number serving in Einsatzgrupp C as 750. See Arad, *The Einsatzgruppen Reports*, vi.
59. Christopher R. Browning, "One Day in Jozefow: Initiation to Mass Murder," in *Lessons and Legacies: The Meaning of the Holocaust in a Changing World*, edited by Peter Hayes (Evanston: NorthwesterN University Press,1991), 197.
60. There are documents that provide grisly and horrifying testimonies of how the SS and SD personnel used and perfected this method of murder first in the Polish campaign back in the fall of 1939. It placed the next group to be executed to lie on top of the already executed: often head to feet. "German Reports on the execution of Jews," in Ungváry, *A második világháború*, 173–77.
61. Testimony of Hermann K., excerpt quoted in *Verbrechen der Wehrmacht*, 135.

62. According to the preference of the Einsatzgruppen's commanders, a number of machine guns and pistols were used. Some preferred the Russian machine gun, while other units preferred the German FWW submachine guns MP 28 and 35.
63. Quoted by Mallmann, *Deutscher Osten 1939–1945. Die Weltanschauungskrieg in Photos und Texten*, 86–87; Klara Moskal, GARF 7021-64-799, copy YVA JM/19711. Deutch, "The Ghetto in Kaminits-Podolsk," 68.
64. Ksenia Prodanchuk GARF 7021-64-799, copy YVA JM/19711. Testimony of N.H. YVA M.49.E/6848.
65. Ksenia Prodanchuk GARF 7021-64-799, copy YVA JM/19711. See Albert Fein's testimony, (February 19, 2005) in Voice/Vision Holocaust Survivor Oral History Archive, University of Michigan-Dearborn.
66. Reserve Police Battalion 320 soon evolved into one of the most ruthless and "productive" killing units in Ukraine, credited with killing more than 45,000 Jews. See Klemp, "Nicht Ermittelt," 289.
67. From the interrogation of Zaloga, a company commander of local Ukrainian auxiliary police: GARF 7021-64-799, copy YVA JM/19711.
68. Emphasis added by author. Burleigh, *Moral Combat: Good and Evil in World War II*, 241. There are numerous reports of policemen and SS personnel who mentally broke down under the psychological burden of committing mass murder.
69. Quoted by Mallmann, *Deutscher Osten 1939–1945. Die Weltanschauungskrieg in Photos und Texten*, 86–87. See also Edward Westermann, "Stone-Cold Killers or Drunk with Murder? Alcohol and Atrocity during the Holocaust," *Holocaust and Genocide Studies* 30, no. 1 (Spring 2016): 7.
70. There is an extensive literature about the process of "conditioning" for mass murder. We can find a good summation for such research in Ungváry, *Magyar megszálló csapatok*, 247–50.
71. GARF 7021-64-799, copy YVA JM/19711.
72. Testimony of Herbert H., former member of Reserve Police Battalion 320, on 15.1.1960. Excerpts quoted in Mallmann, *Deutscher Osten 1939–1945*, 85–86.
73. Rhodes, *Masters of Death: The SS-Einsatzgruppen and the Invention of the Holocaust*, 206–7.
74. This angry exchange was described by Massimo Arico: "Seht euch diesen Mann an," Kamenets-Podolsk, August 27–29, 1941. For a comprehensive account about the role of police battalions on the Eastern Front, see Edward Westermann, "Himmler's Uniformed Police on the Eastern Front: The Reich's Secret Soldiers, 1941–1942," *War in History* 3 (1996): 309–29.
75. SS-Brigadeführer and Generalmajor der Polize, Gerret Korsemann was never appointed to this post. However, he established himself as a formidable mass murderer in Galicia in his own right. In 1941 he was involved in organizing the mass shootings of

17,000 Jews in Rovno. Dieter Pohl, "The Murder of Ukraine's Jews under German Military Administration," 37. See also Breitman, *Official Secrets*, 55.
76. Testimony of Hermann K. during his trial, September 22, 1964. Quoted in *Verbrechen der Wehmacht, Dimensionen des Vernichtungskrieges 1941–1945*, 135. In the Waffen-SS, Sturmbannführer was considered equivalent to a major in the German Wehrmacht. SS-Sturmbannführer Meier was promoted to Obersturmbannführer in 1942.
77. Yaacov Lozowick, "Rollbahn Mord: The Early Activities of Einsatzgruppe C," *Journal of Holocaust and Genocide Studies* 2, no. 2 (1987): 228.
78. Testimony of Albert Fein (February 19, 2005) in Voice/Vision Holocaust Survivor Oral History Archive, University of Michigan-Dearborn. This was not the only time that Jeckeln personally made decision of executing or pardoning individuals. An eyewitness has described Jeckeln's decision to execute two as Jews and spare two he deemed to be non-Jew. "The Riga Ghetto Story," http://www.fold3.com/page/286160993_riga_ghetto.
79. Interrogation of the former auxiliary policemen Ivan Chaykovskiy Report of the ChGK, Kamenets-Podolsk GARF 7021-64-799, copy YVA JM/19711.
80. Quoted by Adam Gopnik, "Blood and Soil," *New Yorker*, September 2, 2015, 100.
81. Testimony of N.H. YVA M.49.E/6848. See also the Interrogation of the former auxiliary policemen Ivan Chaykovskiy, GARF 7021-64-799, copy YVA JM/19711.
82. Interview with Branislava Antonovna Kanarchuk, a seventy-eight-year-old women selling flowers next to the mass grave (April 28, 2008, and September 6, 2012, in Kamenets-Podolsk).
83. Jeckeln was tried and executed in Riga in 1946 for his crime in the destruction of Latvian Jewry. At the time, the tribunal did not know about his role in the Kamenets-Podolsk and other massacres across Galicia. See G. H. Bennett, "Exploring the World of the Second and Third Tier Men in the Holocaust: The Interrogation of Friedrich Jeckeln: Engineer and Executioner," *Liverpool Law Review* 32 (2011): 1–18.
84. For the August 29, 1941, report, see YVA M.36/22.2. For September 11, 1941, report, see Yitzhak Arad, *The Einsatzgruppen Reports* (New York: Holocaust Library, 1989), 129. Operational Situation Report, USSR #80. YVA TR.3/1468.
85. See Yad Vashem, http://www1.yadvashem.org/untoldstories/database/hyperlinks/police_battalion_320.html.
86. Klemp, *"Nichtermittelt" Polizeibataillone und die Nachkriegsjustiz*, 285. Breitman, *Official Secrets*, 64–65.
87. György Ránki, et al., *A Wilhelmstrasse és Magyarország* (Budapest: Kossuth Könykiadó, 1968), 431–32. See also Christopher R. Browning, *The Final Solution and the German Foreign Office: A Study of Referat D III of Abteilung Deutschland, 1940–43* (New York: Holmes & Meier, 1978), 73. Wendy Lower, "Axis Collaboration, Operation Barbarossa, and the Holocaust in Ukraine," in *Nazi Policy on the Eastern Front, 1941*, edited by Alex J. Kay,

Jeff Rutherford, and David Stahel (Rochester: University of Rochester Press, 2012), 199.
88. The pioneering study of Randolph Braham goes one step further in pinpointing the active involvement of a Hungarian sappers' platoon in the mass shooting. The idea that it might have been a Volksdeutsche unit (Schwabian) has also been mentioned by him. Unfortunately, he provided no source for this claim. Based on this article, though, Hungarian participation as cordon personnel, sealing the area of the mass shooting, as well as playing an active role in the extermination itself have repeatedly surfaced—all quoting Braham's statement. A Hungarian witness, himself a deportee, specifically "heard" about two soldiers "from Subcarpathia [who] refused to shoot on command, because they did not want to raise their guns to women and children." This provides another conundrum to this mystery. Braham, "The Kamenets-Podolsk and Délvidék Massacre: Prelude to the Holocaust in Hungary," 141.
89. A tantalizing possibility was provided by Ivan Sved, the son of Gyula Spitz, who took four photographs on the murder site. He recalled the stories of Spitz who insisted on Hungarian participation. Miklós Gábor, "Örökre fülébe csengenek a jajkiáltások," *Népszabadság,* October 12, 1996. Deutsch, "The Ghetto in Kaminits-Podolsk," 68–69. Another survivor, Gábor Mermelstein, a driver and a direct witness to the carnage, doesn't mention Hungarian involvement. Randolph Braham, ed., *The Wartime System of Labor Service in Hungary: Varieties of Experiences* (New York: Columbia University Press, 1995), 1–13. Pohl, "The Murder of Ukraine's Jews under German Military Administration," 30.
90. See Arājs Trial Records, deposition of Botor, October 26, 1977, 9227–28, http://www.nizkor.org/ ftp.cgi/people/ftp.py?people//h/holman.eugene/2005/holman.0405.
91. Gabriel Mermall (Gábor Mermelstein), *By the Grace of Strangers: Two Boys' Rescue During the Holocaust* (Jerusalem: Yad Vashem, 2006), 126–27.
92. It was dated almost a week after the massacre. MNL K-774 1 cs.-1941. September 5, 1941.
93. Testimony of Izidor Salzer, in *Sárga Könyv, Adatok a Magyar Zsidóság Háborus Szenvedéseiből,* 12–14.
94. The word *yahrzeit* (in Yiddish) designates a special day and special observances to commemorate the anniversary of the death of loved ones as well as those who sacrificed their live for their religious belief. Quoted by Majsai, "A kőrösmezei deportálás 1941-ben," 229.
95. It's amazing how accurate are these estimates. Jewish Telegraphic Agency, October 23, 1941.
96. . "Bericht über die Vernichtung des Judentums in Kolomea," Letter of testimony written by Joseph Stern from Hungary, 20 October 1943, regarding the murder of Jews from Kolomea in the forests and in Belzec, 1941–1942. Yad Vashem, Item ID 3728526, Record Group: 0.33, File #2796.
97. "Slaying of Jews in Galicia depicted; Thousands Living There and Others Sent From

Hungary Reported Massacred," *New York Times*, October 26, 1941; "Ghastly Pogroms in Ukraine," *Jewish Chronicle*, October 24, 1941. See also David Cesarani, *The Jewish Chronicle and Anglo-Jewry 1841–1991* (Cambridge: Cambridge University Press, 1994), 175. Also the Yiddish papers such as *Forwarts* and *Der Tag* reported the atrocities. The Hungarian-language *Amerikai Magyar Népszava* and the *Egyleti Élet*, both published in New York, on October 28 and November 1, 1941, respectively, also provided detailed information.

98. Testimony of Dr. Ferenc Vásárhelyi, Trial of Ámon Pásztóy, Budapest Főváros Levéltára, Fond XXV, fond:4, állag A. 2890/51.

99. My own family was informed by a Hungarian soldier with precise details about the final fate of my two uncles. See also the presentation of Éva Gábor, "Személyes Emlékek 70 Év Multán," in a Conference for the 70th Anniversary of the "Körösmező-Kameniec-Podolsky" Deportations, Budapest, John Wesley Theological College (JWTC), October 12–13, 2011. "Testimony of Dezső Weiser" HIL, TGY 2962. László Karsai, "1941. Augusztus 27–28," *Élet és Irodalom* (September 11, 2009): 1–7. Christopher R. Browning, *The Final Solution and the German Foreign Office*, 73.

100. The British government declined to publish the Jeckeln reports with the rationale that it would alert the Nazi authorities about its ability of decoding German communications. Breitman, *Official Secrets*, 63–65. The American Jewish press was especially well informed about the atrocities committed in Galicia. The World Zionist Organization received reliable reports about the massacres. See Burleigh, *Moral Combat*, 449.

101. N. Blumenthal, ed., *Sefer Borszczow* (Tel Aviv: 1960), 287.

102. *Trials of War Criminals Before the Nuremberg Military Tribunal*, 363.

103. Von Roques' headquarter was in close proximity to that of Jeckeln's in Berdichev. *Trials of War Criminals Before the Nuremberg Military Tribunals October 1946–April 1949*, 363. See (BArchB) 162/1564pp.172073. Interrogation of Josef Meiler, September 25, 1959. On the relationship between von Roques and Jeckeln and the attitude of Karl von Roques to the murder of Jews, see Jörn Hasenclever, *Wehrmacht und Occupationpolitik in der Sowjetunion* (Paderborn: Ferdinand Schöningh, 2010), 522–42.

104. Richard Breitman, "Friedrich Jeckeln, Specialist für die 'Endlösung' im Osten," in *Die SS: Elite Unter dem Totenkopf* (Paderborn: Ferdinand Schöningh, 2000), 267–75.

105. Emphasis added by author. Bennett, "Exploring the World of the Second and Third Tier Men in the Holocaust," 32:1.

106. Lozowick, "Rollbahn Mord," 228.

107. Eugene Holman, "Friedrich Jeckeln—An Unsung Holocaust figure," http://motlc.wiesenthal.org/specialcol/instdoc/do9c12/jec228z3.html.

108. Bennett, "Exploring the World of the Second and Third Tier Men in the Holocaust," 15.

109. A unique find from a forty-five-minute documentary film about his daughter, Renata Jeckeln, includes rare footage of Jeckeln and personal recollections by the official

translator from his trial in Riga. "A Child for Hitler, 1992," https://www.youtube.com/watch?v=eDiOYLbiyp8.
110. Breitman, "Friedrich Jeckeln, Specialist für die 'Endlösung' im Osten," 267–75. See for his trial in Riga, Bennett "Exploring the World of the Second and Third Tier Men in the Holocaust," 1–18.
111. In perusing his SS record, one is impressed by his meteoric rise in the ranks. Friedrich Jeckeln became Nazi Party member number 163378 on October 10, 1929. He joined the SS shortly after on December 1, 1930, and rose quickly to the ranks of Standartenführer (June 22, 1931), Oberführer (September 22, 1931), and Gruppenführer (February 4, 1933). See http://motlc.wiesenthal.org/specialcol/instdoc/d09c12/jec228z3.html.
112. He married Charlotte, the daughter of Paul Hirsch, who owned the estate that Jeckeln managed. Jeckeln would later claim that it was only after being married that he became aware that the Hirsch family was Jewish. Problems with alcohol seem to have played a key role in the breakdown of Jeckeln's marriage in the mid-1920s, by which time the couple had three children. Bennett, "Exploring the World of the Second and Third Tier Men in the Holocaust," 3.
113. Erik Larson, *In the Garden of Beasts* (New York: Crown, 2011), 119.
114. Max Hastings, "The Most Terrible of Hitler's Creatures," *New York Review of Books*, January 9, 2012, 36.
115. Felix Kersten, the personal masseur of Himmler, played a rather interesting role during the Nazi years. See Longerich, *Heinrich Himmler*, 619.
116. Quoted by Breitman, *Official Secrets*, 64. Rhodes, *Masters of Death: The SS-Einsatzgruppen and the Invention of the Holocaust*, 100–1.
117. See the documentary "A Child for Hitler, 1992."
118. Interrogation of Hans Wiemer on August 19, 1959. BArch B 162/1564, 32. Mentioned in Gellért, "Egy tömeggyilkosság anatómiája," 6.
119. Testimony of Albert Fein, Voice/Vision Holocaust Survivor Oral History Archive. Gheorgheni, or Gyergyószentmiklós, is in northern Transylvania.
120. B. F. Sabrin, *Alliance for Murder: The Nazi-Ukrainian Nationalist Partnership in Genocide*, 278–79.
121. The "former Polish cemetery" might have been located in the vicinity of the munition's depot. Testimony of Nikolai Tupenko, Report of the ChGK, Kamenets-Podolsk (May 19, 1944), GARF 7021-64-799, copy YVA JM/19711; USHMM, RG-22.002M \7021\64\64-799\,799-0186.TIF.
122. Testimony of V. Chernavskiy, Report of the ChGK, Kamenets-Podolsk (May 15, 1944), USHMM, RG-22.002M\7021\64\64-799\,799-0186.TIF.
123. Testimony of Mikhail Lyubinetski, Report of the ChGK, Kamenets-Podolsk (May 19, 1944), USHMM, RG-22.002M\7021\64\64-799\,799-0341.TIF.
124. Pohl, *Verfolgung und Massenmord in der NS-Zeit 1933–1945*, 7.

5

1. He was born on March 11, 1920, and brought to the United States as a ten-month-old child. Karen Heller, "The Improbable Story of the Man Who Won History's 'Biggest Murder Trial' at Nuremberg," *Washington Post*, August 31, 2016.
2. Thomas Sandkühler, "Endlösung" in *Galizien: der Judenmord in Ostpolen und die Rettungsinitiativen von Berthold Beit: 1941–1944* (Bonn: Dietz, 1996), 132. See also Raul Hilberg, "The Destruction," Vol. 2, 812. For the history of the SS-*Einsatzgruppen* see Richard Rhodes, *Masters of Death: The SS-Einsatzgruppen and the Invention of the Holocaust* (New York: Vintage, 2002).
3. Sandkühler, "Endlösung" in *Galizien*, 132, 493, note 68.
4. While the Wannsee Conference on January 20, 1942, attracted much scholarly attention as the "start" of the Final Solution, I tend to agree with Browning that the launching of the official policy of mass extermination in the East has started earlier, in September and October, 1941. See Christopher R. Browning, "When Did They Decide?," *New York Review of Books*, LXIX #5, March 24, 2022, 29–31.
5. See Wendy Lower, *Nazi Empire Building and the Holocaust in Ukraine* (Chapel Hill: University of North Carolina, 2005), 76. Ukrainian auxiliaries were routinely relegated to support roles in the extermination by Nazi security agencies. Finder, "Collaboration in Eastern Galicia: The Ukrainian police and the Holocaust," 95–118.
6. Adam Gopnick, "Faces, Places, Spaces," *New Yorker*, October 29–November 5, 2012, 115. A comprehensive work was written by Christoph Mick, *Lemberg, Lwów, Lviv, 1914–1947: Violence and Ethnicity in a Contested City* (West Lafayette, IN: Purdue University Press, 2015). See also "Incompatible Experiences: Poles, Ukrainians and Jews in Lviv under Soviet and German Occupation, 1939-44," 2011, http://dx.doi.org/10.1177/0022009410392409.
7. Browning, *The Origins of the Final Solution*, 275. See also Snyder, *Bloodlands*, 204.
8. See the testimony of Leslie Gordon during the trial of Adolf Eichmann, June 1, 1961, about the massacre of Hungarian Jews in Buczacz. *The Nizkor Project*, www.nizkor.org.
9. Katzmann vanished after the war, living in Darmstadt as Bruno Albrecht. His wife and five children never heard from him. He revealed his identity to a hospital priest chaplain shortly before his death on September 19, 1957. Thomas Sandkuehler, *Endlösung in Galizien. Der Judenmord in Ostpolen und die Rettungsinitiativen von Berthold Beitz 1941–1944* (Bonn 1996), 426ff.
10. While not too common, two SS men refused to kill Jews. Consequently, they were driven to commit suicide by Schöngarth. "Murder of the Lvov Professors," http://www.jewishgen.org/yizkor/Galicia3/gal041.html#f146r. According to Peter Hayes, one-third of the SS leaders had PhDs. *Why: Explaining the Holocaust*, 147.
11. Sipo-Sicherheitspolizei and SD (Sicherheitsdienst), the intelligence arm of the SS,

in Stanisławów. The Sipo consisted of the Gestapo, SD, Schipo (Schutzolizei), Kripo (Kriminal Polizei. They were assisted by ORPO (Ordnung Polizei Battalions) and local collaborationists auxiliary like Schuma (Schutzmannschaft) and Hipo (Hilfspolizei).

12. They arrived in Stanisławów on July 20, 1941. Our understanding of the Holocaust in Stanislawów and Kolomea is indebted to the work of Dieter Pohl, "Hans Krueger and the Murder of Jews in the Stanislawów Region (Galicia)," *Yad Vashem Studies* 26 (1998): 240–41, http//www1.yadvashem.org.il/ odot_pdf/Microsoft Word – 2292. pdf. While the Gestapo is the best-known name within the Nazi security apparatus, it played a minor role in the genocide. Among the various branches of the security establishment, we can list *Sicherheitspolizei* (security police, *Sipo*), the *Sicherheitsdienst* (security service, SD), *Feldgendarmerie* (military gendarmerie), *Schutzpolizei* (municipal police, *Schupo*), and *Schutzstaffel* (protection squad, SS). In addition, support services were provided by the border police units (*Grenzpolizei*), railway police (*Bahnschutzpolizei*), and various Ukrainian auxiliary and voluntary police forces such as *Hilfspolizei*, *Hilswillige* (*Hiwis*), and *Selbschutz* (ethnic German militia). Although perhaps least brainwashed by Nazi ideology, the "Ordinary Men," as Christopher Browning coined them, were the backbone of the murder apparatus of Hungarian Jews, as seen in Kamenets-Podolsk. They remained the members of the Order (also called Reserve) Police Battalions, *Ordnungspolizei* (ORPO).

13. He was fighting on two fronts: (1) the liquidation of the Jews until the autumn of 1942, and (2) Polish Armia Krajowa, and Ukrainian Nationalists at the end of 1942. In addition to this, he had the border passes of Tatarow and Wyszkow to contend with. Pohl, "Hans Krüger and the Murder of the Jews," 248.

14. As we have mentioned, *Sipo* is somewhat misleading for it is used often loosely to connote a web of security offices that also included, Kripo, SD, Gestapo, and so forht. SS-First Lieutenant Peter Leideritz arrived in Kolomea in the first week of September. See "Extermination of the Jews of Kolomyja and District," http://www.jewishgen.org /yizkor/galicia/gal002.html.

15. SS officer Rudolf Müller orchestrated this mass shooting. In Tatarow, Seargant Ernst Varchmin implemented this policy. See Sandkühler, "Endlösung," in *Galizien*, 153, notes 120, 121, and 123. See also Dieter Pohl, *Nationalsozialistische Judenverfolgung in Ostgalizien 1941–1944*, 110.

16. Dieter Pohl, "Hans Krüger and the Murder of the Jews," 247.

17. The term *Aktion* (plural: *Aktionen*) was used to refer to the brutal roundup of Jews for forced labor, deportation to ghettos and death camps, or to be killed in shooting operations. Liebesman, *With the Jews of Stanisławów During the Holocaust*, 28. See Lizzi Collingham *The Taste of War: World War Two and the Battle for Food* (London: Allen Lane, 2011), 30–37.

18. Christian Gerlach, *The Extermination of the European Jews* (Cambridge: Cambridge

University Press, 2015). The constant and enduring hunger in the ghettos is well documented by Peninah Kaufman-Blum, *Paamayim Shoah*, 46–50.
19. Browning, *The Origins of the Final Solution*, 351.
20. Richard J. Evans, "What the War Was Really About," *New York Review of Books*, December 5, 2013, 18–20. See also his book about the war, *The Third Reich at War* (New York: Penguin Press, 2010).
21. *Skala on the Brucz*, 63-4. See also "Skala" chapter from *Pinkas Hakehillot Polin*, Vol. II (Jerusalem: Yad Vashem), 395–400. The diary of a Hungarian soldier, Bela Somlo, confirmed the shocking appearance of the Hungarian Jews in Skala.
22. Majsai, "Iratok a Körösmezei Zsidódeportálás Történetéhez," 236.
23. Emphasis added by author. Thomas Sandkühler, "Anti-Jewish Policy and the Murder of Jews in the District of Galicia, 1941–42," in *National Socialist Extermination Policies: Contemporary German Perspectives and Controversies*, edited by Ulrich Herbert, (New York: Berghahn Books, 2000), 113.
24. Several Hungarian witnesses described the slaughter in Dnepropetrovsk and Krivoy Rog. Judit Pihurik, "Magyar katonák és zsidók a keleti hadszíntéren 1941–1943," *Múltunk*, 2007, (52. évf.) 3. sz. 45–47. Even small settlements, where Ukrainian policemen were forced to kill their own neighbors, were not spared. In Miropol, eastern Ukraine, ninety-four Jews, among them forty-nine children, were killed on October 13, 1941. Reserve Police Battalion 303 supervised the murder. Interestingly enough, Battalion 303 was subordinated to Friedrich Jeckeln, the Higher SS and Police Leader (HSS-PF) for army group south in Ukraine, https://www.facebook.com/groups/342757449166582/permalink/1770875176354795.
25. This situation was pervasive not only in Galicia, but in all ghettos across Eastern Europe. See Cesarani, *Final Solution*, 346–48.
26. Milch, *Can Heaven be Void?*, 80–81.
27. The Diary of Elza Binder, "Stanisławów diaries and testimonies," *USHMM 1995.A.0140*, 27.
28. Testimony of Michael Jackson (Jakubowics) in USC Shoah Foundation Visual History Archives, #26142. The construction of the western part of this gigantic "trans-Ukrainian" highway was done almost entirely by Jewish labor from Galicia. Andrej Angrick, "Annihilation and Labor: Jews and Thoroughfare IV in Central Ukraine," in *The Shoah in Ukraine, edited by* Brandon and Lower, 190–223. See also G. H. Bennett, *The Nazi, The Painter and the Forgotten Story of the SS Road* (Chicago: University of Chicago Press: 2012). For life in the labor camp, see the recollections of Rabbi Nathan Blum, "Girush Yehudim Netulai-Ezrahut M'hungaria L'galicia B'shnat 1941," *Yalkut Moreshet* 43–44 (1987): 39–64.
29. See Mendelsohn, *The Search for Six of Six Million Lost*, 327.
30. Blanca Rosenberg, *To Tell at Last, Survival under False Identity, 1941–45* (Urbana:

University of Illinois Press, 1995), 30.
31. Cesarani analyzed well the extreme situation of refugees, be they from Germany, Hungary, or even the neighboring villages. See *Final Solution*, 347–50.
32. A good example was the killing of 350 men, mostly the better educated, in Buczacz on July 28, 1941. Martin Rudner, "The Holocaust in Buczacz," in *Buczacz Origins* (Carleton University, Ottawa, Canada: 1993), http://www.ibiblio.org/yiddish/Places/Buczacz/bucz-tc.htm. A general overview of murder in Ukraine was provided by Krisztina Kurdi, "Az 1941-es Lvovi Pogromok a legujabb Hisztográfia Tükrében," in *Antiszemitizmus történeti formái a cári birodalomban és a Szovjetunió területein*, edited by Tamás Krausz and Tamás Barta (Budapest: Russica Pannonica, 2014), 207–29.
33. We need to note that Stanislawów had the largest number of Ukrainian policemen, 502, in eastern Galicia. In turn, eastern Galicia had the largest number in the whole General Government—over 4,000 policemen. See Finder, "Collaboration in Eastern Galicia," 105–9.
34. Ethnic German death squads, *Selbstschutz*, were implicated in numerous atrocities in Poland and Ukraine. See Dieter Pohl, "Hans Krueger and the Murder of the Jews," 249–50. Sandkühler, "Anti-Jewish Policy and the Murder of the Jews in the District of Galicia," 113. A survivor's account by Norman and Amalie Petranker Salsitz, *Against All Odds: A Tale of Two Survivors* (New York: Holocaust Library, 1990). Statement of Isak Volski-Kuten, December 3, 1947, reported in T. Friedmann's collection of Stanislawów Reports (Haifa, 1957), 30.
35. The short history of Reserve Police Battalion 133 is provided by Stefan Klemp, *Nicht ermittelt: Polizeibattailon und die Nachkriegsjustiz Ein Handbuch* (Essen: Klartext Verlag, 2005), 227–28. Wendy Lower, "The Holocaust and Colonialism in Ukraine: A Case Study of the Generalbezirk Zhytomyr, Ukraine, 1941–1944," *The Holocaust in the Soviet Union*, Symposium by the Center for Advanced Holocaust Studies USHMM, 2005.
36. Leideritz arrived in Kolomea on September 8, 1941. The documents from the Stanislawów trial in Münster against Hans Krüger and others can be found in the Zentrale Stelle Dortmund (ZSt Dortmund), the Bundesarchiv-Aussenstelle Ludwigsburg (BA-L), and also in the Institut für Zeitgeschichte, Munich (IfZ).
37. A detailed account of Krüger's modus operandi was provided by Countess Karolina Lanckoronska, *Michelangelo in Ravensbrück: One Woman's War Against the Nazis* (London: De Capo Press, 2005). She was arrested by Krüger as a member of the Polish Resistance. Thanks to the intervention of the Italian royal family, the countess survived and testified in Krüger's trial in 1963. An equally valuable account was provided by Abraham Liebesman in his diary, *With the Jews of Stanislawów During the Holocaust*, 7.
38. The nightmarish beating, humiliation, and murder was described by two witnesses in their diaries: "A Diary from Stanislawów (1941–1943)" by Juliusz Feuerman in

USHMM 1995.A.0140, and Liebesman, *With the Jews of Stanislawów During the Holocaust*, 3–6. See also "Hans Krueger in Stanislawów, Kolomyja and District," http://www.jewishgen.org/yizkor/Galicia3/gal107.html#f239r. The Polish intelligentsia was fully annihilated by the end of August 1941.

39. He had a special animus against professors. In Stanislawów he was hunting for them among the Jewish intelligentsia. Countess Karolina Lanckoronska was a member of the resistance. *Michelangelo in Ravensbrück*, 125. The most notorious and earliest "*Intelligenz Aktion*" was that of the murder of the "Lvov Professors" on July 4, 1941. See chapter 5 of Robin O'Neil, *Yizkor Book Project*, 2011, http://www.jewishgen.org/yizkor/Galicia3/gal041.html.

40. He was loathed and detested by his fellow officers in Lwów. This interorganizational rivalry finally caught up with him in 1943. In addition, an investigation found inexplicably large sums of foreign currency and gold looted from his victims. Karolina Lanckoronska, *Michelangelo in Ravensbrück*, 125, 297. Pohl, "Hans Krüger and the Murder of the Jews," 258–59.

41. Penina Kaufman Blum *Paamayim Shoah*, 51–52.

42. "Trial of Peter Leideritz," Warsaw, August 7, 1947, USHMM, RG-14.101M3050.00 001581, 15. By some estimates, the number of Hungarian Jews ranged between 1,000 and 2,000, RG-14.101M3050.00001660, 88. Pohl places the murder of Hungarian Jews to December 4–5, 1941. *Nationalsozialistische Judenverfolgung in Ostgalizien 1941–1944*, 149.

43. Szeparowce Forest became the central location for the extermination of the Jews of Kolomea and the surrounding area. "Trial of Peter Leideritz," USHMM, RG-14.101M.3050.00001581. See also http://www.jewishgen.org/Yizkor/kolomyya/kol357.html; http://www.jewishgen.org/Yizkor/Kolomyya/kol375.html; and http://www.yadvashem.org/yv/en/about/institute/killing_sites_catalog_details_full.asp?region=Stanislawów. While some sources quote 1,200, these three sources provide information about 2,000 Hungarian Jews killed.

44. Emphasis added by author. Rosenberg, *To Tell at Last*, 29–30. This eerie scene was magnified by the fictional portrayal of German Jewish society in Hitler's Germany by Hans Fallada, *Every Man Dies Alone* (New York: Melville House, 2009). A nonfiction work by Andrew Nagorski provides a realistic depiction of this illusion. See *Hitlerland: American Eyewitnesses to the Nazi Rise to Power*.

45. http://www.rein-edelstein.com/01-eins_And_Edelsteins/Holocaust/Kolomyja_Ghetto.htm. Sefer Zikaron L'Kehilat Kolomyia mentions this mass murder on page 284. See also "Bericht über die Vernichtung des Judentums in Kolomea," by Joseph Stern from Hungary, October 20, 1943, regarding the murder of Jews from Kolomea in the forests and in Belzec, 1941–1942, Yad Vashem Archives Item ID 3728526, Record Group: 0.33, File #2796, http://www.yadvashem.org/yv/en/about/institute

/killing_sites_catalog_details_full.asp?region=Stanislawów. One source places the murder on December 23, 1941. See *Memorial Book of Kolomey* (Kolomyya, Ukraine), edited by Shlomo Bickel (New York: Rausen Bros., 1957) and http://www.jewish gen.org/Yizkor/kolomyya/kol375.html. There is some discrepancy as to the date, the December 26, and the number of victims. It quotes only 200. Jehoshua Gertner and Danek Gertner, *Home Is No More: The Destruction of the Jews of Kosów and Zabie* (Jerusalem: Yad Vashem, 2000), 98.

46. Lanckoronska, *Michelangelo in Ravensbrück*, 136–37. It's worth remembering, though, that German reports to Berlin often accused the Royal Hungarian Army of close collaboration with Jews and the Polish minority. "Operational Situation Report, USSR #23 (July 15, 1941)," in Yitzhak Arad, *The Einsatzgruppen Reports*, 26.
47. *Sefer Nadwórna*, edited by Israel Carmi (Tel Aviv: Nadwórna Community in Israel and America, 1975), 20–21.
48. *Sefer Nadwórna*, 22–25.
49. Edward B. Westermann, *Hitler's Police Battalion: Enforcing Racial War in the East* (Lawrence: University Press of Kansas, 2005), 221. Statement of Isak Volski-Kuten, December 3, 1947, reported in T. Friedmann's collection of "Stanislawów Reports" (Haifa, 1957), 29.
50. During the trial of Hans Krüger and members of Reserve Police Battalion 133, the general number of the executed in Nadwórna in October 6, 1941, was also placed at around 2,000. "Nadwórna," in *Pinkas Hakehillot Polin, edited by* Ada Green (Jerusalem: Yad Vashem, n.d.), 328–31, file:///H:/Kamanetsk%20Podolsk/nadworna/pol2_00328.htlm, and http://www.yadvashem.org/yv/en/exhibitions/valley/nadworna/german_occupation.asp.
51. *Sefer Nadwórna*, 21.
52. Edward B. Westermann, "Stone-Cold Killers or Drunk with Murder? Alcohol and Atrocity during the Holocaust," *Holocaust and Genocide Studies* 30, no. 1 (Spring 2016): 1–19.
53. *Nadwórna Memorial and Records*, edited by Israel Carmi (Israel & America, 1975).
54. Traditionally, Ukrainians were coerced to do this work. For the most comprehensive account of the extermination in Nadwórna, see Elisabeth Freundlich, *Die Ermordnung einer Stadt namens Stanislau* (Vienna: Osterreichischer Bundesverlag, 1986), 148–54.
55. Pohl, "Hans Krueger and the Murder of the Jews," 251; "Nadwórna," *Encyclopedia of Jewish Communities in Poland*, Vol. II (Nadvirna, Ukraine), trans. of "Nadwórna" chapter from *Pinkas Hakehillot Polin* (Jerusalem: Yad Vashem).
56. Quoted by Pohl, *Nationalsozialistische Judenverfolgung in Ostgalizien 1941–1944*, 46. Sandkühler uses a different quotation, see *"Endlösung," in Galizien*, 152.
57. Liebesman, *With the Jews of Stanislawów During the Holocaust*, 8.
58. Testimony of Marion Samuel, USC #40972.

59. Liebesman, *With the Jews of Stanislawów During the Holocaust*, 8. See also Salsitz, *Against All Odds: A Tale of Two Survivors* (New York: Holocaust Library, 1990), and *Pinkas Hakehillot*, Vol. 11, 359–76. This building was to remain the central feature of the occupation, and served the Germans as a temporary prison and execution site guarded by Ukrainian and Jewish auxiliaries (police and fire brigade). See "III. Der Übergang zur 'Endlösung' von Oktober 1941 bis Juni 1942," 194, in https://www.degruyter.com/downloadpdf/books/9783486706505/9783486706505.139/9783486706505.139.pdf.

60. "Stanislawów," *Pinkas Hakehillot Polin*, 368–76. See also, http://www.jewishgen.org/yizkor/pinkas_poland/pol2_00359.html. Directly under the control of the *Judenreferent* (official for Jewish affairs) Schott, Rudolf's Mill was a place of terror and mass murder. Schott personally took part in many of the shootings. Schupo Lieutnant Ludwig Grimm often joined him in carrying out the shootings. After the first deportations to Belzec, Jews were regularly taken to Rudolf's Mill and shot there. Up to July 1942, most killings were carried out in Rudolf's Mill, and from August onward, in the courtyard of the *Sipo* headquarters.

61. Majsai, "A Stanislaui Zsidó Tanács Báró Weiss Edithnek," in "Iratok a Körösmezei Zsidódeportálás Történetéhez," 20, 227.

62. Juliusz Feuerman, "A Diary from Stanislawów (1941–1943)," 9. Some sources place the start of the carnage around 10 or 11 a.m.

63. Edward B. Westermann, "Drinking Rituals, Masculinity, and Mass Murder in Nazi Germany," *Central European History* 51, no. 3 (September 2018): 367–89. In the opening of a mass grave of the Hungarian victims in Orinin, numerous empty schnapps bottles were found, which could have been thrown away by members of the SS murder squads. See "elaludt az Isten," 2018.

64. Krüger's penchant for riding a horse in the ghetto was corraborated by Cipora Brenner, a Hungarian survivor. There are several versions as to who gave the instruction to dig the mass graves, the Jews or Ukrainians. See Liebesman, *With the Jews of Stanislawów During the Holocaust*, 10. See Klemp, "Nicht ermittelt," 227.

65. Testimony of Cipora Brenner, USC #279. The only additional account about the mass murder in the Jewish cemetery of Stanislawów was given by a woman from Budapest. She might have been in the same transport. See *Sefer Marmarosh; mea ve-shishim kehilot kedoshot be- yishuvan u-ve-hurbanah* (The Marmaros Book; In Memory of 160 Jewish Communities), 380–81.

66. Liebesman, *With the Jews of Stanislawów During the Holocaust*, 11.

67. The eyewitness is mistaken. Ukrainians were not selected to the murder squads. Elisabeth Freundlich, *Die Ermordung einer Stadt namens Stanislau*, 158–60.

68. Liebesman, *With the Jews of Stanislawów During the Holocaust*, 11.

69. Testimony of Cipora Brenner, USC #279.

70. There were numerous instances in the annals of the Holocaust when, during mass executions, Nazi offices were also shot by drunken comrades. See Westermann, "Stone-Cold Killers or Drunk with Murder? Alcohol and Atrocity during the Holocaust," 1–19.
71. Testimony of Cipora Brenner, USC #279. She was the sole survivor from her entire family and was saved by a Jewish forced labor man serving in the Hungarian Army.
72. Juliusz Feuerman, "A Diary from Stanislawów (1941–1943)," 11, USHMM, DS135.U43 A134 2015. He wrote this diary in the prison. Although he escaped the ghetto, he was killed around 1943.
73. Statement of Marek Langer, January 28, 1948, reported in T. Friedmann's collection of "Stanislawów reports," (Haifa, 1957), 37–39. Also statement of Marie Durr in same collection. Sent to RO by Friedmann in December 1997.
74. A comprehensive account was provided by Christopher R. Browning, *Ordinary Men: Reserve Police Battalion 101 and the Final Solution in Poland* (New York: Harper, 1998), 30–33.
75. http://www.digplanet.com/wiki/Deliatyn#cite_note-shtetl-1.
76. See Gertner, *Home Is No More*, 86, 113. Browning, *The Origins of the Final Solution*, 349–50. See the testimony of Leslie Gordon during the trial of Adolf Eichmann, June 1, 1961, regarding the massacre of Hungarian Jews in Buczacz. *The Nizkor Project*, www.nizkor.org. There was often confusion about who these "Romanian" Jews were. Sometimes, Jews from northern Transylvania were labeled "Romanian."
77. "Online Guide of Murder Sites of Jews in the Holocaust, Galicia," Yad Vashem, http://www.yadvashem.org/yv/en/about/institute/killing_sites_catalog_details_full.asp?region=Stanislawów.
78. Volkmann was a civilian administrator. See also "Kolomyja Ghetto," http://www.deathcamps.org/occupation/kolomyja%20ghetto.html.
79. Joseph Stern, "Bericht über die Vernichtung des Judentums in Kolomea," October 20, 1943, Yad Vashem, Item ID 3728526, Record Group: O.33, File #2796.
80. *Sefer Zikaron L'Kehilat Kolomyia*, 287.
81. Albert Warmann served parallel to Leideritz, though reporting to him, as the head of *Kripo* in Kolomea. He was sentenced to death and executed by Polish authorities on December 10, 1948. See "Interrogation of Albert Warmann," July 5, 1946, USHMM. RG-15.155M.0012.00000.662.
82. "Trial of Peter Leideritz," USHMM. RG-14.101M.3050.00001582, and "Interrogation of Alfred Kiefer," June 19, 1946, USHMM, RG-15.155M.0012.00000658.
83. Volkmann was removed because of corruption. He escaped punishment by assuming a new identity, in the name of Peter Grubbe, after the war. "Aktion gegen den ehemaligen kommissarischen Kreishauptmann von Kolomyia und Nazimörder Claus Volkmann/Peter Grubbe," http://www.ecn.org/radikal/154/86.html. See Bogdan Musial, *Deutsche Zivilverwaltung und Judenverfolgung im Generalgouvernement* (Wiesbaden,

1999), 395f, and "Es oft auch recht lustig," *Der Spiegel* 42 (1995): 92–101. Also Pohl, *Nationalsozialistische Judenverfolgung in Ostgalizien 1941–1944*, 82.

84. Wendy Lower, *Hitler's Furies: German Women in the Nazi Killing Fields* (New York: Houghton Mifflin, 2013), 166. See also, Daniel. J. Goldhagen, *Hitler's Willing Executioners: Ordinary Germans and the Holocaust* (New York: Alfred A. Knopf, 1996), 241–44.

85. "Interrogation of Alfred Kiefer," May 31, 1946, USHMM, RG-15.155M.0012.00000.671, 13–14. Kiefer recalled that during the evacuation of the outpost in the spring of 1944, because of the Soviet advance, Leideritz ordered "about 20 boxes that were specially made for the purpose" of transferring the plundered goods back to Germany.

86. "Testimony of Leon Wolfberg," July 31, 1946, USHMM, RG-15.155M,0012.00000638. See also the "Testimony of Jonas Axelrad," August 6, 1947, USHMM, RG-14.101M 3050.00001584.

87. Only one source mentioned specifically Anneilies Leideritz's name. Knackendoeffel was sentenced for seven years for the murder of these fifteen children. Darmstaedter Echo, July 29, 1967, 7. See also Volker Karl Hoffmann, *Die Strafverfolgung der NS-Kriminalität am Landgericht Darmstadt* (Erich Schmidt Verlag, 2013), 263.

88. During Knackendoeffel's trial in 1967, Anneliese Leideritz was not mentioned "Kolomyja and District Transports to Belzec," http://www.jewishgen.org/yizkor/Galicia/gal003.html#63%29. See also Yad Vashem report dated 3.9.1962 (0-4/32), http://www.deathcamps.org/occupation/kolomyja%20ghetto.html, http://www.jewishgen.org/yizkor/Galicia/gal003.html#(63). Some researchers place the time of this action on October 8, 1942.

89. INR-INP, GK_296_129, 95. The murders in the orphanage were extensively discussed during the trial of Peter Leideritz, but Anneliese was not mentioned in conjunction with this crime.

90. Upon hearing about her exploits, Gorgon removed Herta Abicht from her position. She was transferred to southern Russia. Interestingly, after the war, she became involved in the black market and was murdered by her lover. Information provided by Hans Peter Trautmann, July 11, 2021.

91. Hessisches Hauptstaatsarchiv, (HHS) D-65187 Wiesbaden, Germany HHStAW Bestand 520-05-29153—0049, Anneliese Leideritz. Also, Institute of National Remembrance, GK-296-131, 7–9.

92. Hessisches Hauptstaatsarchiv, (HHS) D-65187 Wiesbaden, Germany HHStAW Bestand 520-05-29153—0049, Anneliese Leideritz. This episode of the Holocaust deserves a thorough scholarly investigation. In reading the original German and Polish files, there are serious questions about Anneliese Leideritz's guilt. See in a later discussion, 327–28.

93. Browning, *The Origins of the Final Solution*, 352. We should add to it the region of

Czortków-Buczacz where Sargent Kurt Köllner reigned supreme in murder. See Bartov, *Anatomy of a Genocide*, 185–200.
94. "Interrogation of Albert Warmann," 26. Only one officer from these two outposts refused to take part in the extermination, Lieutenant Franz Gross. While he had a heated argument with his superior, he did not suffer any negative consequences. "Kolomyja Ghetto," http://www.deathcamps.org/occupation/kolomyja%20ghetto.html.
95. Quoted by Peter Hayes, *Why? Explaining the Holocaust*, 242.
96. Quoted by Cesarini, *Final Solution: The Fate of the Jews*, 399.
97. Testimony of Samuel Eisen, YIVO, RG 1187, S No. 1187, Box 1, Folder 19. Quoted also by Bartov, *Anatomy of a Genocide*, 259.
98. "List of Charges Against Peter Leideritz," 32, and "Interrogation of Albert Warmann," July 5, 1946, USHMM. RG-15.155M.0012.00000.671, 17. The large number of SS trials, and even executions of SS men caught in bribery and plunder in Galicia, can attest to the fact that Krüger, Leideritz, and their associates were not the exception but the norm. Claus Volkmann, the *Kreishauptmann* of Kolomea, was removed from his post because of corruption in June 1942.
99. "Interrogation of Alfred Kiefer," May 31, 1946, USHMM, RG-15.155M.0012.00000.671, 13.
100. Gertner, *Home Is No More*, 114. Browning, *The Origins of the Final Solution*, 349–50. See also *Sefer Zikaron L'Kehilat Kolomyia*, which mentions 7,500 zlotys, 288–89. Testimony of Moshe Tauber from Tluste, Ghetto Fighters' Museum, #4484. In the trial of Leideritz, the number of killed was quoted as 2,600. Bartov wrote about the killing of the Jews in Buczacz, *Anatomy of a Genocide*, 182. For Bolechow, see Mendelsohn, *The Lost*, 210.
101. Peter Hayes, *Why? Explaining the Holocaust*, 89, 132. "Testimony of Rebeka Mondschein, August 20, 1956," quoted by Daniel Mendelsohn, *The Search for Six of Six Million Lost* (New York: Harper Collin, 2006), 208–10. The large number of SS trials, and even executions of SS men caught in the wave of bribery and plunder in Galicia, can testify to the fact that Krüger and Leideritz were not the exception but the norm.
102. Lanckoronska, *Michelangelo in Ravensbrück*, 136. The plunder undertaken by Hans Frank in Cracow well described by Philippe Sands, *East West Street*.
103. He made this comment in an informal discussion with the author. A case study by Frank Bajohr discuss this topic in Germany. "The Beneficiaries of 'Aryanization' Hamburg as a Case Study," Yad Vashem, https://www.yadvashem.org/download/about_holocaust/studies/bajohr_full.pdf.
104. Communication by Hans Peter Trautmann to the author, March 10, 2020. He and his wife were arrested at the end of July and early August, respectively. See Institute of National Remembrance (INR), File GK 296-129, 95–97.
105. "Interrogation of Alfred Kiefer," June 19, 1946, USHMM, RG-15.155M.0012.00000660.
106. "The Trial of Peter Leideritz," USHMM, RG-14.101M.3050.0000.1600-04.

107. "The Trial of Peter Leideritz," RG-14.101.M3050.00001615. Among his staff, the main coactors in murder were brought to justice only in 1967 in West Germany. Erwin Gay, deputy of Leideritz, received a verdict of eight years and six months in prison. Friedrich Knackendoeffel was convicted of the murder of fifteen children with a verdict of seven years in prison. Gerhard Goede was sentenced for life imprisonment for the murder of the eighteen-year-old girl, Gisela Glazer. Communication by Hans Peter Trautmann to the author, March 29, 2021. See also "Kolomea: ein Stück Zeitgeschichte," *Darmstedter Echo*, July 29, 1967, 7.
108. This question was posed by Hans Peter Trautmann in an email discussion, August 13, 2021.
109. While Leideritz was extradited already in December 18, 1941, his wife followed him a year later, December 10, 1947. See Hans Peter Trautmann, *Jahre Ende des II. Weltkriegs am 8./ 9. Mai 1945-Reichelsheim in der Zeit des Nationalsozialismus und nach dem Kriegsende*. (Reichelsheim: Self Published, 2015), and Instytut Pamięci Narodowej (INP), GK_256_129, 23. Hessisches Staatsarchiv Wiesbaden, Bestand 520/05 Nr. 29153 (denazification files Anneliese Leideritz). See also, Institute of National Remembrance, GK_286_130, 66.
110. Lanckoronska, *Michelangelo in Ravensbrück*, 136.
111. Dieter Pohl, and Thomas Sandkühler come to mind. See bibliography.
112. Peter Longerich, *Heinrich Himmler*, 15. See *New York Review of Books*, January 9, 2012, 38.
113. Dieter Pohl, "The Murder of Jews in the General Government," in *National Socialist Extermination Policies: Contemporary Perspectives and Controversies. Volume 2, War and Genocide*, edited by Ulrich Herbert (New York and Oxford: Berghahn Books, 2000), 90–91.
114. Waitman Wade Beorn chronicled the extensive and multilevel participation of regular German soldiers in the extermination of Jews. *Marching into Darkness* (Cambridge: Harvard University Press, 2014), 238–41.
115. Christopher Browning, *Ordinary Men: Reserve Police Battalion*, 162–63.
116. Waitman Wade Beorn, *Marching into Darkness*, 63.
117. In the history of the Galician genocide, only one Gestapo officer stands out who refused to engage in killing actions—Lieutenant Karl Gross in Kolomea. After a contentious argument with his superior, no disciplinary action was taken against him, http://www.deathcamps.org/occupation/kolomyja%20ghetto.html.
118. Erik Larson, *In the Garden of Beasts*, 117. Göring was especially notorious for misappropriating artwork all over Nazi-controlled Europe. See Jonathan Petropoulos, *Goering's Man in Paris: The Story of a Nazi Art Plunderer and His World* (New Haven: Yale University Press, 2021).
119. See http://www.deathcamps.org/occupation/kolomyja%20ghetto.html.

120. "Der Kommandeur der Gendarmerie, Shitomir, Kommandobefehl Nr. 8/42 [March 18, 1942]," United States Holocaust Memorial Museum Archive, RG-53.002M. Quoted by Westermann, "Stone-Cold Killers or Drunk with Murder? Alcohol and Atrocity during the Holocaust," 8.
121. See "The Professors of Lwów," https://jkorowicz.wordpress.com/tag/hans-krueger. Michael Wildt discusses this stratum of the Nazi leadership. See *An Uncompromising Generation: The Nazi Leadership of the Reich Security Main Office*, trans. Tom Lampert (Madison: University of Wisconsin Press, 2010).
122. Quoted by Pohl, *Nationalsozialistische Judenverfolgung in Ostgalizien 1941–1944*, 303.
123. Dieter Pohl documented extensively the thievery of both SS officers and civilian authorities. *Nationalsozialistische Judenverfolgung in Ostgalizien 1941–1944*, 303. See also the case of SS-Untersturmführer Paul Elsner: Gertner, *Home Is No More*, 77. See www.jewishgen.org/Yizkor/Pinkas_poland/pol2_00320.html, and https://www.geni.com/people/Beril-Bronislaw-Bruno-Dov-Lieblein-Krumholz-Dr/6000000009588971959, and https://www.jewishgen.org/yizkor/galicia/gal005.html#33.
124. Testimony of Marion Samuel, USC #40972. She and her mother escaped from the ghetto around April 1942. Her mother wasb murdered in Auschwitz in 1944.
125. Liebesman, *With the Jews of Stanislawów During the Holocaust*, 30.
126. "Stanisławów diaries and testimonies," USHMM 1995.A.0140. See also http://www.jewishgen.org/yizkor/pinkas_poland/pol2_00368.html#part4.
127. Sometimes we have a number and sometimes a general estimate. We know, however, that at least 434,000 people were killed in Belzec. Testimony of Cipora Brenner, #279. See Hayes, *Why? Explaining the Holocaust*, 187. "Stanislawów," *Encyclopedia of Jewish Communities in Poland, Vol. II*, 368–69. See also "Stanislawów," *Pinkas Hakehillot Polin, edited by* Joyce Landau (Jerusalem: Yad Vashem, 1975), 368–69, http://www.jewishgen.org/yizkor/belzec/bel004.html#n024; http://www.jewishgen.org/yizkor/pinkas_poland/pol2_00359.html.
128. County of Stanisławów (Galicia), MG, Map 111. See also YA (5000 31. 3. 42), Yad Vashem Archives O-1/32; and TB, table 9 (5000 31. 3. 42). County of Czortków (Galicia), MG, Map 139, YA (2000), 27. 8. 42), TB, table 3. 28.8.2942. See also Yad Vashem Archives, LL/6 26. 8. 42, (2800).
129. Reuben Prifer, "My Walk Through Seven Levels of Hell," Meyer Sukher, "Destruction of the Jews of Horodenka," and Chaim Karl Kaufman, "In the Time of Murder," in *Sefer Horodenka*, edited by Sh. Meltzer (Tel Aviv, 1963), 273–365. See also http://www.jewishgen.org/yizkor/belzec/bel004.html#n024.
130. Mila Sandberg-Mesner, *Light from the Shadows* (Montreal: Polish-Jewish Heritage Foundation in Montreal and the Polish Socio-Cultural Foundation in Montreal, 2005), 124–25.

6

1. "Interrogation of Alfred Kiefer," June 19, 1946, USHMM, RG-15.155M.0012.00000658. Alfred Kiefer was sentenced to death and executed by Polish authorities on December 10, 1948. See also "Trial of Peter Leideritz," USHMM. RG-14.101M.3050.00001582.
2. Marta Havryshko, "Sexual Violence in the Holocaust: Perspectives from Ghettos and Camps in Ukraine," https://www.boell.de/en/2020/05/18/sexual-violence-holocaust-perspectives-ghettos-and-camps-ukraine?dimension1=division_osoe#_ftn20. Later we find similar practices by Hungarian troops in executing prisoners who are naked and forced to dig their own graves. See Tamás Krausz and Tamás Barta, eds., *Az antiszemitizmus történeti formái a cári birodalomban és a Szovjetunió területein* (Budapest: Russica Pannonicana, 2014), 353.
3. Beorn uses the term "sexualized violence." *Marching into Darkness*, 167.
4. Perhaps the most comprehensive work on rape and sexual violence during the war was written by Wendy Jo Gertjejanssen, "Victims, Heroes, Survivors: Sexual Violence on the Eastern Front during World War II" (dissertation, University of Minnesota, 2004). A recent book by Andrea Pető, *Elmondani az Elmondhatatlant* (To Speak about the Unspeakable) is a trailblazer in this genre and an apt title for the mass rape of Hungarian women during World War II by Soviet soldiers (Budapest: Jaffa, 2018).
5. David Cesarani is one of the rare voices wrote extensively about rape of Jewish women in various countries. *Final Solution The Fate of the Jews 1933–1949* (New York: St. Martin, 2016), XXXVIII–IX. A specific chapter about the rape of Jewish women in Ukraine was written by Anatoly Podolsky, "The Tragic Fate of Ukrainian Jewish Women under Nazi Occupation, 1941–1944," in *Sexual Violence against Jewish Women during the Holocaust*, edited by Sonja M. Hedgepeth and Rochelle G. Saidel (Waltham: Brandeis University Press, 2010).
6. James C. McKinley, Jr., "Legacy of Rwanda Violence: The Thousands Born of Rape," *New York Times*, September 23, 1996.
7. Keith Lowe, *Savage Continent: Europe in the Aftermath of World War II* (New York: St. Martin's Press, 2012), 51. One cannot ignore the horrendous wave of rapes by Soviet soldiers in the occupied territories.
8. Lowe, *Savage Continent*, 52.
9. Cesarani, *Final Solution*, 408.
10. Randy Thornhill, "Why Men Rape," *The Sciences* 40, no. 1 (2000).
11. Emphasis added by author. We have already quoted from this report earlier for this was the first account to reach Budapest about the Kamenets-Podolsk massacre itself, almost contemporaneous with the horrifying event. Unfortunately, we were unable to ascertain the identity of this source. See Majsai, "A kőrösmezei deportálás 1941-ben," 229. Majsai presented perhaps the largest depository of original documents from eyewitnesses.

12. Testimony of Marion Samuel in USC Shoah Foundation Visual History Archives #40972.
13. "Testimony of S.G." in DEGOB Protocol #2067.
14. Testimonies of Marion Samuel in USC Shoah Foundation Visual History Archives #40972 and Yaffa Rosenthal #16308. See also the Testimony of Mosheh Zelmanovits, USC, # 48229 and Testimony of S. G. Deportáltak Gondozó Országos Bizottsága—National Committee for Attending Deportees (DEGOB) Protocol #2067.
15. The Hungarians were joined by Romanian refugees along the way. Testimony of Yaffa Rosenthal in USC #16308.
16. Recent studies show almost three times higher suicide rate comparing female and male survivors. It's also markedly higher than the general population. See "High Suicide Rate among Jewish Women Who Escaped Holocaust," *Jerusalem Post*, https://www.jpost.com/Business-and-Innovation/Health-and-Science/High-suicide-rate-among-Jewish-women-who-escaped-Holocaust-451769; "Study: Holocaust Survivors 3 Times More Likely to Attempt Suicide," *Haaretz*, https://www.haaretz.com/1.4929773.
17. Testimony of C. B., USC, #279.
18. Beorn, *Marching into Darkness*, 171.
19. Interview with Elizabeth Lubell, March 2, 1992, USHMM. RG-50.233.0077. Myrna Goldberg called "sex for survival." Myrna Goldenberg, "Rape during the Holocaust," in *The Legacy of the Holocaust: Women and the Holocaust,* edited by Zygmunt Mazur, Jay T. Lees, Arnold Krammer, and Władysław Witalisz (Kraków: Jagiellonian University Press, 2007), 109.
20. Cesarani, *Final Solution*, 347. Gertjejanssen, "Victims, Heroes, Survivors: Sexual Violence on the Eastern Front during World War II," 303–18. The interview with Bözsi Yakobovits about her displaced persons camp experiences was conducted by the author in Israel, May 15, 2012.
21. Testimony of Cipora Brenner, USC, #279. A revealing article about sexual coercion was written recently by Anna Hájková, "The Holocaust Is Having a #MeToo Moment, 'How should we handle Holocaust victims who also suffered sexual violence—at the hands of other Holocaust victims?'" *The Tablet,* October 8, 2019, https://www.tabletmag.com/jewish-arts-and-culture/292226/holocaust-metoo-moment.
22. Gertjejanssen, "Victims, Heroes, Survivors: Sexual Violence on the Eastern Front during World War II," 220.
23. An entire chapter is dedicated by Gertjejanssen on this subject. See "Victims, Heroes, Survivors: Sexual Violence on the Eastern Front during World War II," 153–223.
24. Evans, *The Third Reich at War*, 193.
25. Gertjejanssen, "Victims, Heroes, Survivors: Sexual Violence on the Eastern Front during World War II," 54.
26. Father Patrick Desbois, *In Broad Daylight: The Secret procedures behind the Holocaust*

by Bullets (New York: Arcade Publishing, 2018), 126, 167–68.
27. Ilya Ehrenburg and Konstantin Simonov, *In One Newspaper: A Chronicle of Unforgettable Years*, trans. Anatol Kagan (New York: Sphinx Press, 1985), 412–13.
28. Gertner, *Home Is No More*, 77.
29. See www.jewishgen.org/Yizkor/Pinkas_poland/pol2_00320.html, https://www.geni.com/people/Beril-Bronislaw-Bruno-Dov-Lieblein-Krumholz-Dr/6000000000958 8971959, "Encyclopedia of Camps and Ghettos 1933–1945," by Alexander Kruglov, see http://www.ushmm.org/research/center/encyclopedia/.
30. Thomanek was an especially odious character in the ongoing genocide in Galicia. Bartov, *Anatomy of a Genocide*, 193–95.
31. Liebesman, *With the Jews of Stanislawów during the Holocaust*, 24–25, 28, 38.
32. We were not able to identify or find a trace of SS Officer Schindler.
33. His body was found after the war. "Testimony of Rebeka Mondschein," August 1946. Quoted by Daniel Mendelsohn, *The Lost: A Search for Six of Six Million*, 208–10.
34. There were some instances, not too often, when regional administrators, with impeccable Nazi credentials, objected to the killings of the newly deported German Jews to Eastern ghettos, because they were, after all, "culturally German" and not enough degraded for indiscriminate slaughter.
35. International Military Tribunal, Trials of the Major War Criminals before the International Military Tribunal (Nuremberg: Secretariat of the Military Tribunal, 1948) (hereafter, IMT), 29: 165. Quoted by Westermann, "Stone-Cold Killers or Drunk with Murder? Alcohol and Atrocity during the Holocaust," 4.
36. See Beorn, *Marching into Darkness*; Gertjejanssen, "Victims, Heroes, Survivors: Sexual Violence On The Eastern Front during World War II"; Westermann, "Drinking Rituals, Masculinity, and Mass Murder in Nazi Germany"; and "Stone-Cold Killers or Drunk with Murder? Alcohol and Atrocity during the Holocaust."
37. Polish women were also abused by Krüger and his staff. The rape of Jewish women was widespread across the the former Soviet territories. See "Liquidation of the Jews in Mstislavl," in Cesarani, *Final Solution*, 399–400; William Tannenzaph, *Memories from the Abyss* (Toronto: Azrieli Foundation, 2009), 17; also "Stanisławów," *Encyclopedia of Jewish Communities in Poland. II* (Jerusalem: Yad Vashem), 368.
38. See "Leitender Sanitäts Offizier OFK 365," Az.: 49.s. (I), Monatsbericht, St. Qu., November 18, 1941, NARA, RG 242, T 501, R. 214, Fr. 1240-1243. Quoted in Gertjejanssen, "Victims, Heroes, Survivors: Sexual Violence on the Eastern Front during World War II," 201. At least two brothels were in Drohobycz and one was in Tarnopol.
39. There are some indications that Jewish women were excluded from military brothels by March 1942. Gertjejanssen, "Victims, Heroes, Survivors: Sexual Violence on the Eastern Front during World War II," 188, 282.
40. Testimony of Michael Jackson, USC, #26142.

7

1. This letter is dated on August 4, 1941, and sent from Kamenets-Podolsk. Tamás Majsai, Attachment #13. "Iratok a kőrösmezei zsidódeportálás történetéhez 1941," in *Ráday Gyüjtemény Évkönyve*, Vol. IV-V (1984-85),: 215. It's important to note that an account of the escape and rescue of the deportees was published only recently by Ádám Gellért and János Gellért, "Menekülés a népirtás elől," *BETEKINTŐ* (Az Állambiztonsági Szolgálatok Történeti Levéltárának internetes folyóirata) 4 (2015).
2. MNL Telegram to the Kárpátaljai Területi Kormányzói Biztosának Hivatala. K-774, 1941. We also have a copy that specifically was sent to chief administrator of another county. MNL, K-149 BM Res, 785. 13120.VII. res. 1941.
3. MNL, K-149, 130. d. 1941-6-6891. sz. akta, 1011. 201/7-1941. biz. A határvidéki magyar királyi rendőrkapitányság és alárendelt kirendeltségek 1941. harmadik negyedévi működéséről szóló jelentés. Quoted by Gellért, "Menekülés a népirtás elől," n.p.
4. A clear warning by Margit Slachta to the regent about the disregard of the minister's instruction was dated August 13, 1941.
5. "Hermann Miklós Beszámolója a máramarosi Közigazgatási Kirendeltség 1941, évi tevékenységéről," Kárpátaljai Területi Állami Levéltár KTÁL Fond 1961, op. 3, od. 2b.1113, 1-4p. -A. Beregovo Archives, Ukraine.
6. "Krissfalussy Ezredes Urnak," MNL K-382, August 12, 1941. Colonel Hrabar Kissfalussy served as liason betwen the office of the government commissioner for Carpathian Ruthenia and the Hungarian military in Galicia.
7. The two directives were dated August 15 and 17, 1941, respectively. MNL K-150-4529 . Also quoted by Majsai, "A kőrösmezei deportálás," 71.
8. Letter of Miklos Kozma to the minister of interior, Ferenc Keresztes Fischer. October 22, 1941. MNL K-149 BM Res, 1941-6-12103. 844-845. Quoted also in Ádám and János Gellért, "Menekülés a Népirtás elől," *Betekintő* 4 (2015), http://epa.oszk. hu/01200/01268/00027/pdf/EPA01268_betekinto_2013_3_gellert_gellert.pdf.
9. This directive by Keresztes-Fischer was issued only in 1942. Imre Leibovits, *Zsidótörvények Zsidómentők* (Budapest: Ex Libris, 2007), 327-28. For his role in saving thousands of Jews during the Holocaust, Lieutenant-Colonel Imre Reviczky was inducted into The Righteous Among the Nations by Yad Vashem. Ádám Revitczky, *Vesztes háborúk megnyert csaták* (Budapest: Magvető, 1985), 356-61.
10. Emphasis added by author. The Hungarian term is *"tisztogatási akció."* "Feljegyzés a deportálás körülményeiről és a közben elkövetett jogi visszaélésekről," Budapest, July 23, 1941. See also "Gróf Apponyi György, Slachta Margit, dr. Szabó Imre és Gróf Szapáry Erzsébet úti beszámolója Budapest, 20 august 1941," in "Iratok a Kőrösmezei Zsidódeportálás Történetéhez 1941," edited by Tamás Majsai, 195-237.
11. We can infer of what the August 15 memorandum said from its mention in the telegram

dated on August 17, which explicitly mentions it. ÁBTL, V-138271. MNL K-149. Box 107 1941-8. See also Majsai, "A Kőrösmezei Zsidó Deportálás 1941-ben," 71.
12. Testimony of László Zobel. USC, #51784.
13. Testimony of Dr. Aurél Kern from the Trial of Ámon Pásztóy, BudapestI Fővárosi Levéltár (BFL thereafter), Fond XXV, fond:4, állag A. 2890/51.
14. Hansi and Joel Brand later became key figures in the 1944 unsuccessful rescue efforts of Hungarian Jewry in their desperate negotiation with Adolf Eichmann.
15. www.nizkor.org/hweb/people/e/eichmann-adolf/transcripts/Sessions/Session-056-01.html. 10,000 pengő was equivalent to $2,000 in 1941 and $33,000 in today's exchange rate. József Krem, a drinker and a womanizer, made tidy profits from this and a string of trips to Galicia. It might have been him, who smuggled László Zobel from Kolomea to Budapest six weeks later. See Testimony of László Zobel. USC, #51784. See also Andreas Biss, *Der Stopp der Endloesung.* (Stuttgart: Seewald Verlag, 1995), 45–47, and Ronald Florence, *Emissary of the Doomed* (New York: Viking, 1993), 39–47. Similar rescue efforts by Romanian officers were also prevalent during these years. See Marcus Lecker, *I Remember: Odyssey of a Jewish Teenager in Eastern Europe* (Montreal: Concordia University Chair in Canadian Jewish Studies and the Montreal Institute for Genocide and Human Rights Studies, 1999).
16. Despite his crucial work in rescuing Jews in Hungary during the Holocaust, we know very little about Springmann. Yehuda Bauer, *Jews For Sale? Nazi-Jewish Negotiations, 1933–1945* (New Haven: Yale University Press, 1994), 152–53. See also Szabolcs Szita and Sean Lambert, *Trading Lives?: Operations of the Jewish Relief and Rescue Committee in Budapest, 1944-1945* (Budapest: Central European University, 2004). See also Randolph L. Braham, *A Magyar Holocaust*, 2 vols. (Budapest: Gondolat, 1988), 91.
17. Majsai rightly attributes Slachta's intersession with the wife of the regent as a crucial factor in the cessation of the cross-border transfer. See "Iratok a Kőrösmezei Zsidódeportálás Történetéhez 1941," Doc. 7 and 17. "Red-Cross," USHMM, RG-19.045, Reel 12, File G-59/8-346 and C40-42.
18. The deputy was Gáspár Kóczián, ministerial councilor in the office of Kozma. MNL, K-774. *Képviselőházi Napló,* 1939–1944, Vol. XII, 62. See, "Red-Cross," USHMM, RG-19.045, Reel 12, File G-59/8-346 and C40-42.
19. While Zobel didn't remember the name of the agent, József Krem might have been the individual who rescued him. See the Testimony of László Zobel, USC #51784.
20. *The Diary of Éva Heyman*, trans. by Moshe M. Kohn (New York: Shapolsky Publishers, 1988), 33.
21. A *mezuzah* is fastened on the doorpost of a Jewish household. It is a piece of parchment inscribed with specific Hebrew verses from the Torah (Deuteronomy 6:4–9 and 11:13–21). The Testimony of Mosheh Zelikovits, USC #48229 and the testimony of Fanny Gunzenberger describes the long wandering during the nights, looking for a

Jewish home. DEGOB, Protocol #594.
22. Kaufman, *Paamayim Shoah*, 51–53. DEGOB Protocol #129, http://www.big meathammer.com/aushwitz115.htm; http://www.clevelandjewishnews.com/archives /helen-dub/article_1d8d0a15-8b0d-5e94-b889-1b6b4d2e5fda.html.
23. Max Solomon, USHMM, Oral History Accession Number: 1993.A.0087.48, RG Number: RG-50.091.0048.
24. *Sefer Marmarosh; mea ve-shishim kehilot kedoshot be- yishuvan u-ve-hurbanah* (The Marmaros Book; In Memory of 160 Jewish Communities), 380–81.
25. Majsai, "*Iratok a körösmezői zsidódeportálás töténetéhez 1941*," #30, 236–37. The person mentioned by the writer, Rozsi, was a Hungarian citizen who might have joined the family voluntarily.
26. Interview with Elizabeth Lubell (March 2, 1992), MM, Oral History Accession Number: 1992.A.0125.77, RG Number: RG-50.233.0077.
27. Lea Solowitz, who understood Ukrainian, overheard a discussion among the smugglers of their intentions to throw the refugees overboard. Testimony of Lea Solowitz, USC #6227.
28. This estimate is based on both Hungarian and Galcian Jewish escapees. See *Sefer Zikaron L'Kehilat Kolomiya V'Haseviva*, 313–15. See also the account of Jehoschua Gertner, *Home Is No More*, 73–75.
29. Testimony of Marion Samuel, in USC Shoah, #40972. In one recollection, quoted by Kinga Frojimovics, the witness described a mass killing of escapees in the forests around Körösmező, Hungary. See Frojimovics, *I Have Been a Stranger in a Strange Land*, 150, n. 288.
30. His letter to Keresztes-Fischer was dated on October 22, 1941.MNL K-149 BM Res, 1941-6-12103, 844–45. Maria Ormos masterfully conveys the tortuous inner struggle of Kozma with his conscience regarding the murder of the deported Jews. *Egy Média Vezér*, 766–77.
31. Interview with Elizabeth Lubell, USHMM. RG-50.233.0077.
32. Sniatyn border post was under the command of Peter Leideritz, the murderer of the Kolomea Ghetto. The Yizkor book for Mielnitsa Podolsk (also called Mielnica) can be found at www.jewishgen.org/Yizkor/Pinkas_poland/pol2_00320.html. A dispatch from the military informed the Hungarian foreign minister about the executions of Hungarian deportees that escaped to Chernowitz by the Gestapo. Quoted by Flóris "A zsidók agyonlövése," 203.
33. Gertner, *Home Is No More*, 76.
34. Majsai, "*Iratok a körösmezői zsidódeportálás töténetéhez 1941*," #29, 235.
35. "Report by Naray Antal," October 14, 1941. From the Legfelső Honvédelmi Tanács. HTL. 2749.
36. "Kozma's letter to the Prime Minister." He also forwarded it five days later to Keresztes-

Fischer. MNL K-774-1941, September 13, 1941, and Kárpátaljai Kormányzói Biztosának Hivatala, "Galiciában kiutasitott zsidók vissza-szivárgásának megakadályozása," September 5 and 10, 1941. See also Thomas Sandkühler, "Anti-Jewish Policy," 110–11.
37. He borrowed this idea from a military report by Dr. Bánki, a captain, who also proposed the thirty-kilometer zone. MNL K- 774 1921 1 cs. September 3, 1941. See also HTL 2749.
38. MNL K-83 9. cs. 149/pol-1941. Report from Berlin, dated on November 7, 1941. Also quoted by Flóris, "A zsidók agyonlövése," 204–5.
39. "Zsidók beszivárgásának megakadályozása." Again from Dr. Bánki. MNL K-774 1921 1 cs. October 28, 1941.
40. One of the indirect clues that he was deported might be that his father Markus Joel Adler, a baker by occupation, was born in Jawornik, Galicia, on January 13, 1871. *Sefer Zikaron L'Kehilat Kolomiya V'hasevivah*, edited by Dov Noy and Mordechai Shutzman (Tel Aviv: 1972), 284. A returnee hid nine months for the fear of internment. See the Testimony of K.H. in DEGOB, Protocol #651.
41. We know about this radio announcement from a report by the Jewish Telegraphic Agency in New York, October 22, 1941. See László Karsai, "A Holokausztról szóló információk a magyar sajtóban, 1941–1944," *Századok* 6 (2014): 1365–74.
42. Irene Weiss, "Kiraktak minket a semmi közepére," *Népszabadság*, February 1, 2014. Testimony of Lea Solowitz, USC Shoah Foundation Oral History Archives #6227.
43. Testimony of Gertler Imre. "From the Trial of Ámon Pásztóy," Budapest Fővárosi Levéltár (BFL), Fond XXV, fond:4, állag A. 2890/51.
44. Testimony of László Zobel, USC #51784.
45. Testimony of Mosheh Zelmanovits, USC #48229.
46. The president, Dr. Pásztor József, was one of the leading advocate for the rescue of the unfortunate deportees. László Zobel, USC #51784.
47. Elie Wiesel, *Night*, trans. Marion Wiesel (New York: Hill and Wang, 1958), 12–13.
48. A set of four communications from Krakow and Lwów to Berlin was given to the author by Sándor Szakály, director of the Historical Institute Veritas. Unfortunately, no source was given to these documents.
49. Emphasis added by author. Gertner, *Home Is No More*, 76.
50. Hungarian Jewish Museum and Archives, Pásztor József Hagyatéka.
51. The original group that was saved from the bloodbath included also Jews from Bukovina who escaped separately. See the testimony of Albert Fein, 25. Major László Darnay was the commanding officer of the 16th Bicycle Battalion. A memoir mentions a different commander, Colonel Károly Petrovay. See http://gallai.net/ami-minket-illet/nagyapam-naploja.
52. Testimony of Michael Jackson, USC #26142. Following the intervention of the Judenrat in Horodenka, the German commandant provided travel papers for Jackson and his family. Colonel Meiler provided the permission to eighteen Hungarian Jews,

among them the entire Fein family, to proceed to the border in a military vehicle. The Testimony of Yakov Hintschuk in USC Shoah Foundation, Oral History Archives, #19556 and the Testimony of Dezső Weiser, HIL, TGY. 2962.

53. Quote from the Katzmann report by Jonathan Harrison. See http://holocaustcontroversies.blogspot.com/2008/07/galicia.html. See also The Testimony of Yakov Hintschuk, USC #19556.

54. Gyula Vargyai, *Magyarország a Második Világháboruban* (Budapest: Korona, 2001), 203. See Ungváry, "Kitelepítés, lakosságcsere és a holokauszt egyes összefüggései," 94. He played a proactive and cardinal role in involving Hungary, alongside the German military, in the war against the Soviet Union.

55. Testimony of Moshe Tauber, Ghetto Fighters Archives #4484. The widespread looting by Hungarian soldiers is well documented by Ákos Fóris, *A magyar megszálló politika a szovjet területeken 1941–1944*, 284–92.

56. Mila Sandberg-Mesner, *Light From the Shadows* (Montreal: Polish-Jewish Heritage Foundation, 2005). See Krisztián Ungváry, "Hungarian Occupation Forces in Ukraine 1941-1942: Historiographical Context," *Journal of Slavic Military Studies* 20 (2007): 81–120.

57. HIL II. Carpathian Group Box 2. 16. sz. mell. 120. Carpathian Group. I.b.41.VII.9. H. and K.) (HIL, HM 72345/eln.13.–1941. Carpathian Group. Ákos Fóris brought this information to my attention.

58. Arad, *The Einsatzgruppen Reports*, 26, Operational Situation Report, USSR #23 (July 15, 1941). Also, Christopher R. Browning, *The Final Solution and the German Foreign Office* (New York: Holmes & Meier, 1978), 73. See Ray Brandon and Wendy Lower, eds., *The Shoah in Ukraine: History, Testimony, Memorialization* (Bloomington: Indiana University Press, 2010), 132–33. *A City and the Dead; Zablotow Alive and Destroyed Memorial Book of Zabolotov (Zablotow) (Ukraine)*, edited by Former Residents of Zablotow in Israel and the USA (Published in Tel-Aviv Israel, 1949). See also, http://www.jewishgen.org/yizkor/zabolotov/zab005.html.

59. OL, K 744 no. 1078, B. 1941 on October 28, 1941. In spite of this tenuous agreement, however, Hungarian authorities continued to again and again expel returning refugees.

60. Raul Hilberg, *Destruction of European Jewry* (New York: Harper, 1992), 870. About Romanian policies relating the Jews see Jean Ancel, "The German-Romanian Relationship and the Final Solution," *Holocaust and Genocide Studies* 19, no. 2 (Fall 2005), 252–75; Angrick, "The Escalation of German-Rumanian Anti-Jewish Policy," 203–38.

61. Arad, *The Einsatzgruppen Reports*, 112. Operational Situation Report, USSR #66 (August 28, 1941).

62. "Aurél Salamon Katonia Naplója," HIL, TGZ, 3213, and Alajos Alapi Salamon, "Katona Naplóm, Orosz Föld, 1941," HIL, TGY 3212. Perhaps the best work on this subject was done by Judit Pihurik, "Hungarian Soldiers and Jews on the Eastern Front, 1941–1943," *Yad Vashem Studies* 2 (2007): 71–102.

63. Hilberg, *The Destruction of the European Jews*, 199, 518–20; see also Ronald Headland, *Messages of Murder: A Study of Reports of the Einsatzgruppen of the Security Police and the Security Service, 1941–1943* (Cranbury, NJ: Fairleigh Dickinson University Press, 1992), 132.
64. Gertner, *Home Is No More*, 72–73. Similar accounts were recorded from various towns and villages across Galicia. See also Ronald Headland, *Messages of Murder*, 132–33.
65. Yitzhak Arad, *The Einsatzgruppen Reports: Selections from the Dispatches of the Nazi Death Squads' Campaign Against the Jews July 1941–January 1943* (New York: Holocaust Library, 1989), report #23.
66. The modest size of the forces deployed in the execution of the tasks of occupation and the organization of the administration is demonstrated by the fact that the district under the authority of a single platoon often included as many as 20 to 30 settlements. *HIL Carpathian Group, Box 2, Carpathian Group Doing Service in Occupation IV/1, 4.* Szombathelyi was considered to be pro-Jewish by many of his colleagues. At the time of the launching of the military campaign against the Soviet Union, proceedings were initiated against him by disgruntled officers which were dismissed by the chief of staff.
67. *Szombathelyi Ferenc Visszaemlékezése, 1945,* edited by Péter Gosztonyi (Budapest, Zrinyi Kiadó, 1990), 40.
68. This attempt was probably also at Krueger's initiative, since the Gestapo detachment for Kolomea did not arrive there until the first week in September 1941. See Blanca Rosenberg, *To Tell at Last: Survival under False Identity 1941–45* (Urbana: University of Illinois Press, 1995), 18, 22. This episode can be found also in German sources. See "Ereignismeldung UdSSR des Chefs der Sipo and des SD," no. 23 (July 15, 1941), Bundesarchiv Berlin (BAP) R 58/214, fol. 172. In the second half of August 1941, Hungarians prevented a massacre of Jews in Kolomea, see "Tagebuch S.A," ZStL 208 AR-Z 277/60.
69. The entire episode was described in details by Colonel Pál Lieszkovszky, HIL, TGY 2833. Quoted also by József Kaló, "Szombathelyi Ferenc és a galiciai deportálás," *Magyar Napló* 8 (2008): 29. Another Hungarian contemporary source differs significantly from Lieszkovszky in the details of the rescue, but puts the number of the victims at forty. See Colonel Endre Siegler HIL, TGY 3255.
70. The main headquarter of the Hungarian forces was located at this time in Kolomea. There are several accounts corroborating this story. Jewish testimonies after the war placed the number around 105 Jews. USHMM, RG-14.101M.3050.00001658, 86. See, *Sefer Zikaron L'Kehilat Kolomyia V'hasevivah*, edited by Dov Noy and Mordechai Shutzman (Tel Aviv, 1972), 275–76. *Ir u-metim; Zablotow ha-melea ve-ha-hareva* (City of the Dead: Zablotow Alive and Destroyed. Memorial Book of Zablotow), trans. Schmuel Kahati (Tel Aviv: Former Residents of Zablotow, 1949); "Extermination of the Jews of Kolomyia and District," http://www.jewishgen.org/yizkor/galicia/gal002

.htl. Tuvia Friedmann, "Police Battalion 24/Company 7, to the Order Police in Galicia, September, 24, 1942," in Zentrale Stelle der Landesjustizverwaltugen, Collection UdSSR, Vol. 410, 508–10. See also, *Sefer Zikaron L'Kehilat Kolomyia V'hasevivah*, edited by Dov Noy and Mordechai Shutzman (Tel Aviv, 1972), 275–76, and József Kaló, "Szombathelyi Ferenc és a galíciai deportálás," in *Magyar Napló* (August 2008) 27–32.

71. In the Dniester river flood between September 1–6, 1941, all bridges were destroyed. Testimony of László Zobel, USC #51784.

72. HIL, Combined General Staff, Situation reports to the 1ˢᵗ section of the Combined General Staff, 208.

73. A well-balanced portrait of Ferenc Szombathelyi and his views about the deportation to Galicia belong to Kaló, "Szombathelyi Ferenc és a galiciai deportálás," 27–32.

74. The smuggling attempt took place on October 22, 1941, from Kolomea. Dr. Béla Deák was court-martialed and sentenced to prison. HTL. 4333 csomo, 1941, #13.77709. A copy of the court file is also found in the Holokaust Emlékközpont, Budapest.

75. The report was dated on December 18, 1941. Quoted by Elek Karsai, ed., *Fegyvertelen álltak az aknamezőkön* (Budapest: A Magyar Izraeliták Országos Képviselete, 1962), 403–4, 406.

76. The experience of Cipora Brenner, who was saved by a forced labor company, and its compassionate commanding officer, also shows the rescue effort of Jewish servicemen. *Sefer Zikaron L'Kehilat Kolomiya*, 276.

77. Max Eisen, *By Chance Alone*, 41–49. Because of higher education and economic levels, Jewish drivers were overrepresented in the Royal Hungarian Army. They served as regular soldiers in uniform and not as forced laborers—at least until 1942. See Mermall, *By the Grace of Strangers*, 127. Also the "Testimony of Morris Hershkovits," USC #34346.

78. Testimony of Samuel Gottesman, Access #199.8.10, USHMM RG-50.63.0010.

79. Quoted by Elek Karsai, *Fegyvertelen álltak az aknamezőkön*, 429–30. See DEGOB, Protocol #3031. Also, Testimony of László Zobel, USC #51784.

80. As early as April 17, 1941, several months before the onset of the deportation, MIPI justified its role by focusing on preventing the deportation while OMZSA tended to social issues.

81. It was one of the justifications for the enactment of the Second Jewish Law in 1939. Képviselő Irományok, Vol. 12 (1935), 306. Quoted by Ádám Gellért, "Menekülés a népirtás elől," n.p. In this context, the term "Hungarian compatriot" meant "gentile Hungarians."

82. Parliamentary debate on December 3, 1940. Quoted by Nathaniel, Katzburg, *Zsidó Politika Magyarországon, 1919–1943* (Budapest: Bábel, 2002), 269. Teleki committed suicide in April 3, 1941, in protest of the Hungarian collaboration with Germany in dismembering Yugoslavia.

83. The debate took place on April 17, 1939. Quoted by Katzburg, *Zsidó Politika*

Magyarországon, 123–24.
84. After their escape from Galicia, he and his father were interned in the infamous Toloncház in Budapest. "Girush Yehudim Netulai-Ezrahut M'hungaria L'galicia B'shnat 1941," *Yalkut Moreshet* 43–44 (1987): 42.
85. Besides Edith Weiss, other members were György Polgár, manager, and József Pásztor, secretary general of MIPI.
86. MNL, K-149 BM Res, 105; Box, 1941-6-12103, 780. Thanks to Tamás Stark for this information. Samu Stern was the president of the Neolog (equivalent to Conservative Judaism) community of Pest. Nathaniel Katzburg, "Stern Samu," in the *Yivo Encyclopedia of Jews in Eastern Europe*, http://www.yivoencyclopedia.org/article.aspx/Stern_Samu.
87. Testimony of György Polgár, "Trial of Ámon Pásztóy," Budapest Főváros Levéltára, Fond XXV, fond:4, állag A. 2890/51.
88. My family was in this situation. Samu's wife, Matild, was Christian with three young daughters. This was the practice in Budapest. We have no reports from the provinces.
89. See Majsai, "*Iratok a kőrösmezei zsidódeportálás történetéhez 1941*," no. 3, 201.
90. A glaring example was the village of Irhóc (Vilhiv'ce in Ukrainian), where the local administration called on the Jews to settle their citizenship papers four months before the expulsion. Only two families succeeded, because most cases were deliberately blocked by the notary's office.
91. Only the response of Kozma survived with a summary of the original petition. The main initiator of this petition was Dr. Gyula László, a leader of Carpathian Ruthenia's Jewry. "Feljegyzés," September 13, 1941, MNL K-149, Box 107, 1941-8, 5048-18646.
92. The American Jewish JDC Distribution Committee (JDC) was founded on November 27, 1914. It is an American aid organization headquartered in New York, but with a worldwide network of offices.
93. Emphasis added by author. Communications from MIPI refused to label the expulsion as "deportation." Instead they doggedly adhered to the official line of "relocation" or "evacuation." While, it is highly likely that the Hungarian Red Cross assisted in this endeavor, no communication from this organization survived—its archives were destroyed during the Hungarian Revolution of 1956.
94. In our research, there were only two instances that confirmed the transfer of letters, packages, and money. One was from Kolomea and the other from Kalush. *Sefer Marmarosh; mea ve-shishim kehilot kedoshot be- yishuvan u-ve-hurbanah* (The Marmaros Book; In Memory of 160 Jewish Communities), eds. S. Y. Gross and Y. Yosef Cohen (Tel Aviv: Beit Marmaros, 1983, 1996), 380–81. See also Majsai, "*Iratok a kőrösmezői zsidódeportálás tötéhetéhez 1941*," no. 30, 236–37.
95. Majsai, "*Iratok a kőrösmezei zsidódeportálás történetéhez 1941*," Document #10, July 31, 1941, and #30, November 13, 1941, 236–37.
96. Coincidentally, the same personalities, mainly from the upper crust of aristocratic

circles, played a crucial role in both organizations, which, in some ways, overlapped in their mission. Edith Weiss was also a leading member of the Hungarian–Polish Refugee Committee. Ibid, Document # 6, July 29, 1941.

97. See Elek Karsai, *Fegyvertelen álltak az aknamezőkön* (Budapest: Magyar Izraelita Országos Képviselete, 1962), 406, 414, and 429.

98. The communication was based on the report sent by the representatives of JDC in Budapest, Joseph Blum and C. W. J. Newcomb, "Communication from Paul T. Culbertson, Assistant Chief of the Division of European Affairs," September 26, 1941, JDC Archives, Collection 1933–1944, File 708. However, S. Bertrand Jacobson, the head of the JDC branch office in Budapest, also communicated with the State Department.

99. "Red-Cross," USHMM. RG-19.045, Reel 12 File G-59/8-346, C40-42. The two communications were dated, respectively, on December 3 and 5, 1941.

100. "Red-Cross," USHMM. RG-19.045, Reel 12 File G-59/8-346, C40-42. In the allusion of such "regime change," the name of the extreme right-wing former prime minister, Béla Imrédy, is specifically mentioned. While the signature at the end of the letter is illegible, it seems that the title of the two countesses is readable.

101. The telegram from JDC to the State Department on September 26, 1941, quote these numbers and even the verbiage of a report originating from Galicia. NARA, RG-59, M1206, 864.4016/170.

102. The four communications are dated on July 25; August 1; August 8; and September 26. They are found in the US National Archives, NARA, RG-59, M1206, 864.4016/157; RG-59, M1206, 864.4016/158; RG-59, M1206, 864.4016/163); and RG-59, M1206, 864.4016/170.

103. The British broke off diplomatic reations in 1939. Michael Steward Blayney, *Democracy's Aristocrat: The Life of Herbert C. Pell* (New York: University Press of America, 1986), 105.

104. He made an effort to prevent the Holocaust, and was able to aid in holding the perpetrators responsible as the principal US sponsor of and US representative to the War Crimes Commission. Leonard Baker, *Brahmin in Revolt: A Biography of Herbert C. Pell* (New York: Doubleday, 1972), 34.

105. Szapáry briefed Howard Trawers, the First Secretary of the US Legation. See "Telegram #374 from the Legation to the State Department," July 17, 1941. MNL, K-63 85. cs. 10.t 10/7 4808/pol. 1941. Also NARA RG-59 M1284-840-48/2644-30-552. We can gain some understanding about the role of American diplomatic activities during the interwar years from L. Nagy Zsuzsa, "Amerikai diplomaták Horthy Miklósról, 1920-1944," *Történelmi Szemle*, Vol. XXXII (1990), 174–96. See also Tibor Frank, ed., *Discussing Hitler* (Budapest/New York: Central European University, 2003).

106. National Archives and Records Administration (NARA), roll 12,840.48,

Refugees/2644. See also Pell's communication with Cordell Hull about the deportations, "Expulsion of Jews from Subcarpathia," August 7, 1941. Herbert Pell Papers, reel 8, no. 111/0029.

107. "Expulsion of the Jews from Subcarpathia," USHMM, Herbert Pell Papers, Box 4, 0029 Cordell Hull 1941 and 1943-1944. He was equally critical of the approach by the representatives of the JDC.

108. It seems likely that the State Department was represented by Paul T. Culbertson, assistant chief, Division of European Affairs. He was instrumental in disseminating information about the expulsion to Jewish organizations in America. MNL, K-6385.cs.10.t 10/7 4808/pol.1941.

109. Blayney, *Democracy's Aristocrat: The Life of Herbert C. Pell*, 102-5. See also, György Ránki, et.al., eds., *A Wilhelmstrasse és Magyarország* (Kossuth Könyvkiadó, 1968), 611-12.

110. The sequence of reporting about the Galician situation, including the Hungarian Jews, by JTA was extensive starting on June 26, July 22, July 23, August 3, August 8, August 14, August 22, October 22, and October 23.

111. The Yiddish newspapers: *Der Tog*, and *Forwarts*, October 23, 1941. The Hungarian publications: *Egyleti Élet*, August 23, 1941, and November 1, 1941; *Az Ember,* October 11 and 18, 1941. *Amerikai Magyar Népszava*, October 28, 1941. In English language, *New York Times,* October 26, 1941, and *Contemporary Jewish Record*, December 1941; in London, *The Jewish Chronicle*, October 24, 1941.

112. Blum was a Slovakian citizen and survived the concetration camp.

113. Sally M. Rogow, *They Must Not Be Forgotten* (Martinsburg, WV: Holy Fire Publishers, 2005), 53.

114. Tamas Majsai's work on this episode is trailblazing in Holocaust scholarship. "The Deportation of of Jews from Csikszereda and Margit Slachta's Intervention in Their Behalf," in *Studies in the Holocaust in Hungary*, edited by Randolph L. Braham (New York: Columbia University Press, 1990), 113-63, and Zoltán Tibori Szabó, "Csík vármegye zsidósága a betelepüléstől a megsemmisítésig," in *Tanulmányok a holokausztról*, edited by Randolph L. Braham (Budapest: Balassi, 2004), 115-23.

115. Ilona Mona, *Slachta Margit* (Budapest: Pázmány Péter Elektronikus Könyvtár, 1993), 115 . See also Majsai, *Iratok a kőrösmezei zsidódeportálás történetéhez,* Document #7, 205-6.

116. Majsai, "A körösmezei zsidódeportálás 1941-ben," 73.

117. Perhaps the most trenchant yet sympathetic picture of Slachta was drawn by Krisztián Nyáry, "Egy régi vágású kereszténydemokrata: Slachta Margit," May 5, 2019, https://www.facebook.com/search/str/attila+jakab/keywords_blended_post?filters_rp_author =stories-feed-friends.

118. One of the definitive works about the history of the Polish refugees in Hungary belongs

to Karoly Kapronczay, *Refugees in Hungary*, trans. Eva Barcza-Bessenyey (Toronto: Matthias Corvinus, 1999). Frojimovics' chapter about the Polish rescue gives an in-depth view from a Jewish angel. *I Have Been a Stranger in a Strange Land*, 172–209.
119. Balázs Lengyel, "A gyilkolás kezdete Körösmező-Kamenyec Podolszkij," *Élet és Irodalom*, LXII, no. 10 (March 9, 2018).
120. A biography or a documentary about this remarkable woman is still needed to be written.
121. "Slachta Margit Levele Gróf Károlyi Józsefnének," 203–5; "A Magyarországi Izraeliták Országos 26, July 22, Levele a Magyar Vörös Kereszt Egyletnek," 208–9.
122. In the opinion of Majsai, Ravasz contacted another central personality, József Cavallier, a representative of Christian circles. See Majsai, "Báró Weiss Edith Levele Ravasz Lászlónak," in *Iratok a kőrösmezei zsidódeportálás történetéhez 1941*, no. 20, 227, and no. 29, 234.
123. This was one of the reasons. See Braham, *A Magyar Holocaust*, Vol. I, 181.
124. Some of these thoughts were expressed well by Frank Golczewski, "Shades of Grey: Reflections on Jewish-Ukrainian and German-Ukrainian Relations in Galicia," in *The Shoah in Ukraine: History, Testimony, Memorialization*, edited by Ray Brandon and Wendy Lower (Bloomington: Indiana University Press, 2010), 143–47.

8

1. The testimony of Leslie Gordon during the trial of Adolf Eichmann, June 1, 1961, about the massacre of Hungarian Jews in Buczacz in August 1941. *The Nizkor Project*, www.nizkor.org. Christopher R. Browning, *Ordinary Men: Reserve Police Battalion 101*, 58.
2. Emphasis added by author. Somló Béla File, HIL, TGY 2811.
3. Emphasis added by author. Majsai, "Iratok a kőrösmezei zsidódeportálás történetéhez 1941," Document #19, 219–26.
4. Quoted by Fóris, "A zsidók agyonlövése," 202.
5. Memorandum, dated on January 17, 1942, was composed by the Hungarian general staff. A follow up document from February 10, 1942, also mentioned this joint committee. Quoted by Elek Karsai, *Fegyvertelen álltak az aknamezőkön*, 407–8, 410.
6. He was investigated for exempting the son of a Jewish businessman from the labor service on medical grounds. See Káló, "Szombathelyi Ferenc és a galiciai deportálás," 30.
7. Quoted by Káló, "Szombathelyi Ferenc és a galiciai deportálás," 30. He was tried and executed by a Yugoslavian court in 1946.
8. According to him, retired Gendarmerie Colonel Endre Kricsfalussy-Hrabár was in charge of the administrative direction, headquartered in Kolomyia. See HIL, Combined

General Staff, Reports coming in to the first section of the Combined General of Staff 208.
9. Batizfalvy's role in the 1941 deportation was always shrouded in controversy. Majsai, "Iratok a Kőrösmezei Zsidódeportálás Történetéhez 1941," 219–26. Batizfalvy's recollection and trial testimony reconfirms this story.
10. Memorandum by Miklós Kozma to the prime minister, MNL K-429, Kozma Files, Box 39.
11. Majsai, "Iratok a Kőrösmezei Zsidódeportálás Történetéhez 1941," 222.
12. MOL K 149-1941-8-1626, SZTTI 1130/1. Quoted also by Ilona Mona, *Slachta Margit* (Budapest: Pázmány Péter Elektronikus Könyvtár (PPEK), 1993), http://www.ppek.hu/konyvek/Mona_Ilona_Slachta_Margit_1.pdf, p. 116.
13. Perényi, *More Was Lost*, 169. Some of the perpetrators were put to trial after the war.
14. Aly Götz. *Why the Germans? Why the Jews?: Envy, Race Hatred, and the Prehistory of the Holocaust* (New York: Metropolitan Books, 2014).
15. Márai, *A Teljes Napló, 1943–1944*, 111.
16. Peter Bihari, *Lövészárkok a hátországban* (Budapest: Napvilág, 2008), 252. A recently published "hybrid-novel" by Rudolf Ungvary discusses the issue of a never-resolved inter middle-class conflict. *Balatoni Nyaralo* (Budpest: Jelenkor, 2020). See also Pál Várnay, "Nem Bocsájtják Meg a Zsidóknak az Életben Maradást," *Szombat*, January 22, 2020.
17. Special thanks to Gyula Kosztyó for bringing to my attention this document. It might be appropriate to mention the name of László Megay, the vice mayor of Uzhgorod, for he played a crucial and brutal role in the ghettoization and plunder of the Jews of his city in the spring of 1944, which was 34 percent of the town's population. Kárpátaljai Területi Állami Levéltár, KTÁL Fond 42., op. 1., od. zb. 2918.
18. "Hermann Miklós Beszámolója a máramarosi Közigazgatási Kirendeltség 1941, évi tevékenységéről," KTAL Fond 1961, op. 3., od. 2b.1113, 1-4p. -A. Beregszász, Ukraine.
19. I am thankful again to Gyula Kosztyo for his incisive and in-depth work on the economic destruction of the Jews and consequently the regional economy in Carpathian Ruthenia. See "*Mit vesztett Kárpátalja a holokauszttal? Egy minisztériumi állapotfelmérés elemzése (1939, augusztus).*"
20. Jews in Uzhhorod (Ungvar) and Mukachevo (Munkacs), the two largest towns of the region, constituted 27.2 and 48 percent of the population, respectively, http://www.yivoencyclopedia.org/article.aspx/Uzhhorod. Yet, we have to point out that a large segment of the Jewish population also engaged in agriculture.
21. "Hermann Miklós Beszámolója," KTÁL Fond 1961, op. 3., od. 2b.1113, 1-4p.
22. Katzburg, *Zsidó Politika Magyarországon*, 135.
23. Perényi, *More Was Lost*, 159. Sándor Márai described the same situation in Upper Hungary where the "Jews unwaiveringly supported Hungarian interests." *Hallgatni akartam*, 88.

24. An excellent analysis is presented by Gyula Kosztyó, "Az iskolapadtól a gázkamráig—A kárpátaljai zsidó népiskolai oktatás története," *Neokohn*, August 19, 2019, https://neokohn.hu/2019/08/18/az-iskolapadtol-a-gazkamraig-a-karpataljai-zsido-nepiskolai-oktatas-tortenete. See also Ágnes Ságvári, "Holokauszt Kárpatalján," in *Tanulmányok a magyarországi holokauszt történetéből* (Budapest: Napvilág, 2002), 33–66.
25. Ságvári mentions that the Hungarian authorities confiscated the land of several thousand Ruthenians (Ukrainians), and replaced it with less productive properties. "Holokauszt Kárpatalján," 48–49.
26. Gábor Kádár and Zoltán Vágó, *Self-Financing Genocide* (Budapest: Central European University Press, 2001), 63. Perhaps the most comprehensive work on the economic destruction of Hungarian Jewry during the Holocaust belongs to Gábor Kádár and Zoltán Vágó, *Hullarablás, a Magyar Zsidók Gazdasági Megsemmmisítése* (Budapest: Jaffa, 2005).
27. Emphasis added by author. OL. K-774, Kárpátaljai Kormányzói Biztosának Hivatala, 646/41/eln. Judit Fejes draws a direct line between the economic opportunism and the deportation. See "On the History of the Mass Deportation from Carpatho-Ruthenia in 1941," 305–27. Also quoted in László Karsai, *Holokauszt* (Budapest: Pannonica Kiadó, 2001), 230.
28. Somló Béla File, HIL, TGY 2811, 10.
29. Alajos Alapi Salamon, "Katona naplóm. Orosz föld 1941," HL, TGY 3212.
30. Numerous witnesses and survivors recalled this recurring phrase. Moshe Deutsch, "The Ghetto in Kaminits-Podolsk," 66. See also interview with Iren Weiss, "Kiraktak minket a semmi közepén," *Népszabadság*, February 1, 2014.
31. The event was recorded in Carpathian Ruthenia. Angelika Orgona, *The American Countess: Memories of the Szápárz and Széchényi Families* (Budapest: Magyar Nemzeti Muzeum, 2020), 122.
32. This fact was mentioned during the trial of Reserve Police Battalion 320. It might also be pertinent to mention that Hungarian forces were in no shape to mount any rescue operation, which could involve combat. See http://gallai.net/ami-minket-illet/nagyapam-naploja. Hungarian participation in leading the Hungarian Jews to the killing fields. See Vihar, *Sárga Könyv*, 12–13.
33. Because of the similarity in uniform, witnesses might have misidentified the various military units such as the field gendarmerie or the border guards who perpetrated atrocities. Thanks to Sándor Szakály for pointing out this fact. See "Testimony of Dezső Weiser," HIL, TGY.2962; Testimony of Michael Jackson, USC #26142; and Gertner, *Home Is No More*, 131–35. One recollection, quoted by Kinga Frojimovics, has elicited some doubt about its veracity: the witness described a mass killing of escapees in the forests around Kőrösmező, Hungary. Frojimovics, *I Have Been a Stranger in a Strange Land*, 150, n. 288.

34. Somló Béla File, HIL, TGY 2811. See also the testimony of Leslie Gordon during the trial of Adolf Eichmann, June 1, 1961, about the massacre of Hungarian Jews in Buczacz. *The Nizkor Project*, www.nizkor.org. This was reinforced by László Zobel in his interview. Shoah Foundation Oral History Archives, USC #51784. For more details about tragedies in the Dniester crossing, see DEGOB Collection, Protocol No. 447 in the Hungarian Jewish Museum and Archives.

35. Testimony of F.H. (Hermann Frimmer) in DEGOB, Protocol #447 and Baruch Milch diary on events in Tłuste (Galicia district of Generalgouvernement) after the start of the German occupation in summer 1941, written July/August 1943; USHMMA RG-02.208M (ŻIH 302/98, translated from Polish). See also the letter of a deported family in Majsai, "Iratok a kőrösmezei zsidódeportálás történetéhez 1941," 230. The reputation of sapper battalions for toughness, bordering on cruelty, is well established in the lore of the Hungarian Holocaust. A similar experience was recorded by László Zobel Shoah, USC #51784. Also for the recollection of Ferenc Gallai, see http://gallai.net/ami-minket-illet/nagyapam-naploja.

36. Majsai, "A kőrösmezői zsidódeportálás 1941-ben," Document #29, 235.

37. HIL, Kárpát Csoport, Box II. The command from the chief of general staff was dated September 15, 1941. A similar directive ordered the destruction of all such communication in front of the forced laborers on January 13, 1942. A follow-up report on February 2, 1942, mentiones similar issues. Quoted by Elek Karsai, *Fegyvertelen álltak az aknamezőkön*, 406, 414, and 429.

38. The testimony of László Zobel about his accidental rescue by a Hungarian counter-intelligence agent in Kolomea is a case in point. Shoah Foundation Oral History Archives, USC #51784. Another survivor was rescued by two gentile peasants from his village in Carpathian Ruthenia, who smuggled him and his family across the border. Testimony by Frida Landau, USC Shoah Foundation Oral History Archives, #43849. See also the court proceedings against Lieutenant Béla Deák, who was courtmartialed for the smuggling of Mária Bartal and her son, both Christians, on October 21, 1941. The author found this file in a box containing material about Kamenets-Podolsk, Holocaust Központ, Budapest.

39. We only have to remember the Hungarian participation in the mass murder of 1,500 Jews in the village of Gajsin. See "Pápa Nándor és Társai," court proceedings, in Budapest Fővárosi Levéltár B 7555-1950.

40. The directive, dated on February 10, 1942, came from the Hungarian general staff. Quoted by Elek Karsai, *Fegyvertelen álltak az aknamezőkön*, 411.

41. The best source for such a relationship is Beorn.

42. It might have been Lieutenant Colonel Josef Meiler. Deutsch, "The Ghetto in Kaminits-Podolsk," 67.

43. The testimony of Leslie Gordon during the trial of Adolf Eichmann, June 1, 1961. It is

notable that only one officer in Kolomea refused to participate in the extermination. Lieutenant Karl Gross was not disciplined and was exempted from participating in executions. See http://www.deathcamps.org/occupation/kolomyja%20ghetto.html.
44. Finder, "Collaboration in Eastern Galicia," 106.
45. Again, Father Desbois' book, *In Broad Daylight*, sheds a stark light on the whole process of extermination and the central role of the Ukrainian auxiliaries in it.
46. The two main works documenting the role that Reserve Police Battalions played in the Holocaust are Westermann, *Hitler's Police Battalion: Enforcing Racial War in the East*, and Browning, *Ordinary Men: Reserve Police Battalion 101 and the Final Solution in Poland*. Unfortunately, neither of them provides an account about these two battalions.
47. We know that Jeckeln's trial did not mention his role in the murder of 23,600 people in Kamenets-Podolsk. Massimo Arico, "'Seht euch diesen Mann an'; Kamenec-Podolski, 27–29 August 1941."
48. Quoted by Hayes, *Why*, 257.
49. Veszprémy, *Gyilkos Irodák a Magyar Közigazgatás, a Német megszállás és a Holokauszt*, 23, 68. See also Rigó Máté, "Hétköznapi emberek," in *1944/1945. Társadalom a háborúban. Folytonosság és változás Magyarországon*, edited by Bódy Zsombor and Horváth Sándor (Budapest: MTA BTK TTI, 2015).
50. The central representative from KEOKH, mentioned during the postwar trials, was Ödön Martinidesz, chief of the detective attachment. See Frojimovics, *I Have Been Stranger in a Strange Land*, 107–9. Little is known about Arisztid Meskó, the police commissioner of Carpathian Ruthenia, but his pronouncements and deeds are damning testimony for the destruction of the region.
51. As the commander of the transit camp in Kőrösmező, Lieutenant Colonel Rudolf Orbán conveniently omitted his role in the management of this infamous camp after the war. HIL, AKVI 1770/-1890. See also testimony of Samuel Marion, in USC #40972.
52. Keresztes-Fischer made me realize that Hungarian reality during the war is not a black-and-white picture. He brought forth a hard-to-comprehend contradiction that the Hungarian regime was not a homogeneous entity and perpetrators sometimes turned into rescuers during the Holocaust—of course, in the later phases of the war, when its outcome was predictable. See Veszprémy László Bernát, *Gyilkos Irodák a Magyar Közigazgatás, a Német megszállás és a Holokauszt* (Budapest: Jaffa, 2019).
53. A balanced account about his role in the 1941 deportation is still awaiting to be written. About his pronouncements in front of the Parliament, see *Képviselőházi Napló, 1939–1944*, Vol. XII, 62. Also quoted by Frojimovics, *I Have Been a Stranger in a Strange Land*, 107. George Orwell, "Politics and the English Language," *Horizon* (April 1946): 252–65.
54. MNL K-491.2. cs. K 491-1942-369, October 28, 1942. Quoted by Fóris, "A zsidók agyonlövése," 204.

55. Although I could not find its origin, the quip is attributed to Krisztián Ungváry.
56. Around 4,000 Jews from Budapest were transported to Galicia. See *Társadalmi Konfliktusok*, http://konfliktuskutato.hu/index.php?option=com_maps&view=topicevents&map_id=13&tmpl=dka&full=0&Itemid=204. Werth often kept the cabinet in the dark about momentous decisions, which he made unilaterally.
57. The participants of the trip included Jenő Sándor and Nándor Batizfalvy, representing KEOKH, Arisztid Meskó from Carpathian Ruthenia, and two military officers. "The Interrogation of dr. Árkád Kiss," Állambiztonsági Szolgálatok Történelmi Levéltára 3. I. 9. V-104139.
58. Quoted by Snyder, *Bloodlands*, 387.
59. Longerich, *Heinrich Himmler*, 619. See also, Braham, *The Politics of Genocide*, 284, ff. Of course, the Romanians would have rejected such a proposal outright.
60. See Elek Karsai, ed., *Fegyvertelenül álltak az aknamezőkön* (Budapest: A Magyar Izraeliták Országos Képviselete, 1962), 407–8. MNL K-149 130. dob. 1942—6-6892-50/1952, January 12, 1942. The groundbreaking study of Kinga Frojimovics well demonstrates the lawlessness within KEOKH. "Deportálás Galiciába A Kamenyec-Podolszkiji Vérengzés Után," https://docplayer.hu/15748211-Deportalas-galiciaba-a-kamenyec-podolszkiji-verengzes-utan-1941-1942.html. Sandkühler, "Endlösung," 153, fn. 120 and 121.
61. A curious document surfaced almost at the end of the war, which revoked his and his son's membership in the "Order of Vitéz," a form of knighthood bestowed upon faithful members of Horthy's circle. The justification stated his Jewish background. "Országos Vitézi Szék," March 14, 1945. A copy of the original document was provided to the author by Sándor Szakály. This is also mentioned by Elek Karsai, *fegyvertelenül álltak az aknamezőkön*, CIX-CX. Another document supports this, MNL K-429-35-507. See Majsai, "A körösmezei zsidódeportálás 1941-ben," 22, n. 52.
62. Pál Teleki, from the rank of the nobility, served as prime minister until 1941. He harbored strong reservation about a pro-German political orientation. András D. Bán, *Hungarian-British Diplomacy 1938–1941* (New York: Rutledge, 2004), 88.
63. Gyula Kádár well sums up Werth's responsibility in precipitating Hungary's entry onto the war. *A Ludovikától Sopronkőhidáig* (Budapest: Magveto, 1984), 384–402.
64. Emphasis added by author. Karsai, *Holokauszt*, 228. See Pál Pritz, *The War Crimes Trial of Hungarian Prime Minister László Bárdossy*, trans. Thomas J. DeKornfeld and Helen D. Hiltabidle (New York: Columbia University Press, 2004), 40. Miklós Horthy, *Horthy Miklós titkos iratai* [The Secret Papers of Miklós Horthy], edited by. Miklós Szinai and László Szücs (Budapest: Kossuth Könyvkiadó, 1962), 302–7.
65. Emphasis added by author. It was sent to the prime minister and the minister of interior. MNL Kárpátaljai Kormányzói Biztosának Hivatala. Memorandum, K-774, 646/1941. eln.sz. file 1, on September 10, 1941. Eight days later Miklós Kozma directly informed

the prime minister and the minister of interior about this decision. See Kárpátaljai Kormányzói Biztosának Hivatala. K-774, 646/1941 on September 18, 1941.
66. Memorandum to László Bárdossy, September 16, 1941, MNL K-774-1941 I. cs.
67. "A Letter from Margit Slachta to Baroness Edith Weiss," February 23, 1951. Archives of the Convent of the Hungarian Social Sisters, Buffalo, NY. Also quoted by Ilona Mona, *Slachta Margit*, 116.
68. "Herbert Pell Papers," (undated), 0029, Box. 4, Reel 8, United States Holocaust Memorial Museum (USHMM). See a comment by Márai about the responsibility vs. guilt of Bárdossy. *Hallgatni Akartam*, 135.
69. István Bibó, "Zsidókérdés Magyarországon 1944 után," in *Válogatott tanulmányok. Második kötet 1945–1949*, edited by István Vida (Budapest: Magvető Könyvkiadó, 1986). The most comprehensive account about the trial was provided by Pál Pritz, *Bárdossy László a népbíróság előtt* (Budapest: Maecenas, 1991), 59.
70. As history would confirm his recklessness, his decision in entering the war on Germany's side proved disastrous for Hungary. Quoted by Marianne Szegedy-Maszák, *I Kiss Your Hands Many Times* (New York: Spiegel & Grau, 2013), 56.
71. "Jelentés a Galíciába kitolocolt zsidók németek általi kitoloncolásáról, Berlin, November 7, 1941," MNL K-83 9. Cs.149/pol. 1941. Thanks to Ákos Fóris for bringing this report to my attention. See "A zsidók agyonlövése a megszállt területen köztudomású," *Eszmélet* 115 (2007): 204–5. The trains carrying Jews from Germany and the Protectorate to the East started to roll in October 1941. See Cesarani, *Final Solution*, 416–32. For the Hungarian-German exchange, see MNL K-83 9. Cs. 149/pol.-1941, dated November 7, 1941. It was quoted by Fóris, "A zsidók agyonlövése," 204–5.
72. *Képviselőházi Napló, 1939–1944*, Vol. XI, November 21, 1941, 537. The admission by the minister of interior, Ferenc Keresztes-Fischer, provides another angle to this puzzle. He assumed publicly responsibility for the deportation on November 26, 1941, in stating that "as soon as our troops advanced in Galicia sufficiently to transfer Jews there, I ordered the Galician Jews (…) to be transferred to their native land." *Képviselőházi Napló, 1939–1944*, Vol. XII, November 21, 1941, 60–62. See László Karsai, *Holokauszt*, 230.
73. See Pál Pritz, *Bárdossy László a népbíróság előtt*, 87, 152, 183. See also Márai, *Hallgatni Akartam*, 127–37. See also Braham L. Randolph, *A Magyar Holocaust*, Vol. 1 (Budapest: Gondolat, 1988), 163–67. For the trial of Hans Frank, see Sands, *East West Street*, 345. Hans was executed by hanging nine months later, on October 16, 1946.
74. Quoted by Ádám Gellért, "A gyomrom összeszorult, bekövetkezett, amitől tartottunk," *INDEX*, September, 20, 2017. It seems that the author quoted a report by a delegation of parliamentarians and clerical personaliites, led by Margit Slachta.
75. "Memorandum to László Bárdossy from Herbert Pell," July 24, 1941 in MNL K-6385. cs. 10. T. 10/7 4808/pol. 1941.
76. A recent attempt to find a culprit for the deportation, and specifically the guilt of

László Bárdossy, belongs to Zsuzsa Korn Horváth, "Adalék a magyar holokauszt első szakaszának történetéhez és a Bárdossy-kormány felelősségéhez," *Élet és Irodalom*, Vol. XLIV #1, January 7, 2000.
77. Mária Ormos masterfully conveys Kozma's tortuous inner struggle with his conscience about the murder of the deported Jews. *Egy Média Vezér*, 766–77.
78. This curious document announcing the annulment, and simultaneously, revoking his son's membership in the Order, was issued almost at the end of the war, March 14, 1945. A copy of the original document was provided to the author by Sándor Szakály. This is also mentioned by Elek Karsai, *fegyvertelenül álltak az aknamezőkön*, CIX–CX. Another document that supports this, MNL K-429-35-507. See Majsai, "A körösmezei zsidódeportálás 1941-ben," 22, n. 52.
79. Henry Eaton, *The Origins and Onset of the Romanian Holocaust* (Detroit: Wayne State University Press, 2013); Dennis Deletant, *Hitler's Forgotten Ally: Ion Antonescu and His Regime, Romania 1940–1944* (London: Palgrave, 2006); Frederick B. Chary, *The Bulgarian Jews and the Final Solution, 1940–1944* (Pittsburgh: University of Pittsburgh Press, 1972); Peter Longerich, *Holocaust: The Nazi Persecution and Murder of the Jews* (New York: Oxford University Press, 2012); Jacques Sémelin, *Persécutions et entraides dans la France occupée: comment 75% des Juifs en France ont échappé à la mort* [Persecutions and Mutual Help in Occupied France: How 75 Percent of the Jews of France Escaped Death] (Paris: Seuil-Les Arènes, 2012).
80. The deportation and killing of German, Czech, and Austrian Jews had started already in October and November 1941. Rather, the Wannsee Conference was the place where the "Final Solution" was formally revealed to non-Nazi leaders who would help arrange for Jews to be transported from all over German-occupied Europe to SS-operated "extermination" camps in Poland.

9

1. This rhetorical question was posed by Elza Binder in her diary in the Stanislawów ghetto. "Stanisławów diaries and testimonies," *USHMM 1995.A.0140*, 38.
2. Kershaw, *To Hell and Back*, 369.
3. This was on October 16, 1941, after the massacre. Somló Béla File, HIL, TGY 2811, 51. Dr. Béla Somló was a driver in the transport compasny IV/2 attached to the Rapid Deployment Force.
4. Recollection of Schaje Schmerler in *Sefer Nadwórna*, edited by Israel Carmi (Tel Aviv: Nadwórna Community in Israel and America, 1975), 21.
5. The testimony of Professor V. Chernyovsky, May 20, 1944, United States Holocaust

Memorial Museum, RG-22.002M\7021\64\64-799\,799-0186.TIF. Such a ghastly scene was not the sole domain of Kamenets-Podolsk. Similar testimony was given from Berdichev, and Krupki in Belarus, where the soil of the dense, impervious clay could not absorb the blood. Cesarini, *Final Solution*, 403. See also Beorn, *Marching into Darkness*, 79.

6. Westernmann, "Stone-Cold Killers or Drunk with Murder? Alcohol and Atrocity during the Holocaust," 7.
7. It was within an informal discussion with Professor James Hatley, January 10, 2019.
8. Patrick Desbois, *In Broad Daylight*, 254.
9. Following mass executions, this process was common all across Eastern Europe. See Father Desbois, *In Broad Daylight*, 197–220. The testimony of the process was given by Zaloga Fiodor Alexandrovitch, a Ukrainian policeman in Kamenets-Podolsk, to the Soviet Extraordinary State Commission, USHMM, RG-31.018M. See also http://www1.yadvashem.org/untoldstories/database/chgkSovietReports.asp?cid=278&site_id=288. He was executed for his crimes in 1944.
10. "Situational Report," by István Simonyi, November 3, 1941. HIL, HM 4927. cs. 54861/eln.1.b–1942. Quoted also by Ákos Fóris, "Zsákmányjog a keleti hadszíntéren," January 1, 2018, http://ujkor.hu/content/zsakmanyjog-keleti-hadszinteren.
11. Snyder, *Bloodlands*, 204.
12. Timothy D. Snyder, "Germany Must Own Up To Past Atrocities in Ukraine," *Kyiv Post*, July 7, 2017.
13. Eleanor Perényi, *More Was Lost: A Memoir* (New York: New York Review Books, 1946), 95.
14. It was dated on September 26, 1941. KTAL, Fond 258, op. 1, od.zb 165, 2p. A general overview of this process was provided by Janos Botos, *A Magyarországi Zsidóság Vagyonának Sorsa 1938–1949* (Budapest: Verirtas, 2015).
15. Elie Wiesel was quoted by Carol Rittner and Sandra Meyers, *Courage to Care—Rescuers of Jews during the Holocaust* (New York: New York University Press, 1986), 2. "Testimony of Michael Jackson," USC, #26142. Marion Samuel bitterly recalled this childhood memory forty years later. See "Testimony of Marion Samuel," USC #40972.
16. Patrick Leigh Fermor, *Between the Woods and the Water* (New York: New York Review of Books, 1986), 215, and Márai, *Hallgatni Akartam*, 88.
17. Joyce Carol Oates, "Not All There," *New Yorker*, February 13 and 20, 2017, 93.
18. "Testimony of Tsipora Krauss-Engelman," USC #39642.
19. Baruch Milch diary on events in Tłuste (Galicia district of Generalgouvernement) after the start of the German occupation in summer 1941, written July/August 1943; USHMMA RG-02.208M (ŻIH 302/98), translated from Polish.
20. Kershaw, *To Hell and Back*, 415.
21. The memo from Pásztóy to the minister of foreign affairs found, MNL, K-149 Box 107,

141-8, 5048-18646. Similar number was used in his directive to border police units. MOL OL K-149, 6. t, 250. bundle, 130. d., 6891. File, 1011. 201/7-1941. The report is dated on October 14 and reflects the third quarter of 1941.
22. See the testimony of S.G, in DEGOB Protocol #2067. See also MNL K-774 1941 1cs. September 3, 1941. Some reports also mention the town of Voloc as a transit point. Yaffa Rosenthal's family was loaded up on military tracks at the train station. In USC #16308.
23. American Joint Distribution Committee Archives, New York, "Countries and Regions, 1933–1944," Reel 50. It also places the number of Jewish refugees from German dominated countries as 2,800.
24. The story of Shmuel Milo is unique. He was deported with his family to Galicia. In an attempt to return to Hungary with his father, he was captured by German security forces and transported to Auschwitz in 1942. See "Oral history interview with Shmuel Milo," USHMM, Accession Number: 1995.A.1272.332, RG Number: RG-50.120.0332.
25. Aris Folley "Auschwitz museum: Important to Remember Holocaust 'Did Not Start from Gas Chambers,'" *The Hill*, November 27, 2018, https://thehill.com/blogs/blog-briefing-room/news/418487-auschwitz-museum-says-its-important-to-remember-holocaust-did.
26. "Testimony of Max Solomon," USHMM, RG-50.091.0048. His account was corroborated by a recollection in a video, Ágnes Moldova, "elaludt az Isten," 2018.
27. Höss was quoted by Sands, *East West Street*, 308.
28. They were handed over to the German military for slave labor in various industrial enterprises. My father was transferred to Mauthausen, a notorious concentration camp, around November 1944.
29. The testimony of S.G. in DEGOB Protocol 2067 from Ilosva.
30. The testimony of S.G. in DEGOB Protocol 2067 from Ilosva. Another testimony reinforces the tragedy: "I am alone, my wife and children were killed in Auschwitz." See the Testimony of B.J. in GEGOB Protocol 69.
31. Documentary about Rabbi Hugo Gryn's return to his birthplace in Berehovo, (Beregszasz in Hungarian) Carpathian Ruthenia, Transcarpathia, https://www.youtube.com/watch?v=5bezFjUzgms. He mistakenly identified the deportees as Hungarian Jews. This comment was made by Margit Shlachta, who visited the transit camp on August 10, 1941. Majsai, "Iratok a kőrösmezei zsidódeportálás történetéhez 1941," document #19, 221.
32. The two villages were Iszka and Alsóhidegpatak. Many reports were sent by various school principals in the region. Kárpátaljai Területi Állami Levéltár, KTAL Fond 42, op 5, od.zb.116, p.1 & 6p and KTAL Fond 162, op. 3, od.zb 1826, 2p. I should thank to Gyula Kosztyó for bringing to my attention these important documents.
33. Ian Kershaw, *Hitler, the Germans and the Final Solution* (New Haven: Yale University Press, 2008), 184, 199.
34. Kershaw, *Hitler, the Germans and the Final Solution*.

35. Éva Heyman and Agnes Zsolt, eds., *The Diary of Éva Heyman*, trans. Moshe M. Kohn (New York: Shapolsky Publishers, 1988).
36. The Hinchuck family survived as Christians until the liberation and immigrated to Israel after the war. May 26, 1944, Yad Vashem Archives, YVA JM/19711. See also United States Holocaust Memorial Museum, RD-22.002M\7021\64\64-799\,799-0116.TIF.
37. Margit Slachta and Countess Erzsébet Szapáry were inducted in The Righteous Among the Nations in Yad Vashem, Jerusalem, for saving many lives during the Holocaust. Unfortunately, the story of Edith Weiss still needs to be told.
38. Testimony of Yaffa Rosenthal, in USC #16308.
39. Kaufman-Blum, *Paamayim Shoah*, 54.

EPILOGUE

1. In spite of the mother being Christian, they went into hiding in 1944. Interview with Katalin Gyürke, December 18, 2020.
2. There are no traces of the town, even in the archival material of Yad Vashem.
3. Testimony of Mosheh Zelmanovits, USC, # 48229, and testimony of Max Solomon, USHMM, RG-50.091.0048.
4. The importance and relevance of survivors' testimonies is undisputable in modern Holocaust education and scholarship. The holdings of the Steven Spielberg Film and Video Archive, (USC Shoah Foundation Institute for Visual History and Education) are in use and accessible all across the globe. Quoted by Grace Wermenbol, "Why Must Holocaust Survivors Tell Their Stories?," *Haaretz*, Aug. 11, 2009. See Joanne Weiner Rudof, "Research Use of Holocaust Testimonies," *Poetics Today* 27, no. 2 (2006): 451–46; Lawrence L. Langer, *Using and Abusing the Holocaust* (Bloomington: Indiana University Press, 2006).

ACKNOWLEDGMENTS

1. The groundbreaking work of Leon Goldensohn provides a well-rounded picture of the main architects of the Nazi Holocaust. Leon Goldensohn, *The Nuremberg Interviews* (New York: Alfred A. Knopf, 2004). See also Sand, *East West Street*. Save the United States Holocaust Memorial Museum and some German archives, almost no material can be found about Leideritz and Krüger in major Holocaust archives.
2. *The New Yorker*, November 6, 2018, 22.

BIBLIOGRAPHY

PRIMARY SOURCES

Interviews and Testimonies

Axelrad, Jonas. Testimony. August 6, 1947. USHMM, G-14.101M 3050.00001584.
Binder, Elza. Diary. Stanisławów Diaries and Testimonies. USHMM, accession number 1995.A.0140.
Brenner, Cipora. Testimony. USC Shoah Foundation Visual History Archives, number 279, November, 22, 1994.
Chaykovskiy, Ivan. Interrogation of Ivan Chaykovskiy, former auxiliary policeman. Yad Vashem Archives, YVA JM/19711.
Chernavskiy, V. Testimony. May 15, 1944. USHMM, RG-22.002M\7021\64\64-799\,799-0186.TIF.
Drimer, Gabriel. Testimony. USHMM, accession number 1977.A.0441.56, RG number RG-50.462.0056.
Fein, Albert. Interview. February 19, 2005. Voice/Vision Holocaust Survivor Oral History Archive, University of Michigan–Dearborn. http://holocaust.umd.umich.edu/.
Feuerman, Juliusz. A diary from Stanislawów (1941–1943). USHMM, accession number 1995.A.0140.
Ginchuk, Katarina (Ekaterina). Testimony (in German; Hintschuk in Russian). May 26, 1944, Yad Vashem Archives, YVA JM/19711.
Gordon, Leslie. Testimony during the trial of Adolf Eichmann. June 1, 1961. The Nizkor Project, www.nizkor.org.
Gottesman, Samuel. Testimony. August 22, 1989. USHMM, Oral History, accession number 1990.8.10, RG number RG-50.063.0010.
Hintschuk, Yakov. Testimony (September 4, 1996) USC Shoah Foundation, Visual History Archives, # number 19556.
Jackson (Jakubowics), Michael. Testimony. June 22, 1997. USC Shoah Foundation Visual History Archives, number 26142.
Kanarchuk, Valentina Branislava Antonovna. Interviews. April 28, 2008, and September 6, 2012, in Kamenets-Podolsk.

Kelmanovich, Ilya. Testimony, "Murder of Kamenets-Podolsk Jews at the Munitions Depot." April 8, 2014. Yad Vashem Archives, http://www.youtube.com/watch?v=XYolUFgfFIA.

Kiefer, Alfred. Interrogation. June 19, 1946. USHMM, RG-15.155M.0012.00000658.

Krauss, Tzipora Testimony, February. 26, 1998. USC Shoah Foundation Visual History Archives, # number 39642.

Leideritz, Anneliese. Denazification files. Hessisches Staatsarchiv Wiesbaden, Bestand 520/05, number 29153.

Leideritz, Peter. Trial of Peter Leideritz. Warsaw, August 7, 1947. USHMM, RG-14.101 M3050.00001581 and RG-14.101M3050.00001660.

Lubell, Elizabeth. Interview. March 2, 1992. USHMM, Oral History, accession number 1992.A.0125.77, RG number RG-50.233.0077. https://collections.ushmm.org/search/catalog/irn509160.

Lyubinetski, Mikhail. Testimony. May 19, 1944. USHMM, RG-22.002M\7021\64\64-799\,799-0341.TIF.

Milo, Shmuel. Interview. USHMM, Oral History, accession number 1995.A.1272.332, RG number RG-50.120.0332.

Moldova, Ágnes. "elaludt az Isten..." Video 2018.

Moskal, Klara. Testimony. May 16, 1944. Yad Vashem Archives, YVA JM/19711.

N. H. Testimony (in Yiddish). Yad Vashem Archives, YVA M.49.E/6848.

Prodanchuk, Ksenia. Testimony. May 13, 1944. Yad Vashem Archives, YVA JM/19711.

Rosenthal, Yaffa. Testimony. USC Shoah Foundation Visual History Archives, number 16308. June 17, 1996.

Samuel, Marion. Testimony. USC Shoah Foundation Visual History Archives, number 40972. May 10, 1998.

Solomon, Max. Testimony. USHMM, Oral History, accession number 1993.A.0087.48, RG number RG-50.091.0048.

Stanisławów Diaries and Testimonies. USHMM, accession number 1995.A.0140.

Stern, Joseph. "Bericht über die Vernichtung des Judentums in Kolomea." Letter of testimony written October 20, 1943, regarding the murder of Jews from Kolomea in the forests and in Belzec, 1941–1942. Yad Vashem Archives, YVA, item ID 3728526, record group 0.33, file number 2796.

Trautmann, Hans Peter. Correspondence. March 10, 2020.

Tupenko, Nikolai. Testimony. May 19, 1944. Yad Vashem Archives, YVA JM/19711; USHMM, RG-22.002M\7021\64\64-799\,799-0186.TIF.

Vásárhelyi, Ferenc. Testimony. Trial of Ámon Pásztóy, Budapest Főváros Levéltára, Fond XXV, fond:4, állag A. 2890/51.

Warmann, Albert. Interrogation. July 5, 1946. USHMM, RG-15.155M.0012.00000.662.

Weiser, Dezső. Testimony. HIL, TGY 2962.

Wiemer, Hans. Interrogation. August 19, 1959. BArch B 162/1564, 32.

Wohlberg, Miriam. Testimony. Interview by Szirtes Andras. https://www.youtube.com/watch?v=YONYnpXS1p8&t=16s.
Wolfberg, Leon. Testimony. August 1, 1946. USHMM RG-15.155M,0012.00000638.
Zaloga. Interrogation of Zaloga, a company commander of local Ukrainian auxiliary police. Yad Vashem Archives, YVA JM/19711.
Zelmanovits, Mosheh. Testimony. USC Shoah Foundation Visual History Archives, number 48229. December 14, 1998.
Zobel, László. Testimony. USC Shoah Foundation Visual History Archives, number 51784. October 12, 1998.

Archives Consulted

Állambiztonsági Szolgálatok Történelmi Levéltára (Historical Archives of State Security Services), Budapest – ÁBTL
American Joint Distribution Committee (JDC) Archives, New York
Archives of the Convent of the Hungarian Social Sisters, Buffalo, NY
Budapest Fővárosi Levéltár (Budapest City Archives, BFL)
Bundesarchiv, Ludwigsburg – BArchB, Germany
Deportáltak Gondozó Országos Bizottsága (National Committee for Attending Deportees), Budapest – DEGOB
Galicia Jewish Museum, Cracow
Ghetto Fighters' House Museum, Israel
Hadtörténelmi Irattár és Levéltár, Budapest – HIL
Hessisches Staatsarchiv Wiesbaden, Germany – HSYAW
Historical Institute Veritas, Budapest
Holokauszt Emlékközpont (Holocaust Memorial Center), Budapest
Hungarian Jewish Museum and Archives, Budapest
Institute of National Remembrance (Instytut Pamięci Narodowej), Warsaw – INR
Jewish Historical Institute Archives (Żydowski Instytut Historyczny im. Emanuela Ringelbluma), Warsaw
Kárpátaljai Területi Állami Levéltár, Beregovo (Beregszász), Ukraine – KTAL
Lochamei Hagetaot Museum and Archives, Israel
Magyar Nemzeti Levéltár, Budapest – MNL
Memoir La Shoah, Paris
National Archives, Washington, DC – NARA
Steven Spielberg Film and Video Archive, USC Shoah Foundation Institute for Visual History and Education USC Spielberg Archives, Los Angeles
United Sates Holocaust Memorial Museum, Washington, DC – USHMM

Voice/Vision Holocaust Survivor Oral History Archive, University of Michigan-Dearborn, http://holocaust.umd.umich.edu/

Yad Vashem Archives, Jerusalem – YVA

Yahad-in Unum https://yahadmap.org/#village/kamyanets-podilskyi-khmelnytskyi-ukraine.107

Yale University

YIVO Institute Archives, New York

Books and Dissertations

Ágoston, Péter. *A zsidók útja*, Nagyvárad: Társadalomtudományi Társaság Kiadása, 1917.

Applebaum, Anne. *East and West: Across the Borderlands of Europe*. New York: Pantheon Books, 1994.

Arad, Yitzhak. *The Einsatzgruppen Reports: Selections from the Dispatches of the Nazi Death Squads' Campaign against the Jews July 1941–January 1943*. New York: Holocaust Library, 1989.

Asbrink, Elisabeth. *1947: Where Now Begins*. Translated by Fiona Graham. New York: Other Press, 2018.

Baker, Leonard. *Brahmin in Revolt: A Biography of Herbert C. Pell*. New York: Doubleday, 1972.

Bán, András D. *Hungarian-British Diplomacy 1938–1941: The Attempt to Maintain Relations*. New York: Rutledge, 2004.

Bartha, Miklós. *Kazár földön*. Kolozsvár: Ellenzék Könyvnyomda, 1901.

Bartov, Omer. *Anatomy of a Genocide: Life and Death of a Town Called Buczacz*. New York: Simon & Schuster, 2018.

Bauer, Yehuda. *Jews for Sale? Nazi-Jewish Negotiations, 1933–1945*. New Haven, CT: Yale University Press, 1994.

Bennett, G. H. *The Nazi, the Painter and the Forgotten Story of the SS Road*. Chicago, IL: University of Chicago Press, 2012.

Beorn, Waitman Wade. *Marching into Darkness: The Wehrmacht and the Holocaust in Belarus*. Cambridge, MA: Harvard University Press, 2014.

Bickel, Shlomo, ed. *Memorial Book of Kolomey* (Kolomyya, Ukraine). New York: Rausen Brothers, 1957.

Bihari, Péter. *Lövészárkok a hátországban. Középosztály, zsidókérdés, antiszemitizmus az első világháború Magyarországán*. Budapest: Napvilág, 2008.

Bikont, Anna. *The Crime and the Silence: Confronting the Massacre of Jews in Wartime Jedwabne*. Translated by Alissa Valles. New York: Farrar, Straus and Giroux, 2014.

Blayney, Michael Steward. *Democracy's Aristocrat: The Life of Herbert C. Pell*. New York: University Press of America, 1986.

Blumenthal, N., ed. *Sefer Borszczow*. Tel Aviv, 1960.

Bond, Shlomo, et al., eds. *Memorial Book of Tlumacz*. Translation of *Tlumacz-Tlomitsch Sefer Edut-Ve-Zkaron*. Tel Aviv: Tlumacz Society, 1976.

Boyd, Julia. *Travellers in the Third Reich: The Rise of Fascism through the Eyes of Everyday People*. London: Elliot and Thompson, 2017.

Braham, Randolph L. *A Magyar Holocaust*. 2 vols. Budapest: Gondolat, 1988.

———, ed. *The Wartime System of Labor Service in Hungary: Varieties of Experiences*. New York: Columbia University Press, 1995.

Brandon, Ray, and Wendy Lower, eds. *The Shoah in Ukraine: History, Testimony, Memorialization*. Bloomington: Indiana University Press, 2010.

Breitman, Richard. *Official Secrets*. New York: Hill and Wang, 1998.

Browning, Christopher R. *The Final Solution and the German Foreign Office: A Study of Referat D III of Abteilung Deutschland, 1940–43*. New York: Holmes & Meier, 1978.

———. *Ordinary Men: Reserve Police Battalion 101 and the Final Solution in Poland*. New York: Harper Perennial, 1998.

Browning, Christopher R., and Jürgen Matthäus. *The Origins of the Final Solution: The Evolution of Nazi Jewish Policy, September 1939–March 1942*. Lincoln: University of Nebraska Press, 2004.

Burds, Jeffry. *Holocaust in Rovno: The Massacre at Sosenki Forest, November 1941*. New York: Palgrave Pivot, 2013.

Burleigh, Michael. *Moral Combat: Good and Evil in World War II*. New York: Harper Perennial, 2011.

Carmi, Israel, ed. *Sefer Nadwórna*. Tel Aviv: Nadwórna Community in Israel and America, 1975.

Cesarani, David. *Final Solution: The Fate of the Jews 1933–1949*. New York: St. Martin's Press, 2016.

———. *The Jewish Chronicle and Anglo-Jewry 1841–1991*. Cambridge: Cambridge University Press, 1994.

Chary, Frederick B. *The Bulgarian Jews and the Final Solution, 1940–1944*. Pittsburgh: University of Pittsburgh Press, 1972.

Collingham, Lizzi. *The Taste of War: World War Two and the Battle for Food*. London: Allen Lane, 2011.

Deák, István. *Volt egyszer egy tisztikar: A Habsburg-monarchia katonatisztjeinek társadalmi és politikai története*. Budapest: Gondolat, 1993.

Dean, Martin. *Collaboration in the Holocaust: Crimes of Local Police in Belorussia and Ukraine, 1941–44*. New York: St. Martin's Press, 2000.

Deletant, Dennis. *Hitler's Forgotten Ally: Ion Antonescu and His Regime, Romania 1940–1944*. London: Palgrave, 2006.

Desbois, Patrick. *The Holocaust by Bullets: A Priest's Journey to Uncover the Truth behind the Murder of 1.5 Million Jews*. Translated by Catherine Spencer. New York: Palgrave Macmillan, 2008.

Desbois, Patrick, and Andrej Umansky. *In Broad Daylight: The Secret Procedures behind the Holocaust by Bullets*. New York: Arcade Publishing, 2018.

Dupka, György. *Ne ítéljetek el... Zsidó népírtás, antiszemita üldözés Kárpátalján a náci és a kommunista eszmék nevében, 1938–1991*. Ungvár-Budapest: Intermix Kiadó, 2015.

Eaton, Henry. *The Origins and Onset of the Romanian Holocaust*. Detroit: Wayne State University Press, 2013.

Evans, Richard J. *The Third Reich at War*. New York: Penguin Press, 2010.

Fallada, Hans. *Every Man Dies Alone*. New York: Melville House, 2009.

Farkas, Klaudia. *Jogok nélkül. A zsidó lét Magyarországon, 1920–1944*. Budapest: Napvilág, 2010.

Fedinec, Csilla. *A kárpátaljai magyarság történeti kronológiája 1918–1944*. Galánta–Dunaszerdahely: Fórum Intézet, Lilium Aurum, 2002.

Fejtő, Ferenc. *Magyarság, zsidóság*. Budapest: MTA Történettudományi Intézete, 2000.

Fermor, Patrick Leigh. *Between the Woods and the Water*. New York: New York Review of Books Classics, 1986.

Fóris, Ákos. "A magyar megszálló politika a szovjet területeken 1941–1944." Diss., Eötvös Loránd Tudományegyetem, 2021.

Freundlich, Elisabeth. *Die Ermordung einer Stadt namens Stanislau: NS Vernichtungs-politikin Polen 1939–1945*. Vienna: Österreichischer Bundesverlag, 1986.

Friedman, Tuvia, ed. *Report by SS-General Fritz Katzmann on the Killing of the Half Million Jews in Eastern Galicia*. Haifa, Israel: Documentation Institute, 1993.

Frojmovics, Kinga. *I have been a stranger in a strange land*. Jerusalem: Yad Vashem, 2007.

Gergely, Jenő. *Prohászka Ottokár*. Budapest: Gondolat, 1994.

Gerlach, Christian. *The Extermination of the European Jews*. New York: Cambridge University Press, 2015.

Gertjejanssen, Wendy Jo. "Victims, Heroes, Survivors: Sexual Violence on the Eastern Front during World War II." Diss., University of Minnesota, 2004.

Gertner, Yehoshua, and Danek Gertner. *Home Is No More: The Destruction of the Jews of Kosów and Zabie*. Jerusalem: Yad Vashem, 2000.

Geyer, Arthur. "Az első magyarországi deportálás." In *Új Élet naptár 1960/61*. Budapest: MIOK Kiadása, 1960.

Goldensohn, Leon. *The Nuremberg Interviews*. New York: Alfred A. Knopf, 2004.

Goldhagen, Jonah Daniel. *Hitler's Willing Executioners: Ordinary Germans and the Holocaust*. New York: Alfred A. Knopf, 1996.

Gömbös, Gyula. *Válogatott politikai beszédek és írások*. Edited by József Vonyó. Budapest: Osiris Kiadó, 2004.

Gottesfeld Heller, Fanya. *Love in a World of Sorrow*. New York: Gefen, 2015.

Götz, Aly. *Why the Germans? Why the Jews? Envy, Race Hatred, and the Prehistory of the Holocaust*. New York: Metropolitan Books, 2014.

Grabowski, Jan. *Hunt for the Jews: Betrayal and Murder in German-Occupied Poland*. Bloomington: Indiana University Press, 2013.

Gross, Jan Tomasz. *Neighbors: The Destruction of the Jewish Community in Jedwabne, Poland*. Princeton: Princeton University Press, 2001.

Gross, S. Y., and Y. Yosef Cohen, eds. *Sefer Marmarosh: mea ve-shishim kehilot kedoshot be- yishuvan u-ve-hurbanah* (The Marmaros Book: In Memory of 160 Jewish Communities). Tel Aviv: Beit Marmaros, 1983, 1996.

Gyurgyák, János. *A zsidókérdés Magyarországon*. Budapest: Osiris Kiadó, 2001.

Hasenclever, Jörn. *Wehrmacht und Occupationpolitik in der Sowjetunion*. Paderborn: Ferdinand Schöningh, 2010.

Hayes, Peter. *Why? Explaining the Holocaust*. New York: W. W. Norton, 2017.

Headland, Ronald. *Messages of Murder: A Study of Reports of the Einsatzgruppen of the Security Police and the Security Service, 1941–1943*. Cranbury, NJ: Fairleigh Dickinson University Press, 1992.

Herbert, Ulrich. ed. *National Socialist Extermination Policies: Contemporary Perspectives and Controversies*. Vol. 2, *War and Genocide*. New York: Berghahn Books, 2000.

Herczl. Moshe Y. *Christianity and the Holocaust of Hungarian Jewry*. New York University Press, 1993.

Heyman, Éva, and Agnes Zsolt, eds. *The Diary of Éva Heyman*.Translated by Moshe M. Kohn. New York: Shapolsky Publishers, 1988.

Hilberg, Raul. *Destruction of European Jewry*. New York: Harper, 1992.

Howe, Irving. *World of Our Fathers*. New York: Harcourt Brace Jovanovich, 1976.

Ioanid, Radu. *The Holocaust in Romania: The Destruction of Jews and Gypsies Under the Antonescu Regime, 1940–1944*. Chicago: Ivan R. Dee Publishers, 2000.

Judson, Pieter M. *The Habsburg Empire: A New History*. Boston: Harvard University Press, 2016.

Juhász, Gyula, ed. *Magyarország külpolitikája a második világháború kitörésének időszakában*. Budapest: Akadémia Kiadó, 1962.

Julius, Anthony. *T.S. Eliot, Anti-Semitism and Literary Form*. Cambridge: Cambrdge University Press, 1996.

Kádár, Gábor, and Zoltán Vági. *Hullarablás, a Magyar Zsidók Gazdasági Megsemmmisitése*. Budapest: Jaffa, 2005.

———. *Self-Financing Genocide*. Budapest: CEU Press, 2001.

Kádár, Gyula. *A Ludovikától Sopronkőhidáig*. Budapest: Magvető, 1978.

Kapronczay, Karoly. *Refugees in Hungary*. Translated by Eva Barcza-Bessenyey. Toronto: Matthias Corvinus, 1999.

Karády, Viktor. *Zsidóság, modernizáció, polgárosodás*. Budapest: Cserépfalvi, 1997.

Karsai, László. *Holokauszt*. Budapest: Pannonica Kiadó, 2001.

Katzburg, Nathaniel. *Anti-Semitism in Hungary*. Tel Aviv: Dvir, 1969.

———. *Hungary and the Jews: Policy and Legislation 1920–1943*. Tel Aviv: Bar-Ilan University Press, 1981.

———. *Zsidápolitika Magyarországon, 1919–1943*. Budapest: Bábel, 2002.

Kaufman Blum, Pninah. *Paamayim B'Shoah*. Jerusalem: Yad Vashem, 2006.

Keegan, John. *The First World War*. New York: Vintage, 2000.

Kennedy, Paul. *Engineers of Victory: The Problem Solvers Who Turned the Tide in the Second World War*. New York: Random House, 2013.

Képviselőházi Napló, 1939–1944, Vol. XII.

Kershaw, Ian. *Hitler: 1936–1945 Nemesis*. New York: W.W. Norton, 2000.

———. *To Hell and Back: Europe 1914–1949*. New York: Viking, 2015.

Klee, Ernst, Willi Dressen, and Volker Riess, eds. *The Good Old Days: The Holocaust as Seen by Its Perpetrators and Bystanders*. New York: Konecky, 1991.

Klemp, Stefan. *"Nicht Ermittelt" Polizeibataillone und die Nachkriegsjustiz Ein Handbuch*. Essen: Klartext Verlag, 2005.

Kocsis, Károly, and Eszter Kocsisné Hodosi. *Magyarok a határainkon túl: a Kárpát-medencében*. Budapest: Tankönyvkiadó, 1991.

Kovács, Alajos. *A zsidóság térfoglalása Magyarországon*. Budapest: Self-published, 1922.

Kovács, Mária M. *Törvénytől sújtva: a numerus clausus Magyarországon, 1920–1945*. Budapest: Napvilág, 2012.

Krausz, Tamás, ed. *A Magyar Megszálló Csapatok a Szovietunióban*. Budapest: L'Harmattan, 2013.

Lackó, Miklós. *Arrow-Cross Men: National Socialists 1935–1944*. Budapest: Akadémiai Kiadó, 1969.

Lanckoronska, Karolina. *Michelangelo in Ravensbrück: One Woman's War Against the Nazis*. London: De Capo Press, 2005.

Landauer, Gustav. *Ostjuden und Deutsches Reich. Zu Juden gesagt*. In *Im Scheunenviertel. Bilder, Texte und Dokumente*. Edited by Eike Geisel. Berlin: Siedler, 1986.

Langlet, Valdemar. *On Horseback through Hungary*. Translated by Barnard Balogh. London: Hutchinson, 1935.

Larson, Erik. *In the Garden of Beasts: Love, Terror, and an American Family in Hitler's Berlin*. New York: Crown, 2011.

László, Lugosi L. *A zsidó Budapest*. Budapest: Vince Kiadó, 2002.

Lecker, Marcus. *I Remember: Odyssey of a Jewish Teenager in Eastern Europe*. Vol. 5, *Memoirs of Holocaust Survivors in Canada*. Montreal: Concordia University Chair in Canadian Jewish Studies and the Montreal Institute for Genocide and Human Rights Studies, 1999.

Liebesman, Abraham. *During the Russian Administration: With the Jews of Stanisławów during the Holocaust*. Translated by Sigmund Graubart. Atlanta, 1990.

Lindemann, Albert S. *Esau's Tears, Modern Anti-Semitism and the Rise of the Jews*. Cambridge: Cambridge University Press, 1997.

Longerich, Peter. *Heinrich Himmler: A Life*. Translated by Jeremy Noakes and Lesley Sharpe. New York: Oxford University Press, 2012.

———. *Holocaust: The Nazi Persecution and Murder of the Jews*. Oxford: Oxford University Press, 2010.

Lower, Wendy. *Hitler's Furies: German Women in the Nazi Killing Fields*. New York: Houghton Mifflin, 2013.

Malinowski, Stephan. *Nazis and Nobles: The History of a Misalliance*. Oxford: Oxford University Press, 2021.

Mallmann, Klaus-Michael, Volker Riess, and Wolfram Pyta, eds. *Deutscher Osten 1939–1945: Die Weltanschauungskrieg in Photos und Texten*. Darmstadt: Wissenschaftliche Buchgesellschaft, 2003.

Márai, Sándor. *Hallgatni Akartam*. Budapest: Helikon, 2016.

———. *A Teljes Napló, 1943–1944*. Budapest: Helikon, 1971.

Mazur, Zygmunt, ed. *The Legacy of the Holocaust: Women and the Holocaust*. Kraków: Jagiellonian University Press, 2007.

McAuley, James. *The House of Fragile Things: Jewish Art Collectors and the Fall of France*. New Haven: Yale University Press, 2021.

Meltzer, Sh., ed. *Sefer Horodenka*. Tel Aviv: Irgun yots'e Horodenkah, 1963. http://www.jewishgen.org/yizkor/belzec/bel004.html#n024.

Mendelsohn, Daniel. *The Search for Six of Six Million Lost*. New York: Harper Collins, 2006.

Méray-Horváth, Károly. *Társadalomtudomány mint természettudomány*. Budapest: Athenaeum RT, 1912.

Mermall, Gabriel (Gabor Mermelstein). *By the Grace of Strangers: Two Boys' Rescue during the Holocaust*. Jerusalem: Yad Vashem, 2006.

Mermelstein, Max, and Tony Hausner, eds. *Skala on the Zbrucz: A History of the Former Skala Jewish Community*. New York: Skala Benevolent Society, 2009.

Mick, Christoph. *Lemberg, Lwów, Lviv, 1914–1947: Violence and Ethnicity in a Contested City*. West Lafayette, IN: Purdue University Press, 2015.

Mona, Ilona. *Slachta Margit*. Budapest: Pázmány Péter Elektronikus Könyvtár, (PPEK), 1993. http://www.ppek.hu/konyvek/Mona_Ilona_Slachta_Margit_1.pdf.

Musial, Bogdan. *Deutsche Zivilverwaltung und Judenverfolgung im Generalgouvernement*. Wiesbaden: Harrassowitz, 1999.

Nagorski, Andrew. *Hitlerland: American Eyewitnesses to the Nazi Rise to Power*. New York: Simon & Schuster, 2015.

Nazi Conspiracy and Aggression. Washington DC: United States Government Printing Office, 1946.

Naziskiy Okupatziyniy Regime na Hmelnitziny 1941–1944, Dokumenty I Materiali. Kamenets-Podolsk: Oyum, 2009.

Noy, Dov, and Mordechai Shutzman, eds. *Sefer Zikaron L'Kehilat Kolomiya V'hasevivah*. Tel Aviv, 1972.
Orgona, Angelika. *The American Countess: Memories of the Szapáry and Széchényi Families*. Budapest: Magyar Nemzeti Muzeum, 2020.
Ormos, Mária. *Egy Magyar Médiavezér: Kozma Miklós*. Budapest: Polgár, 2000.
———. *Magyarország a két világháború korában (1914–1945)*. Debrecen: Csokonai Kiadó, 1998.
Orosz, Ildikó, and István Csernicskó. *The Hungarians in Transcarpathia*. Budapest: Tinta Publishers, 1999.
Paksa, Rudolf. *A magyar szélsőjobboldal története*. Budapest: Jaffa Kiadó, 2012.
Paksy, Zoltán, ed. *Az antiszemitizmus alakváltozatai. Tanulmányok*. Zalaegerszeg: Zala megyei Levéltár, 2005.
Perényi, Eleanor. *More Was Lost: A Memoir*. New York: New York Review of Books Classis, 2016.
Petranker Salsitz, Norman, and Amalie Petranker Salsitz. *Against All Odds: A tale of Two Survivors*. New York: Holocaust Library, 1990.
Pinkas Hakehillot — Encyclopedia of Jewish Communities, Poland. Vol. II, *Eastern Galicia*. Jerusalem: Yad Vashem, 1980. https://www.jewishgen.org/yizkor/pinkas_poland/pol2_00320.html.
Pohl, Dieter. *Nationalsozialistische Judenverfolgung in Ostgalizien 1941–1944*. Berlin: Walter de Gruyter, 1997.
———. *Verfolgung und Massenmord in der NS-Zeit 1933–1945*. Darmstadt: Wissenschaftliche Buchgesellschaft, 2011.
Pritz, Pál. *Bárdossy László a népbíróság előtt*. Budapest: Maecenas, 1991.
Ránki, György, et al. *A Wilhelmstrasse és Magyarország*. Budapest: Kossuth Könykiadó, 1968.
Redlich, Shimon. *Together and Apart in Brzeżany: Poles, Jews, and Ukrainians, 1919–1945*. Bloomington: Indiana University Press, 2002.
Rhodes, Richard. *Masters of Death: The SS-Einsatzgruppen and the Invention of the Holocaust*. New York: Random House, 2002.
Ringel, Abraham. *A Time to Speak: The Story of My Life*. Jerusalem: Yad Vashem, 2003.
Rittner, Carol, and Sandra Meyers. *The Courage to Care: Rescuers of Jews during the Holocaust*. New York University Press, 1986.
Romsics, Ignác. *Magyarország története a XX. században*. Budapest: Osiris Kiadó, 1999.
Rosenberg, Blanca. *To Tell at Last: Survival under False Identity, 1941–45*. Urbana: University of Illinois Press, 1995.
Sabrin, B. F., ed. *Alliance for Murder: The Nazi–Ukrainian Nationalist Partnership in Genocide*. New York: Sarpedon, 1991.
Sandberg-Mesner, Mila. *Light from the Shadows*. Montreal: Polish-Jewish Heritage Foundation and the Polish Socio-Cultural Foundation in Montreal, 2005.
Sandkühler, Thomas. *"Endlösung" in Galizien: der Judenmord in Ostpolen und die Rettungsinitiativen von Berthold Beitz: 1941–1944*. Bonn: Dietz, 1996.

Sands, Philippe. *East West Street, On the Origins of Genocide and Crimes against Humanity*. London: Weidenfeld & Nicolson, 2016.

Segal, Raz. *Genocide in the Carpathians: War, Social Breakdown, and Mass Violence, 1914–1945*. Stanford: Stanford University Press, 2016.

Semelin, Jacques. *Persécutions et entraides dans la France occupée: comment 75% des Juifs en France ont échappé à la mort* [Persecutions and Mutual Help in Occupied France: How 75 Percent of the Jews of France Escaped Death]. Paris: Seuil-Les Arènes, 2012.

Snyder, Timothy. *Black Earth: The Holocaust as History and Warning*. New York: Crown, 2015.

———. *Bloodlands: Europe between Hitler and Stalin*. New York: Basic Books, 2010.

Sós, Endre. *Európai Fasizmus és Antiszemitizmus*. Budapest: Magyar Teka, n.d.

Steiner, John Michael. *Power Politics and Social Change in National Socialist Germany: A Process of Escalation into Mass Destruction*. The Hague: Mouton, 1975.

Struve, Kai. *Deutsche Herrschaft, ukrainischer Nationalismus, antijüdische Gewalt: Der Sommer 1941 in der Westukraine*. Berlin: Walter de Gruyter, 2015.

Szabolcsi, Lajos. *Két emberöltő. Az Egyenlőség évtizedei (1881–1931). Emlékezések, dokumentumok*. Budapest: MTA Judaisztikai Kutatócsoport, 1993.

Szegedy-Maszák, Aladár. *Az ember ősszel visszanéz*. Budapest: Európa Könyvkiadó, 1996.

Szegedy-Maszák, Marianne. *I Kiss Your Hands Many Times*. New York: Spiegel & Grau, 2013.

Szekfű, Gyula. *Három nemzedék, és ami utána következik*. Budapest: Királyi Magyar Egyetemi Nyomda, 1935.

Szinai, Miklós, and László Szűcs, eds. *Horthy Miklós Titkos Iratai*. Budapest: Kossuth, 1963.

Szita, Szabolcs, and Sean Lambert. *Trading Lives: Operations of the Jewish Relief and Rescue Committee in Budapest, 1944–1945*. Budapest: Central European University, 2004.

Teleki, Paul. *The Evolution of Hungary and Its Place in European History*. New York: Macmillan, 1923.

Tooze, Adam. *The Wages of Destruction*. New York: Viking, 2007.

Trautmann, Hans Peter. *70 Jahre Ende des II. Weltkriegs am 8./ 9. Mai 1945-Reichelsheim in der Zeit des Nationalsozialismus und nach dem Kriegsende*. Reichelsheim: Self-published, 2015.

Trials of War Criminals before the Nuremberg Military Tribunals October 1946–April 1949. Vol. XI. Washington, DC: United States Government Printing Office, 1950.

Vargyai, Gyula. *Magyarország a Második Világháboruban*. Budapest: Korona, 2001.

Vihar, Béla. *Sárga Könyv*. Budapest: Hechaluc, 1946.

———. *Zsidók a magyar tájban*. In *Ararát*. Budapest: Országos Izraelita Leányárvaház, 1942.

Ungváry, Krisztián. *A Horthy-rendszer mérlege. Diszkrimináció, szociálpolitika és antiszemitizmus Magyarországon*. Budapest: Jelenkor, 2012.

———. *Magyar megszálló csapatok a Szovjetunióban, 1941–1944*. Budapest: Osiris, 2015.

———. *Magyarország a második világháboruban*. Budapest: Kossuth Kiadó, 2010.

———. *A második világháboru*. Budapest: Osiris, 2005.

Ungváry, Rudolf. *Balatoni Nyaralo*. Budpest: Jelenkor, 2020.

Váry, Albert. *A vörös uralom áldozatai Magyarországon. Hivatalos jelentések és bírói ítéletek alapján*. Budapest: A Váci Kir. Orsz. Fegyintézet Könyvnyomdája, 1922.

Veszprémy, László Bernát. *Gyilkos Irodák a Magyar Közigazgatás, a Német megszállás és a Holokauszt*. Budapest: Jaffa, 2019.

Wasserstein, Bernard. *On the Eve: The Jews of Europe before the Second World War*. New York: Simon & Schuster, 2012.

Weiss, Arie Baruch. *Ha-dunah ha-adumah, massa el he-avar derekh ha-tebach be-Kamenets-Podolsk, 1941*. Jerusalem: Yad Vashem, 2008.

Westermann, Edward B. *Hitler's Police Battalion: Enforcing Racial War in the East*. Lawrence: University Press of Kansas, 2005.

Wiesel, Elie. *Night*. Translated by Marion Wiesel. New York: Hill and Wang, 1958.

Wildt, Michael. *An Uncompromising Generation: The Nazi Leadership of the Reich Security Main Office*. Translated by Tom Lampert. Madison: University of Wisconsin Press, 2010.

Wolff, Larry. *The Idea of Galicia: History and Fantasy in Habsburg Political Culture*. Stanford: Stanford University Press, 2011.

Wynne, Suzan. *The Galittzianers: The Jews of Galicia, 1772–1918*. Tucson: Wheatmark, 2006.

Zelikovitch, Zvi. *The First to the Slaughter at Orania, Ukraine 2 elul 5701 26 August 1941*. Translated by Marc Zell. Rana'ana, Israel: Docostory Ltd., 2005.

Zinner, Tibor. *Az ébredők fénykora, 1919–1923*. Budapest: Akadémiai Kiadó, 1989.

A Zsidókérdés Magyarországon: A Huszadik Század Körkérdése, 2nd ed. Publication by *Huszadik Század*. Budapest: Társadalomtudományi Társaság, 1917.

Periodicals and Proceedings

Ancel, Jean. "The German-Romanian Relationship and the Final Solution." *Journal of Holocaust and Genocide Studies* 19 (Fall 2005): 252–75.

Angrick, Andrej. "Annihilation and Labor: Jews and Thoroughfare IV in Central Ukraine." In *The Shoah in Ukraine: History, Testimony, Memorialization*, edited by Ray Brandon and Wendy Lower, 190–223. Bloomington: Indiana University Press, 2010.

Bajohr, Frank. "The Beneficiaries of 'Aryanization': Hamburg as a Case Study." Yad Vashem, https://www.yadvashem.org/download/about_holocaust/studies/bajohr_full.pdf.

Bennett, G. H. "Exploring the World of the Second and Third Tier Men in the Holocaust: The Interrogation of Friedrich Jeckeln: Engineer and Executioner." *Liverpool Law Review* 32 (2011): 1–18.

Blum, Natan. "Girush Yehudim Netulai-Ezrahut M'hungaria L'galicia B'shnat 1941." *Yalkut Moreshet* 43–44 (1987): 39–64.

Bodó, Béla. "Paramilitary Violence in Hungary after the First World War." *East European Quarterly* 38, no. 2 (2004).

Borsányi, György. "Zsidók a Munkásmozgalomban." *Világosság* 2 (1992).

Cseh, Edit K. *A Békés megyei zsidóság történetének levéltári forrásai: Dokumentumok a Békés Megyei Levéltárból.* Gyula: Forráskiadványok a Békés Megyei Levéltárból, 2002.

Braham, Randolph L. "The Kamenets-Podolsk and Délvidék Massacres: Prelude to the Holocaust in Hungary." *Yad Vashem Studies* 9 (1973): 133–56.

Breitman, Richard. "Friedrich Jeckeln, Specialist für 'Endlösung' im Osten." In *Die SS: Elite Unter dem Totenkopf,* edited by Enrico Syring and Ronald Smelser, 267–75. Paderborn: Ferdinand Schöningh, 2000.

Buchler, Yehoshua. "Kommandostab Reichsführer-SS: Himmler's Personal Murder Brigades in 1941." *Journal of Holocaust and Genocide Studies* 1 (1986): 11–25.

Csapody, Tamás. "A Naplóíró Somló Béla." *FONS,* no. 3 (2019): 339–402.

Deák, István. "A Hungarian Admiral on Horseback." In *Essays on Hitler's Europe.* Lincoln: University of Nebraska Press, 2001.

Deutsch, Moshe. "The Ghetto in Kaminits-Podolsk." In *Kaminits-Podolsk & Its Environs,* edited by Abraham Rosen. Tel Aviv: Organization of Emigrants from Kaminits-Podolsk and Its Environs, 1965.

Don, Yehuda. "Economic Implications of the Anti-Jewish Legislation in Hungary." In *Genocide and Rescue: The Holocaust in Hungary 1944,* edited by David Cesarani. Oxford: Berg Publishers, 1997.

Eisen, George, and Tamás Stark. "The 1941 Galician Deportation and the Kamenets-Podolsk Massacre: A Prologue to the Hungarian Holocaust." *Journal of Holocaust and Genocide Studies* 23 (2013): 207–41.

Evans, Richard J. "What the War Was Really About." *New York Review of Books,* December 5, 2013, 18–20.

Fejes, Judit. "On the History of the Mass Deportation from Carpatho-Ruthenia in 1941." In *The Holocaust in Hungary: Fifty Years Later,* edited by Randolph L. Braham and Attila Pók, 305–27. New York: Columbia University Press, 1997.

Finder, Gabriel N., and Alexander V. Prusin, "Collaboration in Eastern Galicia: The Ukrainian Police and the Holocaust." *East European Jewish Affairs* 34, no. 2 (2004).

Fóris, Ákos. "A megszállt szovjet területek kérdése a magyar polgári kormányszerveknél." In *Az Első Világháború Irodalmi és Történelmi Aspektusai a Kelet-európai Régióban,* edited by József Péter Fodor, Renáta Marosi, Dániel Miklós, Krisztina Péró, and Roland Szabó. Budapest: ELTE, 2017.

———. "A zsidók agyonlövése a megszállt területeken köztudomású." *Eszmélet* 115 (2007).

Gábor, Éva. "Személyes Emlékek 70 Év Multán." Paper presented at the Conference for the 70th Anniversary of the 'Körösmező-Kameniec-Podolsky' Deportations, Budapest, John Wesley Theological College (JWTC), October 12–13, 2011.

"Ghastly Pogroms in Ukraine." *Jewish Chronicle,* October 24, 1941.

Gopnik, Adam. "Blood and Soil." *New Yorker,* September 2, 2015, 100.

———. "Faces, Places, Spaces." *New Yorker,* October 29–November 5, 2012, 115.

Hastings, Max. "The Most Terrible of Hitler's Creatures." *New York Review of Books*, January 9, 2012.

Havryshko, Marta. "Sexual Violence in the Holocaust: Perspectives from Ghettos and Camps in Ukraine." Heinrich Böll Stiftung, May 18, 2020. https://www.boell.de/en/2020/05/18 /sexual-violence-holocaust-perspectives-ghettos-and-camps-ukraine?dimension1=division _osoe#_ftn20.

Heller, Karen. "The Improbable Story of the Man Who Won History's 'Biggest Murder Trial' at Nuremberg." *Washington Post*, August 31, 2016.

Kaló, Jozsef. "Szombathelyi Ferenc és a galiciai deportálás." *Magyar Naplo* 8 (2008): 27–32.

Karsai, László. "A Holokausztról szóló információk a magyar sajtóban, 1941–1944." *Századok*. (2014/6): 1365–74.

———. "A magyarországi zsidótörvények és—rendeletek." In *A Holokauszt Magyarországon európai perspektivában*, edited by Judit Molnár, 140–63. Budapest: Balassi, 2004.

———. "1941. Augusztus 27–28." *Élet és Irodalom*, September 11, 2009, 1–7.

Kay, Alex J. "'The Purpose of the Russian Campaign is the Decimation of the Slavic Population by Thirty Million': The Radicalization of German Food Policy in Early 1941." In *Nazi Policy on the Eastern Front, 1941: Total War, Genocide, and Radicalization*, edited by Alex J. Kay, Jeff Rutherford, and David Stahel, 101–29. Rochester: University of Rochester Press, 2012.

"Kolomea: ein Stuck Zeitgeschichte." *Darmstedter Echo*, July 29, 1967, 7.

Komoróczy, Géza. "Zsidók a Tanácsköztársaságban." *Szombat*, February 8, 2012.

Kosztyó, Gyula. "Mit vesztett Kárpátalja a holokauszttal? Egy minisztériumi állapotfelmérés elemzése (1939, augusztus)." Forthcoming.

Kovács, Mária M. "A kisebbségek nemzetközi jogvédelmének csapdája. Vázsonyi Vilmos és a numerus clauses." *Beszélő*, April 7, 1994.

Kovács, Tamás. "A Belügyminisztérium rendészeti és karhatalmi feladatai, 1920 és 1944 között." In *Pécsi Határőr Tudományos Közlemények*, Vol. X, 2009.

Kruglov, Alexander. "*Yevreiskaya Actzia*" *v KamenetsPodolskom*. Scientific bulletin, Ukrainian Center for Holocaust Studies, 2005.

Kurdi, Krisztina. "Az 1941-es Lvovi Pogromok a legujabb Hisztográfia Tükrében." In *Antiszemitizmus történeti formái a cári birodalomban és a Szovjetunió területein*, edited by Tamás Krausz and Tamás Barta, 207–29. Budapest: Russica Pannonica, 2014.

Ladányi, Andor. "Az első zsidótörvény megszületése." *Múlt és Jövő* 2 (2010): 102–21.

Lagzi, István. "Forgószél a délvidéken 1941-ben (A délvidéki jugoszláv hadsereg katonáinak hazatérése a német hadifogoly táborokból)." *Valóság*, no. 3 (March 2007).

Lower, Wendy. "Axis Collaboration, Operation Barbarossa, and the Holocaust in Ukraine." In *Nazi Policy on the Eastern Front, 1941: Total War, Genocide, and Radicalization*, edited by Alex J. Kay, Jeff Rutherford, and David Stahel, 186–219. Rochester: University of Rochester Press, 2012.

―――. "Facilitating Genocide: Nazi Ghettoization Practices in Occupied Ukraine, 1941–1942." In *Life in the Ghettos during the Holocaust*, edited by Eric J. Sterling, 237–51. Syracuse: Syracuse University Press, 2005.

―――. "The Holocaust and Colonialism in Ukraine: A Case Study of the Generalbezirk Zhytomyr, Ukraine, 1941–1944." In *The Holocaust in the Soviet Union: Symposium Presentations*, 1–20. Washington, DC: Center for Advanced Holocaust Studies, United States Holocaust Memorial Museum, 2005. https://www.ushmm.org/m/pdfs/20050908-holocaust-soviet-union-symposium.pdf.

Lozowick, Yaacov. "Rollbahn Mord: The Early Activities of Einsatzgruppe C." *Journal of Holocaust and Genocide Studies* 2, no. 2 (1987): 221–41. https://doi.org/10.1093/hgs/2.2.221.

Majsai, Tamás. "The Deportation of Jews from Csíkszereda and Margit Slachta's Intervention on Their Behalf." In *Studies on the Holocaust in Hungary*, edited by Randolph L. Braham, 113–63. New York: Social Science Monographs, 1990.

―――. "A körösmezei zsidódeportálás 1941-ben." In *Ráday Gyűjtemény Évkönyve*. Vol. IV–V, 59–86. 1984–1985.

―――. "A magyar holocaust első felvonása, 1941." In *Holocaust Emlékkönyv*, 75–98. Budapest: Tedisz, 2008.

―――. "Iratok a kőrösmezei zsidódeportálás történetéhez 1941." In *Ráday Gyűjtemény Évkönyve*. Vol. IV–V, 195–237. 1984–1985.

Mallmann, Klaus-Michael. "Der qualitative Sprung im Vernichtungsprozeß. Das Massaker von Kamenez-Podolsk Ende August 1941." *Jahrbuch für Antisemitismusforschung* 10 (2001).

"Nadwórna." In *Pinkas Hakehillot Polin*, edited by Ada Green. Jerusalem: Yad Vashem, n.d.

Nagy, L. Zsuzsa. "Amerikai diplomaták Horthy Miklósról, 1920–1944." *Történelmi Szemle* 32 (1990): 174–96.

Nagy, Tibor Péter. "Antiszemitizmus és felsőoktatás-politika—a numerus clausus törvény jelentősége." In *A Zsidó Iskolaügytörténete Magyarországon*, edited by Laszlo Balogh, 35–47. Budapest: Országos Pedagógiai Könyvtár és Muzeum, 1996.

"Örökre fülébe csengtek a jajkiáltások." *Népszabadság*, October 12, 1996.

Petropoulos, Jonathan. *Goering's Man in Paris: The Story of a Nazi Art Plunderer and His World*. New Haven, CT: Yale University Press, 2021.

Pietsch, Walter. "A Zsidók bevándorlása Galíciából." *Valóság*, no. 11 (1988).

Pihurik, Judit. "Hungarian Soldiers and Jews on the Eastern Front, 1941–1943." *Yad Vashem Studies* 2 (2007): 71–102.

Pohl, Dieter. "The Murder of Ukraine's Jews under German Military Administration and in the Reich Commissariat Ukraine." In *The Shoah in Ukraine*, edited by Ray Brandon and Wendy Lower. Bloomington: Indiana University Press, 2008.

―――. "The Murder of Jews in the General Government." In *National Socialist Extermination Policies: Contemporary Perspectives and Controversies*. Vol. 2, *War and Genocide*, edited by Ulrich Herbert. New York: Berghahn Books, 2000.

Prohászka, Ottokár. "Pro juventute catholica." *Alkotmány*, May 26, 1918.
Rudner, Martin, trans. and ed. "The Holocaust in Buczacz." In *Buczacz Origins*. Ottawa, Canada: Carleton University, 1993. http://www.ibiblio.org/yiddish/Places/Buczacz/bucz-tc.htm.
Sandkuehler, Thomas. "Anti-Jewish Policy and the Murder of the Jews in the District of Galicia, 1941/42." In *National Socialist Extermination Policies: Contemporary Perspectives and Controversies*. Vol. 2, *War and Genocide*, edited by Ulrich Herbert, 273–89. New York: Berghahn Books, 2000.
"Skala." In *Pinkas Hakehillot Polin*. Vol. II, 395–400. Jerusalem: Yad Vashem.
"Slaying of Jews in Galicia Depicted; Thousands Living There and Others Sent From Hungary Reported Massacred." *New York Times*, October 26, 1941.
Snyder, Timothy D. "Germany Must Own Up to Past Atrocities in Ukraine." *Kyiv Post*, July 7, 2017.
"Stanisławów." In *Pinkas Hakehillot Polin*, edited by Joyce Landau. Jerusalem: Yad Vashem, 1975.
Stark, Tamás. "Adatok a holocaust magyarországi áldozatainak számáról." In *Visszatérés— újrakezdés*, edited by János Botos and Tamás Kovács. Budapest: Holocaust Dokumentációs Központ és Emlékgyűjtemény Közalapítvány, 2007.
Steiner, John Michael. *Power Politics and Social Change in National Socialist Germany: A Process of Escalation into Mass Destruction*. The Hague: Mouton, 1975.
Szabó, Zoltán Tibori. "Csík vármegye zsidósága a betelepüléstől a megsemmisítésig." In *Tanulmányok a holokausztról*. Vol. 3, edited by Randolph L. Braham. Budapest: Balassi, 2004.
———. "Zsidók deportálása Észak-Erdélyből 1940-1942-ben." Manuscript form, 2021.
Thirring, Lajos. "Magyarország Trianontól napjainkig." *Magyar Statisztikai Szemle*, no. 4 (1938).
Tomaszewski, Jerzy. "The Civil Rights of Jews in Poland, 1918–1939." In *Polin: Studies in Polish Jewry*. Vol. 8, edited by Antony Polonsky, Ezra Mendelsohn, and Jerzy Tomaszewski, 79–101. London: Littmann, 1994.
Trials of War Criminals Before the Nuremberg Military Tribunals October 1946–April 1949. Vol. XI. Washington, DC: United States Government Printing Office, 1950.
Ungváry, Krisztián. "Hungarian Occupation Forces in Ukraine 1941–1942: Historiographical Context." *Journal of Slavic Military Studies* 20(2007): 81–120.
———. "Kitelepítés, lakosságcsere és a holokauszt egyes összefüggései." In *A holokauszt Magyarországon európai perspektívában*, edited by Judit Molnár, 84–99. Budapest: Balassi Kiadó, 2005.
Verbrechen der Wehrmacht: Dimensionen des Vernichtungskrieges 1941–1945, edited by Hamburger Institut für Sozialforschung, 132. Hamburg, 2002.
Westermann, Edward B. "Drinking Rituals, Masculinity, and Mass Murder in Nazi Germany." *Central European History* 51, Special Issue 3 (Masculinity and the Third Reich) (September 2018): 367–89.
———. "Himmler's Uniformed Police on the Eastern Front: The Reich's Secret Soldiers, 1941–1942." *War in History* 3 (1996): 309–29.

———. "Stone-Cold Killers or Drunk with Murder? Alcohol and Atrocity during the Holocaust." *Holocaust and Genocide Studies* 30, no. 1 (Spring 2016): 1–19.

Internet Sources

Ákos, Fóris. "Zsákmányjog a keleti hadszíntéren." Újkor, January 1, 2018. http://ujkor.hu/content/zsakmanyjog-keleti-hadszinteren.

"Aktion gegen den ehemaligen kommissarischen Kreishauptmann von Kolomyia und Nazimörder Claus Volkmann/Peter Grubbe." ECN.org, May 17, 1996. http://www.ecn.org/radikal/154/86.html.

Angrick, Andrej. "The Escalation of German-Rumanian Anti-Jewish Policy after the Attack on the Soviet Union." Translated by William Templer (Source: *Yad Vashem Studies*, Vol. XXVI, 203–38. Jerusalem, 1998.). Yad Veshem. https://www.yadvashem.org/articles/academic/the-escalation-of-german-rumanian-anti-jewish-policy.html.

"Arâjs Trial Records, Deposition of Botor, 26 October 1977, pp. 9227–28." The Nizkor Project. http://dx.doi.org/10.1007/978-3-319-57672-5_4.

Arico, Massimo. "'Seht euch diesen Mann an'; Kamenec-Podolski, 27–29 August 1941." Abruf: August 14, 2011. https://de.wikipedia.org/wiki/Massaker_von_Kamenez-Podolsk.

Braham, Randolph L. "The Christian Churches of Hungary and the Holocaust." (Source: *Yad Vashem Studies*, Vol. 29, 241–80. Jerusalem, 2001). Yad Vashem. https://www.yadvashem.org/articles/academic/the-christian-churches-of-hungary-and-the-holocaust.html.

"A Child for Hitler 1992." YouTube video. Posted September 20, 2014. https://www.youtube.com/watch?v=eDiOYLbiyp8.

A City and the Dead; Zablotow Alive and Destroyed: Memorial Book of Zabolotov (Zablotow) (Zabolotive, Ukraine), edited by former residents of Zablotow in Israel and the USA, translated by Schmuel Kahati. Tel-Aviv Israel, 1949. https://collections.ushmm.org/search/catalog/bib26944.

Gellért, Ádám. "A gyomrom összeszorult, bekövetkezett, amitől tartottunk." Index, September, 20, 2017. https://index.hu/tudomany/tortenelem/2017/09/14/magyar_zsidok_deportalasa_1941-ben/.

Gellért, Ádám, and János Gellért. "Az 1941. Évi kőrösmezői deportálások, A kitolocolásokat jóváhagyó minisztertanácsi döntés háttere." *Betekintő*, no. 2 (2012). https://www.academia.edu/5886307 .

———. "Egy tömeggyilkosság anatómiája—Kamenyec-Podolszkij, 1941. Augusztus." *Betekintő*, no. 4 (2015). https://www.academia.edu/21392834/Egy_tömeggyilkosság_anatómiája_Kamenyec-Podolszkij_1941._augusztus._Betekintő_2015_4.

———. "Menekülés a népirtás elől." Az Állambiztonsági Szolgálatok Történeti Levéltárának internetes folyóirata." *Betekintő*, no. 4 (2015). http://epa.oszk.hu/01200/01268/00027/pdf/EPA01268_betekinto_2013_3_gellert_gellert.pdf.

"Helen Dub." *Cleveland Jewish News*, December 17, 2009. http://www.clevelandjewishnews.com/archives/helen-dub/article_1d8d0a15-8b0d-5e94-b889-1b6b4d2e5fda.html.

Holman, Eugene. "Friedrich Jeckeln—An Unsung Holocaust Figure." Simon Wiesenthal Center, July 14, 2000. https://groups.google.com/g/alt.revisionism/c/Wy9MWCtnFos.

Holocaust Controversies (blog). "Galicia." Posted by Jonathan Harrison on July 16, 2008. http://holocaustcontroversies.blogspot.com/2008/07/galicia.html.

"Interview with Efrossinia from Ukraine." Interview by Yahad-in Unum, shared by Father Patrick Desbois. https://www.facebook.com/patrick.desbois.71.

Kádár, Gábor, and Zoltán Vági. "Törvényen kívül: fehérterror és lakossági pogromhullám 1919–1921." Társadalmi Konfliktusok Kutatóközpont, n.d. Konfliktuskutato.hu/index.php?option=com_content&view=article&id=146:toervenyen-kivuel-feherterror-es-lakossagi-pogromhullam-1919-1921-&catid=15:tanulmanyok.

Karády, Viktor. "Jewish Over-Schooling Revisited: The Case of Hungarian Secondary Education under the Old Regime (1900–1941)." Central European University, n.d. http://web.ceu.hu/jewishstudies/pdf/01_karady.pdf.

Karsai, László. "Magyarországi zsidótörvények és rendeletek 1938–1945." In *A magyarországi zsidótörvények és -rendeletek, 1920–1944*, edited by Róbert Vértes. Budapest: Polgár, 2002). https://adoc.pub/a-magyarorszagi-zsidotrvenyek-es-rendeletek-html.

Képviselőházi Napló, 1939–1944, Vol. XI, 537. https://library.hungaricana.hu/en/view/OGYK_KN-1939_06/?pg=6&layout=s.

Kibédi Varga, Sándor. "Horthy mint Pilátus." Review of *A Horthy-rendszer mérlege* by Ungváry Krisztián. *Olvass bele*, January 28, 2013. https://olvassbele.com/2013/01/28/horthy-mint-pilatus-ungvary-krisztian-a-horthy-rendszer-merlege/.

"Killings in Miropol." https://www.facebook.com/groups/342757449166582/permalink/1770875176354795/.

Klettner, Csilla, and Tamás Kovács. "A Lengyel Menekültek Magyarországi Fogadtatása 1939 Őszén." Archivnet XX. *Századi Történeti Források* 16, no. 4 (2016). http://archivnet.hu/menekultkerdes_migracio_magyarorszagon_a_20_szazadban/2._a_lengyel_menekultek_magyarorszagi_fogadtatasa_1939_oszen.html.

"Kolomyja Ghetto." Aktion Reinhard Camps. Last updated May 28, 2006. http://www.deathcamps.org/occupation/kolomyja%20ghetto.html.

Kovacs, Andras. "Terror és pogrom, vörös és fehér." *Múlt és Jövő*, no. 3 (2014): 28–33. http://www.academia.edu/19607504/Terror_és_pogrom_vörös_és_fehér.

"Mielnica." In *Pinkas Hakehillot Polin*, translated by E. Jeanne Andelman. Yizkor Book Project, JewishGen. Page last updated April 1, 2011. www.jewishgen.org/Yizkor/Pinkas_poland/pol2_00320.html.

Monori, Áron. "A numerus clausus és a magyar katolikus sajtó 1919–1920." Mediakutato, 2003. http://www.mediakutato.hu/cikk/2003_02_nyar/03_numerus_clausus.

"The Nadwórna Jewish Community during the Holocaust." Yad Vashem. https://www.yad vashem.org/yv/en/exhibitions/valley/nadworna/ghetto_liquidation.asp.

"Nagyapám-naplója." 2015. http://gallai.net/ami-minket-illet/nagyapam-naploja.

"1941—a zsidók deportálása Kárpátaljáról." Társadalmi Konfliktusok. http://konfliktuskutato.hu/index.php?option=com_maps&view=topicevents&map_id=13&tmpl=dka&full=0&Itemid=204.

O'Neil, Robin. *Extermination of the Jews of Galicia (Galicia Poland)*. Yizkor Book Project, JewishGen. Page last updated July 11, 2009. https://www.jewishgen.org/Yizkor/galicia/galicia.html.

———. "Extermination of the Jews of Kolomyja and District." In *Extermination of the Jews of Galicia (Galicia, Poland)*. Yizkor Book Project, JewishGen. Page last updated August 28, 2005. https://www.jewishgen.org/yizkor/galicia/gal005.html.

———. "Hans Krueger in Stanislawów, Kolomyja and District." In *The Rabka Four Instruments of Genocide and Grand Larceny (Poland)*. Yizkor Book Project, JewishGen. Page last updated April 8, 2016. http://www.jewishgen.org/yizkor/Galicia3/gal107.html#f239r.

———. "Kolomyja and District Transports to Belzec." In *Extermination of the Jews of Galicia (Galicia, Poland)*. Yizkor Book Project, JewishGen. Page last updated August 28, 2005. http://www.jewishgen.org/yizkor/Galicia/gal003.html#63%29.

———. "Murder of the Lvov Professors." In *The Rabka Four Instruments of Genocide and Grand Larceny (Poland)*. Yizkor Book Project, JewishGen. Page last updated July 25, 2012. http://www.jewishgen.org/yizkor/Galicia3/gal041.html#f146r.

"Online Guide of Murder Sites of Jews in the Holocaust, Galicia." Yad Vashem.

Pohl, Dieter. "Hans Krueger and the Murder of Jews in the Stanislawów Region (Galicia)." *Yad Vashem Studies* 26 (1998). https://www.yadvashem.org/articles/academic/hans-krueger-and-the-murder-of-the-jews-in-the-stanislawow-region.html.

"Police Battalion 320." Yad Vashem. http://www1.yadvashem.org/untoldstories/database/hyperlinks/police_battalion_320.html.

"'Seht euch diesen Mann an'; Kamenec-Podolski, 27–29 Agosto 1941." http://www.ordnungspolizei.org/j259/it/articles/5-kamenec-podolski.html.

Wrobel, Piotr. "The Jews of Galicia under Austrian-Polish Rule, 1867-1918." Topographic Maps of Eastern Europe. n.d. http://easteurotopo.org/articles/wrobel/wrobel.pdf.

INDEX

Pages numbers in italics indicate Figures and Photos

Abicht, Herta, 151, 156–57, 312n90
Act II of 1939, 287n29
Act XVII of 1867, 18, 275n7
Adler, Zsiga, 189, 322n40
Ágoston, Péter, 27, 277n33
agriculture, 18, 21, 52–53, 222–23, 330n20
air raids, 2, 144
Ajtay, Gábor, 53, 286n13
Aktionen (rounding up of Jews), xxiv, 81, 143, 155, 162–63, 170, 193; in Bolechow/Bolekhiv, 173–74; defined, 269n8, 292n100, 305n17; Final Solution beginning and, 141; *Gross Aktion* as, 131, 144; *Intelligenz Aktion* as, 133–39, 196; Leideritz, P., and, 147–49. *See also* forced collection
Albrecht, Heinz, 145
alcohol, 140–41, 154, 172, 174, 311n70; role in mass murders of, xxv, 109–10, 143–45, 244, 253. *See also* schnapps
"alien" Jews, xvii, 3, 17, 27, 34, 37, 41, 43, 180, 282n83
Altenstadt, Hans Georg Schmidt von, 95, 228, 295n24
ambivalence, 6, 11, 17, 21, 79, 110, 193, 219
American ambassador to Hungary, Pell as, xii, 11, 118, 178, 181–82, 206–10, 237–39
American Embassy in Budapest, xii, 118, 190, 206–7
American Jewish Joint Distribution Committee (JDC), 45–46, 118, 202, 205–11, 215–16, 251, 280n65, 289n50, 326n91
ammunition/bullets, xvii, xxiv, 11, 14, 108, 129, 134–40, 147, 154, 159, 228

anglophile, 32, 199, 207, 212
anti-Semitism/anti-Semitic, 20–23, 31–35, 39–41, 157, 172–75, 197, 207–8, 238, 241; legislation, 7, 35–36, 38, 40, 42, 223, 280n61, 281n67; of Orbán, 220; role of, 222–23, 233; of Ukrainian irregulars, 73–75, 193–94; of Werth, 233–35. *See also specific topics*
Antonescu, Ion, 85
Applebaum, Anne, 8, 14
Apponyi, György, 59
Arendt, Hannah, 121, 236
aristocracy, Hungarian, 12, 18–20, 29–35, 37, 39, 205, 207, 216, 278n41, 327n96; Szapáry as, xii, 59, 212–13, *213*
armed youth groups (*leventék*), 188
arrests, 136, 151, 187, 200, 210, 251, 255, 311n72; during deportations, 59–61, 64–65, 85; of Jackson, 254; of Lanckoronska, 136, 138; of Leideritz, P., 155–56; of Szapáry, 213; of Zobel, 190, 254. *See also* raids
Arrow Cross movement, 281n66
Åsbrink, Elisabeth, 68
assimilated Jews, 6, 17, 19–27; Hungarian Jews, 31–34, 37–40, 42, 199–200, 222–23
Association of Awakening Hungarians (Ébredő Magyarok Egyesülete), 35, 279n54
asylum, 10, 38, 239
Auschwitz, xi, xxii–xxiii, 2, 14, 246, 252–55, 315n124, 338n24, 338n30
Auschwitz-Birkenau Memorial and Museum, 252–53
Austrian Jews, 6, 25–26, 148–49, 336n80

INDEX

Austro-Hungarian Monarchy, xxiii, 8, 18, 23, 42, 249
authority/discretion, 8, 43, 111, 192–93, 195–97, 285n4, 286n13; jurisdiction and, 56, 176, 179–80, 205; Minister of the Interior, 219–20; of Pásztóy, 188–89; regional, 128–30, 132, 158–59, 178; of Royal Hungarian Army, 179–80; of Werth, 179, 232–34, 271n15, 285n8

Babi Yar massacre, xiii, 108, 120, 129
Bach-Zelewski, Erich von dem, 98, 100
"backwards," Eastern Jews considered, 7, 16–18, 21, 25, 134, 222–23
"bad Jews" stereotypes, 23–34, 39
Bahnschutzpolizei. See railway police
Bajcsy-Zsilinszky, Endre, 200
Baltic region, 88, 98, 100, 116
Bárdossy, László, 13, 51–52, 55, 233, *237*, 250–51, 336n76; death penalty for, xii, 237–38; as Hungarian prime minister, xii, 4, 179, 208–9, 215, *237*, 237–39, 247; Pell communicating with, 69, 208–10, 216
Bartha, Károly, 52
Batizfalvy, Nándor, 56–57, 66, *67*, 200, 232, 289n55, 289n56, 330n9, 334n57
Belzec (extermination camp), xvii, 9, 158, 170, 173–75, 186–87, 227; casualty statistics, 315n127; deportation to Belzec, 147, 150–51, 159; gas chambers in, 128, 147, 161–63
Bennett, G. H., 120–21
Beorn, Waitman Wade, 159, 170, 316n3
Beregovo (Beregszász), 256
Berlin, Germany, 47, 189, 209, 238
Bethlen, István, 34
Bierut, Boleslaw, 156
Bihari, Péter, 25
Binder, Eliza, 134, 162, 336n1
birth certificates, 180, 225
births, 18, 101
Blaschek, Fritz, 121
"bloodland," Galicia as, 7–9, 249, 274n36
"Bloody Sunday" massacre, xi, 127, 141, 144, 228, 244, 247; Krüger overseeing, 143, 145–46, 149. *See also* Rudolfmühle

Blum, Natan, 200, 211
Bolechow/Bolekhiv ghetto, 134 147, 154, 173–74
Bolshevism, Jews associated with, 31, 73, 84, 96, 98, 128, 153, 238
border police (*Grenzpolizei*), 99, 129–30, 172, 187–88, 227, 305n12
borders/borderland, 43, *44*, 45, 129–30, 147–48, 254–55, 258; deportations around, 54–58; Galicia as, 7–9, 249, 269n2, 274n36, 291n96; "Jew-free," 189, 224, 236; rescues along, 184–99; Sniatyn, Ukraine, 321n32
Braham, Randolph, 301n88
Brand, Hansi, 181
Brand, Joel, 181–82
Brandt, Oskar, 129
Brautigam, Otto, 95
Breitman, Richard, 119
Brenner, Cipora, xi, 77, 144–46, 154–55, 161, 170, 310n64, 310n65, 311n71
bribes/bribery, 63–64, 134, 153, 159, 188, 190, 283n95; of Batizfalvy, 289n55, 289n56; fees for human smuggling as, 181, 183–88, 227, 320n15
bridges, 3, 70, 78, 88, 197, 226, 291n92, 325n71
Britain, 100, 116, 118, 213, 238, 302n100, 327n103
brothels, German military, 166, 171–72, 175–77, *176*, 318n39
Browning, Christopher, 85, 100, 107, 128, 152, 159, 304n4, 305n12
Brusilov Offensive (Russian Campaign), 26, 227n29
Buchsbaum, Brona, *186*, 186–87
Budapest: law enforcement agencies, 4, 8, 28, 36, 219–20, 227
Budapest, Hungary, xxiii, 7, 22–25, 40, 184, 213–14, 260, 287n20; American Embassy in, xii, 118, 190, 206–7; deportations from, 4, 63–66, 88–90, 247–48; human smuggling to, 185, 254; internment camps in, 56–58, 190, 200, 222, 260, 326n83; law enforcement agencies, 4, 8, 28, 36, 219–20, 227

INDEX

Bukovina, Romania, 25–27, 80–82, 167–68, 188, 247, 322n51; deportation/expulsions from, 79, 85, 129–30, 195, 293n3, 311n76
Bukowinka Forest, Nadwórna, 139, 243–44
Bulgaria, 242
Burckhard, C. J., 205
bureaucrats, Hungarian, xxiii, xxv, 96, 219, 232–33, 235–36
Burleigh, Michael, 110
burying alive, xxi, 77, 113, 154; in "Bloody Sunday massacre," 145; Jewish children, 11, 124, 145, 152, 244; in Kamenets-Podolsk massacre, 124–25, 244; in Nadwórna massacre, 140
Busk, Galicia, 171–72
bystanders, 14, 116, 189–91, 249

"caftan-wearing Jews" stereotypes, 40, 199
capitalism, 22–23, 27, 276n19
Carpathian Corps (*Kárpát Csoport*), 3, 51–52, 54–55, 85, 219, 226–27
Carpathian Group, 196, 285n7
Carpathian Mountains, 17, 25, 129–30, 148, 154, 179–80, 184–85, 248–49; as natural barrier, 68–71, 187
Carpathian Ruthenia, xviii, 39, 222–24, 263, 270n9, 271n14; deportation from, 4–6, 63–64, 79–82, 239–40, 248–49, *252*, 254–55; Kárpátalja and Zakarpats'ka, 363 Kozma as government commissioner of, xii, 3, 46–47, 51–58, 178–79, 240, *240*, 285n4; Meskó as police commissioner of, 46, 59, 66, 180, 230, 333n50, 334n57; refugees from, 131–34, 139–41, 250; Slachta on, 58–68, 201–2, 205, 207, 217; Uzhgorod, 90, 112, 221, 330n17. *See also* Körösmező, Ukraine
casualty statistics, 10, 120–21, 148, 210, 244, 278n44; in Belzec, 315n127; Kamenets-Podolsk massacre, 83, 113–15, *114*, 118, 246, 294n18, 296n41; Kolomea, 137; Nadwórna, 243, 309n50
Catholic Church, 18, 20, 22, 27, 30, 215, 281n70

cattle cars, xvii, 48, *61*, 287n34
celebration dinners, Nazi, 140–41, 146–47, 225
cemeteries, 124, 147, 246, 303n121, 310n65; New Jewish Cemetery, xi, 128, 141, 143–46, 162
censorship, 190, 203, 206, 210
Cesarani, David, xxii, 166–67
Chesed Besht (organization), 261
children/youths, Jewish, 45, 61–62, *72*, 140–42, 192–93, 250, *252*, 254, 256, 314n107; buried alive, 11, 124, 145, 152, 244; forced undressing of, *165*; human smuggling of, 185; killed in Auschwitz, 255; killed in Kamenets-Podolsk massacre, 109–10, 112, 244, 257; killed in Orinin massacre, 253; orphans/orphanages, 31, 65, 69, 80, 133, 150–51, 157, 162–63, 312n89; sexual violence against, 166–69, 171
Christian church/Christianity, 33–35, 182, 211, 214–15, 217–18, 222–23, 281n70; documents proving, xxii, 192–93, 212, 254; families of Hungarian Jews, xxiii, 3, 7, 113, 188–89, 201, 256, 326n87; Hungarian values as, 22, 27, 30, 230, 239, 247; middle class, 20, 30, 38, 221, 238, 248–49, 330n16; priests/clergymen, 23, 59, 76, 258
Christian Jews. *See* religious conversion
citizens/citizenship: documents, xvii, 7, 57, 61, 63–65, 199–201, 230, 253–55, 326n89; of Hungarian Jews, xii, 26, 51–58, 139, 188, 201–2, 213, 220, 239, 240–41, 250; status, 36, 43, 45, 50–58, 230, 272n20
civil administration, German, 85, 128, 131–35, 139–40, 143, 149–52, 158–61, 183, 191, 228
civil administration, Hungarian, 7, 46, 57, 128, 227–30
class, 32, 207–8. *See also* middle class
clergy. *See* priests/clergymen
code of conduct, SS, 152–53, 158, 160, 169, 175
communications, xi–xii, 88–91, 133, 154, 188–89, 204–7, 218, 238, 240; by Bárdossy, 69, 208–10, 216; by forced labor companies, 197–98, 203; by Jeckeln, 95, 113–19, *114*, 122; by Keresztes-Fischer, 178–84, 187, 230–31; by letters, 142–43, 202–3, 214,

communications (*continued*)
219, 226–27, 236, 239, 241–42, 321n36;
MIPI, 326n93; radio, 94, 113, 115, 172, 190,
194, 210, 322n41; by telegram, 178, 180,
319n11, 327n101

Communism, 14, 29–30, 32–33, 73, 156,
215–16

competition/rivalry, 98–99, 121, 135–36, 152–
61, 308n40

complicity. *See* participation

concentrations camps, 90–91, 113, 157, 176–
77, 254; Mauthausen, xxii, 297n48,
338n28

"conditioning" of executioners, 139, 141,
299n68, 299n70

consensual sexual relations, 169–70

contradictions, 22, 63, 108, 159–60, 192–93,
217, 223, 333n52

cordon personnel, 106–8, 110, 116, 135, 158,
229, 301n88

coreligionists, Jewish, xvii, 21, 27, 111, 132, 148,
188, 198, 202

corruption, 27, 62, 127, 152–61, 311n83,
313n98; bribes and, 63–64, 134, 159, 188,
190, 283n95, 289n55, 289n56

Council of Ministers, Hungarian, xii, 51–52,
56, 224, 234–35, 285n8

counterintelligence, xi, 181, 183, 320n15,
320n19, 332n38

covering of mass graves, 112–13, 117, 124–25,
229; local Jewish communities forced to,
10–11, 140–41, 244

crimes, war, xxii, 13, 116, 119, 150, 171–72, 239,
296n34, 297n49

cross-border transfers. *See* deportation/
expulsion; deportation/expulsion of
Hungarian Jews to Galicia

Culbertson, Paul T., 207, 328n107

"culling" actions, xvii, 75, 132, 133–37, 148. *See
also* "ethnic cleansing"/cleaning actions

cultural divides, 134, 167

currencies, 67, 203, 262, 288n38, 308n40, 320n15

Czechoslovakia/Czech Jews, xiii, 7, 137, 251,
285n6, 336n80

Czortków, Ukraine, 91–92, 132, 137, 162–63,
168, 172, 185, 313n93

Dall, Kurt, 106–7, 111
Daluege, Kurt, 111
Danckwert, Justus, 95
Dargel, Paul, 95
Darnay, László, 192, 322n51
Deák, Béla, 197, 325n73
death camps, 245–46, 252–55
death/deaths, xi, 290n67; of Kozma, xii, 239,
241; of Werth, xii, 235. *See also* casualty
statistics; mass murders
death marches, 77, *102*, 102–4, *104*, *105*
death penalty, 155, 311n81, 316n1; for Bárdossy,
xii, 237–38; for Jeckeln, xiii, 120, 300n83;
for Leideritz, P., xiii, 155–57; for Pásztóy,
xii, 236–37
death squads. *See* murder squads
degradation, sexual, 164, 166
dehumanization, 50, 164, 174, 253
Delatyn, Ukraine, 132, 147, 169, 305n15
demographics, 4–5, 24, 28, 36–37, 43, 88, 139,
221–23, 247–49, 256; Jewish populations
in, 79, 85–86, 148, 275n6, 275n8, 330n20,
339n32
denial, 151, 230, 236, 260
deportation/expulsion, 78–83, 84, 127–
28; to Belzec, 147, 150–51, 159; from
Budapest, 4, 63–66, 88–90, 247–48;
from Carpathian Ruthenia, 4–6, 63–64,
79–82, 239–40, 248–49, *252*, 254–55; of
foreign nationals, 51–58, 232–33, 239, 242,
247–48; from Romania, 79, 85, 129–30,
195, 242, 293n3, 311n76; statistics, 4, 192,
242, 250–51, 334n56
deportation/expulsion of Hungarian Jews
to Galicia, xi, xix–xx, 2, 9–15, 135, 191–98,
218, 230, 245–47; arrests during, 59–61,
64–65, 85; of Bárdossy involved in, 233,
237; demographics of, 4, 247–49; families separated by, 60–66, 69, 184–91, *186*,
250, 254–55; framed as "resettlement,"
3, 144, 199–200, 219, 223–24, 326n92;

identity checks in, 50, 65, 254–55; intercession requested for, 90–91, 187, 191–92, 203–5, 236–39, 320n17; Keresztes-Fischer curtailing, 178–84, 187, 215–16, 230–32; Kozma initiating, xii, 239–41, 321n30, 336n77; legal framework for, 4, 50–58, 232, 235–36; local Jewish communities responding to, 198–204; MIPI on, 69, 75, 290n73; perpetrators of, 164, 214, 218–19, 223–24, 226, 229–41; role of KEOKH in, xii, 4, 50–58, 230–36; role of Pásztóy in, xii, 52–58, 235–36; Royal Hungarian Army facilitating, 49–58, 68–71, 78–82, 178–79; scope of, 12, 67–68, 209, 216, 232–32; survivors of, 184–85, 226, 252; Werth supporting, xii, 51–58. *See also* marches/wandering of deported Jews; trucks/trucking in deportation, military

Desbois, Patrick, xxiv, 171, 246, 333n45

Deutsch, Moshe, 71, 73

Dezső, László, 4, 54–55, 270n10

diaries, xi, 73, 80–81, 143–46, 152, 192, 196, 249–50, 257, 338n19; of Hungarian soldiers, 74, 77–78, 225–26; of Hyman, 184, 257; of Kozma, 54–55, 58, 91; of Milch, 70–71; of Pásztóy, 63; of survivors, 243–44

Diel, Rudolf, 121

dinners, Nazi, 140–41, 144, 146–47, 225, 228, 232

diplomats, US, 207, 210, 270n5, 284n105, 327n104

diseases, 90, 133, 142–43; venereal, 175, 177

Dniester River, 4–5, 228–29; Jewish corpses in, 7, 73–79, 117–18, 167–68, 197, 226; as natural barrier, 70, 82, 187, 192, 224–25

Dobrzensky, Mary, 204

doctors/physicians, 70, 77, 136, 173, 175, 192

documents, *87, 114, 150,* 183, 197, 283n95; birth certificate, 180, 225; Christian papers as, xxii, 192–93, 212, 254; citizenship, xvii, 7, 57, 61, 63–65, 199–201, 230, 253–55, 326n89; Nansen passports as, 7, 54, 209, 250, 271n19, 286n17; travel, 191–92, 271n19

Dodd, Martha, 121

Dodd, William, 121

dogs, 142, 172

Dolina (border town), 147, 194, 225

drafts/drafting, Royal Hungarian Army, 177, 243–54, 297n48

Dreyfus Affair, 22, 275n3, 276n16

drivers, Jewish, xi, 103, 116–17, 198, 243, 297n48, 325n76; photographs by, xi, *102, 103, 104, 105,* 243, 301n89

drowning, 76, 226

drunkenness, 145, 244, 253, 311n70

"dual loyalty" trope, 27, 33, 39–40, 199

Dub, Helen, 185

"Eastern" Jews (*Ostjuden*), 20–23, 32–35, 39–41; considered "backwards," 7, 16–18, 21, 25, 134, 222–23. *See also* "Galicianers"/Galician Jews

Ébredő Magyarok Egyesülete (Association of Awakening Hungarians), 35, 279n54

economic motivations/opportunism, 7, 17, 46, 153, 221–24, 248–49, 331n27

economic restrictions, 38–40, 199

educated Jews, 19, 29, 32, 34–35, 39, 126, 223, 279n54, 307n32, 308n39; Intelligenz Aktion targeting, 133–39, 196; sexual violence against, 173–74

educated Nazis, 128–29, 160

efficiency. *See* productivity

Eichmann, Adolf, 121, 181–82, 228

Einsatzgruppen, SS (mobile killing units), 9, 11, 95, 97, 107, 111–12, 115, 126, 130, 135, 158, 195, 294n21, 298n58

elderly people, Jewish, 141–42, 168–69, 254

Elsner, Paul, 172

emancipation, Jewish, 18, 275n2, 275n7

employment, promises of, 52–53, 64, 234

Englisch, Gustav, 139

epidemics, 83, 90–91, 142, 175

Erdély. *See* Transylvania

escapes, 59–60, 93, 184–89, 218, 227, 254–55, 322n51

"ethnic cleansing"/cleaning actions, xvii, 2–8, 76, 127–28, 136–37, 180, 221, 233

Éva (daughter of Samu), 260–61
Evans, Richard, 132, 171
exclusion, legal, 50, 253
execution (phase of mass murder), 98, *104*, 106–12, 149–50, *165*, 185–87, 196–97, 228, 233; sites of, 102–3, 108, 142, 246, 310n59
executioners, Nazi, xx, xxiv, 14, 106–12, 140, 144–47, 149, 229, 244, 266; "conditioning" of, 139, 141, 299n68, 299n70; plundering by, 164, 246; psychology of, 84, 100, 139, 141, 299n68, 299n70
exile. *See* deportation/expulsion of Hungarian Jews
expropriation, 29, 59–62, 71, 73, 128, 223–24, 238
expulsion. *See* deportation/expulsion of Hungarian Jews
extermination. *See* mass murders

family/families, Jewish, 56–57, 145–46, 192–93, 211–15, 227, *252*, 259–61; Christian members of, xxiii, 3, 7, 113, 188–89, 201, 256, 326n87; deportation separating, 60–66, 69, 184–91, *186*, 250, 254–55; of forced labor companies, 197–98; murdered in Kamenets-Podolsk, 124–25, 257. *See also* children/youths, Jewish
famine, 91, 133, 143, 194
Farkas, Ferenc, 226
Farkas, Pál, 277n33
fees, human smuggling, 181, 183–88, 227, 320n15
Fein, Albert, 112, 123, 192–93, 293n3, 300n78, 322n52
Feldgendarmerie (military gendarmerie), 305n12
Felvidék. *See* Upper Hungary (Slovakia)
Fényes, László, 277n33
Ferencz, Benjamin Berrell, 126
Fermor, Patrick Leigh, 249
Feuerman, Juliusz, 143, 146, 307n38, 310n62, 311n72
Final Solution (Nazi campaign), xvii, 5, 13, 96, 119–20, 127, 133, 147, 161, 246–47, 256, 336n80

financial aid for refugees, 57, 202, 212
Finder, Gabriel N., 228
First Jewish Law, 37–38, 50, 281n70, 282n75
first wave (Nazi exterminations), 8, 14
food supplies, 60, 66, 75–79, 131, 136, 142–43, 161, 194, 198, 203–6; for Kamenets-Podolsk ghetto, 86, 88, *89*, 96–98
forced collection, xvii, 25–26, *57*, 60–65, *165*, 185–86, 200–202, 206, 251; gendarmerie participation in, 225; in Kamenets-Podolsk massacre, 101–2, *102*, 116; by Reserve Police Battalion 133, 135
forced labor companies, Jewish men in, xi, 55, 58, 61–62, 78–79, 113, 134, 169, 177, 225–26, 253–54, 287n29; communications by, 197–98, 203; rescues by, 184, 325n75
"foreign Jews," 36, 39, 50, 134, 137, 148–49, 170, 198–200, 220, 280n65
foreign nationals, 137, 285n6; deportation of, 51–58, 232–33, 239, 242, 247–48; in internment camps, 189, 247–48, 251, 254–55. *See also* refugees
forests, 168, 241, 254, 321n29; Bukowinka Forest, 139, 243–44; Rumbula Forest, xiii, 108, 120; Szeparowce Forest, 137, 149, 151, 308n43
France, 22, 38, 157, 160–61, 242, 275n3, 276n16
Frank, Hans, 154, 239, 313n102, 335n73
Fremden Büro (Swiss immigration agency), 41
Frojimovics, Kinga, 321n29, 331n33

Galicia, xi–xii, xviii, 16–17, 25, 161, 246, 253; as borderland, 7–9, 249, 269n2, 274n36, 291n96; German military control of, 3, 8, 15, 81, 182–83, 242, 332n35, 338n19; Hungarian occupation of, 51, 81, 183, 191, 194, 247–48, 290n76; incorporation into General Government of, 128–29, 131–32, 158, 182–83, 307n33; mass murders in, 131–39, 157–60; sexual violence in, 166–68, 171–77; survivors of, 184–85, 189–91,

226, 252, 254–55. *See also* deportation/expulsion of Hungarian Jews to Galicia; marches/wandering (of deported Jews); Nadwórna, Ukraine; Stanisławów
"Galicianers"/ Galician Jews stereotypes, 12, 26–34, 50, 130–34, 187, 199, 210, 219, 220, 227, 252–53, 270n4, 285n2, 335n72; considered "backwards," 7, 16–18, 21, 25, 134, 222–23; Second Jewish Law impacting, 41–42
gas/gas chambers, 5, 11, 128, 147, 161–63, 253, 255
Gay, Erwin, 314n107
gendarmerie, Hungarian (*táboric sendőrség*), 187–88, 220, 250, 289n57, 331n33; plundering by, 193–94, 224–26, 246
General Government, xiii, 130, 152–61, 191–92; Galicia incorporated into, 128–29, 131–32, 158, 182–83, 307n33
general staff (Royal Hungarian Army), 2, 47, 188, 193–94, 204, 219, 224–27, 232–35, 329n5, 332n40
genocide, xvii, xxii, 5, 10, 119, 128–31, 218, 245–46. *See also specific topics*
gentile. *See* non-Jewish/gentile Hungarians
geography, *xviii*, 2, 4, 6, *44*, 147, 152–53, 222–23, 247–48, 270n9, 337n5. *See also* natural barriers
Gerlach, Christian, 131
German Army, 97, 116, 193, 295n24
German Foreign Office, 194
German – Hungarian joint committee, 219, 238
German Jews, xiii, 137, 318n34
German military, 191–98, 224–29, 270n8; brothels, 166, 171–72, 175–77, *176*, 318n39; control of Galicia, 3, 8, 15, 81, 182–83, 242, 332n35, 338n19. *See also specific divisions*
German Operational Situation Reports, 95, 113, 115, 123–24, 126, 138, 194–95
German travel permits (*Passierschein*), 191, 214–15
Gertjejanssen, Wendy Jo, 171, 176–77
Gerwarth, Robert, 24
Gestapo (secret police), xiii, 99, 175, *176*, 191–98, 213, 305n12, 314n117. *See also* executioners; *Schutzstaffel*

ghettoization, 8–9, 86, 128, 138, 141–43, 221, 330n17
ghettos, xvii, 10–11, 80–81, 132–33, 254; Bolechow/Bolekhiv, 134 147, 154, 173–74; Kamenets-Podolsk, 86, *87*, 88, *89*, 90–92, 257; liquidation of, 96, 147, 150–51, 162, 176, 213, 228; Meiler creating, 86, 88, 91, 192–93; Old Town, 82–83, 86, *87*, 88, *89*, 90–92, 95, 101, 116; sexual violence in, 166, 168–69, 170–72; Stanisławów, xi, 36n1, 69, 155, 162, 170, 172–75. *See also* Kolomea/Kolomea Ghetto
Goebbels, Joseph, 13, 121–22, 160, 266
Goede, Gerhard, 314n107
gold, 67, 160, 164, 166, 308n40
Gömbös, Gyula, 37, 281n68, 281n70, 281n71
gonorrhea, 175
"good Jews," 23–34, 39
Gopnick, Adam, 113, 128
Gorgon, Herbert, 151–52, 312n90
Göring, Hermann, 13, 121–22, 160, 266, 314n18
Gottesman, Samuel, 198
Götz, Aly, 7, 221
government. *See* Hungarian Parliament
Grabowski, Jan, 274n39
grave digging, xxiv, 196, 229, 246, 316n2
Grenzpolizei. *See* border police
Grimm, Ludwig, 310n60
Gross, Franz, 313n94
Gross, Karl, 314n117
Gross Aktion, 131, 144
Grossman, Vasily, 232
Gryn, Hugo, 228n31
guilt, 40–41, 151, 155–56, 230, 236; of Bárdossy, 237–42, 335n68, 336n76

Habsburg Empire, 17–18, 85, 194, 275n7
Hague Convention, 110–11
Hartl, Albert, 100
Hasidic Jews, 19, 21, 26, 249. *See also* Orthodox Jews
Haus, Franz, 152
Havryshko, Marta, 164, 171, 316n2
Hayes, Peter, 2, 154, 159, 247–48

Hazai, Samu, 275n10
Hermann, Miklós, 222
Heydrich, Reinhard, 97
hierarchies, 51, 166; Nazi, 96, 120–22, 132, 148, 150–52, 154–55
Higher SS and Police Leaders (HSS-PF), 97–99, 111, 113–15, 128–29, 145, 272n21, 296n33
Hilfspolizei (Ukrainian police), 99, 301n12
Himer, Kurt, 91, 293n13
Himmler, Heinrich (SS-Reichsführer), xix, 8, *99*, 127, 154, 160–61, 171, 236, 296n33; Jeckeln communicating with, 95, 113–19, *114*, 122; on Kamenets-Podolsk massacre, 98, 100; "virtues of the SS man," 174–75
Hincsuk, Katalin, 257, 339n36
Hitler, Adolf, 2, 37, 84, 98, 122, 156, 212
Hitler's Furies (Lower), 150
Holocaust/shoah, xvii, xxi–xxii, 9–15, 129, 133, 229, 246–47. *See also specific topics*
homosexuality, 169–70
Horowitz (Rabbi), 173
horses, xxi, xxiii, 76, 113, 144, 151, 155, 310n64
Horthy, Miklós, 12, 30, 32, 182, 233–34, 241, 270n9; Kozma reporting to, 47, 179
Höss, Rudolf, 253
houses. *See* property, confiscation of Jewish
Hull, Cordell, 207–9
humanitarian aid, 79, 199, 202–6, 211–15
humanitarian disasters, 79, 91, 99
human resources, 109, 135, 139, 147, 149, 153–54, 235, 244
humiliation, 60, 138, 145, 164, 166, 174, 287n29
Hungarian (language), 19, 34, 169, 249, 251
Hungarian Embassy, 47, 189, 209, 238
Hungarian – German relations, 86, 207
Hungarian Holocaust (1941), 10, 13, 46, 83, 178, 238, 241–42, 252–53, 257, 266. *See also specific topics*
Hungarian Holocaust (1944), xix, 2, 46, 63, 218, 221, 241–42, 252–53
Hungarian-Jewish Assistance Committee (*Magyar Izraeliták Pártfogó Irodája*) (MIPI), 182, 191, 209, 211, 214–16, 292n102, 326n93; reports on on deportations, 69, 75, 290n73; role of, 42, 66, 199–206, 325n80
Hungarian-Jewish National Aid Action (*Országos Magyar Zsidó Segitő Akció*) (OMZSA), 42, 190–91, 199, 216, 325n79, 325n80
Hungarian Jews. *See specific topics*
Hungarian Parliament, 12, 33–36, 206–9, 212, 241–42, 248, 277n33; intercession on deportations requested of, 90–91, 187, 191–92, 203–5, 236–39, 320n17. *See also* Jewish Laws; *specific offices of Parliament*
Hungarian-Polish Refugee Committee, 59, 204, 208, 211–13
Hungarian soldiers, xiii, 102n99, 197, 243, 254, 258; diaries of, 74, 77–78, 225–26
Hungarian Soviet Republic, 29
Hungary, *xviii, 44*. *See also specific topics*
hunger, 5, 49, 56, 68, 77, 81–83, 90, 133–34, 142, 163, 187, 203, 224
Hunger Plan *(der Hunger plan)*, 97–98
Hyman, Éva, 184, 257

identity checks, 50, 65, 254–55
identity/identities, xxii, 8, 20–23, 40, 151, 156–57, 249–50, 286n17; sexual violence affecting, 164, 166
ideology, xxv, 2, 36, 152, 159, 218–24, 246; of deportation, 231–32, 247–48
ideology, Nazi, xix, 36–37, 84–85, 107, 112–13, 174, 305n12; racial, 2, 6–7, 121, 127, 154–55, 164, 171, 176; SS code of conduct, 152–53, 158, 160, 169, 175
Imrédy, Béla, 283n91, 327n100
industrialization/modernization, 18–23
institutionalization of sexual violence, 175–77, *176*
intelligentsia, Jewish, 128, 133–39, 173–74, 196, 308n39
Intelligenz Aktion, 133–39, 196
intercession on deportations, 90–91, 187, 191–92, 203–5, 236–39, 320n17

intermarriage, 7, 17, 19–20, 32, 43
international reactions, 64–66, 204–12, 214–16
International Red Cross, xi–xii, 58, 81, 182, 202, 204–5, 214, 216, 250–51
international refugees, 10, 41, 134, 209, 232–35, 247–48
internment camps, 41, 49, 134, 136, 180, 195, 227, 288n49; in Budapest, 56–58, 190, 200, 222, 260, 326n83; foreign nationals at, 189, 232–33, 239, 247–48, 251, 254–55. *See also specific camps*
interwar period, 2, 30–31, 34, 36–37, 272n20, 281n71, 327n104
Irhóc (Vilhiv'ce), 60, 326n36
Israel, xxii, 263
Italian royal family, 136, 307n37

Jackson, Michael, 177, 254
Jacobson, Bertrand S., 210–11
Jagow, Dietrich von, 209
Jászi, Oszkár, 22–23, 27
JDC. *See* American Jewish Joint Distribution Committee
Jeckeln, Friedrich (General), xiii, *99*, *120*, 152, 229, 290n74, 300n78, 303n111, 303n112; communicating with Himmler, 95, 113–19, *114*, 122; death penalty for, xiii, 120, 300n83; Kamenets-Podolsk massacre overseen by, xiii, 83, 101–15, *114*, 192, 246, 300n83, 333n47; mass murders overseen by, xiii, 126–27, 129, 246–47; postwar trial of, 84, 98, 108, 116, 120–22, 300n83, 333n47; rationalizations of, 84–85, 95–100, 119–25
"Jew-free" border zone, 189, 224, 236
Jewish Councils. *See Judenrat*
Jewish Laws, 7, 199, 212, 222, 248–49, 281n72, 281n73; First, 37–38, 50, 281n70, 282n75; Second, 39–42, 248, 282n74, 282n80, 283n94, 325n81
Jewish leaders/leadership, 49, 52, 60, 64–65, 80, 198–204, 213
Jewish organizations, 189–204, 211–16. *See also specific organizations*

Jewish people/Jewry. *See specific topics*
"Jewish Question," 6, 25, 27, 31, 37, 130–31, 223, 253; Himmler on, 98; Kozma on, 47, 51–52; Szombathelyi on, 219; Wehrmacht on, 228
Jewish Telegraphic Agency (JTA), 64–65, 117, 210, 328n110
József, Pásztor, 322n46, 326n85
JTA. *See* Jewish Telegraphic Agency
"*Judenfrei*," 136, 138, 176
Judenrat (Jewish Councils), 80–81, 86, 134, 136, 142–43, 145–46, 153–54, 170
Judson, Pieter, 42
Julius, Antony, 24
jurisdiction, 56, 176, 179–80, 205. *See also* authority/discretion

Kaddish (Jewish memorial prayer), 257, 264
Kamenets-Podolsk, Ukraine, xix–xx, 1, 68–71, 157, 192–93, *245*, 259–62; deportation to, 78–83, 84–85
Kamenets-Podolsk massacre, xvii, 1, 5, 8, 10, *102*, 126, 202, 210, 246, 251, 305n12; burying alive in, 124–25, 244; casualty statistics, 83, 113–15, *114*, 118, 246, 293n18, 296n41; children/youths killed in, 109–10, 112, 244, 257; as "liquidation" campaign, 96, 101–15, *114*, 122–23; mass grave from, xx, *105*, 106, 108–11, 124–25, 244, *245*, 256, 259; Meiler unaware of, 95–96; Old Town ghetto, 82–83, 86, *87*, 88, *89*, 90–92, 95, 101, 116; role of Jeckeln in, xiii, 83, 101–15, *114*, 192, 246, 300n83, 333n47; Royal Hungarian Army role in, 103, 227, 297n47; schnapps at, 109–10, 244; survivors of, 108–9, 123; von Roque role in, 228–29; Wehrmacht role in, 227–28; witnesses of, xi, 106, 108–9, 116–19, 124–25, 244, 256–57
Karcsi (uncle), xx, xxiii, *xxiii*, 1, 106, 124, 261, 269n1 (chap. 1)
Károlyi, Mihály, 29, 278n41
Kárpát Csoport. See Carpathian Corps
"*Karpatoros*". *See* Carpathian-Ruthenia

Kassa (Kosice), Hungary, 2–3, 64, 101, 137, 270n6
Katzburg, Nathaniel, 222
Katzmann, Fritz (SS-Gruppenführer), 8, 128–29, 145, 193, 272n21, 304n9
Kaufman-Blum, Peninah, 254–55, 258, 288n49
Kelman, Herbert C., 155
KEOKH. *See* National Central Authority for Controlling Aliens (Külföldieket Ellenőrző Országos Központi Hatóság)
Keresztes-Fischer, Ferenc, xii, 52, 54, 57, 189, 209, 221, 333n52; deportations curtailed by, 178–84, 187, 215–16, 230–32; as Hungarian Minister of Interior, xii, 178–84, 187, 335n72
Kern, Aurel, 181
Kershaw, Ian, xxii, 28, 250, 256
Kersten, Felix, 122, 303n115
Khazars (multiethnitc peoples), 25, 227n26
Kiefer, Alfred, 149, 164, 312n85, 316n1
killing, industrialized, 245–46
killing fields, 106, 113, 123, 251, 253
Király, Jenő, 226
Kiss, Árkád, 255
Kissfalussy, Hrabar, 319n6
Knackendoeffel, Friedrich, 151, 312n87, 312n88, 314n107
Koch, Erich, 95
Köllner, Kurt, 154, 313n93
Kolomea/Kolomea Ghetto, xi, 70, 73, 129–30, 172, 186–87, 193, 196, 228; as Royal Hungarian Army headquarters, 80, 137, 148–49, 194
Kolomea massacre, 127–28, 164, 251, 314n117, 333n43; overseen by Leideritz, P., 84, 135, 148–49, 172, 321n32; in Szeparowce Forest, 137, 149, 151, 308n43
Körösmező, Ukraine, 227, 238, 321n29; Yasina, 370
Körösmező transit camp, 4, 48, 50, 59–60, *61*, 62–66, 179, 180, 251, 256, 287n25; humanitarian aid for, 203; Jewish drivers at, 198; Orbán overseeing, 230, 333n51; plundering at, 246; Slachta on, 58–68, 201–2, 205, 207; Szapáry on, 213

Korsemann, Gerret, 111, 299n75
Kosów, Ukraine, 80, 132, 137, 148, 188, 192
Kosztyo, Gyula, 284n101
Kovács, Alajos, 33–34
Kozma, Miklós, xii, 4, 13, 202, 220, 335n65; diaries of, 54–55, 58, 91; as government commissioner of Carpathian Ruthenia, xii, 3, 46–47, 51–58, 178–79, 240, *240*, 285n4; Keresztes-Fischer communicating with, 178–84, 187, 230–31; responsibility of, 239–41, 321n30, 336n77; role of, 51–58, 61–62, 70, 222, 224, 233, 239–40
Krem, József, 181, 183, 320n15, 320n19
Kricsfalussy-Hrabár, Endre, 329n8
Kriminal Polizei (*Kripo*), Ukrainian, 147, 149, 152–53, 156, 305n11, 305n14, 311n81
Kripo. *See* Kriminal Polizei
Krivoy Rog, Ukraine, 243
Krosigk, Ernst-Anton von, 95
Krüger, Hans (Captain), xiii, 129–31, 162, 189, 229, 232–33, 244, 305n13, 308n40; "Bloody Sunday" massacre overseen by, 143, 145–46, 149; Galician murders overseen by, 134–39; Leideritz, P., rivalry with, 150–58; Nadwórna massacre overseen by, 138–42; postwar trial of, 129, 131, 149, 157, 309n50; sexual violence enacted by, 172–75
Külföldieket Ellenőrző Országos Központi Hatóság. *See* National Central Authority for Controlling Aliens
Kun, Béla, 29–30

Labs, Walter, 95
Lanckoronska, Karolina, 136, 138, 154, 157, 160, 308n39
Landau, Saul, 154
Landauer, Gustav, 21
Landler, Jenő, 278n43
Láng, Lajos, 40, 199
Langlet, Valdemar, 31, 279n47
Larson, Eric, 160
law enforcement agencies, Budapest, 4, 8, 28, 36, 219–20, 227

laws. *See specific laws*
League of Nations, 43, 271n19
legal exclusion of Jews, 50, 253
legal framework for deportation, 4, 50–58, 232, 235–36
Leideritz, Anneliese, 150, 155–57, 312n87, 312n88, 312n89
Leideritz, Peter (First Lieutenant), xii, 129–30, 138, 147, 172, 229, 305n14; arrest of, 155–56; death penalty, xiii, 155–57; Kolomea massacre overseen by, 84, 135, 148–49, 172, 321n32; Krüger rivalry with, 150–58; mass murders by, xiii, 147–48, 321n32; postwar trials for, 312n89, 313n100
Leiser (grandfather), xxiii, 269n6
Lepore, Jill, xx
lesbianism, 169–70
letters, 142–43, 202–3, 214, 219, 226–27, 236, 239, 241–42, 321n36
levénték (armed youth groups), 188
Levi, Primo, xxiv, 263
Lieberman, Moshe, 191
Liebesman, Abraham, 162, 173, 175
"liquidation" campaigns, 138–43, 161, 176, 213, 228, 246, 305n13; for ghettos, 96, 147, 150–51, 162, 176, 213, 228; *Intelligenz Aktion* as, 133–39, 196; Kamenets-Podolsk massacre as, 96, 101–15, *114*, 122–23
local Jewish communities, xii, xxi, 45, 63–66, 122–23, 142–43, 171, 198–204; from Bukovina, 79, 247, 322n51; from Carpathian Ruthenia, 222–24; coreligionists in, xvii, 21, 27, 111, 132, 148, 188, 198, 202; deportation of, 127–28; forced to cover mass graves, 10–11, 140–41, 244; from Galicia, 130–34, 194; in Kamenets-Podolsk, 79–83, 92, 102–3, 261
Longerich, Peter, 100, 122, 158
looting. *See* plundering
The Lost (Mendelsohn), xxi
Lowe, Keith, 167
Lower, Wendy, 127, 150
Lubell, Elizabeth, xi, *186*, 186–88

Lwów, Ukraine (Lviv), 85, 98, 128, 139, 147, 159, 191–92, 195, 308n40; Tanzmann overseeing, 129–31, 138, 143, 160, 187–88

machine guns, 92–93, 103, 109, 117, 145, 154, 299n62; submachine guns, 73–74, 104–5, 108–9, 117, 228, 246, 299n62
Magyarization, 19, 222–23
Magyar Izraeliták Pártfogó Irodája. *See* Hungarian-Jewish Assistance Committee
Majsai, Tamás, 212, 320n17, 329n122
Mallmann, Klaus-Michael, 100, 295n23, 296n41
Márai, Sándor, 16, 221, 249, 330n23, 335n68
Máramaros County, Transylvania, 53, 80, 92, 132, 141, 191, 222
marches/wandering of deported Jews, 1, 63, 72, 75–82, 141–42, 184–89, 218, 224, 228; sexual violence during, 166–70
marriage, 7, 17, 19–20, 32, 43, 283n93, 303n112; Jewish, 61, 288n41; mixed, 3, 201, 250. *See also* intermarriage
Martinidesz, Ödön, 333n50
massacres, 126–27, 130–31, 133, 192–93, 246–47. *See also* mass murders; *specific massacres*
mass graves, 4–5, 7–8, 191, 231n31; in "Bloody Sunday massacre," 144–47; in Kamenets-Podolsk, xx, *105*, 106, 108–11, 124–25, 244, *245*, 256, 259; Nadwórna, 243–45; at Orinin, 92–94, *94*, 259–60, 262–64, *264*, 310n63. *See also* covering of mass graves
mass murders, xix–xx, 1, 4–5, 7, 12–15, 210, 218, 225, 252, 272n22, 298n90, 305n12; alcohol use in, xxv, 109–10, 143–45, 244, 253; border police aiding in, 225; in Galicia, 131–39, 157–60; injunction against deportation and, 181; by Jeckeln, xiii, 126–27, 129, 246–47; at Krivoy Rog, 243; by Krüger, xiii, 135, 244; by Leideritz, P., xiii, 147–48, 321n32; perpetrators of, 101, 128–29, 138, 229–41, 305n12; refusal to participate in, 100, 110–11, 193,

mass murders (*continued*)
  296n38, 304n10, 313n94, 314n117, 333n43;
  by Reserve Police Battalion 133, 135, 139–40; role of Bárdossy in, 233, 237; role of Wehrmacht in, 128, 227–28; roles of Pásztóy in, 233, 235–36. *See also Aktionen* (rounding up of Jews); casualty statistics; execution; forced collection; participation in mass murders; undressing, forced; *specific massacres*
mass shootings, xxi, 107–9, 115, 145, 159, 217, 301n88, 305n12. *See also specific massacres*
Mauthausen concentration camp, xxii, 297n48, 338n28
Mechlowitz, Chaim Simcha, *252*
media. *See* press/news
medicine/medical treatment, 198, 203–6, 212
meetings, 91, 200–201, 214, 238, 295n23;
  Council of Ministers, 51–52, 56, 224, 235;
  Nazi, 95–98, 100, 122–23, 140–41, 189
Megay, László, 330n17
Meier, August, 111–12, 300n76
Meiler, Josef (Lieutenant Colonel), 95–97, 119, 195n26, 229, 293n5, 294n16, 295n26;
  Kamenets-Podolsk ghetto established by, 86, 88, 91, 192–93; rescues aided by, 192–93, 197, 322n52
memories, 49, 168, 225, 245, 259–63
men, Jewish, 168, 170, 253–54; forced undressing of, 164, 173, 196; sexual violence against, 166, 172–74. *See also* forced labor companies, Jewish men in
Mendelsohn, Daniel, xxi, xxiv, 173–74
menstruation, 168
Mermelstein, Gábor, 116–17
Meskó, Arisztid, 46, 59, 66, 180, 230, 333n50, 334n57
mezuzahs, 184, 320n21
Michnik, Adam, 242
middle class: Christian, 20, 30, 38, 221, 238, 248–49, 330n16; Jewish, 7, 17–23, 26, 29, 32, 221–23, 248, 330n16
Mielnica, Ukraine, 80, 172, 188
Milch, Baruch, 70–71, 133, 332n35, 338n19

military zones, 55, 66, 204
Milo, Shmuel, 338n24
Minister of Interior, Hungarian, 219–20, 233, 239, 270n11, 283n90; Keresztes-Fischer as, xii, 178–84, 187, 335n72
minorities, 2, 6, 28, 34, 37–38, 51, 221–23, 247, 309n46; non-Jewish Hungarians as, 248–49
MIPI. *See* Hungarian-Jewish Assistance Committee (*Magyar Izraeliták Pártfogó Irodája*)
misinformation campaigns, 52–53, 64, 101, 231
mixed marriage, 3, 201, 250
Moishe the Beadle (character), 12, 191
Moldova, Ágnes, 263
Mukachevo (Munkács), 60, 330n20
Müller, Rudolf, 147, 305n15
Münzer, Márta, 184, 257
murders, 127, 187–88, 192, 206–7, 224–25, 226–27; industrialized, 9, 113, 161; by Leideritz, A., 150–51; rates of, 100, 133, 145, 149, 158, 244; sexual violence and, 172–75; systematic, 5, 8–9, 93–94, 96, 128, 130–31, 133–34, 181, 207. *See also* mass murders
murder squads, 4–5, 7, 11, 107–13, 130, 148, 172, 203, 251, 310n67 94; plundering by, 246

Nadwórna, Ukraine, 80, 127, 132, 139, 161, 309n54; mass murder in, 10–11, 138–43, 147, 243–45, 309n50
names/lists of deportees, 60, 136, 204–5, 223–24
Nansen passports, 7, 54, 209, 250, 271n19, 286n17
National Central Authority for Controlling Aliens (*Külföldieket Ellenőrző Országos Központi Hatóság*) (KEOKH), 41, 215, 227, 235, 250–51, 255; Batizfalvy in, 56–57, 66, 67, 200, 232, 289n55, 289n56, 330n9, 334n57; on injunction against, 179, 209, 230–31; international refugees expelled

by, 247–48; Keresztes-Fischer communicating with, 230–31; legal framework for deportation by, xii, 4, 50–58, 230–36; Pásztóy heading, xii, 45–46, 52–58, 233, *235*; Siménfalvy as director, 50, 55, 58, 65, 118, 180, 214, 230, 232, 285n3
nationalism, 54, 73, 128; Hungarian, 19, 22, 32–33, 35
natural barriers: Carpathian Mountains as, 68–71, 187; Dniester River as, 70, 82, 187, 192, 224–25
naturalization/naturalization documents, 42, 254
Nazis/Nazi Germany. *See specific topics*
"necessary evils," 31, 199–200
neighbors, xxiv–xxv, 10, 14, 106, 249, 257, 262, 274n39, 306n25
Neolog Jews, 17, 19, 21. *See also* assimilated Jews
New Jewish Cemetery, Stanisławów, xi, 128, 141, 143–46, 162
news. *See* press/news
newspapers, 27, 65, 190, 210, 216
non-Jewish/gentile Hungarians, 227, 248–49
nudity. *See* undressing, forced (phase of mass murder)
Nuremberg Laws, 86, 171
Nuremberg trials, 13, 119, 126, 239, 253

Oates, Joyce Carol, 249
Old Town ghetto, Kamenets-Podolsk, 82–83, 86, *87*, 88, *89*, 90–92, 95, 101, 116
OMZSA. *See* Hungarian-Jewish National Aid Action (*Országos Magyar Zsidó Segitő Akció*)
Orbán, Rudolf, 33n51, 66, 179, 220, 230
Order of the Sisters of Social Service, xi, 182, *211*, 212, 215, 217
Ordnungspolizei. See reserve police battalions
Orinin, mass murder/massacre at, 92–94, *94*, 126–27, 185, 251–53, 259–60, 262–64, *264*, 310n63
Ormos, Mária, 240, 321n30, 336n77
orphans/orphanages, 31, 65, 69, 80, 133, 150–51, 157, 162–63, 312n89

ORPO. *See* reserve police battalions (*Ordnungspolizei*)
Országos Magyar Zsidó Segitő Akció. See Hungarian-Jewish National Aid Action
Orthodox Jews, xxii, 17, 19–23, 223
Orwell, George, 231
Ostjuden. See Eastern Jews
"other," 20–23, 248

Paamayim Shoah (Kaufman-Blum), 254–55
"pacification" actions. *See* mass murders
Pakocs, Károly, 287n33
participation in mass murders, xxv, 2–3, 96–100, 119, 128–29, 225, 301n89; refusals of, 100, 192–93, 296n38, 304n10, 313n94, 314n117, 333n43; of Royal Hungarian Army, 103, 117, 225, 297n47, 331n32, 332n39; of Wehrmacht, 95, 158
Passierschein (German travel permits), 191, 214–15
Pásztóy, Ámon, 3, 13, 63, 188–89, 200–201, 214, 250–51; as head of KEOKH, xii, 45–46, 52–58, 233, *235*; role in mass murders of, 233, 235–36
Patai, József, 278n39
peasants, 70–71, 77, 185, 248
Pell, Herbert C., xii, 11, 118, 178, 181–82, 206–10, *208*, 213, 215–16, 237–39
People's Court, Hungarian, xii, 13, 230, 232, 283n95
Perényi, Eleanor, 19, 220, 223, 248, 275n11
perpetrators, 9–13, 217–18; of deportation, 164, 214, 218–19, 223–24, 226, 229–41; of mass murder, 101, 128–29, 138, 229–41, 305n12
photographs, 175, 287n34; by Jewish drivers, xi, *102*, 103, *104*, *105*, 243, 301n89. *See also specific photos*
Pietsch, Walter, 34, 280n55
plundering/looting, 30, 135, 145, 150, 154–61, 187, 221, 290n73, 293n8; during deportation, 59–62, 71, 73, 79–82; by executioners, 164, 246; expropriation as, 29, 128, 223–24, 238; facilitated by Jewish Laws,

plundering/looting (*continued*)
    223–24, 248–49; by Frank, 154, 313n102; by Hungarian gendarmerie, 193–94, 224–26, 246; during Kamenets-Podolsk massacre, 101, 112; by neighbors, 248–49; rivalry in, 150–58; during sexual violence, 164, 166, 172; by Ukrainian irregulars, xvii, 73–79, 140, 152–53, 224–26, 246
Podolia (region), xix–xx, 69, 82, 85–86, 229, 262–63, 291n96. *See also* Kamenets-Podolsk, Ukraine; Orinin, mass murder/massacre at
pogroms, anti-Jewish, 16, 73, 80, 119, 194, 201, 239, 274n36, 290n76
Pohl, Dieter, 107, 116, 125, 158
Poland/Polish people, xiii, 36, 85, 138, 152, 156, 174, 242, 274n39, 285n2, 336n80; reclassification of, 43; refugees, 127, 203, 212; as stateless, 56–58; women, 177, 318n37. *See also* Belzec (extermination camp)
Polgár, György, 201
police: Hungarian, 219–20, 246; Jewish, 134, 143, 162, 170; Ukrainian, 7, 9, 99, 101, 105–13, 115, 144, 175, 228–29, 305n12, 306n24, 307n33
policies, Hungarian, 199–201, 222–27, 240; against repatriation, xii, 191–98, 236–39
policies, Nazi, 4, 8, 15, 94, 96–97
Polish Jews, 43, 64–65, 134, 208, 285n6
postwar trials, 10–11, 150, 152, 155–56, 166, 171, 314n107; of Bárdossy, 237–38; of Eichmann, 182; of Jeckeln, 84, 98, 108, 116, 120–22, 300n83, 333n47; of Krüger, 129, 131, 149, 157, 309n50; Leideritz, P., 312n89, 313n100; Nuremberg trials as, 13, 119, 126, 239, 253; of Pásztóy, 52, 201, 236; of Reserve Police Battalion 320, 107–8; of von Roque, 119, 293n12
poverty, 16–17, 83, 222–24
power, 30, 132, 136, 138, 152–55, 164, 212, 228, 235–36; sexual violence and, 166–70
pregnancies, 171–72
press/news, 24, 64–65, 117–19, 182; Jewish, 190, 210; newspapers, 27, 65, 190, 210, 216

priests/clergymen, 23, 59, 76, 258
prime minister, Hungarian, 34, 37, 218–19, 271n15, 278n38, 283n91, 327n99; Bárdossy as, xii, 4, 179, 208–9, 215, *237*, 237–39, 247; Teleki as, 31, 35, 39, 334n62
prison, xii, 142, 144, 254, 311n72
"productivity," Nazi, xiii, xxiv, 100–101, 129, 135, 189, 299n66
professionals, Jewish, 18–19, 38–39, 134–39, 173
profitability/war profiteering, 7, 22, 24–26, 153–54, 159, 320n15
Prohászka, Ottokár, 22, 27, 32, 35
pro-Hungarian, 19, 223, 248
pro-Jewish, 194, 219, 324n66
pro-Nazi, 4, 54, 193–94, 219, 234, 260
property: confiscation of Jewish, 29, 55–56, 59–62, 67–68, 128, 150, 152–61, 221, 223–24, 238, 287n34, 331n25; promises of, 52–53, 64, 234. *See also* plundering/looting
prostitution, 170
Protestant churches, 18
Prützmann, Hans-Adolf, 98, 100
psychology, 14, 109–10, 120–21, 140–41, 145–46, 154, 247–48, 299n68, 299n70; of sexual violence, 143–44, 167–68, 174
public opinion/knowledge, 116–19, 207, 210

rabbis, 1, 26, 61, 83, 101, 173–74, 288n41, 338n31
racial ideology, 279n54; Nazi, 2, 6–7, 121, 127, 154–55, 164, 171, 176
racial-national designation, "Jew" as, xxii, 6, 27, 32, 34–39, 41–42, 293n4
racial purification, 246
radio communications, 94, 113, 115, 172, 190, 194, 210, 322n41
Radnóti, Miklós, 75, 291n82
raids, 28, 36, 41, 59–60, 64–65, 173, 189, 270n6, 278n38, 281n71; air, 2, 144
railway police (*Bahnschutzpolizei*), 99, 135, 305n12
rapes, 9, 75–76, 166–69, 171–73, 175, 224–25, 316n7, 318n37
Rassay, Károly, 200

rationalizations, xxv, 52–53, 84–85, 95–101, 129–31, 152–53, 159, 218–24, 238–39. *See also* ideology, Nazi
Ravasz, László, 37, 214, 281n70, 329n122
reannexed territories, Hungarian, 2, 36–38, 41, 180, 230, 247, 249
Red Army (Soviet Army), 1, 73, 85, 88, 106, 166
Red Cross, Hungarian, xi–xii, 58–59, 202–5, 211–12, 214, 292n102, 326n92
Red Cross, International, xi–xii, 204–5, 250–51
redeportations, 118, 215–16
refugees, 3–5, 26, 30, 36–38, 129–30, 202, 281n67, 317n15; from Carpathian-Ruthenia, 79–81, 131–34; defined, 249–50; financial aid for, 57, 202, 212; Hungarian Jewish, 139–41, 148, 168–69, 184–89, 192–93; international, 10, 41–43, 134, 209, 232–35, 247–48; Nansen passports for, 7, 54, 209, 250, 271n19, 286n17; Polish, 127, 203, 212. *See also* statelessness/"stateless" Jews
refusal to participate in mass murders, 100, 110–11, 193, 296n38, 304n10, 313n94, 314n117, 333n43
regional authority, 128–30, 132, 158–59, 178
"registration," in deportation, 4, 50, 55, 137, 251
religious conversion, xii, 19, 29, 76, 214, 297n43, 339n36
repatriation, xii, 1, 3, 92–93, 191–98, 200, 214–16, 230–31, 236–39
rescue work/efforts, 66, 169, 181, 191–99, 204–5, *213*, *214*, 258, 322n46; along borderlands, 184–89; by forced labor companies, 184, 325n75; by Slachta, xi–xii, 180, 182, 202–5, *211*, 211–18, 257, 320n17. *See also* smuggling, human
Reserve Police Battalion 101, 107, 159, 217
Reserve Police Battalion 133, 135, 139–40, 144, 146–47, *148*, 149, 158, 229, 309n50
Reserve Police Battalion 320, 99–100, 103–4, 106–11, 113–16, 118, 123, 158, 229, 298n56, 299n66, 331n32

Reserve Police Battalions (*Ordnungspolizei*) (ORPO), 7, 9, 99, 166, 229, 305n12, 306n24
"resettlement," deportations framed as, 3, 144, 199–200, 219, 223–24, 326n92
responsibility, 11–13, 40–41, 49, 97, 122, 180–81, 217–18, 233–42, 335n68; Bárdossy, 233, 237–39; of Keresztes-Fischer, 230–31, 335n72; of Kozma, 239–41, 321n30, 336n77; of Royal Hungarian Army, 227–28
Reviczky, Imre, 180, 257, 319n9
Riga, Rumbula Forest massacre, xiii, 108, 120
Righteous Among the Nations, Yad Vashem, xii, *211*, 212–13, *213*, 279n47, 319n9, 339n37
right-wing movements, 29, 33, 36–37, 205, 286n11, 327n99
rivalry. *See* competition/rivalry
roles, of mass murderers and participants, 11, 36–37, 305n12; of alcohol in mass murders, xxv, 109–10, 143–45, 244, 253; of Bárdossy, 233, 237–39; Jeckeln, xiii, 83, 101–15, *114*, 192, 246, 300n83, 333n47; of KEOKH, xii, 4, 50–58, 230–36, *235*, 235–36; of Kozma, 51–58, 61–62, 70, 222, 224, 233, 239–40; of OMZSA, 199, 325n79; of Orbán, 33n51, 220; Pásztóy, xii, 52–58, 233, 235–36; of rescuers, 211–15; of Royal Hungarian Army, 9–10, 103, 218–19, 224–33, 297n47; Ukrainian irregular forces/paramilitary, 101–13, 117, 228–29; of von Roque, 228; of Wehrmacht, 95–98, 128, 227–29; of Werth, 223–24, 233
Romanian Army, 26, 30, 167, 227
Romania/Romanians, xviii, 2, 5–6, *44*, 45–46, 135, 242, 271n14; deportation/expulsion from, 79, 85, 129–30, 195, 242, 293n3, 311n76; Jews, 50, 79, 85, 195, 293n3, 311n76, 317n15. *See also* Bukovina, Romania; Transylvania, Romania
Roque, Karl von, 90–91, 95–99, 119, 158, 228–29, 293n12, 296n34, 302n103
Rosenberg, Blanca, 63, 134, 137, 155
Rosenthal, Yaffa, 77–78, 168, 258, 338n22

376 INDEX

Rosh Hashanah, 192
Rougemont, Denis de, 16
Rousso, Henry, 245
Royal Hungarian Army, 2–3, 9–10, 149, 166, 184, 187, 191–98, 224–35, 309n46; deportations facilitated by, 49–58, 68–71, 78–82, 178–79; drafts by, 177, 243–54, 297n48; forced labor used by, 253–54; headquarters in Kolomea, 80, 137, 148–49, 194; Jewish drivers for, xi, 84, 198, 243, 297n48, 325n76; participation in mass murders by, 103–13, 116–19, 225, 297n47, 331n32, 332n39; plundering by, 152–53, 246. *See also* forced labor companies, Jewish men in; Hungarian soldiers; Werth, Henrik
Rudolfmühle (Rudolf's Mill), 81, 136–37, 142–44, 161–63, 310n59, 310n60; Hungarian Jews imprisoned in, 131, 170, 247
Rumbula Forest massacre, xiii, 108, 120
Russia, Czarist, 16, 24
Russian Civil War, 274n36
Rusyn people, 79, 198, 222, 271n14

sadism, xix, 121–22, 127, 149; sexual violence as, 167–68, 173
Salamon, Alajos Alapi, 69, 224
Salzer, Izidor, 117
Samu (uncle), xx, xxiii, *xxiii*, 1, 64, 106, 257–58, 259–61, 269n1, 326n87
Samuel, Marion, 79, 142, 161–62, 168
Sandkuehler, Thomas, 132–33
Scharwey, Heinrich, 107, 110–11
Schindler (SS Officer), 173, 318n32
schnapps, xxv, 159, 246; present at Kamenets-Podolsk massacre, 109–10, 244; present at Orinin massacre, 310n63
Schöngarth, Karl Eberhard, 128–29, 135, 140, 160, 304n10
schools for Jewish children, 256
Schupo. See Schutzpolizei
Schutzmann (Ukranian police), 99, 105–6
Schutzmannschaft (Ukrainian auxiliaries), 106–7, 228, 305n11

Schutzpolizei (municipal police)(*Schupo*), 99, 130, 151, 305n12
Schutzstaffel (protection squad)(SS), 92–100, 126, 227, 232–33, 298n60, 304n10, 305n12, 313n98; code of conduct, 152–53, 158, 160, 169, 175; sexual violence by, 166, 171–77, *176*; Wehrmacht as separate from, 10, 97. *See also specific branches of SS*
scope of deportations, 12, 67–68, 209, 216, 232–33
SD. *See Sicherheitsdienst*
Second Jewish Law, 39–42, 248, 282n74, 282n80, 283n94, 325n81
second wave (Nazi exterminations), 8, 14, 132, 134–36
Secretary of State, US, 207–9
secret police. *See* Gestapo
secret service, British, 116, 118
Selbschutz (ethnic German militia), 305n12
"self-financing" mass murders, 153–54, 159
Serbia/Serbians, 5, 38, 270n8, 271n13
sexual violence, 9, 143–44, 164, *165*, 167, 169, 318n37; sexual slavery as, 166, 168, 171, 175–77
shelter, 77, 80–82, 133, 139, 184, 212, 320n21
Shoah (Holocaust/genocide), xxi, xxii
shtetls, 6, 86, 127, 132, 262–63
Shulyk, Alexandr, 263
sichacks. See Ukrainian irregular forces/paramilitary
Sicherheitsdienst (German security service) (SD), 95, 97, 99, 115, 298n60, 304n11, 305n12
Sicherheitspolizei (German security police) (*Sipo*), 99, 130, 136–37, 149, 156, 304n11, 305n12, 305n14
silence, xxii, 9, 12, 166, 189–91, 249
Silva (Jewish girl), 171
Siménfalvy, Sándor, 50, 55, 58, 65, 118, 180, 200, 214, 230, 232, 285n3
Simon (Lieutenant), 226
Sipo. See Sicherheitspolizei
Skala, Ukraine, 71, *72*, 80, 132, 290n70, 306n21

Slachta, Margit, 12, 45–46, 230, 236–37, 241–42, 292n102, 319n4; on Körösmező transit camp, 58–68, 201–2, 205, 207; rescue work by, xi–xii, 180, 182, 201–4, 205, *211*, 211–18, 220, 257, 320n17
slaves/slavery: labor, 106, 134, 161, 170, 200, 254, 338n28; sexual, 166, 168, 171, 175–77, *176*
Slovakia, xviii, 37–38, 43, *44*, 45, 80, 198, 212, 242, 271n14, 281n67. See also Upper Hungary (Slovakia)
smuggling, human, *186*, 197–98, 254, 321n27, 325n73, 332n38; fees for, 181, 183–88, 227, 320n15; sexual violence and, 169
Sniatyn, Ukraine, 172, 188, 321n32
Snyder, Timothy, 8, 14, 96, 246–47
socialism, 20, 29, 84
Solomon, Max, 60–61, 70, 93, 185, 253, 263
Solowitz, Lea, 321n27
Somló, Béla, xi, *72*, 243, 289n54, 290n70, 306n21, 336n3
Soviet Army. See Red Army
Soviet Extraordinary State Commission, 103, 124–25, 257, 297n41
Soviet Union (U.S.S.R.), xii, 2–3, 8, 45–48, *94*, 212, 237, 253; Soviet Extraordinary State Commission, 103, 124–25, 257, 297n41
Spitz, Gyula, 103, 297n48, 301n89
Springmann, Samuel, 182–83, 320n16
SS. See *Schutzstaffel*
SS-Gruppenführer (Major Generals): Katzmann as, 8, 128–29, 145, 193, 272n21, 304n9; Prützmann as, 98, 100
Stalin, Joseph, 99–100, 263
Stanisławów, 80–81, 128–43, 161–62, 189, 244, 251. See also "Bloody Sunday" massacre; Rudolfmühle
starvation, 75–79, 97–98, 131, 142, 161, 187
State Department, US, 214, 118, 181, 204, 206–10, 328n107
statelessness/"stateless" Jews, 3, 43, 50–51, 56, 68, 200, 249–50; Nansen passports for, 7, 54, 209, 250, 271n19, 286n17

statistics, 184–85, 222, 277n28; deportation, 4, 192, 242, 250–51, 334n56. See also casualty statistics
stereotypes, 2, 16, 20–34, 39, 40, 199, 252–53. See also "Galicianers"/ Galician Jews
Stern, Joseph, 301n96
Stern, Lajos, 182, 201
Stern, Samu, 200
Subcarpathia. See Carpathian Ruthenia
submachine guns, 73–74, 104–5, 108–9, 117, 228, 246, 299n62
suicides, 168, 170, 304n10, 317n16; by Teleki, 282n79, 282n80, 325n82
surveillance of Slachta, 205, 220
survivors, 78, 140, 155–57, 168–70, 202–3, 250, 257, 260, 294n20; diaries of, 243–44; of Galicia/Galician deportation, 184–85, 189–91, 226, 252, 254–55; of Kamenets-Podolsk massacre, 108–9, 123; memories of, 68, 168, 225; Rosenberg as, 134, 137, 155; Solomon as, 253, 263; testimony/testimonies, 168–70, 257; Zobel as, xi, 49–50, 75, 180
Swabian (German) ancestry, 233–34, 249
Sweden, 31, 279n47
Swintek, Josef, 123
Switzerland, 213
synagogues, 66, 77, 81, 139, 191, 260
syphilis, 175
systematic murder, 5, 8–9, 93–94, 96, 128, 130–31, 133–34, 181, 207
Szabó, Imre, 59
Szabolcsi, Lajos, 277n28
Szapáry, Erzsébet (Countess), xii, 58–59, 204, 208, 211–14, *213*, 225, 257, 287n34
Szegedi, Csanád, 269n1
Szekfű, Gyula, 33
Szeparowce Forest, 137, 149, 151, 308n43
Szombathelyi, Ferenc (Lieutenant General), 54–55, 58, 69, 138, 193, 196–97, 219, 324n66
Sztójay, Döme, 47

taboos, 169, 216

tábori csendőrség. See gendarmerie, Hungarian

Tamás (Hungarian soldier), 258

Tanzmann, Helmut (SS-Lieutenant Colonel), 129–31, 138, 143, 160, 187–88, 233

telegrams, 178, 180, 319n11, 327n101

Teleki, Pál, 32, 40, 233–34, 238, 279n48; as Hungarian prime minister, 31, 35, 39, 334n62; suicide of, 282n79, 282n80, 325n82

Teleszky, János, 275n10

territories, Hungarian, *xviii*, 3–4, 21, 24, 28, 43, *44*, 45–48; Hungarian occupation of Galicia, 51, 81, 183, 191, 194, 247–48, 290n76; reannexed, 2, 36–38, 41, 180, 230, 247, 249

testimony/testimonies, xi, 103, 124–25, 251–52, 263; about sexual violence, 166, 168–70; of survivors, 168–70, 257; by Zobel, 56–57, 73, 191, 285n1, 290n67, 291n92

Third Jewish Law, 39

Third Reich, 97, 120–21, 127, 175

third wave (Nazi exterminations), 8, 9, 14, 132, 134–36

Tildi (wife of Samu), 260

Tisza, István, 22–23, 27–28

Tłuste, Galicia, 70, 152–54, 194, 250, 332n35, 338n19

torture, 30, 127, 137, 140, 145, 167–68, 205

trains, 1, 26, 56, 62–63, 66, 70, 101–6, 113, 128, 251, 288n46, 335n71, 338n22

Transcarpathia. See Carpathian Ruthenia

transit camps. *See* Kőrösmező transit camp

Transnistria, 167, 227, 233

"trans-Ukrainian highway," 134, 306n28

Transylvania, Romania, 4, 6, 45–46, 123, 248, 271n14; Máramaros County, 53, 80, 92, 132, 141, 191, 222

Trapp, Wilhelm, 217

trauma, 14, 23–24, 29, 60–65, 108–13, 191, 215, 260; of sexual violence, 164, 166–69

travel documents, 191–92, 214–15, 271n19

Treaty of Trianon, 24, 30

Troper, Morris C., 207

trucks/trucking in deportation, military, 4, 59, 68–70, 224, 228, 250–51; following injunction, 90, 179; to Kamenetsk Podolsk, 82, 90–92

Tupenko, Nikolai, 124–25

Ukraine/Ukrainians, xviii, 3, 167, 193–94, 201, 245–47, 271n14, 309n54; Jews, 79, 97, 103, 107. *See also specific topics*

Ukrainian (language), xix, 261, 321n27

Ukrainian auxiliaries (*Schutzmannschaft*), 106–7, 228, 305n11

Ukrainian irregular forces/paramilitary, xxv, 158, 184, 195–97, 201–3, 206–7, 251, 290n74, 304n5, 305n12; murders by, xvii, 4–5, 7, 73–79, 127–28, 147, 152–53, 224–25; plundering by, xvii, 73–79, 140, 152–53, 224–26, 246; role in Kamenets-Podolsk massacre of, 101–13, 117, 228–29; sexual violence by, 166–69, 173

"undesirable" populations, 4, 36, 55

undressing, forced (phase of mass murder), 108–9, 116–17, 139, 145, 164, *165*, 172–74, 196, 316n2

Ungvary, Rudolf, 330n16

United States (US), 6, 16, 34, 163, 215, 304n1, 327n103; diplomats, 207, 210, 270n5, 284n105, 327n104; State Department, 214, 118, 181, 204, 206–10, 328n107

Upper Hungary (Slovakia), 2–3, 6, 38, 59, 61–62, 222, 247, 249, 271n14, 278n38

US. *See* United States

U.S.S.R. *See* Soviet Union

Uzhgorod, Carpathian Ruthenia, 90, 112, 221, 330n17; Ungvár, 378

Valentina (Kamenets-Podolsk witness), xi, xx–xxi, 256–57, 259, 261–62, *262*

Varchmin, Ernst, 147, 305n15

Vázsonyi, Vilmos, 278n36

de Végh, Hanna, 205

venereal diseases, 175, 177

Veres, Éva, 261–62
Vernichtungskrieg, 246–47
veterans, World War I, 45, 230
Volkdeutsche units (ethnic Germans), 135, 144, 301n88
Volkmann, Claus (*Kreishauptmann*), 128, 148–49, 161, 228, 311n78, 311n83

Wagner (Major), 95–97, 295n24
wandering. *See* marches/wandering
Wannsee Conference (1942), 242, 304n4, 336n80
war, declarations of, 47–48, 51, 210–12, 236
war crimes/criminals, 13, 116, 119, 150, 239, 296n34, 297n49
Warmann, Albert, 149, 153, 311n81
Warsaw, Poland, 149, 156–57, 170, 267
Wasserstein, Bernard, 16–17
water supply, 56, 63, 71, 90, 288n46
Weber, Alfred, 107, 111
Wehrmacht, 8–10, 97, 138, 158, 183, 191–98; in Kamenetsk Podolsk massacre, 86, 95–98, 111, 125; role of, 95–98, 128, 227–29; sexual violence by, 166, 171, 174–77, *176*
Weiss, Edith (Countess), xii, 12, 142–43, 200, 203–4, 211–15, *214*, 236, 257
Weiss, Irene, 60
Weiss, Manfred, xii
Wekerle, Sándor, 28
Werth, Henrik (General), 3–4, 6, 13, 35, 47–48, 223–24, 226, *234*, 234–35; authority of, 179, 232–34, 271n15, 285n8; deportations pursued by, xii, 51–58; foreign nationals deported by, 232–33; international refugees expelled by, 247–49
Westermann, Edward, 140, 144, 174
Western Europe, xxiv, 7, 17, 20, 34, 208, 242
West Germany, xiii, 155, 157, 229, 314n107
White Terror, 24, 30, 279n46
Wiemer, Hans, 107, 111

Wiesel, Elie, 12, 191, 249
witnesses, 11, 162, 218, 253, 263, 273n31, 306n24, 331n33; of "Bloody Sunday" massacre, 144–47; Hungarian soldiers as, 217, 243; of Kamenets-Podolsk massacre, xi, 106, 108–9, 116–19, 124–25, 244, 256–57; of sexual violence, 167–68, 171–72; silence of, 189–91
women, xxiii, 140–42; German, 150, 169–70; Polish, 177, 318n37; rescue efforts by, xi–xii, 180, 182, 202–4, *211*, 211–15, *213*, *214*, 257
women, Jewish, 45, *72*, 173, 181, 254, 317n16, 318n39; forced undressing of, 61–62, 109, 164, *165*, 172–73; sexual violence against, 164, *165*, 166–77
World War I, 13, 20, 23, 25, 27–31, 34–37, 42, 45, 230, 298n55; Brusilov Offensive, 26, 227n29; Treaty of Trianon, 24, 30
World War II, 5, 13–14, 158, 212, 241–42, 247–48; sexual violence during, 166–67, 171
Wunnenberg, Alfred, *99*
Wyszkow Pass, 130, 147

Yazlovet, Ukraine, 197, 291n92
Yiddish (language), 19–21, 79, 118, 169, 177, 210, 249, 301n94
Yugoslavia, 5, 28, 43, 167, 282n79, 325n82

Zaslawski (physician), 173
Zelikovitch, Zvi (Hermann), 92–93
Zelmanovits, Moshe, 76–77
Zobel, László, xi, *183*, 197; arrest of, 65, 190, 254–55; expulsion of, 66, 73, 75; human smuggling of, 183, 332n38; as survivor, xi, 49–50, 75, 180; testimony of, 56–57, 73, 191, 285n1, 290n67, 291n92
Zsuzsa (daughter of Samu), 260–61

ABOUT THE AUTHOR

GEORGE EISEN IS A PROFESSOR OF HISTORY AND POLITICAL SCIENCE, AND the author of numerous books and articles about the Holocaust and other subjects. He is the product of three educational systems—Hungary, Israel, and the United States—and his scholarly works have been translated into a multitude of languages, with corresponding awards. His book, *Children and Play in the Holocaust*, received the American Library Association's Outstanding Academic Book of the Year Award (*Choice*, 1990–1991). In 1993, he received the Fulbright Scholar appointment in Estonia. As a scholar, Eisen served as keynote speaker and organizer of major international conferences, workshops, and art projects commemorating the Holocaust. Fulfilling his commitment to increase international awareness of the tragedy of the Holocaust, he has spoken extensively to community and student groups all over the world. He received the Dr. Martin Luther King Jr. Award for Leadership from Nazareth College in 2013. As an internationally recognized author and educator, Eisen is the recipient of three honorary doctorates from Hungary, Chile, and Ukraine.

www.ingramcontent.com/pod-product-compliance
Lightning Source LLC
Chambersburg PA
CBHW071437300426
44114CB00013B/1472